June 25–28, 2012
Milwaukee, WI, USA

I0060984

**Association for
Computing Machinery**

Advancing Computing as a Science & Profession

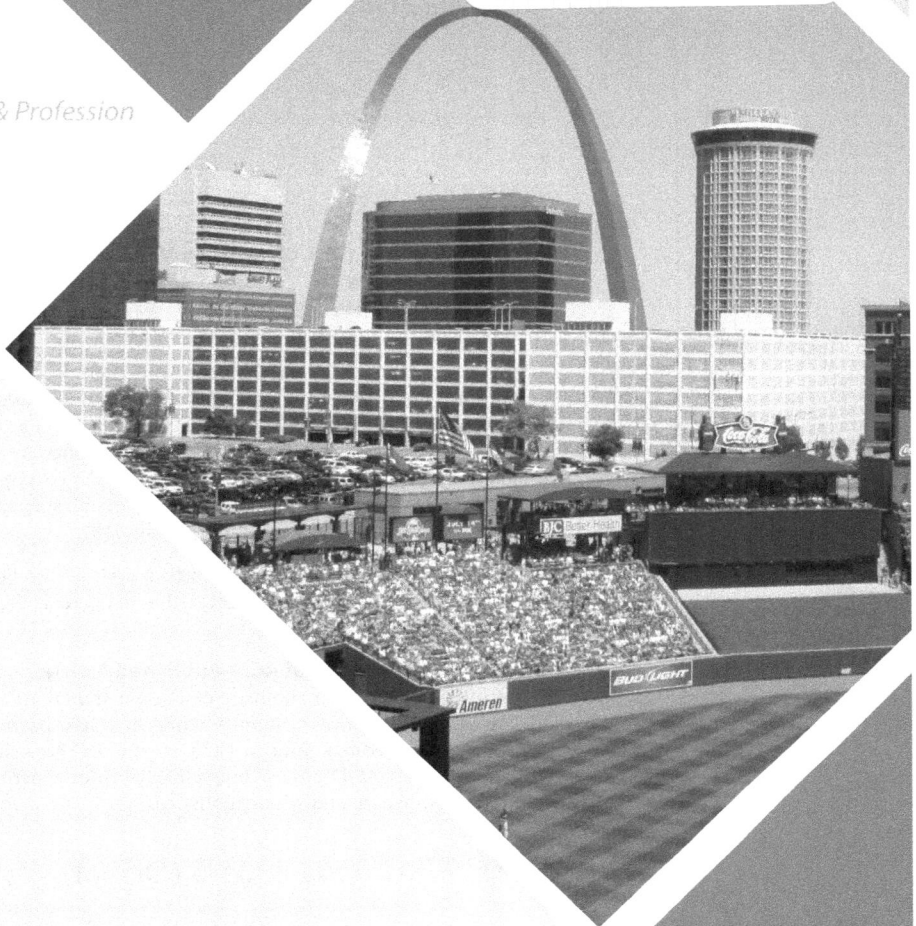

HT'12

The Proceedings of 23rd ACM Conference on

Hypertext and Social Media

Sponsored by:
ACM SIGWEB

Association for Computing Machinery

Advancing Computing as a Science & Profession

The Association for Computing Machinery
2 Penn Plaza, Suite 701
New York, New York 10121-0701

Notice to Past Authors of ACM-Published Articles
ACM intends to create a complete electronic archive of all articles and/or other material previously published by ACM. If you have written a work that has been previously published by ACM in any journal or conference proceedings prior to 1978, or any SIG Newsletter at any time, and you do NOT want this work to appear in the ACM Digital Library, please inform permissions@acm.org, stating the title of the work, the author(s), and where and when published.

ISBN: 978-1-4503-1335-3 (Digital)

ISBN: 978-1-4503-1880-8 (Print)

Additional copies may be ordered prepaid from:

ACM Order Department
PO Box 30777
New York, NY 10087-0777, USA

Phone: 1-800-342-6626 (USA and Canada)
+1-212-626-0500 (Global)
Fax: +1-212-944-1318
E-mail: acmhelp@acm.org
Hours of Operation: 8:30 am – 4:30 pm ET

Printed in the USA

Chairs' Welcome

It is our great pleasure to welcome you to *ACM Hypertext 2012,* the 23rd ACM Conference on Hypertext and Social Media (HT'2012) which is held at the campus of the University of Wisconsin-Milwaukee in Milwaukee, Wisconsin, from June 25–28, 2012.

The ACM Hypertext and Social Media conference is a premium venue for high quality peer-reviewed research on hypertext theory, systems and applications. It is concerned with all aspects of modern hypertext research including social media, semantic web, dynamic and computed hypertext and hypermedia as well as narrative systems and applications. This year's HT'12 conference focuses on exploring, studying and shaping relationships between four important dimensions of links in hypertextual systems and the World Wide Web: *people, data, resources and stories.* This focus is reflected in the four tracks we have:

- **Social Media (Linking people)**
  chaired by Claudia Müller-Birn and Munmun De Choudhury
- **Semantic Data (Linking data)**
  chaired by Harith Alani and Alexandre Passant
- **Adaptive Hypertext and Hypermedia (Linking resources)**
  chaired by Jill Freyne and Shlomo Berkovsky
- **Hypertext and Narrative Connections (Linking stories)**
  chaired by Andrew S. Gordon and Frank Nack

Three keynote speakers for HT'12 present novel and stimulating ideas in this context: Steffen Staab, Jure Leskovec and Sinan Aral. Steffen Staab is a professor for databases and information systems at the University of Koblenz-Landau and director of the institute for Web-Science and Technologies (WeST). His interests lie in researching core technology for ontologies and semantic web as well as in applied research for exploiting these technologies for knowledge management, multimedia and software technology. Jure Leskovec is an assistant professor of Computer Science at Stanford University. His research focuses on mining and modeling large social and information networks, their evolution, and diffusion of information and influence over them. Sinan Aral is an Assistant Professor and Microsoft Faculty Fellow at the NYU Stern School of Business. His research focuses on social contagion and measuring and managing how information diffusion in massive social networks affects information, worker productivity, consumer demand and viral marketing.

HT'12 received 120 submissions in total, with 89 full paper and 31 short paper submissions. Each submission was reviewed by at least three reviewers, discussed by the track program committee, and finally discussed among the program chair Markus Strohmaier and the track co-chairs Claudia Müller-Birn, Munmun De Choudhury, Harith Alani, Alexandre Passant, Jill Freyne, Shlomo Berkovsky. Andrew S. Gordon and Frank Nack. We were able to accept 33 full and short papers for oral presentation and publication in the proceedings (27 full papers, 6 short papers). Thus, the overall paper acceptance rate for HT'2012 is 27.5%. In addition to this program, we have accepted a number of posters and we will also feature an exciting program of workshops and tutorials thanks to the effort of Arkaitz Zubiaga and Carlos Solis. Thanks to Alvin Chin, we have disseminated all information about important HT'12 deadlines and activities through online social media.

The program with (free) workshops and tutorials, three keynotes, social activities and generous student grants has been made possible through the sponsorship of ACM SIGWEB. In addition, to SIGWEB's support, Hypertext 2012 has received generous support from Taylor & Francis, the publisher of the New Review of Hypermedia and Multimedia, and from our host institution, the College of Engineering and Applied Science of the University of Wisconsin-Milwaukee.

We hope that this program provides interesting ideas and novel stimuli for the attendees of HT'12, and we are looking forward to an exciting event.

Ethan Munson   **Markus Strohmaier**

HT'12 General Chair   *HT'12 Program Chair*

University of Wisconsin - Milwaukee, USA   *Graz University of Technology, Austria*

Table of Contents

HT 2012: Hypertext and Social Media

General Chair: Ethan Munson, University of Wisconsin - Milwaukee, USA

Program Chair: Markus Strohmaier, Graz University of Technology, Austria

Publicity Chair: Alvin Chin, Nokia Research Center, Beijing

Workshop Chairs: Arkaitz Zubiaga, Queens College, City University of New York, USA
Carlos Solis, FEXCO, Ireland

**Semantic Data Track
Co-chairs:** Harith Alani, Open University, UK
Alexandre Passant, DERI, Ireland

Program Committee Members: Fabian Abel, TU Delft, Netherlands
Lora Aroyo, VU University Amsterdam, Netherlands
Sören Auer, Universität Leipzig, Germany
Ivan Cantador, Universidad Autonoma de Madrid, Spain
Gianluca Correndo, University of Southampton
Klaas Dellschaft, University of Koblenz
Ying Ding, Indiana University, USA
Miriam Fernandez, Knowledge Media Institute, OU, UK
Fabien Gandon, INRIA, France
Tudor Groza, University of Queensland, Australia
Andreas Harth, AIFB, Karlsruhe Institute of Technology
Michael Hausenblas, NUIG, Ireland
Conor Hayes, NUIG, Ireland
Pascal Hitzler, Kno.e.sis, Wright State University
Andreas Hotho, University of Würzburg, Germany
Geert-Jan Houben, TU Delft, Netherlands
Vanessa Lopez, IBM, Ireland
Natasha Noy, SMI, Stanford University
Matthew Rowe, Knowledge Media Institute, OU, UK
Marta Sabou, MODUL University, Austria
Milan Stankovic, Hypios, France
Thanassis Tiropanis, University of Southampton, UK
Tania Tudorache, SMI, Stanford University
Mischa Tuffield, PeerIndex, UK
Fouad Zablith, Knowledge Media Institute, OU, UK

HT 2012 Sponsor & Supporters

Sponsor:

Supporters:

Taylor & Francis Group
an **informa** business

UNIVERSITY of WISCONSIN
UWMILWAUKEE

How To Do Things With Triples

Steffen Staab
Institute for Web Science and Technologies (WeST)
Universität Koblenz-Landau
Koblenz, Germany
staab@uni-koblenz.de

ABSTRACT

Representing and computing pragmatics for linked data requires the usage of various models, including ontology patterns and navigation models, as well as new programming language constructs.

Categories and Subject Descriptors

E.2 [**Data Storage Representations**]: Linked Representations

Keywords

Semantic Web, Linked Data, Ontology Patterns

1. EXTENDED ABSTRACT

In his famous book Austin [1] asked how to do things with words. He has argued convincingly that beyond the sheer representation of words for concepts, objects, events or relationships, the words in a sentence may fulfill very different roles, i.e. beyond the semantics of words their pragmatic use of of utmost importance. Indeed the same sentence can imply very different actions performed by the speaker when uttering this sentence. For instance, a sentence like

> "Berlin is the capital of Germany."

could imply different things depending on who says it in which context with which pronounciation.

1. The president has made a declaration and by that declaration Berlin became the capital of Germany.

2. A teacher has communicated a piece of information for students to learn.

3. A participant in a quiz show has answered a question about which is the capital of Germany or about which country Berlin is a capital of.

In linked data, we can easily represent the words and the semantics of the above example sentence. However, is there also a necessity and a possibility to explore the pragmatics of linked data? What kind of pragmatics of linked data exist? I.e. how do we use linked data to perform an act or to let users perform an act?

I will argue that while people speak words to perform speech acts, we run programs to act on linked data (satisfying some underlying user need). The programs interact with linked data to create, read and update data. However, as the pragmatics of an utterance can usually not be confined to a single word, the pragmatics of linked data is typically tied to a configuration of triples. Our own research [4] and others [2] have illustrated that the pragmatics of linked data can be described through patterns in the underlying ontologies. These patterns can be content patterns as used in ontology engineering [3, 5] or other patterns, e.g. models for hypertext navigation [2].

In order to facilitate the expression of pragmatics we need explicit means for representing and programming with such patterns and for a tighter interaction between linked data and the programming paradigms in use. We find that novel approaches such as type providers[1] are a promising step towards better doing things with triples.

Acknowledgments

I thank Daniel Schwabe for fruitful discussions about Sync [2] and the useage aspects of linked data. I thank the participants of the Spring MindSwap on Information Rich Programming (http://west.uni-koblenz.de/events/springmindswap) for their discussions. This research has been co-funded by the EU in FP7 in the SocialSensor project (287975) and by the EU IRSES project Net2.

2. REFERENCES

[1] J. L. Austin. How to do Things with Words. 1962.
[2] M. H. de Souza Bomfim and D. Schwabe. Design and implementation of linked data applications using shdm and synth. In S. Auer, O. Díaz, and G. A. Papadopoulos, editors, *ICWE*, volume 6757 of *LNCS*, pages 121–136. Springer, 2011.
[3] V. Presutti and A. Gangemi. Content ontology design patterns as practical building blocks for web ontologies. In Q. Li, S. Spaccapietra, E. S. K. Yu, and A. Olivé, editors, *ER*, volume 5231 of *LNCS*, pages 128–141. Springer, 2008.
[4] S. Scheglmann, A. Scherp, and S. Staab. Declarative representation of programming access to ontologies. In *9th Extended Semantic Web Conference, ESWC 2012*. Springer, 2012.

---

[1]http://msdn.microsoft.com/en-us/library/hh156509%28v=vs.110%29.aspx

[5] A. Scherp, C. Saathoff, T. Franz, and S. Staab. Designing core ontologies. *Applied Ontology*, 6(3):177–221, 2011.

CV

Steffen Staab is professor for databases and information systems at the University of Koblenz-Landau and director of the institute for Web Science and Technologies (WeST). His interests lie in Web Science research including core technologies for social media, linked data and ontologies. He is Editor-in-Chief of the Journal of Web Semantics and has been PC Chair of WWW-2012.

Reverts Revisited – Accurate Revert Detection in Wikipedia

Fabian Flöck
Institute AIFB
Karlsruhe Institute of
Technology
Karlsruhe, Germany
fabian.floeck@kit.edu

Denny Vrandečić
Institute AIFB
Karlsruhe Institute of
Technology
Karlsruhe, Germany
denny.vrandecic@kit.edu

Elena Simperl
Institute AIFB
Karlsruhe Institute of
Technology
Karlsruhe, Germany
elena.simperl@kit.edu

ABSTRACT

Wikipedia is commonly used as a proving ground for research in collaborative systems. This is likely due to its popularity and scale, but also to the fact that large amounts of data about its formation and evolution are freely available to inform and validate theories and models of online collaboration. As part of the development of such approaches, revert detection is often performed as an important pre-processing step in tasks as diverse as the extraction of implicit networks of editors, the analysis of edit or editor features and the removal of noise when analyzing the emergence of the content of an article. The current state of the art in revert detection is based on a rather naïve approach, which identifies revision duplicates based on MD5 hash values. This is an efficient, but not very precise technique that forms the basis for the majority of research based on revert relations in Wikipedia. In this paper we prove that this method has a number of important drawbacks - it only detects a limited number of reverts, while simultaneously misclassifying too many edits as reverts, and not distinguishing between complete and partial reverts. This is very likely to hamper the accurate interpretation of the findings of revert-related research. We introduce an improved algorithm for the detection of reverts based on word tokens added or deleted to adresses these drawbacks. We report on the results of a user study and other tests demonstrating the considerable gains in accuracy and coverage by our method, and argue for a positive trade-off, in certain research scenarios, between these improvements and our algorithm's increased runtime.

Categories and Subject Descriptors

H.5 [**Information Interfaces and Presentation**]: Group and Organization Interfaces—*Collaborative computing, Computer-supported cooperative work, Web-based interaction*; H.1 [**Models and Principles**]: User/Machine Systems—*Human factors*

Keywords

Wikipedia, revert detection, editing behavior, user modeling, collaboration systems, community-driven content creation, social dynamics

1. INTRODUCTION

Wikipedia is a prime example of what can be achieved by mass collaboration on the Web. Its open, participatory policies supported by user-friendly collaboration technology have encouraged millions of Internet users to turn into Wikipedia editors, and dedicate themselves to the creation and continuous improvement of what has become the world's largest (online) encyclopedia. The same principles guide Wikipedia's handling of information, enabling and inspiring a great number of research studies about its content, community and processes, which lead to new insights in the fields of collaborative systems and user behavior. In addition to its primary content, Wikipedia grants free access to a huge amount of historical metadata concerning a large share of its editing activities.[1] This wealth of resources, including detailed usage and edit logs, are often used by scholars to inform and validate their theories and models of online collaboration.[2]

One of the basic tools when analyzing Wikipedia editor behavior is referred to as 'revert detection', which is typically defined as the task of finding edits that undo one or more previous edits (a full discussion about the notion of a revert is given in Section 2). In practice, and taking into account the very nature of the editing process in Wikipedia, revert detection forms a foundational step for many (more elaborated) research ideas, and its purposeful handling leads to a superior understanding of wiki-like systems of collaboration in general. It is used as input and filter for a variety of analysis tasks, including the extraction of implicit networks of editors, the analysis of edit or editor features that influence the chance of a given edit to be reverted, and the removal of noise when analyzing the emergence of the content of an article.

Despite its importance as a pre-processing step, most research work capitalizing on reverts-related information relies on a rather naïve revert-detection approach. In a nutshell, the approach discovers identical revisions of an article based on the MD5 hash values of the corresponding changes, and considers all edits lying between two consecutive revision duplicates as being reverted. Although its coarseness is discussed in some work (see Section 3), the extend of its oversimplification of revert behavior has not yet been acknowledged in its full range of implications. We argue that this approach is neither sound nor complete; it detects only a (in some cases very limited, see Section 5) share of the actual reverts - as they are defined and understood in Wikipedia editing practice, cf. Section 2 - and falsely classifies many co-occurring editing activities as reverts, thus leading to lower-quality analysis data which is

---

[1] A small number of edits is not made available due to legal reasons such as, for instance, copyright laws.
[2] The datasets are available at http://download.wikimedia.org.

very likely to hamper the accurate interpretation of the findings of Wikipedia-related research in areas as those mentioned earlier.

In this paper, we introduce an algorithm improving the detection of reverts in terms of accuracy and coverage. This is achieved by comparing edits based on the actions they perform, which are measured by means of the word tokens they add or delete.[3] To evaluate its performance against the naïve approach currently in use, we conducted a user study and other tests, which clearly provide evidence of significant gains in accuracy and coverage, in particular when considering full (as opposed to partial, see Section 2) reverts giving substance to in-depth studies of editing behavior at the level of individual articles.

The remainder of this paper is organized as follows. Section 2 first introduces the terminology used in the paper, elaborating on the definition of reverts and edits, and motivating the need for revisiting revert detection in Wikipedia. Section 3 gives an overview of the current state of the art in the field and discusses the deficiencies of existing approaches in more detail. Section 4 explains our revert-detection algorithm. Section 5 presents the results of the evaluation, including the positive trade-off between the benefits in accuracy and coverage achieved by the improved method and its potentially increased computational costs compared to the baseline approach. The paper is concluded by a summary of the findings and an outline of planned future work in Sections 6 and 7, respectively.

2. REVERTS AS BASIS FOR USER BEHAVIOR MODELING

In the official Wikipedia guidelines the definition of a 'revert' reads as follows: *"**Reverting** means undoing the effects of one or more edits, which normally results in the page being restored to a version that existed sometime previously. More broadly, reverting may also refer to any action that reverses the actions of other editors, in whole or in part."*[4] Text passages from other Wikipedia pages concur with this definition, see *"A revert means undoing the actions of another editor."* on the Wikipedia:Edit_warring page.[5] The notion of a 'revert' is further discussed and established in the following section. Furthermore, we would like to define a set of basic terms used in the remainder of this paper as follows:

- An 'edit' is the act of changing the content of an article followed by saving these changes to a new version of the article.

- A 'revision' is a version of the article created by an edit. That is, edit 1 creates revision 1, edit 2 creates revision 2, and so on.

- A 'reverting edit' is an edit that carries out a revert, i.e., reverts one or more other edits.

- A 'reverted edit' is an edit whose changes to an article are undone partly or completely by a reverting edit ex post. The article version that is changed by the reverting edit is the 'reverted revision'.

Within Wikipedia, reverting can be carried out in different ways:[6]

1. Manual reverting, which means deleting text from or adding text to an article by hand.

2. Activating the 'undo' button next to an edit in the article history dialog. It enables to undo the actions performed by only that specific edit.

3. Using the 'rollback' feature, which immediately reverts all top consequent edits made by the last editor, going back to a previous version of the corresponding article. It is available to administrators and editors who have been explicitly granted the right to use this function.

Article editing is one of the most frequent user activities in Wikipedia. As of September 2011, 10.9 million edits are made on a monthly basis, with 3.5 million alone in the English Wikipedia.[7] The edits logged in the Wikipedia article-history dumps provide a rich footprint of previous and ongoing user activities, which can be leveraged in a variety of behavioral studies. The research reported here is based on data from the English Wikipedia. However, the method we present should be applicable to most other language Wikipedia's, provided a means to split Wikitext into word tokens, which are the unit on which our method operates.

Editing in Wikipedia refers to the actual encyclopedic articles, to the pages discussing other aspects of the overall collaborative project, as well as to the talk pages associated with the articles. In our work we focus on the first of the three Wikipedia-namespaces, due to its predominance in Wikipedia-related research.[8] For each edit the system logs a variety of metadata, including the name and ID of the article, the date- and timestamp, the username or IP of the editor, the content of the revision in wiki syntax, and a short comment. However, there is much more, potentially relevant insight to be gained by looking at indirectly gathered information; in particular, to analyze the social dynamics among editors, it is essential to study their (direct or indirect) inter-actions in terms of, for instance, specific user activities and their effects on the activities of other users. There are a few user actions that potentially inform such editor relations and can be derived from the editing logs available. One of the most prominent examples is probably 'co-editing', which refers to editing by multiple editors that content-wise steers an article in a similar direction: for example, two editors making edits that introduce similar statements into an article in different subsections. Nevertheless, measuring this type of activities assumes knowledge of the actual meaning of the edits undertaken, in order to identify those which are in agreement with the overall direction of the article. By contrast, reverts may reliably yield evidence of the relation of the actions (edits) of editors indirectly, even without having to take into account the semantics of the content. Let us illustrate how inferences about editor interrelations could be drawn based on rather shallow knowledge of the content of an edit through a simple example: If edit 1 establishes an article consisting only of the

---

[3]The algorithm is available for further usage by interested researchers at http://people.aifb.kit.edu/ffl/reverts/

[4]http://en.wikipedia.org/wiki/Wikipedia:Reverting, also compare http://en.wikipedia.org/wiki/Help:Reverting (accessed 13.09.11, bold from original, italics added).

[5]http://en.wikipedia.org/wiki/Wikipedia:Edit_warring (accessed 13.09.11, italics added).

[6]http://en.wikipedia.org/wiki/Help:Reverting, (accessed 13.09.11)

[7]http://stats.wikimedia.org/reportcard/RC_2011_09_detailed.html and http://stats.wikimedia.org/EN/TablesDatabaseEdits.htm (both accessed 03.11.2011).

[8]Reverts in the discussion namespace are rare as the goal is not to produce a single collaborative piece of content. For other namespaces of Wikipedia besides articles, the question of how to model reverts, in particular the applicability of an approach analogue to the one which is subject of this paper, remains to be investigated in future work.

word apple', edit 2 adds 'pie' after apple' and edit 3 deletes only the word 'pie', we can conclude intuitively that edit 3 deleted the content introduced by edit 2. If these were edits by two different editors, we can further assume that the editor of edit 3 wanted to delete the content introduced by the editor of edit 2 without considering the meaning conveyed by the words that are added and deleted in the process.

As briefly explained through the example above, reverts are relatively easy to extract and interpret compared to other types of editing activities, while providing an essential insight into the behavior of editors. A number of works on Wikipedia have been using reverts as a metric in their studies, be it on general trends involving reverts [16], correlation of the chances of getting reverted with specific editor or edit characteristics [7], using reverts as an indicator of damage repair and vandalism fighting [10, 13], or considering them in some other ways when analyzing editing behavior [8]. By looking into the user interaction modeled through the detected reverts and combining the reverts with additional data generated from the article history and other available sources, it is possible to extract the behavioral interrelations of editors in various ways, for instance by building a social network graph of editors inside an article, as it has been done by Kittur et al.[11]. In the case of social network modeling, it is especially important to not only detect who was reverted or who was reverting, but also *who was reverted by whom*, i.e., to model the antagonistic dynamics in an article on a detailed and accurate level to unveil the fine-grained conflicts and interrelations between users.

Data quality is always a relevant issue when it comes to interpreting reverts, but it is essential in making sense of the social dynamics a the level of individual articles, which can sometimes mean interpreting conflicts among only a handful of users who influence the direction of the entire article. We specifically aim to devise a revert detection method that is suited to deliver data to understand and model these intra-article socio-technical mechanisms in Wikipedia, as discussed in earlier work of ours [6]. Achieving this aim poses, however, higher demands on the quality of the method as is currently delivered by available techniques, as a large number of false-positives and -negatives in the results might lead to grave misinterpretations of editor relations. We give examples for this in Section 3. It is for these reasons necessary to be able to rely on the accuracy and completeness of the identification of edits as 'reverts'. This, in turn, requires a precise and purposeful notion of what a 're-vert' is, and a revision of existing methods operationalizing revert detection to accommodate this theoretical understanding.

3. STATE-OF-THE-ART IN REVERT DETECTION

Wikipedia-related research using reverts as a metric [5, 7, 8, 11, 13, 16, 12] almost invariably deems only so called 'identity reverts' as an appropriate means to investigate revert behavior.[9] This approach relies on finding two revisions containing exactly the same content via MD5 hashes [15].[10] Subsequently, all edits lying between two identical revisions are considered as *reverted*, with the

second identical revision as the *reverting* edit, and the first one as the one *reverted to*. As defined by Halfaker et al. in [7]: "A revert is a special kind of edit that restores the content of an article to a previous revision by removing the effects of intervening edits.". Table 1 shows an example of how reverts are detected in this manner.

Beside such work using identic revisions to detect reverts, there is research discussing types of reverts and actions to be considered reverts more in-depth, as well as the implications and complexity of reverts in Wikipedia (e.g. [14]). But those publications do not introduce an algorithm evaluated to detect reverts in a more accurate way. The work by Adler, Chatterjee and de Alfaro [1, 2] implements very elaborated approaches for keeping track of addition and removal of words in an article by different editors. But it is neither aimed at, nor evaluated in respect to precisely detecting revert relations between editors.

Where used in the research literature mentioned above, the basic identity revert detection method (SIRD) is never explicitly ex ante motivated by a theoretical concept of revert behavior or by any definition established by the Wikipedia editor community. Rather, the motivation for using SIRD as stated (representatively) by Halfaker et al. is that it "is computationally simple and determining exactly which editors' revisions were lost due to the revert is straightforward." [7]. The underlying (implicit) notion of what a revert is can be seen as a simplification of how Wikipedia defines the concept ("[...]which normally results in the page being restored to a version that existed sometimes previously.", see Section 2). It does not require the reverting edit to actually *undo the actions* of an edit identified as reverted (compare the indicated revert of edit 4 by edit 5 in Table 1). As such the revert detection method is also not able to make distinctions concerning the relationship between reverting and reverted edit: It is not possible to indicate if the reverting edit fully, partly or not at all undo the actions of the reverted edit (again, compare the example in Table 1). It also does not require the intention of the reverting edit to revert any other edit.

SIRD supposedly detects most of the existing reverts: Kittur et al. showed that by combining a method based on edit comments, (looking for the keywords 'revert' and 'rv') and SIRD, 95% of the *reverting edits* found as a result could be found using only identity reverts [11].[11] In a number of subsequent papers [7, 13, 16], this finding was used to conclude that the mere 5% additional reverting edits found by looking at comments do not justify the effort of using this additional source of information on top of the SIRD method. Still, to our knowledge, there was no dedicated investigation so far if other detection methods might find even more reverts,[12] as many users do not attach comments to their edits [11, 13, 16] and MD5 hashes cannot be used to find partial reverts that do not produce identical revisions [7].

In terms of a 'real-world-check' of the conceptualization underlying the SIRD method, there has not been any testing of the false-positive-rate of the delivered results, in the sense of evaluating it

---

[9]There is some other work that identifies reverts solely based on regular expressions (e.g., using keywords such as 'rv','revert') in edit comments, calling it a 'reasonable proxy' for revert detection [10] (also [9]). But this is to be neglected here as the work cited as source for this statement clearly states that "MD5 (identity) reverts actually capture more revisions than user-labeled (comment) reverts (3.7M vs. 2.4M), suggesting that a substantial number of reverts are not labeled as such" [11].

[10]The MD5 hash sum is commonly used to check if two file or text contents are identical.

[11]In the paper, the authors refer to such edit pairs as the found 'reverts' while actually they report the number of found reverting edits that either have an identical previous version or a comment mentioning the two keywords [11]. Where identified by comments, it cannot be in all cases concluded *what* revisions were actually reverted when there is no identical version (i.e., in the case of a partial revert) and no indicator in the comment (e.g., in the case of a comment consisting only of one of the keywords).

[12]Ekstrand et al. [5] compared cosine similarity and adoption coefficient approaches with the SIRD for finding revision history "trees". They come to the conclusion that the SIRD algorithm is a better solution for representing revision relationships than the other two approaches.

Table 1: Example of the result of the simple identity revert detection method

Edit number	Revision content (text)	Words deleted/added (actions taken) in the edit	MD5 hash (simplified)	Detected reverts
1	Zero	+'Zero'	Hash1	(Reverted-to by edit 5)
2	Zero Apple Banana	+'Apple' +'Banana'	Hash2	Reverted by edit 5
3	Zero Apple Banana Coconut Date	+'Coconut' +'Date'	Hash3	Reverted by edit 5
4	Zero Coconut Date	-'Apple' -'Banana'	Hash4	Reverted by edit 5
5	Zero	-'Coconut' -'Date'	Hash1	Reverting edits 2, 3, 4

against the Wikipedia definition of a revert or what is perceived as a revert by Wikipedia users. This means there was no evaluation, for instance, if the actions of identified *reverted* edits are really undone in subsequent *reverting* edits. This is a crucial issue especially in the light of the very simplistic, technology-driven definition of a revert the SIRD method implicitly builds upon. Although we know of at least one analysis toolkit (pyMWDat)[13] that extends to some degree the above described basic definition of reverting and reverted edits, we are so far not aware of an elaborate and working algorithm modeling revert behavior, which is designed to capture reverts based on a more realistic definition of how reverting and reverted edits are related.[14]

The inability of the SIRD method to detect reverts that do not create a duplicate revision is acknowledged by Priedhorsky et al., who state that beside the identity revert exists the "*effective revert*, where the effects of prior edits are removed (perhaps only partially)." [13]. Such cases cannot be fully detected using only MD5 hashes [7]. In Table 1, this is exemplified by the actions of revision 4, which deletes all words introduced by revision 2, while still generating a completely new revision content. Intuitively, one could say that revision 4 is *effectively* reverting revision 2, as it undoes all its actions; this interpretation conforms with the Wikipedia revert definition. The SIRD method, however, will not detect the revert relationship in this way, but instead, as shown in the example, detect revision 5 as reverting revision 2, because it (incidentally) lies between two identical revisions. In a scenario where revision 5 would be non-identical to revision 1, the method would not even detect any revert of revision 2. This illustrates the logical inconsistencies of the conceptual model on which SIRD implicitly operates. Note that this is only one of a number of many example scenarios in an edit history we found, where the SIRD method leads to a questionable result. Additional examples are given in Section 4.

The coarseness of SIRD is further discussed by Priedhorsky et al. [13], who note that understanding and taking into account the intention of a revert is challenging (and thus not feasible), while the method already covers one of the most common types of reverts (producing identical revisions) at an, arguably, sufficient level of quality. This statement is, however, neither proved, nor is it necessary an acceptable argument considering the current features of Wikipedia: The manual revert and the undo feature as accessible to common registered Wikipedians do not automatically generate an identical revision, but can, and presumably often do, generate partial reverts. This leads to the likely assumption that they make up the vast majority of non-bot reverts. The rollback feature, which

undoes all edits after a specified revision, on the other hand, is available only to a few editors with the corresponding access rights, including administrators.

As a conclusion, when setting the Wikipedia revert definition as a benchmark for the understanding of revert behavior in current Wikipedia editing practice, the coverage (finding all actual reverts) and accuracy (finding only true-positives) of the SIRD method are suboptimal. Edits are always and only detected as reverted if they lie between two identical revisions for reasons which are not further taken into account. This has a number of important consequences:

- Edit pairs are detected as reverts that cannot be seen as reverts when compared to known edit behavior in Wikipedia and the general understanding of editing practice of the contributors;

- there might be many reverts still to be found by untested methods; and

- for those reverts that are found by the current approach, it cannot be distinguished to which extent a revert took place (full revert, 20%, 70% partial revert, and so on).

Partial reverts are more complicated to use in modeling social interactions than full reverts; for the latter, it is at least known that *all* actions of an editor have been undone, while for the former, the range of possible interpretations of the revert action is comparatively much wider.[15] When using the results of a revert analysis in scientific work, it should therefore at least be possible to in- or exclude partial reverts or select down to which degree of undoing the detected edits should be treated as reverts. This applies in particular to those scenarios where a thorough analysis based on a comparatively smaller data corpus is of interest, such as the editing behavior in one specific Wikipedia article. These scenarios motivated the development of the method presented in the next section.

4. AN IMPROVED REVERT DETECTION METHOD

4.1 Revert definition

The first step towards devising a more accurate revert detection method was to establish a clear conceptual foundation of what a revert is, followed by an algorithm that detects all and only those edits that fit the corresponding definition.

The Wikipedia revert definition was used as a reference point, as it states what actions constitute a revert as a behavior of an editor, and as it is grounded in the common editing practice of the Wikipedia community. For assessing the results of our method versus SIRD, we gave priority to detecting edits that are

---

[13] Available at http://code.google.com/p/pymwdat/ (accessed on 06.11.11)

[14] As noted in the documentation of the tool, pyMWDat works as the described by SIRD method, but differentiates between the revisions marked as 'reverted', in other words, those made by the first editor after the 'reverted-to' revision is marked as 'possible vandalism', while the remaining reverted edits are classified as a separate group of 'good-will edits'.

[15] To give an example, the removal of a word from a 600-word-entry could mean only a small correction, while adding the word 'not' in a certain position could change the meaning of the whole entry.

1. No false-positives, i.e., only reverts fitting the used definition; and

2. Full reverts, as only for those edits we can safely assume they were fully undone and thus unambiguously indicate an reverted-reverting relationship to be leveraged in social-graph-modeling and interpreting the results.[16]

According to these pre-requisites and taking into account what kind of data can be reliably used to identify reverts, the following definition was set up:

"An edit A is reverted if all of the actions of that edit are completely undone in one subsequent edit B. Edit B has then reverted edit A."

Note that this definition does not rule out that edit B performs other actions on top of undoing A's actions or the actions by a number of different edits (for an example see Table 2, where edit 8 is reverting edits 6 and 7). In addition, if A's actions have been undone only partially, this is not counted as a partial revert according to the used definition. Accordingly, if all of A's actions have been undone in a collective effort by many partly reverts, A is not counted as reverted (although all its actions were undone) An example is given in Table 2 (edits 9 to 11 are not reverting edit 8). This is due to the fact that, in this case, it would not be possible to assign a single reverting edit B, and thus not unambiguously determine the reverting and the reverted edit in every case. Those two restrictions do not comply with the Wikipedia concept of a revert, as it comprises partial reverts as well. Still, they were introduced to account for the aforementioned prerequisites. In doing so, our approach trades some of its coverage (of detecting all reverts as stated in the Wikipedia definition) for ease of computational and interpretational processing. Still, the approach is superior - assuming the Wikipedia definition - to the state of the art method in accuracy, coverage and the meaningfulness of the found reverts, as we will discuss in Section 5.

4.2 Algorithm

To operationalize the actions of the editors we use added and deleted word tokens, i.e., character chains separated by white spaces. We operate on the wiki syntax, not on the front-end article content.

Before taking a look at the specific word changes of an edit, we eliminate unchanged paragraphs from the preceding and current revision in order to reduce the amount of text that has to be collated via rather costly text difference comparisons (DIFFs). We first split up the syntax text into paragraphs via double line breaks. Each paragraph is assigned an MD5 hash value. When comparing the preceding and current revision, all paragraphs with matches in their hash values are discarded for the next step, as they were not altered by the edit leading to the current revision.[17] As most edits change no more than one or two paragraphs, this pre-filtering step proved to yield significant runtime improvement during testing of our algorithm.

To compare the remaining (edited) paragraphs, text difference comparisons are used.[18] The location of the word tokens within the article text is not taken into account, i.e., the revision content

is treated as a bag-of-words. For every edit B_n in the article history, we check via text DIFFs if its previous i edits A_{n-1} to A_{n-i}, performed the exact opposite of a subset of actions of B_n, starting with A_{n-1}. The maximum scan-range i is in our example set to 20 previous revisions (we discuss the size of i in Section 5). If a negative matching subset is found in A_{n-1} we do not look for the same subset in the following A_{n-2} to A_{n-20}, as the action of A_{n-1} can only be undone once. In the next step, a content list for B is generated, containing the revision identifiers of all revisions still part of the article text. If no negated subset was found in the previous 20 edits, solely the ID of the revision produced by edit B is added to the content list. If one or more of the previous 20 edits contain a negated subset of B, then the revision ID of those edits A_{n-i} is removed from the content list for B. If B, on top of reverting other edits, added or deleted additional content that does not have a matching negative subset in the previous 20 edits, its revision ID is also added to the content list. Table 2 illustrates the procedure.

When performing the computation discussed above, we filter out so called 'blankers' from the list of possible reverting edits. Blankers are edits deleting the whole content of an article, which should not be treated as common reverting edits, as their behavior cannot be interpreted as an intentional act aimed at undoing the specific edits whose added content they delete. Rather, the vandalistic intention is aimed at harming the article as a whole.

Comparing revisions 1 to 5 in Table 2 with the example in Table 1 shows that, with our method and adhering to our definition, revision 5 is only reverting revision 3, while revision 4 is reverting revision 2. This indicates higher accuracy (according to Wikipedia's definition) in comparison to SIRD. With our method, we additionally detect the revert by revision 8 of revisions 6 and 7, where no duplicate revisions can be found. This means our method is potentially able to find more reverts than SIRD.

There are many other examples of reverts where our method can extract much more meaningful revert information compared to the baseline approach.[19] One very frequently occurring scenario is the repair of a vandalistic revision by several subsequent revisions, all trying to recreate the revision before the vandalism occurred. If the last one in this row of repair edits recreates the last vandalism-free revision, all other repair edits will be marked as reverted with the SIRD method, although each of the edits did only a partial revert. With the DIFF method and the definition introduced earlier in this section, we do not incorrectly assign reverts in this setting.[20]

Note as well that, if using a different definition (e.g., the full Wikipedia definition), our algorithm can be adapted to find partial reverts in addition to full reverts, covering scenarios as the revert of edit 8 in Table 2. As the DIFFs between revisions are already calculated in the current implementation of the method, it is only

---

[16]As noted earlier, the modeling of a social network at the level of individual articles was the main motivation for devising a new revert detection method.

[17]According to our definition, we do not count simple rearrangements of text as reverts.

[18]To find reverts adhering to our definition using DIFFs does suffice. We do not rule out adding other methods in a next step to increase the performance of our method further. We discuss this shortly in Section 7.

[19]We identified a large number of theoretical and practical cases by hand, where reverts do not produce identic revisions or where the simple SIRD approach is imprecise. They are not all listed here because of space constraints.

[20]An example: let the actions by edit 8 in Table 2 be considered vandalism. We then assume that edits 9, 10 and 11 are trying to repair damage caused by edit 8. While edits 9 and 10 overlooked some vandalistic effects, edit 11 eventually restores the last vandalism-free revision 7. In this case, the SIRD algorithm would have assigned edit 11 as the reverting edit of edits 8, 9 and 10, although, according to Wikipedia's definition, at least the actions of edits 9 and 10 were not undone. That means that we, on the one hand, do not detect the revert of edit 8 (false negative), but on the other hand, avoid detecting false-positives, i.e., the revert of 9 and 10 by edit 11. As vandalism reverting is a very common activity in Wikipedia, we assume the trade-off is positive.

Table 2: Example of the result of the improved revert detection method

Edit number	Revision content (text)	Words deleted/added (actions taken) in the edit	Content list (revision ##)	Detected reverts
1	Zero	+'Zero'	1	
2	Zero Apple Banana	+'Apple' +'Banana'	1;2	Reverted by 4
3	Zero Apple Banana Coconut Date	+'Coconut' +'Date'	1;2;3	Reverted by 5
4	Zero Coconut Date	-'Apple' -'Banana'	1;3	Reverting 2
5	Zero	-'Coconut' -'Date'	1	Reverting 3
6	Zero Fig	+'Fig'	1;6	Reverted by 8
7	Zero Fig Grape	+'Grape'	1;6;7	Reverted by 8
8	Zero Huckleberry	-'Fig' -'Grape' +'Huckleberry'	1;8	Reverting 6, 7
9	Zero Huckleberry Grape	+'Grape'	1;6;8	
10	Zero Huckleberry Fig Grape	+'Fig'	1;6;7;8	
11	Zero Fig Grape	-'Huckleberry'	1;6;7	

necessary to build the content list on a word token basis instead of a revision ID basis.

4.3 Implementation

We implemented the SIRD approach and our new algorithm in Python.[21] To decrease runtime, we parallelized the algorithms using the Wikimedia Utilities by Aaron Halfaker, which provide a high-performance framework for analyzing large amounts of Wikipedia data.[22]

The input for both algorithms is a list of all revisions for a given article, consisting of the revision ID and the text of the revision. Both scripts also implement the detection of blankers, as noted earlier. For generating the text DIFFs, the "difflib" library of Python is used, as it correctly produces the needed revision differences.

Whereas the hashing algorithm as part of SIRD runs very efficiently (new content hashes are compared to previous ones), the new algorithm produces results much slower (it is quadratic over the number of words in the DIFFs). As in this work, we focused on showing the qualitative differences of the detected revert relations between the two methods, we optimized the runtime of our algorithm only to a certain extent. There are a number of pre-filtering techniques we are about to implement in future work, as pointed out in Section 7, which will potentially decrease the execution time further. Also, the algorithm needs to be executed only once for each revision and the resulting DIFFs can be saved and made accessible as metadata to the Wikipedia article revisions, so that repeated calculations (for example with a different revert definition) can be performed at much shorter runtimes, as the DIFF execution is the most computationally expensive part.

5. EVALUATION

We evaluated both the accuracy and the coverage of the reverts found by the DIFF method against the baseline SIRD approach.

5.1 Accuracy evaluation

For comparing the accuracy of the revert detection we set up a revert assessment survey with Wikipedia editors.[23] Only Wikipedia editors were chosen as we are interested in results that conform with what the Wikipedia community perceives as a revert. The survey was conducted for 11 days in October 2011. Participants were recruited through several internal Wikipedia outlets such as the Community Portal and the Village Pump.[24] We set up two samples of 20 assessment steps to be evaluated by the participants.[25]

The first sample (referred to as sample A) of 20 assessment steps consisted of 9 edit pairs detected as a revert only by the DIFF method, 9 detected only by the SIRD method and, as a control group, 2 pairs detected by both methods in the same way. 29 users completed this first sample and all assessment steps.[26] The second sample (sample B) consisted of 8 edit pairs detected as a revert solely by the DIFF method, 8 detected only by the SIRD method and 4 pairs detected by both methods. 16 participants, distinct from the assessors of the first sample, completed all steps in this sample.[27]

The samples were designed to include more SIRD- and DIFF-only edit pairs than results identified by both approaches, because the aim of the evaluation was to compare them against each other. The samples of 9, 9, 2 (A) and 8, 8, 4 (B) edit pairs, respectively, were randomly drawn from the pool of all unique revert-pairs detected by the two methods in five randomly selected Wikipedia articles. To generate the edit pairs, the number of i previous revisions to be scanned for reverted edits (as explained in Section 4.2) was set to 20.[28]

---

[21] Both scripts are available under an open-source license from http://people.aifb.kit.edu/ffl/reverts/

[22] https://bitbucket.org/halfak/wikimedia-utilities/wiki/Home

[23] All participants were asked if and how long they had been an editor. All were editors who performed reverts on a regular basis themselves. We asked for the length of their tenure as editor and their experience with reverts, which both had no significant impact on the answers. We also have no reason to believe the self-selection of participants introduced a bias in the answers.

[24] Community Portal: http://en.wikipedia.org/wiki/Wikipedia:Community_Portal
Village Pump: http://en.wikipedia.org/wiki/Wikipedia:Village_pump (both accessed 25.10.11).

[25] We preferred to restrict the number of assessment steps to 20, as first tests showed that participants did otherwise abort the survey prematurely due to its perceived over-length.

[26] Nine users were excluded in total from the two samples, as they aborted the survey after only one or two questions. This was done to prevent a potential bias in more and possibly different answers for earlier questions.

[27] Unfortunately, no more than 16 participants volunteered to complete the assessment steps for sample B, which was set up after 29 users completed sample A. The number of edit pairs detected by both methods was raised slightly sample B to get assessments for a bigger sub-sample of these edits.

[28] The rationale behind this design decision was that an intentional revert targeting specific content is likely to happen within a limited window of edits after the original edit took place, as changes stay in focus of the community (and the change logs) for a limited amount

Was edit 1 reverted by edit 2 according to the Wikipedia definition?

EDIT 1

Version BEFORE edit 1:

Line 21:

Most songs off this album, merge both [[metal]] and [[hip hop music|hip hop]] (although the former is quite prevalent, especially in "One Step Closer" and "Runaway").

"Hybrid Theory" is also notable for its absence of
− profanity, in contrast to many other nu metal bands' records.

==Miscellaneous==

Version AFTER edit 1:

Line 21:

Most songs off this album, merge both [[metal]] and [[hip hop music|hip hop]] (although the former is quite prevalent, especially in "One Step Closer" and "Runaway").

"Hybrid Theory" is also notable for its absence of profanity, in contrast to many other nu metal bands'
+ records. It is also based largely on the life of the Marvel Comics superhero Spider-Man.

==Miscellaneous==

EDIT 2

Version BEFORE edit 2:

Line 21:

Most songs off this album, merge both [[metal]] and [[hip hop music|hip hop]] (although the former is quite prevalent, especially in "One Step Closer" and "Runaway").

"Hybrid Theory" is also notable for its absence of profanity, in contrast to many other nu metal bands'
− records. It is also based largely on the life of the Marvel Comics superhero Spider-Man.

==Miscellaneous==

Version AFTER edit 2:

Line 21:

Most songs off this album, merge both [[metal]] and [[hip hop music|hip hop]] (although the former is quite prevalent, especially in "One Step Closer" and "Runaway").

"Hybrid Theory" is also notable for its absence of
+ profanity, in contrast to many other nu metal bands' records.

==Miscellaneous==

- ○ FULL REVERT of edit 1 BY edit 2
- ○ PARTIAL REVERT of edit 1 BY edit 2
- ○ NO REVERT
- ○ I have no clue.

Figure 1: Screenshot of an assessment step in the survey

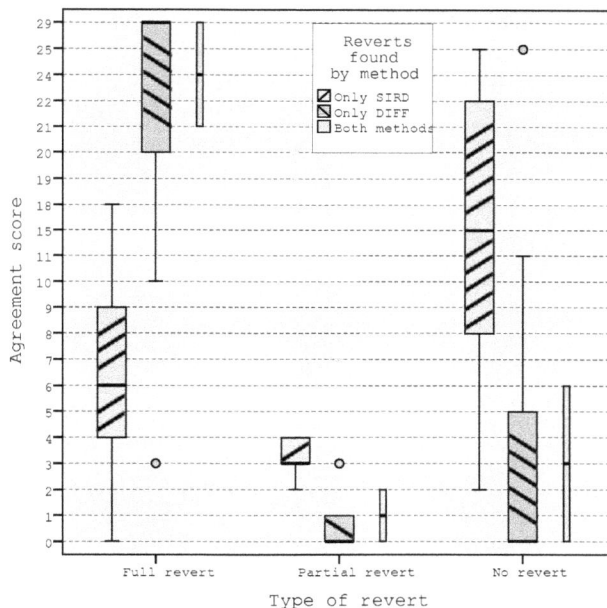

Figure 2: Boxplot comparison of the means of agreement score between all three methods, grouped by indicated type of revert for sample A (25th and 75th percentiles as box, 1.5x interquartile range (IQR) as whiskers, outliers > 1.5*IQR, extremes > 3*IQR)

An assessment step consisted of two text DIFFs, exactly as known from the Wikipedia revision history feature.[29] Figure 1 depicts a sample assessment step. The first DIFF, shown on the top of the page, represented edit 1 (the DIFF showed what was changed by edit 1). The second DIFF depicted edit 2, which was a subsequent edit from the same article identified as the reverting edit of edit 1 by one of the revert detection methods. The use of colors and the "+/-" signs were adapted without changes from Wikipedia, as explained on the respective "Help:Diff" page.[29]

Participants were asked if, according to the Wikipedia definition of a revert, edit 2 had reverted edit 1. The answer options included 'Full revert', 'Partial revert', 'No revert' and 'I don't have a clue.'. The participants were provided with the Wikipedia revert definition in each assessment step (omitted in Figure 1) and were particularly asked to apply this definition in their assessment, and not their own definition, if different. At the end of the survey we asked the respondents if the Wikipedia definition conformed with their own definition of a revert, on a Likert-scale from 1 (no agreement) to 5 (full agreement). 17 editors answered this question, with 15 voicing full agreement and two agreeing only partly (scores 2 and 3).

For each of the two samples, containing 20 edit pairs each, the overall agreement of the participants that the corresponding pair was either a full revert, a partial revert or no revert, was computed. The assessed edit pairs received 29 (16) votes, distributed over the three revert types (or "I don't have a clue.").[30] Consequently, the

revert types could achieve a score from 0 up to all 29 (16) participants agreeing in each assessment step. Figure 2 and Table 3 show the average agreement of participants over all edit pairs for each of the two methods and each of the three types of revert.[31] When asked if the displayed edit-pair was a full revert, in the mean 22.4 (12.6) of the participants expressed their agreement for the pairs found only by the DIFF method, while only 7.4 (3.8) did so for the edit pairs detected only by the SIRD method. This difference in the agreement score means was significant at $p < 0.01$ ($p < 0.01$).[32] When asked if an edit pair was a partial revert, the agreement was at a mean of 6.7 (3.9) for the SIRD method and at 1.2 (1.1) for the DIFF method. With $p < 0.1$, this difference was, however, not significant for sample A, but significant at $p < 0.01$ for sample B. When asked if an edit-pair was no revert at all, i.e., a false positive, a mean of 14.3 (8) participants agreed for the edit pairs detected only by the SIRD, while only a mean of 5 (2.3) said so for the pairs detected solely by our DIFF method. This difference was significant, at $p < 0.05$ ($p < 0.05$). The means of agreement for the control group of the edit pairs found by both methods were generally aligned with those of the new-method-only edit pairs in both samples, as they revealed no significant differences (therefore excluded from the summary of results in Table 3). They were not aligned with the means of the SIRD-only sample, as can be observed in Table 3. For sample A, only the difference in the agreement scores

---

of edits. This was confirmed through additional evidence collected by manual assessment we conducted. From this assessment, we had good reason to assume maximum accuracy at $i = 20$.

[29] http://en.wikipedia.org/wiki/Help:Diff (accessed 01.11.11).

[30] Numbers of sample B are put in brackets, henceforth.

[31] The raw data of the survey answers can be found at http://people.aifb.kit.edu/ffl/reverts/
The box plot for sample B was omitted as it showed very similar agreement scores to sample A, thus yielding no additional information other than confirming our previous findings.

[32] The mean agreement for the pairs found by both methods was 25 (14.8). It was significantly different from the SIRD-method-only sample at $p < 0.01$, but not significantly different from the new-method-only sample.

for full reverts differed significantly ($p < 0.01$), but for sample B, all differences were significant. The means of agreement for the answer "no clue" are not listed here as they were very low (< 0.6) for both methods and samples and all revert types, and there were no significant differences.

Table 3: Means of agreement scores for different methods and revert types, for both survey samples

Sample A	n	Full revert	Partial revert	No revert
DIFF only	9	22.4	1.2	5
Difference		$p < 0.01$		$p < 0.05$
SIRD only	9	7.4	6.7	14.3
Difference		$p < 0.01$		
Both methods	2	25	1	3
Sample B	n	Full revert	Partial revert	No revert
DIFF only	8	12.6	1.1	2.3
Difference		$p < 0.01$	$p < 0.05$	$p < 0.05$
SIRD only	8	3.8	3.9	8
Difference		$p < 0.01$	$p < 0.05$	$p < 0.01$
Both methods	4	14.8	0.8	0.3

Differences tested via Student's T-test. P-values only shown where significant with $p < 0.05$ and always depicting the differences between means below and above. n stands for the number of assessment steps/ edit pairs.

5.2 Coverage of revert detection

To evaluate the performance of our method against SIRD with respect to the number of reverts detected, we analyzed a sample of 5000 randomly selected articles, which were no redirect pages. They contained a total of 392724 edits, which equals 77.116 billion possible combinations of edit pairs. The results were generated via two scripts implementing the two methods under evaluation, as described in Section 4.3. First, we report on the results produced with a maximum scan-range of $i = 20$ previous revisions for identic hashes and, respectively, corresponding DIFFs, as used for the accuracy evaluation in Section 5.1.

In total, 75278 unique edit pairs were detected as reverts in the articles by the two methods. Of those reverts, 39816 were found by both methods in the exact same manner, 14495 were found only by the SIRD method, and 20976 were found only by the new method. Table 4 gives an overview of the results. Thus, for 27% of the reverts found by the SIRD, the new method found different reverts. On top, the new method found about 12% more reverts than the SIRD method. The runtime on a 2.80 GHz Intel Xeon, 4 core, Debian Squeeze 64bit system with 8GB RAM, running with four threads and measured with the Unix 'time' command was 4 min 16 sec for SIRD and 51 min 52 sec for the new method, respectively.

When carried out with a maximum scan-range of $i = 50$ and $i = 100$, the number of reverts found by both methods as well as the difference between the two methods grew considerably. The new method found 19% and 24% more reverts, respectively, as can be seen in Table 4. The table also shows the increase in runtime for a larger size of the edit window.

5.3 Discussion of the evaluation results

Regarding accuracy, participants of the revert assessment agreed that in the mean, for the new method, the found edit pairs are (1) less often false positives, i.e., no actual reverts and (2) more often full reverts than those pairs found only by SIRD.

When we consider the basic definition of a revert SIRD operates with, and the scenarios in which this oversimplification can lead to suboptimal revert classification, as demonstrated in Section 4, the results make a strong case for the more accurate revert detection offered by our method. The explanatory power of the results might be to some extent impaired by the relatively small sample of assessment steps and survey participants. Nevertheless, the high significance of the key findings, and the fact that two distinct groups of Wikipedians assessed two distinct sets of edit pairs in an almost identical fashion speaks for the generalizability of the observations. The survey results for the new DIFF method appear to be in accordance with the part of the detected reverts which both methods are able to find. It becomes clear from the answers of the editors that the share of reverts that is solely identified by the SIRD method is in the mean significantly more often wrong and finds considerably fewer full reverts compared to the total number of reverts detected.

Looking at this number, the new method is able to detect from 12% (at $i = 20$) up to 24% (at $i = 100$) more reverts than SIRD. When operating on larger editing windows the accuracy might decrease because the new method will more likely match negative subsets of word tokens that were not meant to be reverted by the potential reverting edit. An example would be the deletion of the common word 'a' in such a case. If 'a' was introduced 6 edits ago, it is more likely that this is the same 'a' that was deleted. If the addition of 'a' is found, say, 99 edits ago, the likelihood of being a revert target of the current edit is comparatively lower, as this token could, for instance, be from a completely other part of the text, could have been missed in a previous step of the DIFF calculation, and so on. This means that decreasing the window size in this example would increase the likelihood to find an actual revert.

Nevertheless, at least for $i = 20$, we can postulate the following based on the analysis of the evaluation: Given the result of a revert analysis with the SIRD method on a set of edits, our method is able to detect different revert-pairs that are significantly less likely to be false-positives and more likely to be full reverts for 27% of the revert-pairs detected by the baseline approach. In addition, the new method finds 12% more revert-pairs of the same, higher accuracy than does the SIRD method. Note that we excluded partial reverts from the detection for this evaluation. The resulting number of detected reverts would increase considerably when including these.

Another aspect that speaks in favor of the new method is the following: SIRD gives preference to detecting reverts that produce an identical revision. This is more likely to happen when the rollback function (see Section 2) is used, as rollbacks invariably return an article to a pre-existing revision. It is less likely to happen for undo-based and manual reverting. As the rollback function is available only to administrators and editors with special rights, the majority of editors has to make use of the remaining two procedures in order to revert. It is therefore plausible that reverts detected via identical revisions were conducted by a disproportionately high number of users with special rights and administrators. In turn, the reverts left undiscovered by SIRD are more prone to being carried out by 'common' editors. In this manner, SIRD introduces a bias towards a special user group. So, even given a theoretical high accuracy in detecting reverts that can be identified with identical hashes, this bias would exists when relying solely on this method.

Looking at these results, it must be concluded that Wikipedia research work that bases its inferences on data derived via the SIRD method runs the danger of being missguided. Not fully acknowledging these impairments or dismissing them as ignorable noise in the data is more than tenuous; at least if the aim is to model the complex dynamics in specific articles on a detailed and accurate level.

Table 4: Number of detected reverts (edit pairs) in article sample by methods, with runtimes, for different levels of i

i		Pairs detected by		Gain by DIFF	Total unique detected pairs	Detected by both methods	Det. only by SIRD	Det. only by DIFF	Runtime SIRD	Runtime DIFF
		SIRD	DIFF							
20	Absolute	54311	60783	6472	75278	39816	14495	20967	4m 16s	61m 52s
	%	-	-	12	100	52.2	19.3	27.9		
50	Absolute	55647	66115	10468	81714	40048	15599	26067	4m 27s	74m 22s
	%	-	-	19	100	49.0	19.1	31.9		
100	Absolute	56101	69549	13448	85604	40076	16025	29503	4m 45s	79m 01s
	%	-	-	24	100	46.8	18.7	34.5		

6. CONCLUSION

In this paper, we provided new substantial evidence that simple revert detection via MD5 hash values is not sufficient to accurately capture all relevant revert relationships between Wikipedia editors and that these shortcomings seem to be more grave than generally suspected in the research work that applies this method[33]. We presented a new method for the detection of reverts in Wikipedia which compares edits based on the actions they undertake at the level of word tokens added or deleted. Our method relies on a revert notion which is closer to the official Wikipedia guidelines, and to the general understanding of the Wikipedia community with respect to reverting behavior.

As revealed by a user study, our method, without implementing a very complex algorithm, is more accurate in identifying full reverts as understood by Wikipedia editors. More importantly, our method detects significantly fewer false positives than the SIRD method; this is due to the simplified revert model the SIRD method operates on, which does not perform optimally in practice when extracting revert data for realistically modeling editor behavior in Wikipedia. A limiting factor for these encouraging results is the fact that the assessed samples of edit pairs and editors were by no means large. However, the answers of two distinct groups of Wikipedians on two distinct samples of edit pairs showed almost identical assessments. Given these oberservations, combined with the key findings being highly significant and an algorithm built on a solid theoretical foundation, rooted in the Wikipedia community's revert definition, we are confident that our results can be further generalized. Concerning the number of identified reverts, we found that an average 27% of the revert pairs detected by SIRD are not accurate in the above regard and that the DIFF method we developed can not only detect the same amount of reverts with better accuracy, but on top finds 12% more revert pairs than the baseline approach.

While outperforming the baseline approach in terms of quality of results, the major drawback of our algorithm is the increased computational cost. As it is quadratic over the number of words in the DIFFs, in its current implementation it might not be the tool of choice if larger amounts of articles are to be analyzed; especially in the case of complete history dumps of the large Wikipedias, e.g., English, German or Spanish.[34] For this purpose, SIRD has the clear advantage of a shorter runtime. When used to compare revert trends over time for a complete Wikipedia history dump or large batches of articles to each other, the lack of accuracy may for some research scenarios prove negligible in favor of computational efficiency.[35] Still, when calculating relations between editors at the article level and dealing with other tasks that require a in-depth look on reverts, using SIRD introduces the risk of misinterpreting and wrongly modeling revert actions. In particular, the editorial social system of an article, to be studied via social network analysis or visualization, requires an accurate and complete capturing and depiction of what is happening among key editors and editor camps. We are confident that research relying on SIRD for that purpose due to the lack of alternatives [11] or proposing similar modeling [6] will profit from the accuracy and coverage gain of our method.

We believe that our findings can be transferred to any other wiki system that shows editor characteristics and functionalities similar to Wikipedia, given the Wikitext can be split into word tokens. This, of course, has to be subject of further research.

7. FUTURE WORK

In order to improve the efficiency of our algorithm, we are experimenting with additional pre-filtering techniques such as W-Shingling[4] and Bloom filters[3], which we yet have to evaluate regarding the quality of the results.

We are planning to continue our experiments investigating the effects of an increased maximum scan-range of revisions i (see Section 4) on accuracy and coverage. Preliminary insights revealed that choosing an edit frame size of 20 is likely to yield optimal results.

Acknowledgements

The research leading to these results has received funding from the European Union's Seventh Framework Programme (FP7/2007-2013) under grant agreement no. 257790, project RENDER.[36] Special thanks go to Andriy Rodchenko and Maribel Acosta of the KIT Karlsruhe for their efforts regarding the implementation work.

8. REFERENCES

[1] T. Adler and L. Alfaro. A content-driven reputation system for the Wikipedia. In *WWW '07: Proceedings of the 16th international conference on World Wide Web*, pages 261–270, 2007.

[2] T. Adler, K. Chatterjee, L. Alfaro, M. Faella, I. Pye, and V. Raman. Assigning trust to Wikipedia content. In *International Symposium on Wikis*, 2008.

---

[33] It of course depends on the specific research work if and what actual effect these shortcomings have on the eventual outcome of that research.

[34] Of course, the calculated DIFFs (which require the majority of the computational effort) can be reused once generated. But this is of little practical implication as they are not available for many articles yet.

[35] Given the generation of identical revisions through reverts stays almost the same over time, which is not necessary the case when new revert-features are introduced or abolished, as it is the case with the rollback feature. In inter-article comparison, one has to assume an equal production rate of identity reverts per revert in all articles, in turn.

[36] http://www.render-project.eu

[3] F. Bonomi, M. Mitzenmacher, R. Panigrahy, S. Singh, and G. Varghese. An improved construction for counting bloom filters. In *Algorithms – ESA 2006*, volume 4168 of *Lecture Notes in Computer Science*, pages 684–695, 2006.

[4] A. Z. Broder, S. C. Glassman, M. S. Manasse, and G. Zweig. Syntactic clustering of the web. *Computer Networks and ISDN Systems*, 29(8–13):1157–1166, 9 1997.

[5] M. D. Ekstrand and J. T. Riedl. rv you're dumb: Identifying discarded work in wiki article history. In *The Fifth International Symposium on Wiki's and Open Collaboration*, Orlando, FL, Oct. 2009.

[6] F. Flöck, D. Vrandečić, and E. Simperl. Towards a diversity-minded Wikipedia. In E. Munson, D. W. Hall, D. de Roure, and S. Staab, editors, *Proceedings of the ACM 3rd International Conference on Web Science 2011*, 06 2011.

[7] A. Halfaker, A. Kittur, R. Kraut, and J. Riedl. A jury of your peers: quality, experience and ownership in Wikipedia. In D. Riehle and A. Bruckman, editors, *Int. Sym. Wikis*. ACM, 2009.

[8] A. Kittur, E. H. Chi, B. A. Pendleton, B. Suh, and T. Mytkowicz. Power of the few vs. wisdom of the crowd: Wikipedia and the rise of the bourgeoisie. In *Proceedings of the 25th Annual ACM Conference on Human Factors in Computing Systems (CHI 2007)*, 2007.

[9] A. Kittur and R. E. Kraut. Beyond wikipedia: coordination and conflict in online production groups. In *Proceedings of the 2010 ACM conference on Computer supported cooperative work*, CSCW '10, pages 215–224, New York, NY, USA, 2010. ACM.

[10] A. Kittur, B. A. Pendleton, and R. E. Kraut. Herding the cats: the influence of groups in coordinating peer production. In D. Riehle and A. Bruckman, editors, *Int. Symposium on Wikis '09*. ACM, 2009.

[11] A. Kittur, B. Suh, B. A. Pendleton, and E. H. Chi. He says, she says: conflict and coordination in Wikipedia. In *Proceedings of the SIGCHI conference on Human factors in computing systems*, CHI '07, pages 453–462, New York, NY, USA, 2007. ACM.

[12] S. K. Lam, A. Uduwage, Z. Dong, S. Sen, D. R. Musicant, L. Terveen, and J. Riedl. Wp:clubhouse? an exploration of wikipedia's gender imbalance. In *WikiSym 2011*, Mountain View, CA, 10/2011 2011. ACM, ACM.

[13] R. Priedhorsky, J. Chen, S. T. K. Lam, K. Panciera, L. Terveen, and J. Riedl. Creating, destroying, and restoring value in Wikipedia. In *GROUP '07: Proceedings of the 2007 international ACM conference on Supporting group work*, pages 259–268, New York, NY, USA, 2007. ACM.

[14] R. Priedhorsky and L. Terveen. Wiki grows up: arbitrary data models, access control, and beyond. In *7th International Symposium on Wikis and Open Collaboration*, pages 63–71, Mountain View, CA, 10/2011 2011. Association for Computing Machinery (ACM).

[15] R. Rivest. The MD5 Message-Digest Algorithm, 1992.

[16] B. Suh, G. Convertino, E. H. Chi, and P. Pirolli. The singularity is not near: slowing growth of Wikipedia. In *Proceedings of the 5th International Symposium on Wikis and Open Collaboration*, WikiSym '09, pages 8:1–8:10, New York, NY, USA, 2009. ACM.

Leveraging Editor Collaboration Patterns in Wikipedia

Hoda Sepehri Rad   Aibek Makazhanov   Davood Rafiei   Denilson Barbosa

Department of Computing Science
University of Alberta,Edmonton,Canada
{sepehrir,makazhan,drafiei,denilson}@ualberta.ca

ABSTRACT

Predicting the positive or negative attitude of individuals towards each other in a social environment has long been of interest, with applications in many domains. We investigate this problem in the context of the collaborative editing of articles in Wikipedia, showing that there is enough information in the edit history of the articles that can be utilized for predicting the attitude of co-editors. We train a model using a distant supervision approach, by labeling interactions between editors as positive or negative depending on how these editors vote for each other in Wikipedia admin elections. We use the model to predict the attitude among other editors, who have neither run nor voted in an election. We validate our model by assessing its accuracy in the tasks of predicting the results of the actual elections, and identifying controversial articles. Our analysis reveals that the interactions in co-editing articles can accurately predict votes, although there are differences between positive and negative votes. For instance, the accuracy when predicting negative votes substantially increases by considering longer traces of the edit history. As for predicting controversial articles, we show that exploiting positive and negative interactions during the production of an article provides substantial improvements on previous attempts at detecting controversial articles in Wikipedia.

Categories and Subject Descriptors

H.4 [**Information Systems Applications**]: Miscellaneous

Keywords

Wikipedia, Admin Election, Social Interactions, Controversial Articles

1. INTRODUCTION

The recent proliferation of social technologies such as Weblogs, Wikis, social networking sites, etc. has been met with widespread adoption by a large fraction of the general

time	editor	action	Δ	comment
3:55	Infinity0	Rv	—	revert weasel words and pov
4:06	RJII	Rv	412	revert to rjii infinity is misleading the readers to think that tucker opposes employee employer relations...
4:09	Infinity0	Rv	-412	it says that tucker supported private mop please read your version uses many weasel words
4:12	RJII	Del	-131	anarcho capitalism tag
4:15	RJII	Ins	382	noting that tucker supports liberty of people to engage in employee employer relationships don't censor this fact
4:29	Infinity0	Del	-12	anarcho capitalism what's dubious it's a direct quote
5:21	Infinity0	Del	-264	anarcho capitalism
12:03	*other*[†]	Ins	41	ruined it

[†] Different user, with id VolatileChemical.

Figure 1: Partial edit history of article on Anarchism.

population, who have crossed the line from consumers to producers of content. This phenomenon, which now seems irreversible, has had a tremendous impact on how large segments of society get informed and educated. One particular example of this trend is Wikipedia, which has become one of the 5 most visited websites [4] (up from 500-th in 2004). Anecdotal evidence points to problems and virtues of relying on Wikipedia [9], but the trend seems to be that Wikipedia will indeed become the primary source of reference for most common knowledge in the world.

One of the major strengths of Wikipedia, its openness, is also one of its main sources of criticism. The argument is that virtually anyone can edit any Wikipedia article, regardless of their intentions and/or knowledge about the topic of said article. Even for articles where all editors are well intentioned and knowledgeable, the diversity of opinions and points of view will lead to disagreement during the editing process. Since editing is a continuous process, it is possible that consecutive visits to the same article return drastically different material, possibly reflecting the different biases and opinions of different editors. Quality control in this model is delegated to the crowd—if the topic is important to a large enough group of editors, the collaborative editing process will (eventually) lead to a high-quality article. Also, the entire *edit history* of the article is made available to the reader—who could in principle inspect it before deciding whether or not to trust the content (see, e.g., Figure 1). Finally, articles whose editing process deteriorate into flagrant disputes are explicitly marked as controversial by a group of *administrators*, most of whom are elected by their peers (other editors), warning the readers about the contentious or disputable nature of the content that they may read.

A question that arises in this context is whether or not one can detect the attitude (positive or negative) of editors towards each other from the recorded history of interactions between them, in the articles they co-edit. This would be useful to automate the identification of controversial articles, for instance. Figure 1 shows a small fragment of the edit history of the article on Anarchism around March of 2006 (the "Δ" column indicates the net change in length of the article, measured in characters between consecutive versions). At the time of writing, the article contained 15,767 edits. We focus on the interactions between two editors: *RJII*, who contributed 1,544 edits, and *Infinity0*, who made 433 edits. The disagreement between these editors is evidenced by their direct mutual accusations and the difference in their use of language: in this article, on average, *RJII* writes longer comments than *Infinity0* (70.6 characters vs 49.3 characters) and also uses more *positive* terms in his comments (423 versus 115). The sequence and timing of the actions is also revealing. The two editors are working concurrently, sometimes *fully* undoing each other's work (called *reverting* versions and indicated as Rv or revert action in the Wikipedia logs) and other times doing so *partially*, by deleting or inserting content to the previous version (indicated as Del and Ins actions, respectively).

While the history snippet above is clear evidence that these two editors did not collaborate, it should be clear that analyzing the edit history of articles in search of disagreements and potential controversies would be virtually impossible for the reader. The sheer volume of data and the frequency with which the edit histories change make such an approach impractical. Moreover, not every editor writes descriptive comments. In fact, there were several examples in further interactions involving *Infinity0* in which he/she would simply revert back to a previous version without any justification. Another issue is that focusing on individual editors is unlikely to lead to good results as well. Again in this example, several editors "teamed up" with *RJII* against *Infinity0*.

1.1 Our Contribution

We propose a method to predict the attitude (positive or negative) between two editors based on the edit history of their interactions. Using this method, we build a signed network [23] of all editors of an article which allows us to infer whether or not the said article contained controversial material.

Our methods are based on machine learning, using classifiers. To obtain labeled training data, we resort to a *distant supervision* approach, using the *records* of Wikipedia administrator elections. For every vote of editor e_1 for editor e_2, we extract all interactions between them and label such interactions according to the vote. Our intuition is that a vote for administrator is an unequivocal declaration of *agreement* or *disagreement* among editors. Indeed, in our motivating example, *RJII* voted against *Infinity0* when he ran for administrator, emphatically voicing his opinion with comments such as "NO WAY! The kid is OUT OF CONTROL... [his] philosophy is to ban an editor whose edits would otherwise prevail... EXTREMELY unethical".

We validate our model in two ways. First we use it to predict actual votes in the administrator elections. Our results show an interesting contrast: overall, one can predict *positive votes* among editors with a markedly higher accuracy. However, the accuracy when predicting negative votes increases more as we increase the number of interactions in the edit history. This suggests that positive interactions and attitudes between editors are the norm, and that negative interactions are not easily forgotten by editors. We also validate our classifier for controversial content on a sample of 480 articles (240 marked as controversial by the administrators). Our results are very encouraging, leading to 84% accuracy overall. We compare our method against other alternatives, including a classifier based on a completely different set of features, and whose accuracy is around 75%. We combine both classifiers as well, increasing the accuracy further to almost 90% in our tests.

2. RELATED WORK

Our work relates to the following areas.

Trust management in Wikipedia. Among the large body of work on Wikipedia, our work mostly relates to trust and reputation management, where a trust score is assigned to an article [6,16,34], to selected parts of an article [2], or even to contributors [3,7,17]. These works often use information from the edit history (or the so-called revision history) of an article, including edit operations and the way the article evolves in response to an edit, for their scoring. For instance, *reverts* (undoing an edit) and *restores* (changing back to an earlier version) are treated as direct indications of respectively distrust and trust in most of these work; depending on the reputation of the initiator editor, the reputation of the recipient editor is identified.

Text stability is exploited by other authors, [2,3,21] with the intuition that an edit or text that remains longer as part of the article has been approved implicitly by other editors compared to an edit that is undone very soon, hence implying some notion of trust. Having access to visit log data, the number of visits is another metric used as the notion of the quality or impact of a contribution in [26].

Other features that are used to establish some notion of trust are the reputation of the editors of previous versions [10,34], interactions in other contexts such as admin elections and barnstars [24], and finally the degree of intervention of admins in monitoring and improving articles [17].

Our work is also related to coordination and conflict modeling in Wikipedia. For instance, Kittur et al. [20] uses several article-level metrics such as the number of authors, the number of versions, the number of anonymous edits, etc. to train a model for predicting the number of controversial tags assigned to an article. Similarly, using these tags as the ground truth, Vuong et al. [31] built a model to assign a controversy score to articles assuming a mutual reinforcing relationship between controversy score of articles and their contributors.

Identifying attitudes in other domains. Considerable work has been done in *sentiment analysis* in many different domains, ranging from product reviews [25] to forum discussions and news [8,29]. Sentiment analysis aims at classifying statements about a topic, event or product as either positive or negative, but does not directly extract relationships between people. However, it can be used to classify people based on the similarity of their stated opinions to supporting or opposing camps [29].

On a more related level, there is also work on extracting agreement or disagreement relationships in conversational meetings or discussion forums [11, 14, 15]. For meetings in particular, these relationships are learned from a wide range of features such as the number of words in the utterance of the first speaker, the number of common n-grams in their utterances [11, 15], and the previous history of agreement or disagreement between the two speakers [11]. For forums, the attitudes of participants are inferred from the sentences that contain second person pronouns and a sentiment word [14]. Depending on the sentiment expressed in these sentences, a positive or negative attitude is assigned between the corresponding participants of each sentence.

Social Network Analysis. Our work is also related to link prediction or inference in both unsigned and signed networks. Gilbert et al. [12] used seven different categories of features and a linear regression model to learn the strength of links between users in Facebook. The model was trained on a dataset with 2000 links collected from responses of 35 participants about the strength of their relationships with random members of their friends list. In another work [32], a notion of link strength between users was established based on the pairwise similarity of their profiles and their interaction histories and was tested in both Facebook and LinkedIn.

Finally, the link prediction was studied in a more recent work [23] in the context of two well-known theories from social psychology, namely *balance*, and *status*, and was tested on three different domains: Slashdot, Epinions, and Wikipedia admin election.

3. TERMINOLOGY

In this section, we define some of the key technical terms that we use later in the paper.

DEFINITION 1. *We say an interaction happens between two editors e_1 and e_2 if they both edit the same article and their edits are related.*

Two edits may be considered related under multiple circumstances. For example, two edits may be considered related if they are applied to the same or near-by sections of an article; also one would expect related edits to happen within some temporal proximity with not many other edits falling between them. This is on the basis that an edit may be triggered by or may rectify to improve an earlier edit, and with a large gap between two edits, this hypothesis may not hold. For our purpose of inferring interactions between editors, the following gives a more clear and workable definition of relatedness.

DEFINITION 2. *Two edits are related if they are both applied to the same article and the distance between the edits in terms of the number of intermediate versions is less than a threshold.*

The distance between edits is defined in terms of the number of versions the article goes through between the edits, instead of elapsed time, to account for the variance that exists in activity rate of different articles. To set the threshold

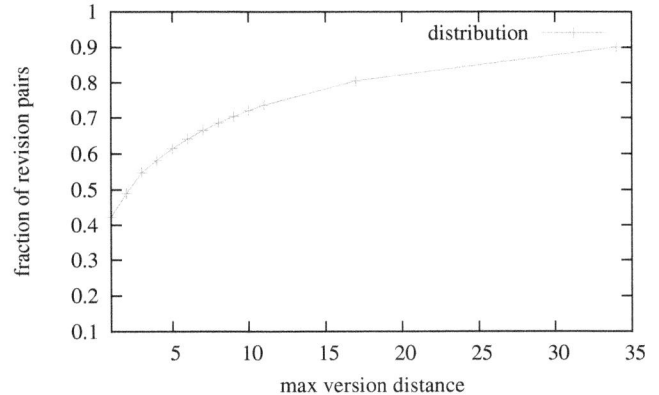

Figure 2: Distance distribution of revision pairs editing the same section

for related edits, we look at the maximum distance of all pairs of edits that modify the same *section*[1] of the same Wikipedia article. Intuitively, two versions editing the same section are more likely to be the result of a collaboration interaction and be related than two edits on different parts of the same article or different articles.

Figure 2 shows the cumulative distribution of the pairs of revisions editing the same section in terms of the maximum distance (i.e. number of versions) in between. The data for this plot comes from a random sample of 100 Wikipedia articles. As one can see, these revisions in about 40% of times are happened in two consecutive versions, while 70% are applied within 9 or less versions, and finally over 90% of them are at most 34 versions apart. Thus, we set the threshold for edits to be related at 34.

DEFINITION 3. *Collaboration profile is an ordered summary of a set of statistics about the individual activities of each of the e_1 and e_2 editors on editing Wikipedia articles, along with their pairwise interactions on the set of their co-edited articles.*

For each collaboration profile, cp_{e_1,e_2}, a sign (positive or negative) can be assigned denoting the supporting or opposing attitude of editor e_1 toward editor e_2. This attitude can be potentially different from the attitude of e_2 toward e_1 (cp_{e_2,e_1}). Hence, in the profile of cp_{e_1,e_2}, we refer to e_1, and e_2 as the *source* and the *target* editors respectively.

DEFINITION 4. *A collaboration network is a directed, signed graph $G = (V, E)$ associated with a Wikipedia article a, where V is the set of all editors who contributed in creating at least one revision for a, and $E \subset V \times V \times W$ is the set of weighted edges connecting editors with non empty collaboration profiles.*

A directed edge from e_1 towards e_2 with weight w represents an existence of a cp_{e_1,e_2}, and w is a number that can be positive or negative depending on the type of the collaboration profile. In a *binary* signed collaboration network, $w \in \{-1, +1\}$, while in a *weighted* signed collaboration network, w can be any real number, often normalized within $[-1, +1]$.

---

[1]Every article in each of its versions can be broken down into shorter units, called sections, where each section discusses the article from a different aspect.

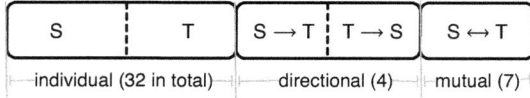

Figure 3: Three groups of features in collaboration profile representing the attitude of editor S (Source) towards T (Target)

4. INFERRING ATTITUDES

With a large number of revisions associated to an editor, and an even larger number of words, expressions or clues that may indicate some form of sentiment in those revisions, it becomes a challenge to infer the attitude of one editor towards another. In this section, we describe our approach for inferring attitudes using a set of features and statistics obtained from revision history of edited pages. These statistics are used in a form of a collaboration profile, which we learn to classify them as positive or negative denoting the corresponding attitude of one editor towards another. In the following two sections, we first describe how we build these profiles, and then how we learn to classify them.

4.1 Building collaboration profiles

The features used in our collaboration profiles are grouped into three parts, as shown in Figure 3. As the names suggest, individual features are derived from each editor individually based on his/her revisions, and represent the general behavior of that editor, while the directional and mutual features represent the behavior of an editor with respect to another editor, describing how this editor (referred to as source editor) interacts or collaborates with the other editor (referred to as target editor). Hence, individual features are assigned to each editor, the directional group features are assigned to an ordered pairs of editors, whereas the mutual features are assigned to an unordered pairs of editors. In the following, we describe each of these groups of features in more detail.

Individual features. To describe the general activity level of an editor, our individual features include for each editor the number of articles edited, total number of revisions, and the average contribution size over articles edited, where the contribution size of an editor in an article is the ratio of revisions made by the editor to all revisions made to the article. As a base to see the type of articles an editor edits, the average concentration ratio of all articles edited by the editor is also kept (i.e. concentration ratio of an article is defined as the ratio of unique editors to all revisions of that article). The intuition here is that a high concentration ratio might cause bias and information censoring compared to a low concentration ratio where the contribution is shared among all editors more evenly.

To characterize the general writing tone of an editor, our features include the number of agreement terms and the number of disagreement terms both in comments of revisions made by the editor, selected from the most frequent words including uni-grams, bi-grams and tri-grams that appear in the comment lines of a set of manually-tagged agreement and disagreement edits. Prominent examples of terms indicating agreement are "add", "fix", "spellcheck", "copyedit", "clarify", and "move". On the other hand, terms such as "uncited", "fact", "is not", "bias", "claim", "revert", and "see talk page" are indicators of disagreement. Similar statis-

tics are also extracted from revisions immediately after an editor's revisions, which are likely to contain responses.

Other features we consider are based on revert and restore actions, for example whether or not other editors like an editor's revisions. Specifically, we keep for each editor the number of reverted revisions, the number of restored revisions and also the number of revisions made by others but reverted by that editor. We also keep track of the average Δ size of an editor's revisions and the average Δ size of revisions immediately after his revisions. The Δ size of a revision is the net change in length of the article, measured in characters between consecutive revisions , hence it can be negative if an edit simply removes some content.

In order to capture *a priori* tendency of an editor to get into conflicts, we also compute the average conflict score of all articles which the editor has been involved with, where the conflict score of an article is simply the fraction of *conflicting* interactions in that article.

DEFINITION 5. *An interaction is* conflicting *if any one of these conditions are met:*

1. *the revisions are consecutive and the edit length of the later revision is negative,*
2. *the revisions are consecutive and the later revision uses more negative terms than positive terms in its comment line, or*
3. *the revisions are related and the later revision reverts the earlier revision.*

Finally, we also compute the average time it takes an editor to respond as well as the average time before the editor gets a response. Intuitively, these can help gauge if an editor engages in so-called "revision wars", characterized by rapid fire of disagreement responses.

Directional features. As for directional features, we have separate statistics for each pair of editors (one in each direction). For these features, we use the ratio of co-edited articles to all articles edited by one editor, and the ratio of revisions by one editor in co-edited articles to the edits of that editor across all articles he edited.

Mutual features. Finally, for the class of mutual statistics we treat the pair undirected by considering the following features: the number of co-edited articles; the number of interactions; ratio of conflicts over all interactions; the average number of versions between related revisions in corresponding interactions; and the fraction of interactions corresponding of consecutive revisions; Also as a base for comparison, we compute the average concentration ratio, and conflict score of all co-revised articles for the pair of editors.

4.2 Classifying collaboration profiles

Given the profiles of editors and their collaborations, our goal is to classify each collaboration into one of *agreement* or *disagreement*. In the absence of labeled data, one needs to resort to heuristics to infer labels for collaborations. For instance, Maniu et al. [24] use features such as the number of deleted, inserted, and replaced words, and whether an editor has given barn-star award to another and label each feature intuitively as a sign of a positive or negative relationship. Then, the final sign of the relationship of a pair of editors is determined based on the sign of the majority

Table 1: Statistics of election dataset

number of elections	3713
number of unique editors	9541
positive votes	130193
negative votes	36239
repeated votes	5601
conflict votes	1420

Table 2: Number of votes in extracted and mapped election data

	extracted data	mapped data
total	166432	89652
positive	130193	75168
negative	36239	14484

class. The authors in [5] develop a content-based method, by building a topic model of edits. In their method, the relationship of a pair of editors, for instance, editing the same paragraph takes a value in the range [-1,1] depending on whether one editor changes the topic distribution of the paragraph towards the changes made by the other editor of that paragraph or not. This approach again relies on a heuristic which is limited to interactions that can change the topic distribution of an article; the method also has not been evaluated.

Our work takes a more systematic approach by leveraging the strong relationship that exists between the way Wikipedia editors collaborate in editing pages, and the way they later vote in admin elections; the intuition here is that an editor who casts, for example, a negative vote to a candidate is more likely to have a negative than a positive interaction with the candidate. In fact, this dataset is used in the work of [24] with votes being a deciding feature in the sign of relationships between two editors. However, they could only use this feature for pairs who participate in elections, and the number of those pairs is much smaller than the number of pairs who interact.

In this paper, we use the election data to learn the weight of features that contribute to positive or negative collaborations. More specifically, we use the election data and tag a limited set of interactions as positive or negative; a classifier is built on this labeled data, which can then be used to predict the sign of collaboration profiles for other editors who may or may not appear in the elections dataset. Our results show that such a classifier can be built with a high accuracy which is evident of the influence of collaboration interactions on votes.

5. PREDICTING ADMIN ELECTIONS

In this section, we describe how we can learn collaboration profiles from admin elections and how these profiles can be useful in predicting votes. In our discussions, *administrators* (shorten as admins) refer to a set of editors in Wikipedia with certain, higher (than ordinary editor) privileges who are chosen by regular elections. In particular, in each election, an editor becomes a candidate for promotion into an admin editor and other editors can cast supporting, opposing or neutral votes towards that candidate. The information about admin elections is available from Wikipedia and is also used in some recent work [22, 23]. Our dataset (as explained next) is more up-to-date and includes more elections.

The election data is available in the usual Wikipedia dump in the form of special articles called "Requests for Adminship" (RFA). We collected and parsed all these RFA articles from a recent Wikipedia dump (dated April 5, 2011), resulting in a dataset that covered 3713 elections (compared to 2794 elections extracted up to January 2008 in [23]). More statistics about this dataset are shown in Table 1.

5.1 Learning profiles and predicting votes

With collaboration profiles as our feature vectors and votes in admin elections as the corresponding labels, we train a classifier to learn the relationship between profiles and vote signs. More specifically, for each candidate c and voter v, we build their profile $cp_{v,c}$ and their respective features (as discussed in section 4).

There are a few caveats in building collaboration profiles to predict elections. First, since we want to predict the sign of the votes before they are cast, a time constraint in building collaboration profiles is to use only the information that is available prior to a vote. Second, a candidate and a voter can appear in multiple elections possibly at different times and the vote of the candidate can change from one election to the next. In cases where v casts a vote for c only once in the entire election dataset, all revisions up to the time of casting vote seem to be relevant and are used for building collaboration profiles. Similarly, in cases where v casts the same vote for c multiple times (referred to as *repeated votes*), all revision history up to the time of vote is considered. However, for multiple conflicting votes (referred to as *conflict votes*), as the vote of v casted for c change over time, we consider only the revision history from the time of the most recent vote v casts for c.

5.1.1 Mapping collaboration profiles to votes

Our collaboration network is built over pairs of editors who collaborate in revising articles (or more precisely, have related edits), and these pairs may or may not appear in the election data. Our experiments on predicting elections only considers pairs who have collaboration profiles and also appear in the election data (these pairs are referred to as *mapped data* in Table 2).

Table 2 shows the number of votes that are extracted from the election data, the number of votes that could be mapped to our feature vectors and their break-down to positive and negative votes. The ratio of positive votes to all votes is 78% and 83% in extracted and mapped datasets respectively.

5.2 Results

Table 3 shows the performance results of our approach on predicting votes using a 10-fold cross validation experiment on full and balanced mapped dataset. The balanced-dataset is obtained from the full dataset by randomly sub-sampling positive votes until the number of positive and negative votes are the same. For these results, we tested four classifiers, namely Random Forest, J48, SMO and Logistic using Weka [2] machine learning tool.

As we can see in Table 3, the Random Forest classifier achieves the highest accuracy among the studied classifiers in both datasets. In fact, Random Forest classifiers have a good performance in general and also on imbalanced datasets, as shown in some previous work [19], due to their bagging

---
[2]www.cs.waikato.ac.nz/ml/weka

Table 3: Results of predicting votes on full and balanced datasets.

Model	F-Acc.	F-AUC	B-Acc.	B-AUC
Random Forest	**0.869**	**0.877**	**0.781**	**0.857**
J48	0.842	0.706	0.695	0.707
SMO	0.838	0.5	0.579	0.579
Logistic	0.837	0.626	0.591	0.628
All positive	0.838	0.5	0.5	0.5
Relative-edit	0.82	0.5	0.499	0.5
talk-positive	0.537	0.570	0.583	0.583

Table 4: 15 most important features of the vote classifier

# of candidate's agreement terms
# of candidate's edits
candidate's avg. contrib. size
candidates's avg. time being responded
# of candidate's disagreement terms
avg. Δ size of revisions after candidate's
avg. Δ size of candidate's revisions
candidate's avg. response time
# of candidate's edits reverted
avg Δ size of voter's revisions
# of candidate's edited articles
# of reverts made by the candidate
avg concent. ratio in articles edited by candidate
avg concent. ratio in articles edited by voter
avg version distance of interactions

and internal feature selection methods. Hence, for this classifier, we applied an additional tuning and feature selection method by following the approach proposed in [27]. In particular, for ranking and selecting features, we used the Gini importance metric of the classifier, and removed 7 features with the lowest importance score. These features were 1) number of co-revised articles, 2) number of interactions, 3) fraction of interactions corresponding to consecutive revisions, 4) average conflict score of co-edited articles, 5) average concentration ratio of co-edited articles, 6) ratio of revisions by candidate in co-edited articles to all of his revisions, and 7) same as 6 but for voter. After selecting features, we tuned the two parameters of the classifier which led us to choose 70 trees and 15 random features at each branch.

This additional tuning and feature selection resulted into 86.9% and 78.1% accuracy, an about 1% improvement (which translates to about 1000 more correct predictions in our data) and 8% over the default setting of Random Forest in Weka on full and balanced datasets respectively. Table 4 shows the top 15 features which are ranked by importance according to the Random Forest classifier.

As is shown, the features that are ranked on top are mostly individual features, and are that of the candidate; this is consistent with our intuition as individual activities of the candidate is more influential on the outcome of votes than the characteristics of the voter. Top 15 features include from interaction features only the average version distance of interactions which is representative of the strength of interactions of the two editors modeled by how fast the two editors responded or collaborated with each other in revising the articles.

5.2.1 Comparison with other methods

We also compared our method with three simple baselines: all-positive, relative-edit and talk-positive: all-positive classifies all votes as positive; relative-edit classifies a vote as negative if the number of previous edits of candidate and the voter is in the same range (having the difference of less than 10), and positive otherwise; finally, talk-positive classifies a vote as positive if the candidate and the voter have any previous communication (writing to each other's user pages).

The relative-edit and talk-positive baselines are from [22], where authors speculated that voters in admin elections tend to do a relative assessment of candidate through implicit comparison to their own merits such as comparing their number of edits with the candidate's (as a sort of the level of activity). The authors also found that having previous communication increases the probability of positive votes.

Comparing all these methods on the full dataset, we can see that our best results using the Random Forest classifier shows about 3% and 37% improvement over the strong all-positive baseline in terms of respectively accuracy and area under ROC curve (which is a measure commonly used for imbalanced datasets [19]). On the balanced dataset, the superiority of our method is more pronounced: 25% higher than the best baseline. We observed that relative-edit has almost the same performance as all-positive. This is because while the probability of negative votes increases when the relative edit distance of candidate and voter is small, the number of pairs with such condition is very low, which makes this baseline to act like the all-positive. On the other hand, as about half of all pairs had a prior communication, the talk-positive baseline cannot be very effective in explaining most of the votes. This shows that while there are important factors that increase the probability of giving positive votes, it is unlikely that a single factor can explain different reasons of different positive and negative votes, and thereby a combination of several factors should be used to learn these votes.

We cannot compare our results against those reported by Leskovec et al. [23] as their method is not applicable when the voter or the candidate does not appear in past elections. Even for pairs of candidates and voters that appear in past elections, their method has a tuning parameter called minimum *embededness* (defined as the number of common neighbors) and both their accuracy and the votes they can predict vary with the values of this parameter, whereas in our work, the interaction window-size is a parameter affecting the votes that can be predicted. These differences make a fair comparison very difficult in general. That said, our method on balanced dataset shows 78.1% accuracy, compared to 80.1% reported by Leskovec et al., which supports an argument that the analysis of revision history (as we do) can be as valuable as the analysis of the social network of voters (as they do) for predicting admin elections.

5.2.2 Effect of interaction window size

A parameter used in our method is the size of the window where two interactions are considered related. This parameter is set by default to 34 (as discussed in section 3). However, a question is how our method performs as we vary the window size. With a change in window size, clearly the number of votes that can be mapped will change. Our results show that by increasing the window size up to 40, the number of votes that can be mapped also increases; after this point, an increase in window size has a very small effect. As expected, by considering larger window sizes, we allow editor pairs to have an interaction in farther distances; this in turn increases their chances of having at least one interaction, but after some point, a larger window size does not increase the chance of finding any new interactions, which is consistent with our definition of related edits.

Also, studying the trend of accuracy over different window sizes, we found out that the classifier is quite stable and by increasing the window size from 2 up to 60, there is less than 3% drop in accuracy. Hence, we can conclude that increasing the window size allows more votes to be predicted for the expense of small loss in accuracy, and also a bit longer time for extracting features and training the classifier.

5.2.3 Effect of history length

In previous experiments, we built the profiles of our editors and their collaborations using all interactions before the casting of a vote. A question that arises is if all edits and interactions are relevant when one wants to predict votes. For example, an interaction that happens much before an election may not carry much weight. In this section, we want to limit the length of history that can be used to construct profiles, and to find out how the performance of our method is affected. It should be noted that limiting the relevant history length also changes the set of predictable votes since we need at least one co-edited article in the history to be able to build our profiles.

Figure 4 shows the change in accuracy on the balanced dataset as we vary the history length. A problem here is that as the history length changes, the set of votes that can be predicted also changes and this makes a comparison difficult. To address this problem and to keep the votes the same, as the history length is increased, even though more interactions are used in building our profiles, we limit our prediction only to pairs of editors who show interactions in our shorter windows. Each cluster of bars in our figures shows the prediction result with the votes kept the same but the length of the history varied. For instance, the cluster on the far left shows the results when the votes are restricted for pairs of editors who show interactions within one week before the vote. The label *all* denotes the case where the entire history is used to build our profiles.

Looking at figure 4, our first finding is that even on balanced dataset, the positive accuracy for all history lengths and vote sets is much higher than the negative accuracy. For instance, there is more than 10% difference between positive and negative accuracy of votes of 1 week when they are learned using all interactions. This implies that in general it is harder to explain negative votes based on previous history of interactions, and other hidden factors such as current state of casted votes, and the response of the candidate to asked questions during the election may play a role in the votes that are cast.

The other interesting finding is that using a longer history improves all accuracy metrics for votes of all set of votes. However, this increasing trend usually stops or even gets reversed after one year period. This suggests that one year is a suitable length for capturing most of the collaboration attitudes of Wikipedia editors and any information about the collaboration of editors beyond this time is not vital for predicting votes.

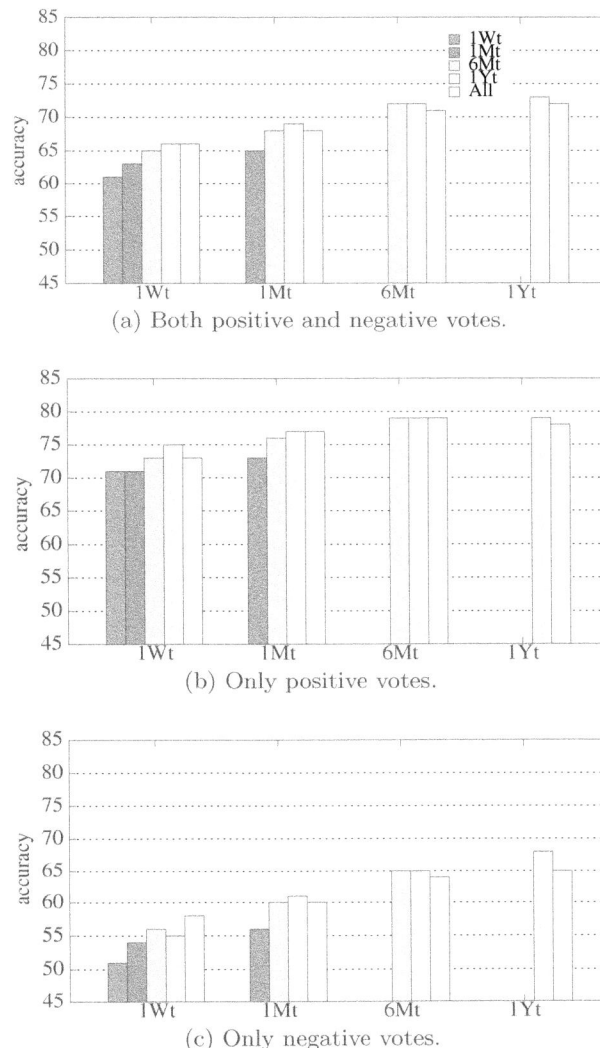

(a) Both positive and negative votes.

(b) Only positive votes.

(c) Only negative votes.

Figure 4: Trend of accuracy over all, positive and negative votes across different time periods. The x-axis represents the vote sets and the bars in each cluster is the prediction result for different history lengths.

Also, we see that whenever longer history improves the overall accuracy, negative votes benefit more than positive votes and the overall difference of bars in each cluster for negative accuracy is higher than positive accuracy. For instance, considering the votes of the first two clusters where we have the most change in metrics, the accuracy of the negative class in overall relatively improves 15% and 8% in each cluster respectively, while the positive accuracy for the same clusters has 5% and 4% relative improvement by using larger history.

This difference in the effect of history length on positive and negative votes might suggest that if the voter casts negative votes based on previous revision history of collaborations, he might remember and refer to negative events from a long time before the vote time. In contrast, positive votes can be explained even by the recent history of collaborations.

6. IDENTIFYING CONTROVERSIES

In this section, we validate our method by showing its usefulness in the task of identifying controversial articles. In particular, for this task, we first build a collaboration profile for each pair of editors who interact in editing the article (based on our discussion in Section 4). We then classify all the collected collaboration profiles associated with each article a by using our vote predictor classifier. The vote classifier trained on admin election data assigns a positive or negative label to each collaboration profile, which represents the sign of the edge connecting the corresponding editors in the collaboration network of each page. Furthermore, for building collaboration profiles and connecting editors in our collaboration networks, we imposed an additional constraint of having at least two edited versions for each editor. This additional constraint aims at removing occasional, non-active editors and giving a more reasonable number of possible collaborating pairs.

Our validation task here is identifying controversial articles, based on the observation that these articles are tagged as controversial by Wikipedia editors themselves. Note that unlike some previous work [20,31], where the number of controversial tags assigned during the history of the page was used as the evaluation method, we consider modeling the problem as a simple binary classification task (whether the page is controversial or not). Controversial tags are tags such as {controversial}, {dispute}, {disputed-section}, etc. that can be added to the text of a version by Wikipedia editors. We avoid using these tags as the ground truth since they can have several problems such as forgetting to remove the tag after the controversy resolves or to add a tag long after the start of controversy as pointed out in [30]. Hence, the number of these tags is not necessarily representative of the controversy degree of pages.

Automatically identifying these articles can benefit both editors and article readers by warning them about the disputed state of the article and how they should interpret the content or manage the collaboration process. Also, due to highly disputed nature of these pages, we expect to have different structure of agreement and disagreement relationships between editors in the corresponding collaboration networks compared to other pages which provides a suitable test set for our method of inferring attitudes.

6.1 Overview

For our purpose, we aim to show that our approach for building collaboration networks leads to different structure between networks of controversial articles and other articles. Previously, Brandes et al [6] showed the structural difference of controversial articles using a metric called *bipolarity*. Bipolarity is a graph-based metric that measures how much a graph is likely to decompose into two opposing groups, where most of disagreement edges will be between the two groups rather than within them. Hence, one approach would be to extract bipolarity from the collaboration networks we build and compare its values over controversial articles and non-controversial articles. However, as bipolarity is defined only for negative edge networks, and was also shown to not provide enough discrimination between controversial and non-controversial pages [28], we extracted some other features from our collaboration networks instead of focusing on a single metric.

More specifically, we set up a classification task where

for each controversial page c, and similarly for each non-controversial page n, we extract a set of features $f_1, f_2,...,f_k$ obtained from the corresponding collaboration networks of each page. Then, we train a classifier to learn to distinguish controversial and non-controversial articles using these features where each page (network) is an instance in our task. We show more accuracy is obtained for this classification task using the features extracted from our built collaboration networks compared to other methods for building collaboration networks.

6.2 Selecting pages

We carefully selected 240 articles for each group of controversial, and non-controversial by the following procedure: We selected controversial articles by randomly selecting pages from all the 15 categories in the list of controversial articles maintained in Wikipedia [3]. When choosing articles, we chose the new title of pages in case of redirected pages. From the 240 selected articles, only 122 articles had controversial tags in their revision history.

For selecting non-controversial pages, we randomly chose 100 pages from the featured article category, and 150 pages from the other quality groups. For each of these pages, we also check that they will not be among controversial articles list. This is because many of the articles in the list of controversial articles later become non-controversial, and even improve to featured articles due to several factors such as limiting the editors access. We avoid choosing such pages for our non-controversial set, and consider only pages without any controversy in any part of their revision histories (i.e. not only in the current state of the page).

6.3 Features extracted from collaboration networks

We extract the following 30 features in total from the graph of collaboration network associated with each controversial or non-controversial article in our test set:

- total number of non-isolated nodes (isolated nodes are nodes not connected to any other node in the graph)

- total, positive, and negative number of edges

- average of total, positive, and negative degrees of nodes

- the percentage of nodes having a in-degree of higher than 90% of maximum in-degree (one feature for each positive and negative in-degree), and similarly for out-degree

- the percentage of nodes having an in-degree of less than 110% of minimum in-degree (one feature for each positive and negative in-degree), and similarly for out-degree

- the percentage of nodes having an in-degree of in the range of 10% lower and 10% higher than the average in-degree (one feature for each positive and negative in-degree), and similarly for out-degree

- the percentage of nodes with higher positive than negative in-degree, and similarly for out-degree

- total number of triads

---

[3]http://en.wikipedia.org/wiki/List_of_controversial_articles

- the relative number of each of the 8 triad types

Triads are directed sub-graphs of size 3, which have been used as important metrics in many recent work such as [13, 18, 23]. We considered 8 different triad types in our work depending on how many negative edges exists (0, 1, 2, or 3) and whether the edges in the triad form a cycle or not.

6.4 Comparison with other methods

The first method that we compared our method with is a simple, and well-known method for building collaboration networks [6], in which authorship is considered at the word level. Based on this notion, whenever editor e_1 deletes some words originally inserted by e_2 in the text of article a, an edge with a negative weight proportional to the number of words deleted will be created from e_1 to e_2. Also, whenever e_1 restores a version created by e_2 to an earlier version created by e_3 (a possibly different editor than e_1), a single unit positive edge will be created from e_1 to e_3, and a single unit negative edge will be created from e_1 to e_2 as e_1 undo the work of e_2 and implicitly agrees with the work of e_3. Note that while we specifically compare our method with this method of building collaboration networks, using delete, and revert actions as disagreements between editors is a common method in other work on Wikipedia [2, 16, 17, 34].

We also compare our method with three baselines: a) Rand50 refers to a method that randomly assigns positive, or negative sign to each of the edges in the network built by our method. b) Rand83 is another baseline that assigns the sign of edges randomly similar to baseline1, but with a probability of 83% positive, and 17% negative, which are the ratio of positive and negative votes in the full mapped admin election. c) NE-count is a method that only uses the number of nodes, and the number of edges in our built networks as features, and does not use any information about the structure of the links.

Finally, we compare our method with a previously proposed method for classifying controversial articles which uses meta features such as the number of versions, the number of reverts, etc. obtained from the revision history of each article [28]. We refer to this method as *Meta* (and exclude two disagreement related features from this method to only focus on meta features).

6.5 Results

Table 5 shows the accuracy of the classifier in detecting controversial articles using each of the methods. The results are based on 10-fold cross validation using Logistic classifier. For our method, collaboration networks built using the vote classifier trained on balanced dataset showed slightly better results than the one trained on the full data-set and hence we report our method based on this better result. Also, the results for Rand50 and Rand83 methods are the average results over 20 runs with different random seeds.

First, as we can see the NE-count baseline has the lowest accuracy among all methods showing that the number of authors and their interactions are not alone enough to distinguish controversial articles from other articles and the actual network structure matters.

Second, comparing our method with other methods for building collaboration networks, we see a substantial improvement. Specifically, our method has more than 20% higher accuracy than the DRR method. This suggests that considering interactions at smaller unit level (word-level au-

Table 5: Results of identifying controversial pages. The same 30 features were used in DRR, Rand50, Rand83 and our method.

Method	Acc
NE-count	56.70%
DRR	64.31%
Rand50	68.67%
Rand83	71.31%
Meta	75.20%
our method	**84.58%**
our method + Meta	**89.12%**

thorship) and also relying only on basic edit operations cannot capture different collaboration relationships between editors, and more extensive global features across all co-edited articles is needed for inferring these relationships. Also, comparing with the two Rand methods, where we have the same network structure and features as our method, and just the sign of edges is different across these methods strongly supports the importance of inferring attitudes and the effectiveness of our method for doing so.

Finally, comparing with the Meta method, we see that while general features about the revision history provide a good discrimination between the two studied classes of articles, they cannot eliminate the important role of the structural properties of the collaboration network of editors. In fact, by taking advantage of these two complementary views (structural and meta features), we are able to boost the performance of both methods and achieve a very promising results of 89.12% for this task.

7. CONCLUSION

In this paper, we showed that revision history of Wikipedia articles contains valuable information that can be utilized in different tasks related to Wikipedia. In particular, we showed that there is a strong correlation between the previous collaboration history of editors and how they vote for each other in admin elections. This new perspective about admin elections in Wikipedia allowed us to not only be able to predict votes with a high accuracy, but to use this dataset as a training environment for inferring attitudes of editors. Besides, studying the relationship of votes and previous history of collaboration of editors showed interesting differences between positive and negative votes, where we found that positive votes usually can be explained by even the recent history of interactions, while negative votes might be associated with negative interactions from long time before the time of the vote.

As an application of inferring attitudes, we tested our method on identifying controversial articles based on the structural properties of the signed collaboration networks of articles, built using our attitude classifier. Comparing with a previous attempt on modeling editors relationships, and also with a method based on meta data of revision history, our promising results suggested that the structural properties of collaboration networks and modeling the attitudes of editors beyond the simple edit operations is indeed crucial for understanding the collaboration nature of Wikipedia articles.

Acknowledgements. This work was supported in part by grants from NSERC.

8. REFERENCES

[1] Spectral analysis of signed graphs for clustering, prediction and visualization. In *SIAM'10*, pages 559–570, 2010.

[2] B. T. Adler, K. Chatterjee, L. de Alfaro, M. Faella, I. Pye, and V. Raman. Assigning trust to wikipedia content. In *WikiSym '08*, pages 1–12, 2008.

[3] B. T. Adler and L. de Alfaro. A content-driven reputation system for the wikipedia. In *WWW '07*, pages 261–270, 2007.

[4] Alexa.com. http://www.alexa.com/topsites. Last visited on Oct 28, 2011.

[5] P. Bogdanov, N. D. Larusso, and A. Singh. Towards community discovery in signed collaborative interaction networks. In *ICDMW'10 workshop*, pages 288–295, 2010.

[6] U. Brandes, P. Kenis, J. Lerner, and D. van Raaij. Network analysis of collaboration structure in wikipedia. In *WWW '09*, pages 731–740, 2009.

[7] K. Chatterjee, L. de Alfaro, and I. Pye. Robust content-driven reputation. In *AISec '08*, pages 33–42, 2008.

[8] Y. Choi, Y. Jung, and S.-H. Myaeng. Identifying controversial issues and their sub-topics in news articles. In *PAISI*, volume 6122, pages 140–153, 2010.

[9] N. Clark. Trust Me! Wikipedia's Credibility Among College Students. *International Journal of Instructional Media*, 38(1):27–36, 2011.

[10] G. M. Druck and A. G. McCallum. Learning to predict the quality of contributions to wikipedia. In *WikiAI08*, pages 7–12, 2008.

[11] M. Galley, K. McKeown, J. Hirschberg, and E. Shriberg. Identifying agreement and disagreement in conversational speech: use of bayesian networks to model pragmatic dependencies. In *ACL'04*, 2004.

[12] E. Gilbert and K. Karahalios. Predicting tie strength with social media. In *CHI'09*, pages 211–220, 2009.

[13] M. Granovetter. The strength of weak ties: A network theory revisited. In *Sociological Theory*, pages 105–130, 1982.

[14] A. Hassan, V. Qazvinian, and D. Radev. What's with the attitude?: identifying sentences with attitude in online discussions. In *Empirical Methods in Natural Language Processing*, pages 1245–1255, 2010.

[15] D. Hillard, M. Ostendorf, and E. Shriberg. Detection of agreement vs. disagreement in meetings: training with unlabeled data. In *HLT-NAACL 200*, pages 34–36, 2003.

[16] M. Hu, E.-P. Lim, A. Sun, H. W. Lauw, and B.-Q. Vuong. Measuring article quality in wikipedia: models and evaluation. In *CIKM '07t*, pages 243–252, 2007.

[17] S. Javanmardi, C. Lopes, and P. Baldi. Modeling user reputation in wikis. *Statistical Analysis and Data Mining*, 3(2):126–139, 2010.

[18] Katherine and Faust. A puzzle concerning triads in social networks: Graph constraints and the triad census. *Social Networks*, 32(3):221 – 233, 2010.

[19] T. M. Khoshgoftaar, M. Golawala, and J. V. Hulse. An Empirical Study of Learning from Imbalanced Data Using Random Forest, volume 2, pages 310–317. 2007.

[20] A. Kittur, B. Suh, B. A. Pendleton, and E. H. Chi. He says, she says: conflict and coordination in wikipedia. In *CHI '07*, pages 453–462, 2007.

[21] T. R. Korsgaard and C. D. Jensen. Reengineering the wikipedia for reputation. *Electronic Notes in Theoretical Computer Science*, 244:81 – 94, 2009.

[22] J. Leskovec, D. Huttenlocher, and J. Kleinberg. Governance in Social Media: A case study of the Wikipedia promotion process. In *ICWSM'10*, 2010.

[23] J. Leskovec, D. Huttenlocher, and J. Kleinberg. Predicting positive and negative links in online social networks. In *WWW'10*, pages 641–650, 2010.

[24] S. Maniu, B. Cautis, and T. Abdessalem. Building a signed network from interactions in wikipedia. In *DBSocial'11 workshop*, 2011.

[25] B. Pang and L. Lee. Opinion mining and sentiment analysis. *Foundations and Trends in Information Retrieval*, 2(1-2):1–135, 2008.

[26] R. Priedhorsky, J. Chen, S. T. K. Lam, K. Panciera, L. Terveen, and J. Riedl. Creating, destroying, and restoring value in wikipedia. In *GROUP'07*, GROUP '07, 2007.

[27] D. M. Reif, A. A. Motsinger, and B. A. McKinney. Feature selection using a random forests classifier for the integrated analysis of multiple data types. In *CIBCB*, pages 1–8, 2006.

[28] H. Sepehri Rad and D. Barbosa. Towards identifying arguments in wikipedia pages. In *WWW'11*, pages 117–118, 2011.

[29] S. Somasundaran and J. Wiebe. Recognizing stances in online debates. In *ACL'09*, pages 226–234, 2009.

[30] R. Sumi, T. Yasseri, A. Rung, A. Kornai, and J. KertÃĺsz. Edit wars in wikipedia. *Technology*, pages 724–727, 2011.

[31] B.-Q. Vuong, E.-P. Lim, A. Sun, M.-T. Le, and H. W. Lauw. On ranking controversies in wikipedia: models and evaluation. In *WSDM'08*, pages 171–182, 2008.

[32] R. Xiang, J. Neville, and M. Rogati. Modeling relationship strength in online social networks. In *WWW'10*, pages 981–990, 2010.

[33] B. Yang, W. Cheung, and J. Liu. Community mining from signed social networks. *IEEE Transactions on Knowledge and Data Engineering*, 19:1333–1348, 2007.

[34] H. Zeng, M. A. Alhossaini, L. Ding, R. Fikes, and D. L. McGuinness. Computing trust from revision history. In *PST '06*, page 1, 2006.

Slicepedia: Providing Customized Reuse of Open-Web Resources for Adaptive Hypermedia

Killian Levacher, Séamus Lawless, Vincent Wade

Centre for Next Generation Localisation, Knowledge and Data Engineering Group

School of Computer Science and Statistics, Trinity College Dublin, Ireland

{Killian.Levacher, Seamus.Lawless, Vincent.Wade}@scss.tcd.ie

ABSTRACT

A key advantage of Adaptive Hypermedia Systems (AHS) is their ability to re-sequence and reintegrate content to satisfy particular user needs. However, this can require large volumes of content, with appropriate granularities and suitable meta-data descriptions. This represents a major impediment to the mainstream adoption of Adaptive Hypermedia. Open Adaptive Hypermedia systems have addressed this challenge by leveraging open corpus content available on the World Wide Web. However, the full reuse potential of such content is yet to be leveraged. Open corpus content is today still mainly available as only one-size-fits-all document-level information objects. Automatically customizing and right-fitting open corpus content with the aim of improving its amenability to reuse would enable AHS to more effectively utilise these resources.

This paper presents a novel architecture and service called Slicepedia, which processes open corpus resources for reuse within AHS. The aim of this service is to improve the reuse of open corpus content by right-fitting it to the specific content requirements of individual systems. Complementary techniques from Information Retrieval, Content Fragmentation, Information Extraction and Semantic Web are leveraged to convert the original resources into information objects called slices. The service has been applied in an authentic language elearning scenario to validate the quality of the slicing and reuse. A user trial, involving language learners, was also conducted. The evidence clearly shows that the reuse of open corpus content in AHS is improved by this approach, with minimal decrease in the quality of the original content harvested.

Categories and Subject Descriptors

H3.3 [**Information Search and Retrieval**]: Information Filtering; Retrieval Models; Selection Process;

H.5.4 [**Hypertext/Hypermedia**]: Architectures; User Issues;

Keywords

Customized Hypertext Content Generation, Open Corpus Content Processing, User Experience

1. INTRODUCTION

Adaptive Hypermedia Systems have traditionally attempted to deliver dynamically adapted and personalised presentations to users through the sequencing of pieces of information. While the effectiveness of such systems and the benefits of their use have been proven in numerous studies [9], the adaptivity offered by

AHS, and thus their widespread adoption, have been restricted by the lack of sufficient content in terms of volume, granularity, style and meta-data. Such systems have traditionally relied upon the manual production [3] of bespoke proprietary content [1], resulting in potentially low volumes and high production costs. Open Adaptive Hypermedia (OAH) research addresses this challenge by leveraging open corpus information available on the Worldwide Web (WWW) and utilising it in AH presentations.

However, when open corpus reuse has been achieved, it is generally performed manually [5] or at best using traditional information retrieval (IR) approaches [1]. The usage of IR approaches has met with very limited success, even when retrieving relevant open web information. These techniques suffer because they only provide one-size-fits-all, untailored delivery of results, with limited control over granularity, content format or associated meta-data. This results in limited and restricted reuse of such resources in AHS. Open corpus material, in its native form, is very heterogeneous. It comes in various formats, languages, is generally very coarse-grained and contains unnecessary noise such as navigation bars, advertisements etc. Hence, there remains a significant barrier to automatically convert native open corpus content into right-fitted information objects meeting the specific content requirements (such as granularity, delivery format, annotations) of individual AHS.

Contribution: In this paper, a novel approach to open corpus reuse through right-fitting is proposed. This novel approach leverages complementary techniques from IR [11], Content Fragmentation [6], Information Extraction (IE) [10] and Semantic Web [4] to improve the reuse of open corpus resources by converting them into information objects called slices. By analysing, fragmenting and re-assembling previously published documents into customized objects, native open corpus resources can be right-fitted to meet a diverse range of content requirements from individual adaptive systems. An implementation of the system architecture, called Slicepedia, is presented, which has been applied in an authentic educational scenario. An evaluation (detailed in section 4) based upon a user-trial was conducted to validate the reuse and appropriateness of the right-sizing. Results provide evidence that this approach improves the reuse of open resources while minimizing any decrease in quality of the original open corpus content harvested. In order to deal with the significant technical challenges of right sizing and reuse, some specific aspects are deemed beyond the scope of this paper; namely copyright and digital rights management issues.

2. BACKGROUND

OAH research has attempted to resolve the closed corpora dependency of traditional AHS by leveraging the wealth of information available over the WWW. These techniques usually consist of incorporating open corpus resources using either i) manual, ii) community-based, iii) automated linkage or iv) IR approaches. Manual incorporation techniques [5] allow users/designers to incorporate documents within an adaptive experience. However these techniques require a significant amount of time and effort due to the difficulty in identifying adequate content and annotating these external resources prior to incorporation within individual systems. Automated linkage [13] and community-based [2] approaches attempt to improve this situation by providing guidance with respect to the relevant content that is available. While the former automatically estimates the semantic relatedness between pages, community-based approaches analyse the quantity of users stepping between various resources in order to derive this information. IR approaches [11], on the other hand, aim to provide pluggable services for AHS by offering various search capabilities to support open corpus content identification and incorporation. The OCCS system [7] for instance, uses focused crawling techniques to harvest large amounts of web resources and identify those most relevant to specific contexts of use, based on arbitrarily pre-selected topic boundaries. All of these approaches focus on dealing with the information overload encountered while leveraging such large quantities of resources; either by improving the identification of suitable content or by connecting resources together. However resources identified by such techniques are still used in their native form, as one-size-fits-all documents, in their original format of delivery. As pointed out by Lawless [7], *"there is an inverse relationship between the potential reusability of content and its granularity"*. The reuse potential of a previously published news page, complete with original menus, advertisements and user comments, is far less than if the article could be reused alone, de-contextualised from its original setting, at various levels of granularity (from a paragraph on a specific topic to the entire article), with associated meta-data and in a delivery format of choice.

Although the field of Personalised Information Retrieval (PIR) has indeed focused on the issue of personalising information delivery, the techniques used by such systems [11] have typically focused on re-ranking the order of resources delivered as opposed to personalising the content itself. Furthermore, the use of such content delivery systems is mostly confined to human "consumption" (which by nature can easily distinguish areas of interest within documents), displayed as entire documents within traditional web browsers. Re-composable information objects, on the other hand, must possess a granularity, scope and discerning meta-data/annotations, specific to each use case, in a format chosen by each individual AHS. If the full reuse potential of open corpus content is to be leveraged, the reuse through right-fitting of these resources represents a necessary preparation step for AHS. This necessity emerges directly from the diversity of formats, page layouts, domains, styles and multilingual nature of open corpus content. A good example of what could be achieved, if open corpus resources were fully available as right-fitted content objects, is the Personal Multilingual Customer Care (PMCC) system developed by Steichen et al. [12]. This system leverages both corporate and user generated resources available in the wild by integrating and re-composing these resources into single coherent presentations to users. Fragments of interest within corporate content and targeted forums are extracted using content specific rule-based algorithms, assigned system specific meta-data and stored in a proprietary format. An ontology is derived from the structure of the corporate content, linked with the forum resources and used as a domain model.

Although this system does reuse these open content resources, it does so by applying manually crafted, content specific rule-based algorithms on targeted resources with a predefined structure. Furthermore, the re-composable content objects which are generated by this system are single purpose, with use case specific format and meta-data as well as pre-defined granularities. If the entire range of open resources available on the WWW is to be fully leveraged and delivered to a diverse range of AHS, a system converting open corpus resources into reusable intelligent content objects, must deal with: i) unknown page structure; ii) multiple languages; and iii) domains. It should also serve a variety of: iv) content requirements (meta-data, granularities); v) delivery formats; and vi) use cases in which content is consumed by an AHS. Additionally, as pointed out by Steichen et al [12], *"OAH systems typically focus on producing educational [...] compositions on predefined needs, rather than [...] informal user need[s] indicated by a query"*. Manually crafted, rule-based content analysis algorithms, for targeted resources, clearly do not scale if the entire open web is to be targeted as a potential resource. Hence the need for: vii) a fully automated solution to open corpus reuse.

As the range of domains available on the open web is unbounded, a content specific ontology provides an inadequate bounded domain model for the purpose of open content object re-composition. Even within a pre-defined domain, various AHS might interpret specific concepts differently. The rise of the semantic web and in particular linked data[1] now provides a wealth of open, shared and interconnected conceptual models, which could provide open content models the ability to anchor fundamental meta-data descriptions of their underlying resources upon linked data concepts within multiple repositories. This approach would also fully disentangle open content models from any particular domain model as well as providing AHS with various domain ontologies to interpret these resources. Semantic searches [4] could then make use of these anchors to manipulate and identify reusable content objects. Such semantic reasoning capabilities could be used for the adaptive selection of open content based on a chosen domain model, unknown by the open content model.

The opportunity in OAH hence lies in the ability to improve the reuse of existing open corpus resources by converting them, into intelligent content objects created on-demand for individual AHS. By focusing on providing a fully automated, independent and pluggable content delivery service, such an approach would enable OAH to fully leverage open resources by providing more control over the granularity, meta-data and delivery of these native resources to individual AHS. The following sections describe the architecture and implementation of such a system called Slicepedia, with an initial evaluation focusing on assessing the reuse improvements of content delivered over native open corpus content.

3. THE WEB DELIVERED AS SLICES
3.1 Slicepedia Architecture
As depicted in Figure 1, a slicer is designed as a pipeline of successive-modules, each analysing open corpus resources and

---

[1] www.linkeddata.org

appending specific layers of meta-data to each document. Resources openly available on the WWW are gathered and then transformed, on demand, into reusable content objects called slices. AHS (or so-called slice consumers) thus use the slicer as a pluggable content provider service, producing slices matching specific unique content requirements (topic, granularity, annotations, format etc.). Although the architecture presented in this paper could of course be implemented over closed corpus resources, the ultimate aim is to provide a pluggable, fully automated service, which can process large volumes of open corpus resources, without any prior knowledge of structure, domain, or language used by each document and with the ability to support diverse AHS content requirements.

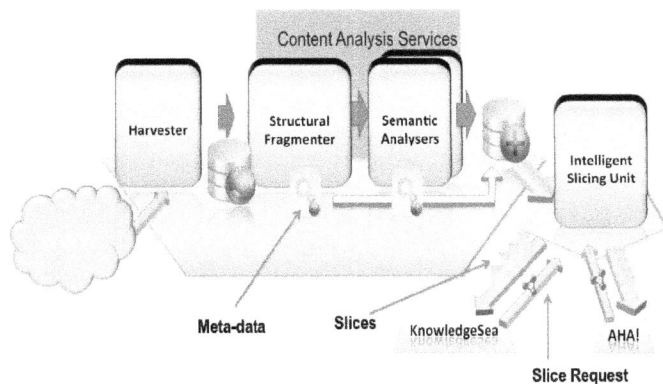

Figure 1 Slicepedia Architecture

Harvesting: The first component of a slicer pipeline aims to acquire open corpus resources, from the web, in their native form. Standard IR systems or focused crawling techniques [7] are used to gather relevant documents, which are then cached locally for further analysis.

Structural Fragmentation: Once resources have been identified, each individual document is analysed and fragmented into structurally coherent atomic pieces (such as menus, advertisements, main article). Structural meta-data, such as the location of each fragment within the original resource, is extracted and stored in the meta-data repository. This phase is critical since, as mentioned previously (section 2), maximising the reuse potential of a resource involves the ability to reuse selected parts of documents, which in turn, depends upon correctly identifying individual sections of pages to produce de-contextualised structurally coherent fragments. Any structural inconsistencies (such as parts of original menus erroneously broken in two and merged with paragraphs or various titles merged together) produced at this stage, will have a direct impact upon the quality of reuse, regardless of the performance of subsequent steps. As mentioned in the previous section, any algorithm used within this component must be fully automated and deal with unknown document structures in multiple languages.

Semantic Analyser: Once an initial set of fragments is produced, each is analysed by standard IE and Natural Language Processing (NLP) algorithms (such as entity extraction [10] and topic detection) with the intention of producing discerning meta-data, supporting the identification and selection of such content for reuse by individual slice consumers. Such meta-data might include, writing style, topic covered or the difficulty level of content. Since what constitutes "discerning" meta-data is highly

dependant upon the reuse intentions of each slice consumer, an inappropriate provision of such data can lead to very low reuse scenarios across consumers. Hence great care must be taken during the selection of suitable annotators in order to support the broadest needs possible of targeted consumer use cases. Additionally, this phase is also essential with respect to the level of granularity control provided to slice consumers. The ability to "focus" (or constrain) a resource to only cover a chosen topic, is clearly dependent upon the capacity to accurately match selected parts of single resources with appropriate concepts. Moreover, as the targeted document space of a slicer is by definition open, the resulting open content model available to slice consumers shouldn't be restrained by any predefined subjective domain model. For this reason, Slicepedia disentangles domain modelling from its open content model and instead provides anchors to linked-data concepts as a foundation for any domain model chosen by individual slice consumers. Additionally, all fragments and annotations produced by Slicepedia are also available as linked-data. The intention is to reduce low reuse effects related to the subjective nature of discerning meta-data, and support collaboration with reusable annotations across institutions.

Slice Creation: Once individual fragments and meta-data annotations are available, the slicer is ready to combine these individual elements into slices. The array of possible adjustments (such as the extent of control over granularity, formats and annotation) a slicer can offer upon an open corpus resource, is referred to as its Content Adaptation Spectrum (CAS). Whenever slice requests are received, an intelligent slicing unit combines atomic fragments together, along with relevant meta-data, into customized slices. Since a slicer is to be used as a pluggable service within a variety of slice consumers, a range of delivery formats should be supported. A slice is therefore defined as: *"Customized content generated on-demand, consisting of fragment(s) (originating from pre-existing document(s)) assembled, combined with appropriate meta-data and right-fitted to the specific content requirements of a slice consumer (with various application-specific content-reuse intentions)".* Slices can contain other slices and can be reused or re-composed with many slices.

3.2 Implementation
The Slicepedia architecture presented in this paper was implemented for the purpose of the experiment described in section 4, in such a way that allows alternative implementations of individual components to be substituted and exchanged with each other to support various measurements. Hence, two alternative implementations of this architecture were implemented. The first implementation supports closed corpus slicing, while the second targets open corpus resources. Both implementations share most components but differ mainly with respect to the fragmentation algorithm selected.

Although IR based harvesting modules (such as the OCCS [7] and Yahoo web search[2]) could easily be plugged into both versions of the slicer, these IR harvesting modules were ignored within the context of this experiment and a simple URL list-harvesting feature was used instead as it was necessary to isolate the components which aim at improving the reuse of these resources as opposed to their identification (see section 4.4). This offered tighter control over the resources supplied to both slicers

---

[2] http://developer.yahoo.com/search/web/V1/webSearch.html

25

simultaneously and allowed for a direct comparison of both slicers over a common subset of resources (see section 4.2). With respect to the fragmentation component, the closed corpus slicer used a rule-based approach to fragmentation (section 4.2). For the purpose of this experiment, Wikipedia pages were downloaded in xml format, converted and stored in a local mysql database. Rules built within the JWPL library[3], developed by Darmstadt University, were subsequently used to ignore any clutter within the pages and fragment each one at various granularities (paragraphs, sections etc…) with ideal accuracy. A densitometric approach [6] to fragmentation was selected for the open corpus version of the slicer. It's ability to fragment pages regardless of the meaning or structure of xml tags used and without the need for any rendering, allows it to process virtually any xml-based documents at very high speed. A prior detailed analysis of this algorithm also revealed that it could fragment parallel corpora in multiple languages with a predictable degree of accuracy. However, limitations of this fragmentation algorithm with respect to content type (such as forum or product pages) were also discovered during this analysis. For this reason, this experiment considered a subset of the WWW as an open corpus target, consisting of any news or encyclopaedia type pages. Although, this clearly represents a limitation with respect to the aim of improving the automated reuse of any open corpus resource available on the WWW, considering the wide diversity and quantity of such pages currently available, this subset was deemed sufficient for the purpose of this experiment. Both slicers used a common set of annotators consisting of the AlchemyApi concept tagging service[4], which identified and associated concepts mentioned within each fragment with Dbpedia instances[5]. The reading-level difficulty expressed as Flesh Reading scores was determined using the open source Flesh annotator[6]. Part of speech[7], noun phrase, and verb phrases[8], were also identified within fragments and annotated with their relevant linguistic attributes. All annotations and fragments were stored as rdf data within a Sesame triple store[9]. The closed corpus slicer additionally associated subject categories as well as content style (ie: bullet point, prose) attributes to individual fragments based on the structure of targeted closed corpus resources (see section 4.2). Finally, the open corpus slicer used a boilerplate detection algorithm[10], annotating to what degree fragments of a page were reusable or not. Slice requests were then converted to SPARQL queries by the slicing unit and submitted to the triple store in order to identify any matching fragment/annotation combinations. Fragments identified were then appended to each other (with an order consistent with their original position in pages) and annotations inserted in the resulting compounded fragment. Since, for the purpose of this experiment, no 3rd party slice consumer was involved, slices were output in xml format.

---

[3] http://code.google.com/p/jwpl/

[4] http://www.alchemyapi.com/api/

[5] http://dbpedia.org/About

[6] http://flesh.sourceforge.net/

[7] Modified version of the Brill Tagger in ANNIE http://gate.ac.uk/

[8] Verb Group and Noun Phrase chunker in http://gate.ac.uk/

[9] http://www.openrdf.org/

[10] http://code.google.com/p/boilerpipe/

The result of these pipeline instances provide an open corpus CAS to slice consumers consisting of 3 right-fitting dimensions (Content Style, Granularity and Annotation Type) including 10 adaptation variables (content style, topics covered, reading difficulty, verb chunk tense, number of annotations, paragraph/word number, topic focus, annotation focus, original sources, delivery format) that can be arbitrarily combined to suit various content requirements over any relevant open corpus resources identified. A slice request could hence consist of the following:

Slice request example: slices should originate from only a specified list of urls and have a granularity ranging from 3 sentences up to 3 paragraphs. They should cover the topics of "whale migration", "atlantic ocean" or "hunting" and should have a Flesh reading score ranging from 45 to 80. They should not contain any tables or bullet points lists but be focused on the specified topics (ie: exclude content not on these topics). Slices should contain between 7 and 15 annotations consisting of verbs conjugated at the past perfect continuous and should be delivered as LOM objects.

4. EVALUATION & RESULTS

Although the reuse of open corpus material is ultimately aimed at large scale reuse and re-composition, this experiment focuses on evaluating the automated reuse of individual open corpus slices. The assumption is that, in order for open corpus content to be reused through re-composition with other slices, the quality of individual slices delivered must be guaranteed to the AHS consumer. Any quality issues arising within individual content objects would subsequently affect any re-composition produced that includes these objects. An experiment investigating the re-composition of slices in an independent third party AHS, as well as scaling performances, is currently in progress. The overall evaluation strategy adopted within this paper consisted in comparing various reuse metrics across open corpus reused i) in its native form, iv) using a manual approach ii) closed corpus approach, or iv) open corpus approach.

4.1 Language eAssessment

In order to evaluate the proposed approach to open corpus reuse along with the two slicer implementations (for open and closed corpora) presented in 3.2, a real life user-trial was performed in the application domain of language e-assessment. In this scenario, native and non-native English speakers assess their personal English grammatical skills using an online e-assessment application, built specifically for the purpose of this experiment, called Slicegap. This simple application presents users with different sets of open/closed corpus resources reused within the context of grammatical exercises. Each resource is sliced, using the various slicing techniques discussed above, and presented individually to users as traditional gap filler exercises. Verb chunks conjugated at specified tenses are removed and replaced by gaps, which users must fill according to particular infinitives and tenses specified for each gap. The answers provided are compared to the original verb chunks and users are assigned a score for this specific grammar point.

The slice consumer application represents an excellent evaluation platform for the purpose of this experiment for many reasons. As this experiment aims to evaluate individual slices as they are delivered to slice consumers (prior to any adaptation or re-composition), the level of re-composition or adaptation performed on these slices needed to be kept at a minimum. Traditional grammar exercises are by nature created using individual pages (or slices) and do not necessarily require any re-composition. Furthermore, the activity involved allows the interface complexity of the application to be kept to a minimum (Figure 2) to avoid any possible interference with the evaluation of the content. Additionally, although component level evaluations are of course necessary, the content consumed by AHSs is ultimately presented to people. Hence, any open corpus reuse measurement should consider as critical, the user-experience aspects of such an evaluation. For this reason, it was necessary to select a "reuse vehicle" where the user needs are very sensitive to: (i) the accuracy of annotations; (ii) the visual layout; and (iii) the linguistic quality of the content presented. A grammatical e-assessment task requires verbal annotations to be precise and the content to be formatted correctly as well as easily readable by groups of users with varying linguistic competencies.

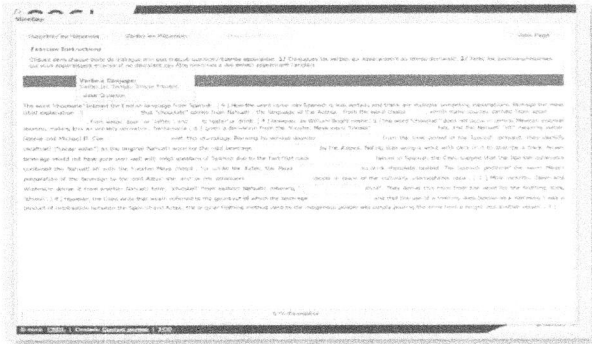

Figure 2 Slicegap Screenshot

4.2 Content Batches

In this experiment, 8 different content batches were presented to users:

1/Content Batch Native (CBN): Content CBN (used as a baseline) consisted of the entire set of open corpus resources used within this experiment in their original native form without any slicing.

2/Content Batch Closed Corpus (CBC): Content CBC consisted of a subset of these resources retrieved as closed corpus content (section 4.4) and sliced using the closed corpus slicer. With the aim of avoiding any confusion, closed corpus content, throughout this research, refers to resources previously known in advance of any slicing performed. Such content, as in the PMCC system described earlier [12], can therefore be sliced with very high precision using a set of manually crafted rule-set algorithms.

3/Content Batch Wikipedia (CBW): Content CBW consisted of the same set of pages available in batch CBC but downloaded in their original form as html web pages.

4/Content Batch Open Corpus (CBO): Content CBO consisted of content batch CBW augmented with a set of random arbitrarily user selected web pages. This content batch represents a true set of open corpus resources since (with the exception of sub-batch group CBW) pages source and structure were unknown in advance of slicing.

The following 4 content batches aimed at evaluating the ability of a slicer to focus native resources upon a topic or set of annotations. For this reason, 2 sets of content were produced both manually and automatically.

5/ Focused Topic Manual (FTM): Batch FTM consisted of pages arbitrarily selected by independent users (section 4.4) on a particular topic T, manually sliced and focused upon content within the original document covering only this specific topic T.

6/ Focused Topic Automated (FTA): Content FTA consisted of the same set of pages independently selected for content batch FTM, sliced and focused automatically upon the same topic T using the open corpus slicer.

7/ Focused Annotation Manual (FAM): Pages within content batch FAM were independently selected in the same way as for FTM but instead focused upon annotations created within this content.

8/ Focused Annotation Automated (FAA): Finally, content FAA consisted of the same set of pages selected for FAM, sliced, annotated and focused upon annotations created using the open corpus slicer.

Furthermore, these 8 content batches can be classified within 4 different content reuse strategies:

1/Manual reuse: As content batch FTM and FAM were produced manually by independent users. These two content batches represent a manual reuse scenario of open corpus content.

2/Native reuse: Since content batch CBN simply consists of unchanged open corpus resources, this content batch represents the equivalent of a traditional IR open corpus reuse strategy (section 2) with resources delivered, in their native form, as one-size-fits-all document objects.

3/Closed corpus reuse: Content batch CBC, on the other hand, represents semi-automated reuse scenarios of content. As part of this reuse strategy, systems (such as the PMCC example in section 2) have full knowledge of the origin and structure of content being reused prior to slicing. For this reason, this form of reuse constitutes the ideal large-scale slicing quality achievable using a form of automated process.

4/Open corpus reuse: Finally, since the origin and structure of pages used to produce content batches CBO, CBW, FTA and FAA was unknown prior to slicing, these content batches represent the equivalent of a large scale, fully automated, reuse of open corpus resources available on the web.

4.3 Aim & Hypothesis

The purpose of the evaluation presented below was to investigate whether the approach to open corpus content reuse, proposed in this paper via slicing, could (H1) improve the reuse of original open corpus resources in their native form (CBN) without (H2) reducing drastically the quality of the original content harvested. In the context of this research, quality refers to the readability and structural coherency of content (for example parts of original page aren't merged with menus from other parts of the page). Finally, assuming the process of automated reuse using closed corpus slicers does indeed improve the reuse of native resources, (H3) can the same performance be achieved using open corpus slicers on any open corpus resources?

The rest of this section lists the hypotheses and sub-hypotheses of the evaluation described previously, followed by the experimental set up and analysis presented in this article.

- H1: Slicing improved the reuse of existing resources
  - o H1.1: The correct removal of original clutter present in the resources improved the reuse appropriateness of such content.

o H1.2: Sliced content retrieve could be correctly focused upon a chosen topic/annotation

o H1.3: The slicer was able to annotate correctly the open corpus content for the purpose of the task being performed.

- H2: Sliced content didn't present any important decrease in quality with respect to the original content

  o H2.1: Sliced content didn't present any important decrease in readability with respect to the original content

  o H2.2: Sliced content didn't present any important decrease with respect to the structural coherence of the original content

- H3: Slicing performance over open corpus content doesn't present any major decrease in performance in comparison to closed corpus.

4.4 Experimental Design

In order to perform an evaluation of the slicer implementations presented in section 3.2, the goal of the following experimental design was to present users with different alternative content, within identical reuse scenarios. This would allow a direct comparison of the four reuse strategies described in section 4.4.1 and thus highlight any differences in content quality perceived by users. These perceived differences would relate to the slicing approach used. Hence, since the aim of this experiment was to focus specifically upon measuring the ability of a slicer to improve the reuse of open corpus resources, as opposed to its ability to identify specific resources, the components of the slicer pipeline built for the purpose of accomplishing such a task were isolated. For this reason, the IR harvesting component of both slicers was omitted from the trial and only the URL list-harvesting feature was used. This ultimately encapsulates the research question as follows: Assuming a correct open corpus resource was initially identified, can slicing improve its reuse?

4.4.1 Content batch creation

As the aim of the experiment is to investigate whether resource reuse improvement, through the use of slicing, is achievable on any open corpus content, the need to initially harvest a truly random set of open corpus pages was necessary. Hence, prior to conducting the experiment, a group of five independent English teachers, from two different schools, were asked to arbitrarily select nine pages of their choice from the web (combined total of 45 pages) and perform a set of tasks. They were first asked to select a set of pages of their choice from Wikipedia. They were then asked to create a second, larger set of pages, harvested from any source of their choice (as along as it consisted of news articles see 3.2). Finally, a third set of pages chosen by teachers was required to be on a specific set of topics T. English teachers were then asked to select fragments of the pages harvested (according to specified granularities and tense requirements) and manually annotate tenses encountered within these extracts. Finally, they were asked to extract fragments from a portion of the pages harvested in tasks 2 and 3 and manually focus these fragments respectively upon tenses annotated and content referring to individual topics T (content not about these topics was discarded). These last two sets of pages created represent content batches FAM and FTM respectively (section 4.2).

Manually produced fragments contained an average of 189 words and 14 annotations.

All of the extracts created were subsequently converted into grammar e-assessment pages. The entire collection of pages collected in each set was then harvested from the web, in their original form, to produce batch CBN. CAS characteristics of extracts manually created, were identified and fed into the open corpus slicer as parameters. The entire content set in its original form was then sliced with these parameters to produce the page set CBO (including set CBW) with similar CAS characteristics as its manual equivalent. The Wikipedia pages downloaded were then matched to the set contained in the database (see section 3.2) and sliced (using again the same CAS parameters as their manually created equivalent) using the closed corpus slicer to produce batch CBC. Since both CBC and CBW, were sliced using respectively closed corpus and open corpus methods from identical source of pages, any improvement in reuse differences detected between the two sets can only be the result of slicing performances between closed corpus and open corpus slicing. Finally, in a similar way, original pages used to create FAM and FTM were fed into the open corpus slicer. The slicer was provided with annotation and topic focused parameters to produce FAA and FTA respectively. As in the previous case, these two parallel content sets are derived from the same original pages. This allows a direct comparison between the performance of manual and automated focused content.

4.4.2 Evaluation scenario

Once the eight content batches had been produced, a user trial was conducted which consisted of a task-based evaluation using real-life linguistic assessment needs. Each user was initially asked to select their interface language of choice and specify their level of ability in the English language. They were subsequently invited to perform successively the same activity eight times in succession, using eight different pages randomly selected from each content batch. Each piece of content was associated with a unique colour and users were unaware of either how the content was created or what content batch was being presented to them at each task. Each original page (regardless of the content batch it belonged to) was only shown once to each user. The trial performed consisted of a traditional language learning activity that is encountered in most textbooks (section 4.1). The activity was divided into four individual tasks:

User Task 1: The first task required users to read the text presented to them and fill in any blanks encountered (there were 10 gaps on average per page) with the appropriate verb and tense specified for each case (Figure 2). If users felt slices were unreadable or inappropriate for this exercise, a "Trash Slice" button could be pressed to select another page. The ability to provide users with accurate grammar assessment questions is highly sensitive to the precision of the annotations delivered by the slicer, therefore this task aimed to evaluate both the annotation quality and overall reuse appropriateness of the slices presented.

User Task 2: The initial task did not necessarily require users to read the entire content presented to them (only the sentences containing gaps). For this reason, users were then asked to summarise what they felt the entire piece of content was about (as in traditional textbooks) in their own native language.

User Task 3: Finally, although previous tasks are clearly dependent upon the quality of the slices presented to users, the ability of a slicer to correctly scope (or focus) an original document on a particular topic or set of annotations certainly was not measured. For this reason, users were asked an additional set of questions, which assess the appropriateness of the scope of each slice. The concepts selected for presentation were chosen to be accessible to as wide an audience as possible. This enabled users to accurately judge the scope of the content presented. Once completed, the answers received for slices that were manually focused (FTM & FAM) were compared to those that had been automatically generated (FTA & FAA) by the open corpus slicer. Although the authors are aware that an activity which was directly dependent upon the scope of slices would have presented a more convincing argument, these results nevertheless provide an initial indication of a slicer's ability to correctly focus native content. A further experiment which is currently in progress, assesses slices that are produced through re-composition and addresses this issue in a different application domain (section 6). Additional questions related to task 1 and 2 were also included in order to reinforce quantitative measurements. All questions presented to users offered a 10 point Likert scale (ranging between "strongly disagree" and "strongly agree"). A scale with no mid-point was was deliberately used to enforce user preference however slight. The order of sentiment in the scales was also randomized between questions in an attempt to ensure that users were genuinely attentive when answering each question..

User Task 4: Finally, users were asked to order a set of colours, corresponding to each content presented, based on their perceived quality. In order to balance any effect of order bias, each user was presented content batches according to a Latin square design distribution. The entire experiment was available online to the public and users were asked to perform the entire set of tasks in a single session without any interruption. Task completion time in addition to user interactions were tracked throughout each activity. Finally, as part of a larger experiment comparing the automated production of language e-assessments with respect to its manual equivalent, non-native English speakers were also invited to perform the experiment. Hence, the interface of the slice consuming application Slicegap (including the questionnaires) was also translated into Spanish and French.

4.5 Results

This section presents a summary of the findings observed throughout this experiment in relation to each hypothesis. The full detailed list of results on the 36 variables measured can be accessed online[11]. A total of 41 users across 7 different countries performed the experiment. Most of these users performed the experiment using the English interface (en=59%, non-en=23%) and rated themselves as native or advanced English speakers (Native=46%, Advance=28%, Intermediate=12%, Beginner=3%, Other=1). Finally, the number of times the "Trash Slice" button (section 4.4) was clicked throughout the experiment was statistically insignificant. For this reason, it is not further discussed within the rest of this paper.

4.5.1 Reuse Improvement (H1)

H1.1: As pointed out in section 2, a part of maximizing the reuse potential of a previously published resource requires the ability to decontextualize this content from its original setting. Hence, users

---

[11] https://www.scss.tcd.ie/~levachk/TCDWebsite/data.html

were asked directly, for each content, whether "*in addition to the main content, a lot of material displayed on the page was irrelevant to the task (such as advertisement, menu bar, user comments..)*". Figure 3 presents the results obtained over a Likert scale ranging from 1 to 10 (section 4.4.2). Content batch CBN, containing pages in their native forms, achieved the worse score with a mean equal to 5.67 while closed corpus (CBC) and open corpus (CBO) content batches achieved much better scores (CBC=1.76, CBO=2.53) with paired t-tests confirming results are indeed significant (p=0.001). Additionally, when comparing closed corpus (CBC) and open corpus (CBW) approaches on an identical set of pages, a mean difference of 0.879 between CBC and CBW was measured (p=0.015). This result suggests that, although the open corpus approach to slicing did achieve a very good performance with respect to its closed corpus equivalent (91% similarity), users did notice a minor performance decrease in it's ability to separate the main content of the original resource. When asked whether "*the level of irrelevant material (e.g: menus, advertisement, user comments etc...) present in the content prevented me from pursuing this task effectively*", CBN again achieved the worse score (3.43) versus closed (CBC=1.48) and open (CBO=1.64) content batches (with paired t-tests confirming these results are statistically significant (p<=0.01)).

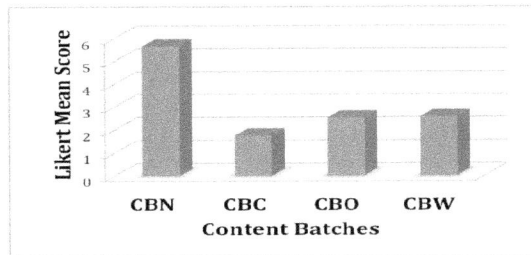

Figure 3 De-contextualisation Performance

This observation, suggesting poor de-contextualisation of original resources impacts the reuse of such content, was confirmed when measuring the average time, per answer provided by users, necessary to complete the exercises. As can be seen in Figure 4, users required an average of 88% more time to complete the exercises using non-decontextualized resources in their native form (CBN) than it did for fully de-contextualised resources (CBC). This finding appears to confirm the assumption stated by Lawless et al [7] earlier (see section 2). Furthermore, differences in results measured between CBC and CBW for both the question and average time measured were insignificant (p=0.77 & p=0.58). This suggests that although a performance decrease in de-contextualising original resources for the slicer using an open corpus approach was noticed by users, this minor performance decrease didn't have any impact upon the reuse of the content produced.

H1.2: As mentioned in section 3.1, the ability to right-fit a resource in its native form into a slice containing only parts of the original document about a specific topic or set of requested annotations, is important with respect to the capacity of a slicer to deliver information objects matching specific content requirements and use cases of various AHS. Content batches FTM and FTA represent such a case of original resources being focused (or scoped) on an arbitrarily chosen topic. When users were asked whether they "*felt parts of the content presented were about topic <T>*" (<T> being the topic in question), the manually focused content batch (FTM) obtained the best score with a mean equal to

9.09 versus the open corpus automated equivalent (FTA) which obtained 8.55. A p value of 0.82 suggests this mean difference between manually and automatically generated contents is insignificant. This result appears to suggest the SOC slicer was capable of automatically identifying which parts of the documents did refer to specific topics.

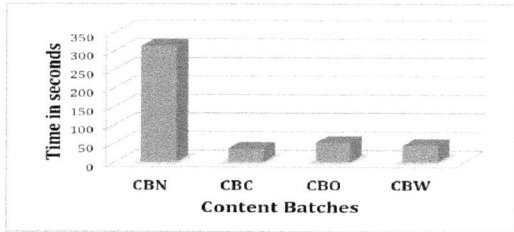

Figure 4 De-contextualisation Impact

Additionally, when asked whether *"a large amount of content delivered was not related to topic <T>"* the manually focused content again achieved the best score in comparison to the open corpus slicing approach with a mean equal to 3.07 and 3.86 respectively for FTM and FTA. The paired t-test (p=0.159) suggests once more that the difference measured between the manual and automated approach is insignificant. As a sanity check, the answers for the same question asked for native content were also measured. Since pages within content batch CBN are presented as entire documents, they are necessarily unfocused; hence a very poor focused performance should be measured. As expected, a mean value equal to 6.43 for CBN suggests users felt this native content wasn't focused correctly on topic T. When asked the reverse (ie:*"all the content presented was related to topic <T>"*), the results lead to the same conclusion with FTA and FTM obtaining respectively 7.36 and 8 (p=0.411) while CBN received a score of only 1.23. These results appear to indicate that not only could the open corpus slicer SOC correctly identify parts of the document on a particular topic, it could also minimize the amount of un-related content delivered, and offer slices with boundaries tightly confined to that specific topic. Moreover, paired t-tests (p=0.159 & p=0.411) do suggest content focused automatically using the SOC slicer achieved similar scores to its manual equivalent. Finally with respect to open corpus content being correctly focused upon annotations requested, a similar pattern can be observed. When asked whether *"apart from any clutter information (advertisements, menus etc...) displayed within the page, I felt a large amount of content delivered to me was un-necessary for the grammar task being performed"*, content manually focused upon annotations (FAM) achieved the best score (3.53) with the automated approach presenting a minor difference (mean=3.73) considered insignificant (p=0.783). A sanity check with CBN again obtained the worse score of 5.87. These results indicate the automated open corpus slicer could correctly focus native content upon annotations requested with a performance similar to it's manual equivalent.

H1.3: In order to measure the accuracy of annotations delivered to slice consumers, a sample set of identical pages annotated by all teachers (section 4.4) was compared to those produced automatically by the open corpus slicer. Individual manual annotations, obtaining the largest agreement among teachers, were used as a golden standard. Precision and recall was calculated for the annotations produced by the open corpus slicer as well as for each manual annotator. An F score equal to 0.88 (precision=0.86, recall =0.92) was measured for the open corpus

slicer. This result suggests the annotator identified most items to be annotated while producing a minority of errors during the process with respect to human annotators. This high correlation between automated and manual annotations hence appears to confirm the quality of annotations produced by the automated open corpus approach to slicing. Additionally, when performing the same measurement for each human annotator individually, with respect to the golden standard, an average F score of 0.77 (Precision=0.89, Recall=0.68) was obtained. This result shows that although human annotators did a better job at correctly annotating the fragments, some disagreements did occur; suggesting mistakes produced by the automated approach could be subject to interpretations. Additionally, the recall score indicates that many human annotators missed several annotations in comparison to the automated approach.

4.5.2 Quality Decrease (H2)

H2.1: As described in section 4.3, the process of structurally fragmenting original resources into individual pieces and subsequently merging selected fragments together to form slices, can lead to structural incoherencies within the final content delivered. For this reason, users were asked directly if *"parts of the original web page presented were merged inappropriately together (eg: end of menu merged with start of a paragraph)"* (Q1). Table 1 depicts the results obtained per content batch. As can be observed, very good performances were measured across all content batches, with t-tests estimating any differences encountered as insignificant. These results suggest that the process of slicing resources didn't produce any significant increase in structural incoherencies in comparison to the original content in its native form. Moreover, a mean difference of 0.688 observed between CBC and CBW was considered insignificant. This would indicate that, although measurements for the open corpus slicing approach were higher than for closed corpus slicing, these results do not provide enough evidence to suggest open corpus slicing leads to any significant decrease in structural coherency of slices produced. When asked the reverse (Q2), opposite values were also measured, with similar t-tests, which confirms these observations.

Table 1 Structural Coherence

		Mean	Comparison	Mean Dif	p
Q1	CBN	3.38	CBN v CBC	0.25	0.734
	CBC	3.13	CBN v CBO	0.28	0.662
	CBO	3.65	CBC v CBW	0.688	0.357
Q2	CBN	8.19	CBN v CBC	0.313	0.608
	CBC	8.5	CBN v CBO	0.531	0.479
	CBO	7.65	CBC v CBW	0.75	0.118

H2.2: While previous measurements aimed at estimating any decrease in quality of the content delivered from the point of view of visual layout, the readability of any content produced for reuse is of course critical. This research defines readability as being composed of two major components, namely i) the ability of content to be easily understood, and ii) the extent to which the flow of reading is broken. The second component refers directly to the notion described by Debasis et al [8], in other words, the extent to which pronouns, for example, referring to earlier subjects missing from a fragment, affect the ease of reading and comprehension of a text. Figure 5, depicts the results obtained for the first component measured. The first pair of questions aimed at asking users directly their opinion with respect to how easily could content presented to them be understood. The second pair relates to measuring any impact upon the difficulty in summarizing content. As can be seen, results obtained across content batches are very similar. While native (CBN) and closed corpus content slicing approaches interchangeably achieved better results across questions, open corpus content sliced using the open corpus slicing approach (CBO) constantly performed lower than the latter two. Paired t-test between CBC and CBW content however estimated any mean differences measured between content produced using closed corpus or open corpus slicers as insignificant (p > 0.06 for all questions). As a sanity check, and in order to make sure all sentences within content presented were read (regardless of whether they contained gaps to be filled), users were asked to summarize the meaning of the content presented to them. Among all the summaries provided by users across content batches, only less than 5% were rated as "weak". Despite being on topic, these answers were too short (less than 5 words) to determine whether the overall meaning of the content was correctly understood or not.

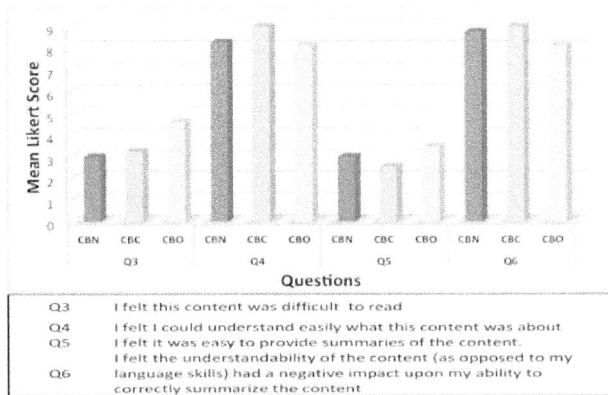

Q3	I felt this content was difficult to read
Q4	I felt I could understand easily what this content was about
Q5	I felt it was easy to provide summaries of the content.
Q6	I felt the understandability of the content (as opposed to my language skills) had a negative impact upon my ability to correctly summarize the content

Figure 5 Slice understandability

Nevertheless, the overall quality of summaries submitted clearly supports previous results obtained. Since close to a third of users, who participated in the trial where non-native speakers, a Pearson correlation analysis between answers submitted to each question and English level of users, was also performed. Correlations measured for each variable combination ranged between -0.2 and 0.2, which indicates no direct correlation between answers provided and the level of users. Additionally, when users were asked whether they felt *"their language skills had any negative impact upon [their] ability to correctly summarize content"*, means measured across content batches were all inferior to 2.30. With respect to the second component of readability, there exists, to the best of our knowledge, no automated mechanism to evaluate whether pronouns or topics mentioned within a fragment referred to earlier subjects mentioned in omitted parts of the original content. Hence users were asked directly whether this situation occurred or not for each content presented to them (Q7). Results depicted in Figure 6, indicate CBN obtained the best results, which is expected since the entire original resource was presented to users. Closed corpus content (CBC) presented no statistically significant differences with its native alternative (CBN) (p=0.685), while results for open corpus approach (CBO) on the other hand, presented a small statistically significant decrease with respect to CBN (mean dif =1.03, p=0.037) for confidence intervals of 95%. This result suggests open corpus slicing can indeed slightly deteriorate the flow of reading of open corpus content, which makes common sense. However when asking users if this situation had a negative impact upon the readability of content presented to them (Q8 & Q9), no statistical difference could be noticed between contents (p>0.300). Hence

although, a slight decrease in the flow of reading for content sliced using an open corpus approach could be noticed, the resulting impact upon the overall readability of content delivered was marginal.

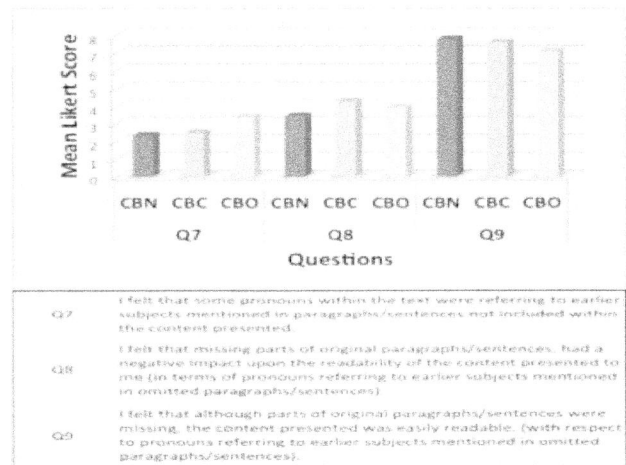

Q7	I felt that some pronouns within the text were referring to earlier subjects mentioned in paragraphs/sentences not included within the content presented
Q8	I felt that missing parts of original paragraphs/sentences, had a negative impact upon the readability of the content presented to me (in terms of pronouns referring to earlier subjects mentioned in omitted paragraphs/sentences)
Q9	I felt that although parts of original paragraphs/sentences were missing, the content presented was easily readable. (with respect to pronouns referring to earlier subjects mentioned in omitted paragraphs/sentences).

Figure 6 Slice reading flow

4.5.3 *Open Corpus Slicing Performance (H3)*
Throughout the results presented previously in section 4.5.1 and section 4.5.2, slices produced by the open corpus slicer consistently depicted lower performances in comparison to their rule based closed corpus or manual equivalent. However, in most cases, differences measured between slices produced by the two closed and open corpus slicers were statistically insignificant. Two exceptions to this rule occurred (both when comparing CBC and CBW content batches): the first occurred with respect to the ability of the SOC slicer to separate the main parts of pages from any clutter (H1.1), while the second occurred when analysing any broken flow in readability (H2.1). Albeit, both cases were anticipated, (since this slicer operates without any prior knowledge in the targeted resources to process) differences measured between slices produced from open and closed content were very small. Moreover, when measuring the effect both cases had upon user experience, no significant differences could be noticed.

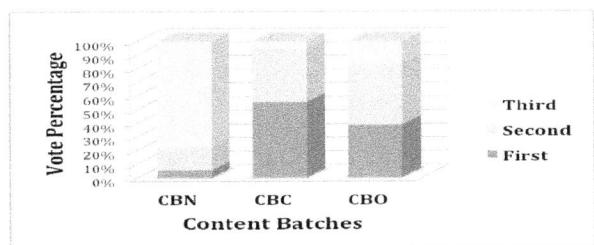

Figure 7 Content batch ordering

4.5.4 *Results Summary*
In summary, the results of the evaluation strongly indicate that the ability of slicers to de-contextualize resources from their original settings and focus this content upon specific topics or annotations, improves the reuse of open corpus resources (H1). Although, the flow of reading in slices produced, deteriorated in comparison to the original resources (H2.2), no significant impact upon the understandability of the content could be measured. These experiments also showed how, although open corpus achieved

lower performances than closed corpus, any difference tended to be very small and its measured impact insignificant. Finally, after being presented with each content, users were asked if *"Overall, [they] felt this content was adequate to perform such an exercise"*. Content semi-automatically (CBC) and automatically (CBO) sliced achieved the best scores, with means respectively equal to 8.89 and 8.57 in comparison to native content (CBN), which only achieved 6.85 (p<0.034) (Figure 8). Moreover, when asked to order contents in order of preference (the lower the value the better), 56% of users placed CBC content in first position (Figure 7), closely followed by CBO, with the overall majority placing content in its native form (CBN) in the last position. This result does confirm a rule-based approach to slicing upon closed corpus offers the best reuse improvement of native content. However, if the source of content to slice is unknown in advance, the open corpus slicing approach will perform with similar performance with very little impact from the point of view of user experience. These overall results reinforce the trend observed across variables, which suggest the reuse of existing resources was improved through the approach of slicing, with open corpus slicing reuse achieving very close performance to its closed corpus equivalent.

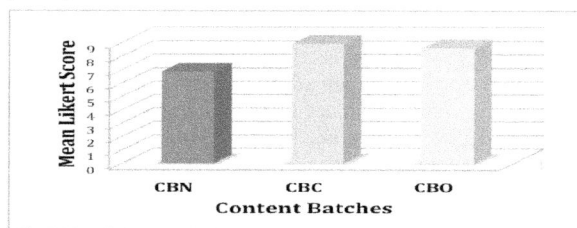

Figure 8 Content batch preferences

5. DISCUSSION

The measurements obtained by the user trial have shown encouraging results for the large-scale full reuse of open corpus material within various OAH systems through an open corpus slicing approach. Despite the identification of minor performance differences between open and closed slicing techniques, the impact upon the user experience appeared to be insignificant. It may be argued that the reuse scenario (including the choice of what constitutes discerning meta-data) selected for the purpose of this experiment only represents one specific use case of open corpus reuse. Indeed, further investigations will be required to determine the range of reuse scenarios possible, which slicing approaches could support. However, this experiment strongly suggests that the ability to go beyond the one-size-fits-all delivery of open corpus content and automate the right fitting of such resources for reuse within various content consumers is possible, with a minimal decrease in quality of this original content. Hence, for at least a selected number of use cases, large scale automated "full" reuse of such resources in AHS is possible. Subsequent steps (section 6) will be required to demonstrate whether these individual slices indeed be re-composed within third party AHS in various reuse scenarios.

6. CONCLUSION

This paper has presented a new approach to open corpus reuse through the automated customization and right fitting of heterogeneous resources available on the web called slicing. An initial implementation of this approach was successfully applied within the application domain of a language e-assessment scenario by reusing random selected resources available on the web. Evaluation results provide evidence that slicing improves the reuse of open corpus resources while minimizing any decrease in the quality of original content delivered. The results also appear to suggest open corpus reuse through slicing achieved very close performance to its closed corpus equivalent with minimal impact upon user perception. This provides evidence that large scale automated reuse of open resource is achievable. Further investigations are currently integrating Slicepedia with third party adaptive eLearning systems targeted at young teenagers in the area of natural sciences.

7. ACKNOWLEDGEMENTS

This research is supported by the Science Foundation Ireland (Grant 07/CE/I1142) as part of the Centre for Next Generation Localisation (www.cngl.ie).

8. REFERENCES

1. Aroyo, L., Bra, P. De Embedding Information Retrieval in Adaptive Hypermedia: IR meets AHA!". *New Review Of Hypermedia And Multimedia 10*, 1 (2004), 53 - 76.
2. Brusilovsky, P., Chavan, G., and Farzan, R. Social adaptive navigation support for open corpus electronic textbooks. *AH'04: Proc. of the 3rd int. conf. on Adaptive Hypermedia and Adaptive Web Based Systems*, (2004).
3. Dieberger, A., Jose, S., CoWeb - Experiences with Collaborative Web spaces. In D. Lueg, Christoph and Fisher, ed., *From Usenet to CoWebs: Interacting with Social Information Spaces*. Springer, 2002, 155 - 166.
4. Fernandez, M., Lopez, V., Sabou, M., et al. Semantic Search Meets the Web. *ICSC'08: Proc. of the int. conf. on Semantic Computing*, (2008), 253 -260.
5. Henze, N. and Nejdl, W. Adaptation in Open Corpus Hypermedia. *IJAIED'01: Int. Journal of Artificial Intellligence in Education*, (2001), 325 - 350.
6. Kohlschütter, C. and Nejdl, W. A Densitometric Approach to Web Page Segmentation. *CIKM'08: Proc. of the 17th int. conf. on Information and knowledge management*, (2008), 1173-1182.
7. Lawless, S. Leveraging Content from Open Corpus Sources for Technology Enhanced Learning., 2009.
8. Leveling, J. and Jones, G.J.F. Utilizing sub-topical structure of documents for Information Retrieval Categories and Subject Descriptors. *Utilizing sub-topical structure of documents for Information Retrieval*, (2011)
9. P, B. and Pesin, L. Adaptive Navigation Support in Educational Hypermedia: An Evaluation of the ISIS-Tutor. *Journal of Computing and Information Technology*, (1998).
10. Pennacchiotti, M. and Pantel, P. Entity extraction via ensemble semantics. *int. conf. on Empirical Methods in Natural Language Processing*, Association for Computational Linguistics (2009), 238.
11. Speretta, M. and Gauch, S. Personalized Search Based on Search Histories. *int. conf. on Web Intelligence*, (2005).
12. Steichen, B., Connor, A.O., Wade, V., and Oconnor, A. Personalisation in the Wild – Providing Personalisation across Semantic , Social and Open-Web Resources. *int. conf. on Hypertext and Hypermedia*, (2011), 73-82.
13. Zhou, D., Goulding, J., and Truran, M. LLAMA: automatic hypertext generation utilizing language models. *Hypertext and Hypermedia*, (2007).

Moving beyond sameAs with PLATO:
Partonomy detection for Linked Data

Prateek Jain
Kno.e.sis Center
Wright State University
Dayton, OH, USA
prateek@knoesis.org

Pascal Hitzler
Kno.e.sis Center
Wright State University
Dayton, OH, USA
pascal.hitzler@wright.edu

Kunal Verma
Accenture Technology Labs
50 West San Fernando Street
San Jose, CA, USA
k.verma@accenture.com

Peter Z. Yeh
Accenture Technology Labs
50 West San Fernando Street
San Jose, CA, USA
peter.z.yeh@accenture.com

Amit Sheth
Kno.e.sis Center
Wright State University
Dayton, OH, USA
amit@knoesis.org

ABSTRACT

The Linked Open Data (LOD) Cloud has gained significant traction over the past few years. With over 275 interlinked datasets across diverse domains such as life science, geography, politics, and more, the LOD Cloud has the potential to support a variety of applications ranging from open domain question answering to drug discovery.

Despite its significant size (approx. 30 billion triples), the data is relatively sparely interlinked (approx. 400 million links). A semantically richer LOD Cloud is needed to fully realize its potential. Data in the LOD Cloud are currently interlinked mainly via the owl:sameAs property, which is inadequate for many applications. Additional properties capturing relations based on causality or partonomy are needed to enable the answering of complex questions and to support applications.

In this paper, we present a solution to enrich the LOD Cloud by automatically detecting partonomic relationships, which are well-established, fundamental properties grounded in linguistics and philosophy. We empirically evaluate our solution across several domains, and show that our approach performs well on detecting partonomic properties between LOD Cloud data.

Categories and Subject Descriptors

I.2 [**Artificial Intelligence**]: Learning; H.3.3 [**Information Storage and Retrieval**]: Online Information Services— *web-based services*

Keywords

Part of Relation, Mereology, Linked Open Data Cloud

1. INTRODUCTION

The LOD Cloud consists of datasets linked primarily by the owl:sameAs property created by different organizations. This has proven to be useful for a number of use cases [4, 15], which combine data from multiple ontologies. The current mechanism for linking entities across datasets is using the *sameAs* relationship to assert that two entities are the same. We believe that using the *sameAs* relationship is not sufficient to capture the rich set of relationships between entities. There are a number of other relationships such as partonomy (part-of), and causality [28], whose presence could allow creating even more intelligent applications such as more sophisticated question answering systems like Watson [12]. One of the main reasons why these relationships are not captured is the issue of scale. As there are millions of entities involved, it is a non-trivial task to manually assert these relationships. While there is some level of automation available for creating the *sameAs* links, there is no automation for creating other kinds of relationships [19].

In this paper, we present *PLATO* (**P**art-Of relation finder on **L**inked Open D**A**ta **TO**ol)[1] for automatically creating part-of relationship between entities in the LOD cloud.

We chose part-of relationship for two reasons: 1) it is a well studied field. In particular we use the partonomy classification created by Winston [33] to guide our work and 2) part-of relationships are freely available on the Web in sources such as Wikipedia. The fundamental premise behind our approach is that the web can be mined to automatically detect part-of relationships between entities. Our approach consists of a combination of heuristics for detecting candidate relationships between any two entities. These heuristics range from detecting bi-directionality of links between articles about these entities to ensuring that the involved entities satisfy domain and range constraints of the relevant partonomic relation. The Web is then mined for evidence to support the candidate relationships with the help of pattern based querying. Using this approach, PLATO is able to discover partonomic relationships between entities in the LOD cloud. For example, PLATO was correctly able to discover that Kurt Cobain was a member of the band Nirvana and that Baked Alaska has ice cream as an ingredient.

---
[1]http://wiki.knoesis.org/index.php/PLATO

These relationships can prove to be extremely useful for the LOD cloud. For example, consider the following query from the National Geographic Bee, "In which county can you find the village of Crook that is full of lakes?". The answer for this query can be successfully retrieved using information present in the LOD cloud dataset (e.g. Geonames), if part-of relationships have been identified and asserted within and between datasets [20].

The key contributions of our work are: 1) To the best of our knowledge, PLATO is the first effort on the automatic detection of part-of relationships in the context of the LOD cloud. 2) We believe that PLATO's approach of mining the Web to detect and validate the relationships for LOD cloud is rather unique and thus extends the existing arsenal of ontology engineering methods. 3) We provide a formal representation of the partonomy classification created by Winston. We furthermore present a comprehensive evaluation in which we automatically detect part-of relationships between hundreds of entities from prominent ontologies in the LOD cloud such as DBpedia and Freebase. We also present precision and recall for our partonomy extraction approach, and the results make us believe ours is a practically useful approach.

The rest of the paper is organized as follows: In Section 2 we present Winston's approach to part-of relation and its conversion into an OWL 2 ontology. In Section 3, we present the PLATO approach, followed by a comprehensive evaluation. We then present the related work, future work and conclusion.

2. WINSTON'S APPROACH TO PART-OF RELATIONSHIPS—ONTOLOGIZED

All entities are fundamentally part of some other entity. Researchers in a number of areas, including philosophy [33, 2], linguistics [14] and geographical information systems (GIS) [29, 20, 7] have investigated partonomy. Our work of identification of partonomic relationships between entities uses well-accepted partonomic relationships, which identify the relationships based on the 'type' of entities involved. The part-whole relation, or partonomy, is an important fundamental relationship which manifests itself across all physical entities such as human made objects (Cup-Handle), social groups (Jurors-Jury) and conceptual entities such as time intervals (5th hour of the day). Its frequent occurrence results in a manifestation of a part-for-whole mismatch and whole-for-part mismatch within many domains, and especially in spatial datasets.

Winston [33] created a categorization of part-whole relations which identifies and covers part-whole relations from a number of domains such as artifacts, geographical entities, food and liquids. It is recognized as one of the most comprehensive categorizations of partonomic relationships, and other work in similar spirit such as [13] analyze his categorization.

Winston's categorization has been created using three relational elements:

1. Functional/Non-Functional (F/NF): Parts are in a specific spatial/temporal relationship with respect to each other and to the whole to which they belong. Example: Belgium is a part of NATO partly because of its specific spatial position.

2. Homeomerous/Non-Homeomerous (H/NH): Parts are the same as each other and as the whole. Example: A slice of a pie is the same as other slices and as the pie itself.

3. Separable/Inseparable (S/IN): Parts are separable/inseparable from the whole. Example: A card can be separated from the deck to which it belongs.

Table 1 illustrates six different types of partonomic relationships based on this categorization, taken from [33], their description using the relational elements and examples of partonomic relationships covered by them.

Using this classification and relational elements, relations between two entities can be marked as partonomic or non-partonomic in nature. If they are partonomic, the category to which they belong can be identified.

In order to use Winston's approach in a Semantic Web context, which is essentially linguistic in nature, we must formalize it by carrying it over to a Semantic Web ontology language. We will thus cast his categorization into an OWL 2 ontology [17] which can then be used in conjunction with a knowledge base of partonomic (and other) information. Let us remark that in [27] a set of best practices have been laid down to deal with straightforward cases for defining classes involving part-whole relations. However their modeling approach is considerably less fine-grained than the one in [33] which we follow here.

For this purpose, we introduce the following OWL property names, which correspond to those listed in Table 1.

- component-integral object: po-component
- member-collection: po-member
- portion-mass: po-portion
- stuff-object: po-stuff
- feature-activity: po-feature
- place-area: po-place

We also use spatially-located-in as the spatial (topological) located-in relationship mentioned in [33], and part-of as the generic part-of (part-whole) relation.

The following axioms can then be drawn from [33]. Let PO = {po-component, po-member, po-portion, po-stuff, po-feature, po-place}.

(P1) [33, Section 5] For all $R \in$ PO, R is transitive, asymmetric, and irreflexive (i.e., a strict partial order).

(P2) For all $R \in$ PO, $R \sqsubseteq$ part-of. Note that this does *not* imply that part-of is transitive, as prescribed in [33].

(P3) spatially-located-in is transitive and reflexive. Note that spatially-located-in should not be understood to be a subproperty of part-of according to [33].

(P4) [33, Section 6] For all $R \in$ PO, we have

$$R \circ \text{spatially-located-in} \sqsubseteq \text{spatially-located-in} \quad \text{and}$$
$$\text{spatially-located-in} \circ R \sqsubseteq \text{spatially-located-in}.$$

(P5) [33, page 435] For all $R \in$ PO $\cup$ {spatially-located-in}, and all classes C, we have the first-order predicate logic axiom

$$(\forall x)(\forall y)(R(x,y) \land C(y) \to (\exists z)(R(x,z) \land C(z)).$$

Note that this is a tautology.

Category	Description	Example	Text Patterns
Component-Integral Object	Parts are functional, non-homeomerous and separable from the whole.	Handle-Cup	part of, component of
Member-Collection	Parts are non functional, non homeomerous and separable from the whole.	Tree-Forest	member of, part-of
Portion-Mass	Parts are non-functional, homeomerous and separable from the whole.	Slice-Pie	of, part-of
Stuff-Object	Parts are non-functional, non-homeomerous and inseparable from the whole.	Gin-Martini	is partly, made of
Feature-Activity	Parts are functional, non-homeomerous and inseparable from the whole.	Paying-Shopping	has, have
Place-Area	Parts are non-functional, homeomerous and inseparable from the whole.	Everglades-Florida	located in, part-of

Table 1: Six type of partonomic relation with relational elements

(P6) [33, page 435] For all $R \in \mathsf{PO} \cup \{\text{spatially-located-in}\}$, and all classes C, we have the first-order predicate logic axiom

$$(\forall x)(\forall y)(C(y) \wedge (C(y) \to R(x,y)) \to R(x,y)).$$

Please note that this is a tautology.

Summarizing, we can axiomatize (P1) to (P4) as the following axioms—we will discuss (P5) and (P6) further below.

- For all $R \in \mathsf{PO}$, R is transitive, antisymmetric, and irreflexive.

- For all $R \in \mathsf{PO}$, $R \sqsubseteq$ part-of.

- spatially-located-in is transitive and reflexive.

- For all $R \in \mathsf{PO}$, we have

  $R \circ$ spatially-located-in $\sqsubseteq$ spatially-located-in   and

  spatially-located-in $\circ\ R \sqsubseteq$ spatially-located-in.

This results in a total of $3 \cdot 6 + 2 \cdot 6 + 2 + 6 \cdot 2 = 44$ axioms, all expressible in OWL 2.

However, there is a catch. While all these axioms are expressible in OWL 2 (more precisely, in OWL 2 Full), the collection of these ontologies does not constitute a valid OWL 2 DL ontology. The reason for this is that (P1) violates a global constraint on OWL 2 DL ontologies given in [24, Section 11]: A property cannot be transitive and irreflexive at the same time.[2] In other words, we cannot specify strict partial orders in OWL 2 DL.[3] The most straightforward way to fix this, is to drop one of the requirements on

R in (P1), and the most obvious candidate would be to drop the irreflexivity axioms. The resulting set of 38 axioms then constitutes a valid OWL 2 DL ontology.

Let us now return to the axioms from (P5) and (P6). They are tautologies in first-order predicate logic, which means that they do not contribute any additional knowledge. As such, they do not need to be added to our ontology.[4] Note that this does not mean that the observations leading to (P5) and (P6) in [33] are void: We obtain tautologies because the use of OWL suggests a particular type of modeling class membership (called class inclusion in [33]) which is probably not obvious or necessary from a more general, linguistic perspective.

It is possible to partially recover irreflexivity of the $R \in \mathsf{PO}$. One way to do this is to use the DL-safe SWRL rule [18, 21, 25] $R(x,y) \wedge R(y,x) \to x \neq y$, which expresses the same as irreflexivity, however its application is restricted to known individuals and is thus weaker than (first-order logic) irreflexivity. Another alternative is to use nominal schemas [21, 22], e.g. by means of the axiom[5]

$$\{x\} \sqcap \exists R.\exists R.\{x\} \sqsubseteq \bot$$

which can actually be understood as a macro that results in n OWL 2 DL axioms, where n is the number of known individuals in the knowledge base.[6] This means that we can incorporate a weak form of irreflexivity *in OWL 2 DL* without having to use DL-safe SWRL (and software which supports the latter).

There is yet another catch: All properties occurring in the above constructed part-of ontology are complex (i.e., non-simple), and OWL 2 DL has global restrictions on the use

---

[2]A transitive property is complex, and thus not simple. However only simple properties are allowed to be irreflexive.

[3]Note that transitivity and irreflexivity of a property R imply that R is also antisymmetric (i.e., a strict partial order): Assume R were transitive and irreflexive, but not antisymmetric. Then, because R is not antisymmetric we must have a, b with $R(a,b)$ and $R(b,a)$ and $a \neq b$. But by transitivity of R, we obtain $R(a,a)$ from $R(a,b)$ and $R(b,a)$ which is impossible by irreflexivity.

[4]In other words, adding them would accomplish nothing.

[5]Nominal schemas could also be used to directly express the just mentioned DL-safe rule [22]. However, this would result in a more complicated axiom with two nominal schemas, which is less favorable in terms of scalability.

[6]The OWL 2 DL axioms are obtained by *grounding*: Replace $\{x\}$ by all available nominals $\{a\}$, a being a known individual, each such replacement resulting in one OWL 2 DL axiom.

of such properties. If this ontology is used in conjunction with a domain ontology, then these global restrictions may be violated. Likewise, usage of properties in OWL 2 DL is globally restricted by the so-called *regularity* condition,[7] which may also be violated if the part-of ontology is used together with a domain ontology. In a way similar to the irreflexivity issue discussed above, it is possible to recover from this by expressing some (or all) of the axioms in the part-of ontology in weaker form, using DL-safe rules or nominal schemas. How this is best done depends on the domain ontology, but it is always possible in principle, and indeed relatively straightforward.

3. APPROACH

Given a LOD Cloud dataset, our solution – PLATO – automatically enriches it with partonomy properties through four key steps.[8]

First, PLATO generates candidate pairs of entities from the dataset. Second, PLATO generates "hypothesis" of possible partonomy properties – represented as linguistic patterns – for each entity pair. Next, PLATO tests the resulting patterns (and hence hypotheses) in a corpus driven manner. Finally, PLATO asserts only those partonomy properties with strong supporting evidence. Figure 1 depicts the workflow, which we describe in more detail in the subsequent sections.

3.1 Candidate Generation

Given a LOD Cloud dataset, PLATO generates all possible pairs between the entities in the dataset. However, the number of entity pairs can be extremely large, which can make the subsequent steps intractable. To address this problem, PLATO filters unpromising entity pairs using a simple heuristic—i.e. entities that are strongly associated are more likely to be related via some property than those that are not. PLATO implements this heuristic by exploiting Wikipedia. The references between Wikipedia pages provide a good proxy for association. Moreover, Wikipedia provides comprehensive coverage across diverse domains. For each entity pair, PLATO retrieves the corresponding Wikipedia page of each entity—using the Mediawiki API[9]—and if these pages refer to each other, then the pair is said to be strongly associated and kept for subsequent processing. Otherwise, the pair is discarded.

For datasets besides DBpedia, such as Freebase, we use the sameAs links present between DBpedia entity (e.g. dbpedia: Cellulose) and entity of other datasets (e.g. fbase: Cellulose). Then we check if the any of the entity refers to the other one. For example, if fbase: Chicken links to dbpedia: Salt. This is just a way to reduce the number of candidate pairs and it is possible to use other techniques to generate these pairs. The use of dataset specific heuristics has been used in other tools such as SILK [31], in order to maximize finding relationships between any two datasets. It is possible to replace this module with another heuristics to generate candidate pairs and use the rest of the system without any modifications.

---

[7]See "Restriction on the Property Hierarchy" in [24, Section 11].

[8]PLATO follows these same four steps for enriching multiple LOD Cloud datasets. For ease of exposition, we will describe PLATO in the context of enriching a single dataset.

[9]http://en.wikipedia.org/w/api.php

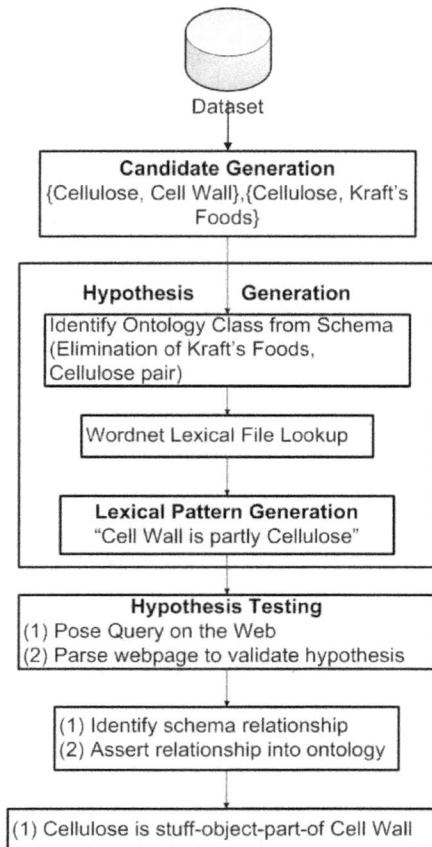

Figure 1: PLATO system flow chart

Please note, in principal it is possible to replace the usage of Mediawiki API with entities directly from DBPedia. However, it may result in the loss of some useful candidate pairs as DBpedia captures limited information from Wikipedia. For example, as of 6th February 2012, the DBpedia page for Cellulose does not refer to Carbon. However, the Wikipedia pages for Carbon and Cellulose do refer to each other, thus making them possible candidate pairs for consideration.

For example, given the DBpedia dataset from the LOD Cloud, some of the entity pairs generated by PLATO will include:

- Cellulose, Cell Wall
- Cellulose, Kraft's Food

PLATO retrieves the Wikipedia pages for Cellulose, Cell Wall, and Kraft's Foods. The Wikipedia pages for Cellulose and Cell Wall refer to each other, so this pair is kept. The Wikipedia page for Cellulose refers to the page for Kraft's Foods, due to usage of Cellulose in cheese manufacturing at Kraft's Foods. However, the page for The Kraft's Foods does not refer back to the page for Cellulose. Hence, this pair is considered to be only weakly associated by PLATO, and thus discarded.

3.2 Hypothesis Generation

PLATO generates hypotheses of possible OWL partonomy properties (described in Section 2) for each entity pair from the previous step. PLATO now determines the type of each entity in the pair using WordNet [11]—a lexical taxonomy that is well suited for this task. Specifically, PLATO retrieves the lexicographer file of the WordNet synset corresponding to each entity to serve as its type.[10] The name of this file has the form *POS.SUFFIX* where *POS* is the part-of-speech (i.e. noun, verb, adv, or adj) and *SUFFIX* is the broader group that the synset (and hence entity) belongs to (e.g. animal, plant, etc.). For example, given the entity pair (*Cell Wall, Cellulose*), lexicographer files of the synsets corresponding to these entities are both noun.body.

PLATO uses this information to determine the applicable OWL partonomy properties. We captured these properties from Winston's taxonomy of part-whole relations [33] (see Section 2), which was chosen for the following reasons:

- Winston's taxonomy is well-established and widely accepted.

- Winston provides guidelines on what types are applicable to each part-whole relationship—e.g. Winston's *Place-Area* relationship applies to only areas, places, and locations. These guidelines can be captured as domain-range axioms for each corresponding OWL partonomy property.

- Winston suggests linguistic cues for each part-whole relationship, which PLATO can use to generate linguistic patterns.

If *POS* is not a noun or verb, then PLATO discards the entity pair because Winton's relationships apply to only nouns and verbs. If so, then PLATO uses the SUFFIX to determine the OWL partonomy properties that are applicable based on their domain and range. Returning to our example, the OWL properties of po-component and po-stuff—corresponding to Winston's *Component-Integral-Object* and *Stuff-Object* relationships respectively—are applicable because the SUFFIXES of Cell Wall and Cellulose satisfy the domain and range of these properties.

Finally, PLATO generates linguistic patterns for each applicable property based on linguistic cues suggested by Winston. For example, the linguistic cues for po-stuff include "is made of" and "is partly." From these cues, the following linguistic patterns are generated for (*Cell Wall, Cellulose*):

- Cell Wall is made of Cellulose

- Cellulose is made of Cell Wall

- Cell Wall is partly Cellulose

- Cellulose is partly Cell Wall

These patterns serve as hypotheses to be validated in the next step.

3.3 Hypothesis Testing

PLATO tests the lexical patterns for each entity pair in a corpus-driven manner. PLATO uses the Web as the corpus because of its coverage, and uses publicly available search

APIs to access its contents. Specifically, PLATO uses the Bing Search API 2.0[11] because it allows unlimited searches.

For each pattern generated for an entity pair, PLATO executes a search of the pattern using the BING API, and takes the top N search results (i.e. URLs for the top N webpages) returned by BING. N can be adjusted by the user; and PLATO sets the default value of N to 50, which we found to produce good results empirically. For each resulting URL, PLATO fetches the page it points to—using off-the-shelf crawling and html parsing technologies, e.g., JSOUP[12]—and determines whether the pattern appears in the page based on exact string match with stemming. This step is necessary because the search results can contain spurious pages—i.e. pages that do not contain the actual pattern. For example, a page containing the string "Is the cell wall of a plant made of cellulose fibers?" may appear in the search result for the pattern "cell wall is made of cellulose"; but this string does not match the pattern (and hence does not support it). The crawling of the page is necessary as the snippet of the page in the result is typically retrieved from the cache, and the actual content may or may not reflect the same content.

Finally, PLATO counts the total number of pages that contain the pattern, and uses this count as the level of support for the OWL partonomy property—associated with the pattern—that could exist between the entity pair. For each entity pair, PLATO asserts the partonomy property whose associated pattern has the strongest supporting evidence, computed from the previous step. Returning to our example for the entity pair (*Cell Wall, Cellulose*), the supporting evidence for each pattern associated with the pair (assuming a search limit of 50) is below:

- Cell Wall is made of Cellulose, 48

- Cellulose is made of Cell Wall, 10

- Cell Wall is partly Cellulose, 50

- Cellulose is partly Cell Wall, 7

Since the pattern 'Cell Wall is partly Cellulose' has the strongest support, the associated property po-stuff—corresponding to Winston's *Stuff-Object* relationships—is asserted, with Cellulose as the part and Cell Wall as the whole.

In addition to adding properties at the instance-level (i.e. between entities), PLATO also enriches the schema by generalizing from the instance level assertions. To explain this step, let C and D be two classes about which we want to find out whether they should be related on the schema level by one of the partonomic relationships R. From the process just described, we obtain a set $M_{R,C,D}$ of instance level assertions of the form $R(a,b)$, where $a \in C$ and $b \in D$.[13] We now add schema level axioms according to the following rules: (1) If, for all $a \in C$, there is a $b \in D$ with $R(a,b) \in M_{R,C,D}$, then add the axiom $C \sqsubseteq \exists R.D$, which can be expressed in OWL/RDF serialization using the *owl:someValuesFrom* property restriction. (2) If, for all $b \in D$, there is a $a \in C$ with $R(a,b) \in M_{R,C,D}$, then add the axiom $D \sqsubseteq \exists R^-.C$, were R^- indicates the inverse (using *owl:inverseOf*) property of R. While this approach seems to be rather crude

---

[10]If a WordNet synset cannot be found for an entity, then PLATO will generalize the entity by looking up its superclass in DBpedia using the JENA ARQ API (http://openjena.org/).

[11]http://msdn.microsoft.com/en-us/library/dd251056.aspx
[12]http://jsoup.org/apidocs/
[13]If we did not obtain any such assertion, then we do not add any schema axiom.

compared to schema learning methods based on inductive paradigms,[14] it already achieves good results, as can be seen from our evaluation in Section 4.3.

4. EVALUATION

We present three experiments to evaluate the performance of PLATO on enriching LOD Cloud dataset with partonomy properties. The first experiment evaluates PLATO's performance on discovering partonomy properties between entities within the same LOD Cloud dataset (i.e. intra-dataset instance-level partonomy discovery). The second experiment evaluates PLATO's performance across different LOD Cloud datasets (i.e. inter-dataset instance-level partonomy discovery). The final experiment evaluates PLATO's performance on discovery partonomy properties at the schema level. All the evaluation components of this work are available for download at the PLATO Project Page[15]

4.1 Intra-Dataset Instance-Level Partonomy Discovery

We evaluated the performance of PLATO on discovering partonomy properties between entities within the same LOD Cloud dataset using the following methodology. First, we chose the DBpedia dataset because: 1) it is one of the largest datasets available on the Linked Open Data Cloud; and 2) it covers diverse domains such as Geography, Science, Politics, History and Arts [5]. The scale and coverage of DBpedia allows us to thoroughly evaluate the performance of PLATO across different partonomy types [33] and domains.

Next, we randomly generated 83,639 entity pairs from DBpedia for evaluation because it was not practical to generate all possible entity pairs given DBpedia's size. We used the Mediawiki API[16] to randomly generate a pair of Wikipedia articles, whose URLs were then translated to the corresponding DBpedia entities. Given that it is not practical to generate all entity pairs within DBpedia, this method provides an unbiased dataset for evaluation.

We then applied PLATO to the resulting dataset to automatically discover partonomy properties between each entity pair. For each partonomy property discovered, the property was randomly assigned to one of three human graders, who validated its correctness. A human grader determined that the partonomy property discovered by PLATO between a pair of entities is correct if the following conditions are all satisfied:

- A part-whole relationship does exist between the entities

- The correct partonomy property is given

- The part-whole roles are correctly assigned to the entities – e.g., given the pair cell and cell wall, cell is the whole and cell wall is the part.

Finally, we report the precision (i.e. the number of correct partonomy properties discovered by PLATO over the total number of partonomy properties discovered) based on the human grader's responses. We did not report the recall for

PLATO because: 1) an existing DBpedia benchmark for this purpose does not exist, and 2) the large number of entity pairs made it difficult to compute the recall manually due to time and resource limitations.

Table 2 shows the results for this experiment. Of the 83,639 entity pairs generated, PLATO discovered partonomy properties for 13,853 pairs. We should note that partonomy relationships do not exist for many of the entity pairs because these pairs were randomly generated – e.g. a random sample of 100 pairs found only 11 to have a valid partonomy relationship. PLATO was able to filter many of these extraneous pairs based on the heuristic that two entities must be strongly associated (see Section 3.1). Overall, PLATO achieved high precision in discovering partonomy properties between entities in DBpedia. Moreover, PLATO discovered partonomy properties across a wide range of entities ranging from places to chemical compounds. However, PLATO did have low precision for a couple of partonomy properties – i.e. 'Portion-Mass' and 'Place-Area'. For 'Portion-Mass', PLATO did not find any entities related to each other. This is understandable as this property deals with very abstract entities such as 'Slice of Lemon', 'Hunk of Clay', etc. and hence it's hard to find entities of this type in DBpedia.

PLATO achieved low precision for the Place-Area property because many places are ambiguous. For example, Athens can refer to either a city in Greece, Georgia, or Ohio. Similarly, Delaware can refer to either the U.S. state of Delaware or Delaware county in the U.S. state of Oklahoma. In the case of the later, given the entity pair of Delaware (State) and Oklahoma, PLATO may find false evidence supporting the hypothesis that the state of Delaware is part of Oklahoma, which can lead to poor precision. This problem can be addressed with richer partonomy semantics such as a state cannot be part of another state. These richer semantics are not captured by Winston's partonomy relationships (and hence the corresponding OWL properties), and offers a possible direction for future research.

Although we could not report recall, we provide preliminary insights into PLATO's performance on this measure. Our random sample of 100 entity pairs (see above) suggests PLATO achieved good performance on this metric. Of the 11 pairs with valid partonomy properties, PLATO discovered 7 of them. Moreover, qualitative observations of sample results further suggest that PLATO performs well on recall. For example, PLATO discovered the correct partonomy property between NATO and 23 of its member states – the total number of NATO member states is 28. Similarly, PLATO discovered the correct partonomy property between the Rock Band 'Nirvana' and all of its members – i.e. Kurt Cobain, Krist Novoselic and Dave Grohl.

The dataset and results used in this experiment are available at the project page[17], and we will continue to provide additional information related to partonomy as it becomes available.

4.2 Inter-Dataset Instance-Level Partonomy Discovery

We evaluated the performance of PLATO on discovering partonomy properties between entities from different LOD Cloud datasets using the following methodology. First, we created two inter-dataset partonomy discovery tasks: 1) discovering partonomy properties between Freebase dishes and

---

[14]such as [23]

[15]http://wiki.knoesis.org/index.php/PLATO

[16]http://en.wikipedia.org/w/api.php
?action=query&list=random&rnnamespace=0

[17]http://wiki.knoesis.org/index.php/PLATO

Relation Type	Distinct Entity Pairs	Correctly Found	Precision
Stuff-Object-Part-Of	4178	3427	0.82
Component-Integral-Part-Of	3126	27931	0.89
Feature-Activity-Part-Of	1287	464	0.85
Member-Collection-Part-Of	1912	803	0.85
Portion-Mass-Part-Of	0	0	NA
Place Area-Part-Of	3350	1248	0.48
Total	13853	10557	0.76

Table 2: Precision of the six different relation types between DBpedia entities

DBpedia ingredients, and 2) discovering partonomy properties between Freebase human anatomy parts and DBpedia organs. We chose these two tasks because:

- Freebase provides a pre-defined list of 2,615 food dishes[18] and 2,916 human anatomy parts,[19] which have well-defined parts (i.e. ingredient) and wholes (i.e. organ) respectively.

- DBpedia provides the corresponding parts and wholes.

- Freebase provides the ingredients for each food dish, which can be used as an independent gold standard for the first task; and experts in the medical domain were readily available to assess PLATO's performance for the second task.

We then applied PLATO to both tasks. For the Dish-Ingredient task, we validated the partonomy properties discovered by PLATO against the ingredients for each dish provided by Freebase to compute both precision (i.e. number of correct partonomy properties discovered by PLATO over all partonomy properties discovered) and recall (i.e. number of actual partonomy properties discovered by PLATO over all partonomy properties). For the Anatomy-Organ task, an independent gold standard does not exist – i.e. Freebase does not provide the organs for each anatomy part. Hence, we employed an expert in human anatomy to grade each partonomy property discovered by PLATO, and reported PLATO's precision based on the expert's response. These experts had no knowledge about PLATO and were presented the results as an exercise to judge if the presented ingredients are used for the given dish. The expert used the same grading criteria described in the previous experiment (see Section 4.1). We did not report the recall for PLATO because of resource and time limitations.

Task	Recall	Precision
Dish-Ingredient Task	0.72	0.53
Anatomy-Organ Task	N/A	0.86

Table 3: This table shows PLATO's performance on precision and recall for the Dish-Ingredient task, and PLATO's performance on precision for the Anatomy-Organ task. Recall was not reported for the second task because of time and resource limitations.

Table 3 shows the results for both tasks. For the Dish-Ingredient task, PLATO achieved high recall and modest

[18]http://www.freebase.com/view/food/views/dish
[19]http://www.freebase.com/view/medicine/views/anatomical_structure

precision. The Freebase dish gold standard consists of 2,615 dishes and a total of 1317 ingredients across these dishes. Many of the dishes do not have ingredients mentioned for them. PLATO discovered a total of 1766 partonomy relationships between Freebase dishes and DBpedia ingredients, of which 936 are valid according to the gold standard – giving a recall of 0.72 and precision of 0.53. This result demonstrates that PLATO can effectively discover partonomy properties across different LOD Cloud datasets. Interestingly, the modest precision was due to PLATO discovering additional, valid partonomy properties not present in the Freebase gold standard. For example, a stuff-object property exists between the ingredient ice cream and the dish 'Baked Alaska', which PLATO correctly discovered. However, the Freebase gold standard overlooked this relationship, resulting in lower precision.

Given this oversight, we employed 2 human graders to independently review each extra result generated (830 in total) to determine whether it's due to a real erroneous result given by PLATO or a gap in the gold standard (i.e. an overlooked ingredient in a food dish). The graders used the same grading criteria described in Section 4.1 We also required that both graders agree that a response is valid in order for it to be counted as correct. The graders responses were then used to adjust the precision. They found 512 correct answers out of 830, which resulted in total correct ingredients of 936+512=1448, an adjusted precision of 0.82 – a significant increase over the original precision.

For the Anatomy-Organ task, PLATO achieved high precision. Of the 8,397 distinct partonomy properties discovered by PLATO, the human expert verified 7,221 as correct, thus leading to a precision of 0.86. The expert in this case, is a researcher in medical science and not related to research and development of PLATO. The expert was presented the results of PLATO as a grading exercise to judge if the assertions are right or wrong. This result further demonstrates – in a different domain – that PLATO can effectively discover partonomy properties across different LOD Cloud datasets. For example, PLATO correctly identified that the entity 'Axon' is a component-integral object part of entities such as 'dorsal root ganglion', 'synapse', 'neuron' and 'nerve'. We plan to enrich Freebase's list of anatomy structures with the partonomy properties discovered by PLATO for this task.

4.3 Assertion of schema level links

Using the instance level assertions which are generated between entities, it becomes possible to identify the schema level relationships, which exist between the classes of these entities, as, described at the end of Section 3.2. For example, using the fact that 'Nirvana has a member Kurt Cobain' and

'Queen has a member Freddie Mercury', and in fact that for all bands some member has been found which is classified as an artist, we are able to identify schema level assertions between DBpedia classes such as

```
dbpedia-owl:Band rdfs:subClassOf  [
    rdf:type            owl:Restriction ;
    owl:onProperty      :hasMember ;
    owl:someValuesFrom  dbpedia-owl:Artist
] .
```

The schema level statement essentially says that 'Bands have members Artists'. Table 4 shows the evaluation of precision for schema level links, which were asserted by PLATO.

Total # of Class Pairs	Correctly Identified	Precision
93	81	0.87

Table 4: Precision as measured on Schema Level Links Between DBpedia entities

The entity in column 1 in Table 4 is the total number of distinct class pairs that were asserted to have a relationship in the file expressing schema level constraints. For example [dbpedia-owl:Artist,dbpediaowl:Organization],[dbpedia-owl:Artist,dbpedia-owl:Artifact]. Thus, a single entity may occur in multiple such combinations, but in each of these pairs, the entity with which it is being related to is unique. Of these 93 different pairs, a total of 81 were found to be correct, leading to a precision of 0.87. The number of class pairs found is low because many entities in the DBpedia dataset do not have any classes associated with them. Identification of schema level relationships can potentially help with improving the precision and recall of instance level relationship identification. This dataset has also been made available on the project page for download.

5. RELATED WORK

To the best of our knowledge, this is the first work which, automatically identifies 'part-of' relationships in the context of the LOD cloud or RDF datasets. The field of Ontology Matching and Instance Matching has been focusing on identifying relationships such as 'sameAs','subClass' and 'equivalentClass.' In [10, 8] the authors present a survey in the area of ontology matching. This helps in cleaning up the data and improving the quality of links at the instance level, but the issue of identifying appropriate relationships at the schema level has not been addressed. voiD [1] provides a vocabulary to represent the relationships between the different datasets. SILK Framework [32] automates the process of link discovery between LOD datasets at the instance level. At the schema level, a notable effort for creating a unified reference point for LOD schemas is UMBEL [3], which is a coherent framework for ontology development and can serve as a reference framework.

There has been a number of efforts in the area of Natural Language Processing for identification of part-of relationships within a text corpora [14, 30]. This includes effort that utilizes the presence of certain lexico-syntactic patterns (Hearst patterns [16]) to indicate a particular semantic relationship between two nouns. However, much of this work

has been confined to ontology learning [9] in the sense of hyponym extraction [16]. A closely related work that also mines the Web for the relations is NELL [6]. There are a few notable differences between our approach and NELL, (1) NELL uses a crawler to crawl the Web and identify relations it can find between entities on the web. We are focused on LOD cloud and for a given pair of entities, PLATO tries to identify the relationship between them. (2) Predicates or properties extracted from NELL are at the surface level and do not convey the semantics of the properties. For example, while NELL does extracts fact such as Athens and Greece are related by the predicate citycapitalofcountry, it does not explicitly provides any semantics to those relationships. We have definitely gained a lot of insight from the work of NELL and it also validates our belief that web can be mined to gain information about relationships. However, it will be extremely difficult to compare PLATO with NELL since, NELL is not available for download and systems have different set up and objectives.

The closest work in this respect is Espresso [26] that again works on a specific text corpus. A key difference of this work from ours is its use of a supervised approach. Further, it disregards any information about the type of entities, which we capture using Winston's patterns.

6. POTENTIAL IMPACT & FUTURE WORK

To the best of our knowledge, this is the only work that can identify partonomic relations between entities in the LOD Cloud. The potential impact of this work is many fold in the context of the LOD Cloud and beyond. Our work suggests that introducing the part-of relationship as a standard ingredient in and between LOD Cloud datasets is viable. This will allow LOD to move beyond the sameAs relationship and allow it to be used for more meaningful purposes. The discovery of individual components of various entities such as body parts or organizations may enable the identification of new scientific facts and the answering of analytical queries. The extension of Freebase to incorporate this information for dishes and human anatomy is something we would like to address in the short term. We would also like to add partonomical relations between entities of other LOD datasets. The additional schema information generated by PLATO will also be made available as a part of the LOD cloud for use by the reasoning community. The low precision on the Place-Area relationship is a matter of concern and we plan to address it in near future. We would also like to evaluate the results for Anatomy-Organ Task using a domain specific ontology such as Foundational Model of Anatomy [20].

We plan on contributing the entire corpus of entities that have been identified to be in part-of relationship as a dataset to the LOD cloud. This will prove useful for researchers who wish to utilize the dataset and also for any comparative evaluation in the future. We have done an initial testing of our approach on identification of other relationships such as 'causality' and it appears promising. We would like to extend it further and develop techniques for the identification of these relations, eventually leading to a rich Relationship Web. There is also plenty of scope for the improvement of our own technique as well. We would like to be able to extend PLATO to identify fundamental relationships. We

---

[20]http://fma.biostr.washington.edu/

would like to further strengthen the schema learning part by adding established inductive methods. We would also like to add additional capabilities for entity disambiguation to improve precision and recall figures. We would also like to explore the use of schema knowledge generated by PLATO to improve instance matching, leading to a system with a feedback loop.

7. CONCLUSION

In this paper we have presented an automatic approach (PLATO) for identification of part-of relation between entities in the LOD cloud. These entities can be part of the same dataset or can belong to different datasets. In addition, the entities can be either instances or classes. Our approach is based on the foundational work by Winston in the area of partonomy and the corresponding taxonomy for the same. Since Winston's work is more tailored towards linguistics, we have expressed the work using OWL constraints in order to operationalize it for the purpose of our work. We described the technical solution used to provide PLATO and also presented a comprehensive evaluation spanning thousands of entities in the LOD cloud. Our results demonstrate that PLATO identifies part-of relationships between entities in the LOD cloud with a fairly high precision.

We believe our solution works well because of the following reasons (1) We utilize a rich datasource 'the Web' to identify the relationship between entities (2) Our approach has a foundational underpinning on a classical work in partonomical relation.

8. ACKNOWLEDGMENTS

This work was supported by the National Science Foundation under award 1143717 "III: EAGER – Expressive Scalable Querying over Linked Open Data."

9. REFERENCES

[1] K. Alexander, R. Cyganiak, M. Hausenblas, and J. Zhao. Describing Linked Datasets – On the Design and Usage of voiD, the 'Vocabulary of Interlinked Datasets'. In *WWW2009 Workshop on Linked Data on the Web (LDOW2009)*, Madrid, Spain, 2009.

[2] A. Artale, E. Franconi, N. Guarino, and L. Pazzi. Part-whole relations in object-centered systems: An overview. *Data & Knowledge Engineering*, 20(3):347–383, 1996.

[3] Michael K. Bergman and Frédérick Giasson. UMBEL ontology, volume 1, technical documentation. Technical Report 1, Structured Dynamics, 2008. Available from: http://umbel.org/doc/UMBELOntology_vA1.pdf.

[4] Christian Bizer, Tom Heath, and Tim Berners Lee. Linked data - the story so far. *International Journal on Semantic Web and Information Systems*, 5(3):1–22, 2009.

[5] Christian Bizer, Jens Lehmann, Georgi Kobilarov, Sören Auer, Christian Becker, Richard Cyganiak, and Sebastian Hellmann. DBpedia—A crystallization point for the Web of Data. *Journal of Web Semantics*, 7(3):154–165, 2009.

[6] Andrew Carlson, Justin Betteridge, Bryan Kisiel, Burr Settles, Estevam R. Hruschka Jr., and Tom M. Mitchell. Toward an architecture for never-ending language learning. In *Proceedings of the Twenty-Fourth Conference on Artificial Intelligence (AAAI 2010)*, 2010.

[7] R. Casati and A.C. Varzi. *Parts and places: The structures of spatial representation.* The MIT Press, 1999.

[8] Namyoun Choi, Il-Yeol Song, and Hyoil Han. A survey on ontology mapping. *SIGMOD Rec.*, 35(3):34–41, 2006.

[9] Philipp Cimiano, Andreas Hotho, and Steffen Staab. Learning concept hierarchies from text corpora using formal concept analysis. *J. Artif. Int. Res.*, 24:305–339, August 2005.

[10] Jérôme Euzenat and Pavel Shvaiko. *Ontology matching.* Springer-Verlag, Heidelberg (DE), 2007.

[11] Christiane Fellbaum, editor. *WordNet: An Electronic Lexical Database (Language, Speech, and Communication).* The MIT Press, illustrated edition edition, May 1998.

[12] David Ferrucci, Eric Brown, Jennifer Chu-Carroll, James Fan, David Gondek, Aditya A Kalyanpur, Adam Lally, J William Murdock, Eric Nyberg, and John Prager. Building watson: An overview of the deepqa project. *AI Magazine*, 31(3):59–79, 2010.

[13] P. Gerstl and S. Pribbenow. A conceptual theory of part-whole relations and its applications. *Data & Knowledge Engineering*, 20(3):305–322, 1996.

[14] R. Girju, A. Badulescu, and D. Moldovan. Automatic discovery of part-whole relations. *Computational Linguistics*, 32(1):83–135, 2006.

[15] Michael Hausenblas. Exploiting linked data to build web applications. *IEEE Internet Computing*, 13:68–73, 2009.

[16] Marti A. Hearst. Automatic acquisition of hyponyms from large text corpora. In *Proceedings of the 14th conference on Computational linguistics – Volume 2*, COLING '92, pages 539–545, Stroudsburg, PA, USA, 1992.

[17] P. Hitzler, M. Krötzsch, B. Parsia, P.F. Patel-Schneider, and S. Rudolph, editors. *OWL 2 Web Ontology Language: Primer.* W3C Recommendation, 27 October 2009. Available at http://www.w3.org/TR/owl2-primer/.

[18] Ian Horrocks, Peter F. Patel-Schneider, Harold Boley, Said Tabet, Benjamin Grosof, and Mike Dean. *SWRL: A Semantic Web Rule Language Combining OWL and RuleML.* W3C Member Submission 21 May 2004, 2004. Available from http://www.w3.org/Submission/SWRL/.

[19] Prateek Jain, Pascal Hitzler, Peter Z. Yeh, Kunal Verma, and Amit P. Sheth. Linked Data is Merely More Data. In *Linked Data Meets Artificial Intelligence*, pages 82–86. AAAI Press, Menlo Park, CA, 2010.

[20] Prateek Jain, Peter Z. Yeh, Kunal Verma, Cory A. Henson, and Amit P. Sheth. SPARQL query re-writing using partonomy based transformation rules. In *Proceedings of the 3rd International Conference on GeoSpatial Semantics*, GeoS '09, pages 140–158, Berlin, Heidelberg, 2009. Springer-Verlag.

[21] Adila Krisnadhi, Frederick Maier, and Pascal Hitzler.

OWL and Rules. In *Reasoning Web. Semantic Technologies for the Web of Data – 7th International Summer School 2011, Galway, Ireland, August 23-27, 2011, Tutorial Lectures*, volume 6848 of *Lecture Notes in Computer Science*, pages 382–415. Springer, Heidelberg, 2011.

[22] Markus Krötzsch, Frederick Maier, Adila A. Krisnadhi, and Pascal Hitzler. A better uncle for OWL: Nominal schemas for integrating rules and ontologies. In *Proceedings of the 20th International World Wide Web Conference, WWW2011, Hyderabad, India, March/April 2011*, pages 645–654. ACM, New York, 2011.

[23] Jens Lehmann and Pascal Hitzler. Concept learning in description logics using refinement operators. *Machine Learning*, 78(1–2):203–250, 2010.

[24] B. Motik, P.F. Patel-Schneider, and B. Parsia, editors. *OWL 2 Web Ontology Language: Structural Specification and Functional-Style Syntax*. W3C Recommendation, 27 October 2009. Available at http://www.w3.org/TR/owl2-syntax/.

[25] Boris Motik, Ulrike Sattler, and Rudi Studer. Query answering for OWL DL with rules. *Journal of Web Semantics*, 3(1):41–60, 2005.

[26] Patrick Pantel and Marco Pennacchiotti. Espresso: leveraging generic patterns for automatically harvesting semantic relations. In *Proceedings of the 21st International Conference on Computational Linguistics and the 44th annual meeting of the Association for Computational Linguistics*, ACL-44, pages 113–120, Stroudsburg, PA, USA, 2006.

[27] Alan Rector, Chris Welty, Natasha Noy, and Evan Wallace. Simple part-whole relations in OWL Ontologies available at http://www.w3.org/2001/sw/bestpractices/oep/simplepartwhole/, August 2005.

[28] Barry Smith. The basic tools of formal ontology. In *Formal Ontology in Information Systems*, 1998.

[29] Nectaria Tryfona and Max J. Egenhofer. Consistency among parts and aggregates: A computational model. *Transactions in GIS*, 1(3):189–206, 1996.

[30] Willem van Hage, Hap Kolb, and Guus Schreiber. A method for learning part-whole relations. In *The Semantic Web - ISWC 2006*, volume 4273 of *Lecture Notes in Computer Science*, pages 723–735. Springer Berlin / Heidelberg, 2006.

[31] J. Volz, C. Bizer, M. Gaedke, and G. Kobilarov. Silk–A Link Discovery Framework for the Web of Data. In *2nd Linked Data on the Web Workshop (LDOW2009)*, Madrid, Spain, 2009. Available from http://ceur-ws.org/Vol-538/ldow2009_paper13.pdf.

[32] Julius Volz, Christian Bizer, Martin Gaedke, and Georgi Kobilarov. Discovering and maintaining links on the web of data. In *ISWC '09: Proceedings of the 8th International Semantic Web Conference*, pages 650–665, Berlin, Heidelberg, 2009. Springer-Verlag.

[33] Morton E. Winston, Roger Chaffin, and Douglas Herrmann. A taxonomy of part-whole relations. *Cognitive Science*, 11(4):417–444, 1987.

Foundations of Traversal Based Query Execution over Linked Data

Olaf Hartig
Humboldt-Universität zu Berlin
Unter den Linden 6, 10099 Berlin, Germany
hartig@informatik.hu-berlin.de

Johann-Christoph Freytag
Humboldt-Universität zu Berlin
Unter den Linden 6, 10099 Berlin, Germany
freytag@informatik.hu-berlin.de

ABSTRACT

Query execution over the Web of Linked Data has attracted much attention recently. A particularly interesting approach is link traversal based query execution which proposes to integrate the traversal of data links into the creation of query results. Hence –in contrast to traditional query execution paradigms– this does not assume a fixed set of relevant data sources beforehand; instead, the traversal process discovers data and data sources on the fly and, thus, enables applications to tap the full potential of the Web.

While several authors have studied possibilities to implement the idea of link traversal based query execution and to optimize query execution in this context, no work exists that discusses theoretical foundations of the approach in general. Our paper fills this gap.

We introduce a well-defined semantics for queries that may be executed using a link traversal based approach. Based on this semantics we formally analyze properties of such queries. In particular, we study the computability of queries as well as the implications of querying a potentially infinite Web of Linked Data. Our results show that query computation in general is not guaranteed to terminate and that for any given query it is undecidable whether the execution terminates. Furthermore, we define an abstract execution model that captures the integration of link traversal into the query execution process. Based on this model we prove the soundness and completeness of link traversal based query execution and analyze an existing implementation approach.

Categories and Subject Descriptors

H.3.3 [**Information Storage and Retrieval**]: Information Search and Retrieval; F.1.1 [**Computation by Abstract Devices**]: Models of Computation

General Terms

Management, Theory

Keywords

link traversal based query execution, query semantics, computability, Web of Data, Linked Data

1. INTRODUCTION

During recent years an increasing number of data providers adopted the Linked Data principles for publishing and interlinking structured data on the World Wide Web (WWW) [10]. The Web of Linked Data that emerges from this process enables users to benefit from a virtually unbounded set of data sources and, thus, opens possibilities not conceivable before. Consequently, the Web of Linked Data has spawned research to execute declarative queries over multiple Linked Data sources. Most approaches adapt techniques that are known from the database literature (e.g. data warehousing or query federation). However, the Web of Linked Data is different from traditional database systems; distinguishing characteristics are its unbounded nature and the lack of a database catalog. Due to these characteristics it is impossible to know all data sources that might contribute to the answer of a query. In this context, traditional query execution paradigms are insufficient because those assume a fixed set of potentially relevant data sources beforehand. This assumption presents a restriction that inhibits applications to tap the full potential of the Web; it prevents a serendipitous discovery and utilization of relevant data from unknown sources.

An alternative to traditional query execution paradigms are exploration approaches that traverse links on the Web of Linked Data. These approaches enable a query execution system to automatically discover the most recent data from initially unknown data sources.

The prevalent example of an exploration based approach is link traversal based query execution. The idea of this approach is to intertwine the traversal of data links with the construction of the query result and, thus, to integrate the discovery of data into the query execution process [7]. This general idea may be implemented in various ways. For instance, Ladwig and Tran introduce an asynchronous implementation that adapts the concept of symmetric hash joins [13, 14]; Schmedding proposes an implementation that incrementally adjusts the answer to a query each time the execution system retrieves additional data [18]; our earlier work focuses on an implementation that uses a synchronous pipeline of iterators, each of which is responsible for a particular part of the query [6, 7]. All existing publications focus on approaches for implementing the idea of link traversal based query execution and on query optimization in the context of such an implementation. To our knowledge, no work exists that provides a general foundation for this new query execution paradigm.

We argue that a well-defined query semantics is essential to compare different query execution approaches and to verify implementations. Furthermore, a proper theoretical foundation enables a formal analysis of fundamental properties of queries and query executions. For instance, studying the computability of queries may answer whether particular query executions are guaranteed to terminate. In addition to these more theoretical questions, an under-

```
1   SELECT ?p ?l WHERE {
2      <http://bob.name>  <http://.../knows>  ?p .
3      ?p  <http://.../currentProject>  ?pr .
4      ?pr  <http://.../label>  ?l . }
```

Figure 1: Sample query presented in the language SPARQL.

standing of fundamental properties and limitations may help to gain new insight into challenges and possibilities for query planning and optimization. Therefore, in this paper we provide such a formal foundation of Linked Data queries and link traversal based query execution. Our contributions are:

1.) As a basis, we introduce a *theoretical framework* that comprises a data model and a computation model. The data model formalizes the idea of a Web of Linked Data; the computation model captures the limited data access capabilities of computations over the Web.

2.) We present a *query model* that introduces a well-defined semantics for conjunctive queries (which is the type of queries supported by existing link traversal based systems). Basically, the result of such a query is the set of all valuations that map the query to a subset of all Linked Data that is reachable, starting with entity identifiers mentioned in the query. We emphasize that our model does not prescribe a specific notion of reachability; instead, it is possible to make the notion of reachability applied to answer a query can be made explicit (by specifying which data links should be followed).

3.) We formally *analyze properties* of our query model. In particular, we study the implications of querying a potentially infinite Web and show that it is undecidable whether a query result will be finite or infinite. Furthermore, we analyze the computability of queries by adopting earlier work on Web queries which distinguishes finitely computable queries, eventually computable queries, and queries that are not even eventually computable. We prove that queries in our model are eventually computable. Hence, a link traversal based query execution system does not have to deal with queries that are not computable at all. However, we also show that it is undecidable whether a particular query execution terminates.

4.) We define an abstract *query execution model* that formalizes the general idea of link traversal based query execution. This model captures the approach of intertwining link traversal and result construction. Based on this model we prove the soundness and completeness of the new query execution paradigm.

5.) Finally, we use our execution model to formally analyze a particular implementation of link traversal based query execution.

This paper is organized as follows: In Section 2 we present an example that demonstrates the idea of link traversal based query execution. Section 3 defines our data model and our computation model. We present our query model in Section 4 and discuss its properties in Section 5. Section 6 introduces the corresponding execution model. Finally, we discuss related work in Section 7 and conclude the paper in Section 8. For all proofs of theorems, lemmas and propositions in this paper we refer to [8].

2. EXAMPLE EXECUTION

Link traversal based query execution is a novel query execution paradigm tailored to the Web of Linked Data. Since adhering to the Linked Data principles is the minimal requirement for publishing Linked Data on the WWW, the link traversal approach relies solely on these principles; it does not assume that each data source provides a data-local query interface (as would be required for query federation). The only way to obtain data is via URI look-ups.

Usually, Linked Data on the WWW is represented using the RDF data model [11] and queries are expressed using SPARQL [17].

$$(\text{ http://}\textbf{bob}.\text{name} , \text{http://.../}\textbf{knows} , \text{http://}\textbf{alice}.\text{name}) \in G_\text{b}$$

$$(\text{http://}\textbf{alice}.\text{name} , \text{http://.../}\textbf{name} , \text{"Alice"}) \in G_\text{a}$$

$$(\text{http://}\textbf{alice}.\text{name} , \text{http://.../}\textbf{currentProject} , \text{http://.../}\textbf{AlicesPrj}) \in G_\text{a}$$

$$(\text{http://.../}\textbf{AlicesPrj} , \text{http://.../}\textbf{label} , \text{"Alice's Project"}) \in G_\text{p}$$

Figure 2: Excerpts from Linked Data retrieved from the Web.

SPARQL queries consist of RDF graph patterns that contain query variables, denoted with the symbol '?'. The semantics of SPARQL is based on pattern matching [16]. Figure 1 provides a SPARQL representation of a query that asks for projects of acquaintances of user Bob, who is identified by URI http://bob.name. In lines 2 to 4 the query contains a conjunctive query represented as a set of three SPARQL triple patterns. In the following we outline a link traversal based execution of this conjunctive query.

Link traversal based query execution usually starts with an empty, query-local dataset. We obtain some seed data by looking up the URIs mentioned in the query: For the URI http://bob.name in our sample query we may retrieve a set G_b of RDF triples (cf. Figure 2), which we add to the local dataset. Now, we alternate between i) constructing valuations from RDF triples that match a pattern of our query in the query-local dataset, and ii) augmenting the dataset by looking up URIs which are part of these valuations. For the triple pattern in line 2 of our sample query the local dataset contains a matching triple, originating from G_b. Hence, we can construct a valuation $\mu_1 = \{?p \rightarrow \text{http://alice.name}\}$ that maps query variable ?p to the URI http://alice.name. By looking up this URI we may retrieve a set G_a of RDF triples, which we also add to the query-local dataset. Based on the augmented dataset we can extend μ_1 by adding a binding for ?pr. We obtain $\mu_2 = \{?p \rightarrow \text{http://alice.name}, ?pr \rightarrow \text{http://.../AlicesPrj}\}$, which already covers the pattern in line 2 and 3. Notice, constructing μ_2 is only possible because we retrieved G_a. However, before we discovered and resolved the URI http://alice.name, we neither knew about G_a nor about the existence of the data source from which we retrieved G_a. Hence, the traversal of data links enables us to answer queries based on data from initially unknown sources.

We proceed with our execution strategy as follows: We discover and retrieve G_p by looking up the URI http://.../AlicesPrj and extend μ_2 to $\mu_3 = \{?p \rightarrow \text{http://alice.name}, ?pr \rightarrow \text{http://.../AlicesPrj}, ?l \rightarrow \text{"Alice's Project"}\}$, which now covers the whole, conjunctive query. Hence, μ_3 can be reported as the result of that query.

3. MODELING A WEB OF LINKED DATA

In this section we introduce theoretical foundations which shall allow us to define and to analyze queries over Linked Data. In particular, we propose a data model and a computation model. For these models we assume a static view of the Web; that is, no changes are made to the data on the Web during the execution of a query.

3.1 Data Model

The WWW is the most prominent implementation of a Web of Linked Data and it shows that the idea of Linked Data scales to a virtually unlimited dataspace. Nonetheless, other implementations are possible (e.g. within the boundaries of a closed, globally distributed corporate network). Such an implementation may be based on the same technologies used for the WWW (i.e. HTTP, URIs, RDF, etc.) or it may use other, similar technologies. Consequently, our data model abstracts from the concrete technologies that implement Linked Data in the WWW and, thus, enables us to study queries over any Web of Linked Data.

As a basis for our model we use a simple, triple based data model for representing the data that is distributed over a Web of Linked

Data (similar to the RDF data model that is used for Linked Data on the WWW). We assume a countably infinite set $\mathcal{I}$ of possible identifiers (e.g. all URIs) and a countably infinite set $\mathcal{L}$ of all possible constant literals (e.g. all possible strings, natural numbers, etc.). $\mathcal{I}$ and $\mathcal{L}$ are disjoint. A *data triple* is a tuple $t \in \mathcal{I} \times \mathcal{I} \times (\mathcal{I} \cup \mathcal{L})$. To denote the set of all identifiers in a data triple t we write $\mathrm{ids}(t)$.

We model a Web of Linked Data as a potentially infinite structure of interlinked documents. Such documents, which we call Linked Data documents, or *LD documents* for short, are accessed via identifiers in $\mathcal{I}$ and contain data that is represented as a set of data triples. The following definition captures our approach:

Definition 1. A **Web of Linked Data** W is a tuple $(D, data, adoc)$ where:

- D is a set of symbols that represent LD documents; D may be finite or countably infinite.

- $data : D \rightarrow 2^{\mathcal{I} \times \mathcal{I} \times (\mathcal{I} \cup \mathcal{L})}$ is a total mapping such that $data(d)$ is finite for all $d \in D$.

- $adoc : \mathcal{I} \rightarrow D$ is a partial, surjective mapping.

While the three elements D, $data$, and $adoc$ completely define a Web of Linked Data in our model, we point out that these elements are not directly available to a query execution system. However, by retrieving LD documents, such a system may gradually obtain information about the Web. Based on this information the system may (partially) materialize these three elements. In the remainder of this section we discuss the three elements and introduce additional concepts that we need to define our query model.

We say a Web of Linked Data $W = (D, data, adoc)$ is *infinite* if and only if D is infinite; otherwise, we say W is *finite*. Our model allows for infinite Webs to cover the possibility that Linked Data about an infinite number of identifiable entities is generated on the fly. The following example illustrates such a case:

Example 1. *Let u_i denote an HTTP scheme based URI that identifies the natural number i. There is a countably infinite number of such URIs. The WWW server which is responsible for these URIs may be set up to provide a document for each natural number. These documents may be generated upon request and may contain RDF data including the RDF triple $(u_i, \text{http://.../next}, u_{i+1})$. This triple associates the natural number i with its successor $i+1$ and, thus, links to the data about $i+1$ [19]. An example for such a server is provided by the Linked Open Numbers project[1].*

Another example were data about an infinite number of entities may be generated is the LinkedGeoData project[2] which provides Linked Data about any circular and rectangular area on Earth [2]. These examples illustrate that an infinite Web of Linked Data is possible in practice. Covering these cases enables us to model queries over such data and analyze the effects of executing such queries.

Even if a Web of Linked Data is infinite, we require countability for D. We shall see that this requirement has nontrivial consequences: It limits the potential size of Webs of Linked Data in our model and, thus, allows us to use a Turing machine based model for analyzing computability of queries over Linked Data (cf. Section 5.2). We emphasize that the requirement of countability does not restrict us in modeling the WWW as a Web of Linked Data: In the WWW we use URIs to locate documents that contain Linked Data. Even if URIs are not limited in length, they are words over a finite alphabet. Thus, the infinite set of all possible URIs is countable, as is the set of all documents that may be retrieved using URIs.

[1] http://km.aifb.kit.edu/projects/numbers/
[2] http://linkedgeodata.org

The mapping $data$ associates each LD document $d \in D$ in a Web of Linked Data $W = (D, data, adoc)$ with a finite set of data triples. In practice, these triples are obtained by parsing d after d has been retrieved from the Web. The actual retrieval mechanism depends on the technologies that are used to implement the Web of Linked Data. To denote the potentially infinite (but countable) set of *all data triples* in W we write $\mathrm{AllData}(W)$; i.e. it holds:

$$\mathrm{AllData}(W) = \bigcup_{d \in D} data(d)$$

Since we use elements in the set $\mathcal{I}$ as identifiers for entities, we say that an LD document $d \in D$ *describes* the entity identified by an identifier $id \in \mathcal{I}$ if $\exists (s, p, o) \in data(d) : (s = id \vee o = id)$. Notice, while there might be multiple LD documents in D that describe an entity identified by id, we do not assume that we can enumerate the set of all these documents; i.e., we cannot discover and retrieve all of them. The possibility to query search engines is out of scope of this paper. It is part of our future work to extend the semantics in our query model in order to take data into account, that is reachable by utilizing search engines. However, according to the Linked Data principles, each $id \in \mathcal{I}$ may also serve as a reference to a specific LD document which is considered as an authoritative source of data about the entity identified by id. We model the relationship between identifiers and authoritative LD documents by mapping $adoc$. Since some LD documents may be authoritative for multiple entities, we do not require injectivity for $adoc$. The "real world" mechanism for dereferencing identifiers (i.e. learning about the location of the corresponding, authoritative LD document) depends on the implementation of the Web of Linked Data and is not relevant for our model. For each identifier $id \in \mathcal{I}$ that cannot be dereferenced (i.e. "broken links") or that is not used in the Web it holds $id \notin \mathrm{dom}(adoc)$.

An identifier $id \in \mathcal{I}$ with $id \in \mathrm{dom}(adoc)$ that is used in the data of an LD document $d_1 \in D$ constitutes a *data link* to the LD document $d_2 = adoc(id) \in D$. To formally represent the graph structure that is formed by such data links, we introduce the notion of a *Web link graph*. The vertices in such a graph represent the LD documents of the corresponding Web of Linked Data; the edges represent data links and are labeled with a data triple that denotes the corresponding link in the source document. Formally:

Definition 2. Let $W = (D, data, adoc)$ be a Web of Linked Data. The **Web link graph for** W, denoted by G^W, is a directed, edge-labeled multigraph (V, E) where $V = D$ and

$$E = \big\{ (d_\mathrm{h}, d_\mathrm{t}, t) \mid d_\mathrm{h}, d_\mathrm{t} \in D \text{ and } t \in data(d_\mathrm{h}) \text{ and }$$
$$\exists id \in \mathrm{ids}(t) : adoc(id) = d_\mathrm{t} \big\}$$

In our query model we introduce the concept of reachable parts of a Web of Linked Data that are relevant for answering queries; similarly, our execution model introduces a concept for those parts of a Web of Linked Data that have been discovered at a certain point in the query execution process. To provide a formal foundation for these concepts we define the notion of an induced subweb which resembles the concept of induced subgraphs in graph theory.

Definition 3. Let $W = (D, data, adoc)$ be a Web of Linked Data. A Web of Linked Data $W' = (D', data', adoc')$ is an **induced subweb** of W if:

1. $D' \subseteq D$,
2. $\forall d \in D' : data'(d) = data(d)$, and
3. $\forall id \in \{ id \in \mathcal{I} \mid adoc(id) \in D' \} : adoc'(id) = adoc(id)$.

It can be easily seen from Definition 3 that specifying D' is sufficient to define an induced subweb $(D', data', adoc')$ of a given Web of Linked Data unambiguously. Furthermore, it is easy to verify that for an induced subweb W' of a Web of Linked Data W it holds $\mathrm{AllData}(W') \subseteq \mathrm{AllData}(W)$.

3.2 Computation Model

Usually, functions are computed over structures that are assumed to be fully (and directly) accessible. A Web of Linked Data, in contrast, is a structure in which accessibility is limited: To discover LD documents and access their data we have to dereference identifiers, but the full set of those identifiers for which we may retrieve documents is unknown. Hence, to properly analyze queries over a Web of Linked Data we require a model for computing functions on such a Web. This section introduces such a model.

In earlier work about computation on the WWW, Abiteboul and Vianu introduce a specific Turing machine called Web machine [1]. Mendelzon and Milo propose a similar machine model [15]. These machines formally capture the limited data access capabilities on the WWW and thus present an adequate abstraction for computations over a structure such as the WWW. We adopt the idea of such a Web machine to our scenario of a Web of Linked Data. We call our machine a *Linked Data machine* (or LD machine, for short).

Encoding (fragments of) a Web of Linked Data $W = (D, data, adoc)$ on the tapes of such a machine is straightforward because all relevant structures, such as the sets D or $\mathcal{I}$, are countably infinite. In the remainder of this paper we write $\mathrm{enc}(x)$ to denote the encoding of some element x (e.g. a single data triple, a set of triples, a full Web of Linked Data, etc.). For a detailed definition of the encodings we use in this paper, we refer to the appendix in [8].

We now define our adaptation of the idea of Web machines:

Definition 4. An **LD machine** is a multi-tape Turing machine with five tapes and a finite set of states, including a special state called *expand*. The five tapes include two, read-only input tapes: i) an ordinary input tape and ii) a right-infinite *Web* tape which can only be accessed in the expand state; two work tapes: iii) an ordinary, two-way infinite work tape and iv) a right-infinite *link traversal* tape; and v) a right-infinite, append-only output tape. Initially, the work tapes and the output tape are empty, the Web tape contains a (potentially infinite) word that encodes a Web of Linked Data, and the ordinary input tape contains an encoding of further input (if any). Any LD machine operates like an ordinary multi-tape Turing machine except when it reaches the expand state. In this case LD machines perform the following *expand procedure*: The machine inspects the word currently stored on the link traversal tape. If the suffix of this word is the encoding $\mathrm{enc}(id)$ of some identifier $id \in \mathcal{I}$ and the word on the Web tape contains $\sharp \mathrm{enc}(id)\, \mathrm{enc}(adoc(id))\, \sharp$, then the machine appends $\mathrm{enc}(adoc(id))\, \sharp$ to the (right) end of the word on the link traversal tape by copying from the Web tape; otherwise, the machine appends $\sharp$ to the word on the link traversal tape.

Notice how an LD machine is limited in the way it may access a Web of Linked Data that is encoded on its Web (input) tape: Any LD document and its data is only available for the computation after the machine performed the expand procedure using a corresponding identifier. Hence, the expand procedure models a URI based lookup which is the (typical) data access method on the WWW.

In the following sections we use the notion of an LD machine for analyzing properties of our query model. In this context we aim to discuss decision problems that shall have a Web of Linked Data W as input. For these problems we assume that the computation may only be performed by an LD machine with $\mathrm{enc}(W)$ on its Web tape:

Definition 5. Let $\mathcal{W}$ be a (potentially infinite) set of Webs of Linked Data; let $\mathcal{X}$ be an arbitrary (potentially infinite) set of finite structures; and let $DP \subseteq \mathcal{W} \times \mathcal{X}$. The decision problem for DP, that is, to decide for any $(W, X) \in \mathcal{W} \times \mathcal{X}$ whether $(W, X) \in DP$, is **LD machine decidable** if there exist an LD machine whose computation on any $W \in \mathcal{W}$ encoded on the Web tape and any $X \in \mathcal{X}$ encoded on the ordinary input tape, has the following property: The machine halts in an accepting state if $(W, X) \in DP$; otherwise the machine halts in a rejecting state.

Obviously, any (Turing) decidable problem that does not have a Web of Linked Data as input, is also LD machine decidable because LD machines are Turing machines; for these problems the corresponding set $\mathcal{W}$ is empty .

4. QUERY MODEL

This section introduces our query model by defining semantics for conjunctive queries over Linked Data.

4.1 Preliminaries

We assume an infinite set $\mathcal{V}$ of possible query variables that is disjoint from the sets $\mathcal{I}$ and $\mathcal{L}$ introduced in the previous section. These variables will be used to range over elements in $\mathcal{I} \cup \mathcal{L}$. Thus, *valuation*s in our context are total mappings from a finite subset of $\mathcal{V}$ to the set $\mathcal{I} \cup \mathcal{L}$. We denote the domain of a particular valuation μ by $\mathrm{dom}(\mu)$. Using valuations we define our general understanding of queries over a Web of Linked Data as follows:

Definition 6. Let $\mathcal{W}$ be a set of all possible Webs of Linked Data (i.e. all 3-tuples that correspond to Definition 1) and let Ω be a set of all possible valuations. A **Linked Data query** q is a total function $q : \mathcal{W} \to 2^{\Omega}$.

To express *conjunctive* Linked Data queries we adapt the notion of a SPARQL basic graph pattern [17] to our data model:

Definition 7. A **basic query pattern (BQP)** is a finite set $B = \{tp_1, \ldots, tp_n\}$ of tuples $tp_i \in (\mathcal{V} \cup \mathcal{I}) \times (\mathcal{V} \cup \mathcal{I}) \times (\mathcal{V} \cup \mathcal{I} \cup \mathcal{L})$ (for $1 \leq i \leq n$). We call such a tuple a **triple pattern**.

In comparison to traditional notions of conjunctive queries, triple patterns are the counterpart of atomic formulas; furthermore, BQPs have no head, hence no bound variables. To denote the set of variables and identifiers that occur in a triple pattern tp we write $\mathrm{vars}(tp)$ and $\mathrm{ids}(tp)$, respectively. Accordingly, the set of variables and identifiers that occur in all triple patterns of a BQP B is denoted by $\mathrm{vars}(B)$ and $\mathrm{ids}(B)$, respectively. For a triple pattern tp and a valuation μ we write $\mu[tp]$ to denote the triple pattern that we obtain by replacing the variables in tp according to μ. Similarly, a valuation μ is applied to a BQP B by $\mu[B] = \{\mu[tp] \mid tp \in B\}$. The result of $\mu[tp]$ is a data triple if $\mathrm{vars}(tp) \subseteq \mathrm{dom}(\mu)$. Accordingly, we introduce the notion of *matching data triples*:

Definition 8. A data triple t **matches** a triple pattern tp if there exists a valuation μ such that $\mu[tp] = t$.

While BQPs are syntactic objects, we shall use them as a representation of Linked Data queries which have a certain semantics. In the remainder of this section we define this semantics. Due to the openness and distributed nature of Webs such as the WWW we cannot guarantee query results that are complete w.r.t. all Linked Data on a Web. Nonetheless, we aim to provide a well-defined semantics. Consequently, we have to limit our understanding of completeness. However, instead of restricting ourselves to data from a fixed set of sources selected or discovered beforehand, we introduce an approach that allows a query to make use of previously unknown data and sources. Our definition of query semantics is based on a two-phase approach: First, we define the part of a Web of Linked Data that is reached by traversing links using the identifiers in a query as a starting point. Then, we formalize the result of such a query as the set of all valuations that map the query to a subset of all data in the reachable part of the Web. Notice, while this two-phase approach provides for a straightforward definition of the query semantics in our model, it does not correspond to the actual query execution strategy of integrating the traversal of data links into the query execution process as illustrated in Section 2.

4.2 Reachability

To introduce the concept of a reachable part of a Web of Linked Data we first define reachability of LD documents. Informally, an LD document is reachable if there exists a (specific) path in the Web link graph of a Web of Linked Data to the document in question; the potential starting points for such a path are LD documents that are authoritative for entities mentioned (via their identifier) in the queries. However, allowing for arbitrary paths might be questionable in practice because it would require following *all* data links (recursively) for answering a query completely. A more restrictive approach is the notion of *query pattern based reachability* where a data link only qualifies as a part of paths to reachable LD documents, if that link corresponds to a triple pattern in the executed query. The link traversal based query execution illustrated in Section 2 applies this notion of query pattern based reachability (as we show in Section 6.3). Our experience in developing a link traversal based query execution system[3] suggests that query pattern based reachability is a good compromise for answering queries without crawling large portions of the Web that are likely to be irrelevant for the queries. However, other criteria for specifying which data links should be followed might prove to be more suitable in certain use cases. For this reason, we do not prescribe a specific criterion in our query model; instead, we enable our model to support any possible criterion by making this concept part of the model.

Definition 9. Let $\mathcal{T}$ be the infinite set of all possible data triples; let $\mathcal{B}$ be the infinite set of all possible BQPs. A **reachability criterion** c is a total computable function $c : \mathcal{T} \times \mathcal{I} \times \mathcal{B} \to \{\text{true}, \text{false}\}$.

An example for such a reachability criterion is c_{All} which corresponds to the approach of allowing for arbitrary paths to reach LD documents; hence, for each tuple $(t, id, B) \in \mathcal{T} \times \mathcal{I} \times \mathcal{B}$ it holds $c_{\text{All}}(t, id, B) = \text{true}$. The complement of c_{All} is c_{None} which *always* returns false. Another example is c_{Match} which corresponds to the aforementioned query pattern based reachability. We define c_{Match} based on the notion of matching data triples:

$$c_{\text{Match}}\big(t, id, B\big) = \begin{cases} \text{true} & \text{if } \exists\, tp \in B : t \text{ matches } tp, \\ \text{false} & \text{else.} \end{cases} \quad (1)$$

We call a reachability criterion c_1 *less restrictive than* another criterion c_2 if i) for each tuple $(t, id, B) \in \mathcal{T} \times \mathcal{I} \times \mathcal{B}$ for which $c_2(t, id, B) = \text{true}$, also holds $c_1(t, id, B) = \text{true}$ and ii) there exist a $(t', id', B') \in \mathcal{T} \times \mathcal{I} \times \mathcal{B}$ such that $c_1(t', id', B') = \text{true}$ but $c_2(t', id', B') = \text{false}$. It can be seen that c_{All} is the least restrictive criterion, whereas c_{None} is the most restrictive criterion.

Using the concept of reachability criteria for data links we formally define reachability of LD documents:

Definition 10. Let $W = (D, data, adoc)$ be a Web of Linked Data; let $S \subset \mathcal{I}$ be a finite set of seed identifiers; let c be a reachability criterion; and let B be a BQP. An LD document $d \in D$ **is** (c, B)**-reachable from** S **in** W if either

---
[3]http://squin.org

1. there exists an $id \in S$ such that $adoc(id) = d$; or
2. there exist another LD document $d' \in D$, a $t \in data(d')$, and an $id \in ids(t)$ such that i) d' is (c, B)-reachable from S in W, ii) $c(t, id, B) = \text{true}$, and iii) $adoc(id) = d$.

We note that each LD document which is authoritative for an entity mentioned (via its identifier) in a finite set of seed identifiers S, is always reachable from S in the corresponding Web of Linked Data, independent of the reachability criterion and the BQP used.

Based on reachability of LD documents we now define reachable parts of a Web of Linked Data. Informally, such a part is an induced subweb covering all reachable LD documents. Formally:

Definition 11. Let $W = (D, data, adoc)$ be a Web of Linked Data; let $S \subset \mathcal{I}$ be a finite set of seed identifiers; let c be a reachability criterion; and let B be a BQP. The (S, c, B)**-reachable part of** W is the induced subweb $W_c^{(S,B)} = (D_\Re, data_\Re, adoc_\Re)$ of W that is defined by

$$D_\Re = \big\{ d \in D \mid d \text{ is } (c, B)\text{-reachable from } S \text{ in } W \big\}$$

4.3 Query Results

Based on the previous definitions we define the semantics of conjunctive Linked Data queries that are expressed via BQPs. Recall that Linked Data queries map from a Web of Linked Data to a set of valuations. Our interpretation of BQPs as Linked Data queries requires that each valuation μ in the result for a particular BQP B satisfies the following requirement: If we replace the variables in B according to μ (i.e. we compute $\mu[B]$), we obtain a set of data triples and this set must be a subset of all data in the part of the Web that is reachable according to the notion of reachability that we apply. Since our model supports a virtually unlimited number of notions of reachability, each of which is defined by a particular reachability criterion, the actual result of a query must depend on such a reachability criterion. The following definition formalizes our understanding of conjunctive Linked Data queries:

Definition 12. Let $S \subset \mathcal{I}$ be a finite set of seed identifiers; let c be a reachability criterion; and let B be a BQP; let W be a Web of Linked Data; let $W_c^{(S,B)}$ denote the (S, c, B)-reachable part of W. The **conjunctive Linked Data query (CLD query)** that uses B, S, and c, denoted by $\mathcal{Q}_c^{B,S}$, is a Linked Data query defined as:

$$\mathcal{Q}_c^{B,S}(W) = \big\{ \mu \mid \mu \text{ is a valuation with } \text{dom}(\mu) = \text{vars}(B)$$
$$\text{and } \mu[B] \subseteq \text{AllData}\big(W_c^{(S,B)}\big) \big\}$$

Each $\mu \in \mathcal{Q}_c^{B,S}(W)$ is a **solution for** $\mathcal{Q}_c^{B,S}$ **in** W.

Since we define the result of queries w.r.t. a reachability criterion, the semantics of such queries depends on this criterion. Thus, strictly speaking, our query model introduces a family of query semantics, each of which is characterized by a reachability criterion. Therefore, we refer to a CLD query for which we use a particular reachability criterion c as a CLD query *under c-semantics*.

5. PROPERTIES OF THE QUERY MODEL

In this section we discuss properties of our query model. In particular, we focus on the implications of querying Webs that are infinite and on the (LD machine based) computability of queries.

5.1 Querying an Infinite Web of Linked Data

From Definitions 10 and 11 in Section 4 it can be easily seen that any reachable part of a *finite* Web of Linked Data must also be finite, independent of the query that we want to answer and the reachability criterion that we use. Consequently, the result of CLD queries over such a finite Web is also guaranteed to be finite. We shall see that a similarly general statement does not exist when the queried Web is infinite such as the WWW.

To study the implications of querying an infinite Web we first take a look at some example queries. For these examples we assume an *infinite* Web of Linked Data $W_{\text{inf}} = (D_{\text{inf}}, data_{\text{inf}}, adoc_{\text{inf}})$ that contains LD documents for all natural numbers (similar to the documents in Example 1). The data in these documents refers to the successor of the corresponding number and to all its divisors. Hence, for each natural number[4] $k \in \mathbb{N}^+$, identified by $\text{no}_k \in \mathcal{I}$, exists an LD document $adoc_{\text{inf}}(\text{no}_k) = d_k \in D_{\text{inf}}$ such that

$$data_{\text{inf}}(d_k) = \Big\{ (\text{no}_k, \text{succ}, \text{no}_{k+1}) \Big\} \cup \bigcup_{y \in \text{Div}(k)} \Big\{ (\text{no}_k, \text{div}, \text{no}_y) \Big\}$$

where $\text{Div}(k)$ denotes the set of all divisors of $k \in \mathbb{N}^+$, $\text{succ} \in \mathcal{I}$ identifies the successor relation for $\mathbb{N}^+$, and $\text{div} \in \mathcal{I}$ identifies the relation that associates a number $k \in \mathbb{N}^+$ with a divisor $y \in \text{Div}(k)$.

Example 2. *Let $B_1 = \big\{ (\text{no}_2, \text{succ}, ?x) \big\}$ be a BQP ($?x \in \mathcal{V}$) that asks for the successor of 2. Recall, $data_{\text{inf}}(d_2)$ contains three data triples: $(\text{no}_2, \text{succ}, \text{no}_3)$, $(\text{no}_2, \text{div}, \text{no}_1)$, and $(\text{no}_2, \text{div}, \text{no}_2)$. We consider reachability criteria c_{All}, c_{Match}, and c_{None} (cf. Section 4.2) and $S_1 = \{\text{no}_2\}$: The $(S_1, c_{\text{All}}, B_1)$-reachable part of W_{inf} is infinite and consists of[5] the LD documents $d_1, \dots, d_k, \dots$. In contrast, the $(S_1, c_{\text{Match}}, B_1)$-reachable part $W_{c_{\text{Match}}}^{(S_1, B_1)}$ and the $(S_1, c_{\text{None}}, B_1)$-reachable part $W_{c_{\text{None}}}^{(S_1, B_1)}$ are finite: $W_{c_{\text{Match}}}^{(S_1, B_1)}$ consists of d_2 and d_3, whereas $W_{c_{\text{None}}}^{(S_1, B_1)}$ only consists of d_2. The query result in all three cases contains a single solution μ for which $\text{dom}(\mu) = \{?x\}$ and $\mu(?x) = \text{no}_3$; i.e. $\mu = \{?x \to \text{no}_3\}$.*

Example 3. *We now consider the BQP $B_2 = \big\{ (\text{no}_2, \text{succ}, ?x), (?x, \text{succ}, ?y), (?z, \text{div}, ?x) \big\}$ with $?x, ?y, ?z \in \mathcal{V}$ and $S_2 = \{\text{no}_2\}$. Under c_{None}-semantics the query result is empty because the $(S_2, c_{\text{None}}, B_2)$-reachable part of W_{inf} only consists of LD document d_2 (as in the previous example). For c_{All} and c_{Match} the reachable parts are infinite (and equal): Both consist of the documents $d_1, \dots, d_k, \dots$ (as was the case for c_{All} but not for c_{Match} in the previous example). While the query result is also equal for both criteria, it differs significantly from the previous example because it is infinite: $\mathcal{Q}_{c_{\text{Match}}}^{B_2, S_2}(W_{\text{inf}}) = \mathcal{Q}_{c_{\text{All}}}^{B_2, S_2}(W_{\text{inf}}) = \{\mu_1, \mu_2, \dots \mu_i, \dots\}$ where*

$$\mu_1 = \{?x \to \text{no}_3, ?y \to \text{no}_4, ?z \to \text{no}_3\},$$
$$\mu_2 = \{?x \to \text{no}_3, ?y \to \text{no}_4, ?z \to \text{no}_6\},$$

and, in general: $\mu_i = \{?x \to \text{no}_3, ?y \to \text{no}_4, ?z \to \text{no}_{(3i)}\}$.

A special type of CLD queries not covered by the examples are queries that use an empty set of seed identifiers. However, it is easily verified that answering such queries is trivial:

Fact 1. *Let W be a Web of Linked Data. For each CLD query $\mathcal{Q}_c^{B,S}$ for which $S = \varnothing$, it holds: The set of LD documents in the (S, c, B)-reachable part of W is empty and, thus, $\mathcal{Q}_c^{B,S}(W) = \varnothing$.*

Due to its triviality, an empty set of seed identifiers presents a special case that we exclude from most of our results. We now summarize the conclusions that we draw from Examples 2 and 3:

Proposition 1. *Let $S \subset \mathcal{I}$ be a finite but nonempty set of seed identifiers; let c and c' be reachability criteria; let B be a BQP; and let W be an* infinite *Web of Linked Data. It holds:*

---

1. *$W_{c_{\text{None}}}^{(S,B)}$ is always finite; so is $\mathcal{Q}_{c_{\text{None}}}^{B,S}(W)$.*

2. *If $W_c^{(S,B)}$ is finite, then $\mathcal{Q}_c^{B,S}(W)$ is finite.*

3. *If $\mathcal{Q}_c^{B,S}(W)$ is infinite, then $W_c^{(S,B)}$ is infinite.*

4. *If c is less restrictive than c' and $W_c^{(S,B)}$ is finite, then $W_{c'}^{(S,B)}$ is finite.*

5. *If c' is less restrictive than c and $W_c^{(S,B)}$ is infinite, then $W_{c'}^{(S,B)}$ is infinite.*

6. *If c' is less restrictive than c, then $\mathcal{Q}_c^{B,S}(W) \subseteq \mathcal{Q}_{c'}^{B,S}(W)$.*

Proposition 1 provides valuable insight into the dependencies between reachability criteria, the (in)finiteness of reachable parts of an infinite Web, and the (in)finiteness of query results. In practice, however, we are primarily interested in the following questions: Does the execution of a given CLD query reach an infinite number of LD documents? Do we have to expect an infinite query result? We formalize these questions as (LD machine) decision problems:

Problem:	FinitenessReachablePart
Web Input:	a (potentially infinite) Web of Linked Data W
Ordin. Input:	a CLD query $\mathcal{Q}_c^{B,S}$ where S is nonempty and c is less restrictive than c_{None}
Question:	Is the (S, c, B)-reachable part of W finite?

Problem:	FinitenessQueryResult
Web Input:	a (potentially infinite) Web of Linked Data W
Ordin. Input:	a CLD query $\mathcal{Q}_c^{B,S}$ where S is nonempty and c is less restrictive than c_{None}
Question:	Is the query result $\mathcal{Q}_c^{B,S}(W)$ finite?

Unfortunately, it is impossible to define a general algorithm for answering these problems as our following result shows.

Theorem 1. *The problems* FinitenessReachablePart *and* FinitenessQueryResult *are not LD machine decidable.*

5.2 Computability of Linked Data Queries

Example 3 illustrates that some CLD queries may have a result that is infinitely large. Even if a query has a finite result it may still be necessary to retrieve infinitely many LD documents to ensure that the computed result is complete. Hence, any attempt to answer such queries completely induces a non-terminating computation.

In what follows, we formally analyze feasibility and limitations for computing CLD queries. For this analysis we adopt notions of computability that Abiteboul and Vianu introduce in the context of queries over a hypertext-centric view of the WWW [1]. These notions are: *finitely computable queries*, which correspond to the traditional notion of computability; and *eventually computable queries* whose computation may not terminate but each element of the query result will eventually be reported during the computation. While Abiteboul and Vianu define these notions of computability using their concept of a Web machine (cf. Section 3.2), our adaptation for Linked Data queries uses an LD machine:

Definition 13. A Linked Data query q is **finitely computable** if there exists an LD machine which, for any Web of Linked Data W encoded on the Web tape, halts after a finite number of steps and produces a possible encoding of $q(W)$ on its output tape.

Definition 14. A Linked Data q query is **eventually computable** if there exists an LD machine whose computation on any Web of Linked Data W encoded on the Web tape has the following two

---

[4]In this paper we write $\mathbb{N}^+$ to denote the set of all natural numbers without zero. $\mathbb{N}^0$ denotes all natural numbers, including zero.

[5]We assume $\text{succ} \notin \text{dom}(adoc_{\text{inf}})$ and $\text{div} \notin \text{dom}(adoc_{\text{inf}})$.

properties: 1.) the word on the output tape at each step of the computation is a prefix of a possible encoding of $q(W)$ and 2.) the encoding $enc(\mu')$ of any $\mu' \in q(W)$ becomes part of the word on the output tape after a finite number of computation steps.

We now analyze the computability of CLD queries. As a preliminary we identify a dependency between the computation of a CLD query over a particular Web of Linked Data and the (in)finiteness of the corresponding reachable part of that Web:

Lemma 1. *The result of a CLD query $\mathcal{Q}_c^{B,S}$ over a (potentially infinite) Web of Linked Data W can be computed by an LD machine that halts after a finite number of computation steps if and only if the (S, c, B)-reachable part of W is finite.*

The following, immediate consequence of Lemma 1 is trivial.

Corollary 1. *CLD queries that use an empty set of seed identifiers and CLD queries under c_{None}-semantics are finitely computable.*

While Corollary 1 covers some special cases, the following result identifies the computability of CLD queries in the general case.

Theorem 2. *Each CLD query is either finitely computable or eventually computable.*

Theorem 2 emphasizes that execution systems for CLD queries do not have to deal with queries that are not even eventually computable. Theorem 2 also shows that query computations in the general case are not guaranteed to terminate. The reason for this result is the potential infiniteness of Webs of Linked Data. However, even if a CLD query is only eventually computable, its computation over a particular Web of Linked Data may still terminate (even if this Web is infinite). Thus, in practice, we are interested in criteria that allow us to decide whether a particular query execution is guaranteed to terminate. We formalize this decision problem:

Problem:	COMPUTABILITYCLD
Web Input:	a (potentially infinite) Web of Linked Data W
Ordin. Input:	a CLD query $\mathcal{Q}_c^{B,S}$ where S is nonempty and c is less restrictive than c_{None}
Question:	Does an LD machine exist that i) computes $\mathcal{Q}_c^{B,S}(W)$ and ii) halts?

Unfortunately:

Theorem 3. COMPUTABILITYCLD *is not LD machine decidable.*

As a consequence of the results in this section we note that any system which executes CLD queries over an infinite Web of Linked Data (such as the WWW) must be prepared for query executions that do not terminate and that discover an infinite amount of data.

6. QUERY EXECUTION MODEL

In Section 4 we use a two-phase approach to define (a family of) semantics for conjunctive queries over Linked Data. A query execution system that would directly implement this two-phase approach would have to retrieve all LD documents before it could generate the result for a query. Hence, the first solutions could only be generated after all data links (that qualify according to the used reachability criterion) have been followed recursively. Retrieving the complete set of reachable documents may exceed the resources of the execution system or it may take a prohibitively long time; it is even possible that this process does not terminate at all (cf. Section 5.2). The link traversal based query execution that we demonstrate in Section 2 applies an alternative strategy: It intertwines the link traversal based retrieval of data with a pattern matching

process that generates solutions incrementally. Due to such an integration of link traversal and result construction it is possible to report first solutions early, even if not all links have been followed and not all data has been retrieved. To describe link traversal based query execution formally, we introduce an abstract query execution model. In this section we present this model and use it for proving soundness and completeness of the modeled approach.

6.1 Preliminaries

Usually, queries are executed over a finite structure of data (e.g. an instance of a relational schema or an RDF dataset) that is assumed to be fully available to the execution system. However, in this paper we are concerned with queries over a Web of Linked Data that may be infinite and that is fully unknown at the beginning of a query execution process. To learn about such a Web we have to dereference identifiers and parse documents that we retrieve. Conceptually, dereferencing an identifier corresponds to achieving partial knowledge of the set D and mapping $adoc$ with which we model the queried Web of Linked Data $W = (D, data, adoc)$. Similarly, parsing documents retrieved from the Web corresponds to learning mapping $data$. To formally represent what we know about a Web of Linked Data at any particular point in a query execution process we introduce the concept of discovered parts.

Definition 15. A **discovered part** of a Web of Linked Data W is an induced subweb of W that is finite.

We require finiteness for discovered parts of a Web of Linked Data W. This requirement models the fact that we obtain information about W only gradually; thus, at any point in a query execution process we only know a finite part of W, even if W is infinite.

The (link traversal based) execution of a CLD query $\mathcal{Q}_c^{B,S}$ over a Web of Linked Data $W = (D, data, adoc)$ starts with a discovered part $\mathfrak{D}_{init}^{S,W}$ (of W) which contains only those LD documents from W that can be retrieved by dereferencing identifiers from S; hence, $\mathfrak{D}_{init}^{S,W} = (D_0, data_0, adoc_0)$ is defined by:

$$D_0 = \left\{ adoc(id) \mid id \in S \text{ and } id \in dom(adoc) \right\} \quad (2)$$

In the remainder of this section we first define how we may use data from a discovered part to construct (partial) solutions for a CLD query in an incremental fashion. Furthermore, we formalize how the link traversal approach expands such a discovered part in order to construct further solutions. Finally, we discuss an abstract procedure that formally captures how the approach intertwines the expansion of discovered parts with the construction of solutions.

6.2 Constructing Solutions

The query execution approach that we aim to capture with our query execution model constructs solutions for a query incrementally (cf. Section 2). To formalize the intermediate products of such a construction we introduce the concept of partial solutions.

Definition 16. A **partial solution** for CLD query $\mathcal{Q}_c^{B,S}$ in a Web of Linked Data W is a pair (P, μ) where $P \subseteq B$ and $\mu \in \mathcal{Q}_c^{P,S}(W)$.

According to Definition 16 each partial solution (P, μ) for a CLD query $\mathcal{Q}_c^{B,S}$ is a solution for the CLD query $\mathcal{Q}_c^{B,S}$ that uses BQP P (instead of B). Since P is a part of B we say that partial solutions *cover* only a part of the queries that we want to answer.

The (link traversal based) execution of a CLD query $\mathcal{Q}_c^{B,S}$ over a Web of Linked Data W starts with an *empty partial solution* $\sigma_0 = (P_0, \mu_0)$ which covers the empty part $P_0 = \varnothing$ of B (i.e. $dom(\mu_0) = \varnothing$). During query execution we (incrementally) extend partial solutions to cover larger parts of B. Those partial solutions that cover the whole query can be reported as solutions for

$\mathcal{Q}_c^{B,S}$ in W. However, to extend a partial solution we may use data only from LD documents that we have already discovered. Consequently, the following definition formalizes the extension of a partial solution based on a discovered part of a Web of Linked Data.

Definition 17. Let $W_\mathfrak{D}$ be a discovered part of a Web of Linked Data W; let $\mathcal{Q}_c^{B,S}$ be a CLD query; and let $\sigma = (P, \mu)$ be a partial solution for $\mathcal{Q}_c^{B,S}$ in W. If there exist a triple pattern $tp \in B \setminus P$ and a data triple $t \in \mathrm{AllData}(W_\mathfrak{D})$ such that t matches tp then the (t, tp)-**augmentation of** σ **in** $W_\mathfrak{D}$, denoted by $aug_{t,tp}^{W_\mathfrak{D}}(\sigma)$, is a pair (P', μ') such that $P' = P \cup \{tp\}$ and μ' extends μ as follows: 1.) $\mathrm{dom}(\mu') = \mathrm{vars}(P')$ and 2.) $\mu'[P'] = \mu[P] \cup \{t\}$.

The following proposition shows that the result of augmenting a partial solution is again a partial solution, as long as the discovered part of the Web that we use for such an augmentation is fully contained in the reachable part of the Web.

Proposition 2. *Let $W_\mathfrak{D}$ be a discovered part of a Web of Linked Data W and let $\mathcal{Q}_c^{B,S}$ be a CLD query. If $W_\mathfrak{D}$ is an induced subweb of the (S, c, B)-reachable part of W and σ is a partial solution for $\mathcal{Q}_c^{B,S}$ in W, then $aug_{t,tp}^{W_\mathfrak{D}}(\sigma)$ is also a partial solution for $\mathcal{Q}_c^{B,S}$ in W, for all possible t and tp.*

6.3 Traversing Data Links

During query execution we may traverse data links to expand the discovered part. Such an expansion may allow us to compute further augmentations for partial solutions. The link traversal based approach implements such an expansion by dereferencing identifiers that occur in valuations μ of partial solutions (cf. Section 2). Formally, we define such a valuation based expansion as follows:

Definition 18. Let $W_\mathfrak{D} = (D_\mathfrak{D}, data_\mathfrak{D}, adoc_\mathfrak{D})$ be a discovered part of a Web of Linked Data $W = (D, data, adoc)$ and let μ be a valuation. The μ-**expansion** of $W_\mathfrak{D}$ in W, denoted by $exp_\mu^W(W_\mathfrak{D})$, is an induced subweb $(D'_\mathfrak{D}, data'_\mathfrak{D}, adoc'_\mathfrak{D})$ of W, defined by $D'_\mathfrak{D} = D_\mathfrak{D} \cup \Delta^W(\mu)$ where

$$\Delta^W(\mu) = \{adoc(\mu(?v)) \mid ?v \in \mathrm{dom}(\mu)$$
$$\text{and } \mu(?v) \in \mathrm{dom}(adoc)\}$$

The following propositions show that expanding discovered parts is a monotonic operation (Proposition 3) and that the set of all possible discovered parts is closed under this operation (Proposition 4).

Proposition 3. *Let $W_\mathfrak{D}$ be a discovered part of a Web of Linked Data W, then $W_\mathfrak{D}$ is an induced subweb of $exp_\mu^W(W_\mathfrak{D})$, for all possible μ.*

Proposition 4. *Let $W_\mathfrak{D}$ be a discovered part of a Web of Linked Data W, then $exp_\mu^W(W_\mathfrak{D})$ is also a discovered part of W, for all possible μ.*

We motivate the expansion of discovered parts of a queried Web of Linked Data by the possibility that data obtained from additionally discovered documents may allow us to construct more (partial) solutions. However, Proposition 2 indicates that the augmentation of partial solutions is only sound if the discovered part that we use for the augmentation is fully contained in the corresponding reachable part of the Web. Thus, in order to use a discovered part that has been expanded based on (previously constructed) partial solutions, it should be guaranteed that the expansion never exceeds the reachable part. Under c_{Match}-semantics we have such a guarantee:

Proposition 5. *Let $\sigma = (P, \mu)$ be a partial solution for a CLD query $\mathcal{Q}_{c_{\mathsf{Match}}}^{B,S}$ (under c_{Match}-semantics) in a Web of Linked Data*

W; *and let $W_{c_{\mathsf{Match}}}^{(S,B)}$ denote the $(S, c_{\mathsf{Match}}, B)$-reachable part of W. If a discovered part $W_\mathfrak{D}$ of W is an induced subweb of $W_{c_{\mathsf{Match}}}^{(S,B)}$, then $exp_\mu^W(W_\mathfrak{D})$ is also an induced subweb of $W_{c_{\mathsf{Match}}}^{(S,B)}$.*

We explain the restriction to c_{Match}-semantics in Proposition 5 as follows: During link traversal based query execution we expand the discovered part of the queried Web only by using valuations that occur in partial solutions (cf. Section 2). Due to this approach, we only dereference identifiers for which there exists a data triple that matches a triple pattern in our query. Hence, this approach indirectly enforces query pattern based reachability (cf. Section 4.2). As a result, link traversal based query execution only supports CLD queries under c_{Match}-semantics; so does our query execution model.

6.4 Combining Construction and Traversal

Although incrementally expanding the discovered part of the reachable subweb and recursively augmenting partial solutions may be understood as separate processes, the idea of link traversal based query execution is to combine these two processes. We now introduce an abstract procedure which captures this idea formally.

As a basis for our formalization we represent the state of a query execution by a pair $(\mathfrak{P}, \mathfrak{D})$; $\mathfrak{P}$ denotes the (finite) set of partial solutions that have already been constructed at the current point in the execution process; $\mathfrak{D}$ denotes the currently discovered part of the queried Web of Linked Data. As discussed before, we initialize $\mathfrak{P}$ with the empty partial solution σ_0 (cf. Section 6.2) and $\mathfrak{D}$ with $\mathfrak{D}_{\mathrm{init}}^{S,W}$ (cf. Section 6.1). During the query execution process $\mathfrak{P}$ and $\mathfrak{D}$ grow monotonically: We augment partial solutions from $\mathfrak{P}$ and add the results back to $\mathfrak{P}$; additionally, we use partial solutions from $\mathfrak{P}$ to expand $\mathfrak{D}$. However, conceptually we combine these two types of tasks, augmentation and expansion, into a single type:

Definition 19. Let $\mathcal{Q}_{c_{\mathsf{Match}}}^{B,S}$ be a CLD query (under c_{Match}-semantics); let $(\mathfrak{P}, \mathfrak{D})$ represent a state of a (link traversal based) execution of $\mathcal{Q}_{c_{\mathsf{Match}}}^{B,S}$. An **AE task** for $(\mathfrak{P}, \mathfrak{D})$ is a tuple (σ, t, tp) for which it holds i) $\sigma = (P, \mu) \in \mathfrak{P}$, ii) $t \in \mathrm{AllData}(\mathfrak{D})$, iii) $tp \in B \setminus P$, and iv) t matches tp.

Performing an AE task (σ, t, tp) for $(\mathfrak{P}, \mathfrak{D})$ comprises two steps: 1.) changing $\mathfrak{P}$ to $\mathfrak{P} \cup \{(P', \mu')\}$, where $(P', \mu') = aug_{t,tp}^\mathfrak{D}(\sigma)$ is the (t, tp)-augmentation of σ in $\mathfrak{D}$, and 2.) expanding $\mathfrak{D}$ to the μ'-expansion of $\mathfrak{D}$ in W. Notice, constructing the augmentation in the first step is always possible because the prerequisites for AE tasks, as given in Definition 19, correspond to the prerequisites for augmentations (cf. Definition 17). However, not all possible AE tasks may actually change $\mathfrak{P}$ and $\mathfrak{D}$; instead, some tasks (σ, t, tp) may produce an augmentation $aug_{t,tp}^\mathfrak{D}(\sigma)$ that turns out to be a partial solution which has already been produced for another task. Thus, to guarantee progress during a query execution process we must only perform those AE tasks that produce new augmentations. To identify such tasks we introduce the concept of *open AE tasks*.

Definition 20. An AE task (σ, t, tp) for the state $(\mathfrak{P}, \mathfrak{D})$ of a link traversal based query execution is **open** if $aug_{t,tp}^\mathfrak{D}(\sigma) \notin \mathfrak{P}$. To denote the set of all open AE tasks for $(\mathfrak{P}, \mathfrak{D})$ we write $Open(\mathfrak{P}, \mathfrak{D})$.

We now use the introduced concepts to present our abstract procedure $ltbExec$ (cf. Algorithm 1) with which we formalize the general idea of link traversal based query execution. After initializing $\mathfrak{P}$ and $\mathfrak{D}$ (lines 1 and 2 in Algorithm 1), the procedure amounts to a continuous execution of open AE tasks. We represent this continuous process by a loop (lines 3 to 9); each iteration of this loop performs an open AE task (lines 5 to 7) and checks whether the newly constructed partial solution (P', μ') covers the executed

Algorithm 1 $ltbExec(S, B, W)$ – Report all $\mu \in \mathcal{Q}_{c_{\mathrm{Match}}}^{B,S}(W)$.

1: $\mathfrak{P} := \{\sigma_0\}$
2: $\mathfrak{D} := \mathfrak{D}_{\mathrm{init}}^{S,W}$

3: **while** $Open(\mathfrak{P}, \mathfrak{D}) \neq \varnothing$ **do**
4:      Choose open AE task $(\sigma, t, tp) \in Open(\mathfrak{P}, \mathfrak{D})$

5:      $(P', \mu') := aug_{t,tp}^{\mathfrak{D}}(\sigma)$
6:      $\mathfrak{P} := \mathfrak{P} \cup \{(P', \mu')\}$ // indirectly changes $Open(\mathfrak{P}, \mathfrak{D})$
7:      $\mathfrak{D} := exp_{\mu'}^{W}(\mathfrak{D})$

8:      **if** $P' = B$ **then** report μ' **endif**

9: **end while**

CLD query as a whole, in which case the valuation μ' in (P', μ') must be reported as a solution for the query (line 8). We emphasize that the set $Open(\mathfrak{P}, \mathfrak{D})$ of all open AE tasks always changes when $ltbExec$ performs such a task. The loop terminates when no more open AE tasks for (the current) $(\mathfrak{P}, \mathfrak{D})$ exist (which may never be the case as we know from Lemma 1).

We emphasize the abstract nature of Algorithm 1. The fact that we model $ltbExec$ as a single loop which performs (open) AE tasks sequentially, does not imply that the link traversal based query execution paradigm has to be implemented in such a form. Instead, different implementation approaches are possible, some of which have already been proposed in the literature [6, 7, 13, 14]. In contrast to the concrete (implementable) algorithms discussed in this earlier work, we understand Algorithm 1 as an instrument for presenting and for studying the general idea that is common to all link traversal based query execution approaches.

6.5 Application of the Model

Based on our query execution model we now show that the idea of link traversal based query execution is sound and complete, that is, the set of all valuations reported by $ltbExec(S, B, W)$ is equivalent to the query result $\mathcal{Q}_{c_{\mathrm{Match}}}^{B,S}(W)$. Formally:

Theorem 4. *Let W be a Web of Linked Data and let $\mathcal{Q}_{c_{\mathrm{Match}}}^{B,S}$ be a CLD query (under c_{Match}-semantics).*

- *Soundness: For any valuation μ reported by an execution of $ltbExec(S, B, W)$ holds $\mu \in \mathcal{Q}_{c_{\mathrm{Match}}}^{B,S}(W)$.*
- *Completeness: Any $\mu \in \mathcal{Q}_{c_{\mathrm{Match}}}^{B,S}(W)$ will eventually be reported by any execution of $ltbExec(S, B, W)$.*

Theorem 4 formally verifies the applicability of link traversal based query execution for answering conjunctive queries over a Web of Linked Data. For experimental evaluations that demonstrate the feasibility of link traversal based execution of queries over Linked Data on the WWW we refer to [6, 7, 13, 14]. We note, however, that the implementation approaches used for these evaluations do not allow for an explicit specification of seed identifiers S. Instead, these approaches use the identifiers in the BQP of a query as seed and, thus, only support CLD queries $\mathcal{Q}_c^{B,S}$ for which $S = \mathrm{ids}(B)$. Theorem 4 highlights that this is a limitation of these particular implementation approaches and not a general property of link traversal based query execution.

In the remainder of this section we use our (abstract) execution model to analyze the iterator based implementation of link traversal based query execution that we introduce in [6, 7]. The analysis of this implementation approach is particularly interesting because this approach trades completeness of query results for the guarantee that all query executions terminate as we shall see.

The implementation approach applies a synchronized pipeline of operators that evaluate the BQP $B = \{tp_1, \ldots, tp_n\}$ of a CLD query in a fixed order. This pipeline is implemented as a chain of iterators $I_1, \ldots, I_n$; iterator I_k is responsible for triple pattern tp_k (for all $1 \leq k \leq n$) from the *ordered* BQP. While the selection of an order for the BQP is an optimization problem [6], we assume a given order for the following analysis (in fact, the order is irrelevant for the analysis). Each iterator I_k provides valuations that are solutions for CLD query $\mathcal{Q}_{c_{\mathrm{Match}}}^{P_k, S}$ where $P_k = \{tp_1, \ldots, tp_k\}$. To determine these solutions each iterator I_k executes the following four steps repetitively: First, I_k consumes a valuation μ' from its direct predecessor and applies this valuation to its triple pattern tp_k, resulting in a triple pattern $tp'_k = \mu'[tp_k]$; second, I_k (tries to) generate solutions by finding matching triples for tp'_k in the query-local dataset; third, I_k uses the generated solutions to expand the query-local dataset; and, fourth, I_k (iteratively) reports each of the generated solutions. For a more detailed description of this implementation approach we refer to [6].

In terms of our abstract execution model, each iterator performs a particular subset of all possible open AE tasks: For each open AE task (σ, t, tp) performed by iterator I_k it holds i) $tp = tp_k$ and ii) $\sigma = (P_{k-1}, \mu)$ where $P_{k-1} = \{tp_1, \ldots, tp_{k-1}\}$. However, I_k may not perform all (open) AE tasks which have these properties.

Lemma 2. *During an iterator execution of an arbitrary CLD query $\mathcal{Q}_{c_{\mathrm{Match}}}^{B,S}$ (that uses c_{Match}) over an arbitrary Web of Linked Data W it holds: The set of AE tasks performed by each iterator is finite.*

Based on Lemma 2 we easily see that an iterator execution of a CLD query $\mathcal{Q}_{c_{\mathrm{Match}}}^{B,S}$ may not perform all possible (open) AE tasks. Thus, we may show the following result as a corollary of Lemma 2.

Theorem 5. *Any iterator based execution of a CLD query $\mathcal{Q}_{c_{\mathrm{Match}}}^{B,S}$ (that uses c_{Match}) over an arbitrary Web of Linked Data W reports a finite subset of $\mathcal{Q}_{c_{\mathrm{Match}}}^{B,S}(W)$ and terminates.*

Theorem 5 shows that the analyzed implementation of link traversal based query execution trades completeness of query results for the guarantee that all query executions terminate. The degree to which the reported subset of a query result is complete depends on the order selected for the BQP of the executed query as our experiments in [6] show. A formal analysis of this dependency is part of our future work.

7. RELATED WORK

Since its emergence the World Wide Web has spawned research to adapt declarative query languages for retrieval of information from the WWW [4]. Most of these works understand the WWW as a graph of objects interconnected by hypertext links; in some models objects have certain attributes (e.g. title, modification date) [15] or an internal structure [5, 12]. Query languages studied in this context allow a user to either ask for specific objects [12], for their attributes [15], or for specific object content [5]. However, there is no explicit connection between data that may be obtained from different objects (in contrast to the more recent idea of Linked Data). Nonetheless, some of the foundational work such as [1] and [15] can be adapted to query execution over a Web of Linked Data. In this paper we analyze the computability of CLD queries by adopting Abiteboul and Vianu's notions of computability [1], for which we have to adapt their machine model of computation on the Web.

In addition to the early work on Web queries, query execution over Linked Data on the WWW has attracted much attention recently. In [9] we provide an overview of different approaches and refer to the relevant literature. However, the only work we are aware of that formally captures the concept of Linked Data and provides a well-defined semantics for queries in this context is Bouquet et al. [3]. In contrast to our more abstract, technology-independent data model, their focus is Linked Data on the WWW, implemented using concrete technologies such as URIs and RDF. They adopt the common understanding of a set of RDF triples as graphs [11]. Consequently, Bouquet et al. model a Web of Linked Data as a "graph space", that is, a set of RDF graphs, each of which is associated with a URI that, when dereferenced on the WWW, allows a system to obtain that graph. Hence, RDF graphs in Bouquet et al.'s graph space correspond to the LD documents in our data model; the URIs associated with RDF graphs in a graph space have a role similar to that of those identifiers in our data model for which the corresponding mapping *adoc* returns an actual LD document (i.e. all identifiers in dom(*adoc*)). Therefore, RDF graphs in a graph space form another type of (higher level) graph, similar to the Web link graph in our model (although, Bouquet et al. do not define that graph explicitly). Based on their data model, Bouquet et al. define three types of query methods for conjunctive queries: a bounded method which only uses those RDF graphs that are referred to in queries, a navigational method which corresponds to our query model, and a direct access method which assumes an oracle that provides all RDF graphs which are "relevant" for a given query. For the navigational method the authors define a notion of reachability that allows a query execution system to follow all data links. Hence, the semantics of queries using this navigational method is equivalent to CLD queries under c_{All}-semantics in our query model. Bouquet et al.'s navigational query model does not support other, more restrictive notions of reachability, as is possible with our model. Furthermore, Bouquet et al. do not discuss the computability of queries and the infiniteness of the WWW.

8. CONCLUSIONS AND FURTHER WORK

Link traversal based query execution is a novel query execution approach tailored to the Web of Linked Data. The ability to discover data from unknown sources is its most distinguishing advantage over traditional query execution paradigms which assume a fixed set of potentially relevant data sources beforehand. In this paper we provide a formal foundation for this new approach.

We introduce a family of well-defined semantics for conjunctive Linked Data queries, taking into account the limited data access capabilities that are typical for the WWW. We show that the execution of such queries may not terminate (cf. Theorem 2) because –due to the existence of data generating servers– the WWW is infinite (at any point in time). Moreover, queries may have a result that is infinitely large. We show that it is impossible to provide an algorithm for deciding whether any given query (in our model) has a finite result (cf. Theorem 1). Furthermore, it is also impossible to decide (in general) whether a query execution terminates (cf. Theorem 3), even if the expected result would be known to be finite.

In addition to our query model we introduce an execution model that formally captures the link traversal based query execution paradigm. This model abstracts from any particular approach to implement this paradigm. Based on this model we prove that the general idea of link traversal based query execution is sound and complete for conjunctive Linked Data queries (cf. Theorem 4).

Our future work focuses on more expressive types of Linked Data queries. In particular, we aim to study which other features of query languages such as SPARQL are feasible in the context of querying a Web of Linked Data and what the implications of supporting such features are. Moreover, we will extend our models to capture the dynamic nature of the Web and, thus, to study the implications of changes in data sources during the execution of a query.

9. ACKNOWLEDGEMENTS

We thank our colleague Matthias Sax for a fruitful discussion that led to one of the proofs in this paper.

10. REFERENCES

[1] S. Abiteboul and V. Vianu. Queries and computation on the Web. *Theoretical Computer Science*, 239(2), 2000.

[2] S. Auer, J. Lehmann, and S. Hellmann. LinkedGeoData – adding a spatial dimension to the Web of Data. In *Proc. of the 8th Int. Semantic Web Conference (ISWC)*, 2009.

[3] P. Bouquet, C. Ghidini, and L. Serafini. Querying the Web of Data: A formal approach. In *Proc of the 4th Asian Semantic Web Conference (ASWC)*, 2009.

[4] D. Florescu, A. Y. Levy, and A. O. Mendelzon. Database techniques for the world-wide Web: A survey. *SIGMOD Record*, 27(3), 1998.

[5] T. Guan, M. Liu, and L. V. Saxton. Structure-based queries over the world wide Web. In *Proc. of the 17th Int. Conference on Conceptual Modeling (ER)*, 1998.

[6] O. Hartig. Zero-knowledge query planning for an iterator implementation of link traversal based query execution. In *Proc. of the 8th Ext. Semantic Web Conference (ESWC)*, 2011.

[7] O. Hartig, C. Bizer, and J.-C. Freytag. Executing SPARQL queries over the Web of Linked Data. In *Proc. of the 8th Int. Semantic Web Conference (ISWC)*, 2009.

[8] O. Hartig and J. C. Freytag. Foundations of traversal based query execution over Linked Data (extended version). *CoRR*, abs/1108.6328, 2011. Online: http://arxiv.org/abs/1108.6328.

[9] O. Hartig and A. Langegger. A database perspective on consuming Linked Data on the Web. *Datenbank-Spektrum*, 10(2), 2010.

[10] T. Heath and C. Bizer. *Linked Data: Evolving the Web into a Global Data Space*. Morgan & Claypool, 1st edition, 2011.

[11] G. Klyne and J. J. Carroll. Resource description framework (RDF): Concepts and abstract syntax. W3C Rec., Online at http://www.w3.org/TR/rdf-concepts/, Feb. 2004.

[12] D. Konopnicki and O. Shmueli. W3qs: A query system for the world-wide Web. In *Proc. of 21th Int. Conference on Very Large Data Bases (VLDB)*, 1995.

[13] G. Ladwig and D. T. Tran. Linked Data query processing strategies. In *Proc. of the 9th Int. Semantic Web Conference (ISWC)*, 2010.

[14] G. Ladwig and D. T. Tran. SIHJoin: Querying remote and local linked data. In *Proc. of the 8th Ext. Semantic Web Conference (ESWC)*, 2011.

[15] A. O. Mendelzon and T. Milo. Formal models of Web queries. *Information Systems*, 23(8), 1998.

[16] J. Pérez, M. Arenas, and C. Gutierrez. Semantics and complexity of SPARQL. *ACM Transactions on Database Systems*, 34, 2009.

[17] E. Prud'hommeaux and A. Seaborne. SPARQL query language for RDF. W3C Rec., Online at http://www.w3.org/TR/rdf-sparql-query/, Jan. 2008.

[18] F. Schmedding. Incremental SPARQL evaluation for query answering on Linked Data. In *Proc. of the 2nd Int. Workshop on Consuming Linked Data (COLD) at ISWC*, 2011.

[19] D. Vrandečić, M. Krötzsch, S. Rudolph, and U. Lösch. Leveraging non-lexical knowledge for the linked open data web. In *RAFT*, 2010.

Building Enriched Web Page Representations using Link Paths

Tim Weninger   ChengXiang Zhai   Jiawei Han
University of Illinois at Urbana-Champaign
weninge1@illinois.edu, czhai@illinois.edu, hanj@illinois.edu

ABSTRACT

Anchor text has a history of enriching documents for a variety of tasks within the World Wide Web. Anchor texts are useful because they are similar to typical Web queries, and because they express the document's context. Therefore, it is a common practice for Web search engines to incorporate incoming anchor text into the document's standard textual representation. However, this approach will not suffice for documents with very few inlinks, and it does not incorporate the document's full context. To mediate these problems, we employ *link paths*, which contain anchor texts from paths through the Web ending at the document in question. We propose and study several different ways to aggregate anchor text from *link paths*, and we show that the information from link paths can be used to (1) improve known item search in site-specific search, and (2) map Web pages to database records. We rigorously evaluate our proposed approach on several real world test collections. We find that our approach significantly improves performance over baseline and existing techniques in both tasks.

Categories and Subject Descriptors

H.3.3 [**Information Storage and Retrieval**]: Information Search and Retrieval; H.2.8 [**Database Management**]: Database applications—*data mining*

General Terms

Algorithms, Experimentation

Keywords

Web, link paths, anchor text, document indexing, record linkage

1. INTRODUCTION

The World Wide Web contains a wealth of information, and it is rapidly expanding in size and scope. Despite the vast complexities of the Web's landscape, billions of people, even young children, are able to navigate the Web with relative ease. This is partly due to the usefulness of modern Web browsers, search engines and Web design techniques, and partly due to the link-based construction of the Web itself. Arguably, the aspect most fundamental and essential to the ongoing operation of the Web is the existence of hyperlinks. These page-to-page links have shown their ability to tame the Web over and over again, and has transformed an otherwise unwieldy mass of documents into information accessible to the World.

Popular search engines commonly index an inbound link's anchor text because "anchors often provide more accurate descriptions of Web pages than the pages themselves" [1]. The idea of indexing incoming anchor text with the page it refers to was initially implemented in the World Wide Web Worm in 1994 [18], and since then dozens of studies have looked at various ways to leverage anchor text information for a variety of tasks. Many reasons for the effectiveness of anchor text have been proposed, and these various proposals are appropriately summed by Eiron and McCurley who note that, "anchor text resembles real-world queries in terms of its term distribution and length" [7]. In other words, anchor text is effective at search because anchor texts resemble searches.

However, the anchor text exploited in previous works is mostly restricted to the directly adjacent inlinks of the Web page [5].

Metzler *et al.* [19] and Dou *et al.* [6] argue that even though a Web page may have several incoming links, the anchor texts of those links are usually the same. Thus, many Web pages (even highly linked Web pages) may only have a small number of *unique* anchor text references. Metzler *et al.* describe this as the *anchor sparsity problem*. The solution proposed by Metzler *et al.* [19] used *aggregated anchor text* made of anchor texts that: (a) originate outside of a Web site, and then (b) link to Web pages inside a Web site, and then (c) link to the Web page in question. This can also be used to help mitigate the problem of navigational, intra-server links with anchor texts like 'next' or 'click here'.

In the link-dependent model (SiteProb), Dou *et al.* discount the re-occurrence of the same anchor text as a solution for multiple non-unique intra-site links. Furthermore, they address the anchor sparsity problem by measuring the relationship between Web sites in their SiteProbEx model.

Contrary to the findings of Metzler *et al.* and Dou *et al.*, Koolen and Kamps [13] demonstrated that the amount of inter-server links does not affect search performance. Moreover, Koolean and Kamps found that the quality of the intra-server links is at least as good as that of inter-server links.

So what do we make of these conflicting reports? These reports agree that the anchor text sparsity problem exists, but they differ on how to best enrich the standard set of adjacent-only anchor texts. On one hand, the propagation of inter-site anchor text is able to enrich the document representation, but on the other hand Koolen and Kamps show that number of inter-site anchors is irrelevant, so long as the total number of anchor texts is not low, *i.e.*, too sparse.

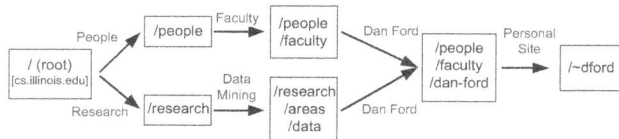

Figure 1: Cropped (real-world) Web site that shows how anchor texts from link paths can be more expressive than adjacent anchor texts.

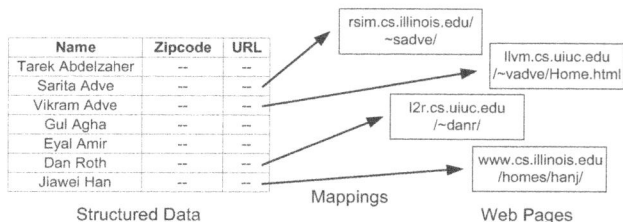

Figure 2: Problem example wherein two columns `Zipcode` and `URL` are added to a database schema, and the `URL` column is mapped to Web pages corresponding to the `Name` column. From this mapping the `Zipcode` column may be populated by extracting data from the Web page.

In this paper, we propose to use a larger scope of anchor text, *i.e.*, anchor text along *link paths* leading to a Web page, in order to solve the anchor text sparsity problem without the need for inter-site anchor texts. Figure 1 shows (via a real-world example) how anchor texts from link paths can be more expressive than the adjacent anchor text.

So we ask the question: can anchor text information from link paths, *i.e.*, non-adjacent Web pages, be used in a straightforward way to enrich Web page representation?

We **hypothesize** that if anchor texts are propagated with our link path model, then the resulting anchor texts will produce better representations of Web documents. To evaluate our hypothesis, we focus our attention on two specific tasks that we believe are most affected by the use of link paths: (1) site-specific known item search, and (2) record linkage.

Site-specific known item search is the task where users expect a single, particular answer in response to a query within an indicated Web site. According to this definition, we also consider navigational queries to be a type of known item search. This is in contrast to more open-ended tasks such as informational or ad hoc search. A recent paper by Dou *et al.*, shows that anchor text is especially useful for known item search, and is actually detrimental to ad hoc search [6]. Therefore, our first task is to use anchor texts from link paths for site specific known item search.

Record linkage, in general, is the task of finding common entities in two or more sets. For our purposes, we aim to map specific Web pages to records in a database. Because this is more of a classification task, matches will be judged on precision and recall metrics instead of ranking evaluation metrics.

Consider the example shown in Figure 2 wherein a structured database holds a list of computer science faculty members with the URL and zipcode fields empty. If we could discover a mapping from each faculty members' record to their personal Web page then we would be able to mine the Web pages for zipcodes in order to fill the missing values in the structured schema. With this information we could perform simple tasks like plotting each professor on a map, or more interesting tasks like examining the geographical density and distribution of computer scientists. Although there has not been much work regarding this specific task, we believe that information from link paths will be useful.

The main contributions of this paper are as follows: (1) We define link paths and show that they are able to represent Web documents more effectively than existing methods; (2) We describe how anchor texts from link paths can be added to the Web page content in the index; (3) We perform a case study on two tasks: (a) site specific known item search and (b) record linkage, which shows that link paths improves performance for both tasks over current methods.

The remainder of this paper is organized as follows. In Section 2 we define link paths and describe how information from link paths can be used to represent Web pages. We perform an experimental evaluation of this method in Sections 3 and 4. In Section 5 we survey related work with special attention paid to the various uses of anchor text. In Section 6 we conclude the paper and offer several avenues for future research.

2. LINK PATHS

On the Web-graph each Web page represents a vertex and each hyperlink represents a directed edge. A *link path*, therefore, is a path through the Web-graph from one Web page to another. Specifically, if a path between page u and page v contains pages x, and y then a link path from u to v is $u \rightarrow x \rightarrow y \rightarrow v$.

Let $G = (V, E)$ denote a given Web site, where $V = \{v_1, \ldots, v_n\}$ is the set of vertices and $E = \{e_1, \ldots, e_m\} \subset V \times V$ is the set of directed edges, where each edge e_k is represented by $\langle v_i, v_j \rangle$. A path $p \in G$ is a sequence of directed edges $p = \langle \langle v_1, v_2 \rangle, \ldots, \langle v_{l-1}, v_l \rangle \rangle$.

Anchor tags along the link path are extremely important. To capture this information we label each edge in the link path with the corresponding anchor text. If the link between pages u and x has the anchor text a, then the link is labeled $u \xrightarrow{a} x$.

Because there are an infinite number of possible paths on the World Wide Web, it is intractable to consider all possible link paths to all Web pages. One way to limit the number of possible paths is to identify a source page u. The source page u, known as the *reference page*, provides context to the indexing task and is therefore task dependent. For instance, if the task is to index Web pages at the University of Missouri then an appropriate reference page would be `missouri.edu`; if the task is to index movie Web pages then an appropriate reference page may be `trailers.apple.com`. In any case, the reference pages should be identified either manually or by some heuristic.

Another way to extract link paths is to navigate backwards from v in G collecting anchor texts for all hyperlinks pointing to v on the first level $x_1 \rightarrow v$, and then all anchor texts from hyperlinks pointing to all x_1 Web pages $x_2 \rightarrow x_1 \rightarrow v$, and so on, up to a certain distance from v. This backwards breadth first enumeration will quickly traverse the entire Web, so a a domain or depth restriction is necessary.

Because path computations on large graphs can be very computationally expensive, special care must be taken to ensure efficient path computation. We intuit that forward link paths (from a reference page) will result in a concise, specific Web document representation, while the backward link paths will result in a broader Web document representation. The computational effort in finding backward link paths is straightforward, but the forward links path method requires special computational considerations. The

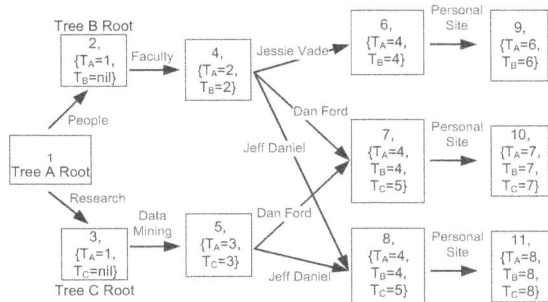

Figure 3: Example Web graph. Vertices are numerically labeled (1-11) by their crawl order. Pointers to link path trees are shown.

Algorithm 1: Forward Link Path Collection

```
input  : Graph G
output: Searchable Web Index

foreach Vertex v ∈ G do
    lp_v ← nil;
    foreach T_x in v do
        lp_{x,v} ← nil;
        /* collect anchors by tree climbing    */
        while ParentOf(v) ≠ nil do
            x ← ParentOf(v);
            lp_{x,v} ← lp_{x,v} + Anchor(G, x, v);
        lp_v ← lp_v + lp_{x,v};
    Index(v, lp_v)
```

next subsection describes the specific method by which forward link paths are collected.

2.1 Collecting forward link paths

Like most Web indexing processes, collecting forward link paths requires a graph of a Web site to be created from Web documents. The creation of such a large graph can easily be incorporated into the Web crawling process itself. If we assume that Web graphs are created and updated during the Web crawl, then a simple extension can be used to efficiently find forward link paths.

Given a set of references pages $u_1, \ldots, u_n = U$ and an existing (*i.e.*, running) Web crawler, when the Web crawler reaches a reference page $u_x \in U$ then a rooted, directed tree T_x called a *link path tree* is initialized with u_x as the root. Tree T_x is updated as the Web crawler expands the horizon in a breadth first manner from u_x. In order to keep the size of the trees manageable we (1) limit the depth of the tree and (2) store directional tree pointers in G rather than storing duplicate data values or tree structures. This will result in n trees, one for each reference page $u_1, \ldots, u_n$ in U while only adding at pointers to the nodes in the graph. The data model described in Figure 3 shows a cropped real world graph where vertices are numerically labeled according to their crawl ordering. There are three reference pages $U = 1, 2, 3$ and each vertex shows the tree representation embedded in the graph.

Note that because of the breadth first nature of the Web crawl the resulting link paths will always result in a directed acyclic graph (DAG). We therefore are not concerned with repetitions due to loops in the graph.

The extra space required for this computation is in the order of $O(n|V|)$ when the depth limit is infinite, and is otherwise bounded by the fanout and tree depth when a depth limit is imposed. The extra computational time is a small constant for common Web crawler and Web graph implementations. Although the fanout cannot be controlled, it seems prudent to limit the maximum tree depth to a reasonable amount; different maximum depths will also affect the search accuracy.

At any time during an existing Web crawl or after a crawl is completed, the trees $T_1, \ldots, T_n$ can be used to calculate forward link paths for each document. The link path trees $T_1, \ldots, T_n$ stored in G allow for the efficient collection of link paths. For each indexable Web document we find its corresponding node v_{idx} in G. For each link path tree reference in v_{idx} we traverse upwards to the root and aggregate the anchor texts stored in G during the upward traversal. Pseudocode for this process is shown in Alg. 1.

Now that the link path trees, and the method by which link paths

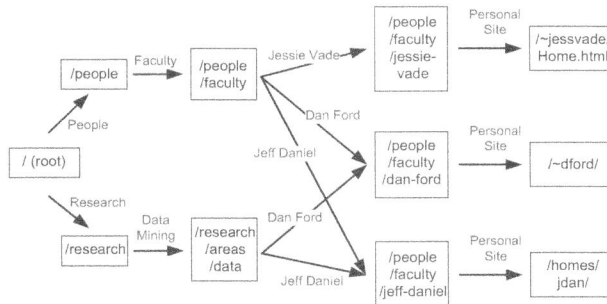

Figure 4: Example Web graph corresponding to the graph in Figure 3. Vertex numerals are replaced by relevant URL suffixes.

are collected are defined we investigate how anchor texts represent documents.

2.2 Anchor Text

The path p from u to v will have edges $\{e_1, \ldots, e_{l-1}\}$ annotated by the anchor text of each edge a_e. The set of anchor texts $\{a_{e_1}, \ldots, a_{e_{l-1}}\}$ for the path p, denoted A_p, typically contains a descriptive text relative to the reference page u of the destination page v.

Following the processing for collecting forward link paths a document may be created or an existing document may be enhanced.

Example. For the vertex /~dford/ in Figure 4 corresponding to vertex 10 in Figure 3, there are three link path trees. The anchor texts retrieved by following Algorithm 1 are: P_{T_A}={*Personal Site, Dan Ford, Faculty, People*}, P_{T_B}={*Personal Site, Dan Ford, Faculty*}, and P_{T_B}={*Personal Site, Dan Ford, Data Mining*}.

From this real world example, we see the utility of anchor texts from link paths because Dan Ford is a *person* and a *faculty* member who does *research* in *data mining*.

The backward link path collection method can also be used to collect link path text.

Example. For the vertex /~dford/ in Figure 4 we can navigate backwards 4 edges to collect anchor texts. The anchor texts retrieved by backward link paths are: *Personal Site, Dan Ford, Faculty, Data Mining, People, Research*}.

In these examples, the backwards and forward results are very similar. However, in non-cropped Web sites the backward link path method collect an order of magnitude more anchor texts than the forward link path method.

Next the link paths $\{P_{T_1} \dots P_{T_n}\}$ are combined into a bag-of-words representation A_v for each of the link paths in n trees. We refer to A_v as a bag-of-anchors.

Example. Forward link paths. The bag-of-anchors from the running example is {*Personal Site:3, Dan Ford:3, Faculty:2, People:1, Data Mining:1*}.

Backward link paths. The bag-of-anchors from the running example is {*Personal Site:1, Dan Ford:2, Faculty:1, People:1, Data Mining:1, Research:1*}.

Finally, the bag of anchors are added to a field in the document of indexing and retrieval.

2.3 Aggregating Link Paths

Ultimately, the output of the crawling and indexing process is two extra fields: (1) aggregated anchors from the backward link paths $A_v(BLP)$ and (2) aggregated anchors from the forward link paths $A_v(FLP)$. When a depth limit of 1 is imposed on the backward link paths method (BLP_1), then the field is similar to the anchor data used in most related work, and is a direct analogue to the data used by Dou *et al* [6].

The fields are created by concatenating all of the the anchor texts from all of the link paths into a single vector. In forward link paths, each Web page $v \in G$ will have its own set of (up to n) link paths and therefore n bags of anchors $\{A_{v_1}, \dots, A_{v_n}\}$. These n bags are aggregated to create a single, bag of anchors for each Web page $A_v(FLP)$. Separately, the backward link path method collects only a single set of anchors, which are similarly aggregated to create a single bag of anchors for each Web page $A_v(BLP)$.

The aggregate anchor texts can be used to enrich the Web page in several ways. We chose to attach the each bag of anchors $A_v(FLP)$ and $A_v(BLP)$ to the Web page as two separate fields in order to maintain flexibility.

From this representation, a ranking function, such as BM25F, can be used to rank documents relative to a query, or normalization methods, such as standard TF-IDF, can be used to compare the importance of a term.

For the sake of discussion, we use a simplified version of TF-IDF to rank the texts within $A_v(FLP)$ so that more descriptive anchor texts are given a higher ranking. In this simplified TF-IDF function, the term frequency is measured by the count of each anchor a in the document's aggregate bag of anchors $f(a, A_v)$ divided by the number of other bags of anchors that also contain a, $|A : a \in A|$. For the record linkage task, we sort the bag of anchors in descending order. The BM25 function is used for actual ranking in the evaluation.

Example. Continuing the example above, with the simplified TF-IDF, the ranked bags of anchors for /~dford/ from forward link paths are:
A_v={*Dan Ford*:3/2=1.5, *Personal Site*:3/3=1.0, *Faculty*:2/7=0.29, *Data Mining*:1/7 =0.14, *People*:1/8=0.13 }
The ranked bags of anchors from backward link paths are:
A_v={*Dan Ford*:1/2=0.50, *Personal Site*:1/3=0.33, *Faculty*:1/7=0.29, *Data Mining*:1/5 =0.20, *Research*:1/6=0.17, *People*:1/8=0.13}

2.4 Link Paths for Known Item Search

The above examples show that the forward and backward link paths methods provide a natural way of describing Web pages with respect to their context. We believe that anchor texts closer to the Web page in question ought to be given a higher weight. Our model

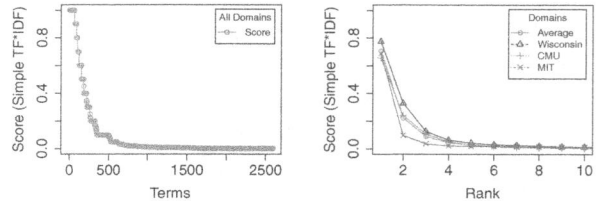

(a) Distribution of scores for forward link paths

(b) Mean scores per rank

Figure 5: Distribution of scores and ranks for forward link paths across three computer science departments' Web sites

incorporates this belief by *inherently* weighting terms by their relative distance from the vertex in question. That is, these models, especially the forward link path model, capture the concept that anchor texts are highly descriptive of the Web page they directly link to, and they are decreasingly less descriptive of its grand-children, great-grandchildren, etc.

By claiming that this distance weighting is *inherent*, we specifically mean that the use of forward link paths dilutes the weight of anchor texts far away from the destination vertex because the as the anchor texts are propagated forward, their document frequency increases. This can be seen in the examples from the previous section where the term *People* is diluted because it has been propagated over many links before reaching /~dford/. Thus, no explicit distance weighting is required.

The weight of anchor texts relative to the distance from the target depends on the inverse document frequency function and the number of link paths reaching the target. If only a single link path tree exists in the target Web page, then the distribution of anchor texts depends solely on the IDF function. When this is the case, the distribution of anchor text weights will resemble a Zipfian distribution (Power-law). The number of link path trees will increase the magnitude of the distribution if the different bags of anchors do not intersect; the distribution will flatten if the different bags of anchors intersect. This intuition is reflected empirically by the real-world distributions shown in Figure 5.

This way we find that the most descriptive terms for each destination page are ranked highest in each list. We especially notice that the anchor text nearest the destination page are not always the most descriptive.

The small example from Figure 4 does not necessarily show the real world distribution of the scores. Figure 5(a) shows the actual distribution of scores, calculated by the simplified TF-IDF described above, from three randomly chosen computer science departments' Web sites (CMU, Wisconsin and MIT). These graphs show that, overall, a relative few anchor texts are highly descriptive. The mean and median score for the distribution is .084 and .010 respectively.

Figure 5(b) shows the mean scores for each rank, that is, the average score for anchor texts ranked first, the average score for anchor texts ranked second, etc. Although this distribution is not guaranteed to be monotonically decreasing, the trend here is that the descriptive value of each rank trails off quickly, and is effectively nil after rank 4 or 5 in this dataset.

2.4.1 Search Function

In the implementation of the actual system, we use the BM25F function to rank the Web documents by a potentially-weighted combination of the documents' various fields. In our evaluations, we consider only three fields: (1) content, (2) backward link paths with a limit of 1 (BLP$_1$), and (3) forward link paths (FLP). When only a single field is selected, the BM25F function essentially becomes normal BM25; however, if more than one field is selected, then the ranking result is dependent upon the weights assigned to each field. For example, a weighting scheme of 1, 1, 1 on content, BLP$_1$ and FLP respectively, equally combines all three fields. A weighting scheme of 0, 1, 2 on content, BLP$_1$ and FLP respectively, will effectively ignore the content field and weight the FLP field twice as much as the BLP$_1$ field.

2.5   Links Paths for Record Linkage

In record linkage task our goal is to use the texts encoded in the link path to map the destination Web page ($v \in V'$) to its corresponding record in a structured database $r \in R$.

To rephrase, given a set of structured database records, we wish to add a new column to the schema labeled URL and populate the new cells of the record with URLs of the corresponding Web pages. This task was described previously in the example from Figure 2 wherein a list of names from, say, DBLP or a phonebook is extended with URL information. The example continues to show the potential benefits of this mapping by showing that extra information from the Web page can be extracted and added to the schema of the database.

Very frequently the text on a link path is not exactly the same as corresponding text in the database. Names, especially, can be represented in several different ways. For example, a person's name can be represented with or without the middle name, with the middle name abbreviated, last name first, and so on. Therefore, an exact byte-by-byte query would rarely return any results. To mitigate this problem, before a query is actually performed, the anchor text is sanitized, that is, all punctuation an extra spaces are removed and all letters are lowercased.

The actual retrieval function should collect records which match terms from the query string, otherwise the ordering of terms would matter (*e.g.*, 'Dan Ford' would not match 'Ford, Dan'). Most database systems have an indexing or search function to handle these types of queries; we use MySQL and its `match against` function to retrieve records as described in the next subsection.

2.5.1   Linkage Function

Searching the selected columns for matches is a straightforward task. For each sorted bag of anchors the database is queried with the top ranked anchor text as the search term. The major difference between byte-by-byte search and our search function is that a full text search on the name 'Ford, Dan' would return 'Dan Ford's record as well as anyone containing the name 'Dan' or 'Ford'. This will likely return at least one result. Unfortunately, there exist 135 Ford's in DBLP, and 'Personal Site' also retrieves a record for 'Luigi Delle Site'.

Obviously, in approximate matching it is necessary to pick a record which most closely resembles the original query string. For this task we use a word alignment algorithm shown in Algorithm 2, which is similar to, but not to be confused with, the character alignment or edit distance algorithm, which attempts to find the string with the fewest *word* differences. Like traditional edit distance algorithms, lower scores denote a closer distance; therefore, lower scores are better.

To illustrate the execution of the approximate matching algorithm let there be a sorted link path {*Personal Site, Ford Dan, Faculty*} – capitalization is maintained for clarity. We first query the database with 'Personal Site' and retrieve the record of 'Luigi Delle Site'. To begin the matching algorithm, we split the shorter string 'Personal Site' into two words 'Personal' and 'Site'. The word

'Personal' is removed from the string 'Luigi Delle Site' resulting in no change; then the word 'Site' is removed from the string 'Luigi Delle Site' resulting in 'Luigi Delle'. The score of this matching is 11/16=.69.

Algorithm 2: Search Function

input : Sorted Bag of Anchors $\mathcal{A}_v$, Set of records R
output: Best Match *best*

foreach *anchor text* $a \in \mathcal{A}_v$ **do**
  $R' \leftarrow$ fulltext query on database R with search term a;
  foreach *record* $r \in R'$ **do**
    $s \leftarrow r_{text}$;   /* text from selected column */
    $t \leftarrow a_{len}$;
    if $s_{len} > a_{len}$ **then**
      Swap(s,a);
      $t \leftarrow a_{len}$; /* a must be longer than s */
    $S \leftarrow$ split s on whitespace;
    for $i \leftarrow 1$ **to** $|S|$ **do**
      if a contains S_i **then**
        remove S_i from a;   /* remove match */
    $res \leftarrow a_{len}/t$; /* percentage not matched */
    $best \leftarrow$ Min($best, res$);   /* fewest diffs */
    if $best = 0.0$ **then**
      return $best$;   /* perfect match */

return $best$;

Next, we query the database with 'Ford Dan' and retrieve two records (in this short example), 'Dan Andresen' and 'Dan Ford'. Starting with 'Dan Andresen', we split the shorter string 'Ford Dan' into two words 'Ford' and 'Dan'. The word 'Ford' is removed from the string 'Dan Andresen' resulting in no change, and the word 'Dan' is removed from the string 'Dan Andresen' resulting in 'Andresen'. The score of this matching is 8/12=.66, and the best matching so far is 'Dan Andresen'. The second record 'Dan Ford' is split into 'Dan' and 'Ford'. The word 'Dan' is removed from 'Ford Dan' resulting in only 'Ford' remaining, and the word 'Ford' is removed from the string 'Ford' resulting in an empty string. The score of this matching is 0/8=0.0, a perfect match so the algorithm stops.

In this way, we can find perfect matches even though the strings are not identical. Furthermore, approximate matches are given scores based on how closely matched they are so that scores above some threshold do not result in a mapping. If, after iterating through the entire link path, an exact match is not found then the best match is used for the mapping.

Searching through the link path in descending order is particularly important because the most descriptive anchor texts will appear at the top of the list, and once a match is found there is no need to continue searching. In fact, we find that it is very likely that the top ranked anchor text will contain a match to the database.

Another important product of the ranked link paths is its use in limiting false positives. In the likely event that the link path contains two or more exact database matches the lower-ranked match will be ignored because the algorithm stops after the first exact match. We observed that in some of our testing domains one or two names frequently appeared on the link paths in addition to the actual, correct name. Fortunately, by searching in a sorted order we reduce the occurrence of false positives because the correct match is likely ranked higher than an incorrect match. In the unlikely event that the correct match is ranked lower than an incorrect match then our method would produce an incorrect mapping.

One potential pitfall of this method is the irreconcilability of misspellings. We realize that misspellings happen, but they will not harm the overall algorithm unless the names are all misspelled in the exact same way. This is because misspellings are not likely to be highly ranked in the sorted link path. Therefore we only need to assume that the number of correctly spelled occurrences outnumber the most frequent misspelling.

2.5.2 Disambiguation

In some domains there will be two or more matches with the same score. In these instances, a tiebreaker is needed to choose between the ambiguous matches otherwise a one-to-many mapping is needed. In our specific problem setting we only consider a single column so disambiguation is difficult because there is no tiebreaker information to consider. If we possessed, for example, not only the list of names from DBLP, but also the abstracts for each author, then some simple extensions to basic approach can be tried. A topic model, for instance, based on the abstracts could be used in concert with the link paths' texts as a tiebreaker. In our experiments, we only allow one-to-one mappings and therefore do not address this problem because, for example, only 0.07% of records in DBLP share the same author name.

2.5.3 Achieving Strict and Approximate Matching with a Threshold

The search function lends itself to multiple variants of the same algorithm based on the adaptation of a threshold on the word distance. This threshold λ does not allow a mapping to occur when the word distance is above the threshold. The word distance threshold is guaranteed to be between 0 and 1 inclusive, $0 \leq \lambda \leq 1$. For our purposes we examine the two possible extremes of λ: strict matching ($\lambda = 0$), and approximate matching ($\lambda = 1$).

In strict matching we map a Web page to a database record if and only if an exact match is found, that is, when the word distance is 0. We hypothesize that the strict matching will result in a high precision and relatively low recall. The recall should be low because this is a strict condition, and there may not be many of these types of matches; however, the precision should be high because the few mappings which do happen should be accurate.

In approximate matching we map a Web page to the database record with the closest word distance. We hypothesize that the approximate matching will result in a slightly lower precision and perfect recall. The recall should be perfect because the closest word will always be mapped to the database record; however, the precision should be lower because more matches provides a larger room for error.

The results section shows how the precision and recall are specifically affected by the threshold.

3. EVALUATION OF KNOWN ITEM FINDING

Because we use the link path model for two different tasks, we evaluate the model with two separate experiments. As such, this paper has a section dedicated to each task: (1) an evaluation of link paths on the Web site-specific known item finding task, and (2) an evaluation of link paths on the record linkage task.

Data Sets

It is not possible to use existing data sets because our method requires the annotation of Web pages *during the crawling process*. Public TREC data sets, such as ClueWeb09, have link-graphs that

Table 1: Known Item Search Task Dataset Characteristics

Domain	Seed Web page	Web pages	Hyperlinks
Illinois	illinois.edu	243,705	1,910,157
Berkeley	berkeley.edu	519,758	10,729,954
ESPN	espn.com	45,846	860,754
US Senate	senate.gov	2,953	183,294
Wikipedia	en.wikipedia.org	5,716,808*	130,160,392

can be re-crawled and annotated. However, these public datasets are multi-domain crawls with multi-domain test queries, which cannot be evaluated with respect to a single domain.

Instead we performed breadth first, site-specific crawls on the domains listed in Table 1 starting at the listed seed Web page to a depth of 4, except the Wikipedia dataset, which was obtained from http://users.on.net/~henry/home/wikipedia.htm.

Preliminary Tests

The first, and arguably most simple benchmark is to use BM25 on the content of the Web pages only.

In order to compare the expressive power of forward link paths to the current method which uses only adjacent links, a second benchmark test was run using only adjacent links. This test is in line with previous works [5, 25, 8].

We directly compare our algorithm to the site-independence model from Dou *et al* [6]. Dou *et al* showed that the intra-Web site anchor texts should not be considered independent of one another because heavy anchor text replication can errantly inflate the weight of non-descriptive anchor text. By discounting this replication, Dou *et al.* show increased retrieval performance.

Finally, we test Google as a black-box; although the inner workings of the Google algorithm are kept secret, Brin and Page have disclosed that directly adjacent anchor texts are included in the algorithm along with several other ranking features [1]. Thus, we do not expect to outperform the Google results.

Setup

We test the forwards and backwards link paths by aggregating the anchor texts from the paths and storing them in an index. Because we only specified a single reference page, there should only be a single link path for each Web page. The backward link paths have a depth limit of 1, 2 and 3 in our experiments. Note that the backward link paths with depth 1 is equivalent to the Craswell *et al*'s paper [5].

To compare these algorithms we obtained the top 50 most common queries from the University of Illinois query logs. We found that most of these queries represent known item searches. We were unable to obtain the query log from the University of Berkeley, but for the sake of experiment we assume that the top 50 queries at Berkeley are semantically equivalent to those at Illinois. Thus, we manually created Berkeley analogues to the Illinois queries. For example, "nessie" represents the human resources department at Illinois, the Berkeley equivalent is "blu web portal"[sic]; so we test "nessie" on the Illinois data set and "blu web portal" on the Berkeley data set.

We created 50 random known item queries for ESPN including 30 athletes, 10 teams, and 10 coaches. Finally, 50 random, known item queries for Senate included 20 senators, 25 states and 5 committees. Although we did judge result relevancy ourselves, it is doubtful that we introduced bias into our results because known item queries typically have a clear answer, and we always annotated the correct answers before we performed the evaluation runs. For all experiments, the BM25 parameters are: $k_1 = 2.0$ and $b = 0.75$, and the maximum depth for forward link paths is 4.

For the Wikipedia dataset we used 40 queries from the 50 query 2009 TREC Web track (the Entity track queries were not avail-

Table 2: MRR results. Significance tests (two-tailed, paired) w.r.t the Content-only run, .95 confidence, are denoted by •; significance tests w.r.t BLP$_1$, .95 confidence are denoted by (†).*Best Combo represents weights of 0.006, 0.497, 0.497 for Content, BLP$_1$ and FLP respectively.

Fields	Illinois	Berkeley	ESPN	Senate	Wiki
Content-only	.212	.159	.252	.364	.482
BLP$_1$ [5]	.558	.551	.545	.645	.905•
FLP-only	.713†•	.549	.645†•	.765†•	.912•
Best Combo*	.728†•	.575	.671†•	.943†•	.988†•
Google	.847†•	.685†•	.754†•	.956†•	.988†•

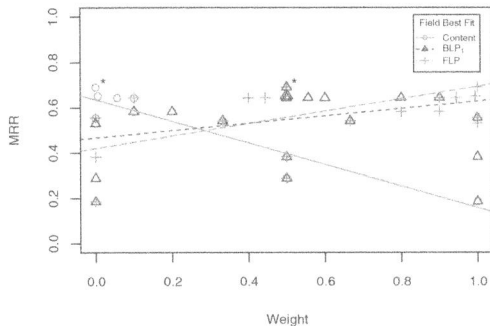

Figure 6: MRR results with respect to normalized field weights. Lines represent linear regression (best fit) lines.

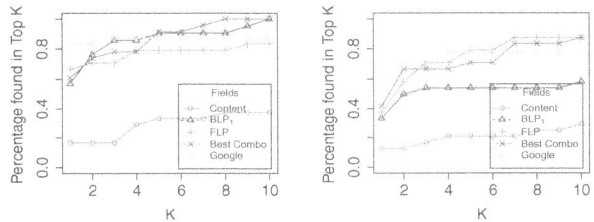

(a) Illinois   (b) Berkeley

Figure 7: Percentage of positive results found in top K results as K varies from 1 to 10.

Table 3: Record Linkage Task Dataset Characteristics

Domain	Seed Web page	Web pages	Hyperlinks
25 CS Depts	cs.*.edu	123,157	1,597,936
AllMovie	allmovie.com	32,258	123,596
Apple	trailers.apple.com	8,862	110,666

able). During evaluation, we assert that there is a single Wikipedia page to answer the query, manually find that page, and evaluate our algorithm using the MRR metric. We found, and removed, 10 non-entity queries, like "wt09-3: getting organized"[1].

3.1 Results: Site-specific Known Item Search

The first three results in Table 2 shows the MRR results of BM25 on individual fields, that is, BM25 on only the content-text, BM25 on only the aggregated BLP$_1$-text, etc.

We are not surprised to see that content-only performs poorly on known item queries. Backward Link Paths with a hop limit of 1 (BLP$_1$) received good results as did our proposed Forward Link Paths method. Not shown are results for Backward Link Paths with a hop limit of 2 (BLP$_2$) which performed poorly with an average MRR of .368. We were able to perform some experiments on BLP$_3$ but the results were rarely correct.

We remind the reader that the queries always used BM25 to rank the results relative to the query. The different results shown in Table 2 represent how the results are affected by varying the document representation, not the ranking function.

Figure 6 shows how ranking is affected when BM25F is used to combine data from multiple fields. These results explore different combinations of the Content, BLP$_1$ and FLP fields. The regression lines clearly show that as the relative weight for the content field increases the MRR scores decrease. As the relative influence of FLP and BLP$_1$ increase so do the MRR scores. Looking closely we see that the regression line for FLP is steeper than the regression line for BLP$_1$; this demonstrates that the FLP field is more tightly correlated to the increase in performance than the BLP$_1$ field.

Table 2 shows that the field combination resulting in the best MRR score used a weighting scheme of 0.006, 0.497, 0.497 on the Content, BLP$_1$ and FLP fields respectively. The corresponding

---

[1]Removed: wt09-3,6,7,10,11,19,38,40,49,50

plots are marked in Figure 6 by an asterisk. We were unable, and did not expect, to find a combination that outperformed Google.

Finally, we investigated the results from Illinois and Berkeley more deeply by plotting the percentage of positive results found in the top K results as K varies from 1 to 10. This metric was used by Ogilvie and Callan during their initial investigation of known item search [21]. Figure 7 shows how the different fields respond as K increases. Specifically, we see that the weighted combination (Best Combo) catches and eventually surpasses the Google results in both data sets. Other fields, especially FLP, are competitive with Google at higher values for K.

3.2 Discussion

Our experiments show that both backwards link paths and forward link paths contain valuable information with respect to an indexable Web page. We find that Web pages indexed with anchor text from forward link paths have higher retrieval scores than Web pages with only anchor text from adjacent links (BLP$_1$). Furthermore, we find that when BLP$_1$ is combined with FLP the document representation is enriched resulting in significantly higher known item search accuracies.

The Wikipedia results show that anchor texts are very influential in search performance. The forward link paths performed slightly better, statistically insignificant, than the BLP$_1$ results in the Wikipedia dataset; we hypothesize that this is because (1) Wikipedia is not a hierarchical structure like most Web sites, and/or (2) Wikilinks are formed by a different cognitive and physical processes than HTML-links. These results deserve further investigation.

Although our results were not able to match Google in the MRR metrics, there are many enhancements that can be made to our model; language models, PageRank-type weighting, click-through training, etc. are all intentionally absent from our model so that a clear evaluation of our specific contribution could be presented. We are especially confident that a PageRank-type weighting would improve known item search results.

4. EVALUATION OF RECORD LINKAGE

Data sets

Like in the known item search task, we are unable to use existing data sets because our method requires the annotation of Web pages during the crawling processes. Therefore, we performed breadth first, site-specific crawls on the domains listed in Table 3 starting at the listed seed Web page.

The first domain is from the departmental Web sites of the top 25 American computer science graduate schools[2]. From the Top 25 computer science department Web pages, the personal homepages of 1,137 computer science faculty members were found with the parallel path finding algorithm [24] and manually verified. The task for this first data set is to map each of the 1,137 faculty homepages to their corresponding record in DBLP using only information from their link paths. Assuming that all computer science faculty members are listed in DBLP is a faulty assumption. Unlisted cases are true negatives that add to the difficulty of the problem and can be represented in the results; for example, returning "not found" for an unlisted faculty member is a positive result.

From the second and third domains, 345 official movie Web pages were found with parallel path finding algorithm [24] and manually verified. The task for the second data set is to map each of the movie homepages to their corresponding records in the Internet Movie Database (IMDB). In this case, assuming that each of these movies will be listed in IMDB is a valid assumption because of each movie's relative popularity and because of the wide coverage of IMDB.

Preliminary Tests

One of the goals of this section is to compare the expressive power of link paths to the current method which uses only adjacent links. With this in mind, we ran two baseline tests using (1) adjacent anchor text only, and (2) Google.

The first baseline uses data from BLP_1 to match against the database via Alg. 2 with $\lambda = 0$ and $\lambda = 1$. The Google baseline queries the title of a movie, and maps the first result to the corresponding record in IMDB, and thus can be evaluated with the Precision@1 metric.

Setup

The link paths were found between the department's homepage and each faculty members' personal Web pages. The paths were combined and ranked as described in Section 2 and mapped to DBLP's author column using the strict and approximate matching methods from Section 2.5.

In the movies domain, the link paths were found between `http://trailers.apple.com` each of the 345 movie Web pages, as well as `allmovie.com` and the 345 movie Web pages. The paths were combined, ranked and mapped to the IMDB title column using the strict and approximate matching methods.

We judge the effectiveness of each method by standard precision and recall methods. Note that the recall metric is only important in the strict matching experiments because mappings are not made where there is not an exact match. In the approximate matching experiments recall is always 100% because the algorithm will always make an attempt resulting in 0 null mappings. In all results the final mean scores are based on total sums and counts, not an average of averages.

4.1 Results: Record Linkage

Although we tested the algorithm on 25 individual computer science departments, in Table 5 only the averages (mean/median) are shown for brevity. The Google baseline is shown in Table 4 and uses Precision at 1 (Prec@1) because, for the sake of comparison, we suppose that the top ranked Google result is linked with the record in the database. The mean reciprocal rank (MRR) metric of the Google results are shown for an implicit, albeit apples-to-oranges, comparison with TREC results.

[2]Rankings from US News 2010

Table 4: Web page record linkage baseline results

Google Baseline	Prec@1	MRR
DBLP 25 dept. avg.	71.58/74.60	.752/.776
IMDB w/ Apple	20.61	.408
IMDB w/ AllMovie	41.18	.505

Table 5: Web page record linkage results. Matching is "Strict" when $\lambda = 0$, "Approx." when $\lambda = 1$

Strict BLP_1	Precision	Recall
DBLP 25 dept. avg.	81.35/91.89	53.50/56.52
IMDB w/ Apple	38.17	36.40
IMDB w/ AllMovie	43.14	63.34
Approx. BLP_1	Precision	Recall
DBLP 25 dept. avg.	74.19/77.35	100
IMDB w/ Apple	38.17	100
IMDB w/ AllMovie	43.14	100
Strict FLP	Precision	Recall
DBLP 25 dept. avg.	98.63/100	54.49/57.89
IMDB w/ Apple	100	37.41
IMDB w/ AllMovie	98.03	64.71
Approx. FLP	Precision	Recall
DBLP 25 dept. avg.	94.32/97.83	100
IMDB w/ Apple	70.99	100
IMDB w/ AllMovie	76.47	100

Table 5 shows the results for the adjacent only baseline, and the two extreme variations of our record linkage algorithm. Under strict matching conditions ($\lambda = 0$) the linkage results show high precision and low recall as expected. Under approximate matching conditions ($\lambda = 1$) the linkage results show a lower precision and perfect recall as expected. Moreover, the overall accuracy under strict conditions confirms our assertion that anchor texts often represent succinct, canonical representations of the referenced Web page.

Comparing the baseline results to our results in Table 5, we see a 36.03% increase in precision over the Google baseline and a 31.24% increase in precision over the BLP_1 approximate matching baseline.

In terms of recall, our algorithm will always return a result when there is no threshold to limit the string distance. For tasks which require a higher level of precision a lower threshold (λ) may be appropriate. Figure 8 shows how the precision and recall of FLP on the DBLP data set fluctuate as λ varies between 0 and 1.

The graph in Figure 8 confirms our assertion that lower thresholds will result in high precision and lower recall. We also see that at its worst the recall is relatively low, but the lowest precision score is not too low. For our purposes we prefer $\lambda = 1$ because the small drop in precision is worth the large gain in recall.

The IMDB data set performed similarly to the DBLP data, and these complimentary results offer reinforcement to the validity of our approach. However, the lower precision and recall scores show that the IMDB task is more difficult than the DBLP task. The results from Google were low because gossip, biography, etc. Web pages were frequently ranked higher than the official movie Web page. Using only adjacent anchor texts also performed poorly because, according to our observation, most of the links to the movie Web page were images, which do not contain anchor text; a finding similar to that of Metzler et al. [19]. For Apple specifically, the recall was particularly low because many movie titles in this data set were shortened to fit on the Web page making strict matching difficult. We believe that data from AllMovie.com obtained a higher

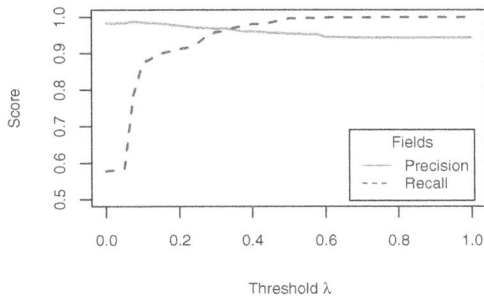

Figure 8: Precision and Recall tradeoff for FLP on the DBLP task as λ varies from 0 to 1.

recall under strict conditions because it does not shorten movie titles.

4.2 Discussion

Overall, the results above show promising results for the difficult task of mapping Web pages to their appropriate record in a structured database. We remind the reader that our algorithm uses *only* data from anchor texts and does not rely on the titles or content of the referenced Web page. Undoubtedly, other information sources could be used to further enhance this task, but we leave that for future research. It is also important to note that the Web pages used in these experiments come from many different sources with a variety of styles and templates. So the traditional wrapper generation approach would not be effective at this task.

Generally, the results show that the task of mapping faculty members to their DBLP record is more precise than the movie data set. This is because the ambiguity among names of computer scientists is (perhaps purposefully) quite low, and a link path to one faculty member typically does not contain the name of another faculty member. On the other hand, the ambiguity among movie titles is quite large and the link paths frequently contained more than one movie title.

5. RELATED WORK

To the best of our knowledge, the use of anchor text from links paths to enrich document representation is a novel concept. However, anchor text has been widely studied and used as an important source of relevant information for many years. McBryan was one of the first to associate anchor texts of incoming links to a Web page in the World Wide Web Worm tool [18]. Later, Brin and Page explained the importance of associating anchor texts with both the Web page it occurs on as well as the Web page it points to [1]. Harmandas *et al.* showed that anchor texts could also be used to annotate Web pages containing only images [10]. We also find that, due to their importance and descriptive ability, anchor texts are currently used in most commercial search engines. Because we evaluate the use of link paths in two separate tasks: (1) known item search, and (2) record linkage, we examine the related works of each task separately.

5.1 Known Item Search

A great deal of work has been done regarding how to best use anchor texts in general Web information retrieval. Dou *et al* [6] evaluate the use of anchor texts on different types of queries and find that anchor texts significantly increase accuracy on *known item queries* and only marginally impact accuracy on *informational queries*.

Anchor texts are combined with the traditional document representation in several different ways. Arguably, the most naive way to use anchor texts is by treating the anchor text as surrogate documents [5] in which the original documents' text is replaced with anchor text. This naive approach comprises the baselines in work by Dou *et al* [6] and Westerveld *et al* [25]. Another less-naive approach is to concatenate the anchor text to the original documents' text so that both anchor texts and content can be searched [7]. In these previous works the BM25 retrieval model is used to score and rank the results.

Most non-baseline proposals use the BM25F [22] retrieval model to store the anchor text and content in separate fields. These fields are then be combined in a weighted fashion to score and rank documents. Westerveld *et al* [25] found that a weighted combination of 0.63, 0.07 and 0.03 on the content, anchor and url fields respectively of the WT10G dataset more than tripled the MRR score of content and anchor text fields that were examined independently. Dou *et al.* extended this work to account for site-specific hyperlinks [6]. Fujii *et al.* broke anchor texts into terms and assigned weights to those terms according to the weight of each term in the anchor text as well as the weight of each term in the referenced Web page [8]. The weighted BM25F is an obvious retrieval model choice for this task, but other combination models may be appropriate for different tasks.

Other studies have examined the similarities between anchor text and common queries. Jin *et al.* demonstrated that document titles bear a close resemblance to common queries because of their succinct, descriptive nature, and because they are typically developed via a similar cognitive process [12]. Eiron and McCurley argue that anchor texts are even more beneficial than Web page titles because (1) Web pages can have only one title while several distinct anchor texts can point to each Web page, and (2) different anchor texts can help with the problem of synonymy. They further show that anchor texts also represent real-world user queries in term distribution and length [7]. Fuijii *et al.* proposed a model to identify synonymous query terms in anchor texts in order to expand queries [9]. Kraft and Zien proposed a method that mines clicked anchor texts in concert with query logs in order to learn query rewriting rules to improve search engine results [14]. Shen *et al.* draw implicit links between certain Web pages by the observation that people who search the Web with the same queries often click on different, yet related documents; these implicit links are then used with explicit anchor texts to aid in document classification [23]. Chakrabarti *et al.* used the link structure and anchor texts to retrieve Web pages which are authoritative for a topic in their Automatic Resource Compilation system [4]. Lu *et al.* showed that they could extract a live translation dictionary for cross-language IR by considering anchor texts referencing the same Web page as 'parallel texts' [17]. What all of the above studies have in common is that only the anchor text directly adjacent to the Web page in question is used, and therefore the various paths of anchor texts are never considered. In sum, these works provide valuable insight into the nature of anchor texts, but are limited in their use of anchor texts.

A recent paper by Metzler *et al.* proposed a method that aggregates anchor texts from the Web pages external to the Web site in question to enrich the individual document representations. However, this work aims to overcome anchor text sparsity and receives its best results when anchor text is only added to documents which do not already have anchors present [19].

5.2 Record Linkage

Unlike the abundance of related work for the retrieval task, Web page to database record linkage is a largely unstudied task, and we find that most of the recent work in bridging structured and unstructured data focuses on information extraction. Information extraction rightly assumes that many Web pages are constructed by merging an HTML template with database records, and the goal, therefore, is to automatically reverse that process in order to extract the structured database records from the semi-structured Web page.

Several methods have been devised to accomplish this task. Liu *et al.*'s Mining Data Records (MDR) algorithm finds patterns in the HTML code of a Web page to extract data records. This work was later extended by Zhai and Liu to extract patterns via partial tree alignments from the Web page's DOM tree [26], and again by Miao *et al.* to extract data records by clustering HTML tags from DOM paths [20]. Unfortunately, these types of algorithms assume that each Web page contains two or more similarly structured records. Cafarella *et al.* showed that Web tables represented database records [2, 3], and Lin *et al.* used these Web tables to discover entity relationships on the Web [15]. For more information on this type of work see Hovey's survey paper [11] or Liu's Web Data Mining book [16]. Each of these information extraction techniques are useful for creating structured database records from Web pages. However, none of these works address the problem of mapping existing database records to their corresponding Web page.

Previous research demonstrates that anchor texts provide critical information to Web search engines, and that, currently, Web search engines only use anchor texts adjacent to the Web page. Our notion of link paths lifts the adjacently-only restriction by aggregating anchor text from specific paths through the Web.

6. CONCLUSIONS

In conclusion, this paper proposes a an enhancement to Web page representations using aggregated anchor texts from *link paths*. We show that by intelligently crawling the Web, forward link paths can be constructed and the data from these paths is useful for known item retrieval and record linkage. Our results also demonstrate that link paths alone (both backwards and forwards) provide for better results than the Web page content, and the inclusion of Web page content actually hurt retrieval accuracy on average. Furthermore, we believe that our method does generalize to other data sets, and we encourage the community to explore this approach on more data sets.

Following this line of work, there exist many opportunities for further research. First, following the intuition of previous research, our evaluation uses only site specific links and anchor text. We are interested to see if link paths extending from references pages outside of the Web domain improve of hinder the retrieval and linkage accuracy. Second, our evaluation only considers a single reference page, and therefore a single link path tree for each evaluation domain. We believe that multiple reference pages are likely to increase the system's accuracy, but too many reference pages may hurt the system's accuracy. Finally, the choice of reference pages is extremely important, and we cannot guarantee that our choice of reference pages (Web site entry page) is optimal; therefore, we are actively investigating how the choice of reference page(s) impacts the document representation and subsequent retrieval and linkage accuracy.

7. ACKNOWLEDGMENTS

This work is funded by an NDSEG Fellowship to the first author. The second and third authors are supported by NSF IIS-09-05215, U.S. Air Force Office of Scientific Research MURI award FA9550-08-1-0265, and by the U.S. Army Research Laboratory under Cooperative Agreement Number W911NF-09-2-0053 (NS-CTA).

8. REFERENCES

[1] S. Brin and L. Page. The anatomy of a large-scale hypertextual web search engine. *Computer Networks and ISDN Systems*, 30(1–7):107–117, 1998.

[2] M. J. Cafarella, A. Halevy, D. Z. Wang, E. Wu, and Y. Zhang. Webtables: exploring the power of tables on the web. *Proc. VLDB Endow.*, 1(1):538–549, 2008.

[3] M. J. Cafarella, J. Madhavan, and A. Halevy. Web-scale extraction of structured data. *SIGMOD Rec.*, 37(4):55–61, 2008.

[4] S. Chakrabarti, B. Dom, P. Raghavan, S. R. D. Gibson, and J. Kleinberg. Automatic resource compilation by analyzing hyperlink structure and associated text. In *WWW*, pages 65–74, Amsterdam, The Netherlands, The Netherlands, 1998. Elsevier Science Publishers B. V.

[5] N. Craswell, D. Hawking, and S. Robertson. Effective site finding using link anchor information. In *SIGIR*, pages 250–257, New York, NY, USA, 2001. ACM.

[6] Z. Dou, R. Song, J.-Y. Nie, and J.-R. Wen. Using anchor texts with their hyperlink structure for web search. In *SIGIR*, pages 227–234, New York, NY, USA, 2009. ACM.

[7] N. Eiron and K. S. McCurley. Analysis of anchor text for web search. In *SIGIR*, pages 459–460, New York, NY, USA, 2003. ACM.

[8] A. Fujii. Modeling anchor text and classifying queries to enhance web document retrieval. In *WWW*, pages 337–346, New York, NY, USA, 2008. ACM.

[9] A. Fujii, K. Itou, T. Akiba, and T. Ishikawa. Exploiting anchor text for the navigationalweb retrieval at ntcir-5. In *NTCIR-5 Workshop*, 2005.

[10] V. Harmandas, M. Sanderson, and M. D. Dunlop. Image retrieval by hypertext links. *SIGIR Forum*, 31(SI):296–303, 1997.

[11] E. H. Hovy. *Natural Language Processing and Information Systems*, chapter 1, pages 1–7. Springer Berlin / Heidelberg, 2010.

[12] R. Jin, A. G. Hauptmann, and C. X. Zhai. Title language model for information retrieval. In *SIGIR*, pages 42–48, New York, NY, USA, 2002. ACM.

[13] M. Koolen and J. Kamps. The importance of anchor text for ad hoc search revisited. In *SIGIR*, pages 122–129, 2010.

[14] R. Kraft and J. Zien. Mining anchor text for query refinement. In *WWW*, pages 666–674, New York, NY, USA, 2004. ACM.

[15] C. X. Lin, B. Zhao, T. Weninger, J. Han, and B. Liu. Entity relation discovery from webtables and links. In *WWW*. ACM, April 2010.

[16] B. Liu. *Web Data Mining – Exploring Hyperlinks, Contents and Usage Data*. Springer, 2006.

[17] W.-H. Lu, L.-F. Chien, and H.-J. Lee. Anchor text mining for translation of web queries: A transitive translation approach. *ACM Trans. Inf. Syst.*, 22(2):242–269, 2004.

[18] O. A. McBryan. Genvl and wwww: tools for taming the web. In *WWW*, 1994.

[19] D. Metzler, J. Novak, H. Cui, and S. Reddy. Building enriched document representations using aggregated anchor text. In *SIGIR*, pages 219–226, New York, NY, USA, 2009. ACM.

[20] G. Miao, J. Tatemura, W.-P. Hsiung, A. Sawires, and L. E. Moser. Extracting data records from the web using tag path clustering. In *WWW*, pages 981–990, New York, NY, USA, 2009. ACM.

[21] P. Ogilvie and J. Callan. Combining document representations for known-item search. In *SIGIR*, pages 143–150, 2003.

[22] S. E. Robertson and S. Walker. Some simple effective approximations to the 2-poisson model for probabilistic weighted retrieval. In *SIGIR*, pages 232–241, New York, NY, USA, 1994. Springer-Verlag New York, Inc.

[23] D. Shen, J.-T. Sun, Q. Yang, and Z. Chen. A comparison of implicit and explicit links for web page classification. In *WWW*, pages 643–650, New York, NY, USA, 2006. ACM.

[24] T. Weninger, F. Fumarola, R. Barber, C. X. Lin, J. Han, and D. Malerba. Growing parallel paths for entity-page discovery. In *WWW*, 2011.

[25] T. Westerveld, W. Kraaij, and D. Hiemstra. Retrieving web pages using content, links, urls and anchors. *TREC*, 10, 2001.

[26] Y. Zhai and B. Liu. Structured data extraction from the web based on partial tree alignment. *IEEE Trans. on Knowl. and Data Eng.*, 18(12):1614–1628, 2006.

Navigational Efficiency of Broad vs. Narrow Folksonomies

Denis Helic
Knowledge Management
Institute
Graz University of Technology
Graz, Austria
dhelic@iicm.org

Christian Körner
Knowledge Management
Institute
Graz University of Technology
Graz, Austria
christian.koerner@tugraz.at

Michael Granitzer
Chair of Media Informatics
University of Passau
Passau, Germany
Michael.Granitzer@uni-passau.de

Markus Strohmaier
Knowledge Management
Institute and Know-Center
Graz University of Technology
Graz, Austria
markus.strohmaier@tugraz.at

Christoph Trattner
Institute for Information
Systems and Computer Media
Graz University of Technology
Graz, Austria
ctrattner@tugraz.at

ABSTRACT

Although many social tagging systems share a common tripartite graph structure, the collaborative processes that are generating these structures can differ significantly. For example, while resources on Delicious are usually tagged by all users who bookmark the web page `cnn.com`, photos on Flickr are usually tagged just by a single user who uploads the photo. In the literature, this distinction has been described as a distinction between *broad vs. narrow folksonomies*. This paper sets out to explore navigational differences between broad and narrow folksonomies in social hypertextual systems. We study both kinds of folksonomies on a dataset provided by Mendeley - a collaborative platform where users can annotate and organize scientific articles with tags. Our experiments suggest that broad folksonomies are more useful for navigation, and that the collaborative processes that are generating folksonomies matter qualitatively. Our findings are relevant for system designers and engineers aiming to improve the navigability of social tagging systems.

Categories and Subject Descriptors

H.5.4 [**Information Interfaces and Presentation**]: Hypertext/Hypermedia—Navigation; H.5.3 [**Information Interfaces and Presentation**]: [Group and Organization Interfaces—Collaborative computing]

General Terms

Experimentation, Measurement, Algorithms

Keywords

Navigation, Folksonomy, Keywords, Tags

1. INTRODUCTION

In social tagging systems, users organize information using so-called *tags* – a set of freely chosen words or concepts – to annotate various resources such as web pages on Delicious, photos on Flickr, or scientific articles on BibSonomy. In addition to using tagging systems for personal organization of information, users can also socially share their annotations with each other. The information structure that emerges through such processes has been typically described as "folksonomies[1]" (**folk**-generated ta**xonomies**). Usually, such folksonomies are represented as tripartite graphs with hyper edges. These structures contain three finite, disjoint sets which are 1) a set of users $u \in U$, 2) a set of resources $r \in R$ and 3) a set of tags $t \in T$ annotating resources R. A folksonomy as a whole is defined as the annotations $F \subseteq U \times T \times R$ (cf. [26]). A *bookmark* or *post* refers to a single resource r and all corresponding tags t of a user u.

Although this tripartite structure of folksonomies can be mapped onto a broad range of different systems in heterogeneous domains (such as Delicious, Flickr, Mendeley and others), the *collaborative processes that are generating these structures can differ significantly*. For example: While resources on Delicious are usually tagged by a larger group of users (e.g. by everybody who has bookmarked the web page `cnn.com`), photos on Flickr are usually tagged just by a single user (e.g. just by the user who has uploaded the photo). In past discussions, this distinction has been described as a distinction between *broad vs. narrow folksonomies[2]*.

Thus, while broad folksonomies are structures that have been generated as a result of aggregating data from *many people tagging the same resource*, narrow folksonomies are structures that have been generated as a result of aggregating data from *single users tagging their own resources*. Although both kinds of folksonomies can be mapped onto

---

[1] http://www.vanderwal.net/folksonomy.html
[2] http://personalinfocloud.com/2005/02/explaining_and_.html

the tripartite structure of folksonomies, it is reasonable to expect that they differ with regard to their overall network characteristics and topology, form and function. In this paper we will argue that without thorough investigations of the different characteristics of different kinds of folksonomies (e.g. broad vs. narrow), our understanding of the potentials and limitations of social tagging systems will be limited. Therefore, understanding the usefulness and utility of different kinds of folksonomies for different tasks - such as navigation, emergent semantics or information retrieval - represents a problem of both theoretical and practical importance.

Similar classifications of metadata have been analyzed in other application areas such as learning objects metadata. In their analysis in [29] the authors distinguish between "authoritative" metadata that is provided by official data descriptors, e.g. learning object authors and "non-authoritative" metadata which emerges through the usage of learning objects in different contexts, e.g. it is created by a user community. In our terminology "authoritative" metadata corresponds to narrow folksonomies and "non-authoritative" metadata to broad folksonomies. The authors argued in their study that there are significant differences in the utility of different types of metadata. For example, they demonstrated that the "non-authoritative" metadata is crucial for effective discovery and reuse of learning objects in different contexts.

In this paper, we aim to systematically compare differences between broad and narrow folksonomies on a large tagging system (Mendeley). Mendeley is a collaborative platform for scientists where users can annotate and organize scientific articles with tags. Because Mendeley not only captures data about the set of tags assigned by users, but also about the set of keywords assigned by the authors of articles (extracted from library and metadata information), *we can generate both broad and narrow folksonomies for the same set of resources* (i.e. scientific articles) at the same time. This means that we can generate broad folksonomies based on the tags users assigned to scientific articles, *and* we can generate narrow folksonomies for the same set of resources based on the keywords that authors assigned to their papers.

In this work, we will compare the usefulness of broad vs. narrow folksonomies for a given *task*: navigation. We start by applying hierarchical clustering algorithms (such as the algorithm by [2] and others) to create hierarchies of tags and keywords as navigational structures between resources. We then use an existing framework for simulating navigation in social tagging systems [13] based on Kleinberg's decentralized search [17] to simulate a hypothetical user navigating the resource space using information provided by keywords vs. tags. In particular, we are going to model a navigational task where the user starts at an arbitrary keyword/tag and navigates to another keyword/tag to reach the list of articles with that keyword/tag. In our simulations, we adopt a greedy routing strategy based on Kleinberg's decentralized search. As a result, we use keyword/tag hierarchies as background knowledge that guides the simulation towards a particular destination by providing information on distances between keywords/tags in the resource network. To reflect the limitations of a real-world user interface, we then repeat the simulations by introducing constraints related to different user interface elements inspired by previous work

[12]. The overall outcome of our investigations allows us to shed light on the differences between broad vs. narrow folksonomies in theoretical but also in practical navigation settings (by considering UI constraints). For our simulations we use a dataset that currently includes about 150 million scientific articles and has a community of about 1,5 million of users who tag articles in an unconstrained manner.

Our results suggest that both broad (tag-based) and narrow (keyword-based) folksonomies support efficient navigation in theory. However, taking some practical limitations of typical user interfaces into account, we find that broad folksonomies outperform narrow folksonomies significantly on our dataset.

In summary, this paper reports on the following findings based on our dataset:

- Narrow folksonomies create less effective navigational structures than broad folksonomies when real-world user interface constraints are considered.
- Our analysis suggests that navigational effectiveness of tags comes from the different viewpoints of readers provided through tagging resources.
- Broad folksonomies provide substantially higher quality of navigational structures than narrow ones. We speculate that with growing numbers of tags in broad folksonomies, their navigational advantage becomes even greater. More research on this question is warranted though.

The remainder of this paper is organized as follows. In Section 2, we discuss related work. In Section 3 we shortly present our simulation model for user navigation. In Section 4, we outline our experimental setup and in Section 5 we present our experimental results. In Section 6 we discuss the results and provide a possible explanation for the observed difference in navigational efficiency.

2. RELATED WORK

Related work in this field of research can be split up into two different parts: *folksonomies*, and *navigation and hierarchies in networks*.

Folksonomies: In the past, folksonomies have been studied from at least two different perspectives – from an ontological and an information retrieval perspective. From the ontological perspective, our community analyzed emergent semantic structures. For example [2, 14, 24] propose algorithms for constructing semantically sound tag hierarchies from social tagging data. A detailed analysis of approaches to semantic relatedness of tags in social tagging systems can be found in e.g. [6]. In our own previous work [20, 21], we investigated the extent to which tag semantics are influenced by user motivation and usage practices. In [31] we investigated the quality of semantic relations in automatically constructed tag hierarchies. By measuring Taxonomic Recall and Precision [9] against a huge number of existing human created concept hierarchies we have shown that algorithms such as e.g. [2] outperform other popular tag hierarchy induction approaches such as Affinity Propagation [11] or Hierarchical K-Means [10].

From the information retrieval perspective, Chi at al. [7] investigated the ability of tags to efficiently encode resources for later retrieval and found out that this ability decreases over time. In [15] and [1] the authors proposed and evaluated search ranking algorithms such as FolkRank and SocialSimilarity Rank. In our own previous work[13], we evaluated the suitability of different tag hierarchies to support navigation in social tagging systems on a theoretical level – not taking user interface constraints into account. There we showed that tag hierarchies created with algorithms such as [2, 14] are able to, at least in theory, provide an efficient support for *navigation* in tagging systems. In subsequent work, we also modeled typical limitations of a standard user interface such as e.g. *directories*, and were able to deduce a new algorithm that produces tag hierarchies that are still able to support efficient navigation even when restricted by a real-world user interface [12]. These hierarchies were evaluated by simulations with the same decentralized approach as it is also used in this paper.

Navigation and hierarchies in networks: Research on navigation in complex networks was initiated by the famous small-world experiment conducted by Milgram [27]. In that experiment randomly selected persons were required to pass a letter to a target person through their social networks. The striking result of the experiment was that the average chain length length was only six. Apart from the findings that humans in that social network are connected by short paths, another conclusion was that humans can efficiently navigate social networks although they have only *local knowledge* of that network – humans can efficiently perform *decentralized search*. Kleinberg concluded that humans possess *background knowledge* of the network structure and that this knowledge allows humans to efficiently find short paths [16, 18, 19]. Kleinberg represented such background knowledge as a hierarchy of nodes, where more similar nodes are situated closer to each other in the hierarchy.

In [30] the authors extend the notion of background knowledge to the notion of *hidden metric spaces*. In such hidden metric spaces nodes are identified by their co-ordinates – distance between nodes is their geometric distance in a particular metric space. Navigation strategies in complex networks are then based on the distances between nodes – an agent always navigates to the node with the smallest distance to a particular destination node. An interesting research question is the structure of such hidden metric spaces that underlie observable networks. In [4], the authors introduce a model with the circle as a hidden metric space and show its effects on routing in the global airport network. In [22] the authors discuss hyperbolic geometry as a hidden metric space (which can be approximated by a node hierarchy) whereas in [5] the authors apply hyperbolic geometry as a model of the hidden metric space of the Internet and design a novel greedy Internet routing algorithm. In [23] the authors describe a novel decentralized search model for efficient navigation in social networks. The model is based on the users interest. By simulating navigation on the co-author network of DBLP[3] they evaluate the model and show the importance of one step lookahead in decentralized search algorithms for social networks.

Hierarchies that are extracted from networks play an important role in many of these network navigation models. Apart from the tag hierarchy induction algorithms based on bipartite networks such as e.g. [14, 2, 12], researchers also proposed hierarchy extraction algorithms for general networks. In [28] the authors discuss an algorithm for hierarchy construction in Wikipedia networks based on metrics for estimating hierarchy level of single nodes. Also,

---

[3]http://dblp.uni-trier.de/

Clauset et al. [8] present a hierarchy induction algorithm based on prediction of hierarchical links. Links prediction problem (in general settings) has been also studied by Liben-Nowell and Kleinberg [25]: They studied the extent to which interactions among members of a social network are likely to occur in the near future.

West and Leskovec [32] performed a study of user navigation behavior. The authors analyzed a collection of click paths of users playing a navigation game in a network of links between the concepts of Wikipedia. In their work they found out that user navigation behavior differs from shortest paths. For example, users typically navigate through high-degree hubs in the early phase and then apply content similarity as a criteria for reaching the destination concept.

3. METHODOLOGY

Our methodology for comparing the usefulness of broad vs. narrow folksonomies for navigation is simulation. We simulate a user who visits a digital library in search for a set of scientific articles and applies thereby a set of standard information seeking strategies. A recent study that investigated user behavior in Web search [33] showed that not many users satisfy their information need with their first search query. Instead, users visit one of the first search results, follow links on that result page, backtrack, follow some other links, then in many cases refine their search, and so on.

Thus, we model a user who starts the inquiry by issuing a search query either at an external search engine or using the integrated search function provided by the digital library. Upon selecting one of the search results the user lands at a particular page in the digital library and explores the links from that page in order to satisfy her information need. We model this first step by randomly selecting words from broad (tags) vs. narrow (keywords) folksonomies from the library. We represent the user information need as another randomly selected destination keyword together with the list of articles for which this destination keyword was assigned. We then simulate the navigation from the starting keyword to the destination keyword. In our previous work we simulated the navigation in tagging systems by simulating a user traversing links between tags from tag clouds [13] or links in a hypothetical directory-like user interface for tags [12]. The former was an assessment of the navigability of tags in an unconstrained settings whereas the latter represents a more realistic settings of a user interface that has limitations in the number of items that are presented to the user. Please note that an important advantage of simulation as an evaluation strategy is the possibility to experiment with various configurations and parameters and in this way cover a wide range of different settings – something that would not be possible in more traditional user studies. Thus, we apply the same methodology in this paper and evaluate different settings in which keywords might be used to support navigation, such as unconstrained navigation, or different variations of navigation limited by constraints of a typical user interface.

In [12, 13] we introduced a simple user navigation model – in this paper we just shortly explain its basic principles. Essentially, user navigation in information networks (such as networks of tags, or networks of keywords and scientific articles) is a kind of so-called decentralized search, or search with local knowledge of the network [16, 17, 18, 19]. At each step of navigation towards a specific destination node the user is aware only of links emanating from the current node. The user does not possess the global knowledge of the network and is therefore required to adopt a navigation strategy that will guide her as fast as possible to the destination node. In his research on the search in social networks inspired by the famous small-world experiment by Milgram [27] Kleinberg introduced a simple greedy strategy [16, 17]. The prerequisite for this strategy is the existence of an external background knowledge on the network that defines the notion of distance or similarity between network nodes. An agent applying the greedy strategy selects from currently available links the link that leads to the most similar, i.e. to the node closest to the destination node. Kleinberg was able to show that such a greedy strategy is a very efficient one and that an agent applying that strategy always finds the destination node in a small number of steps that is bounded poly-logarithmically in the number of nodes.

Thus, we simulate user navigation by applying such a greedy strategy in search from the start to the destination node. In [12, 13] we represented the background knowledge as various tag hierarchies. Clearly, the structure of this hierarchy influences navigational capability. We assessed navigational efficiency provided by those hierarchies by measuring how often the search for the destination node is successful and if successful how fast is it. We were able to show in those papers that tag hierarchies can indeed support efficient navigation. We also designed a new algorithm that induces tag hierarchies that are efficiently navigable even under the restrictions of a realistic user interface. In this paper we apply those same algorithms on collections of keywords and scientific articles, measure the navigability of keywords and compare those results with the results that we obtained for tags on the same set of resources.

Moreover, in this paper we extend our navigation model to account for a situation where the user looks for a specific scientific article. Thus, we are not only interested in how quickly we can find keywords – we also want to know how easy it is to find a particular article once when we reach one of its keywords.

4. EXPERIMENTAL SETUP

4.1 Simulation and Evaluation Metrics

We divide our evaluation into two parts: We compare the usefulness of broad vs. narrow folksonomies by comparing their (i) encoding efficiency and (ii) navigational efficiency.

Encoding efficiency. First, we evaluate how good different folksonomical data is at encoding articles for later retrieval. This evaluation provides an insight in the intermediate exploration steps of the navigation process – the user has already reached a potentially interesting keyword or tag and the system presents a list of articles associated with that keyword or tag. We want to estimate how easy is it to find a specific article in this list. This is typically measured in terms of conditional entropy [7]. Entropy is a measure of uncertainty in a random variable. In information theory entropy is expressed in the number of bits that are needed to encode a random variable. Entropy reaches the maximal value when the random variable is distributed uniformly (uncertainty in the value of that random variable is maximal) and is minimal, i.e. it is equal to zero if the random variable always takes on a single value. Entropy of a single random variable (e.g. tags or keywords) is calculated by:

$$H(X) = - \sum_{x \in X} p(x) log(p(x)) \qquad (1)$$

In turn, conditional entropy quantifies uncertainty in one random variable (articles) once we know a specific value of another random variable (keywords or tags). Thus, conditional entropy of articles measures how difficult is to find a specific article within the presented list. Higher values of conditional entropy mean that there is more uncertainty and it is therefore more difficult to reach a particular article. On the contrary, lower values of conditional entropy mean that the first random variable (keywords or tags) encodes articles more efficiently, decrease uncertainty, and thus it is easier for users to reach a specific article. Conditional entropy of two random variables is given by:

$$H(Y|X) = - \sum_{x \in X} p(x) \sum_{y \in Y} p(y|x) log(p(y|x)) \qquad (2)$$

The navigability evaluation consists of four steps:

Network construction. We start with the datasets that include triples of keywords or tags, articles, and authors or users. From those datasets we construct bipartite networks of keywords (tags) and articles and remove the user information as that information is typically not relevant for navigation. Subsequently, we project the bipartite networks onto keyword-to-keyword and tag-to-tag networks as those networks are available for the user for navigation. We assume that article lists are also presented to the user upon selecting a keyword or a tag but only as a means of satisfying the initial information need, whereas keywords or tags are used for exploration, i.e. as a means of making progress towards the final destination.

Hierarchy construction. We induce broad (tag-based) and narrow (keyword-based) folksonomy hierarchies which we will use as the background knowledge to steer navigation. We use two algorithms for constructing hierarchies. In [14], the authors introduce a generic algorithm for producing hierarchies from bipartite networks such as tag-to-resource networks. The algorithm can be applied to arbitrary bipartite structures. The algorithm takes as input two parameters. The first is a ranked list of tags sorted by their centrality in the projected tag-to-tag network. This centrality ranking acts as a proxy to the generality ranking of tags. Benz et al. [3] showed that the centrality provides a viable approximation to the tag generalities. The second input parameter is the tag similarity matrix. The algorithm starts then by a single node hierarchy with the most general tag as the root node and then iterates through the centrality list. At each iteration step, the algorithm adds the current tag to the hierarchy as a child to its most similar tag. The centrality and similarity measure are exchangeable – in [14] the authors use closeness centrality and cosine similarity, whereas in [2] the authors select degree centrality and co-occurrence similarity measure. As both combinations perform similarly in supporting navigation [13], we select the latter combination because of better computational properties. This algorithm produces unbalanced hierarchies that are typically very broad in the top hierarchy levels. As some of the top nodes in real datasets might end up with hundreds or even thousands of children those hierarchies give us the

	K	T	OK	OT
Bipartite				
Metadata	1,124,260	399,703	469,952	201,651
Links	28,459,841	12,869,137	3,323,787	1,492,217
Articles	5,172,180	3,649,350	523,488	523,488
$\frac{\#Links}{\#Metadata}$	25.3	32.3	140.8	134.72
Eff.Diam	6.92	7.10	8.25	8.65
Projected Dataset				
Metadata	1,092,655	371,044	455,001	166,957
Links	124,690,988	47,760,792	26,450,686	7,877,564
$\frac{\#Links}{\#Metadata}$	114.18	128.7	58.13	47.5
Eff.Diam	4.06	3.94	4.79	4.68

Table 1: Dataset and network statistics of broad (T, OT) vs. narrow (K, OK) folksonomies. Datasets OT and OK only contain articles for which both tags and keywords are available.

	K	T	OK	OT
Entropy	15.09	14.23	12.74	12.39
Cond. Entropy	6.40	5.92	4.18	3.81

Table 2: Entropy and Conditional Entropy for broad (T, OT) vs. narrow (K, OK) folksonomies. Datasets OT and OK only contain articles for which both tags and keywords are available.

insight in the intrinsic, theoretical, and unconstrained navigational support. We obtain a more realistic assessment of navigational efficiency by applying a variant of this algorithm. In [12], we extended that algorithm and introduced an algorithm that takes also the branching factor (the maximal number of children) of the final hierarchy as an input parameter. Through re-balancing of the hierarchy and introduction of nested misc categories we were able to produce hierarchies that support efficient navigation even under realistic limitations imposed by a typical user interface.

Search pairs selection. We randomly select one million of so-called search pairs consisting of a start node and a destination node. Both start and destination nodes are low degree nodes as searching for high degree nodes is a trivial task. For those pairs we calculate the global shortest path that we will use as our metric to assess the navigation efficiency.

Navigation simulation. We run simulation with greedy navigation on those search pairs and measure the success rate s and stretch τ which is the ratio of the number of simulator steps and the global shortest path. We calculate the global averages of both metrics (s_g and τ_g), as well as distribution of both values over the global shortest path. Also we calculate average of the global shortest path ($\bar{l}$), as well as average number of simulator hops ($\bar{h}$), i.e. average number of clicks of the simulated user.

4.2 Datasets

Mendeley[4] claims to be the largest research database, with 150 million papers and 1,5 million users. For our experiments, we used tagging data (dataset **T**) from the system gathered in September 2011 as well as a snapshot from the Mendeley system which includes papers as well as the corresponding keywords provided by the authors (dataset **K**). For dataset **T** we lowercased the tags and removed typos and personal bookmarks, i.e. tags that were used only once by a single user. Lowercasing of the keywords was also performed for dataset **K**. Furthermore we constructed an "overlapped" dataset - a dataset which includes only articles for which both keywords and tags are available. These datasets are called **OT** – overlapped tags and **OK** – overlapped keywords respectively.

Projection of the Dataset: After this preprocessing step, we construct the bipartite networks of keywords and

---
[4] http://www.mendeley.com

articles and tags and articles. From those bipartite networks we extract the largest connected component (which typically contains around 99% of the network nodes). Finally, we project the largest connected component onto keyword-to-keyword and tag-to-tag networks and obtain the final networks on which we perform our analysis. The dataset and network statistics are shown in Table 1.

The first important property here to note is that the quantitative ratio of the number of links and the number of metadata items (i.e. nodes) is comparable between the data set. The second property – the effective diameter (which is the longest shortest path that connects 90% of all network nodes) – is also comparable in all datasets. Thus, this basic *quantitative network-theoretic properties* indicate that all networks possess similar navigational properties. Hence, any differences in navigational efficiency have to be accounted for *qualitative differences in the network topology*.

5. RESULTS

5.1 Tag and Keyword Entropy

Table 2 shows the entropy of articles conditional on keywords and tags in all four datasets. Although it is difficult to interpret absolute values obtained for the conditional entropy, a comparison of entropy values obtained for different datasets provides insight in the relative encoding efficiencies of broad vs. narrow folksonomies. From this analysis we can observe that in our dataset, broad folksonomies (T, OT) encode articles more efficiently than narrow folksonomies (K, OK). In other words, on average we know more about articles annotated by a particular tag than about articles annotated by a particular keyword. This is important when considering that users navigate for resources, not for tags. Our simulation currently does not take into account that users would have to investigate all resources attached to a particular keyword. Hence, the more uncertainty there is on the articles captured by a node, the more time users have to invest for searching the list of articles.

5.2 Unconstrained Navigation

We start our navigational analysis with an estimation of the theoretical navigability of keyword and tag hierarchies. Thus, we construct hierarchies by using Heymann's algorithm [14] which does not consider any user interface constraints. The algorithm produces broad and flat hierarchies in which the nodes from the top hierarchies have hundreds or even thousands of children nodes. Figure 1 shows the degree distributions of the hierarchies depicting the existence of hub nodes.

The results of the simulation with Mendeley tags are comparable with our previous experiments with tagging datasets from Flickr, Delicious, LastFM, BibSonomy, and CiteULike [12, 13]. In such theoretical settings Mendeley tags are efficiently navigable. Keyword networks show similar behavior

$$(a)\ K \qquad (b)\ T \qquad (c)\ OK \qquad (d)\ OT$$

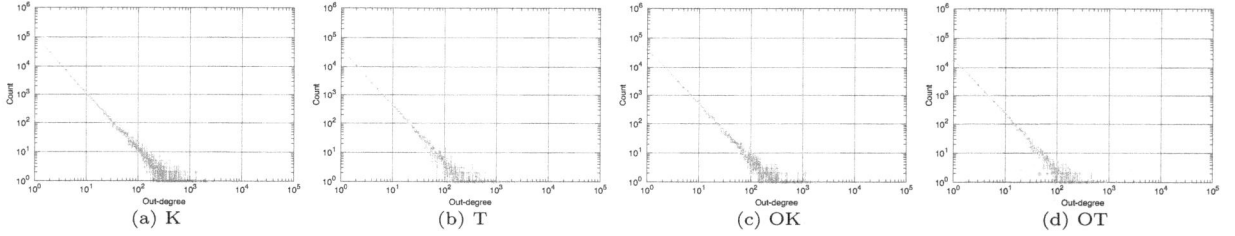

Figure 1: Out degree distribution of unconstrained hierarchies. The top hierarchy levels are populated by high-degree hubs − nodes that have hundreds or even thousands of children nodes. The hierarchies are very broad and flat.

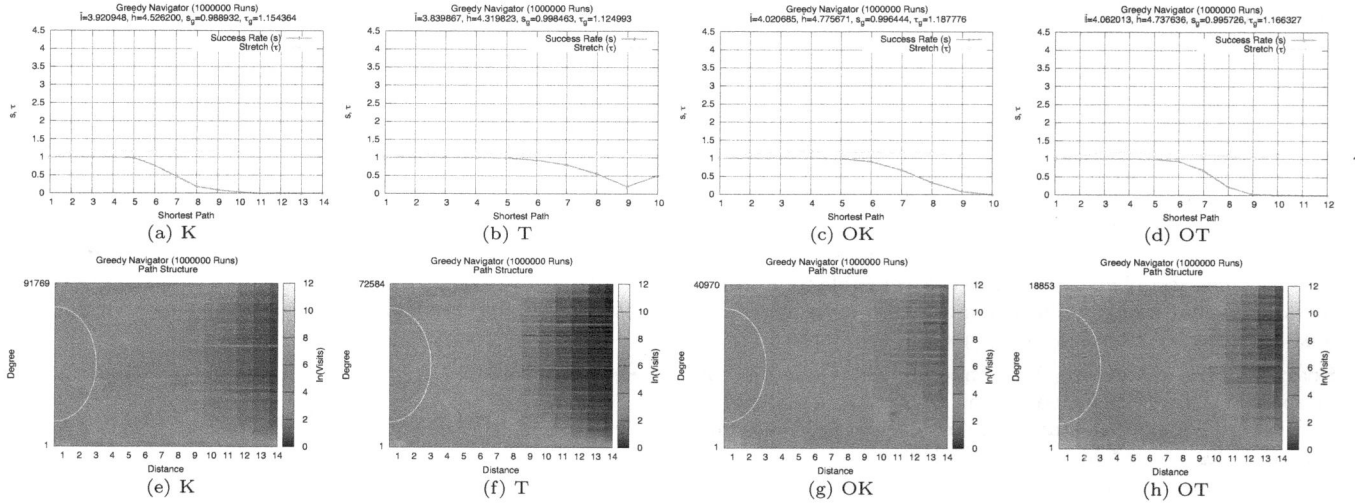

$$(a)\ K \qquad (b)\ T \qquad (c)\ OK \qquad (d)\ OT$$

$$(e)\ K \qquad (f)\ T \qquad (g)\ OK \qquad (h)\ OT$$

Figure 2: Results of the simulation with unconstrained user interface. *Top:* Average shortest path $\bar{l}$, average hop count $\bar{h}$, greedy navigator success rate s and stretch τ − global average values (s_g and τ_g) and distribution over shortest paths. Theoretical evaluation of Mendeley tag hierarchies produces results comparable to other tagging datasets. In theory, tag hierarchies support efficient navigation − both success rate and stretch are close to 1. Similarly, keyword hierarchies aid efficient navigation − success rate and stretch are excellent. *Bottom:* Navigator path structure without user interface constraints. The density maps visualize visit frequency to nodes of a given degree at a given distance to the destination node − the color is logarithm of the visit frequency (black and violet indicating less visits; orange and yellow indicating more visits). As already observed by [4] in e.g. airport network or the Internet, the navigation path structure follows the zoom-out/zoom-in phase pattern. In the zoom-out phase, navigation starts at a low degree node in the network periphery and continues from there by visiting the nodes of increasing degrees into the network core to one the network hubs there. In the second, zoom-in phase, navigation continues over decreasing node degrees to its low-degree destination node in the periphery. Over all datasets, the top nodes are the most visited nodes − these are the nodes from the network core where the phase transition in the navigation process occurs. A specific property of navigation paths in tagging networks are so-called shortcuts between related mid-degree nodes occurring at the smaller distances to the destination node (see e.g. white marked region of a large orange-colored area in 2h). Those shortcuts are taken between sibling tags of a high-degree parent in the cases where the destination node is situated in the sub-hierarchy of one of the siblings. The density maps reveal a slightly different path structures between keyword and tag navigation. The green marked regions of shortcut areas in the keyword navigation (2e and 2g) show that shortcuts between related mid-degree and siblings are taken less frequently in the case of keyword navigation − high-degree hubs are more frequently visited in keyword than in tag networks. Since the global success rate and stretch in both networks are comparable to each other this phenomenon indicates that there exist structural differences between keyword and tag hierarchies − a possible explanation would be that tag hierarchies are somewhat richer in structure, i.e. keyword hierarchies more broad and flat. Nevertheless, in this theoretical navigational settings without any user interface constraints this does not impede the keyword navigation.

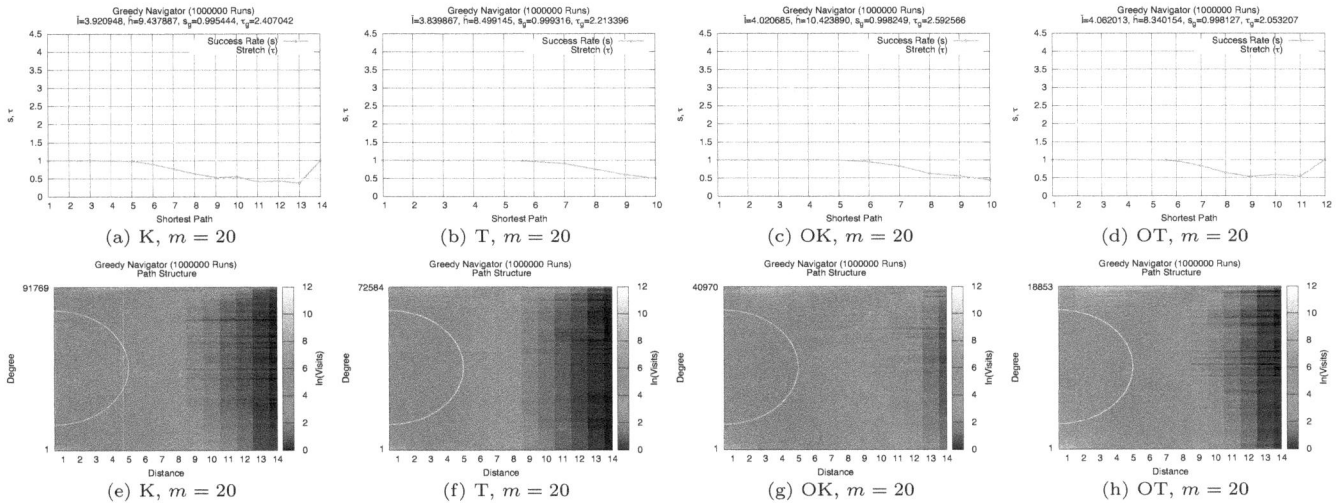

Figure 3: Results of the simulation with constrained user interface. The number of siblings is limited to $m = 20$. *Top:* **Average shortest path $\bar{l}$, average hop count $\bar{h}$, greedy navigator success rate s and stretch τ – global average values (s_g and τ_g) and distribution over shortest paths. Although the success rates remain excellent over all datasets, stretch increases slightly in keyword datasets. This results in path lengths that are on average longer by 1 or 2 in keyword networks.** *Bottom:* **Path structure with user interface constraints. The green marked regions of shortcut areas in keyword networks (3e and 3g) demonstrate less frequent shortcuts than in tag networks (white regions in 3f and 3h) explaining the increased stretch values in keyword networks.**

– in theory, keywords support efficient navigation. The complete results of the experiments are shown in Figure 2.

5.3 Constrained Navigation

In our next experiments we configure the simulator to reflect typical limitations of a standard user interface, e.g. a directory-like interface, such as Yahoo directory[5]. Thus, we model constraints such as limited number of children nodes that are shown (e.g. 20 children), limited number or related items (e.g. 20 siblings), or combination of both restrictions. As we have shown in [12], such restrictions seriously impede the navigation properties of tag hierarchies and we obtain similar results for both keyword and tag hierarchies. The most interesting observation that we make with those experiments is the difference in stretch values for the limitation of the number of related items that are presented to the user. In our experiments, we observe increased stretch values for keyword navigation resulting in one or two more clicks that are needed on average to reach the destination node. This result is consistent over all datasets and it might reflect an intrinsic property of keyword networks and keyword hierarchies. Our explanation for this phenomenon is that within a group of co-occurring keywords there exist a single keyword which "dominates" the group, i.e. other keywords co-occur more frequently with that "dominating" keyword and less frequently with other keywords from the group. The "dominator" becomes a parent node in the hierarchy and all other nodes are attached as children to that node (see also 6). Thus, the limitation of the number of siblings that are presented to the user causes that a longer path over the parent node is taken and increases the path length by 1 or 2 (see Figure 3).

[5] http://dir.yahoo.com/

5.4 Realistic Constrained Navigation

Finally, we want to perform experiments using an alternative algorithm for hierarchy induction to better reflect the realities of user interfaces. We apply the algorithm presented in [12] that produces balanced hierarchies with a maximal number of children (we set e.g. 20 children to reflect a typical user interface limitation). The algorithm produces a nested sub-hierarchy of so-called misc categories in which it inserts nodes with the smallest similarities to their parent node. In a typical case, low-degree nodes from the long tail are inserted into such nested misc categories. In our experiments, we obtain similar results as in experiments limiting the number of siblings. Consistently and over all datasets, keywords perform slightly worse exhibiting increased stretch and an increase of the average number of clicks by 1 (see Figure 4).

Finally, we remove misc categories completely to reflect another situation – a case where users might not navigate within misc categories. In those experiments we obtain smaller success rates that are comparable to each other over all datasets. As before, we observe an increased stretch in keyword networks resulting in the average number of clicks to increase by 1 in those networks (see Figure 5).

6. DISCUSSION

Our results show that in realistic navigational settings - when we take into account user interface limitations - tag navigation is slightly more efficient than keyword navigation. Moreover, tag encoding efficiency is also higher than keyword encoding efficiency. The density maps reveal the reason for this finding – there are more shortcuts taken between mid-degree and high-degree siblings in tag hierarchies than between such keywords in keyword hierarchies. A possible cause for that is a lower average overlap between sib-

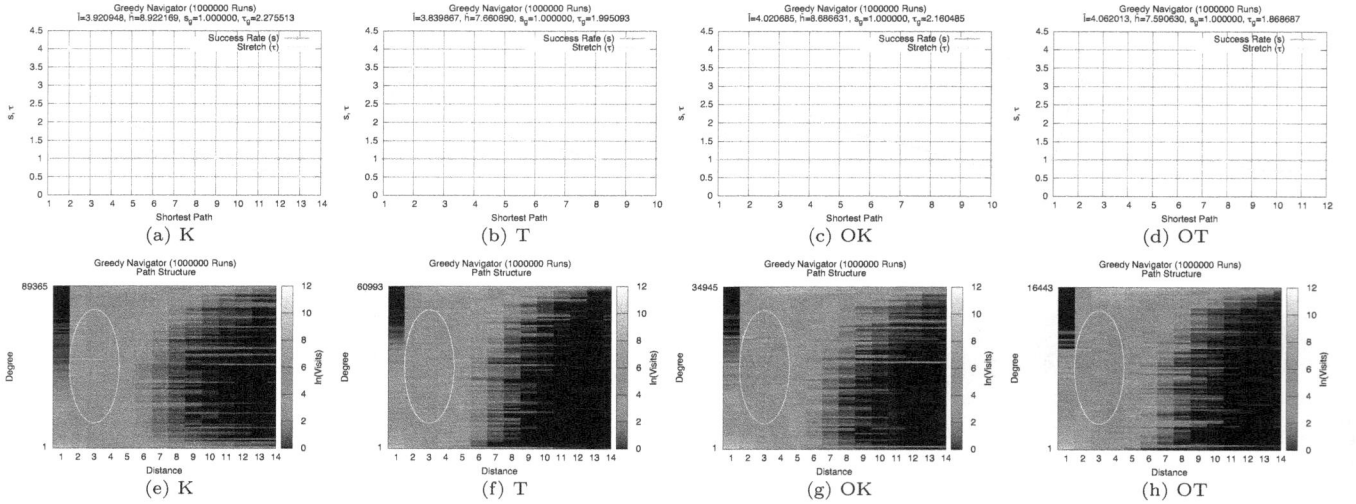

(a) K (b) T (c) OK (d) OT

(e) K (f) T (g) OK (h) OT

Figure 4: Results of the simulation with balanced hierarchies. The number of children and siblings is set to 20. *Top:* Average shortest path $\bar{l}$, average hop count $\bar{h}$, greedy navigator success rate s and stretch τ − global average values (s_g and τ_g) and distribution over shortest paths. As previously observed the success rates remain stable and excellent over all datasets, whereas stretch increases slightly in keyword datasets. This results in path lengths that are on average longer by 1 in keyword networks. *Bottom:* Navigator path structure with balanced hierarchies. Again, the green marked regions of shortcut areas in keyword navigation (4e and 4g) indicate smaller shortcut frequencies than in tag navigation (white ellipses in 4f and 4h).

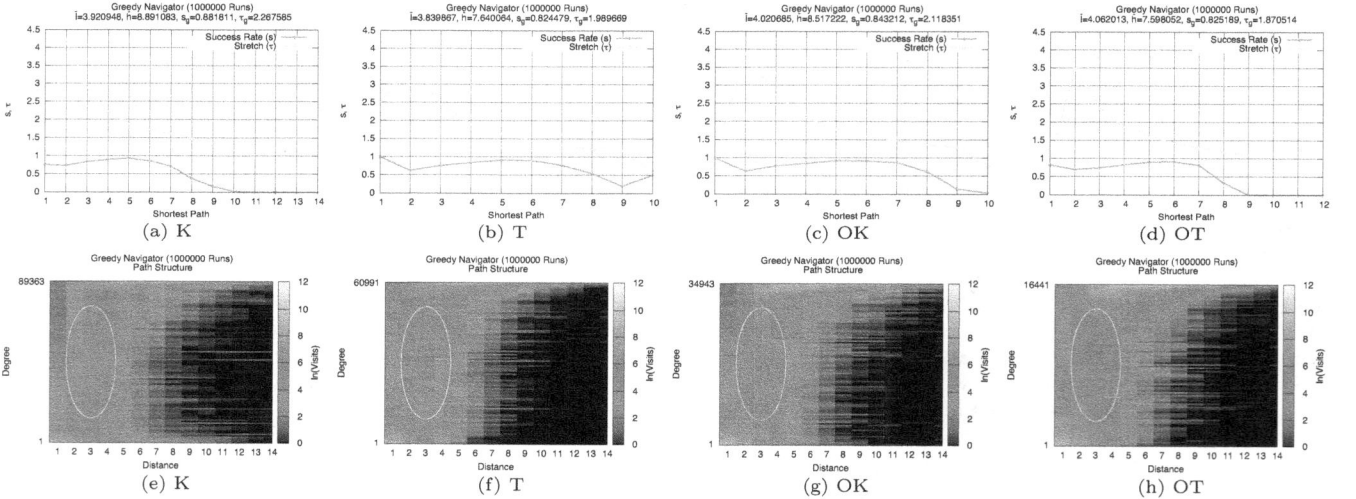

(a) K (b) T (c) OK (d) OT

(e) K (f) T (g) OK (h) OT

Figure 5: Results of the simulation with balanced hierarchies without misc categories. The number of children and siblings is set to 20. *Top:* Average shortest path $\bar{l}$, average hop count $\bar{h}$, greedy navigator success rate s and stretch τ − global average values (s_g and τ_g) and distribution over shortest paths. The success rates is smaller than before over all datasets. Again, stretch increases slightly in keyword datasets. *Bottom:* Navigator path structure with balanced hierarchies. The green marked regions of shortcut areas in the keyword navigation (5e and 5g) and white marked regions in tag datasets (5f and 5h) show differences in the number of shortcuts.

ling keywords compared to sibling tags. We will explain this situation with the following simple example. Suppose we have an article dealing with navigation in tagging systems. The authors define the following keywords for this article: "folksonomy", "tagging", "navigation" (see $r1$ in Figure 6). Suppose also that the authors calculate entropy

in that article, but do not include "entropy" as a keyword in their article. Thus, the authors define their single viewpoint that defines a narrow navigation structure in the proximity of that article and its keywords. Now, suppose that multiple users annotate that article with tags. For example, the first user annotates it with "folksonomy" and "tagging". The

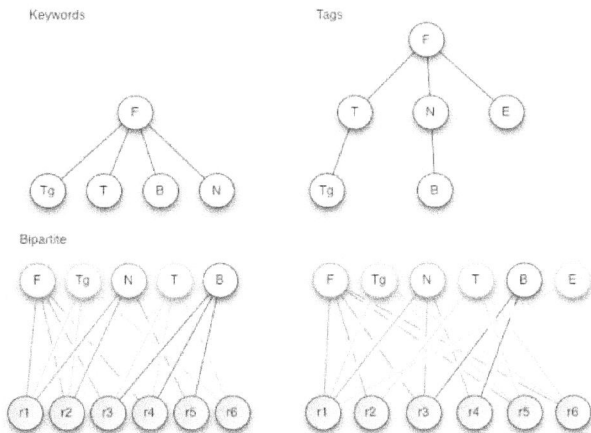

Figure 6: Two simple examples showing the emergence of hierarchies in keyword networks (left) and tag networks (right) with metadata "folksonomy" (F), "tagging" (Tg), "tags" (T), "navigation" (N), "brwosing" (B), and "entropy" (E). In keyword (narrow) folksonomies keywords are applied for grouping of articles. On contrary, in tag (broad) folksonomies tags are assigned by many users with multiple and possible alternative viewpoints. This results in tag distributions that impose richer overlap between similar tags. As a consequence the hierarchies that are based on tag generality and their mutual similarities are richer in structure than keyword hierarchies. Our experiments show that those structurally richer hierarchies are more stable and robust to the negative effects of the user interface constraints.

second user annotates it with "navigation", and the third user with "entropy" (because that is the most interesting part of the article for that user). Now, there are multiple viewpoints on the same article and there are multiple navigational structures that are broader and *overlap* with each other. Suppose now that a user is interested in an article about entropy. Now a user may reach that article in a number of alternative ways – one of these paths leads also over our sample article as its "entropy" tag represents an entrance to a completely different cluster in the network. Thus, the user might come from a cluster related to e.g. social tagging and then upon arriving on the sample article take a *shortcut* over "entropy" tag and enter the entropy cluster. Thus, tags provide different, alternative, and more heterogeneous access paths to articles. In other words, tag folksonomies result in tag distributions whereas keyword folksonomies result in simple almost independent groups of keywords.

Moreover, such multiple viewpoints from many users tagging the same resource collection result in richer hierarchical structures – at least under the algorithms that we applied in our paper. Figure 6 depicts an example with a group of similar articles dealing with e.g. social tagging systems – the constructed hierarchies differ in their structures. Richer structures that emerge in tag hierarchies are more robust to the restrictions imposed by a user interface – less tags

are affected by e.g. limiting the number of related tags as compared to more keywords that are removed when we limit the number of related keywords presented to the user. We can provide a remedy for this problem of keyword networks by e.g. enriching the keywords with additional metadata such as categorizations, or subject descriptors to turn *narrow* keyword folksonomy into a *broad* folksonomy similar to the tag folksonomy.

7. CONCLUSIONS

This paper set out to study differences between broad vs. narrow folksonomies and their usefulness for the task of navigation. Using data from Mendeley, we created both broad (based on tags provided by users) and narrow (based on keywords provided by authors) folksonomies. While our experiments show that broad and narrow folksonomies exhibit comparable quantitive properties, we find interesting qualitative differences with regard to navigation. For example, broad folksonomies create more efficient navigational structures that enable users to find target resources with fewer hops. We find that the reason for better navigational utility of broad folksonomies can be explained by the fact that greater overlap between tags provides better options for users to switch between different parts of the network. Narrow folksonomies are not able to provide this kind of support. While our findings are limited to a single dataset (Mendeley), they warrant future research in this direction. Our results are relevant for designers of social tagging systems and for engineers aiming to improve the navigability of their systems.

8. ACKNOWLEDGMENTS

This work is funded by - BMVIT - the Federal Ministry for Transport, Innovation and Technology (grant no. 829590) to the last author.

9. REFERENCES

[1] S. Bao, G. Xue, X. Wu, Y. Yu, B. Fei, and Z. Su. Optimizing web search using social annotations. In *Proceedings of the 16th international conference on World Wide Web - WWW '07*, page 501, New York, New York, USA, May 2007. ACM Press.

[2] D. Benz, A. Hotho, and G. Stumme. Semantics made by you and me: Self-emerging ontologies can capture the diversity of shared knowledge. In *Proc. of the 2nd Web Science Conference (WebSci10)*, Raleigh, NC, USA, 2010. Web Science Trust.

[3] D. Benz, C. Körner, A. Hotho, G. Stumme, and M. Strohmaier. One tag to bind them all: Measuring term abstractness in social metadata. In *Proceedings of the 8th Extended Semantic Web Conference (ESWC 2011)*, Heraklion, Crete, May 2011.

[4] M. Boguñá, D. Krioukov, and K. C. Claffy. Navigability of complex networks. *Nature Physics*, 5:74–80, Jan. 2009.

[5] M. Boguñá, F. Papadopoulos, and D. Krioukov. Sustaining the Internet with hyperbolic mapping. *Nature Communications*, 1:62, Sept. 2010.

[6] C. Cattuto, D. Benz, A. Hotho, and G. Stumme. Semantic grounding of tag relatedness in social bookmarking systems. In *The Semantic Web – ISWC*

2008, Proc. of International Semantic Web Conference 2008, volume 5318 of *LNAI*, pages 615–631, Heidelberg, 2008. Springer.

[7] E. H. Chi and T. Mytkowicz. Understanding the efficiency of social tagging systems using information theory. In *Proc. of the nineteenth ACM conference on Hypertext and hypermedia, HT '08*, pages 81–88, New York, NY, USA, 2008. ACM.

[8] A. Clauset, C. Moore, and M. E. J. Newman. Hierarchical structure and the prediction of missing links in networks. *Nature*, 453(7191):98–101, 2008.

[9] K. Dellschaft and S. Staab. On how to perform a gold standard based evaluation of ontology learning. In *Proceedings of ISWC-2006 International Semantic Web Conference*, Athens, GA, USA, November 2006. Springer.

[10] I. Dhillon, J. Fan, and Y. Guan. Efficient clustering of very large document collections. In *Data Mining for Scientific and Engineering Applications*. Kluwer Academic Publishers, Heidelberg, 2001.

[11] B. J. J. Frey and D. Dueck. Clustering by passing messages between data points. *Science*, 315(5814):972–976, January 2007.

[12] D. Helic and M. Strohmaier. Building directories for social tagging systems. In *Proceedings of the 20th ACM international conference on Information and knowledge management*, CIKM '11, pages 525–534, New York, NY, USA, 2011. ACM.

[13] D. Helic, M. Strohmaier, C. Trattner, M. Muhr, and K. Lerman. Pragmatic evaluation of folksonomies. In *Proceedings of the 20th international conference on World wide web*, WWW '11, pages 417–426, New York, NY, USA, 2011. ACM.

[14] P. Heymann and H. Garcia-Molina. Collaborative creation of communal hierarchical taxonomies in social tagging systems. Technical Report 2006-10, Stanford InfoLab, April 2006.

[15] A. Hotho, R. J, C. Schmitz, and G. Stumme. Information Retrieval in Folksonomies : Search and Ranking. *Data Engineering*, 4011:411–426, 2006.

[16] J. Kleinberg. The small-world phenomenon: an algorithm perspective. In *Proceedings of the thirty-second annual ACM symposium on Theory of computing*, STOC '00, pages 163–170, New York, NY, USA, 2000. ACM.

[17] J. Kleinberg. Complex networks and decentralized search algorithms. In *International Congress of Mathematicians (ICM)*, pages 1019–1044, Zürich, Switzerland, 2006. European Mathematical Society Publishing House.

[18] J. M. Kleinberg. Navigation in a small world. *Nature*, 406(6798):845, August 2000.

[19] J. M. Kleinberg. Small-world phenomena and the dynamics of information. In *Advances in Neural Information Processing Systems (NIPS) 14*, page 2001, Cambridge, MA, USA, 2001. MIT Press.

[20] C. Körner, D. Benz, M. Strohmaier, A. Hotho, and G. Stumme. Stop thinking, start tagging - tag semantics emerge from collaborative verbosity. In *Proc. of the 19th International World Wide Web Conference (WWW 2010)*, Raleigh, NC, USA, Apr. 2010. ACM.

[21] C. Körner, R. Kern, H. P. Grahsl, and M. Strohmaier. Of categorizers and describers: An evaluation of quantitative measures for tagging motivation. In *21st ACM SIGWEB Conference on Hypertext and Hypermedia (HT 2010)*, Toronto, Canada, ACM, Toronto, Canada, June 2010.

[22] D. Krioukov, F. Papadopoulos, M. Kitsak, A. Vahdat, and M. Boguñá. Hyperbolic geometry of complex networks. *Phys. Rev. E*, 82(3):036106, Sep 2010.

[23] S. Lattanzi, A. Panconesi, and D. Sivakumar. Milgram-routing in social networks. In *Proceedings of the 20th international conference on World wide web*, WWW '11, pages 725–734, New York, NY, USA, 2011. ACM.

[24] R. Li, S. Bao, Y. Yu, B. Fei, and Z. Su. Towards effective browsing of large scale social annotations. In *Proc. of the 16th international conference on World Wide Web, WWW '07*, page 952, New York, NY, USA, 2007. ACM.

[25] D. Liben-Nowell and J. Kleinberg. The link prediction problem for social networks. In *Proceedings of the twelfth international conference on Information and knowledge management*, CIKM '03, pages 556–559, New York, NY, USA, 2003. ACM.

[26] P. Mika. Ontologies are us: A unified model of social networks and semantics. *Web Semantics: Science, Services and Agents on the World Wide Web*, 5(1):5–15, March 2007.

[27] S. Milgram. The small world problem. *Psychology Today*, 1:60–67, 1967.

[28] L. Muchnik, R. Itzhack, S. Solomon, and Y. Louzoun. Self-emergence of knowledge trees: Extraction of the wikipedia hierarchies. *Phys. Rev. E*, 76:016106, Jul 2007.

[29] M. Recker and D. Wiley. A non-authoritative educational metadata ontology for filtering and recommending learning objects. *Journal of Interactive Learning Environments*, 9(3):255–271, 2003.

[30] M. A. Serrano, D. Krioukov, and M. Boguñá. Self-similarity of complex networks and hidden metric spaces. *Phys. Rev. Lett.*, 100(7):078701, Feb 2008.

[31] M. Strohmaier, D. Helic, D. Benz, C. Körner, and R. Kern. Evaluation of folksonomy induction algorithms. *ACM Trans. Intell. Syst. Technol.*, 2012.

[32] R. West and J. Leskovec. Human Wayfinding in Information Networks. In *Proceedings of the 21th international conference on World Wide Web - WWW '12*, New York, New York, USA, 2012. ACM Press.

[33] R. W. White and S. M. Drucker. Investigating behavioral variability in web search. In *Proceedings of the 16th international conference on World Wide Web*, WWW '07, pages 21–30, New York, NY, USA, 2007. ACM.

Measuring the Influence of Tag Recommenders on the Indexing Quality in Tagging Systems

Klaas Dellschaft
Inst. for Web Science and Technologies (WeST)
Universität Koblenz-Landau
Koblenz, Germany
klaasd@uni-koblenz.de

Steffen Staab
Inst. for Web Science and Technologies (WeST)
Universität Koblenz-Landau
Koblenz, Germany
staab@uni-koblenz.de

ABSTRACT

In this paper, we investigate a methodology for measuring the influence of tag recommenders on the indexing quality in collaborative tagging systems. We propose to use the inter-resource consistency as an indicator of indexing quality. The inter-resource consistency measures the degree to which the tag vectors of indexed resources reflect how the users understand the resources. We use this methodology for evaluating how tag recommendations coming from (1) the popular tags at a resource or from (2) the user's own vocabulary influence the indexing quality. We show that recommending popular tags decreases the indexing quality and that recommending the user's own vocabulary increases the indexing quality.

Categories and Subject Descriptors

H.5.3 [**Information Interfaces and Presentation**]: Group and Organization Interfaces—*Collaborative Computing, Evaluation*

Keywords

Collaborative Tagging, Indexing Quality, Tag Recommenders

1. INTRODUCTION

Collaborative tagging systems allow users to organize resources, e.g. photos, bookmarks or BibTeX entries, by assigning tags or keywords to them. Users can freely choose the tags which they want to use for indexing resources. Over time, the tag assignments of the different users lead to the emergence of a loose categorization system for resources, often called a *folksonomy* [11]. One key aspect of tagging systems is the uncontrolled nature of the community's vocabulary. Nevertheless, it has been observed in [5, p. 205] that the combined tag assignments of users "give rise to a stable pattern in which the proportions of each tag are nearly fixed". This is typically taken as an indicator that tagging is successful in collaboratively indexing resources despite of its uncontrolled nature.

During adding tags to resources, in many tagging systems, e.g. in Delicious and Bibsonomy, the users see a set of tag recommendations. It is an often posed question how these tag recommendations influence the users in their tagging decision and whether this influence is rather positive or negative. In the related work (see Section 2), there exist several approaches for analyzing the influence of tag recommendations. In many cases, it is analyzed how tag recommendations influence the inter-indexer consistency [3, 5, 7, 10, 14]. It corresponds to the degree to which the users have agreed on a common vocabulary for describing resources. It is assumed that increasing the inter-indexer consistency is important for dealing with the uncontrolled nature of the vocabulary in tagging systems.

But what does a high inter-indexer consistency mean in terms of indexing quality as it might also be measured by precision and recall during querying resources? The inter-indexer consistency only measures the average consensus of the indexers at the single resources. But precision and recall are influenced by how indexers use the indexing terms across a set of resources. For example, a high recall is achieved if related resources are linked to each other by indexing them with terms which express their common aspects. Furthermore, a high precision is achieved if indexing terms are discriminative enough, i.e. if they only link related but not also unrelated resources.

None of these aspects which influence precision and recall are directly measured by the inter-indexer consistency. Nevertheless, the inter-indexer consistency may be positively correlated with these aspects by introducing the assumption that the indexers reach the same consensus for related resources and a different consensus for unrelated resources.

In contrast, the inter-resource consistency is a more direct way of measuring the aspects which lead to high precision and recall. It measures in how far the indexers are successful in linking related resources by indexing their common aspects. Thus, the inter-resource consistency is directly correlated with the indexing quality and a high precision and recall of query results (cf. Subsection 3.1). Measures of inter-indexer consistency are also positively correlated with the inter-resource consistency are positively correlated, if it can be assumed that the indexing terms are "selected individually and independently by each of the indexers" [19].

However, our investigations show that the assumption of the positive correlation between inter-indexer consistency on the one hand and inter-resource consistency or indexing quality on the other hand does not hold when it comes to investigating the influence of tag recommenders. The rea-

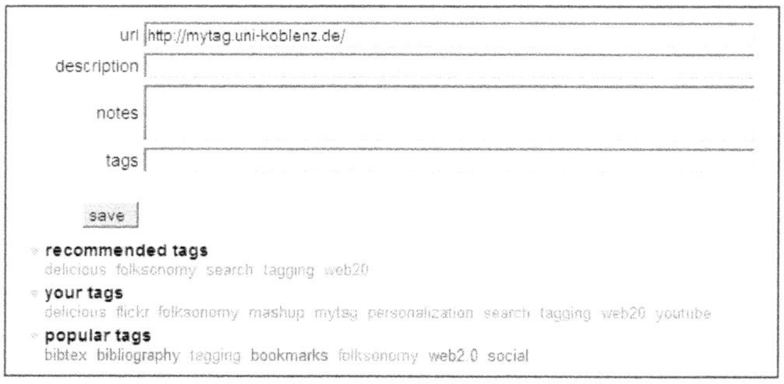

Figure 1: Tagging interface of Delicious. Users can enter free tags in the *tags* input field and/or they can select some of the suggested tags.

son is that the users no longer apply their tags individually and independently of each other. We thus argue that only the inter-resource consistency can be used as an indicator of indexing quality in tagging systems. We support this argument by measuring the inter-resource and the inter-indexer consistency for two exemplary tag recommenders, showing that the two measures are not positively correlated with each other. The rest of this paper is structured as follows:

In Section 3, we provide a methodology for measuring the inter-resource consistency in tagging systems. Furthermore, we take from the related work a method for measuring the inter-indexer consistency. In Section 4, we derive the hypotheses that these two measures are not positively correlated with each other for two exemplary baseline tag recommenders. Then, in Section 5 we describe the user experiment during which we collect the necessary data for measuring the inter-resource and the inter-indexer consistency. The results from Section 6 support our hypotheses that the two measures are not positively correlated with each other if tag recommendations are used and that thus only the inter-resource consistency is a valid measure of indexing quality.

2. RELATED WORK

Given an individual user who is about to tag a given resource, e.g. a web page, there are three basic paradigms of suggesting tags to this user [8]: One can suggest (1) tags based on the tag assignments of other users (either extracted from the tag assignments associated with the current resource or from all tag assignments), (2) tags based on the previous tag assignments of the current user, and (3) tags based on the content of the current resource, e.g. by extracting keywords from the content or title of a web page.

Simple tag recommendation algorithms suggest tags only based on one of the three paradigms. For example, in the tagging interface of Delicious (see Fig. 1) the user sees amongst others the seven most popular tags at the current resource and all his previously used tags. More sophisticated tag recommendation algorithms suggest tags based on several of the paradigms. For example, the recommender in [8] first extracts candidate tags from the local vocabulary and the content of the current resource. Then, the candidate tags are checked against the vocabulary of the current user.

But which effect does a given tag recommendation algorithm have on the indexing quality in collaborative tagging systems? In the introduction, we have explained that one central aspect of indexing quality is the inter-resource consistency, i.e. in how far the indexers are successful in linking

related resources by indexing their common aspects [18]. For measuring the inter-resource consistency, an indicator of relatedness of resources is required which is independent of the indexing to be tested [18]. In [18], the authors use topical clusters of resources for measuring in how far the resources within a cluster are linked by their indexing terms. The higher the inter-resource consistency, the better are precision and recall of queries which use the indexing terms.

Because this independent indicator of resource relatedness is difficult to acquire, many studies concentrate on the inter-indexer consistency instead. The inter-indexer consistency does not require such additional data. But this approach is only valid if the indexing terms are "selected individually and independently by each of the indexers" [19]. An example of a recent study using inter-indexer consistency where this assumption holds is available in [13]. In this study, the authors compare the indexing quality between professional indexers and laymen.

But also in the literature about tagging systems, often some kind of inter-indexer consistency is measured. For example, in [5] it is studied how long it takes until the frequencies of the most popular tags at a resource have reached a stable state. A faster convergence process is ascribed to be an indicator for a higher inter-indexer consistency. Furthermore, in [14] the inter-indexer consistency is measured in terms of the tag reuse rate, i.e. by the average number of users who apply a tag. Finally, in several other studies [3, 6, 7, 10] a smaller size of the final vocabulary is taken as an indicator for the consensus among the users. In all these studies, it has been shown that recommending tags based on the tag assignments of other users leads to a higher inter-indexer consistency. This higher inter-indexer consistency is then taken as an indicator of an improved indexing quality, ignoring the fact that the assumption of individual and independent tag selection does not hold.

But besides the approaches for measuring the inter-indexer consistency, also some alternative measures for indexing quality have been proposed in the literature about tagging systems. For example, in [15, 17] it has been proposed to compare the resulting tag assignments against the true preferences of the users. In [15, 17], the true preferences of the users are defined to be the tag assignments which would occur without the influence of tag suggestions. This methodology judges any deviation from the uninfluenced behavior of users as negative. Thus, from our perspective it seems unsuitable for measuring positive effects of tag recommenders because positive effects can only occur if users deviate from their uninfluenced behavior.

Furthermore, in the literature about tag recommendation algorithms, the quality of tag recommenders is measured by the precision and the recall of the set of recommended tags (see [8, 16] for examples). In these studies, precision and recall compare the tag recommendations against a gold standard. It depends on the chosen gold standard how to interpret precision and recall. For example, if precision and recall are measured in a live system[1], then they measure how often users accept a recommendation. If precision and recall compare the recommendations with the uninfluenced tag assignments of the individual users then the recommendations are compared to the true preferences of the users

---

[1]See the *Online Tag Recommendations* track of the ECML PKDD Discovery Challenge 2009 http://www.kde.cs.uni-kassel.de/ws/dc09/

(like in [15, 17]). The former approach measures in how far users prefer one tag recommender over another. But this aspect of tag recommendations is distinct from the resulting indexing quality. The latter approach of comparing with un-influenced tag assignments has the same drawbacks as the approach in [15, 17] (see above).

3. MEASURING THE INDEXING QUALITY

In this section, we describe the inter-resource and inter-indexer consistency measures in more detail. Furthermore, we explain in Subsection 3.1 how an improved inter-resource consistency might also lead to an improved precision and recall for queries. In Section 4, we then present our hypotheses how inter-resource and inter-indexer consistency are influenced by two exemplary tag recommenders.

3.1 Measuring the Inter-Resource Consistency

In general, the inter-resource consistency measures in how far indexers are successful in linking related resources by indexing their common aspects. We follow the approach from [18], in which the relatedness of resources according to their tag vectors V is compared to their relatedness according to a set of topical clusters C. Given V and C, the idea of inter-resource consistency is as follows: (1) If two resources are contained in the same topical cluster $c \in C$ then this should be reflected by a higher similarity of their tag vectors. (2) If two resources are contained in different topical clusters c_1 and c_2 then this should be reflected by a lower similarity of their tag vectors. The higher the ratio of the similarity within a cluster and the similarity between distinct clusters, the better is the inter-resource consistency.

During ranked retrieval, the similarity of two tag vectors v_1 and v_2 has an important influence on the relevance ranking of the corresponding resources with regard to a query. The more similar two tag vectors, the more likely the corresponding resources will get a similar relevance value and the closer together they will be in the ranked result list. Thus, the first criterion from above ensures that resources from the same topical cluster are in average ranked closer together. The second criterion ensures that resources from distinct clusters are in average ranked farther away from each other.

Overall, combining both criteria leads to a better separation of resources from the different topical clusters in a ranked result list. Thus, resources from the topical cluster which is most relevant for answering a query are intermixed with fewer resources from other, less relevant topical clusters. Assuming the match between indexing terms and query terms which has been shown in [15], then an improved inter-resource consistency finally leads to an improved precision and recall for the top-k results for a query.

Measuring the inter-resource consistency is a two-step process: In a first step, we have to measure the pairwise similarities of the tag vectors in V. In the second step, we then measure the ratio between the similarity of tag vectors within a cluster and the similarity of tag vectors from distinct clusters. In the following, we propose measures applicable for a ranked retrieval model. In [18], measures for a boolean retrieval model are available.

3.1.1 Measuring the Similarity of Tag Vectors

A common model in information retrieval is the vector space model which forms the basis for ranked retrieval. It is the fundamental model for several information retrieval tasks like scoring documents on a query, document classification and document clustering [9]. According to this model, the tag vector of a resource captures the relative importance of tags for this resource. In our case, the tag vector of a resource contains how often the tags $t_1, \ldots, t_n$ have been assigned to it by the users. A standard way for calculating the similarity of resources in the vector space model is the cosine similarity [9]. Given two tag vectors v_i and v_j, their similarity is measured as follows:

$$cosim(v_i, v_j) = \cos \Theta = \frac{v_i \cdot v_j}{\parallel v_i \parallel \cdot \parallel v_j \parallel} \qquad (1)$$

The calculation of the cosine similarity is based on the angle Θ between two tag vectors. Θ itself can also be used for measuring the *dissimilarity* between the tag vectors of two resources.

3.1.2 Within Cluster vs Distinct Clusters Similarity

In order to measure the ratio between the similarity of tag vectors in the same topical cluster and the similarity of tag vectors in distinct topical clusters, we propose to use the Silhouette Coefficient. The Silhouette Coefficient was first introduced in [12] for evaluating clustering algorithms. Given a set of resources $R = \{r_1, \ldots, r_n\}$ and a set of clusters $C = \{c_1, \ldots c_k\}$, so that each resource is contained in only one of the clusters, and a measure of dissimilarity between the resources, the Silhouette Coefficient s_i for a resource r_i is computed as follows:

First, the average dissimilarity a_i of r_i to all other resources in its cluster c is computed. Second, from all clusters not containing r_i, we identify the cluster c' whose resources have in average the lowest dissimilarity to r_i. We call this minimal average dissimilarity b_i. In our case, the average dissimilarity scores a_i and b_i correspond to the average angle Θ between the tag vectors of the resources. Finally, a_i and b_i are set into relation to each other as follows:

$$s_i = \frac{b_i - a_i}{\max(a_i, b_i)} \qquad (2)$$

The Silhouette Coefficient s_i ranges between -1 and 1. s_i will take a positive value if resource r_i is closer to the resources in the same cluster c than to resources in the closest other cluster c'. It reaches its maximal value if the dissimilarity of r_i to the resources in c is 0. In contrast, s_i will take a negative value if r_i is farther away from the resources in c than from the resources in c'. It reaches its minimal value if the dissimilarity of r_i to the resources in cluster c' is 0.

In general, the following relationship between the inter-resource consistency and the precision and recall of queries for resources in cluster c holds: The lower the s_i value, the more likely it gets that resources from cluster c' are ranked as more relevant for the query than the resource r_i. This decreases the precision and recall of queries for resources in cluster c. The same holds for querying resources from cluster c': The lower the s_i value, the more relevant is r_i for such a query, thus leading to a decreased precision.

Given these definitions, we can now use the average Silhouette Coefficient $E(s_i)$ for measuring the inter-resource consistency of a set of tag vectors $V = \{v_1, \ldots, v_n\}$ of the resources in R. The higher the $E(s_i)$-value, the higher the inter-resource consistency of the tag vectors. The $E(s_i)$-values for two sets of tag vectors V_1 and V_2 can be compared given that they describe the same set of resources R

and that they are compared to the same set of clusters C. Only if these two preconditions are fulfilled, we can be sure that a difference in the two $E(s_i)$-values also indicates a difference in the inter-resource consistency for V_1 and/or V_2.

3.2 Measuring the Inter-Indexer Consistency

According to our analysis of the related work in Section 2, many authors assume that a high inter-indexer consistency also indicates a high indexing quality. We argue that this assumption does not hold if the users are influenced by tag recommendations during tagging. In order to support our argument, we compare during our evaluation a traditional measure of inter-indexer consistency to our measure of inter-resource consistency. If our argument is correct, we expect to see no positive correlation between the two measures.

By looking at the literature about tagging systems (see Section 2), two measures related to the inter-indexer consistency can be identified: The tag reuse rate from [14] and the size of the vocabulary [3, 6, 7, 10]. The global vocabulary size is not a good measure for the inter-indexer consistency because it is not only influenced by the overlap of the users' vocabularies or the inter-indexer consistency respectively but also by the average size of the users' vocabularies. Thus, we will only use the tag reuse rate for measuring the inter-indexer consistency in the following. In [14], it is defined as "the average number of users who apply a tag". In our case, we first compute the tag reuse rate tr_i for each resource r_i. The overall tag reuse rate then corresponds to the average $E(tr_i)$ over all resources.

4. RESEARCH HYPOTHESES

In this section, we present two exemplary tag recommenders which are actually used in Delicious. For these two tag recommenders we derive the hypotheses that in their case the inter-resource consistency and the inter-indexer consistency are not positively correlated with each other. The first recommender shows that the inter-resource consistency may increase even if the inter-indexer consistency decreases. The second recommender shows that the inter-resource consistency may decrease even if the inter-indexer consistency increases. If we are able to show in Section 6 that these correlations between inter-resource and inter-indexer consistency hold for the two recommenders then this would support our argument that one has to directly measure the inter-resource consistency instead of the inter-indexer consistency for making conclusions on the indexing quality in tagging systems.

4.1 Increasing the Inter-Resource Consistency

One important way for increasing the inter-resource consistency in a tagging system is to increase the inter-resource consistency of the tag assignments of the individual users. It is the objective of the *User Tags*-based recommender to help the individual user in establishing a consistent tagging vocabulary and to consistently apply it to all resources in his personal collection which have the respective aspects in common. This objective is tried to be achieved by recommending the user all his previously used tags. This recommender is also used in Delicious (see the *Your Tags* suggestions in Fig. 1). These considerations about the *User Tags*-based recommender lead to the following testable hypothesis:

HYPOTHESIS 1. *Suggesting the user his/her own tags in the user interface increases the inter-resource consistency and/or indexing quality in tagging systems.*

Of course, it is unreasonable to assume that the *User Tags* recommender increases the inter-indexer consistency in a tagging system. In reverse, it can be assumed that the inter-indexer consistency either remains unchanged or that it is even decreased. Both cases support our argument that one can not assume a positive correlation between inter-resource and inter-indexer consistency.

HYPOTHESIS 2. *Suggesting the user his/her own tags in the user interface leads to an unchanged or decreased inter-indexer consistency in a tagging system.*

4.2 Increasing the Inter-Indexer Consistency

One important way for increasing the inter-indexer consistency in a tagging system is to show the individual users the tags of the other users. It is a common assumption in the literature that such suggestions reduce the uncontrolled nature of the vocabulary in tagging systems (see Section 2). But in how far do they also help in increasing the inter-resource consistency in a tagging system? A positive correlation between both measures can no longer be automatically assumed because the individual users no longer select the tags individually and independently of each other.

In the following, we argue that in case of the *Popular Tags*-based recommender a decreased inter-resource consistency may be observed although it increases the inter-indexer consistency. Our *Popular Tags* recommender suggests the individual user the seven most popular tags of a resource, , i. e. it mimics the behavior of the corresponding recommender in Delicious (see the *Popular Tags* suggestions in Fig. 1).

In [17], it has been argued with a theoretical model that a recommender based on popular tags may distort the true tagging preferences of a user. Thus, the user applies different tags then he would do without seeing the suggestions. But in itself, distorting the true tagging preferences is not a negative thing: The *User Tags* recommender changes the actual tag assignments of a user, nevertheless we assume in Hypothesis 1 that it helps to increase the indexing quality. But in case of the *Popular Tags* recommender, the tag frequencies converge to a random limit (see [5]). Thus, the tag frequencies no longer only express the important aspects of a resource but they are also influenced by a random process. This influence of the random process decreases the inter-resource consistency:

HYPOTHESIS 3. *Suggesting the user a list with the most popular tags at a resource decreases the inter-resource consistency and/or indexing quality in tagging systems.*

Furthermore, getting feedback about the tags used by other users for describing the same resource increases the inter-indexer consistency:

HYPOTHESIS 4. *Suggesting the user a list with the most popular tags at a resource increases the inter-indexer consistency in a tagging system.*

5. USER EXPERIMENT

In this section, we describe the web-based user experiment which we use for testing the hypotheses from Section 4. The results of the experiment are presented and discussed in Section 6 and 7. The experiment is divided into two phases: During the first phase, screenshots of ten web pages were shown to the users in a random order. To each web page, the

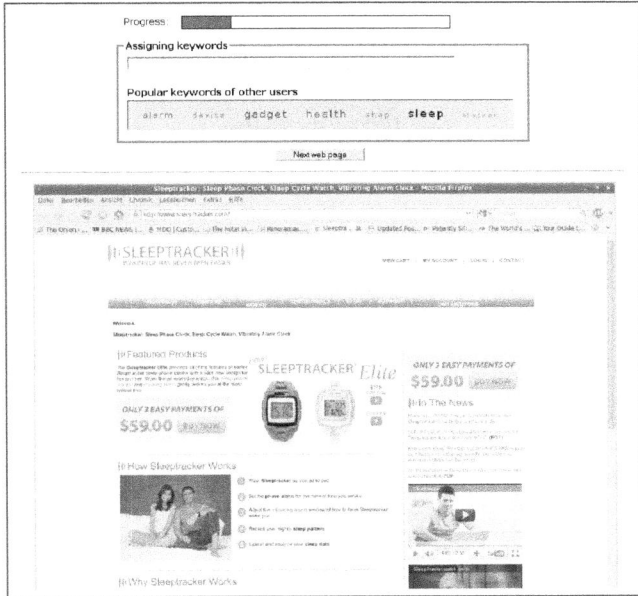

Figure 2: The user interface for assigning keywords to the 10 web pages. The web pages were shown in random order. During tagging, the users saw a screenshot of a browser window showing the web page. The screenshot also included the URL and the title of the web page. Depending on the experimental condition, a tag cloud with the tag suggestions was displayed below the input field for the keywords. Here, the interface for the *Popular Tags* condition is shown. By clicking on one of the suggested tags, the user added it to the input field.

participants should assign any number of tags (see Fig. 2). In a second phase, we asked the participants to group the web pages into topical clusters (see Fig. 3).

For the experiment, we used the same set of web pages as in a previous experiment by Bollen and Halpin [1]. The URLs of the used web pages are shown in Tab. 1. The URLs were selected so that their topics appeal to the general public and not only to participants with a specialized background. In [1] more details are available about how the specific URLs were selected. From the set of eleven web pages used in [1], one web page was removed because a pretest showed that participants had problems in understanding the topic of the web page based on a screenshot of it.

5.1 Experimental Conditions

In order to test our hypotheses from Section 4, we have to distinguish the following three experimental conditions:

Under the **No Suggestions** condition, the users do not get any tag suggestions while tagging the ten web pages. This user group is the control group to which we compare the results of the other two experimental conditions.

Under the **Popular Tags** condition, the users gets suggested the seven most popular tags for the current web page. The most popular tags are based on the tag assignments of the previous users under the same experimental condition for the same web page. Prior to the experiment, each of the web pages got initialized with the tags of a random user from Delicious for the same web page (see Tab. 2). For

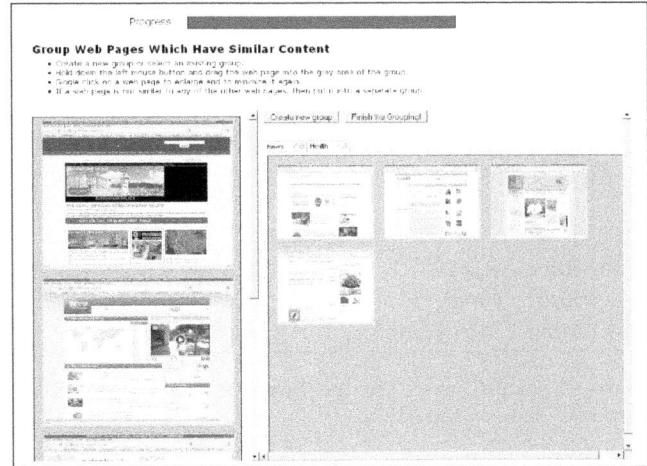

Figure 3: The user interface for grouping the web pages into topical clusters. In the left column, screenshots of the 10 web pages are shown. On the right side, all clusters of the current user are shown. The users were allowed to create any number of clusters. When creating a new cluster, the users were asked to provide a name for it.

ID	URL
1	http://www.theonion.com/
2	http://news.bbc.co.uk/2/hi/uk_news/6057734.stm
3	http://uk.moo.com/
4	http://www.tvtrip.com/
5	http://www.panoramas.dk/
6	http://www.sleeptracker.com/
7	http://blisstree.com/feel/what-happens-to-your-body-if-you-drink-a-coke-right-now/
8	http://www.patentlysilly.com/
9	http://www.whfoods.com/
10	http://www.webmd.com/balance/features/your-guide-to-never-feeling-tired-again/

Table 1: URLs of the 10 web pages used during the experiment.

the German variant, the same tags have been translated to German.

The initialization of the *Popular Tags* condition with a random user is necessary in order to introduce a comparable level of randomness to the tag assignment process as in a real system like Delicious. In a real system, the resources would also be first tagged by different users. Without initializing the resources with a random posting, the first assignments at the resources would all come from the first participant of the *Popular Tags* condition.

Under the **User Tags** condition, each user sees all tags which he/she previously used in the experiment. For the first web page, the users do not get any suggestions.

5.2 Recruiting and Instructing Participants

We used several channels for recruiting participants for the experiment: (1) We approached colleagues and friends. (2) We promoted the experiment during the Web Science Conference 2011. (3) We distributed the call for participation over twitter and several public mailing lists about informa-

ID	URL
1	theonion, news, america
2	bbc, news, evolution, human
3	moo, business cards, post cards, printing
4	tvtrip, travel, hotels, reviews
5	panorama, background image
6	sleep, alarm, shop
7	health, coke, diet
8	funny, patents
9	health, food
10	sleep, health, guide

Table 2: Tags used for bootstrapping the English *Popular Tags* condition.

German	|Users|	|Tags|	|TAS|	|TAS|/|User|
No Suggestions	74	706	2,134	28.84
User Tags	79	466	1,507	19.08
Popular Tags	78	531	2,228	28.56
English	|Users|	|Tags|	|TAS|	|TAS|/|User|
No Suggestions	115	973	3,150	27.39
User Tags	118	819	2,919	24.74
Popular Tags	118	550	3,003	25.45

Table 3: Sizes of the experimental data sets. Only participants who finished tagging all ten web pages are included. (TAS = tag assignments)

tion retrieval. (4) We distributed the call in an internal news group of the University of Koblenz.

All in all, 877 users participated of which 582 finished tagging all 10 web pages. For 530 users, also the grouping of the web pages according to their similarity is available. In Section 6, we only use the tag assignments and groupings of those 582 users who finished tagging all 10 web pages. According to a questionnaire at the end of the experiment, approximately 53% of the participants use tagging systems for searching regularly or sometimes. The rest tried it either once or not all. Furthermore, 45% of the participants upload content to tagging systems regularly or sometimes.

Due to our recruiting strategy, we expected to observe a homogeneous subgroup of native German speakers. Thus, we decided to not only offer an English variant of our experiment but also a German variant. In both variants, the same English web pages were shown but in the German variant we asked the participants to preferably use German keywords. Thus, German participants were able to use their larger and more accurate active German vocabulary during tagging. Each participant decided on his own whether to participate in the German or English variant.

All in all, 231 users finished the experiment in the German variant and 351 users in the English variant (see Tab. 3). It was the objective of our recruiting strategy to recruit around 100 participants for each of our experimental conditions because usually this number of participants is required until the tag vectors reach a stable state (cf. [5]). For the German variant, we recruited slightly less participants than our target value of 100 participants per experimental condition. For the English variant, we recruited slightly more participants. But an a posteriori analysis of our results showed that we nevertheless reached for all experimental conditions the primary objective of having stable tag vectors.

Background of the Experiment

This experiment is part of my PhD thesis in which I'm studying tagging systems (What are tagging systems?). The experiment helps to better understand how keywords are used for organizing collections of web pages. ***Effort: ~15 minutes.***

Running the Experiment

- 10 web pages will be shown to you, one after another.
- Assign any number of keywords to each web page.
- Keywords are like categories and/or they describe the content of a page. **Example**: *You may use the keyword "work" for grouping web pages relevant for your work.*
- The keywords are primarily for yourself, to find your way in your own collection of web pages.

Figure 4: Instructions given to the participants of the English experiment variant.

After choosing between the German or the English variant of the experiment, each participant was randomly assigned to one of the three conditions described in Subsection 5.1. The experimental condition with the most participants was excluded from the random assignment, if it already contained at least 5 participants more than the condition with the fewest participants. This ensured a balanced distribution of participants over the experimental conditions.

The participants were not aware that different experimental conditions exist and that they have to create topical clusters at the end of the experiment. They were only told that the experiment analyses how keywords are used for organizing collections of web pages (see Fig. 4).

6. RESULTS

In this section, we are showing the results of our user experiment. The results help us in validating the hypotheses from Section 4. In a first step, we evaluate in Subsection 6.1 in how far the users from the different experimental conditions have identified similar topical clusters. The identification of similar topical clusters is a precondition for comparing the inter-resource consistency between the different experimental conditions in Subsection 6.2. Finally, in Subsection 6.3 we compare the inter-indexer consistency between the different experimental conditions.

6.1 Similarity of the Topical Clusters

In Subsection 3.1.2, we have described how to use the average Silhouette Coefficient $E(s_i)$ for measuring the inter-resource consistency of the tag assignments. But before we can apply this method on our data, we have to verify that the participants of the different experimental conditions have in average identified the same topical clusters during the second phase of the experiment (see Fig. 3). Otherwise, the differences in the $E(s_i)$-values may not only be caused by the influence of the respective experimental condition but also by differences in the topical clusters.

During the second phase of the experiment, we received feedback from 530 of our participants. A user was only able to finish the second phase if every web page was assigned to one cluster. The participants were allowed to provide a name for each cluster in order to make it easier for them to keep track of their clusters. On average, each participant separated the 10 web pages into 4.76 clusters, i. e. 2,521 clusters have been created. Together, the users identified 140 distinct clusters. Two topical clusters are considered as equal if they contain the same web pages.

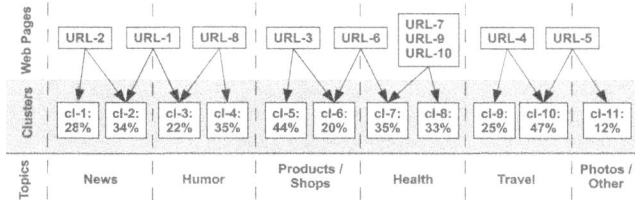

Figure 5: Visualization of the 11 most frequently identified clusters of web pages. Each box in the gray area corresponds to one cluster. Within the box of each cluster it is given, by how many participants the cluster has been identified. For example, 28% of all experiment participants put the *BBC* web page (URL-2) alone into a cluster, leading to cluster *cl-1*. Another 34% of the participants instead decided to group *BBC* (URL-2) together with *The Onion* (URL-1), leading to cluster *cl-2*. The remaining 38% of the participants have put URL-2 into other, less frequent clusters. Nevertheless, an analysis of the names used for *cl-1* and *cl-2* reveals that both clusters are seen as related to the *News* topic.

In Fig. 5, the eleven most frequently identified clusters from the second experiment phase are shown. Altogether, the eleven clusters from Fig. 5 represent 70.25% of all identified topical clusters. According to the names of the clusters, the 10 web pages are roughly related to 6 different topics. URL-1, URL-5 and URL-6 are each on the border between two topics. For example, the web page *The Onion* (URL-1) publishes satirical news articles. 34% of the users think that it is more related to the *News*-topic and thus they group it with an article from the *BBC* web page (URL-2), leading to cluster *cl-2*. In contrast, 22% emphasize more the *Humor*-topic and thus group it with *Patently Silly* (URL-8) which lists funny and strange patents, leading to cluster *cl-3*.

In Fig. 5, the reported cluster probabilities are based on all 530 participants who completed the second phase of the experiment. But in Fig. 6 it can be seen that in the German variant the vast majority of the participants perceive *The Onion* (URL-1) as related to *BBC* (URL-2) and the *News* topic. In contrast, participants of the English variant more prefer to cluster *The Onion* with *Patently Silly* (URL-8) according to the *Humor* topic. This preference for clustering *The Onion* together with *Patently Silly* is even more prevalent for the English *Popular Tags* condition (see Fig. 7).

But in how far are these differences in the cluster probabilities significant? In the following, we use the χ^2-Test [2, p. 199ff] for answering this question.[2] If the χ^2-Test rejects the hypothesis of equal cluster probabilities then we cannot compare $E(s_i)$-values for those experimental conditions.

In a first test, we compare the clusterings from the English variant of the experiment with those from the German variant. The test reveals that the clusterings differ significantly ($T = 161.69$, $n_1 = 1519$, $n_2 = 1002$, $p < 0.01$). Thus, we cannot use the Silhouette Coefficients for comparing the inter-resource consistency across the two language variants.

---

[2]For the χ^2-Test, we counted how often each of the distinct clusters has been identified by the different participants. The probability of all clusters identified by only a single user from either of the compared participant groups is combined in a single cluster "other". This is necessary for preserving the validity of the χ^2-Test (see [2, p. 201f]).

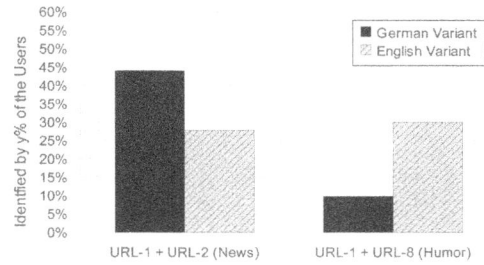

Figure 6: Differences in the clustering of URL-1 between the participants of the English and the German experiment variant. Participants of the German variant see it more as *news* related and thus cluster it with URL-2. In the English variant, the participants more emphasize its humorous aspects by clustering it with URL-8.

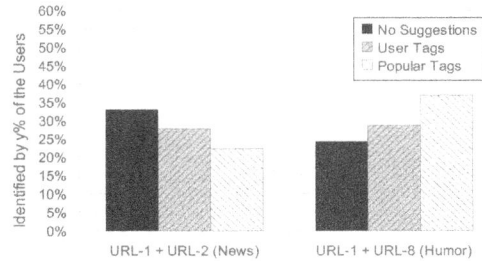

Figure 7: Differences in the clustering of URL-1 between the participants of the English experiment variant. Under the *Popular Tags* condition, more participants see URL-1 as related to *humor* and thus cluster it with URL-8.

But for evaluating our hypotheses from Section 4, it is more important whether we can use the Silhouette Coefficient for comparing the *No Suggestions* condition to the other two experimental conditions within the same language variant:

No Suggestions vs. Popular Tags Only for the German variant of the experiment the clusterings from the *No Suggestions* condition and from the *Popular Tags* condition can be considered as equal. For the English variant, the clusterings from the two conditions differ significantly. Possible explanations for the significant differences are discussed in Subsection 7.
German: $T = 39.25$, $n_1 = 339$, $n_2 = 323$, $p = 0.75$;
English: $T = 63.04$, $n_1 = 489$, $n_2 = 515$, $p = 0.06$

No Suggestions vs. User Tags For the English variant of the experiment as well as for the German variant the clusterings from the *No Suggestions* condition and from the *User Tags* condition can be considered as equal. For the German variant, the differences between the clusterings are smaller than for the English variant.
German: $T = 35.03$, $n_1 = 339$, $n_2 = 340$, $p = 0.86$;
English: $T = 51.99$, $n_1 = 489$, $n_2 = 515$, $p = 0.36$

All in all, the results in this subsection show that there are only minor differences in the cluster probabilities between the three German experimental conditions. Thus, we can compare the $E(s_i)$-values between all three German experimental conditions. In contrast, in the English experiment variant we can only compare the *No Suggestions* and the English *User Tags* condition. The English *No Suggestions*

German	$E(s_{x,i})$	$E(tr_{x,i})$
No Suggestions	0.1847	2.44
User Tags	0.2367	2.39
Popular Tags	0.1474	3.60
English		
No Suggestions	0.1713	2.76
User Tags	0.1915	2.68
Popular Tags	N/A	4.67

Table 4: Influence of the experimental conditions on the inter-resource consistency and on the inter-indexer consistency. The inter-resource consistency is measured by the average Silhouette Coefficient $E(s_{x,i})$. The inter-indexer consistency is measured by the average Tag Reuse Rate $E(tr_{x,i})$.

	German Variant	English Variant
$E(s_{ns,i}) - E(s_{pt,i})$	[0.0337, 0.0582]	N/A
$E(s_{ut,i}) - E(s_{ns,i})$	[0.0584, 0.0955]	[0.0106, 0.0434]
$E(tr_{ns,i}) - E(tr_{pt,i})$	[−1.611, −0.691]	[−2.403, −1.276]
$E(tr_{ut,i}) - E(tr_{ns,i})$	[−0.392, 0.3437]	[−0.392, 0.2804]

Table 5: 95% confidence intervals for the differences between the $E(s_{x,i})$-values and the $E(tr_{x,i})$ values under the experimental conditions.

and the English *Popular Tags* condition cannot be compared because of the differences in the identified topical clusters.

6.2 Measuring the Inter-Resource Consistency

In this subsection, we evaluate the hypotheses from Section 4 which are related to the influence of tag suggestions on the inter-resource consistency. In the following, we use the average Silhouette Coefficient $E(s_{x,i})$ from Subsection 3.1.2 for measuring the inter-resource consistency for a tagging system X. We compare the $E(s_{ns,i})$-value for the *No Suggestions* condition with the $E(s_{pt,i})$-value for the *Popular Tags* condition and/or the $E(s_{ut,i})$-value for the *User Tags* condition. Based on our hypotheses from Section 4, we expect the following order of the $E(s_{x,i})$-values:

$$E(s_{pt,i}) < E(s_{ns,i}) < E(s_{ut,i}) \qquad (3)$$

For the German experiment variant, we compute the $E(s_{x,i})$ values by comparing the tag vectors of the three experimental conditions against the union of all clusters given by participants of the German variant. This way the differences between the $E(s_{x,i})$ values are only caused by differences in the tag vectors and not also by slight differences in the cluster probabilities. For the English variant, we compare the tag vectors from the *No Suggestions* and the *User Tags* condition against the union of the clusters from the respective participants. The clusters and tag vectors from the English *Popular Tags* condition have to be excluded from the evaluation because of the significant differences in the cluster probabilities as it is shown in Subsection 6.1.

For comparing the $E(s_{x,i})$-values of two experimental conditions, we apply a two-tailed Mann-Whitney Test [2, p. 272ff]. It tests the null hypothesis whether two given $E(s_{x,i})$ values have to be considered as equal against the alternative hypothesis that they are not equal. Furthermore, we use the Hodges-Lehmann Estimator of Shift [2, p. 281f] for determining the 95% confidence interval for the difference between the two $E(s_{x,i})$-values.

A summary of the experimental results is shown in Tab. 4 and 5. For these results, we have restricted the number of users so that under each of the experimental conditions the same number of users contributed to the tag vectors. For the German variant, we restricted it to the first 74 users of each of the experimental conditions. For the English variant, we restricted it to the first 115 users. Thus, we control that different numbers of users do not cause the differences in the results. Controlling for vocabulary size and number of tag assignments only led to minor fluctuations in Tab. 4 and 5 so we omit the numbers here.

The exact method for computing the $E(s_{x,i})$-values is as follows: Given a set of clusters which was provided by an individual user, for all ten web pages we compute the respective s_i-value. For example, in case of the German experiment variant we overall have 216 sets of clusters which have been provided by the users in this experiment variant. Thus, the $E(s_{x,i})$-values for the German experiment variant are each based on $10 \cdot 216 = 2160$ s_i-values.

When computing the $E(s_{x,i})$-values, we omit from our analysis the s_i-values of web pages which are in a cluster of size 1 in their respective set of clusters. The reason is that in such a case a_i and subsequently the s_i-value are not well defined (see [12]). For example, in case of the German experiment this excludes 334 of the 2160 s_i-values from our experiment. Nevertheless, the tag vector of the respective web page still takes part in the computation of the b_i-value for the s_i-values of the remaining web pages in the same set of clusters. Furthermore, the s_i-value of the respective web page may still be computed in the context of another set of clusters where it is not in a cluster of size 1.

6.2.1 No Suggestions vs. Popular Tags

In the following, we test the effect of suggesting popular tags on the average Silhouette Coefficient. For this purpose, we compare the $E(s_{ns,i})$-value for the *No Suggestions* condition to the $E(s_{pt,i})$-value for the *Popular Tags* condition as they are shown in Tab. 4. Because of the differences in the perception of the web pages for the English variant of the experiment (see Subsection 6.1) we can test Hypothesis 3 for the German experiment variant only.

For the German experiment variant, we can confirm that $E(s_{pt,i}) < E(s_{ns,i})$. A two-tailed Mann-Whitney Test shows that the difference between the $E(s_{x,i})$-values is significant ($T_1 = 7.4157$, $n = m = 1798$, $p < 0.01$). According to the Hodges-Lehmann Estimator of Shift, suggesting popular tags decreases the average Silhouette Coefficient by 0.0472 with a 95% confidence interval of [0.0337, 0.0582].

Thus, our experimental results show that recommending the seven most popular tags of a resource has a significant influence on the indexing quality. The results support Hypothesis 3 that recommending the popular tags decreases the inter-resource consistency in tagging systems.

6.2.2 No Suggestions vs. User Tags

Now, we test the effect of suggesting the user his/her own previously used tags on the average Silhouette Coefficient. We compare the $E(s_{ns,i})$-value for the *No Suggestions* condition to the $E(s_{ut,i})$-value for the *User Tags* condition as they are shown in Tab. 4. For both language variants of the experiment, we can confirm that $E(s_{ns,i}) < E(s_{ut,i})$.

For both language variants, the two-tailed Mann-Whitney Test shows that the difference between the $E(s_{x,i})$-values is significant (German: $T_1 = -8.11$, $n = m = 1796$, $p < 0.01$;

English: $T_1 = -3.0563$, $n = m = 1721$, $p < 0.01$). For the German variant, suggesting the user his/her own previously used tags increases the average Silhouette Coefficient by 0.0775 with a 95% confidence interval of $[0.0584, 0.0955]$. For the English experiment variant, the average Silhouette Coefficient increases by 0.0306 with a 95% confidence interval of $[0.0106, 0.0434]$.

Thus, our experimental results show that suggesting the user his/her own previously used tags has a significant influence on the indexing quality. The results support Hypothesis 1 that recommending the user's tags increases the inter-resource consistency in tagging systems.

6.3 Measuring the Inter-Indexer Consistency

In this subsection, we evaluate the hypotheses from Section 4 which are related to the influence of tag suggestions on the inter-indexer consistency, as it might be measured by the average tag reuse rate $E(tr_{x,i})$ from Subsection 3.2. We argue that in the presence of tag suggestions one cannot automatically assume a positive correlation between the inter-resource and the inter-indexer consistency. Thus, the inter-indexer consistency is not suitable for measuring the indexing quality in tagging systems if the users have been influenced by tag suggestions. According to our hypotheses from Section 4, we expect that the *Popular Tags* recommender helps to increase the inter-indexer consistency. In contrast, we expect that the *User Tags* recommender either leads to a decreased or unchanged inter-indexer consistency. Overall, we expect the following order of the $E(tr_{x,i})$-values:

$$E(tr_{ut,i}) \le E(tr_{ns,i}) < E(tr_{pt,i}) \quad (4)$$

6.3.1 No Suggestions vs. Popular Tags

In the following, we test the effect of suggesting popular tags on the average Tag Reuse Rate. For this purpose, we compare the $E(tr_{ns,i})$-value of the *No Suggestions* condition to the $E(tr_{pt,i})$-value of the *Popular Tags* condition as they are shown in Tab. 4. For both language variants of the experiment, we can confirm that $E(tr_{pt,i}) > E(tr_{ns,i})$.

For both language variants, the two-tailed Mann-Whitney Test shows that the difference between the $E(tr_{x,i})$-values is significant (German: $T = 58$, $n = m = 10$, $p < 0.01$; English: $T = 55$, $n = m = 10$, $p < 0.01$). For the German variant, suggesting popular tags increases the Tag Reuse Rate by 1.2274 with a 95% confidence interval of $[0.6912, 1.6111]$. For the English variant, the average Tag Reuse Rate increases by 1.7955 with a 95% confidence interval of $[1.2760, 2.4027]$.

Thus, our experimental results show that the suggestion of the seven most popular tags of a resource has a significant influence on the inter-indexer consistency. The results support Hypothesis 4 that suggesting the popular tags increases the inter-indexer consistency.

6.3.2 No Suggestions vs. User Tags

Now, we test the effect of suggesting the user his/her own previously used tags on the average Tag Reuse Rate. We compare the $E(tr_{ns,i})$-value for the *No Suggestions* condition to the $E(tr_{ut,i})$-value for the *User Tags* condition (see Tab. 4). For both language variants of the experiment, we can confirm that $E(tr_{ut,i}) \le E(tr_{ns,i})$.

For the German variant, we cannot reject the hypothesis of observing equal $E(tr_{x,i})$-values for the two conditions (Mann-Whitney, $T = 104$, $n = m = 10$, $p = 0.97$ two-tailed). Accordingly, the 95% confidence interval for

$E(tr_{ut,i}) - E(tr_{ns,i})$ is $[-0.392, 0.3437]$. Also for the English variant, we cannot reject the hypothesis of observing equal $E(tr_{x,i})$-values for the two conditions (Mann-Whitney, $T = 113$, $n = m = 10$, $p = 0.57$ two-tailed). In this case, the 95% confidence interval for $E(tr_{ut,i}) - E(tr_{ns,i})$ is $[-0.392, 0.2804]$.

Thus, our experimental results support Hypothesis 2 that $E(tr_{ut,i}) \le E(tr_{ns,i})$. Given the current data set, $E(tr_{ut,i}) = E(tr_{ns,i})$ has to be favored over $E(tr_{ut,i}) < E(tr_{ns,i})$ because the difference in the $E(tr_{x,i})$-values is not significant.

7. DISCUSSION

In Section 6, we have presented the results how different kinds of tag suggestions influence the inter-resource and the inter-indexer consistency in tagging systems. But in our experiment, we also discovered effects of tag suggestions which cannot be measured by our proposed methodology because in case of the English *Popular Tags* condition the suggestions not only influenced the tag vectors but also the topical clusters of the participants. It has been shown in Fig. 7 that the participants of the *Popular Tags* condition have a significantly higher probability to cluster *The Onion* according to its humorous aspects than the other participants.

It seems plausible that these differences are due to the influence of the tag suggestions. Indeed, under the English *Popular Tags* condition, for 107 participants the list of suggested popular tags contained the tag "satire". Additionally, the tag "fun" was contained 104 times in the list and "humor" 89 times. We assume that these tags helped to increase the likelihood of recognizing the humorous aspects of *The Onion* and of clustering it with *Patently Silly*. It seems that seeing the tags not only changed the users' vocabulary for describing the resource but also how they understood it.

But why didn't we observe a similar effect for the German *Popular Tags* condition? It seems that in the German experiment variant not enough participants recognized the humorous aspects of *The Onion* in order to push such tags into the list of popular tags. A possible reason is the overall lower probability of describing the humorous aspects of *The Onion* in the German experiment variant (see Fig. 6). Indeed, in the German *Popular Tags* condition the list of popular tags contains only for one participant a tag related to the humorous aspects, namely the tag "lustig" (=funny). Consequently, we do not observe an increased probability of clustering *The Onion* with *Patently Silly* when compared to the other German experimental conditions. Quite contrary: The dominance of news related tags in the list of popular tags for the German *Popular Tags* even decreases the probability of clustering *The Onion* with *Patently Silly* from 13% for the other two German experimental conditions to 3%.

All in all, it thus seems that suggesting popular tags has the potential to not only influence the tag vectors but also how users understand web pages, i.e. tag suggestions may lead to permanent learning effects as they are also discussed in [4]. This may potentially have a positive effect on the indexing quality but it is not measurable with our proposed methodology of measuring the inter-resource consistency. But our experiment also suggests that certain preconditions have to be fulfilled for learning effects to occur: We only observed it for a single web page and only in the English experiment variant. It would be subject to further research to identify these preconditions and to study in how far is a regular effect or rather an exception.

8. CONCLUSIONS

In this paper, we have discussed how to measure the influence of tag recommenders on the indexing quality of tagging systems. We have proposed to use the inter-resource consistency as the main target parameter to be optimized by tag recommenders because it influences the precision and recall of queries in a tagging system [19]. Improving the inter-indexer consistency should only be a secondary target of tag recommenders. We have applied our methodology for measuring the inter-resource and inter-indexer consistency for two exemplary baseline recommenders: (1) The *Popular Tags* recommender which recommends the seven most popular tags of a resource, and (2) the *User Tags* recommender which recommends a user his/her previously used tags.

During our user experiment with 582 participants, we have contrasted our measure of the inter-resource consistency with a measure of the inter-indexer consistency. In the literature about tagging systems, the inter-indexer consistency is often used as a measure of indexing quality. But we have shown that the inter-indexer consistency is not positively correlated with the inter-resource consistency if users are influenced by tag recommendations. In case of the popular tags, the recommendations increased the inter-indexer consistency and decreased the inter-resource consistency. For the user tags, the recommendations had no influence on the inter-indexer consistency while they increased the inter-resource consistency.

From these results of the user experiment one can conclude that the tag vectors of related resources get more dissimilar to each other if popular tags are recommended. In contrast, the tag vectors of related resources get more similar to each other if the user tags are recommended. Thus, the user tags would not only improve the retrieval results if a user searches in his own collection, as one might expect, but also if he searches for resources tagged by other users.

The only precondition for this positive effect during retrieval is that users have a similar judgment of the relevance of resources to each other, i. e. that they form similar topical clusters. But our results have also shown that this is reasonable to assume because we couldn't measure significant differences in the topical clusters between our experimental conditions. The only exception was the English *Popular Tags* condition but there this effect is restricted to a single web page for which different ways of looking at it exist.

9. SUPPLEMENTAL MATERIAL

The data set from our user experiment can be downloaded: `http://west.uni-koblenz.de/Research/DataSets/tagging-experiment/`. The experiment interface is still accessible at `http://userpages.uni-koblenz.de/~klaasd/experiment/`.

10. ACKNOWLEDGMENTS

We thank Thomas Gottron, Isabella Peters, Julia Preusse and Ansgar Scherp for their feedback, as well as all participants of the experiment for donating their time. This work has been co-funded by the German Research Foundation (DFG) under the Multipla project (grant 38457858) and by the EU in FP7 in the ROBUST project (grant 257859).

11. REFERENCES

[1] D. Bollen and H. Halpin. An Experimental Analysis of Suggestions in Collaborative Tagging. In *International Joint Conference on Web Intelligence and Intelligent Agent Technologies*, 2009.

[2] W. Conover. *Practical Nonparameteric Statistics*. John Wiley, 3rd edition, 1999.

[3] F. Floeck, J. Putzke, S. Steinfels, and K. Fisch. Imitation and Quality of Tags in Social Bookmarking Systems – Collective Intelligence Leading to Folksonomies. In T. Bastiaens, U. Baumöl, and B. Krämer, editors, *On Collective Intelligence*. Springer, 2010.

[4] W.-T. Fu and W. Dong. From Collaborative Indexing to Knowledge Exploration: A Computational Social Learning Model. *IEEE Intelligent Systems*. In Press.

[5] S. Golder and B. Huberman. Usage Patterns of Collaborative Tagging Systems. *Journal of Information Science*, 32(2):198–208, 2006.

[6] T. Kannampallil and W.-T. Fu. Trail Patterns in Social Tagging Systems: Role of Tags as Digital Pheromones. In *International Conference of Human-Computer Interaction*, 2009.

[7] T. Kowatsch and W. Maass. The Impact of Pre-Defined Terms on the Vocabulary of Collaborative Indexing Systems. In *European Conference on Information Systems*, 2008.

[8] M. Lipczak, Y. Hu, Y. Kollet, and E. Milios. Tag Sources for Recommendation in Collaborative Tagging Systems. In *ECML PKDD Discovery Challenge*, 2009.

[9] C. Manning, P. Raghavan, and H. Schütze. *Introduction to Information Retrieval*. Cambridge University Press, 2008.

[10] C. Marlow, M. Naaman, D. Boyd, and M. Davis. HT06, tagging paper, taxonomy, Flickr, academic article, to read. In *Hypertext Conference*, 2006.

[11] A. Mathes. Folksonomies - Cooperative Classification and Communication Through Shared Metadata. Website, December 2004. http://www.adammathes.com/academic/computer-mediated-communication/folksonomies.html.

[12] P. Rousseeuw. Silhouettes: A Graphical Aid to the Interpretation and Validation of Cluster Analysis. *J. of Comput. and Applied Mathem.*, 20:53 – 65, 1987.

[13] J. Saarti. Consistency of Subject Indexing of Novels by Public Library Professionals and Patrons. *Journal of Documentation*, 58:49–65, 2002.

[14] S. Sen, S. Lam, A. Rashid, D. Cosley, D. Frankowski, J. Osterhouse, M. Harper, and J. Riedl. tagging, communities, vocabulary, evolution. In *Conference on Computer Supported Cooperative Work*, 2006.

[15] F. Suchanek, M. Vojnovic, and D. Gunawardena. Social Tags: Meaning and Suggestions. In *Conference on Information and Knowledge Management*, 2008.

[16] M. Tatu, M. Srikanth, and T. D'Silva. RSDC'08: Tag Recommendations using Bookmark Content. In *ECML PKDD Discovery Challenge*, 2008.

[17] M. Vojnovic, J. Cruise, D. Gunawardena, and P. Marbach. Ranking and suggesting popular items. *IEEE Transactions on Knowledge and Data Engineering*, 21(8):1133–1146, 2009.

[18] H. White and B. Griffith. Quality of Indexing in Online Data Bases. *Information Processing & Management*, 23(3):211–224, 1987.

[19] P. Zunde and M. Dexter. Indexing Consistency and Quality. *American Documentation*, 20:259–267, 1969.

Short Links Under Attack: Geographical Analysis of Spam in a URL Shortener Network

Florian Klien
Graz University of Technology
klien@student.tugraz.at
f@qr.cx

Markus Strohmaier
Knowledge Management Institute
Graz University of Technology and Know-Center
markus.strohmaier@tugraz.at

ABSTRACT

URL shortener services today have come to play an important role in our social media landscape. They direct user attention and disseminate information in online social media such as Twitter or Facebook. Shortener services typically provide short URLs in exchange for long URLs. These short URLs can then be shared and diffused by users via online social media, e-mail or other forms of electronic communication. When another user clicks on the shortened URL, she will be redirected to the underlying long URL. Shortened URLs can serve many legitimate purposes, such as click tracking, but can also serve illicit behavior such as fraud, deceit and spam. Although usage of URL shortener services today is ubiquitous, our research community knows little about how exactly these services are used and what purposes they serve. In this paper, we study usage logs of a URL shortener service that has been operated by our group for more than a year. We expose the extent of spamming taking place in our logs, and provide first insights into the planetary-scale of this problem. Our results are relevant for researchers and engineers interested in understanding the emerging phenomenon and dangers of spamming via URL shortener services.

Categories and Subject Descriptors

H.3.5 [**Information Storage and Retrieval**]: Online Information Services—*Web-based services*; H.3.7 [**Information Storage and Retrieval**]: Digital Libraries—*System issues*

General Terms

Measurement, Experimentation

Keywords

URL Shortener, link analysis, spam

1. INTRODUCTION

URL Shortener services have been available for at least 10 years [1]. Such services i) take a long URL as an input, ii) offer a short URL in return, and iii) permanently redirect traffic from the short

URL to the long URL. One of the first URL shortener services was TinyURL, founded in 2002 [2]. The idea of shortening URLs originated from problems observed with links in emails, where links were often re-wrapped by clients and thus rendered unclickable. However, it has not been until recently that URL shortener services have gained popularity through online social media such as Twitter where space is limited. Although URL shortener services can be used for a multitude of different purposes including link tracking, click analysis or spam, our research community knows little about how exactly these services are used and what purposes they serve. In this paper, we study usage logs of a URL shortener service that has been operated by our group for more than 20 months. During this time, the service has *shortened* more than one million URLs and has *resolved* more than nine million links. At the same time, it has attracted significant attention of spammers. In this work, we expose the extent of spamming taking place on our URL shortener service, and provide first insights into the national and international scale of this problem.

Based on usage log data provided by our URL shortener service, this short paper addresses the following research questions: (i) What is the extent of spam in URL shortener services? (ii) Does usage of URL shortener services differ across countries, and if yes, in what way? (iii) Do shortened URLs "travel" across countries, and if yes, what is the nature of interaction between countries? and (iv) What are promising features for identifying spam in URL shortener services?

While the analysis presented in this paper is based on one dataset only, we believe that our results are interesting to the Hypertext community for at least two reasons: First, they provide unique insights into the use and misuse of a URL shortener service that was operated over a period of more than 20 months. Second, other URL shortener services such as bit.ly do not share usage logs that can be studied openly. Our work therefore provides a rare view into the operation of such services over a significant period of time. We leave the task of applying our analysis to other datasets to future research.

2. RELATED WORK

In [10], Inoue et al. present a study of a URL Shortener that was build right after the Great East Japan Earthquake in March 2011. The authors of this paper use a combination of a CDN (Content Delivery Network) and a URL Shortener to prevent server overload on heavily visited websites. By using CoralCDN, they distribute requests on servers around the world [5]. CoralCDN works on basis of DNS and HTTP mirrors. One can divert the traffic from a website to the mirrors of CoralCDN by inserting ".nyud.net" after the original domain name. The resulting address serves the website via the CoralCDN mirrors. Inoue et al. use the URL Shortener to rewrite long URLs to be *coralized* and thus redirect users to mirrors of the CoralCDN. They analyzed the content users shortened with their own shortener. Their data set is available on-line [3]. Antoniades et al. analyzed a data set of short URLs they obtained through crawling [6]. They crawled Twitter for short URLs of *bit.ly* and *ow.ly*. Further they guessed short URLs via brute forcing hashes. Their results show that the lifetime of 50% of short links exceeds 100 days. Further they investigated the latency of short URL services and show that most request are delayed by about 0.35 seconds. Grier et al. point out that many spammers use shortener services to obfuscate their links in tweets. They find that blacklisting URLs is no optimal solution for fighting spam on Twitter since blacklists often lag Twitter and a spammer's link often reaches the public before it can be blacklisted [9]. Our work is related to this work in a sense that we will present promising features for spam classification that might be helpful to fight spam. Leskovec and Horovitz examined a very large graph of a personal messaging tool. It consisted of millions of links between millions of individuals, where every edge represented one conversation or chat. Users were located all around the world and the resulting connections that could be derived between countries and people led to the insights that most connections seemed to be between countries that had ethnic or historical connections: Germany - Turkey, Portugal - Brazil and China - Korea. We too will focus on the connections that evolve between countries via short URLs [11]. Chhabra et al. did a study concerning the distribution of phishing links across Twitter. Their research analyzes the connection between users and their vulnerability to click malicious links. Further they look into the geographical distribution and the lifetime of phishing URLs [8]. In our own previous work, we have studied the behavior of bots in social networks [12]. Our work builds on and relates to the state-of-the-art by conducting geographical analysis of spam in a usage log created by a URL shortener service that we have operated.

3. EXPERIMENTAL SETUP

We use data from the URL Shortener *qr.cx* that started operating in June 2009. It is a regular HTTP service with an API in place. A *creator* (a user who wants to shorten a URL) can send GET requests with a long URL as an argument and receive a short URL (e.g. `http://qr.cx/1r8`) as a response. Our URL shortener generates one random string as an identifier, which is appended to the base URL and becomes the short link or short URL. This short URL redirects the visitor via a 301 HTTP response to the previously provided long URL. In the following, we will use the term *resolve* whenever we refer to the function of returning a long URL in exchange for a short URL that has been requested by a *resolver*. Other terms that are sometimes used to denote this function include *redirect*, *click* or *expand*. Each provided long URL is only registered once with our service, it cannot be re-registered and the long URL cannot be changed. Unlike other popular URL shortener services like *bit.ly*, our service does not offer user accounts (for privacy concerns) and provides no possibility to get multiple short URLs for an already registered long URL.

	Resolves	Creates	Sum
complete data set	7,919,892	731,624	8,651,516
with location	7,918,221	731,228	8,649,449

Table 1: Data set characteristics: The observation period ranges from 1st of April 2010 to 31st of December 2011. For our evaluation we generated a subset of this data that contains location information.

Our data set ranges from 1st of April 2010 to 31st of December 2011 and contains 7,919,892 *resolves* of short URLs and 731,624 *created* short URLs (see Table 1). A subset of this data contains geographical longitude and latitude information for users which we obtained from geo-locating their IP. There are some limitations and biases in our dataset.

Given that the URL shortener service was operated from within Austria, there might be a local social influence. Furthermore, popular online social media are often hosted in US-based territories, which represents another source of bias. In addition, these services sometimes use bots to *resolve* short URLs and explore the mentioned content. Other biases are possible (e.g. with regard to users' preferences with regard to certain shortener services). In general however, we believe that - based on our comprehensive logs - our URL shortener service reflects certain characteristics of URL shortener services in general.

Figure 1a shows a histogram of *resolves* for our data set and Figure 1b plots the number of *creates* and *resolves* over our observation period. *Resolves* and *creates* correlate strongly in the second half of 2011. The traffic for URL *creates* has increased by two orders of magnitude between December 2010 and December 2011. In the same time period, *resolves* have increased by a factor of about 25. There exist 51,675 links that have only been *resolved* once and one link that has been *resolved* around 30,000 times. A spam wave hit our service in April 2011. This is depicted in Figure 1b, and in a video visualization of our data that we have made available [4].

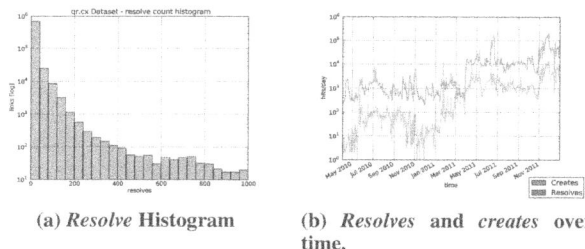

(a) *Resolve* Histogram (b) *Resolves* and *creates* over time.

Figure 1: 1a shows the *Resolve* histogram for the data set including *resolves* up to a limit of 1000. The y-axis shows a logarithmic scale count of links, the x-axis shows the number of *resolves*. 1b: *Resolves* per day are depicted in green (upper line), *creates* per day are depicted in red (lower line). An increase of both *creates* and *resolves* can be observed for April 2011. From a deeper look at our logs, we find that this increase was caused by a spam wave that hit the URL Shortener service at that time.

3.1 The URL Shortener Network

For our following analysis, we define a URL shortener network as a weighted directed network of users, where *resolves* correspond to edges between *creators* and *resolvers*. The number of *resolves* observed corresponds to the weight of the edge. This network gives us the possibility to study network-theoretic characteristics of URL shortener networks. To reduce the number of nodes in the network, one can group users by IP address, IP subnet, country, region or provider. By grouping IPs in different ways, analysis can focus on different levels of granularity and different aspects depending on the data set. In the following, our analysis groups users by country in order to enable us to do geographical analysis of URL shortener service usage on a planetary scale.

	Country	Link Creates	Resolves	IRR	RC Ratio	Outdegree	Indegree	Resolver Pct.	Creator Pct.
1	**US**	81,341	6,250,743	**79.82%**	**98.72%**	148,264	6,209,235	**97.67%**	2.33%
2	**GB**	2,409	699,804	**7.19%**	**99.66%**	33,869	696,590	**95.36%**	4.64%
3	DE	6,544	357,036	22.16%	98.20%	69,520	352,607	83.53%	16.47%
4	RU	7,599	108,996	3.04%	93.48%	119,712	103,572	46.39%	53.61%
5	JP	8,015	102,979	0.75%	92.78%	111,082	101,433	47.73%	52.27%
6	KR	8,967	50,679	1.63%	84.97%	126,600	50,629	28.57%	71.43%
7	FR	26,272	43,886	1.84%	62.55%	179,489	43,613	19.55%	80.45%
8	CA	1,155	34,263	12.4%	96.74%	16,817	33,687	66.70%	33.30%
9	NL	1,686	32,454	2.88%	95.06%	21,185	32,244	60.35%	39.65%
10	CN	907	30,626	17.67%	97.12%	7,705	29,155	79.10%	20.90%
11	GR	1,196	16,293	0.05%	93.16%	15,295	16,243	51.50%	48.50%
12	**IN**	31,798	15,620	**0.54%**	**32.94%**	436,535	14,761	**3.27%**	96.73%
13	IE	283	14,930	0.02%	98.14%	3,390	14,877	81.44%	18.56%
14	AU	278	11,877	2.64%	97.71%	4,408	11,532	72.35%	27.65%
15	AT	1,120	9,580	34.99%	89.53%	75,869	9,428	11.05%	88.95%

Table 2: Top 15 Countries by *resolves*. Note: The Indegree would be the same as the *resolves* column, if the data set would not be limited to the observation period between 04/2010-12/2011. The column Indegree has smaller values because URL creations before 04/2010 have no known creation country and are ignored. India, ranked at 12th place, shows an interesting pattern of link *creates* to *resolves*, where *creates* outnumber *resolves* twice. The U.S. and Great Britain show far more *resolves* than *creates*.

3.2 Metrics

To characterize different countries and their URL Shortener usage, we present and use the following measures: The ratio between *resolves* and *creates*, the *Internal Resolve Rate*, the *Resolver Percentage* and the *Creator Percentage* as the ratio between Indegree and Outdegree [13].

The *RC Ratio* between *resolves* and *creates* tells us if a particular group (in this paper: a country) visited more links than it *created*.

$$RC\ Ratio = \frac{\#\ of\ Resolves}{(\#\ of\ Creates + \#\ of\ Resolves)} \quad (1)$$

This ratio models *resolves* and *creates* as percentage. 100% *RC Ratio* means the group has no link *creates*. If it is lower than 50% it means the group *resolved* fewer links than it *created*. This shows the group as a whole "sends out" more links than it uses (*resolves*). A variation of this metric would be to only count *resolves* of self-*created* short URLs.

The *Internal Resolve Rate* (IRR) is the percentage of link *resolves* by a group that were created by themselves:

$$Internal\ Resolve\ Rate\ (IRR) = \frac{\#\ of\ Resolves\ by\ Group}{\#\ of\ all\ Resolves} \quad (2)$$

The ratios between Indegree and Outdegree show the "consumption" or "broadcasting" activity of a group. In this work, the Indegree is defined as the cumulative *resolve* count of a group. The Outdegree is defined as the cumulative *resolve* count of links *created* by that group. Whenever someone *resolves* a link, the creator's Outdegree is increased by one. The

$$Resolver\ Percentage = \frac{Indegree}{(Indegree + Outdegree)} \quad (3)$$

shows how much a group consumes and the

$$Creator\ Percentage = \frac{Outdegree}{(Indegree + Outdegree)} \quad (4)$$

shows how much a group "broadcasts". The Resolver Percentage differs from the Internal Resolve Rate as it does count link *resolves* that were not *created* locally.

4. RESULTS

In this section, we organize the presentation of our results in correspondence to the research questions introduced before:

4.1 What is the extent of spam?

We annotated a random sample of 5,957 shortened URLs by visiting the long URL and evaluating its content.

Our annotated set contained 4,780 spam and 1,177 non-spam links. This results in a spam rate of 80.24%. We also evaluated whether *creators* had *resolved* their link themselves. The resulting sub set can be seen in Table 3.

	self resolved	not self resolved	Sum
spam	17	4,763	4,780
non-spam	18	1,159	1,177
Sum	35	5,922	**5,957**

Table 3: The annotated sub set of our data set. 80.24% of URLs are labelled as spam.

To visualize temporal and geographical aspects of this data, we plotted all redirects and link creations on a world map for a given time frame, and then assembled the different frames in sequential order into a video that covers the 20 months observation period. Binning our data in frames with a window of 6 hours resulted in a 1 min 40 seconds video, which we have made available for viewing online: http://youtu.be/06MhnOL23Tk [4]. In the video, yellow dots represent *resolves* and pink dots *creates*. Especially noteworthy are "waves" of URL creations around minute 0:57. This nicely illustrates how spammers use bot nets to *create* a lot of URLs in a very short time. Links are *created* all over the world but are *resolved* mostly in the U.S. and Europe, which indicates that the primary targets of spammers are US and Europe based populations or services. The video also suggests that the number of *resolves* in spam attacks using URL shortener services can likely be used as a proxy measure for gauging the success of a spam wave.

4.2 Does usage of URL shorteners differ across countries, and if yes, in what way?

Answering this question would give us insights into the local usage of URL shorteners. Details on usage can potentially be used for tackling a number of problems including marketing, infrastructural planning or abuse detection.

We found that the usage differs significantly between different countries. First, absolute *resolve* counts differ a lot. The U.S. has almost 10 times more *resolves* than the second biggest "consumer", Great Britain, and 200 times more than the 10th place China. In

Table 2 the top 15 Countries by *resolves* are listed in more detail. Second, relative usage numbers differ too. The U.S. has a total *resolve* count of 6,250,743 and a total link *create* count of 81,341. India has a total *create* count of 31,798 short links and a *resolve* count of only 15,620, as seen in Table 2. We use the measures from Section 3.2 to look into these numbers more deeply.

As shown in Figure 4, one can see that a lot of countries *resolve* more links than they *create* (green) but even more *create* more links than they *resolve*, as seen in red. Generally put, a high Outdegree seems to be indicative of creating nations (which might be linked to spamming) and a high Indegree seems to be indicative of spam-receiving countries (the targets of spam campaigns). Looking at the *IRR* of countries we see very different usage types of countries. We picked two countries that differ significantly with regard to usage. For example, our dataset produces a 100% "export" ratio or 0% *IRR* for India. This high external resolve ratio is significant as there are more than 30,000 links that were *created* in India. At the same time, the U.S. has the highest *IRR* distribution. The numbers show that more than half of the links *created* in the U.S. are *resolved* in the U.S.

In addition, we compared countries based on their In- and Out-degree (cf. equations 3 and 4). Taking the absolute values and plotting them in a scatter plot (Figure 2) reveals drastic differences in different countries' usage. Kazakhstan has an extremely high Outdegree compared to it's Indegree. Mexico and Thailand have the highest Outdegree but do not match Germany, Great Britain or the U.S. based on their Indegree.

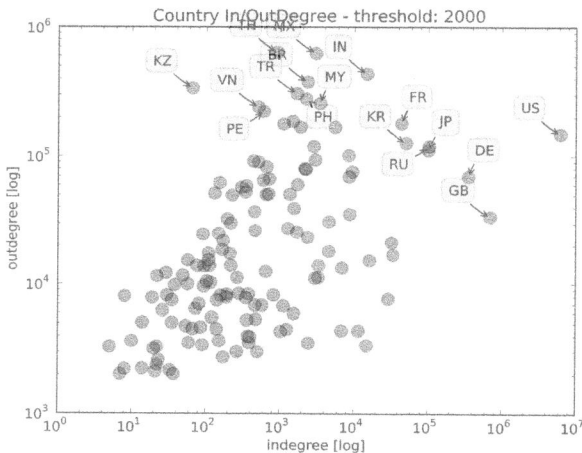

Figure 2: Scatter plot of countries by Indegree and Outdegree on a logarithmic scale. The U.S. has the highest Indegree and Mexico and Thailand have high Outdegrees.

4.3 Do shortened URLs "travel" across countries, and if yes, what is the nature of interaction between different countries?

In order to "travel" across countries, we require a URL to be *created* in country A and be *resolved* in country B. We consider this analysis to be of interest as it might be useful to distinguish locally-relevant from internationally relevant content or identify international flows of information and diffusion.

In Figure 3, we illustrate directionality of *resolves* in a graph of the top 15 countries from Table 2. *Resolves* are edges that start from a *creating* country and point to a *resolving* country. Edges are

weighted according to the number of short URLs that have been *resolved* between two countries. The graph only shows the top 15 countries ranked by *resolves* in our data set and starts displaying edges with a weight higher than 5,000. From this graph, we can observe that the U.S. dominates the consumption of short links in our data set. We also noticed that there are only four countries that appear to be *resolving* their own links (given our thresholds). India accounts for the strongest edge to the U.S. with 340,000 *resolves*.

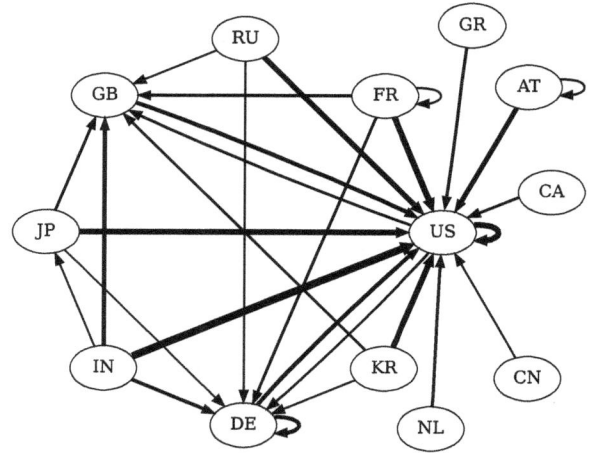

Figure 3: The international flow of shortened URLs: Edges go from countries where links have been *created* to countries that *resolve* them. Edges' widths correspond to logarithms of their *resolve* count. Smallest edge weight is 5,000, biggest 340,000.

4.4 What are promising features for spam identification?

While presenting and evaluating a spam classification method is beyond the scope of this paper, we want to explore the usefulness of initial features for spam identification. While potential features include but are not limited to content-based or behavior-based features, in the following we are interested in behavioral features as they can be assumed to work across languages and work independant of the type of content (e.g. textual vs. images). We evaluate a simple hypothesis that states that spammers would be less likely to verify the shortened URLs or use them themselves. Evaluating a statistical independence between hypothetical non-spammers that *resolve* their links and spammers that do not *resolve* their links we find a significant difference. Using a random subset from our dataset, a little under 1% drawn from each month, we manually labled links to be spam or not (see Table 3). A Pearson's chi-squared test showed that the two variables (self *resolved*, spam) are not independent [7]: $\chi^2_{1,5957} = 20.3091$, $p < 10^{-5}$, this corroborates our intuition.

While these initial investigations are promising and relevant for future work on spam classification algorithms in the context of URL shortener services, more work is warranted.

5. DISCUSSION AND CONCLUSIONS

URL shortener services such as bit.ly and others play a critical role on the web today. While usage of these services is ubiquitous, we know little about how exactly these services are used, and what purposes they serve. The work in this paper exposes that spam represents a pressing problem both for operators and for users

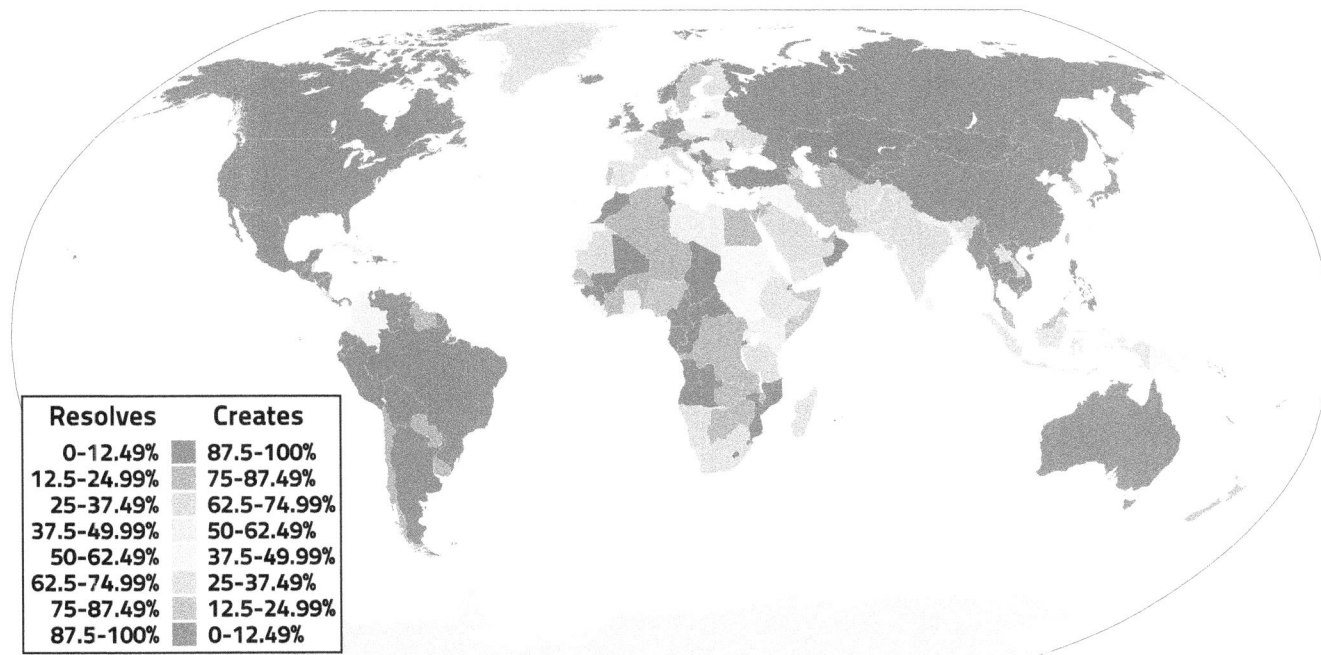

Figure 4: World map showing the ratio between *resolves* and *creates* (*RC Ratio*) by country, as shown in equation 1. Large parts of South America and Africa are identified as mostly *creators* (with small numbers of *resolves*) whereas Northern America, Asia, Australia and (to some extent) Europe are identifed as mostly *resolvers* (with small numbers of *creators*).

of URL shortener services. Based on our investigations of a URL shortener service, we find that around 80% of shortened URLs contained spam-related content. The extent of spam might be larger due to the lack of spam blocking features. Our geographical analysis reveals that this problem has an international scale, suggesting that URL shorteners play a role in spam attacks that cross national borders. The scale of this problem also suggests that in the future, sophisticated approaches and algorithm for identifying URL spam are needed. Our results indicate that different countries differ significantly with regard to the usage of URL shortener services. We find that imbalances between *creating* and *resolving* short URLs exist, and we have visualized the flow of *resolves* between countries based on URL shortener services. Our exploratory work provides first novel insights into global usage patterns of URL shortener services and warrants future research into understanding spam behavior in this new domain.

6. REFERENCES

[1] We want 'em shorter.
    http://www.metafilter.com/8916/, 2001.
[2] TinyURL Shortener. http://tinyurl.com/, 2002.
[3] rcdn data. http://rcdn.info/data.html - rcdn dataset, 2011.
[4] qr.cx usage time analysis video. http://qr.cx/8Ctq or http://youtu.be/06MhnOL23Tk, 2012.
[5] The Coral Content Distribution Network.
    http://www.coralCDN.org/, 2012.
[6] D. Antoniades, I. Polakis, G. Kontaxis, E. Athanasopoulos, S. Ioannidis, E. P. Markatos, and T. Karagiannis. we.b: the web of short urls. In *Proceedings of the 20th international conference on World wide web*, WWW '11, pages 715–724, New York, NY, USA, 2011. ACM.
[7] D. G. Bonett. Pearson chi-square estimator and test for log-linear models with expected frequencies subject to linear constraints. *Statistics & Probability Letters*, 8(2):175–177, June 1989.
[8] S. Chhabra, A. Aggarwal, F. Benevenuto, and P. Kumaraguru. Phi.sh/$ocial: the phishing landscape through short urls. In *Proceedings of the 8th Annual Collaboration, Electronic messaging, Anti-Abuse and Spam Conference*, CEAS '11, pages 92–101, New York, NY, USA, 2011. ACM.
[9] C. Grier, K. Thomas, V. Paxson, and M. Zhang. @spam: the underground on 140 characters or less. In *Proceedings of the 17th ACM conference on Computer and communications security*, CCS '10, pages 27–37, New York, NY, USA, 2010.
[10] T. Inoue, F. Toriumi, Y. Shirai, and S.-i. Minato. Great east japan earthquake viewed from a url shortener. In *Proceedings of the Special Workshop on Internet and Disasters*, SWID '11, pages 8:1–8:8, New York, NY, USA, 2011. ACM.
[11] J. Leskovec and E. Horvitz. Planetary-scale views on a large instant-messaging network. *Proceeding of the 17th international conference on World Wide Web WWW 08*, 393:915, 2008.
[12] C. Wagner, S. Mitter, C. Koerner, and M. Strohmaier. When social bots attack: Modeling susceptibility of users in online social networks. In *Proceedings of the WWW'12 Workshop on 'Making Sense of Microposts' (MSM2012)*, 2012.
[13] S. Wasserman and K. Faust. *Social Network Analysis: Methods and Applications*. Number 8 in Structural analysis in the social sciences. Cambridge University Press, 1994.

Storyspace: a Story-driven Approach for Creating Museum Narratives

Annika Wolff
Knowledge Media Institute
The Open University
Milton Keynes, MK7 6AA
+44 (0)1908 659462

a.l.wolff@open.ac.uk

Paul Mulholland
Knowledge Media Institute
The Open University
Milton Keynes, MK7 6AA
+44 (0)1908 654506

p.mulholland@open.ac.uk

Trevor Collins
Knowledge Media Institute
The Open University
Milton Keynes, MK7 6AA
+44 (0)1908 655731

t.d.collins@open.ac.uk

ABSTRACT

In a curated exhibition of a museum or art gallery, a selection of heritage objects and associated information is presented to a visitor for the purpose of telling a story about them. The same underlying story can be presented in a number of different ways. This paper describes techniques for creating multiple alternative narrative structures from a single underlying story, by selecting different organising principles for the events and plot structures of the story. These authorial decisions can produce different dramatic effects. Storyspace is a web interface to an ontology for describing curatorial narratives. We describe how the narrative component of the Storyspace software can produce multiple narratives from the underlying stories and plots of curated exhibitions. Based on the curator's choice, the narrative module suggests a coherent ordering for the events of a story and its associated heritage objects. Narratives constructed through Storyspace can be tailored to suit different audiences and can be presented in different forms, such as physical exhibitions, museum tours, leaflets and catalogues, or as online experiences.

Categories and Subject Descriptors

H.5.4 [**Information Systems**]:Hypertext/Hypermedia – *architectures, theory, user issues*

General Terms

Algorithms, Design

Keywords

Narrative, story, plot, events, museum, heritage objects, hypertext

1. INTRODUCTION

Current metadata-based schemes for describing cultural content are designed for describing individual heritage objects within a cultural collection, not for describing the stories that span objects. They do not tap into the rich, additional context provided through the knowledge and research efforts of curators as they construct exhibitions. By including these stories along with the standard metadata it becomes possible to create better ways for publishing exhibitions online, providing narratively meaningful links to related content that was not available in the physical space and allowing the user to better explore the underlying stories and

plots that link objects to one another. The curate ontology (http:/decipher.open.ac.uk/curate) represents an approach to modelling heritage content by capturing the underlying stories of both the individual heritage objects and the curated exhibits as a whole. It has been developed to address the limitations of current metadata-based schemes.

The structure of the ontology is reflected in Storyspace, a web based environment for authoring curatorial stories. In Storyspace, curators can add content and information about an exhibition. Both the ontology and software tool have been developed through collaboration with two large Irish heritage institutions, the Irish Museum of Modern Art (IMMA) and the National Gallery of Ireland (NGI). These institutions are currently using the tool to describe two recent exhibitions, one on Gabriel Metsu and one on Irish Modernism. Storyspace [1] assists a curator in constructing stories, plots and narratives. Using timeline visualisations, the curator can explore and plot the story from multiple different angles, using facets that they have defined as being central to the current curatorial story. This in turn leads to richer narrative construction.

This paper will outline how Storyspace can be used to describe stories that span museum objects. Narrative presentations can be created from a specified story and plot, using the described narrative organization methods. We will first look at related work in the field of narrative, museum hypertexts and current approaches to organising and presenting museum content online. Next we will briefly introduce the Curate ontology and the Storyspace web environment including events, plot and facets. The core of the paper will explore in detail the narrative module of Storyspace and the different types of narrative presentations that can be produced.

2. RELATED WORK

2.1 Narrative, plot and drama

The work described in this paper is founded on the principle that far from being a special type of narrative, the curatorial narrative as found in a museum exhibition, is founded on the same principles as other forms of narrative, including the dramatic plot-based narratives found in many fictional books and films. We subscribe to a structuralist view [2, 3] whereby the events of the story are distinct from the telling of it (the narrative). In between lies the plot [4], organising and relating the events of the story according to a particular perspective. The plot identifies a purpose for all the events that it contains, selecting only those which advance the plot in some way [5]. The intensity of the narrative can vary according to the plot selected for that telling of the story.

The most basic narrative form omits the plot altogether, thus imposing no view on the story and merely relating events. In a plotless narrative, where there are no relationships defined between events, it is usually assumed – unless indicated otherwise by some linguistic device – that events are presented chronologically [6]. If an ordering principle other than time is used, then this needs to be indicated to the reader of the narrative otherwise it could lead to a loss of coherence [7]. Plots introduce the ability to add drama to a narrative. The dramatic impact of a plot can be manipulated by choosing when to introduce conflict, when to escalate tension and when to introduce a resolution [8]. When constructing narratives from visual content, coherence is improved by identifying and using themes for content selection, which then provide a sub-text to the narrative presentation [9, 10].

2.2 Narrative, hypertext and the museum

Each heritage objects tells a story about why it is significant, what it shows, where it came from, and how it relates to other items in the collection and elsewhere [11]. For example, a mass-produced clothing item can become interesting when we know that someone famous has worn it. It is the story, as much as the item itself, which captures the imagination. The impact of the story intensifies the more the clothing item is linked to other objects or stories from the person's life. From all of this related information, curatorial narratives are made. Peponis et al. [12], in an analysis of museum exhibitions, used the term narrative to refer to an arrangement of exhibits and their associated information into a sequence that yields more complex insights than could be derived from exhibits individually. They use narrative to refer to the manner in which the contents of the exhibits can be conceptually related. Rowe et al. [13] distinguish between the "big" narrative of the exhibition and the small vernacular narratives associated with it. These small narratives may originate from the visitor, triggered by something in the exhibition. For example, the visitor recalling a personal experience related to an object or event of the exhibition. Museums may also use small narratives themselves to help visitors to relate to the bigger narrative. For example, presenting the (possibly fictional) story of a character who lived at a certain time in order to bring it to life.

In the physical space, some interconnections between objects may be afforded by the layout of the space. Conversely, some items that evidence a story may be separated by distance. In such cases, notes and signs may be used to indicate the linking of such items, to allow the visitor access to that part of the narrative. But unless the visitor is willing to walk backwards and forwards some items are inevitably encountered 'out of sequence' of the intended narrative, as the visitor must follow a linear path through the museum.

The web has long since been offering new ways of exploring curatorial narratives [14]. An early use of hypertext in the museum was Hyperties [15], which provided contextual information about museum objects from a museum's database, linked through a hypertext menu system. Content included both text and pictures and users could easily navigate the topics of their interest. As well as addressing the needs of the end-user, Hyperties aimed at making the authoring process relatively simple. The Ipertecne hypertext [16] aimed to connect objects in a Florence museum to each other, or to people involved in the objects narratives. More recent work moves away from the traditional complex linked hypertexts and examines issues related to helping users to orient themselves within a hypertext and to find information that is targeted towards both their interests and their level of understanding. These offer the facility to present the same story and plot but in different narrative forms (e.g. [17]). ILEX [18] generates dynamic hypertexts, tracking a user's path through online museum content and using this to create hyperlinks for the next stage of exploration which are coherent with respect to the users past navigational choices.

2.3 Tools for sequencing museum content

Many initiatives exist for making cultural content, and related information, available online using a standard, easily searchable metadata description. In addition to the content coming directly from museums, some sites such as Europeana [19], Freebase [20], and the People's Network [21] aggregate large quantities of cultural data. The bigger challenge is how to turn all of this content into a valuable and coherent user experience, one that reflects the types of curatorial narratives that can be found in a professionally curated exhibition. Systems that focus on the metadata tend to produce narratives that sequence items according to common attributes, such as being produced by the same artist, in the same time period, or in the same medium. The CHIP project [22, 23] merges user preferences with metadata to suggest personalized tours through online cultural content. Agora [24] seeks to enrich heritage object metadata by automatically creating a linked thesaurus of related historic events that can connect objects in different collections and allow navigation according to topics and event properties, such as location and person, in addition to the indexed metadata. This increases the potential set of relationships that can be used for connecting content. Culture Sampo [25, 26] annotates content by events, which can be organized into stories that link content. As a user browses the annotated content, the event data is used to suggest semantically related information, e.g. according to people or places described in the events. It has been demonstrated through systems related to the production of ceramics and the typical seasonal farming processes. Similarly, Bletchley Park Text [27] links historical stories based on common properties of their events.

The use of events to describe objects clearly better supports the sequencing of content, for example by time, and location of related items than is possible from metadata matching alone. However, without a representation of plot it is only possible to build certain types of narrative, such as chronicles that simply list events by time. Plot introduces the drama and the tension and imposes a specific viewpoint across the story.

3. STORYSPACE

The following sections contain brief descriptions of the Storyspace components that are used in narrative construction. Figure 1 shows a screenshot of the interface. Storyspace supports curators in creating exhibitions from selections of heritage objects and the stories that link them. The main constituents of Storyspace are as follows.

1) Story layer – this consists of the events of the story. Facets, visualisations (of story events and plots) and references can all be added to a story. This layer contains both heritage object stories (about individual objects) and curatorial stories (containing multiple heritage objects and the events that link them). Stories can be broken into components.

2) Plot layer – describing relationships between the events that move the story forwards.

3) Narrative layer – ordering events and plots for a narrative presentation.

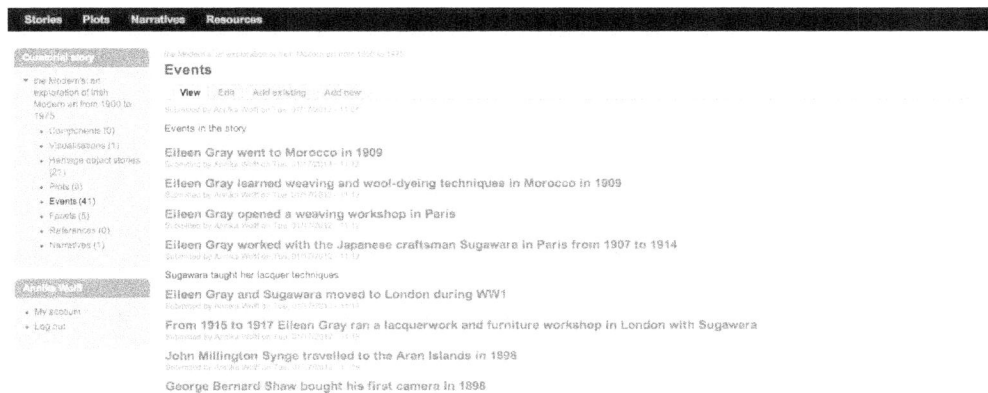

Figure 1. The Storyspace software.

4) Heritage objects - information about heritage objects can be entered into Storyspace, along with uploaded images or links to online sources. The objects can be both those which can be used within a physical exhibition and also external objects that the curator does not have physical access to, but is able to use within online narratives. Heritage objects are used within Heritage Object Stories. When a Heritage Object story (and its associated object) is brought into a Curatorial Story, all of its events become part of the Curatorial story and are then available for emplotment.

The underlying curate ontology was developed with input from the project's museum partners and by analysis of the two focal exhibitions, Metsu and the Moderns. For a fuller explanation of the underlying curate ontology please see [1]. Two workshops were held in Dublin with curators and other museum professionals, to validate the assumptions of the model. Sessions included talks by the curators of the exhibitions, as well as question and answer sessions with the curators, educators, archivists and other museum staff. Finally, there were break out sessions aimed at gathering feedback on possible use-cases using paper-mockups, which also served to validate parts of the model which would have been hard to present out of context. Staff in both institutions have been using an online version of the tool for inputting exhibition content. Feedback has been elicited via structured questionnaire, which has further informed design decisions for both the ontology and the software.

The examples used in the remainder of the paper are taken from the Modern's exhibition that was held by IMMA.

3.1 Defining story events

A curatorial story contains of a set of events. Events come from two sources. The first source is from the heritage object stories relating to the heritage objects that are chosen for the curated exhibition. As an example, these stories might describe when and where an object was created, circumstances that have inspired its creation, or what has happened to it in its lifetime. The second source are the events that relate not to a single object but to a set, or subset, of the exhibited objects. These provide additional context. Some example events - some from heritage object stories and others more general - can be seen in Table 1. The events can be added by a curator or can be pulled in from external sources.

The same event can belong to multiple different stories. An event can be described in different ways for different stories, using facets. Facets are described next.

Table 1. Example events from a story about the Irish Modernist artist Eileen Gray.

Eileen Gray worked with the Japanese craftsman Sugawara
Eileen Gray went to Morocco
Eileen Gray learned weaving and wool-dyeing techniques in Morocco
Eileen Gray opened a weaving workshop in Paris
Eileen Gray ran a lacquerwork and furniture workshop in London with Sugawara
Eileen Gray and Sugawara moved to London during WW1
Eileen Grey designed the St. Tropez rug

3.2 facets

Facets can be defined which describe an important property of a curatorial story. Examples include time, location and theme. Example of facet values are shown in Table 2.

Table 2. Example facets from the Moderns

	Facet name	Values
F1	Theme	Irish women modernists, Early photography/film
F2	Time	value range = 1898-1950
F3	Location	Aran Islands, England, Morocco, France, Peru, Ireland

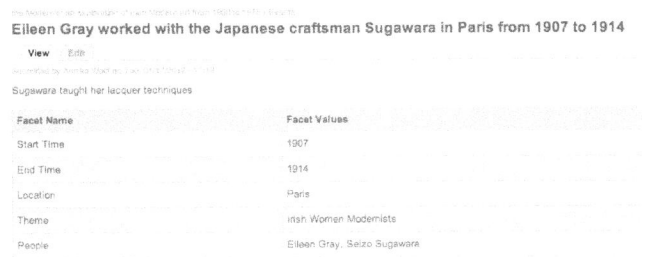

Figure 2. Annotating an event with some facet values.

Events that belong to a curatorial story are annotated according to the defined story facets. (Figure 2) Facets can be used first for interpreting and describing events and then for filtering and colour-coding those events on the timeline visualization, for identifying groups of events that belong together and to identify possible components of the story. Facets are also used in the generation of narratives.

3.3 Emplotting events

Emplotment involves identifying relationships between events, or groups of events. A plot is divided into *plot descriptions*. Each plot description specifies a relationship between some events within the story. Some example plot descriptions are shown in Table 3.

Table 3. Example plot descriptions from the Moderns

	Plot Description	
P1	Eileen grey was influenced by studying and working with Sugawara	
	influential	Eileen Gray worked with the Japanese craftsman Sugawara in 1907
		Eileen Gray ran a lacquerwork and furniture workshop with Sugawara in 1915
		Eileen Gray and Sugawara moved to London during WW1 in 1918
	influenced-by	Eileen Gray designed Green Japanese Style Carpet Template in 1919
		Eileen Gray created lacquer boxes 1 and 2 in 1920
P2	Eileen Grey was influenced by her travels in Morocco	
P3	Eileen Grey was influenced by her travels to America on an ocean liner	
P4	Donegal carpets were influenced by Eileen Grey	
P5	Roger Casement's revolutionary activities were influenced by his photography in Peru	
P6	George Bernard Shaw was a keen photographer	

When creating a plot description, the curator first selects the type of plot they want to create. We refer to this as the *plot type*. A plot type determines the nature of the relationship that is being specified. Examples include *influenced-by, reacted-against,* or the less committal *related-to.* These are structurally similar, but conceptually different plot types. Each plot type has one or more plot elements, which contains the event or events that are being related. These events provide some evidence for the plot relation. For example, in the *influenced-by* plot type, one plot element identifies the event, or set of events, that are influential and the other plot element identifies the event, or set of events, that are influenced. When authoring a plot, the author can decide how to describe the plot type within the plot description, giving the possibility for the curator to select more nuanced terms. Figure 3 shows an example of viewing events on a timeline visualization during emplotment of part of the Moderns story.

3.4 heritage objects

Data pertaining to heritage objects can be entered into Storyspace. Images of objects can either be uploaded, or else linked to via specifying a url. Table 4 shows some examples of objects from the Modern's exhibition. Each object has a linked creation event in its associated heritage object story.

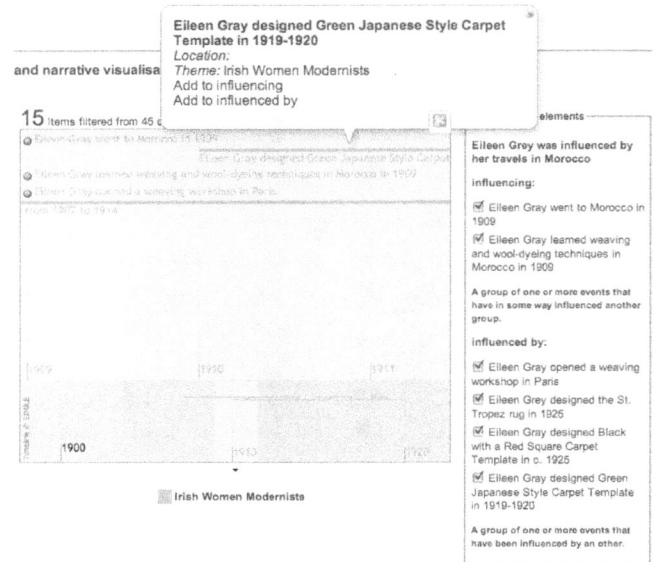

Figure 3. Making a plot on a timeline visualisation.

Table 4. Some heritage objects from the Moderns

	Object description and creation date	Object
o1	Eileen Green Japanese Carpet (1919)	
o2, o3	Eileen Gray lacquer boxes 1 and 2 (1920)	
o4	Eileen Gray designed Black with a Red Square Carpet Template (1925)	
o5	Eileen Grey designed the St. Tropez rug (1925)	
o6	George Bernard Shaw photo of unknown woman (1900)	
o7	George Bernard Shaw photo of ship rigging (1900)	
o8	George Bernard Shaw photo of Bridge (1904)	
o9	George Bernard Shaw photo of Trees (1904)	
o10	Casement and Sealy photo negro overseer (1910)	
o11	Roger Casement photo Group of Putumayo girls (1910)	

o12	Roger Casement Putumayo girl (1910)	
o13	Roger Casement Putumayo man (1910)	
o14	George Bernard Shaw handprint (1920)	

4. NARRATIVE ORGANISATION METHODS

A narrative presents a story for an intended audience and through a chosen medium. Thus, the same story can be presented through both multiple plots and multiple narratives. As previously discussed in section 2.1, the choice of narrative presentation of a story can affect both the coherence and the dramatic impact. As an example, a temporally coherent presentation of an artist's life work would present the work in chronological order. However, the dramatic impact of this ordering is completely different if the artist died at the peak of their career, or if their peak occurred some time earlier.

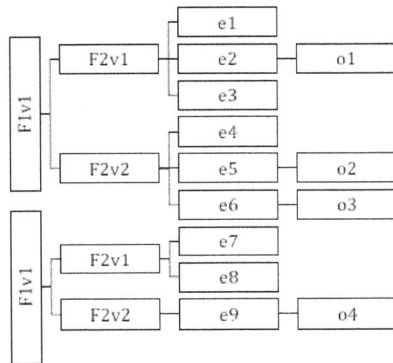

Figure 4. A generic narrative structure.

The rest of the paper focuses on the narrative module of Storyspace and how the curator can alter the effect of a narrative by altering the principles used for organising its elements. The narrative is output as an ordered set of story events and related heritage objects. The ordering is determined according to some stated preference of the curator: a narrative can be created from facet only, from plot only, or a combination of both (facet then plot, or plot then facet). These cases are explored in detail below.

4.1 Create narrative from facet

A narrative can be created from Storyspace by specifying the important facet, or facets, to be used for organising and ordering events. For a selected facet, the events are grouped according to their value for that facet. If multiple facets are selected, then the author also chooses the order in which the facets are used. Some events within the curatorial story will be heritage object story events, which in turn are linked to heritage objects. This association is used to propose an ordering of the heritage objects associated with the story. Figure 4 shows a generic narrative structure. Figure 5 shows the narrative structure instantiated with content from the Moderns example. In this case, the plot is un-used, so there is no interpretation of events, or how they relate. The events are provided simply as a list of what has happened. The coherence of the output and the general look and feel of the narrative is manipulated through the choice of facet ordering.

Changing the primary facet will usually have quite a significant effect, whereas the effect of swapping facets further down the ordering is much more subtle and nuanced. This type of narrative is most useful for grouping objects into categories and to be effective, the facets must be properly defined. These narratives are conceptually similar to the ones produced by the tools described in section 2.3.

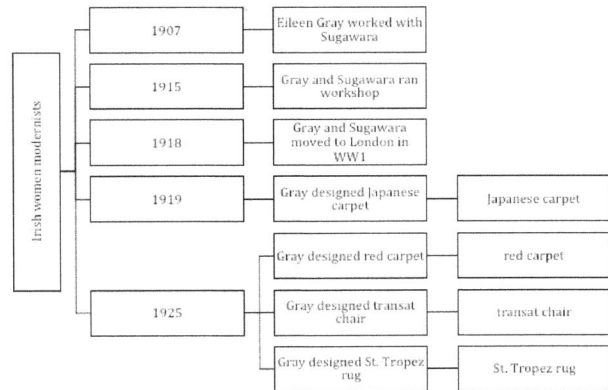

Figure 5. A narrative structure using Irish womenModernists as the primary organisational facet, followed by time.

Figure 6 explores how this output might look when viewed through the heritage objects associated with the curatorial story. The data in Table 4 offers insight into how the narrative ordering of the objects is generated within Storyspace, with the facet ordering *theme* and then *time*. The objects are in the order as given in the table, i.e the first item is '*o1: Japanese style artist template*' and the last item is '*o14: photograph of handprint*'. Objects 1-5 belong to the theme '*Irish women Modernists*' and 6-14 belong to '*Early photography/film*'. It can be seen from this order that the last item in the sequence, the photograph by George Bernard Shaw, is not grouped with his other photographs but appears at the end of a series of photos taken by Roger Casement. In this case, the curator has two options if they wish to group works of the same artist together. They could make a small adjustment to the narrative output, or they could change the underlying story that generates it (e.g. create a facet for 'people' to use as an organising facet). Further options, using plot, are explored next.

Figure 6. Objects ordering by the facets *theme* and *time*.

4.2 Create narrative from plot

As mentioned previously, a plot is used to provide a specific interpretation of events. The narrative presentation of a plot can alter the effect it has towards an audience. Aristotle describes a dramatic arc [5] where the plot is narrated to provide a rising action, a crisis that reaches a climax whereupon the tension falls, before the narrative is brought to a satisfactory conclusion. This same pattern may repeat over several acts of a story, each climax getting higher and higher. The effect of the narrative can be manipulated by changing the order of plot elements, for example by presenting a story outcome before the story unfolds (such as showing an arrest for a crime, before discovering what the crime was and how/why it took place), or narratives that deliberately play with temporal ordering by going backwards and forwards between time periods, or visiting key story components in complete reverse order. In Storyspace, there are three different ways to create a narrative from a plot. The choice depends on the desired effect towards the audience. Figure 7 shows two plot descriptions, of the plot type 'influenced-by'. This plot type contains two plot elements, one contains 'influencing events' (indicated by the *i*) and a set of influenced events (indicated by the letter *ib*). This example is used in the following sections to illustrate the different organising principles for plot-based narratives.

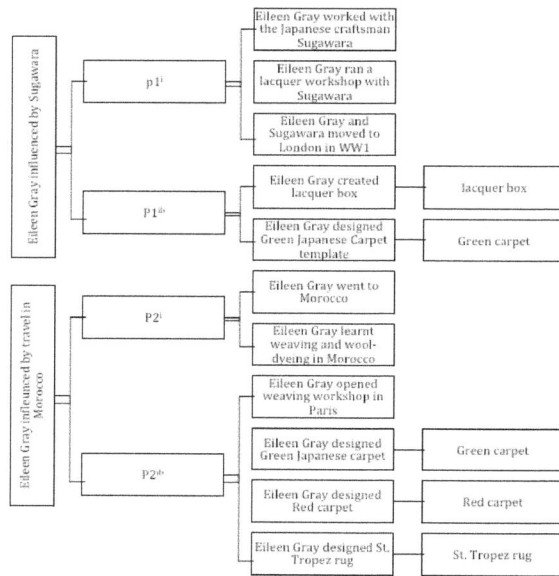

Figure 7. Two plot descriptions, of plot type 'influenced-by' each divided into influencing and influenced by events.

4.2.1.1 *Order by plot description (minimize tension)*
Using this organising principle, events are organized according to their inclusion in plot descriptions. Each individual plot description is treated as a separate entity. This minimizes the number of plot descriptions that are in progress at any one time when reading through the events. The ordering of the individual plot descriptions is determined by the curator. In terms of a dramatic arc, tension is minimized by completing a plot description as soon as possible (Figure 8). For example, in an 'influenced-by' plot, all causes of influence are introduced and then immediately the outcome is presented, before moving on to the next plot description.

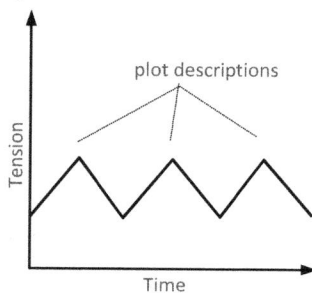

Figure 8. Minimizing tension in a plot-based narrative.

Looking at the Figure 7 example, first the plot description *Eileen Gray was influenced by Sugawara* is introduced in its entirety, before the next plot description *Eileen Gray was influenced by her travel in* Morocco' can start. Figure 9 demonstrates how plot-based ordering can change the ordering of heritage objects. In the first example, one photo by George Bernard Shaw was mixed with those by Roger Casement. Using plot as an organising principle, George Bernard Shaw's photographs are now grouped together, as are Roger Casement's. This is because they have each been described in the same plot description.

In some cases, a conflict must be resolved where the same object appears in two plot descriptions One possibility is that the item can be placed to act as a bridge between two different plots. An example of this is shown in the top row of Figure 9 where the green carpet is used to transition between one plot and the next. If this is not possible, or not desirable, and the exhibition is online then the heritage object can if desired appear in both plots, or else a hyperlink might provide a link from one plot to another. In a physical space, the indication of an alternative plot for an object might be given by text on a wall plaque next to the object, or a comment in an audio guide or tour guide's speech.

Figure 9. Objects ordered according to plot descriptions.

4.2.1.2 *Order by plot elements (maximize tension)*
This narrative style can be used to maximize tension by leaving the plot descriptions unresolved for as long as possible (Figure 10). In the Figure 7 example, this would entail presenting all of the events of p1[i] and P2[i] before moving onto the events of P1[ib] and P2[ib]. This creates suspense where the reader must await the outcome. In a gallery setting, this plot type is fairly common. As an example, the influencing factors for several, often interrelated, plots are explained by way of a wall plaque that the visitor might view before looking at the objects on display. These objects are provided as evidence of the stated influences.

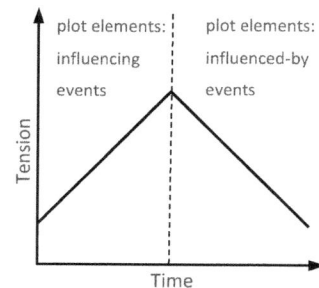

Figure 10. Maximising tension in a plot-based narrative

4.2.1.3 *Order by plot type*
In this case, the author specifies which types of plot they want to show first, for example to show all examples of related-to, then all examples of influenced-by. The nature of the plot relationship defined affects the dramatic arc. Plot descriptions that demonstrate a 'related-to' relation could be seen to be less dramatic than an 'influenced-by' relation. This plot style might be used to increase tension over a period of time (Figure 11) or to decrease it. A narrative of this type might be used to show how

certain plot types tend to repeat, such as showing multiple examples of art being produced in reaction to an important world event.

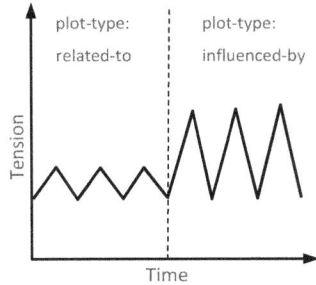

Figure 11. Escalating the tension.

4.3 Create narrative from plot, then facet

In this case, common to many art and museum exhibitions, the elements within an overarching plot are ordered according to the selected facets. For example, an art exhibition might have an overarching plot about an artist's life works, exploring how their experiences have influenced their career and painting. Within this main plot, the exhibition could be organized to show the different time periods in their career, or explore how their work changed as they moved from one location to another. The Modern's exhibition, which explored the development of Modern art in Ireland as the overarching narrative, used themes (such as Irish women modernists) within broad temporal categories to show a progression in style across the span of the exhibition (Figure 12).

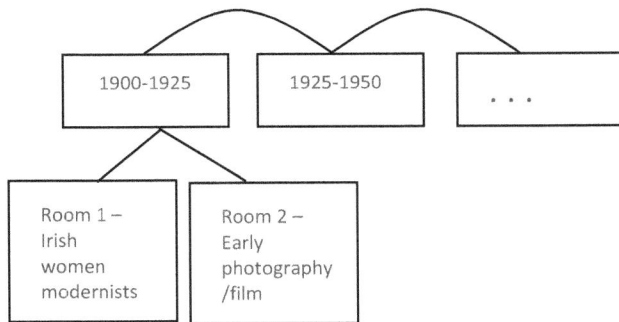

Figure 12. Overarching plot and some themes of the Moderns.

4.4 Create narrative from facet, then plot

Whereas the previous example viewed works organized by theme within an over-arching plot, this organizational principle focuses on the vernacular narratives, within a smaller thematic category. The events are first organized according to the chosen facet, with associated plot structures being secondary. Figure 13 shows an example where events are related in plot structures under the thematic headings *Irish women modernists* and *Early photography/film*. Some plots may relate several objects together, others might be plots of individual heritage object stories. This organizational principle is suitable when the plots are, to a large extent, self-contained within the thematic grouping.

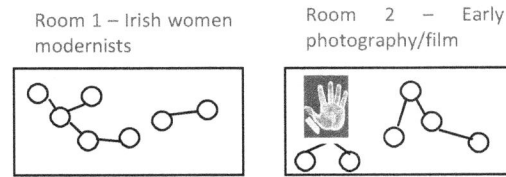

Figure 13. Thematic groupings with plots.

As discussed in section 2.2, most museum narratives use a combination of the grand narrative with some thematic organization (the case discussed in 4.3) and within the themes are smaller vernacular narratives (the case discussed in 4.4). The vernacular narratives collectively help the visitor to see the bigger narrative and to relate on a more personal level to the objects in the exhibition [13].

5. STORYSPACE NARRATIVE INTERFACE

Social curation tools are designed to allow authors to quickly and easily select, organize and edit social content into personalized narratives. In particular, Storify [28] and Bagtheweb [29] both offer intuitive and easy interfaces for ordering narrative components, editing and adding text and for viewing the completed narratives. These features, such as drag and drop ordering and node adding and editing, have informed the design of the Storyspace narrative interface.

A new narrative is added by selecting a story, and therefore the events, facets and plots, from which to create the narrative. The curator then chooses the organising principle, e.g. facet, or plot. Currently the curator must also select the ordering within this initial grouping (see Figure 14). So, if organising by facets, then they must select the primary facet to group by, then the second and so forth. Figure 15 shows a view of a narrative when it is first output. This narrative has been output in plot order and the events that influenced Roger Casement are introduced first, followed by the heritage objects. The narrative is output as in a linear path from which more complex structures can be built.

Within the *edit elements* view of the narrative, the curator can drag and drop items to reorder objects and events. For presenting the narrative, the story events may be replaced by more free-flowing text, or rewritten for a younger audience. This is achieved by inserting a new text node, or by editing existing event text. (see Figure 16). It is important to note that this does not alter the original event only how it is presented in that specific narrative.

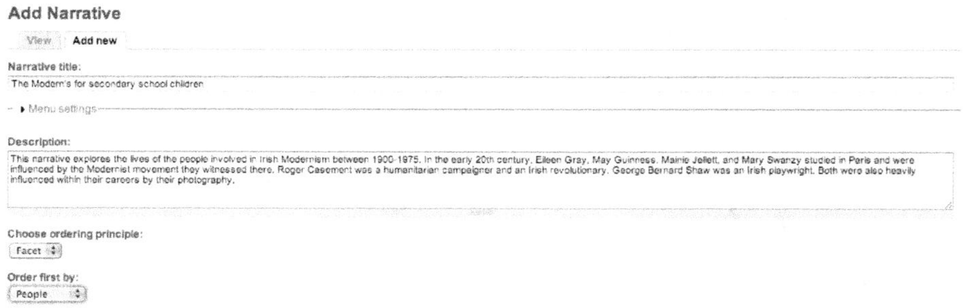

Add Narrative

View | Add new

Narrative title:

The Modern's for secondary school children

– ▸ Menu settings

Description:

This narrative explores the lives of the people involved in Irish Modernism between 1900-1975. In the early 20th century, Eileen Gray, May Guinness, Mainie Jellett, and Mary Swanzy studied in Paris and were influenced by the Modernist movement they witnessed there. Roger Casement was a humanitarian campaigner and an Irish revolutionary. George Bernard Shaw was an Irish playwright. Both were also heavily influenced within their careers by their photography.

Choose ordering principle:

Facet ⬍

Order first by:

People ⬍

Figure 14. Creating a narrative from a curatorial story.

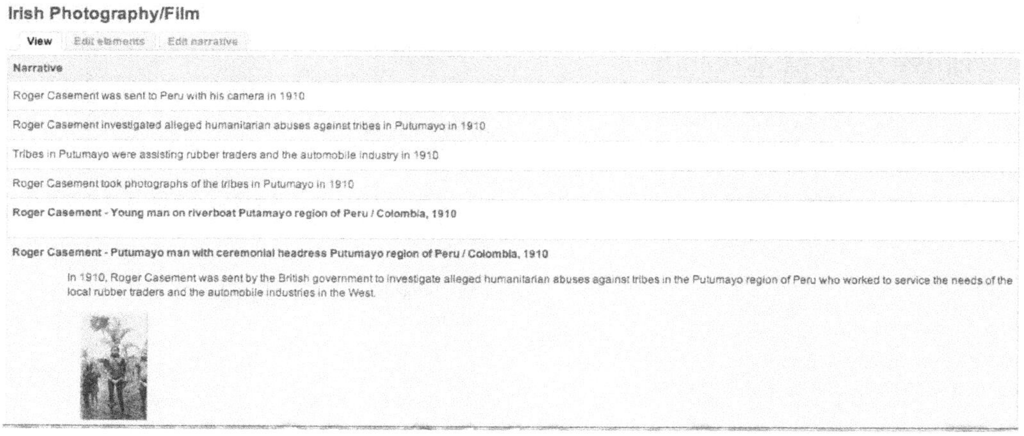

Irish Photography/Film

View | Edit elements | Edit narrative

Narrative

Roger Casement was sent to Peru with his camera in 1910

Roger Casement investigated alleged humanitarian abuses against tribes in Putumayo in 1910

Tribes in Putumayo were assisting rubber traders and the automobile industry in 1910

Roger Casement took photographs of the tribes in Putumayo in 1910

Roger Casement - Young man on riverboat Putamayo region of Peru / Colombia, 1910

Roger Casement - Putumayo man with ceremonial headress Putumayo region of Peru / Colombia, 1910

In 1910, Roger Casement was sent by the British government to investigate alleged humanitarian abuses against tribes in the Putumayo region of Peru who worked to service the needs of the local rubber traders and the automobile industries in the West.

Figure 15. Viewing a narrative constructed from events and related objects of the Irish Photography/Film facet.

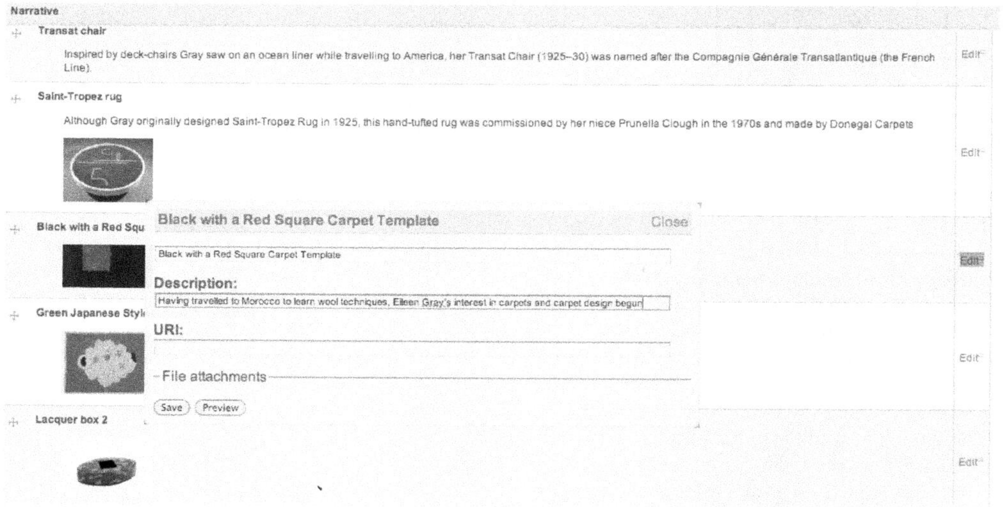

Narrative

⊹ Transat chair

Inspired by deck-chairs Gray saw on an ocean liner while travelling to America, her Transat Chair (1925–30) was named after the Compagnie Générale Transatlantique (the French Line). Edit

⊹ Saint-Tropez rug

Although Gray originally designed Saint-Tropez Rug in 1925, this hand-tufted rug was commissioned by her niece Prunella Clough in the 1970s and made by Donegal Carpets

Edit

⊹ Black with a Red Squ **Black with a Red Square Carpet Template** Close

Black with a Red Square Carpet Template Edit

Description:

Having travelled to Morocco to learn wool techniques, Eileen Gray's interest in carpets and carpet design begun

⊹ Green Japanese Styl

URI:

Edit

– File attachments

⊹ Lacquer box 2 (Save) (Preview)

Edit

Figure 16. Editing a node within a narrative template. The drag handles allow reordering of content.

In addition to the overall organization of the exhibition, the curator must take into account other factors when developing the final narrative. The presentation of objects in terms of the setting (the room, the online canvas), the proximity to other pieces, or to other features of the space such as lifts, cafeteria, interface navigation items etc., can all affect the viewers' interpretation of the pieces. Other curatorial choices include:

- Where to place objects in a physical space to achieve a desired dramatic effect. Placing the exhibition 'highlights' in prominent locations can lead to visitors going straight to them and missing more subtle and less well-known, but no less interesting, pieces.

- How and where to place objects in an online space. Issues include the sizing of objects, e.g. showing pictures in relative sizing or making them all appear the same size, zooming in on detail-views of objects more relevant to a narrative or showing always the whole piece, or the choice of perspective on a 3 dimensional object, such as a sculpture, where 3D views are not an option.

- The extent to which underlying story and plot is revealed to a visitor. Some curators choose to show only the heritage objects as a prompt to visitors to construct the story for themselves, giving the objects the role of sources of evidence for the narrative. This is seen as being consistent with constructivist approaches to learning [30]. Alternatively, stories related to an individual heritage object might be presented alongside it. Stories that link collections might be written as a block of text on the wall close to the set of exhibits it describes.

- How to present the narrative. Who is it for? audio guides, themed tours, or the language used to present the story for children, adults, art professionals. Another important consideration is how to make the most of online technologies when presenting the exhibition online.

- How to handle constraints. In a physical space, constraints might include not having access to desired objects that form part of the narrative, not being able to put story-related items close to each other due to, for example, the nature of the pieces (they need different lighting conditions), the nature of the physical space (they won't both fit), or the necessity to follow the instructions of an artist (they want their piece displayed on its own). In an online space, constraints might include copyright restrictions, or broken links.

- How to use narrative markers to links parts of a story. Narrative markers can be arrows, directions via the audio, text on a wall plaque indicating a relationship between objects, or hyperlinks in an online gallery.

- Similarly, how to inform about the organising principles used for constructing the narrative to ensure that the narrative is coherent to the viewer. In a physical space, the exhibition spaces are often clearly marked with some indicators as to the theme or plot. In an online presentation, where user's have freedom to move beyond the linear presentation, it is equally important that the user is still made aware of the theme.

These issues can if desired be incorporated into a narrative output. For example, if a curator is creating a template for a physical exhibition they may want to include notes about curatorial choices of placement related to their space, or mention an artist's specific instructions for installing a piece.

Storyspace creates linear narratives from which more complex interconnected narrative structures can be built. A Storyspace narrative can be turned into a handout, or an audio guide. It can be used in the process of authoring the curatorial narrative for a physical exhibition, or as a record of the layout and presented information of a physical exhibition. This in turn could be used for recording how a travelling exhibition differs between locations. Finally, the narrative can be used as the basis for create an online exhibition, giving the user flexibility to explore the story plot and narrative for themselves as well as providing access to additional content that may be unavailable in the physical space. The narrative ontology component is compatible with outputting the narrative structure and object descriptions in a METS (Metadata Encoding and Transmission Standard) compatible form, although the export is not yet implemented.

5.1 Technical architecture of storyspace

Storyspace is written in Drupal and uses an SQL database. In addition, content is written to a Sesame triple store according to the associated curate ontology. Custom Drupal modules have been developed to provide the core functions of Storyspace, these modules replicate the underlying curate ontology. Exhibit/Simile [31] are used for creating the visualisations, additional custom functionality has been written to allow plot structures to be entered and edited directly from a timeline view.

6. FUTURE WORK

Future work will focus on the inclusion of heuristics to suggest which organizational principle to use, based on how the events of the story have been annotated by facets or grouped into plots. Heuristics will aim at suggesting an organising principle based on minimizing plot disruption and maintaining temporal ordering. The interface for creating narratives will be extended to allow the curator to combine facet ordering, with plot ordering on multiple levels to create more complex narratives, as described in section 4.6.

Work will also look at flagging possible conflicts to curators, for example where an object appears in more than one plot, and suggest ways to solve the conflict, such as using the object to transition between plots, or to add a hyperlink or marker depending on whether the narrative is intended for an online or physical space. The narrative module will be extended to allow the output of the narrative framework as a METS description for to allow online browsing of the narrative structure. Further evaluation is scheduled in which curation teams will each select a topic of interest and author stories plots and narratives using Storyspace. Initial support will be given during a workshop, followed by a period of supported working at a distance, where the curation teams will keep user diaries of their issues and progress. Support will be via email and telephone contact. A workshop will be held after this period to elicit further feedback. In the second phase, student groups, supported by their regular teachers, will explore the stories created by the curation teams in the first evaluation stage and use these to construct their own narratives.

7. CONCLUSIONS

This paper presents an approach for creating narratives from the stories and plots of museum exhibitions. Authors can influence the shape and impact of a narrative by selecting different organising principles for the events within a story. On the story level, events are organized by facets, such as time or theme. The introduction of plot allows authors to add and alter the dramatic impact of a narrative, by choosing when to introduce and when to resolve plots. Storyspace supports a curator in describing the objects and stories of an exhibition from which they can select the parameters to create a narrative structure. The narrative elements within the structure are re-orderable and editable, new narrative Drupal nodes can be easily added. Therefore, the narrative is fully customizable towards the intended audience or narrative output medium. The narrative module can be used to create multiple curatorial narratives from an exhibition, for catalogues and handouts, for online viewing or within a museum space, for different audiences from school children to art professionals, and in different forms such as audio guides, text presentation or heritage objects only.

8. ACKNOWLEDGMENTS

This work is being conducted as part of DECIPHER, an EU Framework Programme 7 project in the area of Digital Libraries and Digital Preservation.

9. REFERENCES

[1] Mulholland, P., Wolff, A., Collins, T., and Zdrahal, Z. 2011. An event-based approach to describing and understanding museum narratives. *In: Detection, Representation, and Exploitation of Events in the Semantic Web*. Workshop in conjunction with the International Semantic Web Conference.

[2] Chatman, S. 1980. *Story and Discourse: Narrative structure in fiction and film*. Cornell U.

[3] Polkinghorne, D. 1988. *Narrative knowing and the human sciences*. State Univ. NY Press.

[4] Hazel, P. 2008. Narrative and New Media. *In: Narrative in Interactive Learning Environments*.

[5] Aristotle. 1996. *Poetics*. Penguin Classics.

[6] Berman, R. A., and Slobin, D. I. 2003. *Relating events in narrative: Typological and Contextual Perspectives*. Psychology Press.

[7] Walker, J. 1999. Piecing together and tearing apart: finding the story in afternoon. *Hypertext 1999*, Darmstadt, Germany.

[8] Szlias, N. 1999. Interactive drama on the computer: beyond linear narrative. *AAAI Fall Symposium on Narrative Intelligence*, Technical Report FS-99-01, AAAI Press.

[9] Hargood, C., Millard, D., and Weal, M. 2010. A Semiotic Approach for the Generation of Themed Photo Narratives. *Hypertext 2010*, Toronto, Canada.

[10] Wolff, A., Mulholland, P., Zdrahal, Z. and Joiner, R. 2007. Re-using digital narrative content in interactive games. *International Journal of Human-Computer Studies*, 65, 3, pp. 244-272.

[11] Pearce, S. M. 1995. *On collecting: An investigation into collecting in the European tradition*. Routledge: London.

[12] Peponis, J., Dalton, R., Wineman, J., and Dalton, N. 2003. Path, theme and narrative in open plan exhibition settings, *International Space Syntax Symposium*.

[13] Rowe, S., Wertsch, J., and Tatyana, K. 2002. Linking Little Narratives to Big Ones: Narrative and Public Memory in History Museums. *Culture and Psychology*, 16 (2), pp. 96-112.

[14] Nilsson, T. 1997. The Interface of a Museum: Text, Context and Hypertext in Performance Setting, *Archives and Museum Infomatics*, Le Louvre, Paris, France.

[15] Shneiderman, B. 1987. User interface design for the Hyperties electronic encyclopedia. *Hypertext'87 Workshop*, Raleigh, North Carolina, 199-204.

[16] Fresta, G., and Signore O. 1993. A hypertext for an interactive visit to a science and technology museum. (Lees, Diane, Ed.). *Museums and Interactive Multimedia: Selected papers from the second International Conference on Hypermedia and Interactivity in Museums*.

[17] MacKenzie, D. 1996. Beyond Hypertext: Adaptive Interfaces for Virtual Museums, *Proceedings of EVA'96*, Vasari Enterprises.

[18] O'Donnell, M., Mellish, C. Oberlander, J., and Knott, A. 2001. "ILEX: An architecture for a dynamic hypertext generation system". *Natural Language Engineering 7*, 225—250.

[19] http://www.europeana.eu/portal/

[20] http://www.freebase.com/

[21] http://www.peoplesnetwork.gov.uk/discover/simple

[22] Wang, Y., Aroyo, L. and Stash, N. 2007. Interactive User Modeling for Personalized Access to Museum Collections: The Rijksmuseum Case Study. *In: User Modeling*.

[23] Wang, Y., Aroyo, L. and Stash, N. 2009. Cultivating Personalized Museum Tours Online and On-site. *In: Interdisciplinary Science Reviews*, 32 (2), pp. 141-156.

[24] van den Akker, C., Legêne, S.van Erp, M., Aroyo, L. Segers, R. van der Meij, L., van Ossenbruggen, J. Schreiber, G., Wielinga, B., Oomen, J., and Jacobs, G. 2011. Digital hermeneutics: Agora and the online understanding of cultural heritage. *In ACM Web Science Conference '11*, Koblenz.

[25] Hyvönen, E., Makela, E., and Kauppinen, T. 2009. CultureSampo: A national publication system of cultural heritage on the semantic Web 2.0. *In: ESWC*.

[26] Hyvönen, E., Palonen, T., and Takala, J. 2010. Narrative semantic web - Case National Finnish Epic Kalevala. *In: 7th Extended Semantic Web Conference*.

[27] Mulholland, P., Collins, T. and Zdrahal, Z. 2005. Bletchley Park Text. *In: Journal of Interactive Media in Education*, http://jime.open.ac.uk/2005/24.

[28] http://storify.com/

[29] http://bagtheweb.com/bagstream

[30] Hooper-Greenhill, E. 2000. *Museums and the Interpretation of Visual Culture*. London: Routledge.

[31] http://simile.mit.edu/wiki/Exhibit

Story/Story

David Kolb
Charles A. Dana Professor Emeritus of Philosophy
Bates College
Home: 841 W 36th Ave., Eugene, OR
+1 541 345 3110

davkolb@gmail.com

ABSTRACT

This paper starts with an introductory essay stating the issues and discussing the notion of metafiction. Then it continues in an online hypertext narrative demonstration of the interweaving of story and meta-story. The hypertext attempts to show in action how seemingly unified narratives and narrative voices are surrounded and influenced by other voices and meta-stories. No narrative is un-mediated and no narrative voice is alone. The hypertext concludes with some musings on the complexities of narrative reading and writing, also with counterpoint voices. Throughout, the text comments on issues about the reading and writing of hypertext narratives.

Categories and Subject Descriptors

J/5 [**Arts and Humanities: literature**]

General Terms

Design, Experimentation, Human Factors

Keywords

Story, Metastory, Narrative, Hypertext, Links, Levels, Complex pages, Metafiction, Metanarrative

1. INTRODUCTION

This essay comes in two parts, this prose and an online hypertext. This introductory essay explains the issues raised and describes the solution that the hypertext tries to enact. The hypertext itself contains a story and ongoing reflections on the story, plus reflections on those reflections. It is not so much a logical argument for its conclusions as a demonstration of them in action, thus confirming their possibility.

The hypertext contains thirty-eight linked nodes. Thirty-two nodes (7000 words) tell a branching story in the Choose Your Own Adventure style. Each node is a complex page with the story in the left column and in the right a meta-story discussion by two voices, concerning issues about the construction of the story, and the general relations of stories to stories about stories, and the uses of hypertext for narrative. The remaining six nodes (3000 words) offer philosophical reflections about narrative incompleteness, authorial voices, and the possibilities of "constructive hypertext." These reflections are also accompanied by other voices.

The full hypertext can be accessed online (http://www.dkolb.org/dark.site/intro.html), or downloaded locally, in the Hypertext 2012 proceedings on the ACM Digital Library.

2. MAP OF THE HYPERTEXT

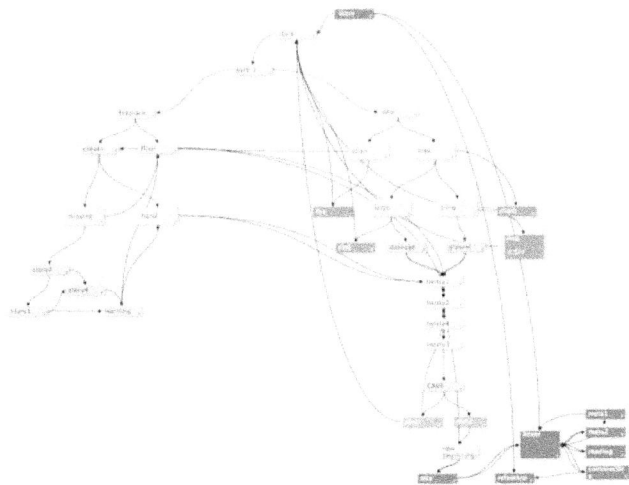

The map shows that the hypertext has a mostly tree-like structure but with some returns to the beginning and with all branches eventually leading to a single conclusion. The story occupies the tree-structure and the final set of nodes contains the philosophical musings.

3. THE ISSUES

In other writings I have argued that we too often rely on the presupposition that a concept, an argument, a place, or a community has a single core identity. I have tried to show how there are multiple layers, relations, and connections that do not nest together in a hierarchy organized around a single core. There are gaps and slidings and self-reflections even in what seems solid identity, especially as those identities endure through time by reproducing and reinterpreting themselves.[1]

---

[1] See [16] for a discussion of the complex unity of places, [11] for the slidings of concepts, [13] for the problem of criticism without a firm meta-platform, and [14] for the different modes of unity in hypertext vs. linear writings.

This essay/hypertext takes up the relation of a story to the meta-stories and discourses that surround narrative. The border between story and meta-story may seem firm: here is the teller and there is the critic. I try to show how in action the hierarchy breaks down and borders are crossed.

In philosophy and logic there can be a sharp distinction between language and meta-language, as long as each language is taken as a finished product formally defined and derived from axioms in a way that "ordinary" language cheerfully ignores. And even with all the technicalities observed, paradoxes of self-reference can still arise and borders be transgressed.

When language is seen in the act of being produced, or a story in the act of being told, then its internal spacings and self-reflections become more available, as do the surrounding meta-stories that grow and guide its production. This hypertext tries to make that evident by telling a story and reflecting on the telling, all at once.

4. METAFICTION

The hypertext is an example of metafiction, fiction that emphasizes and comments on its own fictive character. More precisely, it offers a metanarrative, a narrative that foregrounds and comments on its own act of narration.

The use of the term "metanarrative" in this sense differs from the more familiar post-modern use of "meta-narrative" (deriving from Lyotard [17]) to designate totalizing over-narratives such as the Enlightenment story of Progress, the Marxist story of History, or the Christian story of Salvation History that orient and locate local and smaller stories within their expansive context. Such Lyotardian "meta-narratives" do not necessarily show up in metanarrative gestures, though they may. They are, though, part of the multiplicity of "meta-stories" that this hypertext is concerned with.

In this specialized sense of the terms,

> Metanarration and metafiction are umbrella terms designating self-reflexive utterances, i.e. comments referring to the discourse rather than to the story. Although they are related and often used interchangeably, the terms should be distinguished: metanarration refers to the narrator's reflections on the act or process of narration; metafiction concerns comments on the fictionality and/or constructedness of the narrative.

> Thus, whereas metafictionality designates the quality of disclosing the fictionality of a narrative, metanarration captures those forms of self-reflexive narration in which aspects of narration are addressed in the narratorial discourse, i.e. narrative utterances about narrative rather than fiction about fiction.

> In contrast to metafiction, which can only appear in the context of fiction, types of metanarration can also be found in many non-fictional narrative genres and media. [21]

Given hypertext's ability to exfoliate nodes and links of many kinds in all directions, it is easy for hypertexts to become self-referential. See, for instance, the self-comments in afternoon, the self-analogies in *Patchwork Girl* [7], or the story of its own composition and performance in *The Unknown* [22].

5. HYPERTEXT TECHNIQUES

The hypertext story uses a mildly complex pattern of links, whereby each page is replaced by another that occupies the same place on the screen. But the text also makes each single page complex, with two columns and multiple voices. Both the link pattern and the complex pages do metanarrative, but in different ways.

Link-and-node hypertext that replaces one page with another can enact different kinds of relationships. Links can be arranged to make a text multiple and self-referential, with no clear central text standing over against subordinates such as footnotes.

Complex pages, however, introduce spatial contrasts, and these combine with our spatial habits of perception to relations and centralities and subordinations. One benefit of spatial hypertext is the way these spatial habits and perceptions can be used or played against. But for metanarrative spatially complex pages almost inevitably introduce subordinations that may quite literally marginalize some voices.

Lately on the web, complexly linked hypertext structures that might enact metanarrative gestures have largely given way to simpler Wikipedia-style collections of linked mini-essays [15]. So complex pages then must take up more of the burden in doing metafiction, and new creativity is called for.

6. ILLUSIONS

Metafiction is hardly new. One of its finest examples is the "first" Western novel, *Don Quixote* [18]. But in keeping with a general trend in twentieth-century critical theory, metafiction is now interpreted as trying to break down the illusions of a unified narrator and seamless story world. These illusions are seen as restricting readers' freedom and as supporting potentially or actually oppressive institutions. They need to be "denaturalized" and seen for the constructs they are.

But metanarrative, with its self-referential narrative voice(s), can also be seen as maintaining illusions:

> substantiating the illusion of authenticity that a narrative seeks to create….by accentuating the act of narration, thus triggering a different strategy of naturalization, viz. what Fludernik ([3], p. 341) has called the "frame of storytelling." [21]

Perhaps, though, we should talk less about naturalizing and denaturalizing, which suggest that normal narratives are doing something illegitimate or socially repressive. We should talk of metafiction as making clear how a narrative voice or a story world that appears seamless and immediate is really internally complex and mediated by connections among conflicting internal and external multiplicities. The immediacy and unity of voice and story can be seen for what they are, effects produced in a field of forces and mediations that they do not dominate or control.

We should also question the presupposition that a "normal" narrative produces a single unified cognitive frame in its audience, which metanarrative then disturbs by adding a second frame. For instance:

> Wolf [26] seeks to increase the transmedial applicability of metafiction by reconceptualizing it in a first step as a non media-specific concept, namely as "metareference." Metareference denotes a signifying practice that generates a self-referential meaning and *actualizes a secondary cognitive*

frame in the recipient. On this basis, individual media can be examined with respect to their metareferential capacities. [21, my emphasis].

Notice in the quoted paragraph how talk of a "*secondary cognitive frame*" presupposes a single unified *principal* cognitive frame. In opposition to this, my hypertext story tries to show how both author and reader inhabit multiple levels and frames at the same time, all the time, within the acts of writing or reading.

What I wanted to show in this hypertext was that no voice and no frame exists alone but is always surrounded and supported by other voices [12].

It is wrong in any case to presuppose that most narratives have always produced the illusion of a unified author and seamless story world. The hypertext mentions the case of an endlessly ramifying Indian skein of stories that never reach a conclusion. A seventeenth century reader of *Don Quixote* who was familiar with medieval romances and Italian mock-epics [2], especially Ariosto, would have been used to long narratives that were over-rich and internally inconsistent, or were attributed to multiple and pseudonymous authors, or that ironically commented on themselves. Critics who see oppressive illusions holding sway until being denaturalized by metafiction may be constructing an overly unified picture of the life of narrative. Multiplicity and implicit self-reference may be the rule, not the exception.[2]

7. REFERENCES

(This list includes items referred to in this introductory essay, and also items referred to in the hypertext.)

[1] Bernstein, Mark, "More than Legible", http://www.markbernstein.org/talks/HT00.html

[2] Brand, Peter. *The Cambridge History of Italian Literature.* Cambridge University Press, 1999

[3] Fludernik, Monika. *Towards a 'Natural' Narratology.* London: Routledge, 1996.

[4] Ingarden, Roman. *Cognition of the Literary Work of Art,* translated by Ruth Ann Crowley and Kenneth R. Olson. Evanston: Northwestern University Press, 1973.

[5] Iser, Wolfgang. *The Act of Reading: A Theory of Aesthetic Response.* Baltimore: Johns Hopkins UP, 1978.

[6] "Hypertext Hotel", http://hyperdis.de/hyphotel/ [No longer available on line.]

[7] Jackson, Shelley. *Patchwork Girl,* Watertown, MA: Eastgate Systems, 1995.

[8] Jauss, Hans Robert. *Aesthetic Experience and Literary Hermeneutics,* translated by Michael Shaw. Minneapolis: University of Minnesota Press, 1982.

[9] Joyce, Michael. *afternoon, a story.* Watertown: Eastgate Systems, 1986-2011. http://www.eastgate.com/catalog/Afternoon.html

[10] Joyce, Michael. "Siren Shapes: Exploratory and Constructive Hypertexts". Academic Computing (November, 1988): 10+.

[11] Kolb, David. *The Critique of Pure Modernity: Hegel, Heidegger, and After.* Chicago: University of Chicago Press, 1987.

[12] Kolb, David. *Socrates in the Labyrinth: Hypertext, Argument, Philosophy.* Watertown, MA: Eastgate Systems, 1994.

[13] Kolb, David. "Hegelian Buddhist Hypertextual Media Inhabitation, or, Criticism in the Age of Electronic Immersion", *Adrift in the Technological Matrix, Bucknell Review* 46.2, Autumn 2002, 90-108. Online at http://www.dkolb.org/hegelian.buddhist.media.pdf

[14] Kolb, David. "Twin Media: Hypertext Structure Under Pressure," *Proceedings of the 2004 ACM Hypertext Conference.* Online at http://www.dkolb.org/twin.media.ht04/covershe.html.

[15] Kolb, David. "The Revenge of the Page" http://www.dkolb.org/fp002.kolb.pdf

[16] Kolb, David. *Sprawling Places.* University of Georgia Press, 2008. Also a book-length hypertext at http://www.dkolb.org/sprawlingplaces.

[17] Lyotard, Jean François. *The Postmodern Condition.* Minneapolis: University of Minnesota Press, 1984.

[18] Mancing, Howard. 1981. "Cide Hamete Benengeli vs. Miguel de Cervantes: The Metafictional Dialectic of Don Quijote," in *Cervantes: Bulletin of the Cervantes Society of America* 1.1-2 (1981): 63-81. Online at http://www.h-net.org/~cervant/csa/articf81/mancing.htm

[19] Moulthrop, Stuart. *Victory Garden.* Watertown: Eastgate Systems, 1986-2011. http://www.eastgate.com/catalog/VictoryGarden.html

[20] Moulthrop, Stuart. "Polymers, Paranoia, and the Rhetorics of Hypertext", Writing on the Edge, 1991. Reprinted in *The New Media Reader CD,* edited by Noah Wardrip-Fruin and Nick Montfort, Cambridge, MA: MIT Press, 2003.

[21] Neumann, Birgit and Nünning, Ansgar.. "Metanarration and Metafiction", Paragraph 4. In: Hühn, Peter et al. (eds.): *The Living Handbook of Narratology.* Hamburg: Hamburg University Press, 2012. Online at http://hup.sub.uni-hamburg.de/lhn/index.php/Metanarration_and_Metafiction

[22] Rettberg, Scott, Gillespie, William, Stratton, Dirk, Marquardt, Frank. *The Unknown.* http://collection.eliterature.org/2/works/rettberg_theunknown.html

[23] Ricoeur, Paul. *Time and Narrative,* volume 3, translated by Kathleen Blarney and David Pellauer, University of Chicago press 1988. Abbreviated as TN3.

[24] Somadeva. *Katha☐saritsa☐gara.* (For a discussion of this Indian "ocean of stories", see [9] and http://en.wikipedia.org/wiki/Katha☐saritsa☐gara. An English translation of the Katha☐saritsa☐gara in two volumes can be downloaded from http://www.archive.org/details/oceanofstorybein06somauoft.)

[25] van Buitenen, J. A. B. *Tales of Ancient India,* Chicago: University of Chicago Press, 1959.

[26] Wolf, Werner. "Metareference across Media: The Concept, its Transmedial Potentials and Problems, Main Forms and Functions." Werner Wolf (ed.) in collaboration with Katharina Bantleon and Jeff Thoss. *Metareference across Media. Theory and Case Studies.* Amsterdam: Rodopi, 2009, 1–85.

Reprinted in *The New Media Reader,* edited by Noah Wardrip-Fruin and Nick Montfort, Cambridge, MA: MIT Press, 2003.

---

[2] Even though it ignores European Medieval and Renaissance works, and the whole non-western world, the Wikipedia entry for "Metafiction" still lists dozens of works from the ancient world, the eighteenth and nineteenth centuries, as well as modern metafictions.

The Paradox of Rereading in Hypertext Fiction

Alex Mitchell
Department of Communications and New Media
National University of Singapore
Singapore
alexm@nus.edu.sg

Kevin McGee
Department of Communications and New Media
National University of Singapore
Singapore
mckevin@nus.edu.sg

ABSTRACT

Rereading often involves reading the *same thing* again to see something *new*. This paradox becomes more pronounced in an interactive story, where a reader's choices can *literally* change what the reader sees in each reading. There has been some discussion of rereading in both non-interactive and interactive stories. There has not, however, been any detailed study of what readers think they are doing as they reread hypertext fiction that changes dynamically as the result of reader choice. An understanding of this would help authors/designers of hypertext fiction create better hypertext that is explicitly intended to encourage rereading.

To explore this issue, we conducted semi-structured interviews with participants who repeatedly read a complex hypertext fiction. Participants had trouble describing what they were doing as "rereading", and were looking for either the text, or their understanding of the story, to remain constant between readings. This difficulty highlights the paradoxical nature of rereading in interactive stories, and suggests the need for further research into this phenomenon.

Categories and Subject Descriptors

H.5.4. [**Information Interfaces and Presentation**]: Hypertext/Hypermedia

Keywords

rereading, hypertext fiction, interactive stories, reader response, empirical studies

1. INTRODUCTION

"One cannot read a book: one can only reread it. A good reader, a major reader, an active and creative reader is a rereader" [26]. Whether or not one agrees with Nabokov's observation, it contains an often overlooked tension about rereading. On the one hand, we reread to experience the *same thing* again. On the other hand, we reread the same

thing to get *new perspectives or insights*. There is an inherent tension here between reading the "same thing" again and getting something "new" out of the experience: if the experience is new, how can it be the same?

In a non-interactive story, the *text* remains the same between readings. If the experience of reading the text again is different from previous readings, as Galef observes, "[w]hat changes is the reader, not the invariant text" [8, p. 21]. The unchanging text provides one possible invariant on which we can focus, so that instinctively we can continue to call going back to a story again "rereading", even when that rereading involves looking for something "new". For an interactive story, this is no longer the case. Choices a reader makes during the course of a reading may lead to very different text being encountered on each reading. If the text itself is literally different, what is it that we can point to as being "the same"? In fact, in a story where, as Joyce suggests, "[y]ou can neither always go back above, or in fact count upon the existence of the same 'above' from reading to reading" [13, p. 157], it is not clear what it means to "reread".

In this paper we investigate whether readers feel they are "rereading" when they repeatedly read hypertext fiction. Our observations suggest that readers have difficulty trying to describe whether or not they are "rereading", and struggle to define what it is that they are doing, when repeatedly reading hypertext fiction.

This paper is structured as follows. We begin with an overview of the related work and statement of our research problem. Next we describe the design of our study, and present the results. We then discuss the implications of these results in terms of studying rereading in both non-interactive and interactive stories, and the challenges that these results raise for the design of interactive stories which are intended to be reread.

2. RELATED WORK

In this section, we survey the work that has been done to explore rereading in both non-interactive and interactive stories. We describe work which discusses rereading in non-interactive stories, present the various positions which have been taken on rereading in hypertext fiction and other types of interactive stories, and describe the empirical studies which have investigated rereading in interactive stories.

The first problem facing those who discuss rereading is how to define it, particularly with respect to reading. According to Iser, "during the process of reading, there is an active interweaving of anticipation and retrospection, which on a second reading may turn into a kind of advance retrospection" [12, p. 282]. This potentially changes the way in which the reader approaches the text. Although Calinescu [5] distinguishes between first-time reading and rereading, he stresses the lack of a clear distinction. This suggests that it is difficult to define what, exactly, is meant by rereading. In fact, Leitch [16] feels that "[t]he very term *rereading* is contradictory, since it implies the repetition of a process that by definition cannot be repeated without change" [16, p. 507].

Despite this theoretical difficulty, there have been attempts to understand and categorize motivations for rereading. Bacon [1] distinguishes between two categories of motivation to reread: the desire for *sameness* and the desire for *novelty*. Similarly, Calinescu [5] has categorized rereading into *partial*, *simple*, and *reflective* rereading. Partial rereading, or backtracking, takes place in an effort to recall details or understand information which was missed on the first reading. This implies an incomplete first reading. However, it may be that there were certain details which did not appear important in the first reading which, once the entire text has been read, now appear to be of greater importance. Simple, or unreflective, rereading is an attempt to recapture the experience of the first reading [27, 28]. Simple rereading can prove to be problematic, particularly for texts which involve suspense [8, 9]. Finally, reflective rereading involves stepping back and looking at the text in a more analytical manner [5, 16].

The above research has focused on non-interactive stories. There has also been some discussion of rereading in interactive stories. In terms of hypertext fiction, there are differing opinions about the nature of rereading. Some critics focus on the relationship between variation and rereading. For example, Bernstein [2, 3, 4] stresses the importance of rereading, which he sees as opening up the possibility for multiple meanings to emerge as fragments of text are encountered in different contexts on subsequent readings. For Bernstein, "hypertextuality is perceived through rereading and reflection" [3, p. 2]. Similarly, theorists such as Selig [32] and Peacock [29] suggest that the variations, multiple meanings and challenges that readers face when trying to make sense of hypertext fiction will encourage rereading.

In contrast, researchers such as Harpold [11] and Douglas [6] argue that readers return to hypertext fiction, not to experience variation for its own sake, but rather to seek closure. Harpold does suggest that the opening of new possibilities draws readers back, but he still feels that it is the promise of eventually finding a conclusion which provides the motivation for rereading. Douglas feels that readers are looking for some indication as to when they have reached the end of a text, and that there is some possibility of reaching closure in a hypertext fiction. These close readings suggest a somewhat different model of rereading than the model implied by the theorists who emphasize variation.

The work discussed above refers to the "rereading" of hypertext fiction. However, some of this work focuses, not on the rereading of an entire work, but on repetition and loops within a single reading. For example, Bernstein [3] refers to "recurrence" as a form of rereading, seeing cycles within a hypertext which lead the reader to revisit nodes in different contexts as a way of allowing readers to see the consequence of their choices. Similarly, Joyce suggests that, at times, rereading "becomes dissected (along dotted lines) into varieties of 'backtracking' " [13, p. 161], where nodes are revisited within a single reading session.

Researchers and theorists of AI-based interactive drama have tended to focus on the need for variability and agency for interactive stories to be satisfying, and argue that this requires repeated experiences for readers to be able to see the impact of their choices [17]. For example, Murray [25] has suggested that readers will want to repeatedly experience interactive stories to see different perspectives, and eventually achieve a form of second-order closure when they are able to perceive the larger system underlying the variations. Mitchell [19] suggests several new motivations for rereading of interactive stories, including rereading to find out more, to experiment with different choices, and to figure out how the system works. However, Mitchell and McGee [23] caution that rereading may actually impose limitations on agency and variation.

Although there has been much theoretical discussion of the issue of rereading in interactive stories, most of which is grounded in close readings, there have only been a few empirical studies which directly address the question of rereading. Most of these studies [7, 14, 18] have focused on Mateas and Stern's interactive drama *Façade* (Mateas and Stern, 2005). One exception is Mitchell and McGee [22], whose study of readers rereading two simple hypertext stories found that readers do not want to experience endless variation when rereading interactive stories. Instead, they are looking for some form of closure, either in terms of "understanding the story", reaching the "best ending" for the characters, or finding the "most interesting" version of the story.

3. RESEARCH PROBLEM

Having surveyed the related work, we now identify our research problem. Although rereading is often seen as an essential element of interactive stories, theorists have conflicting opinions as to why people would want to reread: either to experience variation, or for some form of closure. It is also not clear what is meant by rereading: the re-experience of an entire work, or repetition within a reading session. In addition, there have been few empirical studies of rereading in interactive stories. This suggests that not much is known about the experience of rereading, particularly in the context of interactive stories.

To explore this issue, we ask the question: what do readers think they are doing when they repeatedly read an interactive story, and do they consider this to be "rereading"? For this study, we are focusing specifically on one form of interactive story: procedural hypertext fiction which changes dynamically as the result of reader choice.

Developing a clearer understanding of the reader's experience of rereading in interactive stories will provide insight into both rereading and interactive storytelling, and help designers and authors of interactive stories to create better interactive stories which are intended to encourage repeated reading.

4. METHOD

To investigate whether readers think they are rereading when repeatedly reading interactive stories, we created a complex hypertext fiction which presents a conflict between several people from a variety of perspectives, in which the reader is able to make choices related to which perspectives are seen. We conducted an empirical study of readers reading this story, using a semi-structured interview approach [31]. Readers were asked to repeatedly read the story. We now discuss the details of the study.

4.1 Study Design

For this study, we conducted semi-structured interviews with 22 participants, 10 male and 12 female, between the ages of 20 and 24. The participants were drawn from an undergraduate research methods class, and the participants were given academic credit for taking part in the study. The participants were assured that their performance in the study would have no bearing on their academic results, and the researchers were not involved in teaching the class in any way.

4.2 Materials

The hypertext fiction which we created for the study involves the reader making choices about *what to see next*, an approach usually taken by literary hypertext fiction, as opposed to *what happens next*, which is more commonly seen in computer games and "choose-your-own adventure" books. The story revolves around an altercation between a man and a woman at a train station, who appear to be arguing about a young child. The story is told from 10 different perspectives, consists of 69 nodes and 205 links, and is roughly 2500 words in length. Possible paths through the story range from 5 to 25 nodes in length.

The story was designed to be "complex" in terms of the structure of the hypertext, the narrative structure, and the ways in which the system responds procedurally to reader choice. The hypertext structure of the story can be regarded as complex, as it incorporates several of the patterns of hypertext described by Bernstein [2]: counterpoint, split/join, missing link, and navigational feint. The narrative structure is also a complex narrative [33], making use of multiple characters' points-of-view, which at times contradict each other. Finally, the story is procedurally complex, with links enabled or disabled depending on the path taken by the reader through the story.

The story was created using the HypeDyn [21] hypertext fiction authoring tool [1]. We chose to create a new story for the study, rather than use a well-known hypertext fiction such as *afternoon, a story* (Joyce, 1990), as we wanted a story which, while complex, was also short enough to be read several times within a one-hour study session, and which the participants would definitely not have encountered before.

4.3 Protocol

Participants were first asked a set of questions related to their experiences with and preferences for various types of stories, to provide context for the interpretation of their responses to the story. They were then taken through a short tutorial explaining the interface conventions and interaction style for the story. After the tutorial, the researcher answered any questions they may have about the mechanics of the system.

They were next asked to read through the story once, on their own. They were not asked any questions nor were they asked to think aloud during this reading. Following the first reading, the participant was engaged in a semi-structured

interview, where the researcher probed for the participant's reactions to the story and expectations for subsequent readings. They were also asked whether they wanted to go back and read the story from the start.

After the semi-structured interview, the participant was asked to go back to the start of the story and read it. Again they were asked to do this on their own, without any interference. Following the second reading, they were again engaged in a semi-structured interview. This time, they were asked what they were doing as they were reading the story, and were asked to compare this experience with the previous reading. They were then asked whether they would consider this experience to be "rereading". This term was not explained – instead, participants were asked whether this is a term they would use for what they had just done. Then they were probed about their answer.

Following the first two readings, the participants were repeatedly asked to go back and read the story again several more times. After each reading, they were engaged in a short interview, focusing on whether they called the repeated experience "rereading", what they felt was similar and/or different from the previous readings, and whether they wanted to read again.

Once the participant indicated that either they understood the story, or they no longer wanted to reread the story, a final "reframing" or twist-ending passage [15] was shown, which suggests that one of the main characters has a completely different role in the story than has been suggested by the earlier text. After reading this new passage, the participant was asked whether they wanted to read the story again. Regardless of their response, they were then asked to read the story a final time, following which they were again asked whether they considered this experience "rereading". Over all of the 22 participants in the study, the participants read the story a minimum of 3 times, and a maximum of 8 times, with an average of 5.14 readings. The session ended with a brief discussion of their experience.

4.4 Data Collection and Analysis

The sessions were recorded through the use of screen-capture software and audio recordings, to aid with analysis. The researcher also took notes during the session. Analysis took an emergent grounded theory approach [10], with notes taken during the interviews used to highlight key points that emerged during each session. After each session, these key points were reviewed and used to begin to form theories as to what was happening, which were noted down by the researcher in the form of memos. These developing theories were used to refine the questions and probing in subsequent sessions. Concurrently, the audio and screen recordings were coded for key incidents. After each transcription, this coding was also compared with the developing theory, and insights were captured in memos. The coding and memos were then sorted and collated.

5. RESULTS

Participants had difficulty determining whether or not what they were doing could be considered "rereading". We observed a tension between whether it was the *text* or their *understanding of the story* which readers felt must remain the same for their experience to be considered "rereading" (see Table 1). This highlights the problem of reconciling the desire to go back to *get something new* out of the story with

---
[1]HypeDyn, and the story used in this study, are available at *http://www.partechgroup.org/hypedyn*.

Table 1: Participants' views of rereading

View of Rereading	Number of Participants
Text must be the same	6
Understanding must be the same	6
Conflict between text and understanding	
Text *and* understanding must be same	1
Changed after "getting the gist"	6
Uncertain (conflict never resolved)	3

the feeling that what you are going back to is still *the same thing*.

When probed as to whether their experience of repeatedly reading our hypertext fiction could be considered "rereading", participants had a range of responses. Some participants only felt that they were rereading if the text remained unchanged. Others felt that as long as their understanding of the story remained constant, they were rereading. For a third group of participants, however, these two views were in conflict, and they struggled to determine whether or not what they were doing was rereading.

We also observed that some participants changed their view of rereading as their understanding of the story changed. At the point when they claimed that they "got the gist" of the story, these participants changed their opinion and started to call the experience "rereading". Many of those who had previously focused on the text as invariant now started to look to their understanding of the story as what must remain unchanged for the experience to be considered rereading. When this understanding was disrupted by the reframing at the end of the session, however, some of these participants again became uncertain as to whether what they were doing could be called rereading.

We now discuss these observations in more detail.

5.1 Text Must Be the Same

One model of rereading which we observed was focused on whether or not the *text* changed across readings. For these participants, any change in the text encountered meant that they were not rereading. In some cases, even a change to the *order* in which the text was encountered meant they were not rereading.

For example, participant 8 encountered different text on the second reading. When asked if he considered this rereading, he said:

> *P8*: Rereading? uh, no I wouldn't say rereading, because if I reread, right, I'll be looking for things that I might have missed out in the fixed text, right, like for example I have a certain text and I reread that particular text to see if I have missed any little details, but in this sense what I was looking for was new pieces of text.
> (16:05)

Participant 8 was very clear that the text he was reading had to be exactly the same in each reading. Even when some text was reencountered or seemed similar, as long as *any* new text was seen in a reading session, he felt that he was *not* rereading the story. This happened during the third reading, at which point he saw both some text that he had

seen before, and some new text. When asked whether he was rereading, he replied:

> *P8*: I'll still say no, because I was looking at other things that I didn't look at previously.
> *R*: Was there any passages of text that you've seen before?
> *P8*: Uh, I think it went back to the same thing, like when how the girl mentioned that, how Diane mentioned that its all a deliberate plan, yeah.
> *R*: So even though you saw some of the same text you'd say it isn't rereading?
> *P8*: Yeah.
> (20:19)

In addition to seeing the same text again, participant 8 also indicated that he would only consider what he was doing to be rereading if the *order* of the text was the same:

> *R*: What would it take for you to say yes it is rereading?
> *P8*: I would say yes it is rereading if I was given the previous text, and how I read it, arranged how I read it, and then I would read, I would read everything in the same sequence, and then I'll say that's rereading, yeah.
> (32:15)

It is important to note that participant 8, as with all the other participants, was making judgements as to whether he was seeing the same text based on his memory of the text – participants were not given a copy of the previous text for comparison.

For participants such as participant 8, their model of rereading when reading our hypertext fiction was the same as when reading a traditional, non-interactive story. This view allows the reader to feel that what they are doing is rereading because there is very clearly something being held invariant: the text. If this invariant does not hold, then they reject the notion that they are rereading.

5.2 Understanding Must Be the Same

Other participants, however, felt that what was important was their *understanding of the story*, and whether or not they encountered story elements which altered this understanding. As long as they were still trying to figure out what the story was about, most felt that they were *not* rereading. However, if they felt that what they were reading matched their current understanding of the story, they felt that they were rereading, whether or not the text they encountered was the same as in previous readings.

For example, even though she had seen a completely different perspective on the events of the story in her second reading, participant 2 considered this to be rereading:

> *R*: So if I asked you to describe what it meant to go back to the start like that, would you describe it as rereading the story?
> *P2*: Yeah.
> *R*: So what you saw the second time is it the same as what you saw the first time?
> *P2*: Uh, similar, similar yeah, but I read it from the passenger['s perspective], another perspective that I didn't read the first time.
> (14:21)

Similarly participant 1 felt that what he was doing was rereading, even though he encountered different text in the second reading. He explained that the reason it was rereading was that he already understood the story:

> R: So in what sense would you say its rereading?
> P1: In the sense that the whole context is still the same, the train station, it involves the same characters.
> (14:27)

For these participants, there was clearly a concept of "story" which was held invariant across the reading sessions, despite the fact that they saw different text, and possibly different perspectives on the story, each time they read. In this view of rereading, understanding the story has replaced the text as the invariant which allows readers to say that they are rereading.

5.3 Conflict Between Text and Understanding

Some participants did not fall into either of the above groups, as they found it difficult to decide whether or not they were rereading. For these participants, there was a conflict between whether rereading required that the text or that their understanding of the story remain unchanged across readings.

Some of these participants began to see that something was "familiar" across reading sessions, but felt that this was in conflict with their awareness that the text was different in each reading. They saw a conflict between their two different views on what they were doing, but were unable to resolve this conflict. Other participants attempted to overcome the conflict by inventing new terms for what they were doing, such as "additional" reading. Finally, one participant reacted by saying that that he was not rereading as long as he did not understand the story, even if the text did *not* change.

5.3.1 Starting To See Something "Familiar"

For those who were unable to reconcile the conflict between whether the text or their understanding of the story should be held constant, they often began by focusing on the text, but then repeatedly encountered the same story elements, which led them to question this view.

For example, although participant 4 began by focusing on whether or not the text he encountered was "the same", he seemed to be having trouble determining what he meant by this. He initially insisted that he would need to see the same text again, at which point the repeated passage would feel "familiar":

> R: So what would it take for it to be called rereading?
> P4: Um I want to go back and read the same passage again when it feels familiar.
> (17:28)

This suggests that it is seeing the "same passage" again which constitutes rereading.

However, what is interesting about participant 4's remark is that he says the passage should feel "familiar". When the researcher probed this concept, participant 4 struggled to explain what he meant by "familiar":

> P4: As long as its unfamiliar, I haven't read it before, I wouldn't consider it rereading, I only

consider it rereading if I'm reading the same exact slides again.
> R: So even if it completely confirms your understanding of the story, it doesn't add anything to your understanding or experience, its just literally the words are different but there's not additional...
> P4: OK now that's interesting, in that case I might consider it rereading if its exactly the same story but just a different slide [...] I think the primary thing is whether it feels familiar to me, I more or less feel that hey I've sort of read this part before, then I'll think its rereading.
> (21:52)

Participant 4 was trying to come up with some notion of what it means to have "read this part before", and was starting to connect this to whether or not his *understanding of the story* is the same.

In contrast, participant 10 recognized that as she repeatedly read, she was seeing the same story, but continued to insist that she was not rereading because she encountered different text. After the third reading, she continued to hold this position, but was starting to notice that there was actually something constant between readings – the story:

> P10: Yeah there was some stuff I saw before but my definition of rereading is more like reading the exact same text over and over again to gain new perspectives and to gain a better understanding of it, other than changing text but in the same context. The similar thing is that the story plot is ultimately the same but the difference is that each time I read it I know new information based on new text that comes out from the different links.
> (24:37)

At this point, she mentions that the story is the same, but still considers this *not* to be rereading, as each time she reads she gets "new information based on new text".

For these participants, they were starting to see that what was being held constant across readings was the story, but they were still focused on the fact that the text was changing each time they read the story, and therefore were not comfortable calling what they were doing "rereading".

5.3.2 Inventing New Labels

For participant 13, the way to deal with the conflict between her expectation that rereading requires the text to remain unchanged, and her realization that her understanding of the story had stabilized, was to invent a new label for what she was doing. After the second reading, she said she was not rereading. However, she did say that she felt she was reading *the same story*. Eventually she came up with her own term for what she was experiencing:

> P13: I'll take like the definition of rereading as reading the same title or the same thing as a whole, but here even though I read the same thing, the same story, but the content I took in on the second time is different, it was additional information from the first time so I would not really consider that as rereading.

R: What would you call it then?
P13: Additional reading.
(19:10)

Unable to reconcile the fact that the story was the same, but that she was still seeing new information and different text, she created a new category into which this situation could be placed, calling what she was doing "additional reading".

5.3.3 Unchanging Text is Not Enough

One participant, when faced with the conflict between his view that the text must remain the same and the opposing view that the text can change but the story must stay the same, adopted the position that if he has not yet reached an *understanding* of the story, then he is *not* rereading, even if the text remains the same.

Participant 5 initially felt that he was not rereading because he saw different text each time. Later, as he felt that the story was becoming clearer, he changed his opinion and said that he was now rereading "to an extent", regardless of whether or not the text changes:

> *P5*: Yeah its starting to become a bit clearer, and there are certain overlaps that I can make, to an extent its rereading but I'm still getting new information so its rereading to an extent but not completely.
> (23:44)

Participant 5 was trying to reconcile his feeling that an understanding of the story was important to rereading with his initial position that he had to see the same text again to consider what he was doing to be rereading.

He eventually resolved this conflict by deciding that *even if the text didn't change*, he was not rereading if he didn't understand the story:

> *P5*: If I don't understand what's going on I can't consider that rereading.
> *R*: Even though you see exactly the same text each time?
> *P5*: Yeah I don't think I consider that rereading because rereading has to do with some understanding of the elements as well.
> (25:56)

For participant 5, both the text and his understanding of the story had to be invariant for what he was doing to be considered rereading.

5.4 Changed Opinions After "Getting the Gist"

As can be seen from participant 5's experience, there seemed to be a connection between whether readers understood the story, and how they viewed what they were doing. In fact, some participants changed their view of the process of going back over the story after "getting the gist" of the story. Having "got it", they now considered any further readings of the story to be "rereading".

For participant 6, understanding "what's happening" in the story gradually came to be seen as more important than whether the text changed between readings. She was initially uncertain as to whether she could call what she was doing "rereading", given that she wasn't rereading the same text. After the second reading, when asked if she was rereading, she replied that it was "kind of" rereading. When probed as to what she meant by this, she said:

> *P6*: I think when it comes to rereading you sort of expect to read the same text and find out more about the same thing but for this its sort of you're looking at completely different perspectives so you're not, you're finding out new things but not from this original thing that you read the first time.
> (20:20)

At this point she was clearly struggling with the concepts, and was unable to reconcile her expectation that rereading means reading "the same text" with her observation that in our hypertext story she was encountering different text but "its the same story".

After the third reading, she started to change her opinion, saying that now she was beginning to understand the story so it could be considered rereading:

> *P6*: Here you are not really sure about what's going on, so you keep looking out for different perspectives and stuff and you piece things together along the way, but its only at the end that you get the whole story and so now if I go back to the start and reread, like do it from some other perspective, then that would be like rereading cause I know exactly what's happening.
> (25:40)

This clearly shows that her view of rereading has shifted from a focus on reading the same text, to an emphasis on understanding the story.

Similarly, for participant 7, she initially felt that what she was doing was *not* rereading, but then changed her mind after getting the gist. In her case, she was initially not clear if it was changes to the text or the story which determined whether or not she called what she was doing rereading. After the second reading, she did not feel that she was rereading, as she had encountered a different perspective in the first and second readings. However, after the third reading, she changed her mind and said she *was* rereading, even if she saw new text. When probed about the contradiction with her earlier response, she said:

> *P7*: I think because what the witness is saying [her third reading] its similar to the third person account [her first reading], yeah like the general overview, it doesn't really add depth to what the people within the commotion are feeling, yeah so that's why I feel that its a rereading of the general description.
> (17:06)

Interestingly, after the fourth reading, participant 7 decided that she was *not* rereading, as she had encountered new information which *disrupted her understanding* of the story:

> *R*: So would you consider this rereading?
> *P7*: No [laughs] because I know another part that I didn't know about.
> (20:43)

When she encountered new information which challenged her current understanding of the story, she labelled this as *not* rereading, because the story was no longer invariant. This is consistent with her view that rereading requires a constant understanding of the story.

For these participants, there was a developing sense that the concept of rereading was closely tied to their understanding of the story. As long as their understanding of the story remained constant, they could describe their experience as rereading *the story*, whereas when this was lost, they were no longer rereading.

5.5 Rereading Problematized by Reframing

Once the participants indicated that they understood the story, the researcher introduced a "reframing" which was designed to disrupt the reader's understanding of the story. After the reframing was introduced, participants struggled with whether to call this rereading, given that they no longer understood the story but the only thing that had changed was the final passage in the story.

For example, participant 10 had been struggling with the question of whether or not she was rereading, but had started to feel that there was something "familiar" across readings (see 5.3.1). After several readings, she mentioned that she understood the story, and that this meant that she *would* be rereading if she went back again. When the reframing was revealed but *before* going back again, she said:

> *P10*: Now its not rereading as its possible that the storyline has taken a completely different turn, so its not rereading because I might be finding out new stuff about the story rather than new emotions based to a storyline that didn't change.
> (40:05)

This is consistent with the view that rereading depends on an unchanging understanding of the story.

However, after actually going back through the story, she changed her mind again, and said she *was* rereading:

> *P10*: Its still rereading because I'm reading the same thing that she does and says, the action is the same but the only difference is my perspective, so actually I'm rereading it from a different perspective.
> (41:39)

When probed further about her definition of rereading at this point, she struggled to reconcile her use of the term with what she was experiencing, and changed her mind again, now saying that she was *not* rereading:

> *P10*: Its rereading because, as in its the same thing, but that's the technical term to use, its the, the most, its the word that just comes naturally to me, but if you ask me whether I'm rereading it I will still say not really [...] yeah, because its um, I guess its the way I define rereading, I've always thought that rereading is more of like going through the exact same thing rather than in this way where its rather ambiguous, I can't say its the exact same thing but I can't say its entirely new either.
> (49:10)

When asked to compare this experience to rereading a short story with a similar reframing at the end, she said

that she *would* describe the experience of repeatedly reading the short story as rereading, but felt that the experience of repeatedly reading our hypertext story was not the same:

> *P10*: Um because, I guess its there, like I'm reading the exact same thing in the exact same order, whereas if I'm reading it in this way the order keeps changing and everything so its more, its not so much rereading.
> (51:46)

This confusion and constant revision of participant 10's notion of rereading was common, and reflects the difficulty that participants had coming to terms with what could be considered rereading in an interactive story.

A similar confusion can be seen in participant 13's experience. When asked what she would call going back again after the reframing, she thought it would be rereading:

> *P13*: Yes because I already know that there's a bag, I want to make sure, I want to find out the exact details about the bag like where, who was the one carrying it, how did it end up on the train, yeah, so it would be rereading because I know that there's a bag.
> (44:44)

However, she had earlier described this type of reading as "additional" reading, not rereading (see 5.3.1). When probed about this contradiction, she admitted that she was now confused about how to describe the experience:

> *R*: Before you were saying that if its different or additional information...
> *P13*: It will not be rereading, oh OK yeah [laughs], yeah because I don't know where the bag was, hmm. I think, I would say that it depends on the amount of new information that I will take in every time. I dunno what is my own limit but I think when I said that there's a limit, like if its just a little detail about some thing about the bag I wouldn't consider its like a very new information, even though its new information like its not a major thing, yeah.
> (45:07)

What is emerging here is a notion of *how much* the reader's understanding of the story has changed. For both participants 10 and 13, there seemed to be a threshold beyond which they do not consider what they are doing to be rereading. However, they were not able to clearly determine where that threshold lies, and as a result struggled with what to call their experience.

6. DISCUSSION

Our observations suggest that readers hold two different views of their experience of rereading hypertext fiction: for some, the text must remain unchanged for what they are doing to be called rereading, whereas for others, it is their understanding of the story which must remain constant (see Table 2). It is important to note that, without this explanation of the participants' questioning of whether or not they are rereading, the reaction "am I rereading?" would seem

Table 2: What Can Be Considered "Rereading"? (Note: numbers refer to sections in this paper)

	Understanding Stays the Same	Understanding Changes
Text Stays the Same	rereading (5.1)	not rereading (5.3.3), or uncertain (5.5)
Text Changes	not rereading (5.1), rereading (5.2), or uncertain (5.3)	not rereading (5.2)

confusing and contradictory. We now examine these conflicting views in detail.

As mentioned at the start of the paper, there is an inherent paradox in rereading, as it often involves reading the *same thing* again to *see something new*. When faced with this paradox, rereaders of non-interactive stories are able to overcome the contradiction by focusing on the fact that, even if their reading experience is different, *the text is still the same*. In an interactive story, as we have observed in our study, readers often struggle to call what they are doing rereading.

In the case of an interactive story, there is potentially *nothing* which the reader can readily point to as constant between reading sessions. If the reader is going back to see something new, then the story and/or the reader's understanding of the story will most likely *not* be the same. If, in addition, the text that they encounter when going back is literally not the same as what they saw in the previous readings, then it is hard to see what the reader could possibly point to and say that they are "rereading". It is exactly this conflict which we observed in our study. Many of the participants in the study, when faced with changing text and/or changing story, struggle to describe what they were doing as rereading, often flipping back and forth between a focus on text as invariant and story as invariant. The difficulty which participants showed in coming to terms with what is happening as they reexperienced our hypertext fiction demonstrates the complexity of this problem.

Participants initially brought certain expectations to the situation, namely that rereading involves "reading the same text over and over again" (participant 5). When they repeatedly read the story, eventually there was a point where participants noticed that, although the text was changing, they were starting to see or feel that things were "familiar". At this point, many of the participants became confused, and struggled to make sense of what they were experiencing. This confusion, resulting from the clash between their expectations and what they were seeing, can be viewed as a form of cognitive disequilibrium [30]. To deal with this challenge to their expectations, participants had to find a way to reconcile their earlier notion of the text as the invariant with this new feeling that there is something familiar, but they are not seeing the same text.

One response was for participants to *assimilate* this new experience, struggling to make what they were seeing fit into their existing beliefs. For some participants, they did this by sticking with the opinion that the text must remain invariant, and that they were not rereading unless they saw exactly the same text in each reading.

The other response was to *accommodate* the new experience, trying to adapt their existing concepts to fit the new

experience. Some participants struggled with the new concept, and tried to deal with it by inventing new labels, such as "additional" reading or "revisiting" to describe what they are doing. This is a partial accommodation. Other participants were able to accommodate the notion that their understanding of the story, rather than the text, was being held invariant across reading sessions, and changed their concept of "rereading" to include this new situation.

7. IMPLICATIONS

The above discussion has implications for the study and design of both non-interactive and interactive stories which are intended to be reread.

In the study of reading of traditional, static text, the assumption is that the text is invariant, but the reader's understanding may change, both during an initial reading and when rereading. Our observations of rereading in the context of interactive stories suggest that, in addition to the text, readers' understanding of the story is also something which readers eventually come to see as potentially invariant. It may be that, when rereading a static story, readers' conception of what they are doing also changes at the point when they feel that they understand the story. In addition, if further reading disrupts that understanding, they may, again, change their view of whether or not they are "rereading" in the same sense. This may be particularly relevant in, for example, stories where a reframing causes a radical disruption of the reader's understanding of the story. Considering the reader's understanding of the story as a focus of the reader's experience, in addition to or even instead of the text, may shed new light on the differences between partial, simple, and reflective rereading [5]. This may also provide authors with some insight into ways to encourage rereading.

The results discussed above raise a design challenge for authors and designers who want to support rereading in interactive stories: how to deal with the conflicting views which readers have of rereading? Given that in any form of interactive story the text is most likely to be changing between readings, how can the author give the reader the feeling that she is *rereading* the story? One possibility, which we have discussed in more detail elsewhere [22], is that rereading may impose constraints on how much procedural variation authors can introduce *between* reading sessions. Should the events in the story be held constant, but something else, such as the perspective or the amount information presented to the reader, be changed between reading sessions? Or instead, should the events in the story be allowed to change, but something else (such as Murray's "moral physics" [25]) be held constant? In the latter case, what can be done to encourage the reader to feel that the repeated experience involves rereading to some extent, as opposed to experiencing a entirely *new* story? This problem requires further investigation.

8. CONCLUSIONS AND FUTURE WORK

Our observations suggest that there are two different ways in which readers view rereading. One view is that any change to the *text* when a work is revisited means that the reader is *not* rereading. From this perspective, what is invariant between readings, and what is being reread, is the text itself. A second view is that it doesn't matter whether or not the text changes – going back is seen as rereading as long as the reader's *understanding* of the story is the same. This perspective holds the reader's understanding of story as the invariant, with rereading involving seeing the same story again, regardless of any changes to the text. Participants in our study often had trouble deciding whether they were rereading, and struggled with which of these two views of rereading they felt was appropriate to their experience. This difficulty highlights the problematic, paradoxical nature of rereading, particularly in the context of stories which change as the result of reader choice.

An interesting issue is that, when we asked our participants to reread the story, which we phrased as a request to "go back and read the story from the start", readers initially had no problem. It wasn't as if they were unable to conceive of doing this. What they were uncertain about, rather, was how exactly to characterize this activity. By going back and reading "the story from the start", were they reading the *same* story *again*? Were they *still reading* the story, having not yet finished reading it for a first time? Or were they reading a *different* story for the *first* time? This is a complex problem. A deeper understanding of this problem may provide insight into readers' expectations and experience of interactive stories in general.

The results reported in this paper form part of a larger investigation of what it means to reread interactive stories [19, 20, 22, 23, 24]. Our observations have served as a starting point for the development of a model of rereading in interactive stories, and have been used to develop guidelines for designing interactive stories which are intended to support rereading [20]. Future work includes validating this model with various forms of interactive stories, and refining the guidelines through the iterative design, development and study of new interactive stories. A better understanding of the phenomenon of rereading will provide insight into ways to better design and support the creation of interactive stories which encourage repeated satisfying experiences.

9. ACKNOWLEDGMENTS

This work was funded under a Singapore-MIT GAMBIT Game Lab research grant, "Tools for Telling: How Game Development Systems Shape Interactive Storytelling."

10. REFERENCES

[1] H. Bacon. Cognition and the aesthetics of reexperience. In J. D. Anderson and B. F. Anderson, editors, *Narration and spectatorship in moving images*, pages 260–276. Cambridge Scholars Publishing, 2007.

[2] M. Bernstein. Patterns of hypertext. In *Proceedings of Hypertext '98*, pages 21–29. ACM Press, 1998.

[3] M. Bernstein. On hypertext narrative. In *Proceedings of Hypertext '09*. ACM Press, 2009.

[4] M. Bernstein, M. Joyce, and D. Levine. Contours of constructive hypertexts. In *Proceedings of Hypertext '92*, pages 161–170. ACM, 1992.

[5] M. Calinescu. *Rereading*. Yale University Press, 1993.

[6] J. Y. Douglas. *The End of Books - or Books Without End? Reading Interactive Narratives*. University of Michigan Press, 2001.

[7] S. Dow, M. Mehta, E. Harmon, B. MacIntyre, and M. Mateas. Presence and engagement in an interactive drama. In *Proceedings of CHI '07*, pages 1475–1484. ACM Press, 2007.

[8] D. Galef. Observations on rereading. In D. Galef, editor, *Second Thoughts: a Focus on Rereading*, pages 17–33. Wayne State University Press, 1998.

[9] R. J. Gerrig. Suspense in the absence of uncertainty. *Journal of Memory and Language*, 28(6):633–648, 1989.

[10] B. G. Glaser and A. L. Strauss. *The Discovery of Grounded Theory: Strategies for Qualitative Research*. Aldine Publishing, 1967.

[11] T. Harpold. *Links and their vicissitudes: Essays on hypertext*. PhD thesis, University of Pennsylvania, 1994.

[12] W. Iser. *The Act of Reading: A Theory of Aesthetic Response*. The Johns Hopkins University Press, 1980.

[13] M. Joyce. Nonce upon some times: Rereading hypertext fiction. *MFS Modern Fiction Studies*, 43(3):579–597, 1997.

[14] R. L. Knickmeyer and M. Mateas. Preliminary evaluation of the interactive drama *Facade*. In *CHI '05 Extended Abstracts*, pages 1549–1552. ACM Press, 2005.

[15] E. Lavik. Narrative structure in The Sixth Sense: A new twist in "twist movies"? *The Velvet Light Trap*, 58:55–64, 2006.

[16] T. M. Leitch. For (against) a theory of rereading. *Modern Fiction Studies*, 33(3):491–508, Autumn 1987.

[17] M. Mateas. A preliminary poetics for interactive drama and games. *Digital Creativity*, 12(3):140–152, 2001.

[18] D. Milam, M. Seif El-Nasr, and R. Wakkary. Looking at the interactive narrative experience through the eyes of the participants. In U. Spierling and N. Szilas, editors, *Interactive Storytelling*, volume 5334 of *Lecture Notes in Computer Science*, pages 96–107. Springer Berlin / Heidelberg, 2008.

[19] A. Mitchell. Motivations for rereading in interactive stories: A preliminary investigation. In R. Aylett, M. Lim, S. Louchart, P. Petta, and M. Riedl, editors, *Interactive Storytelling*, volume 6432 of *Lecture Notes in Computer Science*, pages 232–235. Springer Berlin / Heidelberg, 2010.

[20] A. Mitchell. *Reading Again for the First Time: Rereading for Closure in Interactive Stories*. PhD thesis, NUS Graduate School for Integrative Sciences and Engineering, National University of Singapore, 2012.

[21] A. Mitchell and K. McGee. Designing hypertext tools to facilitate authoring multiple points-of-view stories. In *Proceedings of Hypertext '09*, pages 309–316. ACM Press, 2009.

[22] A. Mitchell and K. McGee. Limits of rereadability in procedural interactive stories. In *Proceedings of CHI '11*, pages 1939–1948. ACM Press, 2011.

[23] A. Mitchell and K. McGee. Rereading in interactive stories: Constraints on agency and procedural variation. In M. Si, D. Thue, E. Andre, J. Lester, J. Tanenbaum, and V. Zammitto, editors, *Interactive Storytelling*, volume 7069 of *Lecture Notes in Computer Science*, pages 37–42. Springer Berlin / Heidelberg, 2011.

[24] A. Mitchell and K. McGee. Supporting rereadability

through narrative play. In M. Si, D. Thue, E. Andre, J. Lester, J. Tanenbaum, and V. Zammitto, editors, *Interactive Storytelling*, volume 7069 of *Lecture Notes in Computer Science*, pages 67–78. Springer Berlin / Heidelberg, 2011.

[25] J. H. Murray. *Hamlet on the Holodeck: The Future of Narrative in Cyberspace*. The MIT Press, 1998.

[26] V. Nabokov. *Lectures on Literature*. Mariner Books, 2002.

[27] V. Nell. *Lost in a Book: The Psychology of Reading for Pleasure*. Yale University Press, 1988.

[28] K. Odden. Retrieving childhood fantasies: A psychoanalytic look at why we (re)read popular literature. In D. Galef, editor, *Second Thoughts: a Focus on Rereading*, pages 126–151. Wayne State University Press, 1998.

[29] A. Peacock. Towards an aesthetic of 'the interactive'. *Digital Creativity*, 12(4):237–246, 2001.

[30] J. Piaget and M. Cook. *The Origins of Intelligence in Children*. WW Norton & Co, 1952.

[31] I. Seidman. *Interviewing as qualitative research: A guide for researchers in education and the social sciences*. Teachers College Pr, 2006.

[32] R. L. Selig. The endless reading of fiction: Stuart Moulthrop's hypertext novel "Victory Garden". *Contemporary Literature*, 41(4):642–660, Winter 2000.

[33] J. Simons. Complex narratives. *New Review of Film and Television Studies*, 6(2):111–126, 2008.

Evaluating Tag-Based Information Access in Image Collections

Christoph Trattner[*]
ctrattner@iicm.edu

Yi-ling Lin[†]
yil54@pitt.edu

Denis Parra[†]
dap89@pitt.edu

Zhen Yue[†]
zhy18@pitt.edu

William Real[‡]
william.real@gmail.com

Peter Brusilovsky[†]
peterb@pitt.edu

[*]Knowledge Management Institute, Graz University of Technology, Austria
[†] School of Information Sciences, University of Pittsburgh, USA
[‡] Carnegie Museum of Art, Pittsburgh, USA

ABSTRACT

The availability of social tags has greatly enhanced access to information. Tag clouds have emerged as a new "social" way to find and visualize information, providing both one-click access to information and a snapshot of the "aboutness" of a tagged collection. A range of research projects explored and compared different tag artifacts for information access ranging from regular tag clouds to tag hierarchies. At the same time, there is a lack of user studies that compare the effectiveness of different types of tag-based browsing interfaces from the users point of view. This paper contributes to the research on tag-based information access by presenting a controlled user study that compared three types of tag-based interfaces on two recognized types of search tasks – lookup and exploratory search. Our results demonstrate that tag-based browsing interfaces significantly outperform traditional search interfaces in both performance and user satisfaction. At the same time, the differences between the two types of tag-based browsing interfaces explored in our study are not as clear.

Categories and Subject Descriptors

H.5.4 [**Information Interfaces and Presentation**]:
Hypertext/Hypermedia - Navigation

General Terms

Human Factors

Keywords

Tag-Based Search Interfaces, Tag Navigation, Tagging Systems

1. INTRODUCTION

Social tags provide an easy and intuitive way to annotate, organize and retrieve resources from the Web. Promoted by several pi-

oneering systems such as Delicious, Flickr, and CiteULike, social tagging has emerged as one of the most popular technologies of the modern Web. The value of tags was specifically advocated for image collections such as Flickr, where the presence of tags made images searchable and discoverable. While tags help to discover content even with a standard keyword-search, the most innovative feature of social tags was the ability to support browsing-based access to information through so-called "tag clouds". Effectively, tag clouds are a new "social" way to find and visualize information providing both: one-click access to information and a snapshot of the "aboutness" of a tagged collection. Not surprisingly, a large volume of research has been devoted to developing better approaches to construct and visualize tag clouds [5, 30, 18] as well as more advanced tag constructs such as clustered/classified tag clouds [23, 32, 2, 39, 16, 25] and tag hierarchies [10, 19, 34, 35].

The majority of research on tag clouds and hierarchies used an information- or network-theoretical approach to evaluate the quality of different tag constructs in terms of search and navigation while ignoring the user prospective. User studies comparing performance of users applying different tag-based browsing constructs in a set of realistic search tasks are rare. Moreover, there is a lack of user studies that compare the effectiveness of various tag constructs with simple search-based access to tagged collections. This paper attempts to bridge this gap by comparing several types of tag-based information access in a controlled user study. The study has been performed in the context of image search, where the presence of tags is known to be most valuable. To make the study more useful, we compared the performance of three types of tag-based information access interfaces in two commonly recognized types of search tasks – lookup search and exploratory search. The tag-based interfaces explored in the study include a search-based interface that plays the role of a baseline and two types of tag-based browsing interfaces: a regular browsing interface using traditional tag clouds and a faceted browsing interface using classified tag clouds. We selected the faceted tag cloud interface from among other advanced tag-based browsing approaches because our previous study [26] in the image search domain revealed that faceted search interfaces helped users to better explore large collections of images.

2. DATASET

As a dataset for our study, we utilized a collection of images from an archive belonging to the Carnegie Museum of Art in Pittsburgh, Pennsylvania. Overall, the collection contains more than

Figure 1: Screenshots of the three search interfaces - baseline (left), tag cloud (middle) and faceted tag cloud (right).

80,000 images taken by the famous local photographer, Charles Teenie Harris, who captured African-American life in Pittsburgh over a 40-year period. In our study, we used 1,986 of these images, of which 986 have been featured in a current exhibition at the Carnegie Museum of Art. The remaining 1000 images were included in this study as they provide a finer-grained overview of the entire collection. For the 1,986 images, we collected user tags using Amazon Mechanical Turk. Overall, the dataset provides 4,206 unique tags and 16,659 tag assignments applied by 97 users to the 1,986 images.

3. INTERFACES

For the purpose of our study, we implemented three tag-based interfaces to search the collection of Teenie Harris images – one standard "search box" interface and two interfaces that support both search and tag-based browsing. In the following section, we introduce these interfaces and their functionalities.

3.1 The Baseline (Search Only) Interface

As a baseline for our study (see Figure 1), we utilized a simple search box-based interface that offers the look and feel of well-known search engines. Similar to the Google, Yahoo! or Bing image search interfaces, we provide our users with a search box to submit a query, a thumbnail preview of the resulting images sorted by relevance and the functionality to click on the image in order to get a more detailed view of the image resource. The back-end of our search interface is built upon the OpenSource search engine Apache Lucene, which utilizes the tags of each image to create the search index.

3.2 The Tag Cloud Interface

The second interface explored in this paper is referred to as the tag cloud interface. As indicated by its name, this type of search interface extends the baseline search interface with the functionality of a traditional tag cloud. The alphabetically-ordered tag cloud provides the user with a topical overview of the search results and allows the user to search or browse images using the tags displayed in the cloud. This form of tag cloud is currently the most popular type of tag-based browsing in social tagging systems. To generate the tag cloud in this interface, we utilized a simple popularity-based tag cloud algorithm. For each query, we display the top N most frequent co-occurring tags to the user. This approach was shown to be one of the best choices to create a tag cloud from the perspective of tag-based search and browsing [37]. As the number of tags displayed in the tag cloud is an important factor which can negatively affect tag cloud-based search and navigation [33, 20], we also provide the functionality to increase or decrease the number of tags in the tag cloud to suit the user's needs. In Figure 1, a sample screenshot is presented to show how the tag cloud interface appears on

the user's screen. As can be seen in the figure, the interface offers not only the functionality to click on a tag to issue a query, but also the possibility to expand the query by clicking the "+" sign in the tag cloud or shrink the query by utilizing the "x" sign in the query string beneath the search box. Currently, many popular tagging systems such as Delicious or BibSonomy offer similar approaches for query expansion or reduction to give the user a more flexible way to search and navigate in a tag-based information system.

3.3 The Faceted Tag Cloud Interface

The third interface developed for the study is referred to as a faceted tag cloud interface (see Figure 1). It can be considered as one of the most innovative tag-based search interfaces currently available. The interface was first introduced in 2009 by Yahoo! [32] in order to search for images in the social tagging system Flickr. Although there are very few implementations of this type of interface, there is a great deal of current research in this area [29, 38, 8, 7]. Similar to the tag cloud interface, this type of interface provides the user with the functionality to view the tags of the retrieved images in a visually appealing representation. However, contrary to the traditional tag cloud interface, where all tags appear in a tag cloud in an unstructured way, this type of interface classifies tags into several categories.

To decide which classification schema to utilize, we performed an extensive literature survey on currently available tag classification approaches [6, 29, 38, 8, 32, 11]. In the end, we selected a simplified form of the well-known "Editor's 5 Ws" approach that recognizes "Who" (people, groups or individuals), "Where" (location or places), "When" (time, activities or events), "What" (objects, food, animals or plants) and "Other" (unknown, not classified) classification schema. This schema was found to be effective in classifying tags in the image domain [32] as well as in our earlier user studies [26]. To classify our tags for this type of interface, we also used Amazon Mechanical Turk. The classification procedure itself was independent of image context as none of the currently available tag classification approaches take into account context information such as resource information, user information or other tags for the same or similar resources.

To ensure that the workers on Amazon Mechanical Turk (referred to as turkers) would classify our tags in a meaningful way, we provided them with detailed instructions of how to select those tags which fit into the one of the five given categories. The guidance included a sample screenshot of three different types of tags classified into one of the five categories and a detailed explanation of how to use these categories. Overall, three turkers were assigned to classify each particular tag. After the first classification round, we noted that 11% of tags were not classified as the turkers could not agree on which of the five given categories to use. Therefore, we decided to initiate a second classification round with an additional

Search Tasks	Search Task Descriptions
Lookup	Find the following picture!*
Exploratory	1. Find at least 8 different types of stores/shops in Pittsburgh! Each type of store/shop should have at least two images from different locations, i.e. in total you will have to find at least 16 images.
	2. Pittsburgh is a city with many sport teams. Find at least 8 different sport activities! Each type of sport should be represented by at least two pictures. In total, you will have to get at a minimum of 16 pictures.
	3. Pittsburgh has a rich cultural heritage. There were many musicians who worked in Pittsburgh. Find at least 5 different types of music instruments which the musicians played in Pittsburgh. Each instrument needs 2 pictures and all pictures should be taken in different locations. In total, you will have to collect at least 10 pictures.

Table 1: Search tasks and descriptions (*= in the user study, only one image at a time was presented to the user).

six turkers (per tag) to increase the precision of our classification procedure. All in all, 22% of the tags were classified as "Who", 16% as "Where", 23% as "When", 34% as "What" and only 5% of the tags as "Other", which clearly out-performs current automatic tag classification approaches in terms of unclassifiable tags (represented as "Other" tags in our classification schema). We had 86 different turkers for the first classification round and 35 turkers for the second. The mean inter-rater agreement per tag over all turkers was substantial (75%).

In Figure 1, one can see a screenshot of how this type of interface appears on the user's screen. As with the tag cloud interface, users have the opportunity to issue a query by clicking on a tag, to expand a query by clicking on the "+" sign or shrink the query by utilizing the "x" sign in the query string beneath the search box. In addition, the faceted tag cloud can be expanded or collapsed as same as in the tag cloud interface.

4. USER STUDY DESIGN

To compare the three tag-based information access interfaces, we designed a within-subject study. In this design, each of our subjects evaluated the three different search interfaces during one study session. To determine when tag-based support is most effective; each interface was examined in the context of two kinds of search tasks, which are discussed in the following section.

4.1 Search Tasks

It has been shown that search task attributes affect the information seeking behavior of users [13, 36, 9]. The complexity, familiarity, clarity and difficulty of a search task influences how a person searches, browses and uses information systems [13, 17]. To account for the impact of these factors, our study separately evaluated the effectiveness of the three tag-based information access interfaces in the two primary types of search tasks known as lookup search and exploratory search.

As indicated by its name, lookup search is typically performed to find a specific information item in a document collection [27]. Lookup search tasks are considered to be relatively simple and most frequently involve using a traditional search interface (cf. [13, 36, 9]). More complicated search tasks – "beyond lookup"– are typically called exploratory search tasks [27, 9]. Exploratory search assumes that the user has some broader information need that cannot be simply met by a "relevant" information item (as in simple lookup search), but requires multiple searches interwoven with browsing and analysis of the retrieved information [26].

To study lookup search behavior, we created nine different lookup search tasks. All of these tasks were of a similar nature: the subject was given and the user was expected to find relevant images in the collection within a certain time limit. To account for the differences in difficulty [13, 36, 9], a variety of pictures were selected ranging from "easy" to "hard" to find. To classify images by difficulty, we calculated the mean search time for each image in the image collection based on lookup searches performed with Amazon Mechanical Turk. Then, we selected nine images ranging from "easy" to "hard" to find in the Teenie Harries image collection. In Table 1, the nine different images chosen for the user study are presented.

To study exploratory search behavior, we designed three exploratory search tasks as shown in Table 1. To ensure the balance between each type of user interface and also to capture the attribute of difficulty, we designed the exploratory search tasks carefully with a variety of additional search criteria and attributes. For instance, to capture balance with the faceted search interface, we tried to tune our search tasks to utilize as many facets as possible. We did that by asking the subjects to search for several different topics such as music, sports or shops as well as various search criteria such as different locations. To capture the property of familiarity with the search tasks, we asked our subjects in the post-questionnaire to rate their expertise level on the given topic or search item.

To be sure that our search tasks were meaningful, we performed several trial searches with Amazon Mechanical Turk and we conducted a pilot study.

4.2 The Process

As discussed previously, our subjects had to undertake two different kinds of search tasks using three different types of search interfaces within one user study session. During the study, each subject was assigned to perform nine different lookup and three different exploratory search tasks which were the same for the duration of the whole experiment. To counter the impact of fatigue and learning, the order in which the search tasks and system interfaces were used were rotated using a Latin square design. In addition to this, the lookup and the exploratory search tasks were randomized among all three interfaces to make sure that each of them was evaluated under different search interface conditions. The process of the user study was as follows:

1. Each participant was informed of the objective of the study, and asked to complete a consent form and a short questionnaire eliciting background information.

2. For each interface and task, a demonstration was given and the participant was given enough time to familiarize themselves with the interfaces and tasks. 3. For each interface, the user was given three lookup tasks and one exploratory search task.

   (a) Lookup task: An image was presented to the participant and a limit of 3 minutes (+30secs. for task reading)

Task	Measure	Baseline		Tag Cloud		Facet	
		All cases	Successful	All cases	Successful	All cases	Successful
Lookup	Cases	72	59	72	57	72	59
	Total Actions	9.01±.89	6.46±.67	8.58±.94	5.37±.56	8.68±.86	6.12±.63
	Search Time	77.35±7.35	54.19±5.31	75.38±8.03	44.37±4.48	77.67±7.8	52.17±5.32
Exploratory	Cases	24	23	24	20	24	22
	Total Actions	43.67±4.36	**42.17±4.27**	41.04±4.52	**33.50±3.37**[**]	42.58±4.26	40.73±4.44
	Search Time	421.58±38.03	**413.48±38.81**	363.96±35.05	**312.4±30.74**[***]	378.33±33.46	356.91±32.8

Table 2: Descriptives (*mean±SE*) of total actions and search time by search and interface. Each statistic is calculated considering all cases and considering only successful search tasks (**=significant at p<0.01 ; ***=significant at p<0.001).

was given to complete the task. Afterwards, a post-search questionnaire was given to the subject to elicit disposition toward the system interface.

(b) Exploratory task: A description of the task was given to the participant and they were allotted a limit of 10 minutes (+1min. for task reading) to complete the task. A post-search questionnaire was presented as well.

3. A final questionnaire was given to the subject to assess the differences among the three search interfaces.

4. A series of open-ended questions were asked according to the observations made during the study.

4.3 Participants

Our study involved 24 participants (8 females, 16 males), who were recruited via email and flyers distributed throughout the University of Pittsburgh campus. The participants were from a variety of disciplines ranging from law to computer science. Four of them had earned a bachelor's degree, 16 a master's degree and four a PhD degree. The average age of the participants was 30.6 years (min=22, max = 61, SD=7.59 years). Almost all (except 2 participants) reported using computers for more than 5 hours a day. All participants (except two) rated their search engine skills as high and indicated using Google, Yahoo! or Bing frequently. A significant number (19) reported that they were familiar with tagging or used search tagging systems such as BibSonomy, Delicious or Flickr regularly. Four participants reported that they were familiar with the history of Pittsburgh, the rest of our subjects stated that they were not. On average, each user study session lasted 90 minutes.

5. RESULTS

In this section, we present the results of our user study. We start by comparing user performance with different search interfaces and follow with an extensive log analysis that describes how the interfaces were used. After that, we report the findings from our post and final questionnaires and report the participants' subjective opinions about these interfaces.

5.1 Performance Analysis

The main goal of this study was to compare user search performance for two types of search tasks (lookup and exploratory search) and with three different interfaces (with and without tag-based browsing support). To assess user performance, we examined search time and total number of interface actions [24] which are traditionally used in the study of search and browsing interfaces. Shorter search time and fewer actions should indicate a more efficient interface for image search.

While these two performance measures are known to be reliable, they do not allow us to clearly distinguish between several search conditions in the presence of many failed search attempts (i.e., cases where the subjects were not able to complete the task

and were interrupted). Due to the presence of this cap, the time and actions spent on failed attempts flattens the overall differences, making different conditions look more similar than they are in reality. To avoid this problem, we separately measured user performance only on successful tasks. Given comparable success rates (as we observed in the study), user performance on successful tasks enables us to more easily distinguish between several conditions.

Table 2 provides a summary of performance data for our three interfaces and two kinds of search tasks. The table separately reports performance data for all tasks (including failed tasks with capped time) and that for successfully completed search tasks. As the data shows, the main difference in user performance is observed between the task types: exploratory search, as expected, required much more time and actions than lookup tasks. To discover significant performance differences among interfaces, we applied 2 x 3 ANOVA (analysis of variance). The analysis was done separately for search time and for the total number of interface actions as functions of search task and interface. We also separately evaluated data for all cases and for successful cases only. The analysis of successful cases data revealed significant differences between tag cloud and baseline interfaces in terms of search time, $p < .001$, and total actions, $p < .001$, under exploratory search. Likewise, we found a significant difference in the total number of interface interactions between faceted tag cloud and baseline (search only), $p = .037$. No significant differences were discovered for "the data for all cases". We also have not discovered any significant differences between the two kinds of tag-based browsing interfaces under all conditions.

Effect of familiarity and difficulty on performance. Prior research on exploratory search interfaces indicated that the value of advanced information access interfaces might depend not only on the type of task (i.e., lookup vs. exploratory search) but also on task difficulty [13] and user familiarity with the search topic [17]. In the context of our study, we registered some reasonable differences in user familiarity on a Likert scale(1-5) with the topics of the three exploratory search tasks ($M=3.125$, $SE=.15056$, $SD=1.27751$). In other words, it was possible to divide users into two groups for each task - those familiar with the task topic and those not. Moreover, as the study indicated, the level of difficulty in the three exploratory search tasks was considerably different between the one relatively easy task and the two more complicated tasks. These variations allowed us to perform a separate analysis that explored the combined effect of the interface, task difficulty, and task familiarity in the context of exploratory search. We ran a 3 x 3 ANOVA as a function of task difficulty and interface, and also controlling for the two levels of familiarity previously mentioned. As shown in Table 3, the analysis revealed a significant difference between tag cloud and baseline interfaces in search time for those users not familiar with the topic and at a medium level of task difficulty when considering all cases, $p = .014$, and when only considering successful cases, $p = .009$. No other significant differences were found. These results

Difficulty	Measure	Baseline		Tag Cloud		Facet	
		All cases	Successful	All cases	Successful	All cases	Successful
Hard	cases	6	6	7	4	6	4
	Total Actions	67.33±5.94	67.33±5.94	64.43±8.48	51.5±10.9	55.5±6.59	51.75±9.71
	Search Time	603.5±23.05	603.5±23.05	557.43±40.42	507.5±61.4	562.67±38.47	537.0±55.14
Medium	cases	3	3	4	4	3	3
	Total Actions	38.33±5.24	38.33±5.24	35.25±3.09	35.25±3.09	57.33±6.89	57.33±6.89
	Search Time	**494.67±148.17***	**494.67±148.17****	**285.75±16.95**	**285.75±16.95**	382.00±22.11	382.00±22.11
Easy	cases	5	5	5	5	6	6
	Total Actions	25.0±4.24	25.0±4.24	23.6±2.5	23.6±2.5	19.0±1.53	19.0±1.53
	Search Time	308.8±49.31	308.8±49.31	227.8±23.77	227.8±23.77	212.23±25.45	212.33±25.45

Table 3: Descriptives (*mean±SE*) of total actions and search time, by interface at different difficulty levels, when people are not familiar with the topics and under exploratory search tasks (*=significant at p<0.05).

indicate that the tag cloud interface provides the most significant impact in cases where tasks are more complicated and users are less familiar with the topic of the task.

A similar analysis of the impact of difficulty and familiarity was performed for the lookup search context, but we did not find significant differences between interfaces. However, the impact of difficulty and familiarity might be determined by the relatively low level of user task familiarity in this context. Based on the average of the ratings in the lookup search task (M=1.3611, SE=.08463, SD=.71809), our subjects were not as familiar with the images as they were in the exploratory task of the user study. Only two of them reported that they were familiar with the images due to the fact they found an image during a prior search session.

5.2 Looking Deeper: Log Analysis

Although the previous analysis reveals performance differences between interfaces and tasks, it does not show how different usage profiles were created for each of the interfaces and tasks. To look for these differences we performed extensive user log analysis on users' answering specific questions.

The first question was : *How different were usage profiles for different interfaces and tasks?* To build the usage profile, we distinguished several different interface actions: (1) *Search* (inserting a query in the search box); (2) *Click Tag* (issuing a query by clicking on a tag); (3) *Add Tag* (expanding the query with a tag by clicking the "+" sign); (4) *Remove Term* (removing a term from the query by clicking the "x" sign); (5) *Show More Tags* (clicking the show more tags button to increase the number of tags in the tag cloud); (6) *Show Fewer Tags* (clicking the show fewer tags button to reduce the number of tags in the tag cloud); (7) *Show More Results* (clicking the show more results button to increase the number of images in the result list); (8) *Click Image* (clicking on an specific image) and (9) *Total Actions*.

Table 4 presents usage profiles for different interfaces and search tasks. The most visible (albeit trivial) result is that the action *Search* is used more frequently in the baseline interface, $p = .006$. While the *Search* action is also used more frequently in the tag cloud than in the faceted tag cloud interface, this difference is not significant. Another interesting discovery is that the use of *Show More Results* is significantly higher in the baseline interface than in the tag cloud, $p = .015$. The corresponding difference between the baseline and the faceted tag cloud is close to significant at the acceptable level of $p = .055$. Since the use of *Show More Results* is evidence that the top results returned by the last search or tag browsing action were not satisfactory, we can argue that tag browsing was more successful at providing relevant results. We can speculate that this result stems from the tag browsing interface's ability to provide a snapshot of the "aboutness" of the collection, guiding the user to a more successful choice of a search term or tag. In addition, we found

an intriguing difference between the tag cloud and the faceted tag cloud interfaces: the action *Add Tag*, which was used to narrow the results by adding tags to the query, was used significantly more frequently in the faceted interface than in the tag cloud interface, $p = .006$. The difference among interfaces in terms of the usage frequency of other actions (*Click Tag, Remove Term, Show More Tags, Show Less Tags*) was not significant. Table 4 also reports differences in the usage profile between lookup and exploratory search tasks. As we can see, the usage profile was considerably different for the two types of tasks. This emphasizes that lookup and exploratory search tasks are radically different from the user perspective. However, as users had different amounts of time available to complete lookup and exploratory search tasks, we compared percentages instead of the mean number of actions. However, to test for significant differences between these percentages, we run one chi-squared test per each action. As shown in Table 4, we found significant differences for the *Search* action, p < .001, the *Add Tag* action p < .001 , the *Remove Term* Action, p < .001 and the *Show More Results* action p < .001. These indicate that people rely more on the search box, the *Add Tag* and *Remove Term* functionality, and skimming through the paginated results list in lookup tasks than in exploratory search tasks. The significant difference for *Click Image* action, p < .001, shows that people rely more on clicking images in exploratory search than in lookup search.

The second question that we attempted to answer was : *Does tag grouping by semantic category affect the usage of these categories?* As outlined in Section 3.3, we classified tags in our tag corpus into the following five dimensions: Who, Where, When, What and Other. The users in the faceted interface case were able to see which category each tag belonged. However, the users of both the search and regular tag cloud interfaces used the same terms in search and browsing, although without knowing to which category the issued query term or the clicked tag belonged. One could hypothesize that the tag usage profile (i.e., frequencies of using tags in different categories) may be affected by making the categories visible. Table 5 shows the proportion of query terms in each classification category as used by the study participants; each row presents percentages for each type of interface. We analyzed the significant difference in these percentages by running two chi-square goodness of fit tests. Considering overall tag usage, (i.e., aggregating lookup and exploratory search tasks), as well as setting the expected percentages of the tag categories to match those in the faceted tag cloud interface, we found them significantly different than those in the baseline interface ($\chi^2(4,548) = 46.092$, p < .001), and the percentages in the tag cloud interface ($\chi^2(4,683) = 58.612$, p < .001). This data provides evidence that explicit tag categorization does impact user behavior.

	Interface			Task			
	Baseline	Tag Cloud	Facet	Lookup	%	Exploratory.	%
Search	9.24±.96**	5.61±.82	4.81±.63	3.89±.28	44.45%***	14.54±1.36	34.27%
Click Tag	.00	2.88±.46	2.92±.46	.94±.13	10.67%	4.92±.74	11.58%
Add Tag	.00	.61±.14	1.25±.2**	.72±.11	8.19%***	.33±.12	0.78%
Remove Term	.00	.95±.18	1.40±.25	.62±.1	7.08%***	1.26±.3	2.97%
Show More Tags	.00	.17±.07	.11±.05	.07±.02	0.74%	.18±.09	0.42%
Show Less Tags	.00	.02±.01	.00	.01±.0	0.05%	.01±.01	0.03%
Show More Results	1.78±.3**	.86±.18	1.01±.19	1.31±.17	14.90%***	.96±.2	2.25%
Click Image	6.66±1.1	5.59±.86	5.66±.87	1.22±.07	13.90%	20.22±.99	47.65%***
Total Actions	17.68±1.99	16.70±1.95	17.16±1.94	8.76±.52	100%	42.73±2.5	100%

Table 4: Summary of the *mean±SE* **of actions based on each task session in the baseline, tag cloud, faceted tag cloud interfaces and means/percentages of actions based on each task session and interface for lookup and exploratory search tasks (**=significant at p<0.01, ***=significant at p<0.001).**

	Lookup Task			Exploratory Task		
Question	Baseline	Tag Cloud	Facet	Baseline	Tag Cloud	Facet
1. Did the interface provide enough support for that task?	2.88±.24	3.92±.15*	4.04±.15**	2.88±.21	4.21±.13*	4.21±.13*
2. Were some of the interface features unnecessary for that task?	1.33±.12	1.83±.18*	1.92±.2*	1.33±.12	1.54±.13*	2.17±.23*
3. Were you confident in the system's ability to find relevant information on this topic?	-	-	-	3.25±.22	3.92±.2**	3.92±.18**
4. Did you find the tag cloud/faceted tag cloud helpful in finding relevant information?	-	3.79±.2	3.96±.18	-	4.13±.22	3.83±.21
5. Was it helpful to display the tags in different font sizes?	-	3.5±.23	3.54±.23	-	3.17±.27	3.38±.24
6. Was the + useful to add terms to the query?	-	3.77±.25	3.82±.27	-	4.05±.2	3.73±.27
7. Was the x helpful to remove terms from the query?	-	4.09±.23**	3.65±.26	-	4.04±.17	4.04±.18
8. Did you find it distracting that some terms in the faceted tag cloud were not classified correctly?	-	-	2.33±.26	-	-	2.43±.25

Table 6: Response (*mean±SE***) to post questionnaire items (*=significant at p<0.05 ; **=significant at p<0.01 , scale 1-5, higher values indicate more agreement with the statement).**

	Who	Where	When	What	Other
Baseline	9.9%	29.6%	11.7%	42.7%	6.2%
Tag Cloud	13%	28.8%	9.4%	43.2%	5.6%
Facet	16.2%	24%	18.9%	34.6%	6.3%

Table 5: Percentage of search actions in each type of semantic category by search interface.

5.3 Post-Task Questionnaires: Participants' Perceptions of the Interfaces

To better understand the participants' perceptions of each interface, we focus on analyzing user feedback about the different interfaces and their features. In the user study, the participants were asked to compute a post-task questionnaire after each of their search tasks was finished. By analyzing this questionnaire, we could assess the usefulness of each interface and see whether any significant differences could be found among the three interfaces and also between two search tasks (lookup vs. exploratory). Table 6 shows the average user rating for each question in the survey.

In Question 1 and 2, a 2 x 3 ANOVA was conducted on users' ratings in order to examine the effect of interface and search task. There is no significant interaction between interface and search task. For Question 1, a simple main effect analysis showed that there is a significant difference between the interfaces $F(2,46) = 30.113, p < .001$. Participants judged the support provided by the tag cloud interface significantly higher than that provided by the baseline, $p < .001$. They also rated the interface support of the faceted tag cloud interface significantly higher than that of the baseline, $p < .001$.

For Question 2, we also found a significant difference between the interfaces $F(1.406,32.332) = 11.097, p = .001$. Participants felt that the baseline interface had fewer "unnecessary features" than tag cloud, $p < .001$, and the faceted tag cloud, $p < .001$. However, the unnecessary features were a relatively trivial concern to the users of all three interfaces.

Question 3 specially asked about the exploratory search task : "How confident were the participants in the systems' ability to find relevant information". A 1-way ANOVA was used to test for performance differences among the three interfaces. We found a significant difference among the interfaces $F(2,46) = 5.412, p = .008$. The participants were significantly more confident in their ability to find relevant information with the tag cloud interface, $p = .015$, and the faceted tag cloud interface, $p = .037$, as compared to the baseline interface.

In Questions 4–7, we investigated the usefulness of various tag-related features. The 2 x 2 ANOVA as a function of interface (tag cloud and faceted tag cloud interfaces) and search task showed that the only significant difference within this group of questions "Was the x helpful to remove terms from the query", $F(1,20) = 6.450, p = .02$. The result indicated that users found this interface feature significantly more useful in the tag cloud than in the faceted tag cloud interface. No significant difference was found between the lookup and the exploratory search tasks in respect to Question 8.

5.4 Post Questionnaires: Participants' Interface Preferences and Comments

Another useful source of user feedback was a post questionnaire that was administered after each participant completed the entire study. This questionnaire offered us an opportunity to ask users for their opinions about three different interfaces. By this point in time, users had gained practical experience with both types of tasks and all three types of interfaces. As shown in Table 7, when asked a retrospective question "*Which one of the interfaces did you*

	Interface					
Question	Baseline	(freq.)	Tag Cloud	(freq.)	Facet	(freq.)
1. Which one of the interfaces did you like/prefer most?	4.2%	(1)	**54.2%**	**(13)**	41.7%	(10)
2. Which one of the interfaces would you prefer for lookup search?	4.2%	(1)	41.7%	(10)	**54.2%**	**(13)**
3. Which of the interfaces would you prefer for exploratory search?	-	(-)	41.%	(10)	**58.3%**	**(14)**
4. Which of the interfaces would you suggest the Carnegie Museum of Art?	-	(-)	41.%	(10)	**58.3%**	**(14)**

Table 7: Percentages and frequencies (=freq.) about final questionnaire items.

like/prefer most?", 54.2% (13) of subjects preferred the tag cloud interface, 41.7% (10) the faceted tag cloud interface, and only 4.2% (1) preferred the baseline search interface. This data correlates well with the users' actual performance on tasks. At the same time, user feedback differed on "forward looking" questions designed to assess user preferences in future situations (such as *"Which one of the interfaces would you prefer for lookup search?"*). For both tasks, the faceted tag cloud interface emerged as most preferred for future use. In addition, none of the users clearly preferred the baseline interface for exploratory search tasks. It is interesting that our subjects reported divergent results when they were asked about preferences in general and for each specific task.

Further, we found that 58.3% (14) of subjects favored the same interface for both past and future use while the other 41.7% (10) of subjects indicated a preference for a different interface when working on at least one type of tasks in the future. In particular, among the 10 subjects who reported changing preferences, one subject who favored the baseline (search only) interface in the prior tasks switched to the tag cloud interface for exploratory search tasks.

We believe that the most likely explanation for the difference in interface preferences between past and future tasks is the interface complexity. While the baseline search interface is very familiar to our subjects, both the tag-based browsing interfaces were rather novel. Moreover, while the subjects might have had at least some experience with using the traditional tag cloud interface, the faceted tag cloud was new to all of them. It is reasonable that a user's opinion of a more complex interface might be less favorable during their first attempts in using it. At the same time, armed with some experience, the users expressed stronger preferences for the use of more complex and powerful interfaces in the future. This might explain the difference in users' answers to the question *"which of the interfaces they would recommend for Carnegie Museum of Art"* (i.e., to professionals working with images): 58.3% (14) of our subjects recommended the faceted tag cloud interface while only 41.7% (10) of subjects recommended the tag cloud interface; no one recommended the baseline interface. This indicates that tag-based browsing interfaces, particularly the faceted tag cloud interface, were evaluated to be more powerful and more preferred for experienced users.

The data also showed that the main difference in users' perceptions is between the baseline and the two tag-based browsing interfaces. Tag-based interface was preferred almost unanimously for both previous and future situations. At the same time, the difference between the two tag-based browsing interfaces is much less pronounced: the traditional tag cloud interface appeared to be a bit simpler and more preferred during previous tasks (which correlates well with the performance data), while the faceted tag cloud was perceived as a bit more powerful and preferred for future tasks.

Further support for this assessment of users' subjective preferences across the three interfaces is provided by analyzing their explicit rating for each interface (see Table 8). On a Likert scale(1-5), the average rating for the baseline (search only) interface was 2.75, 4.17 for the tag cloud interface and 4.04 for faceted tag cloud interface. From these statistics, we can see that the baseline interface

was rated significantly lower than the tag cloud interface, $p = .002$, and the faceted tag cloud interface, $p < .001$. However, there is no significant difference between the tag cloud and the faceted tag cloud interfaces.

5.5 Looking Deeper: Comment Analysis

To explain differences in users' perceptions of the different interfaces and their features, we examined verbatim comments provided in the post questionnaire. Below, these comments are grouped by the type of the interface preferred by the user:

5.5.1 Preferred Baseline (Search Only) Interface

According to the 24 participants, only 1 subject preferred the baseline search interface. The reason why the user chose this type of interface favorite was the following:

"I liked the search box most, because everything else distracted me. For me it is not necessary to have tags, because I have everything in my mind!" – P20

This subject identified that the simplest interface is the best as it did not distract by adding elements to the interface.

5.5.2 Preferred Tag Cloud Interface

Thirteen subjects preferred the tag cloud interface. Based on the feedback from the interview and open-ended question on why they preferred a particular interface, our subjects attributed their preference for the tag cloud interface to it being more effective than the baseline interface. They also felt that it was easier to use than the faceted tag cloud interface.

"The tag cloud provided more information than search only and was less complex than the facet search interface" – P4

"I think the tag cloud interface was very helpful for exploratory search tasks and the faceted tags are a bit harder because I have to figure out what facet to look at" – P3

"I like tag cloud because it gives me new ideas and it is easier to use" – P21

Sometimes, the poor categorization of tags in the faceted tag cloud interface accounted for why our subjects preferred the non-faceted interface. They either thought the category of the facet was of low quality or irrelevant to the task.

"The facet did not seem to identify tags well" – P1

"I would recommend the faceted interface only if tags are rich enough and categorized correctly, otherwise tag cloud is better" – P8

"I think the categorization was not good, it was not relevant to the task" – P19

Some of the subjects preferred the tag cloud interface because they thought that the different font sizes in the tag clouds made more sense than the categorizing tags. Furthermore, some of them didn't pay attention to the category at all.

Question	Rating
1. Overall how would you rate the Search interface?	2.75±.22
2. Overall how would you rate the Tag Cloud interface?	4.17±.13*
3. Overall how would you rate the Faceted Tag Cloud interface?	4.04±.15*

Table 8: Response (*mean±SE*) to final questionnaire items (*=significant at p<0.05; higher values indicate more agreement with the statement).

"I did not look at the facets at all as I just looked at the terms" – P12

"Font size attracted my attention more than the facets" – P18

"The font size helped me to get most relevant information quickly" – P24

5.5.3 Preferred Faceted Tag Cloud Interface

Overall, we had 10 subjects who preferred the faceted tag cloud interface. The reason for this preference can be categorized into three aspects. First, they thought that the faceted tag cloud interface provided them with more functionality.

"I like faceted tag cloud because the interface provided me with the most functionality" – P6

"For difficult search task the facet is useful and for easy tasks you can just ignore the facet feature" – P7

"The Faceted tag cloud interface seems to be a smarter interface" – P13

Second, our subjects opined that the faceted tag cloud interface organized tags in more meaningful ways than the tag cloud interface.

"I prefer faceted tag cloud interface because it shows more tags in an organized way, so I could find more information faster" – P2

"It is easy to find the tags that I needed in faceted tag cloud" – P11

"I like faceted tag cloud interface, because the interface is clearer and I always know where to find the tag" – P15

The third aspect is that some of our subjects thought that the faceted tag cloud suggested more keywords to them. The interface also inspired them to think of additional relevant key terms.

"I like the faceted tag cloud because it suggest more query options than the tag cloud" – P5

"The faceted tag cloud made me think of more useful keywords than the tag cloud" – P21

6. RELATED WORK

Tagging systems such as Delicious, Flickr, and CiteULike have emerged as one of the most popular technologies of the modern Web era. Tagging behavior has been widely studied with regards to either the structure of tagging systems [15, 31], or qualitative insights about tagging behaviors across small collections [3, 12, 28]. The collective tagging behavior of users seems to offer a strong platform for summarizing and indicating content popularity to improve Web search [1].

In the computer-supported cooperative work (CSCW) domain, researchers have noted that tags could be utilized to offer search signals to others in the community. Several ranking algorithms have been investigated to improve search performance within the tagging space, such as SocialSimilarityRank [4], and FolkRank [21]. In the HCI community, Furnas et al. discovered the similarities in the cognitive processes between generation of search keywords and tags [14]. Kammerer et al. investigated how to apply relevance feedback about tags to indicate users' interests in various topics as well as to enable rapid exploration of the topic space [22]. Although CSCW and HCI both have provided different approaches to improve Web search, the focus of those studies was only on optimizing search ranking algorithms.

To understand how people use tags in reality and to what extent tag-based browsing constructs support users during their information seeking processes, we are interested in exploring the usage and efficiency of tag-based search interfaces. From an interface point of view, several interfaces have been explored. While tags are used to discover content in a traditional keyword-based search context, the innovative usage of social tags also supports browsing-based access to information. For instance, in [30], the authors investigated a visualization technique, a tag cloud, to display tags to support search performance. They applied various dimensions to construct tag clouds for use in information retrieval usage. They explored parameters of constructing tag cloud layouts including font size, quadrant and proximity-to-largest-word during a presentation period or an interpretative period. The study showed that the list ordered by frequency is better for categorizing.

Another tag-based browsing construct is clustered tag clouds [39], which utilizes SOMs for visualization. The proposed approach not only facilitates the discovery of relationships between tags and corresponding content, but also improves tag-based navigation by clustering relevant tags. A similar idea, classified tag clouds, studied by Yahoo! Labs [32] classified tags by utilizing facets such as Wordnet. Their approach enabled Flickr photo browsing through different facets. Their analysis showed that users could effectively deploy query recommendations to explore large sets of images annotated with tags. Other studies [19, 34] explored another advanced tag construct, tag hierarchy, for tag-based navigation. By utilizing a decentralized search framework [34], the authors found that there are significant differences among different approaches to tag hierarchy construction in terms of success rate and average path length.

Since our primary goal intent in this paper is to explore whether the tag-based browsing constructs could provide any additional value to tag-based search, we apply the most popular interface layout, a tag cloud, as our basic tag interface and compare it to a traditional search box interface. Furthermore, according to our previous study [26] on image search, where we discovered that facets help users in exploring a large collection of images, we also investigate a faceted tag cloud interface in this study [32].

A similar study conducted by Sinclair and Cardew-Hall investigated the usefulness of tag clouds in terms of information seeking by analyzing the usage of tag clouds in a traditional search interface [33]. They found that subjects prefer tag clouds when the search task is more general, but favor issuing search queries, when more specific information is needed. Contrary to their study, our work is based on the domain of images where typically no descriptive content (such as page-text or abstract information) is given. Furthermore, we study three separate tag-based interfaces to discover the differences between a traditional search interface, a search interface enriched with tag clouds, and search interface extended with faceted tag clouds. In this setting, we can clearly identify *how people use* each interface and *how they perform*. To the best of our knowledge, this is the first work that compares multiple tag-based search interfaces.

7. DISCUSSION AND CONCLUSIONS

The main goal of the presented study was to perform a comparative user evaluation of tag-based browsing interfaces against simple search-based access to tagged collections. We compared user performance and feedback for three types of tag-based information access interfaces in the context of two recognized types of search tasks – lookup search and exploratory search. As expected, we obtained empirical evidence that the two tag-based browsing interfaces were superior to the baseline (search only) interface. At the same time, the analysis of objective data (performance and action profile) and of subjective data (questionnaires) produced slightly different results.

From the users' perspective, both tag-based browsing interfaces were perceived to be superior to the baseline. The users indicated that these interfaces provided significantly enhanced support for both types of user tasks and reported significantly higher levels of confidence that relevant information would be found. They also ranked both tag-based browsing interfaces significantly higher "overall" than the baseline interface.

From the performance and log analysis, significant differences were found for the traditional tag cloud interface when used in the exploratory search context. The tag cloud interface was found to be significantly more efficient in terms of both time and actions than the baseline interface. We also found that the tag cloud provided the most significant impact upon more difficult tasks and when the user was less familiar with the core topic of the task. A deeper analysis of user actions revealed another argument in favor of the tag cloud interface - with this interface, the "show more results" action was used significantly less often than in the baseline interface. This indicated that, with the tag cloud, the users were more likely to receive useful results at the top of the ranked list. None of these differences appeared to be significant for the faceted tag cloud; its objective performance was inferior to the performance of the traditional tag cloud. In addition, neither objective nor subjective data revealed any significant differences between the traditional tag cloud and the more advanced faceted tag cloud.

Why was the more advanced tag-based browsing interface less effective than the simpler tag-based browsing interface? Why was the faceted tag interface not a significant improvement over the baseline (search only) interface from a performance aspect? The post-session questionnaire provided some answers to these questions. This questionnaire asked users to select their "preferred" interface in light of two aspects : looking at performance in the past and looking forward to potential future uses of these interfaces. While the traditional tag cloud interface was preferred in previous tasks (which correlated with the objective performance data), the faceted tag cloud interface was the most popular for future use. It was also the top choice to be recommended to museum professionals. This was a strong indication that the faceted tag cloud interface was perceived as more powerful in the long run, but too difficult to use at first. This speculation is further confirmed by users' comments. In these comments, subjects stressed several aspects in which the faceted tag cloud interface was superior to the traditional cloud, yet indicated that it was harder to use at first. This data revealed that the faceted tag cloud interface should be assessed in a longer-term study, which would allow users to gain experience and become more proficient in operating with more sophisticated interfaces. We plan to explore this hypothesis in our future studies.

We also should acknowledge that the most noticeable differences observed in the study were not between the interfaces, but between the lookup and exploratory search tasks. Our data further confirmed that these two kinds of tasks are radically different. Exploratory search tasks are much harder; they consume more time and require more actions than lookup search tasks. Moreover, the very structure of user activities was very different between exploratory and lookup search. The occurrence of traditional search decreased considerably perhaps because it was much harder to find right keywords for the query. In contrast, almost 50% of user time in exploratory search context was spent on examining specific documents that were important to understand the domain and identify the most useful terms. These results correlate well with the previous research on exploratory search.

Finally, we should acknowledge a few limitations of our study. First, we focused on the query-to-image part of tag-based information access since it was the most different aspect among the three interfaces. The explicit presence of tags can also also enhance image-to-image navigation and further increase the value of tag-based browsing. Additional studies are required to determine the value of tags in this context. In addition, by the nature of our studies, we were unable to investigate one potential weakness of tag-based browsing in respect to classic search. All tag-based browsing interfaces require some considerable screen space for a tag cloud or other tag browsing artifact. This might reduce the space needed to show search results and decrease the effectiveness of tag-based browsing. In our studies, this effect was minimal: the study was performed on a regular desktop screen and search results were shown as thumbnails, which occupied relatively little space. We believe that, in this context, tag-based browsing interfaces were able to present a sufficient number of results despite the decreased presentation space. As the results shows, the Show More Results action was called upon significantly less frequently for the tag cloud. However, this might be of concern for those cases of mobile search with limited screen space as well as for different kinds of objects that require more space in the results presentation area. This is one of the reasons that we hesitate to generalize the observed results on tag-based information access to non-image resources. This is another aspect that requires additional investigation. We hope to explore some of these issues in our future work.

8. ACKNOWLEDGMENTS

This work is mainly supported by grants from the BMVIT – the Federal Ministry for Transport, Innovation and Technology (grant no. 829590) and the Marshalplan Funding Agency, to the first author. Part of this work is also supported by CONICYT – the National Commission of Scientific and Technological Research, government of the Republic of Chile, to the third author and NSF grant DUE-0840597 to the last author. The authors wish to thank the Carnegie Museum of Art for use of the Teenie Harris image collection.

9. REFERENCES

[1] P. , G. Koutrika, and H. Garcia-Molina. Can social bookmarking improve web search? *Proc. of the international conference on Web search and web data mining*, pages 195–206, 2008.

[2] A. Ammari and V. Zharkova. Combining tag cloud learning with svm classification to achieve intelligent search for relevant blog articles. In *In Proceedings of the 1st International Workshop on Mining Social Media*, 2009.

[3] L. B. Baltussen. *Barbarians versus gatekeepers ? Tagging as a way of defining the ememrgent living archive paradigm*. PhD thesis, 2010.

[4] S. Bao, G. Xue, X. Wu, Y. Yu, B. Fei, and Z. Su. Optimizing web search using social annotations. In *Proceedings of the 16th international conference on World Wide Web - WWW '07*, page 501, New York, New York, USA, May 2007. ACM Press.

[5] S. Bateman, C. Gutwin, and M. Nacenta. Seeing things in the clouds: the effect of visual features on tag cloud selections. *Proc. of the nineteenth ACM conference on Hypertext and hypermedia*, pages 193–202, 2008.

[6] K. Bischoff, C. S. Firan, C. Kadar, W. Nejdl, and R. Paiu. Automatically identifying tag types. In *Proceedings of the 5th International Conference on Advanced Data Mining and Applications*, ADMA '09, pages 31–42, Berlin, Heidelberg, 2009. Springer-Verlag.

[7] K. Bischoff, C. S. Firan, W. Nejdl, and R. Paiu. Can all tags be used for search? In *Proceedings of the 17th ACM conference on Information and knowledge management*, CIKM '08, pages 193–202, New York, NY, USA, 2008. ACM.

[8] D. Böhnstedt, L. Lehmann, C. Rensing, and R. Steinmetz. Automatic identification of tag types in a resource-based learning scenario. In *Proceedings of the 6th European conference on Technology enhanced learning: towards ubiquitous learning*, EC-TEL'11, pages 57–70, Berlin, Heidelberg, 2011. Springer-Verlag.

[9] K. Byström and K. Järvelin. Task complexity affects information seeking and use. *Inf. Process. Manage.*, 31:191–213, March 1995.

[10] K. Candan, L. Di Caro, and M. Sapino. Creating tag hierarchies for effective navigation in social media. *SSM '08: Proc. of the 2008 ACM workshop on Search in social media*, pages 75–82, 2008.

[11] I. Cantador, I. Konstas, and J. M. Jose. Categorising social tags to improve folksonomy-based recommendations. *Web Semantics: Science, Services and Agents on the World Wide Web*, 9(1), 2011.

[12] E. H. Chi and T. Mytkowicz. Understanding the efficiency of social tagging systems using information theory. In *HT '08: Proceedings of the nineteenth ACM conference on Hypertext and hypermedia*, pages 81–88, New York, NY, USA, 2008. ACM.

[13] A. Diriye, A. Blandford, and A. Tombros. When is system support effective? In *Proceedings of the third symposium on Information interaction in context*, IIiX '10, pages 55–64, New York, NY, USA, 2010. ACM.

[14] G. W. Furnas, C. Fake, L. von Ahn, J. Schachter, S. Golder, K. Fox, M. Davis, C. Marlow, and M. Naaman. *Why do tagging systems work?* ACM Press, New York, New York, USA, Apr. 2006.

[15] S. A. Golder and B. A. Huberman. The structure of collaborative tagging systems. *Journal of Information Science*, 32(2):198–208, 2006.

[16] Y. Hassan-Montero and V. Herrero-Solana. Improving tag-clouds as visual information retrieval interfaces. In *InScit2006: International Conference on Multidisciplinary Information Sciences and Technologies*, 2006.

[17] M. A. Hearst. *Search User Interfaces*. Cambridge University Press, 1 edition, 2009.

[18] M. A. Hearst and D. Rosner. Tag clouds: Data analysis tool or social signaller? In *Proc. of the Proceedings of the 41st Annual Hawaii International Conference on System Sciences*, HICSS '08, Washington, DC, USA, 2008. IEEE Computer Society.

[19] D. Helic and M. Strohmaier. Building directories for social tagging systems. In *Proceedings of the 20th ACM international conference on Information and knowledge management*, CIKM '11, pages 525–534, New York, NY, USA, 2011. ACM.

[20] D. Helic, C. Trattner, M. Strohmaier, and K. Andrews. On the navigability of social tagging systems. In *Proc. of 2010 IEEE International Conference on Social Computing*, pages 161–168, Los Alamitos, CA, USA, 2010. IEEE Computer Society.

[21] A. Hotho, R. J, C. Schmitz, and G. Stumme. Information Retrieval in Folksonomies : Search and Ranking. *Data Engineering*, 4011:411–426, 2006.

[22] Y. Kammerer, R. Nairn, P. Pirolli, and E. H. Chi. Signpost from the masses: learning effects in an exploratory social tag search browser. In *Proceedings of the 27th international conference on Human factors in computing systems*, CHI '09, pages 625–634, New York, NY, USA, 2009. ACM.

[23] O. Kaser and D. Lemire. Tag-Cloud Drawing: Algorithms for Cloud Visualization. *Proc. of Tagging and Metadata for Social Information Organization (WWW 2007)*, 2007.

[24] D. Kelly. Methods for evaluating interactive information retrieval systems with users. *Found. Trends Inf. Retr.*, 3:1–224, January 2009.

[25] K. Knautz, S. Soubusta, and W. G. Stock. Tag clusters as information retrieval interfaces. In *Proceedings of the 2010 43rd Hawaii International Conference on System Sciences*, HICSS '10, pages 1–10, Washington, DC, USA, 2010. IEEE Computer Society.

[26] Y. Lin, J.-W. Ahn, P. Brusilovsky, D. He, and W. Real. Imagesieve: Exploratory search of museum archives with named entity-based faceted browsing. *Proceedings of the American Society for Information Science and Technology*, 47(1):1–10, Nov. 2010.

[27] G. Marchionini. Exploratory search: from finding to understanding. *Commun. ACM*, 49:41–46, April 2006.

[28] J. Oomen, L. B. Baltussen, Sander Limonard, M. Brinkerink, A. van Ees, L. Aroyo, J. Vervaart, K. Afsar, and Riste Gligoro. Emerging Practices in the Cultural Heritage Domain - Social Tagging of Audiovisual Heritage. In *Web Science10:Extending the Frontiers of Society On-Line*, Raleigh, NC, USA., 2010.

[29] S. Overell, B. Sigurbjörnsson, and R. van Zwol. Classifying tags using open content resources. In *Proceedings of the Second ACM International Conference on Web Search and Data Mining*, WSDM '09, pages 64–73, New York, NY, USA, 2009. ACM.

[30] A. W. Rivadeneira, D. M. Gruen, M. J. Muller, and D. R. Millen. Getting our head in the clouds: toward evaluation studies of tagclouds. In *Proceedings of the SIGCHI conference on Human factors in computing systems*, CHI '07, pages 995–998, New York, NY, USA, 2007. ACM.

[31] S. Sen, S. K. Lam, A. M. Rashid, D. Cosley, D. Frankowski, J. Osterhouse, F. M. Harper, and J. Riedl. tagging, communities, vocabulary, evolution. In *Proceedings of the 2006 20th anniversary conference on Computer supported cooperative work CSCW 06*, volume 4 of *CSCW '06*, pages 181–190. ACM, ACM Press, 2006.

[32] B. Sigurbjörnsson and R. van Zwol. Tagexplorer: Faceted browsing of flickr photos. In *Technical Report, Yahoo! Research*, 2010.

[33] J. Sinclair and M. Cardew-Hall. The folksonomy tag cloud: when is it useful? *J. Inf. Sci.*, 34:15–29, February 2008.

[34] M. Strohmaier, D. Helic, D. Benz, C. Körner, and R. Kern. Evaluation of folksonomy induction algorithms. *ACM Trans. Intell. Syst. Technol.*, 2012.

[35] C. Trattner, C. Körner, and D. Helic. Enhancing the navigability of social tagging systems with tag taxonomies. In *Proceedings of the 11th International Conference on Knowledge Management and Knowledge Technologies*, i-KNOW '11, pages 18:1–18:8, New York, NY, USA, 2011. ACM.

[36] P. Vakkari, M. Pennanen, and S. Serola. Changes of search terms and tactics while writing a research proposal a longitudinal case study. *Inf. Process. Manage.*, 39:445–463, May 2003.

[37] P. Venetis, G. Koutrika, and H. Garcia-Molina. On the selection of tags for tag clouds. In *Proceedings of the fourth ACM international conference on Web search and data mining*, WSDM '11, pages 835–844, New York, NY, USA, 2011. ACM.

[38] C. Wartena. Automatic classification of social tags. In *Proceedings of the 14th European conference on Research and advanced technology for digital libraries*, ECDL'10, pages 176–183, Berlin, Heidelberg, 2010. Springer-Verlag.

[39] A. Zubiaga, A. P. García-Plaza, V. Fresno, and R. Martínez. Content-based clustering for tag cloud visualization. In *Proceedings of the 2009 International Conference on Advances in Social Network Analysis and Mining*, pages 316–319, Washington, DC, USA, 2009. IEEE Computer Society.

Understanding Factors that Affect Response Rates in Twitter

Giovanni Comarela
Federal University of Minas Gerais, Brazil
giovannicomarela@dcc.ufmg.br

Virgilio Almeida
Federal University of Minas Gerais, Brazil
virgilio@dcc.ufmg.br

Mark Crovella
Boston University, USA
crovella@cs.bu.edu

Fabricio Benevenuto
Federal University of Ouro Preto, Brazil
fabricio@dcc.ufmg.br

ABSTRACT

In information networks where users send messages to one another, the issue of information overload naturally arises: which are the most important messages? In this paper we study the problem of understanding the importance of messages in Twitter. We approach this problem in two stages. First, we perform an extensive characterization of a very large Twitter dataset which includes all users, social relations, and messages posted from the beginning of the service up to August 2009. We show evidence that information overload is present: users sometimes have to search through hundreds of messages to find those that are interesting to reply or retweet. We then identify factors that influence user response or retweet probability: previous responses to the same tweeter, the tweeter's sending rate, the age and some basic text elements of the tweet. In our second stage, we show that some of these factors can be used to improve the presentation order of tweets to the user. First, by inspecting user activity over time, we construct a simple on-off model of user behavior that allows us to infer when a user is actively using Twitter. Then, we explore two methods from machine learning for ranking tweets: a Naive Bayes predictor and a Support Vector Machine classifier. We show that it is possible to reorder tweets to increase the fraction of replied or retweeted messages appearing in the first p positions of the list by as much as 50-60%.

Categories and Subject Descriptors

J.4 [**Computer Applications**]: Social and behavioral sciences Miscellaneous; H.3.5 [**Online Information Services**]: Web-based services

General Terms

Human Factors, Measurement

Keywords

Social Networks, Twitter, timeline

1. INTRODUCTION

Twitter has become a vast network, hosting an immense flow of information passing among its users. According to [1], Twitter users now send more than 140 million messages (*tweets*) per day, meaning that Twitter carries a billion messages every 8 days. As a consequence, a flood of information swamps Twitter users. For instance, according to [7], active users can easily receive more than 1000 tweets a day. It is difficult or impossible for a user to keep up with this amount of tweets. However, many tweets are irrelevant, superfluous, or too difficult to understand without context. For example, the recent study presented in [2] estimates that only 36% of the Twitter's feed are worth reading. Clearly, users can benefit from tools that help them sort the "wheat from the chaff."

To do so, a starting point is to understand how users consume messages and interact with other users in the network. Research on Twitter is newer than on e-mail and Web so we know less about the behavior of users in this information network. A fundamental set of questions then is the following: how do users manage the incoming flood of messages in Twitter? How do users value incoming messages, as evidenced by their generation of message responses (*replies* and *retweets*)? What factors affect whether users reply to or retweet messages? Answers to these questions can help us reason about management strategies to distinguish important or interesting messages.

Our approach to answering these questions begins with an extensive characterization of the behavior of Twitter users. To understand user behavior, we looked at a very large dataset, consisting of all tweets exchanged among Twitter users over more than two years. Our focus is on understanding and improving the timeline of tweets presented to the user. When users log in to Twitter, they typically see a chronological stream of tweets as sent by all of their sources. Users interact with this tweet-stream by replying to tweets, or resending tweets (retweeting). The tweets a user reply to or retweet thus can provide indication of a sense of importance or *interestingness* the user ascribes to the specific tweet. Hence we reconstructed the timeline for a numbers of subsets of users and examined questions related to the reply and retweet behavior of users.

Our first set of findings consists of characterizations of reply and retweet behavior. From the outset it is clear that information overload is a common experience of Twitter users; we show that users sometimes have to search through hundreds of messages to find those that are important. We then identify features that influence user response or retweet probability: previous responses to the same tweeter, the tweeter's sending rate, the age of the tweet, the size of the text message and the presence of *mentions, hash-*

tags or *URLs*. We show that these features are correlated with the likelihood that a user will reply to or retweet a tweet.

These findings not only unveil unique aspects of user behavior and their interactions in Twitter, but they also motivate us to propose an approach to improve a user's interaction with Twitter by reordering the presentation of tweets in a user's timeline. This prompts our second set of findings: by inspecting user activity over time, we construct a simple on-off model of user behavior that allows us to infer when a user is actively using Twitter. Then we investigate the feasibility of applying machine learning methods to rank tweets in a user's timeline in a manner that brings the most important tweets to the top of the timeline. We take two different approaches: a Naive Bayes predictor that combines the empirically observed conditional response probabilities, and a Support Vector Machine classifier. These methods do not make use of the contents of tweets, and so are lightweight enough for implementation in Twitter clients. Using trace-driven simulation we show that employing only three content-independent features, it is possible to reorder tweets to increase the fraction of replied or retweeted messages appearing in the first p positions of the list by as much as 50-60%. These results indicate that our methodology can originate an interesting alternative interface to present tweets instead of the usual reverse chronological order.

The remaining of this work is organized as follows. Section 2 describes related work. In Section 3 we present our dataset. Section 4 discusses characteristics associated with response rates in Twitter. In Section 5 we show machine learning based approaches to reorder the common Twitter *timeline*, and Section 6 provides an evaluation of these algorithms. Finally, Section 7 summarizes the paper and presents the main findings of this work.

2. RELATED WORK

User behavior characterization is fundamental to the understanding and engineering of efficient information networks. Next, we survey studies that are focused on analyzing user characteristics and interactions among users.

There has been a number of studies that provide an overview of Twitter and its users. In [19], the authors present a detailed characterization of Twitter. They gathered three datasets (covering nearly 100,000 users) and identified distinct classes of Twitter users and their behaviors, geographic growth patterns and current size of the network. The work in [17] studies linked structures of social networks and argue the structures do not reveal actual interactions among people. Scarcity of attention and the daily rhythms of life and work drive interaction patterns in social and information networks. This study of social interactions within Twitter reveals that the driver of usage is different from the declared network of friends (i.e., followings). The authors of [18] present a characterization of the Twitter phenomena and study topological and geographical properties of the information network. They show people use messages to talk about their daily activities and to seek or share information. They also analyze user interactions at a community level.

Several authors present data-driven analysis and measured patterns of communications as well as information spreading across social network links. Kwak *et al.* [20] provides an in-depth characterization of different aspects of Twitter. In particular, they found a non-power-law for follower distribution, a short effective diameter, and low reciprocity. These characteristics contrast with known characteristics of human social networks. A prominent model of human behavior related to the amount of information one can process was presented in [5]. Their approach is based on a queuing model with a priority discipline and assumes that every individual prioritizes different activities and executes the corresponding task with the highest priority. With this assumption, this model shows that the waiting time of tasks follows a power-law distribution. In [11] the authors study the reasons that make a conversation to be interesting or what prompts a user to participate in the discussion on a social network. They conjecture that people participate in conversations when they find the conversation theme interesting or when they see comments by people they know or when they observe an engaging dialogue between two or more people. The reference then introduces the concept of *interestingness*. They also propose a mathematical framework to measure the *interestingness* of textual conversations about a certain video on YouTube. They collect commentaries on YouTube videos and show that their method to measure *interestingness* of a conversation provides a better assessment than traditional methods, based on the number of comments, number of new participants, etc.

Bernstein *et al.* [7] presents an approach to group tweets, by identifying a topic a tweet belongs to. Finally, there has been recent efforts on identifying influential users in Twitter [4, 9, 25]. One of the possible use of these efforts is to sort upcoming tweets according to sender's influence score. However, current influence metrics are susceptible to be fooled by spammers [6], bots [8] and social capitalists [14] and do not capture the temporal dynamics of Twitter. One important observation from [9] is that highly influential users are not necessarily the most followed users, meaning that aspects of the Twitter topology are not sufficient to capture one's influence. Regarding the attention that users pay in their Twitter's timeline, a recent effort [13] used eye-tracking techniques to measured which tweets has more user's attention. Among their findings, they show evidence that reply patterns reflect attention interest. They also show that only tweets above a relatively high threshold in terms of attention and interest are considered for retweets.

Compared to this body of work, our work take different directions as our interest is mainly on the study of user interactions in Twitter. We also are interested at finding better mechanisms to organize incoming streams of tweets. To this end, we measure and model user behavior aiming at capturing how interesting a tweet can be for a user and how to use these informations in a simple process in order to reorganize timelines. To keep the procedure simple, we decided do not look at the tweet's content because, in general, topic identification is CPU intensive (not desirable for handheld devices). Moreover, studies of interactions on Twitter are generally more focused on retweets, for example [24], and here we also present an extensive study for replies, which are an important type of interaction, but less explored in the literature.

3. TWITTER DATASET

Our dataset contains extensive data from a previous measurement study that included a complete snapshot of the Twitter network and the complete history of tweets posted by all users from 2006 to July 2009 [9]. Our dataset contains 54,981,152 user accounts connected to each other by 1,963,263,821 social links. Our dataset also contains all tweets ever posted by the collected users, which consists of 1,755,925,520 tweets. For detailed characteristics of this dataset we refer the user to [9, 23].

This dataset is very suitable for the purpose on this work as it contains all tweets exchanged among all users over a long period of time as well as the social links among users. From the tweets in our dataset we can identify two special types of messages that a user can post: *replies* and *retweets*. A *reply* occurs when a user replies other tweet posted by other user. A *retweet* refers to the practice of copying a tweet of someone and post it with a personal comment (optional). In our dataset each *reply* has the IDs of the tweet and

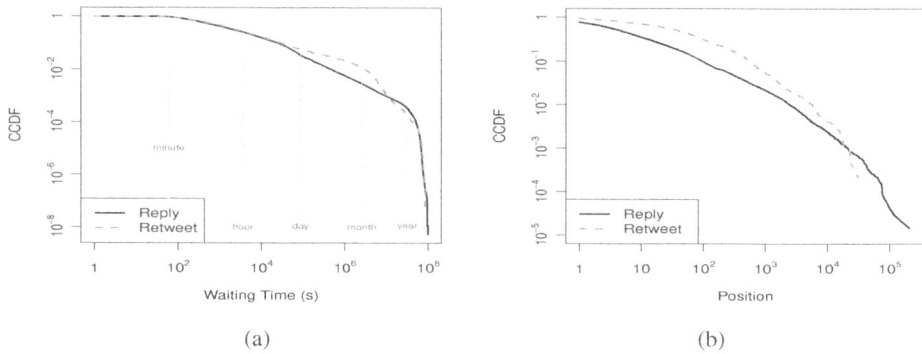

Figure 1: (a) Waiting time and (b) timeline position distributions for replies and retweets.

user that were replied. In the case of *retweets*, on the other hand, we do not have such information, since this type of message was done through a user's convention. In this convention the users used the pattern `RT @user_name` with the content of the original message plus a comment, where `user_name` is a name that is uniquely assigned to each Twitter user. We used this information to identify the origin (user and tweet) of each *retweet* in the dataset. Moreover, a tweet can have two kinds of elements embedded: *mentions* and *hashtags*. A *mention* is a citation of another user and a *hashtag* is a way to mark keywords in a tweet. These elements are respectively used through the patterns `@user_name` and `#keyword`.

4. CHARACTERIZING INTERACTIONS

Our first set of results consists of a characterization study of the behavior of Twitter users. This section presents those results as a foundation for our proposed timeline ordering algorithms, which are presented later.

4.1 Notation and sampling setup

We start by introducing notations and definitions. We use U to denote the set of all Twitter users in the dataset. For each $i \in U$, the total of messages sent by i is T_i, and the j-th message sent by i is $m_{j,i}$. We denote by $M_i = [m_{1,i}, \ldots, m_{T_i,i}]$ the list of all messages posted by i in chronological order, and $M_V = \bigcup_{j \in V} M_j$ (also in chronological order) the list of all messages sent by the set of users V. The set of all users followed by user i is denoted Out_i, and the set of all users followed by any user in set $V \subset U$ is $Out_V = \bigcup_{j \in V} Out_j$. For any user i, the list of messages sent by users in Out_i, presented in reverse chronological order, is user i's timeline, denoted by TL_i.

Many of our characterizations are based on user's timelines. Unfortunately it was not feasible to construct timelines for all users in the dataset (the dataset size has almost 1 TB). Instead we took random samples from U, and built timelines for those users.

Sampling users gave us another advantage. Because the level of user activity varies dramatically from user to user, it is important to consider users with different activity levels separately. Thus, we took four samples, each one comprising 2000 users. These samples, denoted by S_1, S_2, S_3 and S_4 were sampled at random from those users that posted more than 2, 10, 100, and 1000 messages respectively. As it will be seen below, users belonging to different sets often show quite different characteristics. When a result is not associated with one of those specific samples, it refers to the entire dataset (all users in U).

After this step we extracted from the dataset the users that are

followed by users in each of the four samples (Out_{S_k}) as well as their tweets ($M_{Out_{S_k}}$). In this way we were able to build all timelines, TL_i, $\forall\, i \in S_k$. Finally, we also extracted the message sets M_{S_k} from the data for $k = 1, \ldots, 4$.

4.2 Waiting Times

We start our characterization study by looking at evidence that Twitter users experience information overload. We do so by examining the duration between when a tweet arrives in the user's timeline and when it is replied to or retweeted.

Figure 1(a) shows the Complementary Cumulative Distribution Function (CCDF) for the time that a tweet waits to be replied or retweeted, across all replies and retweets in the dataset. We can see that almost all messages wait more than 100 seconds until they are replied or retweeted and that approximately 90% can wait up to 1000 seconds. Figure 1(b) shows the distribution of the position in the user's timeline of replies and retweets for sample S_1. This figure shows that sometimes users must search far back in their timeline to find a tweet that they wish to retweet or reply to. For example, 10% of the retweets are made to tweets that are more than 800 positions back in the user's timeline.

This motivates efforts to change the presentation order of the user's tweets in such way that messages will wait less time before being replied or retweeted.

Figure 1(a) shows other important points. First, it shows that after one day, the behavior of waiting times for replies and retweets becomes different. This shows that message replies tend to occur more quickly than retweets — suggesting that users are more likely to share old information than to reply to old messages. This is confirmed by Figure 1(b) which shows that users do not search as far back in their timelines for tweets to reply to as they do for retweets. Second, this figure suggests a general change in user behavior around the timescale of one day. Finally, we can note that both curves from Figure 1(a) drop off sharply near 10^8 seconds. This corresponds to the age of the Twitter system at the time that the dataset was collected.

4.3 Tweet Age

Having motivated a search for better ordering of tweets, we turn to features that may help in assessing their importance. The first feature we consider is the age of a tweet. In particular, we ask: *are newer messages more likely to be replied or retweeted?*

To answer this question we return to the question of where in the user's timeline each replied (retweeted) message was found. In other words, for $j = 1, \ldots, T_i$, if $m_{j,i}$ is a reply (retweet) we looked for the message it replies to (retweets) in TL_i. We do this

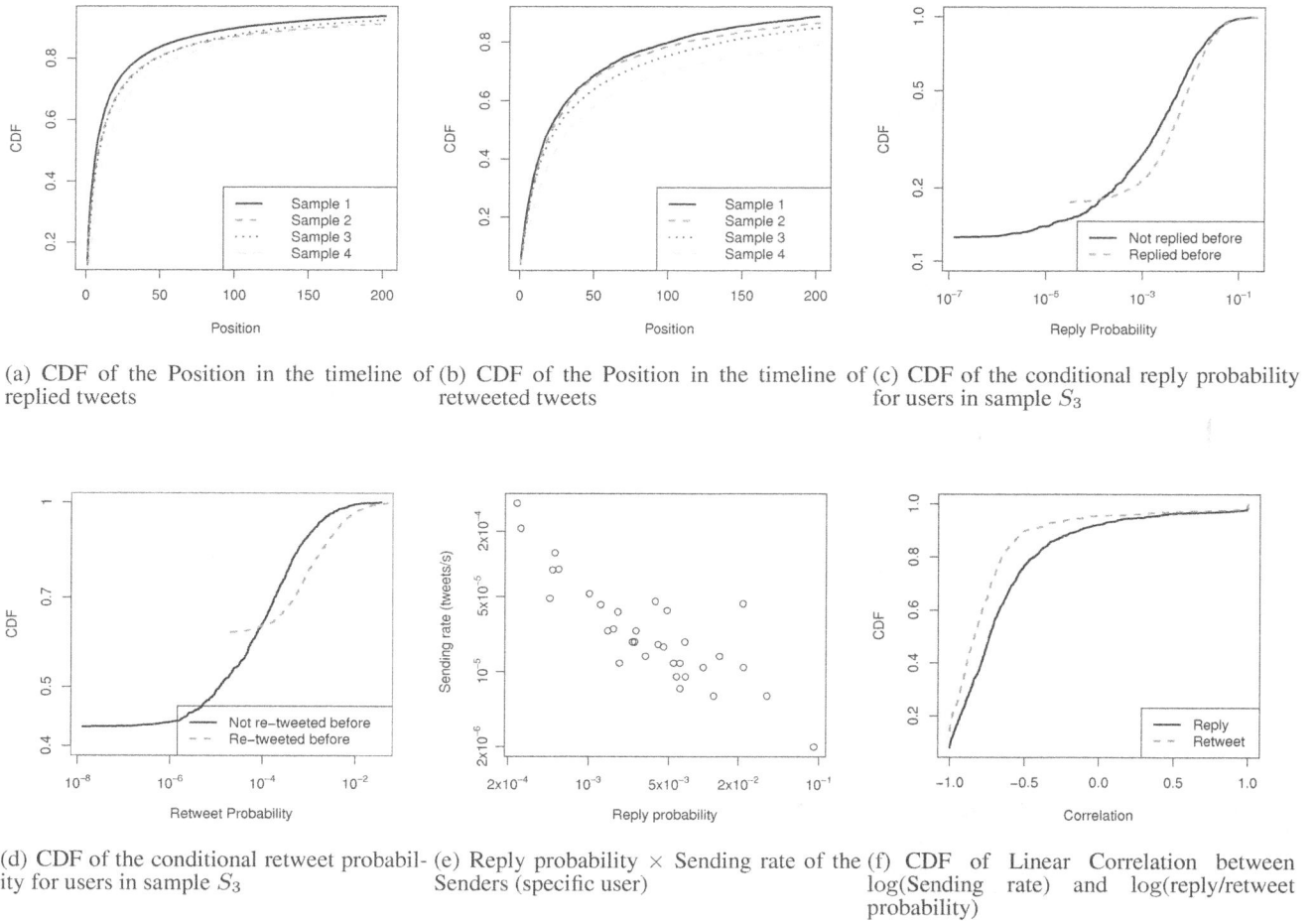

(a) CDF of the Position in the timeline of replied tweets

(b) CDF of the Position in the timeline of retweeted tweets

(c) CDF of the conditional reply probability for users in sample S_3

(d) CDF of the conditional retweet probability for users in sample S_3

(e) Reply probability $\times$ Sending rate of the Senders (specific user)

(f) CDF of Linear Correlation between log(Sending rate) and log(reply/retweet probability)

Figure 2: Characterizations of attributes related with the likelihood of interaction with tweets in the user's timeline.

with respect to the state of TL_i at the moment that $m_{j,i}$ was posted, and note the position of the message (with the newest message assigned position 0, etc.). We compute this quantity for each user $i \in S_k, k = 1, ..., 4$.

Figures 2(a) and 2(b) present the Cumulative Distribution Function (CDF) of the position in the timeline of replied and retweeted messages. The distributions show that newer messages are much more likely to generate responses than older messages. For example, it can be seen that 14% of replies are in position 0 in S_1. This fraction decreases to 12%, 10% and 5% for S_2, S_3 and S_4, respectively. Moreover, 84% (81%, 80%, 77%) of all replies happen in the top 50 for S_1 (S_2, S_3, S_4).

The same phenomenon is found for retweets. The figure shows that 68% (68%, 64%, 58%) of all retweets are in the top 50 for S_1 (S_2, S_3, S_4). Moreover, both figures show that more active users have a higher probability of replying or retweeting messages at higher (older) positions, indicating that users who send more tweets also spend more time reading and interacting with their received messages.

To complement this result we decided to compute the probability that a user i will reply (retweet) a tweet m given it is in position p of his/her timeline. If m is in the position p, then i had the chance to interact with m when it was in the positions $0, \dots, p-1$ and has now the chance to interact with it in the position p. In this way, we

computed the fraction of tweets replied or retweeted in a specific position p from all tweets that could be replied (retweeted) in this position. Figure 3 presents the probability for replies, retweets and for both of them as a function of p for sample S_1. In these three cases we can see two different shapes for the curves, one in the beginning (for $p \leq 10$) and other in the tail ($p > 10$) and that in both cases a linear function can be a good approximation (in logarithmic scale). The parameters of the fitted curves were obtained through a linear regression. This same behavior of two shapes was observed in all other samples.

4.4 Prior Interaction

The next feature we consider is whether the tweet sender has previously sent a tweet that was retweeted or replied to. Thus we ask: *are previously replied (retweeted) users more likely to have their tweets replied to (retweeted) again?* To answer this question we proceed as follows: For each user $i \in S_k$ ($k = 1, \dots, 4$) and for each message $m \in TL_i$ we compute the conditional probability that m will be replied (retweeted) given that the sender of m was replied (retweeted) by i before. We also compute the same probability given the complementary event.

For example, to compute the probability that i replies to a user given that i has replied to that user before, we count two events for each message that i has received: A, the number of times that i

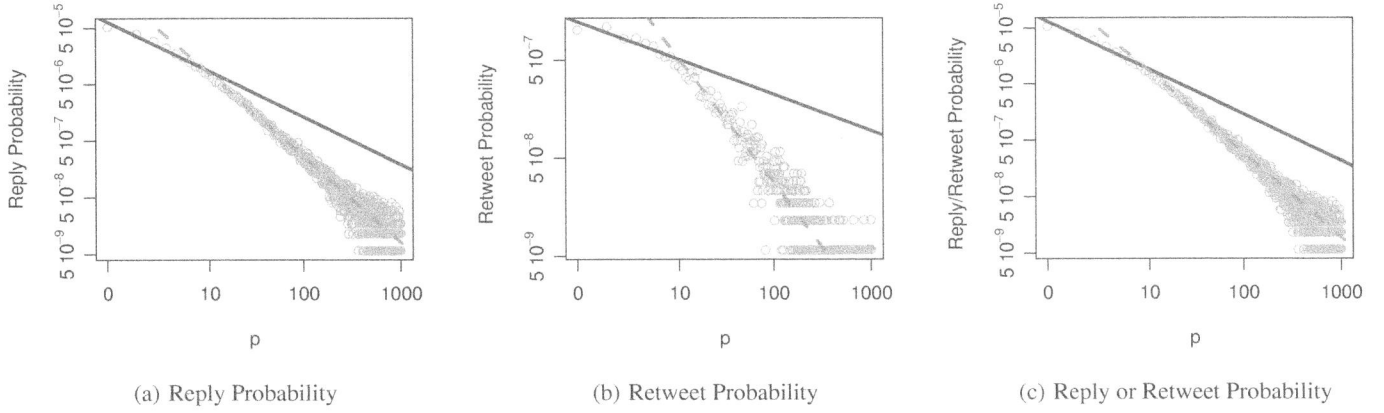

(a) Reply Probability

(b) Retweet Probability

(c) Reply or Retweet Probability

Figure 3: Probability of (a) Reply, (b) Retweet and (c) Reply or Retweet a tweet given that it is in the position p of the user's timeline.

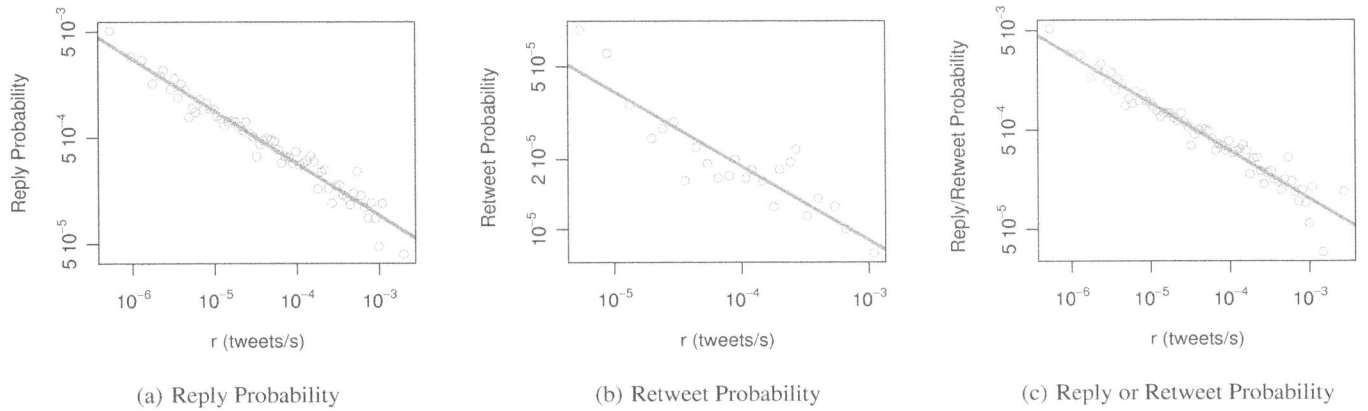

(a) Reply Probability

(b) Retweet Probability

(c) Reply or Retweet Probability

Figure 4: Probability of (a) Reply, (b) Retweet and (c) Reply or Retweet a tweet given that it was sent by a user with sending rate r.

replies to a message that comes from a previously-replied-to user, and B, the number of times that a received message comes from a previously-replied-to user. We then estimate the corresponding probability as $\frac{A}{B}$.

Figures 2(c) and 2(d) show the CDF of the conditional probabilities computed for all users of the sample[1] S_3. The figures show that for replies (retweets), the probability distribution of a reply (retweet) rate increases (shifts to the right) when the sender has been replied-to (retweeted) before. The figure shows that for retweets, this shift is approximately by a factor of 5. In other words, in general, a user is 5 times more likely to retweet a sender that the user has retweeted before, than if the sender has not been retweeted before.

4.5 Sender Rate

The third feature we examine is the activity level of the sender – how prolific the sender is in sending tweets. In this section we seek to answer the question: *Do more active users have a higher chance to be replied (retweeted)?*

To answer this question, we find for each user $i \in S_k$ ($k = 1, \ldots, 4$) the users that i follows, $j \in Out_i$. For each such j, we compare their sending rate with the fraction of their sent messages

that were replied (retweeted) by i. We define the sending rate of user j as T_j divided by the time between the first and last messages posted by user j. It is important to remark that this variable considers at once the number of tweets of a user and the interval of time that the user is active in the network.

Figure 2(e) shows a scatter plot of these variables for an example user i. Each point corresponds to a user $j \in Out_i$. Users who were never replied to by i are omitted due to the log scale. The figure shows that the higher the sending rate of the user, the lower the reply probability. Moreover, this figure shows a strong linear correlation in log scale. To verify if this relationship holds across all users, we repeated this procedure for each $i \in S_k$ and computed the linear correlation between these two variables (sending rate and reply probability) in log scale. Figure 2(f) shows the results for replies and retweets for sample S_2. It can be seen that for replies (retweets) almost 80% (90%) of all users have a correlation coefficient smaller than -0.5, while only 10% (9%) have a positive correlation. Thus, we find that almost all users are more likely to reply or retweet a sender if his/her sending rate is low.

In order to understand better this matter we also computed the probability that a user i will reply (retweet) a tweet m given that it was posted by a user with a sending rate of tweets r. To this end, for all users $i \in S_k$ we computed the fraction of replies (retweets) to users with sending rate of r over the total number of received tweets that came from senders with this same sending rate. As this is a

---

[1]We do not present the figures for all four groups due to space restrictions.

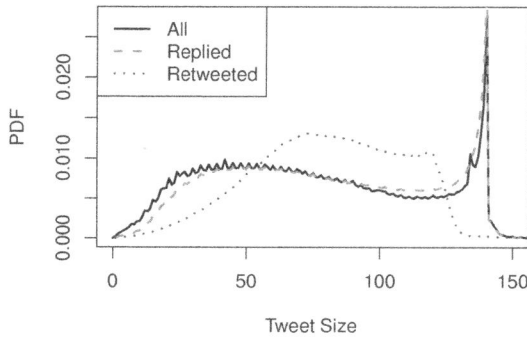

(a) Probability Distribution Function

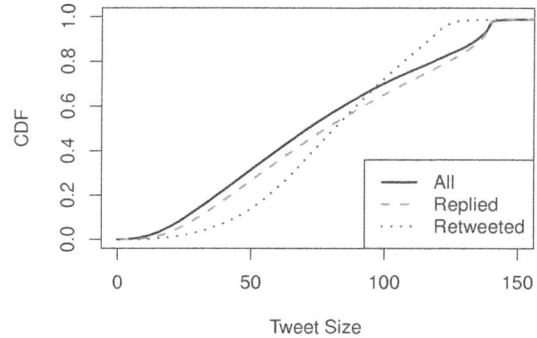

(b) Cumulative Distribution Function

Figure 5: Characterization of the importance of the tweet size in the likelihood of interaction with tweets in the user's timeline.

continuous variable, we aggregated their values in logarithmic bins and grouped bins to ensure that each bin had at least one hundred of replies (retweets). Figure 4 presents probabilities in function of r and the fitted curve for sample S_1. Clearly this figure maintains the conclusions obtained with Figure 2(f).

4.6 Message features

In this section we investigate the influence of intrinsic characteristics of Twitter messages on the interaction among users, represented by replies and retweets. We do not look into the semantic content of tweets. Rather, we analyze the size of tweets, the presence of *hashtags*, *mentions*, and embedded links (i.e., *URLs*). In order to do that we look at such characteristics in all tweets of our data set, i.e. we do not use samples. We considered three separate datasets: *i) Replied* tweets; *ii) Retweeted* tweets; and *iii) All* tweets.

Table 1 displays the fraction of tweets with hashtags, mentions and URLs in these three datasets. On one hand, we see that tweets with hashtags and URLs are more likely to be retweeted. On the other hand, we observe that the same behavior does not hold for tweets with mentions, once only 25% of the retweeted messages contain a specific mention. The characteristics of the Replied dataset are exactly the opposite, the most of the replied tweets (i.e., 55%) contain mentions. Only a small fraction of the replied tweets have hashtags or URLs.

Table 1: Fraction of tweets with hashtags, mentions and URLs.

	Replied	Retweeted	All
Hashtag	0.04	**0.16**	0.05
Mention	**0.55**	0.25	0.36
URL	0.10	**0.51**	0.22

Does size matter for retweets or replies? Tweets can be up to 140 characters in length. Our findings show that retweeted messages have a positive relationship to sizes considerably smaller than 140 characters. Figures 5(a) and 5(b) show the Probability distribution (i.e. PDF) and the Cumulative distribution (i.e., CDF) curves of tweet sizes for the three datasets considered above. The first observation is that we find in the dataset some tweets with more 140 characters. There were only few cases and we conjecture that the reason is some interface failure in the beginning of the service.

By examining figures 5(a) and 5(b) we notice that the PDF and CDF curves for the *Replied* and *All* datasets are similar, which means the size characteristics of replied tweets do not differ from the rest of the tweets. However, the *Retweeted* set shows strong differences when compared to the rest of the tweets. Figure 5(a) shows no specific peak near 140 for retweets. Instead it exhibits a plateau ranging from 50 to 120 characters. Shorter tweets were retweeted much more often than longer tweets. One possible explanation is that shorter tweets leave followers with more room add names or personal comments they want to make. In other words, short tweets make possible the participation of different users in the retweeting process.

5. REORDERING THE TIMELINE

The previous section showed that Twitter users can spend a long time searching through tweets in their timelines until they find one interesting enough to reply to or retweet. It also showed some characteristics that indicate which type of tweets are most interesting to users. Motivated by these results, in this section we present two algorithms to reorganize the Twitter timeline. The goal is to present the most interesting tweets for a user first.

Although we presented seven characteristics related to the interaction rate on Twitter, we use only three in our methodology: tweet age, sending rate of the sender and prior interactions. We proceed in this way once our goal is to have a general methodology, good for replies and retweets and as we saw the text features which we studied are not good for both at the same time. Moreover, the authors of [2] showed through a qualitative study that the "bad" use of some textual elements can make tweets "boring" in the user's opinion.

The two approaches we describe in this section are instances of the general procedure described in Algorithm 1. The main idea is to recognize that users can be in two different states regarding their interaction with Twitter: online (or ON), when they are paying attention in their timelines; and offline (or OFF), otherwise. When a user is in the ON state, the user is viewing all the tweets that have been received during the user's last OFF session, as well as tweets received while in the ON state. Based on this typical user's behavior we perform the timeline reorganization upon occurrence of either of two events: *i)* every change of state from OFF to ON (Line 2); and *ii)* every tweet arrival (Line 5). After the reorganization process the revised timeline TL' is presented to the users instead the old one (TL).

The instances of this algorithm are obtained with two different versions of the procedure *Reorganize*. Both are based in machine learning techniques used to compute score for tweets based on their characteristics discussed in the last section. These techniques are

> **Data**: user u and Tweets of u received in the last OFF
>   session
> **1** $TL \leftarrow$ Set of all Tweets received in the last OFF session
> **2** $TL' \leftarrow$ Reorganize(TL)
> **3** **foreach** *Tweet m received in the current ON session* **do**
> **4** $TL \leftarrow TL \cup \{m\}$
> **5** $TL' \leftarrow$ Reorganize(TL)
> **6** **end**

the *Naive Bayes* predictor (NB) and a *Support Vector Machine* classifier (SVM) and will be presented in Sections 5.2 and 5.3 respectively. After this step of computing scores, the tweets are sorted in such way those that are more likely to interact with will be presented first.

One important characteristic of our methodology is that it considers the change of score that tweets can have over the time, once the *Reorganize* procedure can be performed several times during an ON session. In such way, a tweet which is interesting now may not be in the future. In practical terms, it can be very expensive to reorder the timeline every time that a new tweet arrives. In order to avoid this problem the second type of event can be replaced by some *time out* mechanism or the arrival of at least $l > 0$ tweets in the timeline.

Since our dataset does not allow us to know when each user was ON or OFF we decided to use a simple model to infer this user's behavior. This model is presented in the next section.

5.1 ON-OFF Model

In this section we present a simple model to describe the interaction between Twitter and its users. As described in the last section, each user can be ON or OFF. In our model, an ON session is defined as the interval of time during which the user is actively engaged in posting tweets to Twitter, in such way, that the time between two consecutive messages posted does not exceed a preset threshold T_{OFF}. In the remaining of the time we say that the user is in an OFF session. We observe that our definition of user interaction session does not include passive activities, such as reading messages.

Since the dataset does not explicitly identify the delimiters of a given session, the number of sessions in the Twitter dataset depends on our choice of the T_{OFF} parameter. Following the procedure presented in [21] we varied this timeout value T_{OFF} and counted the total number of sessions. A value extremely small (e.g. 1 minute) could result in a high volume of sessions. As the value of T_{OFF} increases, the number of sessions is reduced continuously until stabilizing. Following this procedure we considered only users with more than a thousand of tweets. We did in this way because users with few tweets could increase the variance of the total number of sessions, leading to a non precise estimate of T_{OFF}. The result of this measurement showed that the number of sessions stabilizes when T_{OFF} is near to 10^4 seconds, which represents almost three hours.

Compared to previous efforts, which characterize sessions in traditional Web sites [3, 22], the timeout values obtained are much longer compared to the 10-45 minutes usually observed. The most intuitive reasons for this behavior are the longer time period that users take on Twitter, keeping a track of real time events all the time. This high value of T_{OFF} is also supported by Figure 6, which presents the Complementary Cumulative Distribution Function (CCDF) of the inter-event (we consider an event any tweet

posted) time of all users in our dataset. In this figure we can see that 70% of all inter-event times are smaller than 10^4 seconds.

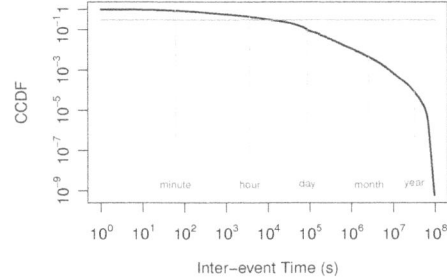

Figure 6: CCDF for inter-event time for all tweets in the dataset. Above the horizontal line we have 70% of the observations.

It is important to remark that this model is an heuristic to infer when users are ON or OFF. We adopted this strategy due to our dataset limitations. In a real situation, if there is better information about the user's state, it should be used.

5.2 Naive Bayes approach

This section aims at presenting how we use the *Naive Bayes* predictor [15] to assign scores to tweets in the procedure *Reorganize* of the Algorithm 1. We represent this score through a probability measure for each tweet, which gives the probability that a user will interact with that tweet given a set of its attributes. As previously said we consider three attributes:

- $Age(m)$, the age of the tweet m represented by its position in the timeline (the newest one has $Age(m) = 0$, the next $Age(m) = 1$ and so on);

- $SR(m)$, the average sending rate of tweets of the users that has sent m; and

- $I(m)$, a binary indicator which can be 1 if the user has interacted with the sender of m before and 0 otherwise.

In this way, for each tweet m, its score, denoted by $P(m)$, is defined as follows:

$$P(m) = P(\text{Interact with } m | \; Age(m) = p, \; SR(m) = r, \; I(m) = b).$$

Under the naive assumption we consider the independence among the events $Age(m) = p$, $SR(m) = r$ and $I(m) = b$, which leads us to:

$$
\begin{aligned}
P(m) \quad = \quad & P(\text{Interact with } m | \; Age(m) = p) \\
\times \quad & P(\text{Interact with } m | \; SR(m) = r) \\
\times \quad & P(\text{Interact with } m | \; I(m) = b).
\end{aligned}
$$

We present next how we estimated each one of these probabilities in the next three sections.

5.2.1 Age score

In Section 4 we presented the probability of replying (retweeting) a message m given $Age(m) = p$ in Figure 3. Motivated by this figure we decided to use the following model:

$$P(\text{Interact with } m \mid Age(m) = p) = \begin{cases} \beta_1 p^{\alpha_1}, & p \leq 10 \\ \beta_2 p^{\alpha_2}, & p > 10. \end{cases} \quad (1)$$

It is important to remark that during the fitting process, in all cases the R^2 of the linear regression were greater than 0.81, for retweets, and 0.95 in the other cases.

5.2.2 *Sending Rate Score*

Proceeding as in the previous section and motivated by Figure 4 we assume for the sending rate probability the following model:

$$P(\text{Interact with } m \mid SR(m) = r) = \beta r^{\alpha}. \qquad (2)$$

The R^2 of the fitted curves in all cases are greater than 0.8, for retweets, and 0.94 in the other cases.

5.2.3 *Interaction Score*

Once $I(m)$ is a binary variable we decided to use the following model for this score:

$$P(\text{Interact with } m \mid I(m) = b) = \begin{cases} \gamma_1, & b = 1 \\ \gamma_2, & b = 0, \end{cases} \qquad (3)$$

where $0 \leq \gamma_1, \gamma_2 \leq 1$.

In order to estimate these parameters, for all u in a subset of U we proceed in the following way: for each arrival in his/her timeline we compute the fraction of tweets m, that were replied (retweeted) and had $I(m) = b$ over all received tweets with $I(m) = b$.

5.3 Support Vector Machine Approach

Support Vector Machine (SVM) is a set of useful methods widely used in data classification to recognize patterns. The most common version of SVM is a binary supervised classifier that maps a vector of attributes in two classes. In this paper we used this SVM version, more specifically the presented in [16], to implement the *Reorganize* procedure of the Algorithm 1. The idea is composed of two steps. First, we consider the same attributes used in the previous section in order to classify the tweets of the timeline in interesting (most likely to interact with) and non interesting. In others words, for each tweet m in the user's timeline we use SVM to map the vector $[Age(m), SR(m), I(m)]$ in 1 (interesting) or 0 (non interesting).

Second, we present for the user all tweets classified as 1, in reverse chronological order, and after, all classified as 0, also in reverse chronological order. It is important to remark that as the attributes of a tweet can change over the time, the same can happen with its class. Details about the training phase of this classifier are presented in Section 6.1.

6. EXPERIMENTS

In this section we present the results of the proposed algorithms. First we show the evaluation methodology and then we present the performance of the algorithms. After, we show the impact of parameter T_{OFF}, of our ON/OFF model, in the results and finally, we discuss the difference in the performance of the algorithm when we apply it for users' classes with different activities' patterns.

6.1 Evaluation Methodology

In order to evaluate whether the proposed algorithms are effective we performed a trace-driven simulation to figure out what would happen if the tweets were presented according to our methodology instead of the reverse chronological order (in the official Twitter interface). The necessary steps for this simulation are presented in Algorithm 2 and explained below.

For each user u, we split all his/her tweets in ON and OFF sessions according to Section 5.1 (Line 1). After that, for each tweet which is an interaction of u (an interaction here can be a reply or

---

Algorithm 2: Simulation Procedure

Data: User u, M_u, TL_u, Out_u
1 Split M_u in two lists, one for ON sessions (on_u) and other for OFF sessions (off_u)
2 **foreach** *session* $s \in on_u$ **do**
3 $\quad$ $t_1 \leftarrow$ time when s begins
4 $\quad$ $t_2 \leftarrow$ time when the last OFF session in off_u that precedes s begins
5 $\quad$ $TL \leftarrow$ list of tweets in TL_u posted after t_1 and before t_2
6 $\quad$ $IT \leftarrow$ list of Interaction Tweets in s
7 $\quad$ **foreach** $m \in IT$ **do**
8 $\quad\quad$ Update TL with messages posted before m
9 $\quad\quad$ $TL' \leftarrow$ Reorganize(TL)
10 $\quad\quad$ Search the origin of m in TL'
11 $\quad\quad$ Return the position of the origin of m in TL'
12 $\quad$ **end**
13 **end**

---

retweet) we look for the original tweet (the replied or retweeted one) in the timeline of u. However, we look only in the most recent tweets, those received since the beginning of the last OFF session up to the time of the actual interaction (Lines 5 and 8). Before this search (Line 10), we perform one of the reorganizations algorithms described in Section 5 (Line 9). If the replied (retweeted) tweet is found in the timeline, its position is returned. It is important remark that not necessarily the tweet will be found in the timeline because it can be a reply or retweet of a non-followed user.

With this procedure we can compare our methodology with the normal Twitter timeline. It is only necessary compute the fraction of replied or retweeted tweets in the first p positions of the timeline when the reorganization method (Line 9) is one of the Section 5 or the simple chronological order.

In order to have a good estimate of these values it is important to perform this simulations for a large number of users. The ideal scenario would be repeating it for all users in U. However, due to the computational cost, we need to use a sample. We extracted a random sample S from U with 10,000 users. In this sample we have 2.25 million tweets, of which 540 thousand are replies and 62 thousand retweets. Associated with this sample we have approximately 500,000 followed users whose were responsible for over 200 million received tweets.

Since we are working with samples, it is important guarantee that we have enough observations to have statistical confidence in the results. So we must be sure that the number of replies and retweets aforementioned are greater than a minimum threshold. According to Cochran [12] an approximation for a pessimist value in this case, with 95% of confidence and absolute error smaller than 0.005, is 38,416, showing that our sample is representative[1].

After this step we divided this sample in five subsamples with 2000 users each and performed a cross validation procedure with them. We retained one subsample for training and used the others to test the machine learning algorithms. We performed this procedure 5 times. In each one, we used a different sample for training and the remaining for tests. For each test phase we computed the fraction of replies and retweets in the top-p position of the timeline for $p = 1$, $p = 5$ and $p = 10$. Finally, we averaged each one of these

---

[1]The same argument can be used for the samples in Section 4. But, using 90% of confidence and an absolute error smaller than 0.01, which are still reasonable.

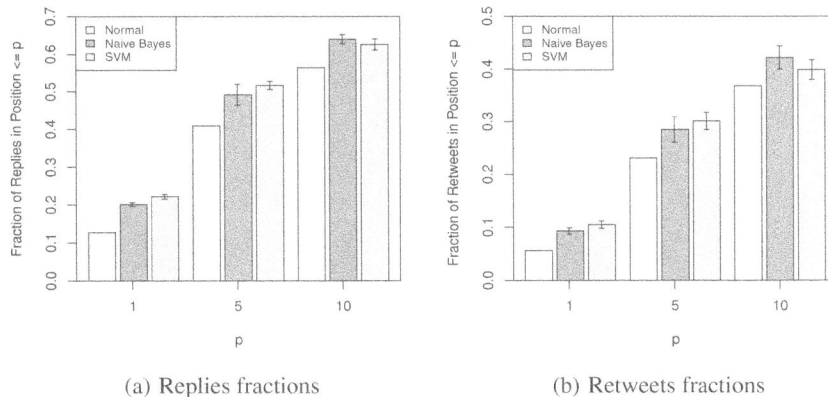

(a) Replies fractions   (b) Retweets fractions

Figure 7: Fraction of Replies/Retweets in the first p positions of the timeline. Errors bars are 95% confidence intervals.

quantities using the results of all combinations of training and test subsamples.

Each machine learning algorithm has different training methodologies. For the NB, the training phase consists basically in estimating the parameters for the probabilities models presented in Section 5.2. For the SVM classifier we extracted a labeled trace of tweets and their attributes used for the classification. To perform this, we analysed our dataset and for each reply (retweet) we noted the data related to the replied (retweeted) tweet and selected other in the user's timeline randomly that were not replied neither retweeted. After that we used this trace to train the classifier. For each sample we trained the classifier with information of replies, retweets and a third composed of the union of both. It is important remark that for the SVM classifier we used the library *Libsvm* [10] as base for simulations. In the training phase we used a tool available in that library to find the best parameters for the model.

6.2 Algorithm Evaluation

In this section we present the results obtained with the algorithms proposed in Section 5. Figure 7 presents the fraction of replies and retweets that are related with the first p tweets in the user timeline. These results were obtained when we trained the algorithms with information of replies and retweets. We proceeded in this way because this combination gave the best results.

We can see that both, NB and SVM algorithms improved significantly the fraction of replied tweets in the first positions of the timeline. Moreover, we have that NB and SVM have almost the same results (statistically equivalent).

In general, with this strategy we have good results in terms of presenting the most important tweets first for both types of interaction, where improvements of more than 50%, 20% and 10% for p equals to 1, 5 and 10 respectively were achieved.

6.3 T_{OFF} parameter Impact

All results presented in the previous section use the parameter T_{OFF} equals to 10^4 s in the ON/OFF model presented in Section 5.1. But, is this value the most appropriate for all kind of Twitter users and situations? To answer this question we conducted one experiment where we varied T_{OFF} for sixteen different values in the range 10^3 s to 10^5 s. In this experiment we trained the algorithms with one sub sample (also used in previous section) with information of replies and retweets together and tested (executed the simulation procedure) in other one.

Table 2 shows the results of this experiment. To have a better

visualization we present only the minimum and maximum fractions among the sixteen values. We can see that for both algorithms (NB and SVM) the variation (difference between the maximum and minimum) is small, indicating that we can choose different values for T_{OFF} without a significant impact on the results.

Table 2: Fractions of replies and retweets for different T_{OFF}.

		SVM		NB	
	p	Min.	Max.	Min.	Max.
Reply	1	0.21	0.22	0.18	0.20
	5	0.50	0.54	0.47	0.51
	10	0.62	0.67	0.61	0.65
Retweet	1	0.07	0.08	0.07	0.08
	5	0.23	0.28	0.23	0.27
	10	0.32	0.38	0.34	0.39

6.4 Active and Passive users

The objective of this section is to show that our algorithm is robust to work in classes of users with different patterns of activity. To that end, we conducted the same simulation procedure presented in last sections in two different classes of U: the first one is composed of active users, those that spend more time ON, and the second one of passive users, who spend less time ON. To divide these classes we defined the variable $R_{ON}(u)$ as the fraction of time that user u is ON between his/her first and last tweets. After that we computed $R_{ON}(u)$ for all users in U and considered the 20% of the users with the higher $R_{ON}(u)$ as the active class and the remaining as the passive class.

We extracted a sample with 2000 users of each class, and used them in the simulation in order to investigate how our algorithms work in both cases. It is important to observe that we trained the algorithms with the same trace obtained of one subsample used in Section 6.2.

Figure 8 shows the results of this experiment. It is important remark that the same conclusions hold for replies, but we do not present the related figures due to space restriction. The fist interesting point is that passive users tend to interact more with messages in the top of the timeline than active users. This is possible explained by the fact that active users spend more time ON and in this way, they spend more time looking at their timelines and interacting with tweets far from the top. Passive users tend to have more contact with tweets in top.

The second point is that improvements were achieved for both classes, especially for active users, where NB and SVM gave good

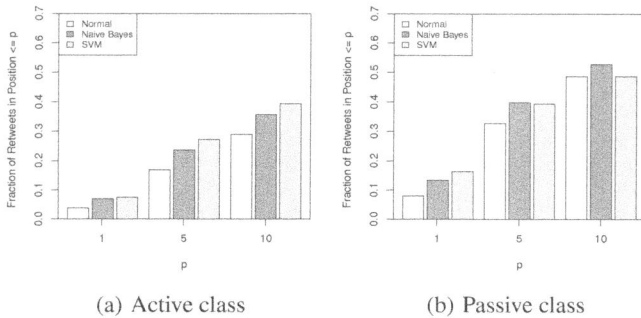

(a) Active class   (b) Passive class

Figure 8: Fraction of retweets in the first p positions of the time-line for active and passive classes.

results. For the passive class, NB and SVM also worked well, except for SVM when $p = 10$ in this last case.

7. CONCLUSIONS

In this paper we addressed the problem of understanding how users in Twitter interact with their timelines. Through an extensive characterization study we showed the importance of this problem and presented a set of relevant characteristics to deal with it. We showed that in general users prefer to interact with newer tweets, with users that they had previously interacted and with users with a lower sending rate (those that do dot fullfill their timelines). Moreover, we showed that some basic textual characteristics such as, message size and the presence of hashtags, mentions and URLs affect interactions patterns, but in a different way, when we consider replies or retweets.

Motivated by these characterizations we proposed an algorithm to change the presentation order of the Twitter's timeline. Our methodology is based on two machine learning techniques, which showed significant improvements through a trace-driven simulation. Our main contribution is achieved when we used information of replies and retweets to train the classifiers. In this case we had good rates of replies and retweets in the top-p positions of the time-line. Moreover, training the algorithms with information of a random sample over all users, we showed that our methodology was capable of working well for users in classes with distinct patterns of activity, showing the robustness of our method.

This is an important contribution once it represents another option of interface for the Twitter users, which can be specially interesting for mobile devices with a small screen. In addition, it is important remark that we used three simple attributes which are easy to compute. This fact makes our approach even more interesting for theses devices once, in general, they have energy and memory constraints. In fact, we are currently building a Twitter client for iOS that implements our tweet-ordering algorithms, which we will distribute as open-source.

8. ACKNOWLEDGEMENTS

This research was funded by the Brazilian National Institute of Science and Technology for the Web (MCT/CNPq/INCT grant number 573871/2008-6) and by the authors' individual grants from CNPq, FAPEMIG and National Science Foundation (grants CNS-0905565, CNS-1018266, CNS-1012910 and CNS-1117039).

9. REFERENCES

[1] Twitter blog. http://blog.twitter.com/.
[2] P. André, M. S. Bernstein, and K. Luther. Who Gives A Tweet? Evaluating Microblog Content Value. In *Proceedings of CSCW 2012*, Feb. 2012.
[3] M. Arlitt. Characterizing web user sessions. *SIGMETRICS Performance Evaluation Review*, 28(2):50–63, 2000.
[4] E. Bakshy, J. M. Hofman, W. A. Madson, and D. J. Watts. Identifying 'Influencers' on Twitter. In *Web Search and Data Mining*, 2011.
[5] A.-L. Bárabási. The origin of bursts and heavy tails in humans dynamics. *Nature*, 435:207, 2005.
[6] F. Benevenuto, G. Magno, T. Rodrigues, and V. Almeida. Detecting spammers on twitter. In *Annual Collaboration, Electronic messaging, Anti-Abuse and Spam Conference (CEAS)*, 2010.
[7] M. S. Bernstein, B. Suh, L. Hong, J. Chen, S. Kairam, and E. H. Chi. Eddi: interactive topic-based browsing of social status streams. In *Proceedings of the 23nd annual ACM symposium on User interface software and technology*, UIST '10, pages 303–312, New York, NY, USA, 2010. ACM.
[8] Y. Boshmaf, I. Muslukhov, K. Beznosov, and M. Ripeanu. The Socialbot Network: When Bots Socialize for Fame and Money. In *Annual Computer Security Applications Conference (ACSAC)*, Austin, TX, December 2010.
[9] M. Cha, H. Haddadi, F. Benevenuto, and K. Gummadi. Measuring User Influence in Twitter: The Million Follower Fallacy. In *Int'l AAAI Conference on Weblogs and Social Media (ICWSM)*, 2010.
[10] C.-C. Chang and C.-J. Lin. LIBSVM: A library for support vector machines. *ACM Transactions on Intelligent Systems and Technology*, 2:27:1–27:27, 2011.
[11] M. Choudhury, H. Sundaram, A. John, and D. Seligmann. What makes conversations interesting? themes, participants and consequences of conversations in online social media. In *World Wide Web Conference (WWW)*, pages 331–340, 2009.
[12] W. G. Cochran. *Sampling Techniques, 3rd Edition*. John Wiley, 1977.
[13] S. Counts and K. Fisher. Taking It All In? Attention in Microblog Consumption. In *AAAI Int'l Conference on Weblogs and Social Media (ICWSM)*, july 2011.
[14] S. Ghosh, B. Viswanath, F. Kooti, N. K. Sharma, K. Gautam, F. Benevenuto, N. Ganguly, and K. P. Gummadi. Understanding and Combating Link Farming in the Twitter Social Network. In *Proceedings of WWW 2012*, April 2012.
[15] T. Hastie, R. Tibshirani, and J. H. Friedman. *The elements of statistical learning: data mining, inference, and prediction*. New York: Springer-Verlag, 2009.
[16] C.-W. Hsu and C.-J. Lin. A simple decomposition method for support vector machines. *IEEE Transactions on Neural Networks*, 12:291–314, 1999.
[17] B. A. Huberman, D. M. Romero, and F. Wu. Social networks that matter: Twitter under the microscope. *ArXiv e-prints*, Dec. 2008.
[18] A. Java, X. Song, T. Finin, and B. Tseng. Why We Twitter: Understanding Microblogging Usage and Communities. *Procedings of the Joint 9th WEBKDD and 1st SNA-KDD Workshop 2007*, August 2007.
[19] B. Krishnamurthy, P. Gill, and M. Arlitt. A few chirps about twitter. In *Proceedings of the first workshop on Online social networks*, WOSN '08, pages 19–24, New York, NY, USA, 2008. ACM.
[20] H. Kwak, C. Lee, H. Park, and S. Moon. What is twitter, a social network or a news media? In *Int'l World Wide Web Conference (WWW)*, pages 591–600, 2010.
[21] D. Menascé, V. Almeida, R. Fonseca, and M. Mendes. A methodology for workload characterization of e-commerce sites. In *ACM conference on Electronic commerce (EC)*, 1999.
[22] A. Oke and R. Bunt. Hierarchical workload characterization for a busy web server. In *Int'l Conference on Computer Performance Evaluation, Modelling Techniques and Tools (TOOLS)*, 2002.
[23] T. Rodrigues, F. Benevenuto, M. Cha, K. P. Gummadi, and V. Almeida. On word-of-mouth based discovery of the web. In *ACM SIGCOMM Internet Measurement Conference (IMC)*, 2011.
[24] B. Suh, L. Hong, P. Pirolli, and E. H. Chi. Want to be retweeted? Large scale analytics on factors impacting retweet in Twitter network. In *Proceedings of the IEEE Second International Conference on Social Computing (SocialCom)*, pages 177–184, 2010.
[25] J. Weng, E.-P. Lim, J. Jiang, and Q. He. Twitterrank: finding topic-sensitive influential twitterers. In *Proceedings of the third ACM international conference on Web search and data mining*, WSDM '10, pages 261–270, New York, NY, USA, 2010. ACM.

Graph and Matrix Metrics to Analyze Ergodic Literature for Children

Eugenia-Maria Kontopoulou
CEID, University of Patras
Rio, Greece
kontopoulo@ceid.upatras.gr

Maria Predari
CEID, University of Patras
Rio, Greece
predari@ceid.upatras.gr

Thymios Kostakis
SEOKO
28, A. Papandreou st.
Halandri, Athens, Greece
kostakth@gmail.com

Efstratios Gallopoulos
CEID, University of Patras
Rio, Greece
stratis@ceid.upatras.gr

ABSTRACT

What can graph and matrix based mathematical models tell us about ergodic literature? A digraph of storylets connected by links and the corresponding adjacency matrix encoding is used to formulate some queries regarding hypertexts of this type. It is reasoned that the Google random surfer provides a useful model for the behavior of the reader of such fiction. This motivates the use of graph and Web based metrics for ranking storylets and some other tasks. A dataset, termed CHILDIF, based on printed books from three series popular with children and young adults and its characteristics are described. Two link-based metrics, SM-rank and versions of PageRank, are described and applied on CHILDIF to rank storylets. It is shown that several characteristics of these stories can be expressed as and computed with matrix operations. An interpretation of the ranking results is provided. Results on some acyclic digraphs indicate that the rankings convey useful information regarding plot development. In conclusion, using matrix and graph theoretic techniques one can extract useful information from this type of ergodic literature that would be harder to obtain by simply reading it or by examining the underlying digraph.

Categories and Subject Descriptors

H.5.4 [**Information Systems**]: Hypertext/Hypermedia

General Terms

Algorithms, Experimentation, Human Factors, Measurement

Keywords

hypertext, ergodic, interactive fiction, storylet, link analysis, directed graph, matrix function, stochastic matrix, path problem, ranking, PageRank, SMRank

1. INTRODUCTION

The recent issue by American Girl of the "Innerstar University books"[1], a series of printed hypertexts, at a time when the modeling and study of "connectedness" is attracting the interest of many researchers, triggered this study.

We consider some metrics based on matrix analysis and graph theory for analyzing large scale networks and study what they tell us regarding such texts. A longer term goal is to study to what extent such metrics can be used to discover interesting information, possibly uncover latent meanings, provide unexpected interpretations and hopefully assist the writer of hypertext readings cope with what is sometimes called "runaway branching".

Following Aarseth, we use the term "ergodic literature" for the genre of these books, underlying that "there is non-trival effort to traverse the text" (p.1 of [1]); cf. [24, 31, 32, 33] for information on this and the related concept of interactive fiction. In our case, when finishing reading a page of these books, one does not simply turn to the next one. Instead, the reader follows one of several possibilities, usually based on some criterion, for instance the reader's answer to one or more questions related to the story, a riddle, etc. So at the very least, the reader has to do some work ("ergon") to accomplish the page hopping necessary to find his way ("hodos") through the text. Since the way is by and large determined by the reader's decisions, these books inevitably offer plot variability.

It is fair to say that ergodic literature, especially in printed form, is not widespread and that with few notable exceptions such texts are mostly experimental and rather esoteric[2]. In

---

[1] http://store.americangirl.com/agshop/html/thumbnail/id/1505/uid/814

[2] An often cited example is Julio Cortázar's "Rayela" (Hopscotch), offering at least two possible readings. The much more recent "A Heartbreaking Work of Staggering Genius" [17] by Dave Eggers offers the reader several choices early on, while making some caustic but humoristic remarks about Interactive Fiction.

Table 1: **The three collections. The first row for each entry shows the title, publisher, number of books in the series and number of books we used in this study. The second row shows years in publication and URL.**

Choose Your Own Adventure (CYOA corp.)	>200 (6)
1979-1998, www.cyoa.com/	
Innerstar University (American Girl)	9 (4)
2010-today, http://web.innerstaru.com/	
Multiclone Tales (Kalendis pub.)	2 (2)
1997-2003, http://www.kalendis.gr/	

fact, it has been proposed by some scholars that this state of affairs might be the downside of offering choices to the reader; see for example [16] and the discussion on page 170 of [1]. On the other hand, since the mid'70s there have been several printed collections from children pre-teens and teens, the one by American Girl being the most recent (for other examples see e.g. (e.g. [12, 34]) that are enjoying considerable success. It thus appears that young readers have been much more appreciative of the genre. Therefore, we make this literature the focus of our investigation, using books from two collections published in English and one in Greek as summarized in Table 1 (cf. Section 3.1).

Details (number of pages, possible readings, etc.) vary but their structure is similar. A plot (cf. [5]) is "woven" by putting together a "valid" sequence of pages, from starting to some terminal page[3]. Hopefully, this stimulates the children to read by engaging them in the "construction" of a plot. Following [5], we call a specific sequence of linked pages "reading". The child can read the book multiple times, from entry to some terminal page, without repeating the same reading twice. Even an adult might be under the impression that the book offers many plots to last for a long time, if not forever. This characteristic is also not lost on publishers, who frequently use it to promote this literature[4].

For the purposes of our discussion we propose the term *storylet* for the material (textual or visual) that is contained within a single page of these books (other than the usual front and back matter). This name, we hope, carries the flavor "children's tales meet computer science". Our "storylets" are a special case of Barthesian "lexias" [2] or "substories" [14]). We focus on printed hypertext books where, with the exception of front and back material, each page consists of a storylet. It is worth noting that the proper choice (content and size) of storylets is an important factor when building hypertexts [14]. In our case, we suspect that the anticipated age of readers played a role in selecting lexias to be delimited by the page boundaries, in contrast to much more aggressive linking that can be found even in early electronic hypertexts[5]. Every storylet can be one of the following: A

---

[3]After all, repeated readings are necessary to perceive hypertextuality, as noted in [5].

[4]From the cited literature, only [34] contains a seemingly plausible number - contained in the title - regarding the total number of possible readings. We have not had the chance to check it but it is interesting that the book also discusses, using computer science terminology some of the difficulties related to its creation.

[5]See e.g. Michael Joyce's "Afternoon, a story", http://www.eastgate.com/catalog/Afternoon.html, one of the first works of hypertext literature.

"starting storylet", marking the beginning of a reading, an "ending storylet" marking the end of one or more readings, or a storylet of intermediate action. All storylets finish with a "branching" statement that links to other storylets, usually based on reader input, or are "endings". Sometimes, an ending storylet is exactly that; it is also possible for an ending storylet to link to the starting storylet, in case the reader wants to start over. Plot, then, is the sequence of events presented in a reading from a starting to an ending storylet. Unless specified otherwise, we consider that the first page in all readings is a starting storylet and the last one an ending storylet.

The contributions of this paper, on the subject of stories written as hypertexts modeled as directed graphs (with special emphasis on a dataset, termed CHILDIF, consisting of 12 books for children as shown in Table 1) are the following: 1) It is reasoned that there is an analogy between the actions of random surfers on the Web and readers of interactive fiction. 2) Several questions related to the characteristics of these hypertexts are shown to be expressed in terms of graph and matrix theory. 3) Because of (1), it is argued that it is sensible to consider ranking storylets. 4) A graph based metric, called SMRank is used to rank storylets and its properties discussed. 5) Because of (1) and the difficulty of computing (3) when graphs contain cycles, it is argued that spectral rankings like PageRank offer a practical alternative for ranking storylets. 6) The storylet rankings for all the stories in the CHILDIF dataset are computed. An interpretation of the ranking results is provided. Results on some acyclic digraphs indicate that the rankings convey useful information regarding plot development.

To the best of our knowledge, this is the first time that a systematic study of link-based analysis is conducted across a variety of literary works of interactive fiction. We note, however, that in early unpublished work Bruckman had considered the combinatorial explosion of possibilities in interactive fiction based on a graph interpretation of such stories, one of which was from the CYOA series [11].

2. DIGRAPH READINGS, SPARSITY AND SURFING

The books under study can be encoded and represented as directed graphs (digraphs)[6]. Digraphs are present in the underlying structure of several hypertext related systems, ranging from author tools (e.g. [4, 13]) to plain plot sketches by fans[7].

In the digraph model of hypertext, storylets correspond to vertices (or nodes); the starting one is a source vertex (of zero indegree), the ending ones are sinks (of zero outdegree) and the edges correspond to valid transitions between storylets. Nodes that have zero in- and outdegree (number of in- and outgoing edges are zero) play no role in the plots (they are usually visual material). Any node that has zero indegree is either a source or the result of an error. It is worth noting that the graph representation helped us in the

---

[6]It is worth noting that a founding member of the group Oulipo (acronym for "Ouvroir de littérature potentielle"), that has been experimenting since 1960 with novel types of writing, some resembling the ergodic genre, was the distinguished graph theorist Claude Berge. Raymond Queneau, Georges Perec and Italo Calvino were some of the well-known authors of Oulipo [7].

[7]http://www.gamebooks.org/

past to locate non-starting storylets whose nodes had zero indegree and thus were unreachable from the source; this was not what the author had in mind, and a correction was necessary.

We remind the reader (cf. [21]) that walks between two distinct vertices of a digraph are sequences of edges, where every edge and the one immediately following it share a common vertex. If the initial and last vertices in a walk are the same, the walk is closed. Trails are walks that do not repeat edges. Paths are trails without repetition of internal vertices. A cycle is a closed path of length at least 1.

Let $G = (V, E)$ be a digraph consisting of the set of vertices (nodes) V and the set of directed edges E. We assume that the digraph is simple, that is it contains no self-loops or multi-edges. For each digraph we can construct its adjacency matrix A that is a square matrix of order n, where $n = |V|$ is the number of nodes, and such that it contains 1 in position (i, j) if there is an edge from node i to node j. It has long been known that for any k, the kth power of A, that is A^k, reveals in each position (i, j) the number of walks of length k between nodes i and j of the digraph; cf. [18] and [10, 29]. For all books under consideration in this study, there are only few edges leaving every node, therefore all graphs and their adjacency matrices are sparse. We denote by $\texttt{nnz} = |E|$ the total number of edges in the graph, that is the number of nonzeros in A and use $A^\top$ to denote the transpose of A.

Digraphs and sparse matrices are used to represent the connectivity and analyze the World Wide Web [9, 23], social and other networks, as well as for purposes of information retrieval; see e.g. the recent monograph [29]. Sparse matrix technology, of course, is an important topic in high performance scientific computing and can be used for the analysis of large scale networks. It is thus of interest to find out if this technology as well as tools from graph theory can be leveraged in order to learn more about the underlying books.

To this effect, we enumerate some issues, relevant to readers and storytellers, authors and publishers, in lay terms as well as in the technical language used for graphs. The list is certainly not exhaustive, there are many more interesting questions, but illustrates that one could apply the mature armory of graph and matrix theory (e.g. [20, 21, 28, 29]) to reveal the complexity of some of these questions and the means for computing exact or approximate answers.

1. How many different readings are there?
2. What is the length of each reading? Which readings are shortest/longest?
3. Is any storylet repeated in a single reading?
4. Can we rank storylets?

In this work we focus on the last question. Nonetheless, before initiating our discussion on ranking methods, let us consider for a moment some of the preceding ones. Let G be the digraph corresponding to the book under study. We assume throughout, as is the case with all books in CHILDIF, that all digraphs are simple and that there is a single source node. Regarding question (1), we need to compute how many walks are contained in G. Without additional constraints for the digraph, the walks can be many (an infinite number, if we permit cycle repetition) and counting them is hard or pointless. If G is a directed acyclic graph (DAG), however, counting walks is the same as counting paths. We

will show one method shortly. Regarding (2), for general digraphs the first part is at least as hard as the previous question. However, the shortest readings amount to computing the shortest paths from the source to the sinks, a problem that can be solved with a variety of algorithms, see e.g. [19]. Finding the shortest and longest paths of a DAG with single source can also be done efficiently. Regarding question (3), it amounts to detecting cycles in the digraph, which can be accomplished, for example, by depth-first search to compute the strongly connected components of the digraph or by considering powers of the adjacency matrix, e.g. [27, 35]. Note that a nonzero diagonal element in any A^k implies the presence of a cycle. Without loss of generality in this section we assume that the nodes are numbered in such a way that the last $f \geq 1$ of them are sinks (that is ending storylets). For DAGs, this can be the result of an easy to perform relabeling of the nodes after a topological sort. Therefore, assuming that the (possibly reordered) nodes are labeled $V = \{v_1, ..., v_n\}$, then v_1 is the source (it usually is, that is the starting storylet is the first page right after the introductory material that we do not count anyway) and the last f nodes are the sinks. Then the adjacency matrix can be partitioned to have the following block form (the 0 submatrices indicate that the sinks have 0 outdegree), that is sustained when taking powers, as the right term shows:

$$A = \left(\begin{array}{cc} A_{11} & A_{12} \\ 0 & 0 \end{array} \right), \quad A^k = \left(\begin{array}{cc} A_{11}^k & A_{11}^{k-1} A_{12} \\ 0 & 0 \end{array} \right),$$

where A_{11}, A_{22} are both square of order $n - f$ and f respectively. The first shows the connections strictly between all nodes that are not sinks, the latter between sinks. Because $A_{11}^k = 0$ for $k \geq n - f$, the number of paths from source to each sink are readily available and denoted below by p_f, in locations $n - n_f + 1$ up to n of the first row of

$$B := \sum_{j=1}^{n-f} A^j = \left(\begin{array}{cc} \sum_{j=1}^{n-f-1} A_{11}^j & (\sum_{j=0}^{n-f-1} A_{11}^j) A_{12} \\ 0 & 0 \end{array} \right),$$

while the total number of paths from source to the sinks is the sum of these values. Because the DAG's adjacency matrix is nilpotent, we can write $B = (I - A)^{-1}$ and thus

$$p_f^\top = [\pi_{n-f+1}, ..., \pi_n] = e_1^\top (I - A)^{-1} \left(\begin{array}{c} 0 \\ I_f \end{array} \right),$$

where I_f is the identity matrix of order f, $e_1 = [1, 0, \ldots, 0]^\top$ of order n. Therefore, the number of paths from source to the sinks is equal to $p_f^\top e^{(f)}$, where $e^{(f)}$ is the f-size vector of all 1's. Moreover

$$(I - A)^{-1} = \left(\begin{array}{cc} (I - A_{11})^{-1} & (I - A_{11})^{-1} A_{12} \\ 0 & I_f \end{array} \right) \quad (1)$$

where we abuse notation slightly and do not put a subscript to the identity of similar order as A_{11}.

3. STORYLET RANKING: DAGS, SMRANK AND PAGERANK

Ranking graph nodes using matrix methods is an important topic today because of the Web and other large scale networks, though, the topic has been of interest in the social sciences much before the advent of the Internet; cf. [36]. Ranking of Web nodes is based on a complex combination of "signals", that includes the result of link-based algorithms, such as Google's PageRank, or others [25]. Typically, this result could be represented as a nonnegative vector (sometimes stochastic[8]) with each element containing the rank of the node corresponding to that location. The question is whether ranking storylets is meaningful; and if it is, how to produce a "correct" ranking? The rest of the paper is devoted to these issues. We do this by presenting ranking methods and applying them on CHILDIF.

One way to rank nodes is by counting the in- and outdegrees of each node. These are easy to compute (in matrix terms, a simple summation of the columns and rows of the adjacency matrix provides the result, that is $A^\top e$ or Ae where e is the vector of all 1's). Since the maximum indegree for all and the maximum outdegree for all but 2 of the books in the collection was 5, this type of ranking would be too coarse to be useful. Another class of methods is based on metrics for hypertexts using distance matrices [6].

For the ergodic literature hypertexts that we consider, an alternative idea is to consider ranking schemes based on the level of storylet participation in all possible plots. So let us define a scheme in which the rank of every storylet is determined by the number of plots containing it. After normalization, we call this ranking SMRank.

DEFINITION 1. Let $G = (V, E)$ be a DAG. For every $v_j \in V$ with $n = |V|$ let

$$\tau_j := \#(paths\ in\ G\ containing\ v_j).$$

Then SMRank : $V \to \mathbb{R}$ is defined by

$$\mathtt{SMRank}(v_j) = \frac{\tau_j}{\sum_{j=1}^n \tau_j}.$$

As mentioned earlier, we assume single source digraphs. When these are DAGs, since every plot must terminate at some sink, the rank of any node can be computed by counting the total number of paths from that node to all sinks and multiplying by the total number of paths from the source to that node. If the DAG is topologically sorted making sure that all f sinks are numbered last, then $e_1^\top (I - A_{11})^{-1} e_1 = 1$ from (1) and thus SMRank(v_1) is the sum of all the paths to the sinks. Also if $n \geq j > n - f$ (that is the node is a sink) then SMRank(v_j) is the first element in column $j - (n - f)$ of matrix $(I - A_{11})^{-1} A_{12}$. All these results facilitate the computation of this ranking on DAGs. The following can be shown easily:

PROPOSITION 1. Assume that the graph $G = (V, E)$ is a DAG with a single source, and that there are f sink nodes, labeled v_1 and $v_{n-f+1}, ..., v_n$ respectively, where $n = |V|$. Then it holds that for any $v_j \in V$

$$\tau_j = e_1^\top (I - A)^{-1} e_j e_j^\top (I - A)^{-1} \begin{pmatrix} 0 \\ I_f \end{pmatrix} e^{(f)}. \quad (2)$$

Moreover

$$\mathtt{SMRank}(v_j) \leq \mathtt{SMRank}(v_1).$$

Unfortunately, computing SMRank for an arbitrary digraph would be much more expensive (see the discussion regarding question (1) in the previous page) since we must count walks (cycles are allowed). It is reasonable to prevent traversing a cycle more than once, but still, the cost of computing the

---

[8]Meaning that its elements add to 1 so that they can be interpreted as probabilities.

rank is prohibitive. Also, expression (2) relies on $I - A$ being invertible. This cannot be guaranteed for general digraphs (e.g. when cycles are present). Another idea is to modify the matrix by introducing a positive scaling attenuation factor say γ, such that the inverse of $I - \gamma A$ exists. Such a γ always exists for non-trivial A, by selecting any value $\gamma < 1/\rho(A)$, where $\rho(A)$ is the spectral radius of A. Then

$$(I - \gamma A)^{-1} = \sum_{j=0}^\infty \gamma^j A^j$$

and γ penalizes longer paths by damping their effect as powers increase. This metric was proposed early on in the field of sociometrics by Katz to rank the status of individuals in a community [22], except that he was interested in column sums of $(I - \gamma A)^{-1}$ to account for the indegrees of nodes. Thus the ranking vector was based on solving the linear system $(I - \gamma A^\top)^{-1} e$. Instead, our goal here is to rank based on the direct or indirect role of each storylet in readings, rewarding storylets that participate by providing one more step towards one or more endings (the more, the better). Notice that the attenuation factor also penalizes cycles. Their contribution is especially discounted when these are taken multiple times. In fact, even though at first sight, the penalty imposed on longer walks might seem questionable (after all we are talking about readings, not distant acquaintances), we argue that it is justified in the hypertext context. Specifically, longer stories are more likely to be stopped prematurely because the young reader rapidly loses patience or is distracted. The above metric is based on the matrix resolvent $(I - \gamma A^\top)^{-1}$. It would be natural to consider other functions as well; cf. [3, 15].

Our next goal is to propose spectral ranking and in particular a PageRank approach to rank storylets. We first describe three important modifications that are made to the graph adjacency matrix. These are standard in PageRank (cf. [25]) but we need to examine their role and justify them for the problem under study. The first is designed to prevent problems caused by "dangling nodes" (in PageRank terminology), that is sink nodes, which in our case are the ending storylets. Specifically, unless we compute SMRank (which is not affected by dangling nodes), we assume that from every ending storylet, the reader is offered the option to start again reading from the beginning and thus the graph is adjusted to include a link from all sink nodes to the source; the adjacency matrix is also adjusted to reflect these new links. We believe that this adjustment is reasonable and justified; it is worth noting, for example, that these "backlinks" actually exist in the text of the "Multiclone Tales".

More significantly, this modification makes the digraphs strongly connected (any node is accessible from any other node). This means the modified matrix irreducible which has important consequences as we will soon see. The second modification is to normalize the adjusted matrix to make it stochastic. This can be accomplished by dividing each row by the sum of the corresponding nodal outdegree; the resulting matrix is $D^{-1}A$, where D is the diagonal matrix of nodal outdegrees while now A is the modified matrix. Since S is stochastic, it can be considered as a transition probability matrix for a discrete-time, finite-state, stationary, irreducible Markov chain. In the sequel we also prefer to work with the transpose $S := (D^{-1}A)^\top$. Because S is column stochastic and irreducible, it has a unique positive eigenvalue equal to 1. From Perron-Frobenius theory, the corresponding (right) eigenvector normalized to be stochastic, is unique and positive; cf. [28]. This is called the Perron vector of S and can be used to rank nodes of the graph [25] thus, in our case, the storylets of the book. Note that unlike the case of matrices representing large scale network connectivity and the Web, the matrices we are confronted with only needed a small and natural modification to guarantee irreducibility and hence the existence of a unique Perron vector. Moreover, their size is such that the vector can be computed easily using direct or iterative methods that are available in high quality numerical libraries and environnments such as MATLAB[9], our preferred package in this work. As we note in the next section, the irreducible matrices, S, resulting following the above adjustments for all the books we considered have only one eigenvalue of modulus 1 (actually real positive and equal to 1 as discussed above), therefore all matrices are primitive.

Therefore, at first sight, there appears to be no need to undertake the third proposed modification, that is to construct and use (as in PageRank) the parametric Google matrix $G(\mu) = \mu S + (1 - \mu)H$, where H is the teleportation matrix and $0 < \mu < 1$ the damping coefficient that was used to guarantee that the Perron vector of $G(\mu)$ is well defined (even if S were irreducible). On the other hand, we recall that one ingenuity in PageRank was that working with G rather than S for μ strictly less than 1 also provided an interpretation of PageRank in terms of a "random surfer". In the words of Google's Brin and Page ([8]) the random surfer "is given a web page at random and keeps clicking on links, never hitting 'back' but eventually gets bored and starts on another random page. The probability that the random surfer visits a page is its PageRank." We observe that this pattern of behavior resembles that children reading this type of ergodic literature and illustrate the proposed analogy in Table 2. We thus consider the random surfer to be a suitable model for our young readers and will use the Perron vector of $G(\mu)$ to rank the storylets. It is also known that when computing PageRank, μ can be interpreted as a damping factor on distant connections, as the previously mentioned attenuation parameter by Katz; cf. [25, 36].

Another indication that this approach is justified is that the overall concept behind PageRank makes sense in our context. Specifically, it is natural to reward storylets that immediatly follow an important storylet (signifying a sequence of important events broken in storylets) but if a storylet branches out to several other ones, the rewards to storylets that follow are reduced.

It is worth noting that more detailed models could be formed by utilizing probabilistic finite automata (cf. [26]) but this is left for future investigation. Some brief comments in [30] is the closest available to the mathematical modeling of the literature we are discussing herein.

In the remainder of this paper we will apply and study the results of these rankings to determine experimentally how they work in practice. Of course, the ranking of storylets (or websites), by people or automatically (using algorithms designed by people) are inherently subjective endeavors. In evaluating the methods discussed, we need to "understand the data" well, in this case the books in CHILDIF, in order to be able to comment upon and possibly interpret the results.

After all, we have an advantage over evaluating ranking results from websites, in that storylets consist of narrative elements that are part of one or more plots as opposed to website chains.

3.1 The CHILDIF collection

We describe in some detail the books in the collection tabulated in Table 1.

Innerstar University This is a recent entry in the realm of ergodic children's literature. We analyzed 4 books from this collection. All of them claimed more than 20 endings in their cover. The digraphs from all the books we considered were acyclic, with a single starting storylet and several ending storylets (around 25).

Choose Your Own adventure (CYOA) The blueprint for this series was "Sugarcane Island" by E. Packard, published in 1976[10] (not included). All the books we considered were authored by R.A. Montgomery. Apparently, the series was very successful and widely translated[11]. We analyzed 6 books from this collection, 3 of which were DAGs. The number of endings in each book is shown on the cover page but no estimate of the number of stories is provided.

Multiclone Tales The last two books in our set were authored by Dr. Eugene Trivizas, one of the most prolific and beloved authors of children's literature in Greece. Trivizas, whose passion for word coinage and play is evident throughout his oeuvre, refers to these books as ΠΑΡΑπολυΜύθια (PARApolyMythia, a contrived term which could mean "too much fabling" or "polyfabling", amongst other things) while the inside cover informs us that they belong to the series "Πολύκλωνα Παραμύθια" (Multiclone Tales). Both books carry the subtitle "A magic tale with one thousand tales hidden in the same tale" and inform readers that "it is a strange and rare book that every time you read it, it tells you another story". In all respects, these two books were the most complex (none of them were DAGs) of our dataset. The smaller of the two contained two sink nodes that did not correspond to ending storylets; we did not attempt to introduce links to amend this omission. As is apparent from Fig. 3 as well as the counts in Table 5, "33 Pink Rubies" was the most complex book, providing the reader with over 220,000 possible stories[12].

We analyzed 12 books in total (a little over 1500 pages) whose titles are listed in Table 3 and created the corresponding adjacency matrices and graphs and computed several of their characteristics. We call the collection CHILDIF. In all cases we did not account for pages corresponding to nodes of zero degree (these were invariably drawings whose removal

---

[9] http://www.mathworks.com/products/matlab/

[10] See http://www.gamebooks.org/show_item.php?id=162 and D. Katz's http://www.gamebooks.org/.

[11] According to the Wikipedia entry for CYOA, more than 250 million copies were sold between 1979 and 1998.

[12] This is corroborated from anecdotal, "user experience": As one parent posted (in Greek) at http://www.greekbooks.gr/books/pedika/pedika/ta-33-roz-rubinia.product, "My daughter and I began this book when she was three and got bored when she was seven. Incredible imagination!".

Table 2: Reader-surfer analogy

reader	surfer
open book	turn browser on
goto starting storylet	open homepage
choose "next" storylet	click on existing link
reached ending, go to starting storylet	reached sought page, click homepage
reached ending, stop	reached sought page, stop
choose any storylet	enter URL, click preferred website

did not affect the readings). We also computed the top few eigenvalues. The second largest (in modulus) eigenvalues ranged in size from 0.88 up to 0.97, whereas the largest eigenvalue was always 1, as expected. Fig. 1 depicts the

Table 3: Book titles, abbreviated name and adjacency matrix characteristics (order n and number of nonzeros nnz) in CHILDIF. Zero degree nodes are omitted.

title	name	n	nnz
Choose Your Own Adventure			
Abominable Snowman	CYOA_AS	91	93
Journey Under the Sea	CYOA_JU	101	109
Space and Beyond	CYOA_SB	115	119
Lost Jewels of Nabooti	CYOA_LJ	110	114
Mystery of the Maya	CYOA_MM	113	116
House of Danger	CYOA_HD	91	90
Innerstar University			
Girl's Best Friend	INUN_GB	110	116
Taking the Reins	INUN_TR	103	107
Into the Spotlight	INUN_IS	112	115
Fork in the Trail	INUN_FT	110	122
Multiclone Tales			
88 Dolmadakia	MUTA_ED	154	265
33 Pink Rubies	MUTA_TP	211	386

sparse matrices INUN_GB and CYOA_SB that correspond to the two graphs shown in Fig. 1 but adjusted for the use of PageRank, that is adding links from the sinks back to the root.

Table 4: Books from CHILDIF that are DAGs and their characteristics. DAGness tested with MATLAB function test_dag.m from MatlabBGL.

title	storylets	ends	plots	lengths (min, max, avg)
CYOA_AS	91 (+25)	28	36	(7,20,11.8)
CYOA_MM	113 (+18)	39	106	(8,30,19.7)
CYOA_HD	91 (+17)	20	20	(9,19,14.4)
INUN_GB	110 (+11)	24	68	(8,24,17.5)
INUN_TR	103 (+19)	24	37	(10,25,16.3)
INUN_IS	112 (+11)	24	40	(7,27,17.8)
INUN_FT	110 (+11)	23	511	(7,34,25.9)

Table 5: Books from CHILDIF that are not DAG and their characteristics.

title	storylets	links	ends	plots
CYOA_JU	101 (+16)	109	42	(>202)
CYOA_SB	115 (+16)	119	43	(>98)
CYOA_LJ	110 (+21)	114	38	(>92)
MUTA_ED	154	265	41	(>1349)
MUTA_TR	211	386	53	(>220431)

alization package GraphViz[13] and the following MATLAB toolboxes: a) Toolbox MatlabBGL[14] b) GraphViz [15] library. c) Brain Connectivity Toolbox[16]. This was used to compute lower bounds to the number of walks in graphs that were not DAGs. The graphs for some books from the collection are depicted in Fig. 2, 3 and 5.

4. EXPERIMENTS

In the sequel, we denote the PageRank ranking with value μ by PR(μ). As explained in Section 3, when running PR all matrices were adjusted to include links from every sink to the source. In all experiments the teleportation matrix was chosen to be $H = \frac{1}{n}ee^{\top}$ modeling an (impatient or bored) child that prefers to go to any other page in the book with probability $1 - \mu$. We used the values $\mu = 0.85$ and 1. The latter case is simply ranking based on the Perron vector of S (thus the "bored" attitude is not captured).

Our first experiment is with "Girl's Best Friend" which is

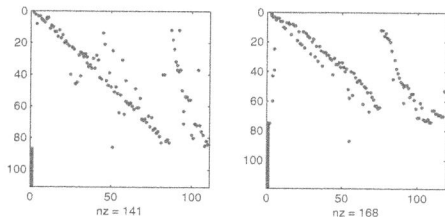

Figure 1: Matrices INUN_GB and CYOA_SB.

We next illustrate some of the books using their digraph and adjacency matrix representations. We used the visu-

---

[13] http://www.graphviz.org/

[14] Authored by D. Gleich; http://www.mathworks.com/matlabcentral/fileexchange/10922.

[15] Function graph_to_dot.m; toolbox authored by L. Peshkin; http://www.mathworks.com/matlabcentral/fileexchange/4518-matlab-graphviz-interface.

[16] Function findpaths.m; toolbox authored by O. Sporns; http://www.indiana.edu/~cortex/connectivity.html.

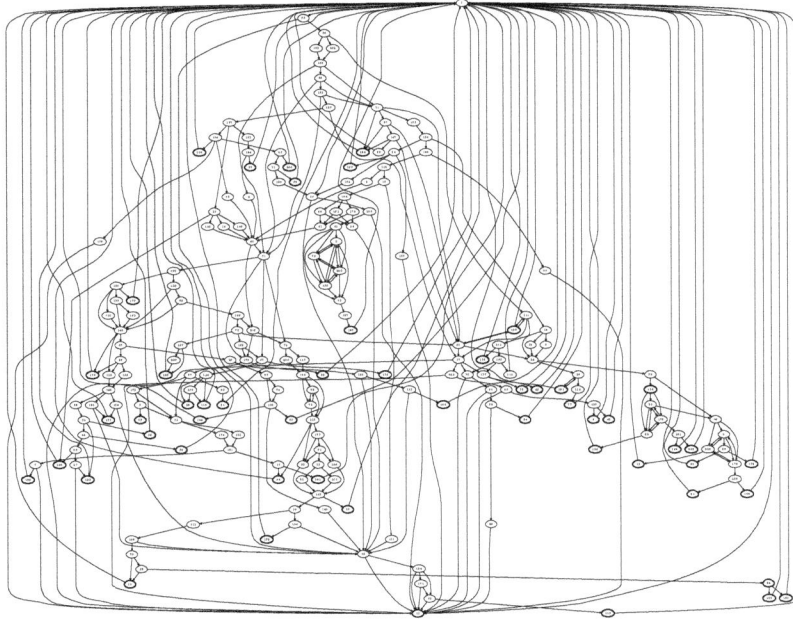

Figure 3: Graph for MUTA_TP ("33 Pink Rubies"). Sink nodes (endings) are marked with bold.

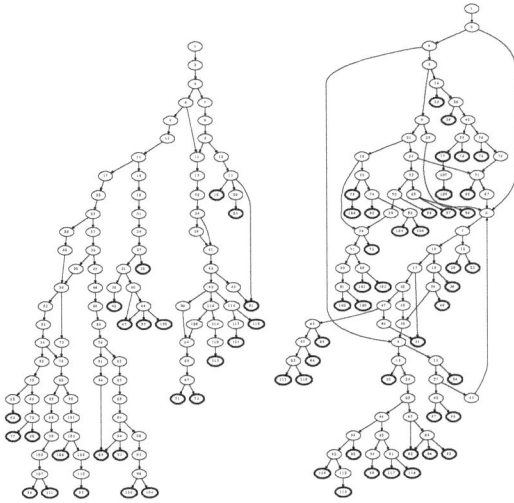

Figure 2: Digraphs for INUN_GB (DAG, left) and CYOA_JU (right) with nodes of degree 0 removed. Sink nodes (endings) are marked with bold.

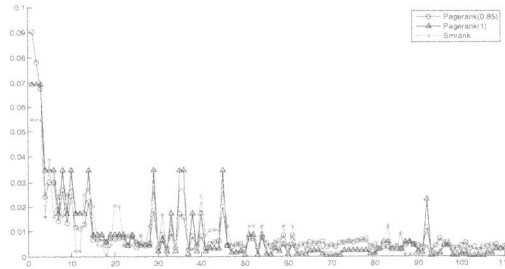

Figure 4: Rankings for all nodes of INUN_GB as computed for each ranking method. The x-axis numbers the nodes, the y-axis the ranking value.

a DAG, therefore we computed SMRank using the formulas of Section 3. For comparison we also computed the values for PR(μ) for $\mu = 0.85, 1$. The resulting rankings are shown in Fig. 4 while a more detailed view of the top results for each ranking is tabulated in Table 6. In the discussion that follows for this book the node labels are shifted down by 8 positions relative to the actual page numbers because the first storylet in the book is on page 9. Thus, node 1 corresponds to page 9, etc. As expected, the top nodes are storylets that would be part of every valid reading of any plot. Indeed, the first group of nodes may be interpreted as an initial substory,

shared by all stories derived from the same novel, and for that reason it could have been written (or summarized) as a single, first, page. The second group contains node 6 (corresponding to p14). Its importance was corroborated by our "independent readers"[17]. Reading all plots, it becomes evident that node 6 takes the reader to node 11 (if one chooses for the protagonist to take Pepper the dog straight to the dog-shelter) or to node 8 (if one chooses the protagonist to walk Pepper home). This choice in some sense reveals the personality of the protagonist (that is the kid making the choice); it is therefore important, therefore the ranking algorithms were right to place the storylet higly. On the other hand, the storylets that were ranked last usually were either ending storylets or storylets directly preceding ending sto-

---

[17]When we refer to "independent readers" we mean friends that accepted to read the stories and mark the pages that they thought were most important, *before knowing* the results of our ranking experiments.

rylets and linked to them with a single link. Observe that in Fig. 4, there are some peaks in the PageRank values far to the right, specifically at positions 92 and 95 (the latter only for PR(0.85)). These positions correspond to nodes 51 and 68 in the graph and are both terminal nodes. The fact that their ranks are substantially higher than those of other terminal nodes (as we showed above and is validated in the figure, SMRank ranks terminal nodes last) is because they are linked directly to nodes 13 and 84, both of which lie near the root, and thus have high ranks that pump up the PageRank of their immediate descendants. Such "link jumps" exist in several of the books and manifested themselves with a similar pattern of peaks in the ranking plots.

Table 6: Top ranked results for INUN_GB. Actual page numbers have been shifted by 8 so that the initial book page of 9 is listed as 1.

SmRank		Pagerank			
		$\mu = 0.85$		$\mu = 1$	
value	node	value	node	rank	node
0.0547	4	0.0903	1	0.0695	4
	2	0.0781	2		1
	1	0.0677	4		2
0.0388	6	0.0302	6	0.0347	43
0.0274	56		7		41
	43	0.0270	9		11
	41	0.0245	11		5
	34	0.0243	5		56
	15	0.0222	15		6
	11	0.0202	56		15
0.0251	14	0.0186	34		7
	10	0.0171	41		9
	8	0.0159	43		34

We next consider "Mystery of the Maya" (CYOA_MM), also a DAG; cf. Fig. 5. As before, the first few pages ($1 \rightarrow 2 \rightarrow$

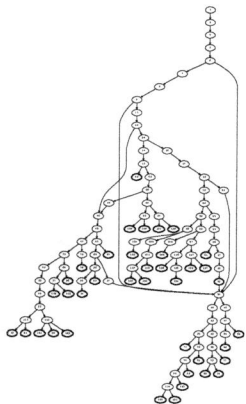

Figure 5: Graph for CYOA_MM (DAG). Nodes of zero degree are not depicted. Sink nodes (endings) are marked with bold.

$3 \rightarrow 5 \rightarrow 6$) are supposed to be read in sequence. These introduce some background to the story ("a friend of the hero has disappeared while on assignment in Mexico and the hero decides to search for him"). Not surprisingly, all

ranking algorithms identify these pages as being the most important. Also, sinks were consistently ranked very low. The groupings in SMRank and PR(1) for the top nodes are similar, while PR(0.85) appears to provide a more refined view, placing the source above the others. P6 contains the first decision for the reader. Moreover, after reading the book it became clear that p6 was quite special because it divides the book into two "conceptual directions". These directions are further divided in the sequel as in the concept map shown in Fig. 6. After reading all the plots in the book, three storylets (on pages 6, 12 and 38) that were judged by the readers to be important, were also assigned a high SMRank value. From the readings, it became clear that at those nodes there were "conceptual" directions that opened up. It is also worth noting that p12 and p38 are at the same level, but have very different ranks. This can be exlained by the fact that p12 leads to 24 endings whereas p38 to only 10. We show the ranks for all the nodes in Fig. 7.

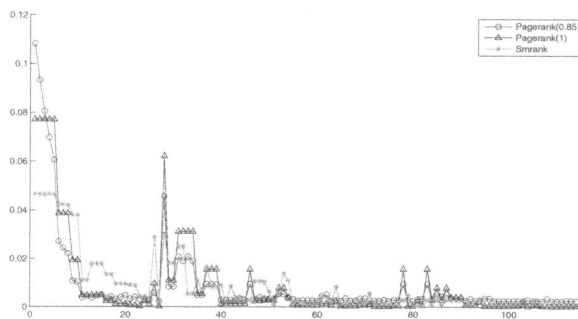

Figure 7: Rankings for all nodes of CYOA_MM.

Table 7: Top ranked results for CYOA_MM.

SmRank		Pagerank			
		$\mu = 0.85$		$\mu = 1$	
rank	node	rank	node	rank	node
0.0466	6	0.1082	1	0.0772	1
	5	0.0933	2		5
	3	0.0806	3		2
	2	0.0698	5		6
	1	0.0607	6		3
0.0422	9	0.0457	38	0.0621	38
	8	0.0271	7	0.0386	7
	7	0.0244	8		8
0.0379	12	0.0220	9		9
	11	0.0207	44	0.0310	46
0.0304	38		46		44
0.0288	34	0.0189	45		45
0.0249	45		47		47
	44	0.0107	11	0.0193	12
0.0182	43	0.0104	12		11

Another observation is that SMRank and PR(1) gave similar orderings in all DAG books under evaluation.

We next consider one book that is not a DAG, specifically CYOA_JU, and the ranking obtained by PageRank. Results are shown in Fig. 8 and Table 8. It can be seen from the

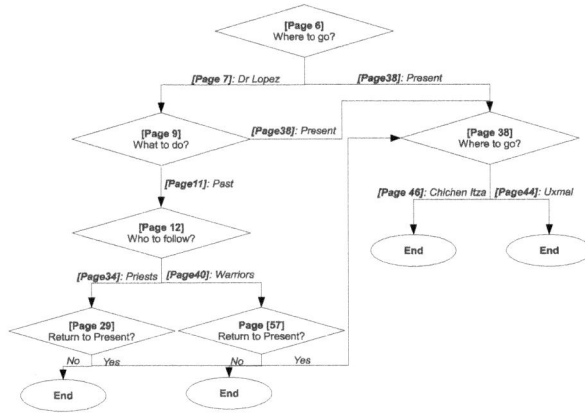

Figure 6: Concept map for `CYOA_MM`. Each box represents several storylets and possible plots (endings included), but sharing the marked concept.

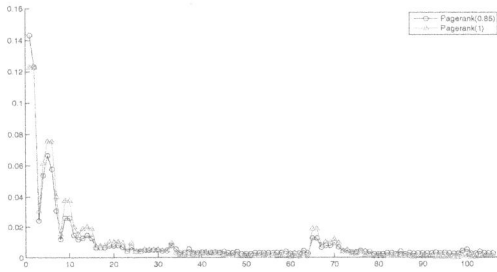

Figure 8: Rankings for all nodes of `CYOA_JU`.

Table 8: Top ranked results for `CYOA_JU`.

Pagerank			
$\mu = 0.85$		$\mu = 1$	
rank	node	rank	node
0.1431	1	0.1226	1
0.1231	2		2
0.0663	6	0.0754	7
0.0578	7		6
0.0537	4	0.0613	4
0.0310	8	0.0401	8
0.0260	12	0.0377	10
	10		12
0.0242	3	0.0307	3
0.0146	18	0.0200	13
	13		18
0.0125	20	0.0189	22
	19		20
	17		17
	22		19

table that a significant number of storylets that are ranked as important belong to a cycle (pages 6, 8, 7,10,13 etc). To see why this is so, we examine the rankings at the nodes where cycles begin. Consider for instance the cycle $6 \rightarrow 7 \rightarrow 10 \rightarrow 17 \rightarrow \cdots \rightarrow 27 \rightarrow 43 \rightarrow 6$. Pages 6 and 8 can be viewed as entry nodes to the cycle since any path entering the cycle has to include them. PageRank recognizes this and assigns these pages relatively higher values than the rest of the cycle nodes. For the same reason, if the entry nodes had low rank, then the rank of the remaining nodes in the cycle would be even lower. There is also no difference for the tabulated nodes between the rankings computed with `PR(1)` and `PR(0.85)`.

Finally, it is interesting to note that none of the books had more than one starting storylet. This would have made the rankings more interesting as there would be more candidates for the top position (currently occupied by the single source).

5. CONCLUSIONS

From the above discussion and experiments it appears that the `SMRank` (for DAGs) and PageRank can be used to obtain interpretable and useful information from the `CHILDIF` collection. This opens the way for further analysis of hypertexts of this kind using graph and matrix tools developed for link based analysis, including recent methods developed for digraphs; see e.g. [3]. There are also interesting educational avenues, such as the use of this "literary framework" to introduce modern computer science and mathematical concepts for data analysis. A further challenge would be to apply matrix and graph tools online, on ergodic literature that cannot be readily leafed through[18]. The bigger quest, of course, is to incorporate such methods into tools that can assist readers, authors, and even publishers of ergodic literature, printed or digital.

6. ACKNOWLEDGMENTS

We are grateful to: Markus Strohmaier and the reviewers for considering our work and for constructive comments;

---

[18] As in the interactive fiction "Choice Of" series; cf. `http://www.choiceofgames.com/`.

Michele Benzi for discussions on the topic of matrix functions for network analysis and Oulipo; Giorgos Kollias for helpful discussions and advice on tools for graph manipulation; Christos Zaroliagis and Panagiotis Mihail for discussions on graph algorithms; Aristoula Georgiadou for advice on philological matters. We also thank Eugenios Trivizas (who has been Professor of Criminology at the Department of Sociology of University of Reading, UK, since 1978) for his comments on a very early version of this work presented at a local student workshop in Patras[19]. The current paper represents a major advancement over that work. We also thank our "independent readers team", Ioanna Gazi and Angeliki Rapti. Our discovery of children's hypertext literature in Greece was the result of some serendipity having to do with parenting and storytelling. So it is appropriate to also thank Anabella for causing it!

7. REFERENCES

[1] E. Aarseth. *Ergodic Literature*. The Johns Hopkins University Press., Baltimore, MD, 1997.

[2] R. Barthes. *S/Z: Essais*. Seuil, Paris, 1970.

[3] M. Benzi, E. Estrada, and C. Klymko. Ranking hubs and authorities using matrix functions. Technical Report Math/CS TR-2012-003, Emory University, 2012.

[4] M. Bernstein. Storyspace 1. In *Proc. 13th ACM Conf. Hypertext and Hypermedia*, HT'02, pages 172–181, New York, NY, USA, 2002. ACM.

[5] M. Bernstein. On hypertext narrative. In *Proc. 20th ACM Conf. Hypertext and Hypermedia*, HT'09, pages 5–14, New York, NY, USA, 2009. ACM.

[6] R. A. Botafogo, E. Rivlin, and B. Shneiderman. Structural analysis of hypertexts: Identifying hierarchies and useful metrics. *ACM Trans. Inf. Syst.*, 10:142–180, April 1992.

[7] D. Bouyssou, D. de Werra, and O. Hudry. Claude Berge and the "Oulipo". *EURO Newsletter*, (6), 2006.

[8] S. Brin and L. Page. The anatomy of a large-scale hypertextual Web search engine. *Computer Networks and ISDN Systems*, 33:107–117, 1998.

[9] A. Broder, R. Kumar, F. Maghoul, P. Raghavan, S. Rajagopalan, R. Stata, A. Tomkins, and J. Wiener. Graph structure in the Web. *Comput. Netw.*, 33(1-6):309–320, 2000.

[10] R. Brualdi and D. Cvetkovic. *A Combinatorial Approach to Matrix Theory and its Applications*. Chapman & Hall/CRC, 2009.

[11] A. Bruckman. The combinatorics of storytelling: Mystery train interactive. Unpublished paper, MIT Media Lab in http://www.cc.gatech.edu/~asb/papers/misc/combinatorics-bruckman-90.pdf, 1990.

[12] K. Casey. *The Runaway Game*. May Davenport Publishers, Los Altos Hills, CA, 2001.

[13] M. P. Consens and A. O. Mendelzon. Expressing structural hypertext queries in Graphlog. In *Proc. 2nd Annual ACM Conf. on Hypertext*, HT'89, pages 269–292, New York, NY, USA, 1989. ACM.

[14] C. Crawford. *On interactive storytelling*. New Riders Games, Berkeley, CA, 2005.

[15] J. Crofts, E. Estrada, D. Higham, and A. Taylor. Mapping directed networks. *Electronic Transactions on Numerical Analysis*, 37:337–350, 2010.

[16] A. Doxiadis. The mathematical logic of narrative. In M. Manaresi, editor, *Matematica e cultura in Europa*, pages 171–181. Springer, Milan, 2005.

[17] D. Eggers. *A Heartbreaking Work of Staggering Genius*. Simon & Schuster, New York, 2000.

[18] L. Festinger. The analysis of sociograms using matrix algebra. *Human Relations*, 2:153 – 158, 1949.

[19] M. Fredman and R. Tarjan. Fibonacci heaps and their uses in improved network optimization algorithms. *J. ACM*, 34(3):596–615, July 1987.

[20] I. Gessel and R. Stanley. Algebraic enumeration. In R.L. Graham et al., editor, *Handbook of Combinatorics*, volume 2, pages 1021–1061. Elsevier, 1995.

[21] J. Gross and J. Yellen, editors. *Handbook of Graph Theory*. CRC Press, 2004.

[22] L. Katz. A new status index derived from sociometric analysis. *Psychometrika*, 18:39–43, 1953.

[23] J. Kleinberg. Authoritative Sources in a Hyperlinked Environment. *Journal of the ACM*, 46(5):604–632, 1999.

[24] G. Landow. *Hypertext 3.0*. Johns Hopkins University Press, 2006.

[25] A. Langville and C. Meyer. *Google's PageRank and Beyond: The Science of Search Engine Rankings*. Princeton Univ. Press, 2006.

[26] M. Levene and G. Loizou. Web interaction and the navigation problem in hypertext. In *Encyclopedia of Microcomputers*, volume 28 (suppl. 7), pages 381–398. Marcel Dekker, New York, 2002.

[27] P. Mateti and N. Deo. On algorithms for enumerating all circuits of a graph. *SIAM Journal on Computing*, 5(1):90–99, 1976.

[28] C. Meyer. *Matrix Analysis and Applied Linear Algebra*. SIAM, Philadelphia, 2001.

[29] R. Mihalcea and D. Radev. *Graph-based Natural Language Processing and Information Retrieval*. Cambridge University Press, 2011.

[30] N. Montfort. Cybertext killed the hypertext star: The hypertext murder case. *Electronic Book Rev.*, 2000.

[31] N. Montfort. *Twisty Little Passages*. MIT Press, 2003.

[32] A. Saemmer. Littératures numériques: tendances, perspectives, outils d'analyse. *Études Françaises*, 43:111–131, 2007.

[33] S. Schreibman, R. Siemens, and J. Unsworth, editors. *A Companion to Digital Humanities*. Blackwell, Oxford, 2004.

[34] J. Shiga. *Meanwhile: Pick Any Path. 3,856 Story Possibilities*. Amulet Books, 2010.

[35] R. Tarjan. Depth-first search and linear graph algorithms. *SIAM Journal on Computing*, 1(2):146–160, 1972.

[36] S. Vigna. Spectral ranking. *CoRR*, abs/0912.0238, 2009.

---

[19]T. Kostakis and E. Gallopoulos, "The 88 dolmadakia eigenvector: Link analysis and linear algebra in children's books", Eureka Conf. presentation, Patras, 2007.

Human Navigation in Networks

Jure Leskovec
Stanford University
jure@cs.stanford.edu

ABSTRACT

World around us interconnected in giant networks and we are daily navigating and finding paths through such networks. For example, we browse the Web [2], search for connections among friends in social networks [6, 3], follow leads in citation networks of scientific literature, and look up things in cross-referenced dictionaries and encyclopedias [9]. Even though navigating networks is an essential part of our everyday lives, little is known about the mechanisms humans use to navigate networks as well as the properties of networks that allow for efficient navigation.

We conduct two large scale studies of human navigation in networks. First, we present a study an instance of Milgram's small-world experiment where the task is to navigate from a given source to a given target node using only the local network information [5]. We perform a computational analysis of a planetary-scale social network of 240 million people and 1.3 billion edges and investigate the importance of geographic cues for navigating the network. Second, we also discuss a large-scale study of human wayfinding, in which, given a network of links between the concepts of Wikipedia, people play a game of finding a short path from a given start to a given target concept by following hyperlinks (Figure 1) [7]. We study more than 30,000 goal-directed human search paths through Wikipedia network and identify strategies people use when navigating information spaces [8, 9].

Even though the domains of social and information networks are very different, we find many commonalities in navigation of the two networks. Humans tend to be good at finding short paths, despite the fact that the networks are very large [8]. Human paths differ from shortest paths in characteristic ways. At the early stages of the search navigating to a high-degree hub node helps, while in the later stage, content features and geography provide the most important clues. We also observe a trade-off between simplicity and efficiency: conceptually simple solutions are more common but tend to be less efficient than more complex ones [9].

One potential reason for good human performance could be that humans possess vast amounts of background knowledge about the network, which they leverage to make good guesses about possible paths. So we ask the question: Are human-like high-level reasoning skills really necessary for finding short paths? To answer this question, we design a number of navigation agents without such skills, which use only simple numerical features [8]. We evaluate the agents on the task of navigating both networks. We observe that the agents find shorter paths than humans on average

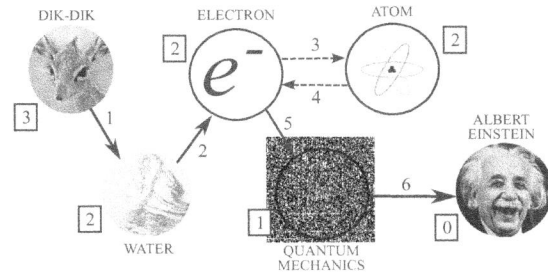

Figure 1: A human example path between the concepts DIK-DIK and ALBERT EINSTEIN in the Wikipedia network. Nodes represent Wikipedia articles and edges the hyperlinks clicked by the human. Edge labels indicate the order of clicks, the framed numbers the shortest-path length to the target. One of several optimal solutions would be ⟨DIK-DIK, WATER, GERMANY, ALBERT EINSTEIN⟩.

and therefore conclude that, perhaps surprisingly, no sophisticated background knowledge or high-level reasoning is required for navigating a complex network.

The talk is based on joint work with Robert West and Eric Horvitz.

Categories and Subject Descriptors

H.5.4 [**Information Interfaces and Presentation**]: Hypertext / Hypermedia—*Navigation*

General Terms

Algorithms, Experimentation, Human Factors

Keywords

Navigation, decentralized search, information networks, small-world.

1. REFERENCES

[1] L. Adamic and E. Adar. How to search a social network. *Social Networks*, 27(3):187–203, 2005.

[2] E. H. Chi, P. Pirolli, K. Chen, and J. Pitkow. Using information scent to model user information needs and actions and the web. In *Proceedings of the SIGCHI conference on Human factors in computing systems*, CHI '01, pages 490–497, 2001.

[3] P. S. Dodds, R. Muhamad, and D. J. Watts. An experimental study of search in global social networks. *Science*, 301(5634):827, 2003.

[4] J. M. Kleinberg. Navigation in a small world. *Nature*, 406(6798):845–845, 2000.

[5] J. Leskovec and E. Horvitz. Planetary-scale views on a large instant-messaging network. In *Proceedings of the 17th international conference on World Wide Web*, WWW '08, pages 915–924, 2008.

[6] S. Milgram. The small-world problem. *Psychology Today*, 2(1):60–67, 1967.

[7] R. West. Wikispeedia. Website, 2009. http://www.wikispeedia.net.

[8] R. West and J. Leskovec. Automatic versus human navigation in information networks. In *Proceedings of the AAAI International Conference on Weblogs and Social Media*, ICWSM '12, 2012.

[9] R. West and J. Leskovec. Human wayfinding in information networks. In *Proceedings of the 21st International Conference on the World Wide Web*, WWW '11, 2012.

TrustSplit: Usable Confidentiality for Social Network Messaging

Sascha Fahl, Marian Harbach, Thomas Muders and Matthew Smith
Leibniz University of Hannover
Distributed Computing & Security Group
Hannover, Germany
{fahl,harbach,muders,smith}@dcsec.uni-hannover.de

ABSTRACT

It is well known that online social networking sites (OSNs) such as Facebook pose risks to their users' privacy. OSNs store vast amounts of users' private data and activities and therefore subject the user to the risk of undesired disclosure. The regular non tech-savvy Facebook user either has little awareness of his privacy needs or is not willing or capable to invest much extra effort into securing his online activities.

In this paper, we present a non-disruptive and easy to-use service that helps to protect users' most private information, namely their private messages and chats against the OSN provider itself and external adversaries. Our novel Confidentiality as a Service paradigm was designed with usability and non-obtrusiveness in mind and requires little to no additional knowledge on the part of the users. The simplicity of the service is achieved through a novel trust splitting approach integrated into the Confidentiality as a Service paradigm. To show the feasibility of our approach we present a fully-working prototype for Facebook and an initial usability study. All of the participating subjects completed the study successfully without any problems or errors and only required three minutes on average for the entire installation and setup procedure.

Categories and Subject Descriptors

H.3.5 [**Information Storage and Retrieval**]: Online Information Services—*Data Sharing*; E.3 [**Data**]: Data Encryption

General Terms

Security, Human Factors

Keywords

Confidentiality, Usability, Privacy, Social Networks, Symmetric Encryption

1. INTRODUCTION

Social networks currently play an important role in many people's daily lives. The amount of social interaction taking place on the Internet is growing rapidly and benefits from new technology. In 2011, around 2 billion people around the world were using Social Networks (SNs), such as Facebook (750 million users)[1]. However, this also poses a risk to a user's information in terms of privacy and trust [5]. Studies have shown that users value their privacy in general, but act the opposite in social networks [1, 14, 27].

Previous work has proposed measures to improve privacy concerning unwanted disclosure to other SN users (e.g. [25, 12, 16]). While the privacy implications of publicly sharing information is slowly finding its way into the users' minds, the problem of giving the SN provider all their (possibly highly private) information without any means of control has not been properly recognised by the general public yet.

Generally, the business model of SN providers (make money with advertisements based on the users' content) collides with the users' need for privacy. However, this is so easily forgotten over flashy games and catchy features. It is only in Facebook's interest to protect its users' information for publicity reasons. While this might be acceptable for many users in principle, we believe that there should be a clear distinction between content that obviously is intended to be public or at least semi-public (e.g. wall posts, likes, or fan site memberships) and information that is thought to be personal and confidential (e.g. private messages and chats). Semi-public content does not need to be protected to the same extent as private content, since its purpose is to be consumable by a higher number of users. For private content, on the other hand, we argue that there needs to be a solution to effectively protect a user's privacy, even from the SN providers themselves, without burdening the users with security related workflows or requiring specialised knowledge.

Lucas et al. [18] actually argue that the current legal framework in the U.S. does not protect a user's privacy at all when interacting with Facebook, because the users have "no reasonable expectation of privacy" when using the service. Additionally, since Facebook is based in Menlo Park, Ca, USA, all the users' data stored on Facebook's servers is subject to the US Electronic Communications Privacy Act[2]. Hence, there is a need for external digital measures to pro-

---

[1]http://www.socialnomics.net/2011/08/16/social-network-users-statistics/
[2]http://cpsr.org/issues/privacy/ecpa86/

tect a user's privacy, which has been recognised in several previous approaches [18, 3, 4, 17, 11, 21].

While the idea of cryptographically securing messages and other SN content is no novelty, previous approaches often suffer from a lack of usability by impeding the user's regular workflow. Especially because privacy in SNs is often outweighed by the perceived utility [6], users are not willing to invest considerable effort into additional measures. Furthermore, many of the proposed solutions are still susceptible to unauthorised access by foreign governments. Therefore, we propose a novel and above all user-friendly approach to add confidentiality to social networks: Confidentiality as a Service (CaaS). By utilising existing infrastructure, this approach will allow us to conserve the existing user experience, scale well to the sizes of current social networks and overcome the legal problems many other approaches still have.

Our core contributions to confidentiality in social networks are:

- We demonstrate that many existing confidentiality-enhancing approaches for private SN messaging suffer from limitations, due to limited usability and legal issues.

- We introduce the CaaS paradigm that splits trust between a number of entities or organisations to overcome administrative and legal problems with confidentiality, often causing undesired access by foreign governments.

- We provide an easy-to-use prototype for Facebook that integrates seamlessly with the normal workflow and raises awareness for (un)protected information.

One may argue that encrypting the private messages of social network users may subvert the OSN provider's business model. But, in contrast to other users' content such as wall posts, Facebook explicitly mentions in their general business terms that users' private messages are not analysed for targeted advertising purposes.

Organisation of this paper. In the next section, we will present the problems with privacy in modern online social networks and how other measures fail to address these. Section 3 will subsequently introduce the Confidentiality as a Service (CaaS) paradigm and how it integrates with social networks. In Section 4 we analyse the security of the CaaS approach before Section 5 gives details on the implementation and evaluation of a fully functional CaaS prototype for Facebook. Section 6 discusses related work, before Section 7 concludes this paper and outlines future work.

2. PROBLEM STATEMENT

In the following, we illustrate why privacy concerns are often neglected by users of Social Networks and outline how these needs could be satisfied. We will argue why existing paradigms, such as Public Key Infrastructures (PKI) and PGP (Pretty Good Privacy), are not widely deployed for end-to-end encryption between end users and furthermore which general shortcomings need to be overcome. We will use Facebook's messaging service as an example for today's social network communication mechanisms.

Social Networks changed the way users perceive communication on the Internet. Communication partners use the SN regularly (or get notified of new activity on their profile automatically) and perceive their interactions as natural.

There is no more need to consider the size of one's inbox or how to remember a friend's email-address. Modern Internet communication through Social Networks offers great general usability and makes the user's life a lot easier, but there is a fundamental difference to the early days of simple emails: While communication was previously using the Internet only for transport and short-term storage, it is nowadays using the Internet as a long-term information archive as well. The user is often not aware of or does not care about potential privacy implications of this scenario and is generally not willing to switch to another (possibly more laborious) communication mechanism to achieve confidentiality for his data.

Moreover, with Facebook, the problem is that the service stores all communication that has ever taken place on the platform and also has the right to use it for whatever purposes[3]. On top of that, the business model of Facebook and many other services relies on mining the users' personal information in order to sell targeted advertisements. Since privacy is not in the provider's interest, there is often hardly a chance to effectively protect or delete content with or without the provider's help. Over time, this becomes an immense privacy problem, because the user has lost all control over his data and may not know who else has gained access to his information, possibly under a foreign legislation and political system. Hence, confidentiality of data must be managed by the users themselves or in cooperation with a trusted third-party.

Existing paradigms, such as PKI and PGP, heavily involve the user in preparing appropriate cryptographic keys for the exchange in order to provide end-to-end security. With a PKI, all communication partners have to obtain a (potentially costly) certificate and trust one arbitrary central authority to vouch for the identity of a given communication partner. Using PGP, one either has to manually verify the validity of the partners' public key or the Web of Trust needs to be extensive enough to obtain a meaningful trust statement. Both approaches require a higher level of technical knowledge than that required for using a SN site and thus are not practically usable by most SN users. They are also not easily compatible with many users' habit of using the SN with multiple devices. Most importantly however, they are burdensome to use, mainly due to key-management issues. Also, there generally is no support for these technologies by social network providers, due to the reasons outlined in the previous paragraph.

Since today's highly mobile Internet users access services from multiple devices and are not willing to invest additional effort into confidentiality measures, an effective solution for the message confidentiality problem must integrate well into this environment.

Based on the above problem statement, we derive the following usability requirements for an easy-to-use confidentiality and integrity mechanism for OSN messages.

Usability Requirements

UsabReq1. Confidentiality and integrity for OSN messages must be unobtrusively integrated into the users' usage patterns, causing minimal extra effort. This includes the following sub-requirements:

---

[3]cf. `http://www.facebook.com/terms.php`

- There should be no visible key-management for the user.

- Security mechanisms that are visible to the user should be limited to familiar concepts such as usernames and passwords.

- Encryption and decryption of data should be handled automatically by the software.

UsabReq2. Users must be able to recover access to their message history, in case decryption credentials were forgotten or lost.

UsabReq3. Users must be able to access encrypted data from multiple devices without needing to move digital artefacts.

2.1 Legal Problems

An entirely different risk to a user's privacy stems from legal requirements. Many countries require telecommunication providers to allow national intelligence and law enforcement agencies access to their users' communications. This prevents SN providers from offering complete privacy, since there is a requirement to be able to recover the cleartext of arbitrary users and there can be no guarantee that this recovery mechanism cannot be abused. A prominent example is Hushmail [17], who was forced to disclose personal emails (which the users believed to be fully confidential) from their web-based service after moving encryption from the client-side to the server-side. Because they were technically able to provide the plaintext (since they were then encrypting the emails on the server), they were legally required and forced to do so [24].

Hence, in order to ensure confidentiality for users, the storage of content and any corresponding confidentiality mechanisms should be managed by separated service providers, ideally subject to different legal systems. Involving multiple legal systems greatly improves the confidentiality of the users' data. While data can be stored in a country with lower privacy standards such as the US, using a confidentiality provider residing in a legislation with strong privacy protection provides an effective means to avoid undesired disclosure.

3. CONFIDENTIALITY AS A SERVICE

The Confidentiality as a Service (CaaS) paradigm promotes the idea of outsourcing the provision of confidentiality for digital content. While traditional paradigms only involve the immediately participating parties (i.e. the communication partners in a private message exchange) into cryptographic operations, the CaaS paradigm proposes a third-party service provider who caters for encryption and decryption for the end users without itself being able to access the content being protected. The CaaS provider transparently provides key management and encryption/decryption of user content by linking a CaaS identity with the social network identity of that user. This link is used to effortlessly integrate confidentiality mechanisms into the traditional SN operations of the users, effectively freeing them from any security-related overhead. A CaaS provider can be run by a company, a non-profit organisation, a private person or any other entity that is interested in being a trust partner of the Social Network users. The CaaS provider is entirely oblivious to which kind of information is being protected. Its only task is to facilitate confidentiality and not to store, transport or access the users' messages in any way. This is fully orthogonal to a SN provider's interests and business model (cf. **Req3** below).

We postulate that this separation of interests provides a powerful means to effectively protect data from undesired disclosure. Furthermore, this paradigm solves the legal problems described above, based on the sovereignty of countries and the ubiquitous nature of the Internet.

There are three requirements to successfully apply the CaaS paradigm:

Req1: The CaaS provider must be able to identify and authenticate SN users through an out-of-band channel, such as an Email address, to bind the SN identity to a CaaS identity.

Req2: The SN offers sharing of data between multiple users protected by an access control list mechanism.

Req3: The SN provider and the CaaS provider must not have any incentive to collude.

While Requirement 1 addresses the linking of service identities to prevent identity theft and will be discussed in Section 3.3.1, Requirements 2 and 3 outline the basic characteristics of a service that can leverage CaaS functionality.

3.1 The CaaS Workflow

Before delving into details of the CaaS paradigm, this section will outline a typical CaaS-enhanced message exchange, using Facebook as an example. In order to protect the privacy of a user's message against a SN provider and the CaaS provider, multiple commutative layers of encryption – referred to as *cLayer* in the following – are applied. cLayers are layers of encryption that can be added and removed from data in an arbitrary order. For example, if two layers l_1 and l_2 are added consecutively, either l_1 or l_2 can be removed first. Subsequently, we will use the following user-centric naming convention for the cLayers. Layers added locally by the SN user's client are called local cLayers. Layers added by the CaaS provider on the remote CaaS server are called remote cLayers.

In a typical CaaS-encrypted communication session, one user – the sender – intends to confidentially send messages to one or more users – the recipients – over a SN platform. Figure 1 illustrates the CaaS paradigm and all involved parties.

The following describes the steps transparently and automatically executed in the CaaS workflow. First, the sender's software adds a local cLayer to the message and sends it to the CaaS provider. Second, the CaaS provider adds a remote cLayer, that will remain in place until the recipients remove it. Before actually sending the encrypted message to all recipients over the SN platform, the sender's software removes the local cLayer. Subsequently, the CaaS-cLayer-protected data can be transferred to the SN platform.

To recover the plaintext data, one recipient's software again adds a local cLayer and sends the twice-encrypted data to the CaaS provider. At this point, the CaaS provider removes the remote cLayer and transfers the result back to the recipient. Finally, the recipient's software removes the local cLayer to display the plaintext to the user. Since each user-to-CaaS-provider request is protected by a commutative en-

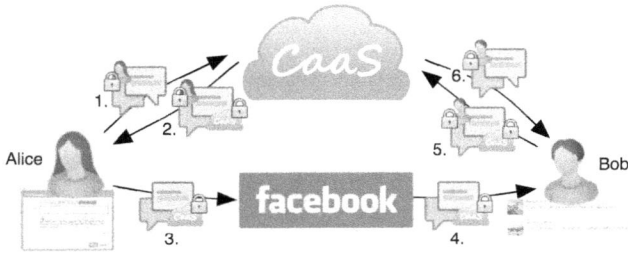

Figure 1: A CaaS provider encrypts a message for Alice before it is sent to Bob through Facebook (Steps 1., 2. and 3.). On the other side, Bob receives the encrypted data and sends it to the CaaS service for decryption (Steps 4., 5. and 6.). The different types of locks on the exchanged messages indicate the key(s) the messages are protected with.

cryption layer, the CaaS provider is not able to eavesdrop on the users' data. These six steps use encryption and decryption methods on the client- (+cLayerLocal/-cLayerLocal) and the server-side (+cLayerRemote/-cLayerRemote). The following subsections elaborate on details of the CaaS environment.

3.2 CaaS Provider

Setting up a CaaS provider is simple. The provider's initialisation phase consists of an algorithm called Global Setup:

3.2.1 Global Setup

The software chooses the following primitives:

- a symmetric stream cipher: Sym_{stream}^p, e.g. AES [20] in CTR mode. For further encryption and decryption operations, this cipher is used to generate a pseudo-random key stream based on a given symmetric encryption key k and a random initialisation vector iv;

- a cryptographic hash function: H_p (e.g. SHA-2);

- a HMAC-based Key Derivation function: $HKDF_p$[4].

- a random master secret X_p of appropriate length (making a brute force attack infeasible);

- and a cryptographic hash function H_u for all users in the CaaS provider's domain and publish H_u as a public parameter.

Based on these parameters and primitives, the CaaS provider can cryptographically secure messages for registered users before they are sent to the SN.

3.3 CaaS Client-side Integration

Today's social network users are used to viewing websites using web browsers and are familiar with identifying and authenticating using a tuple of username and password to access services online. The past has shown that further measures are often only accepted for transactions that are perceived as being particularly sensitive (e.g. online banking). Studies have indicated that the use of a SN is not perceived

---

[4]cf. http://www.ietf.org/rfc/rfc5869.txt

---

as a sensitive application (cf. [1, 14, 27]) and users will therefore not accept complicated security measures. Hence, the CaaS paradigm maintains the familiar usability experience of a SN, in order to allow adoption by regular users. The integration of CaaS into the daily SN routine only requires one noticeable change, namely entering an additional CaaS password after logging into the SN and triggering the first encryption/decryption sequence. This password is sent directly and securely to the CaaS provider and cannot be intercepted by the SN provider.

3.3.1 Registration

The Registration procedure is the initial user-driven step to create a new CaaS account. This process requires the user to identify and register with an email address and a password. To confirm that information, a validation email is sent. As described by Garfinkel [13], email based identification and authentication (EBIA) is an attractive alternative to public-key infrastructure on the one hand and simultaneously provides functional security on the other. Internet users are used to this sort of workflow and therefore easily accept this measure. The EBIA scheme identifies and authenticates a user by sending a validation secret to the given email address. If the user is able to read the secret (i.e. to receive the email), the EBIA scheme was completed successfully and a new active CaaS credential set $Cred_{CaaS} = \langle email, ids = [], password \rangle$ is created.

To provide the necessary integration with Social Networks, the CaaS approach binds an existing SN identity to a previously registered CaaS account (cf. **Req1**). We adopt a quick and simple out-of-band procedure to confirm the identity's ownership before creating a binding. Most SN providers require an external identification token (in form of an email address) during their registration process. After the SN's registration procedure, the internal SN identification (e.g. the Facebook UID) is bound to the user's external identification. During registration for a CaaS account, this mapping can be leveraged to send a confirmation email to the future CaaS user using the EBIA scheme.

Using Facebook as an example, registration works as follows: The user logs into his CaaS account and clicks a button to log into his Facebook account using Facebook's Authentication API. After Facebook has confirmed the authentication – through Facebook's OAuth mechanism – the user agrees to allow the CaaS provider to see the email address he uses with Facebook. The CaaS provider uses this email address to send a validation link, which establishes that the currently logged-in CaaS user also has access to the Facebook account in question and can furthermore read email sent to that account. This process only proves that the current CaaS user has access to the SN account, but does not give the CaaS provider access to the SN account.

After the binding of a SN identity to a CaaS account was successful, the CaaS credential set is extended with the SN identity $Cred_{CaaS} = \langle email, ids = [sn_{id_1}], password \rangle$. When using Facebook, sn_{id_1} is a large numerical UID. Subsequently, the user is able to use the CaaS provider's services with all identities in ids, since he has successfully proven that he is their owner.

The registration process has two requirements to ensure safe and correct functionality of the CaaS services:

RegReq1 A user must choose different passwords for the CaaS and Social Network accounts – This prevents a malicious SN provider from using the SN password to login to the CaaS service and vice versa.

ReqReq2 The registration and binding procedure must be finished successfully before a user is able to participate in a CaaS-protected conversation – This prevents the pre-registration attack described in Section 4.1.

After the registration process has been completed, the user interaction to successfully encrypt and decrypt data with the CaaS is reduced to a minimum. The user only needs to install a web-browser plugin, which is a known point-and-click use case for many Internet users. The plugin transparently communicates with the CaaS provider and handles all the cryptographic operations without requiring any more user involvement, except entering the CaaS password once per session. The duration of a session is configurable and can be based on a SN login or a timeframe.

After a successful registration, the account binding, and the installation of the plugin, the next step is to actually encrypt and decrypt Social Network messages. The next section will outline the algorithms used for the actual data encryption and decryption on the client- as well as the server-side.

3.3.2 +cLayerLocal

The +cLayerLocal procedure is applied each time before a message is sent to the CaaS provider from the client-side. As input parameters, it takes the cleartext message $clear_{u_1}$ as well as the list of recipients R and subsequently runs the following steps without any user involvement:

1. Choose a random initialisation vector iv_{u_1} and temporarily store it.

2. Choose a random symmetric encryption key k_{u_1} and temporarily store it.

3. Calculate the message digest $dig_{u_1} = H_u(clear_{u_1})$. H_u is a public parameter published by the corresponding CaaS provider.

4. Calculate a key stream $kstr_{u_1} = Sym^u_{stream}(iv_{u_1}, k_{u_1})$. Sym^U_{stream} is a stream cipher chosen by the client software.

5. Add a first cLayer to the plain text message: $enc_{u_1} = clear_{u_1} \oplus kstr_{u_1}$.

The result of the +cLayerLocal procedure is a first cLayer of encryption on the original message. This ciphertext is sent to the CaaS provider for the next step in the process.

3.3.3 +cLayerRemote

The +cLayerRemote procedure adds the remote cLayer to the message and is applied after a CaaS user successfully authenticated with his CaaS credentials. Because of the previous binding, the social network user ID in combination with the CaaS password is sufficient. The input for the +cLayerRemote procedure are the sender's credentials for authentication, the ciphertext enc_{u_1} that was created by +cLayerLocal and the list of recipients R (which is automatically extracted from the SN). In case the authentication of the sender was successful, the CaaS provider software runs the following steps to add a remote cLayer to the ciphertext enc_{u_1}:

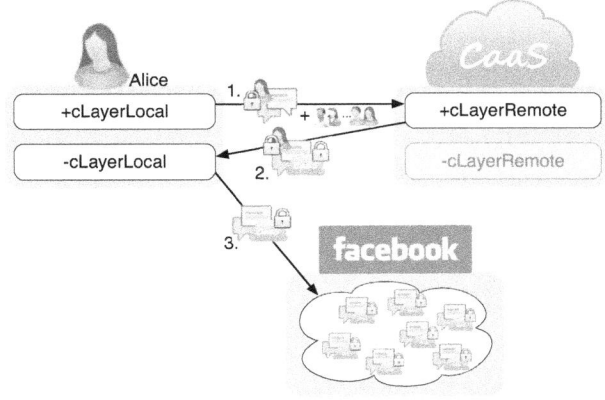

Figure 2: The preparation sequence. First, Alice locally encrypts the message (+cLayerLocal), then sends it with the participants list to the CaaS service to add a remote layer of encryption (+cLayerRemote), then removes her encryption layer (-cLayerLocal) and finally sends the CaaS encrypted data to the SN provider.

1. Check if all recipients in R are registered CaaS users. Abort if not (cf. **RegReq2**)

2. Add the sender's identity to R and sort the list to obtain R'.

3. For $r_j \in R'$ run $H_p(r_j) = H_p(H_p(r_{j-1}))$ with $j \in \{1, \ldots, i = |R'|\}$ to obtain an iterative hash h_i of all participating users.

4. Calculate the symmetric secret encryption key $k_p = HKDF_p(h_i, X_p)$.

5. Choose a random initialisation vector iv_p.

6. Calculate $kstr_p = Sym^p_{stream}(iv_p, k_p)$, the key stream used to encrypt the message.

7. Add a remote cLayer to the sender's input: $enc_p = enc_{u_1} \oplus kstr_p$.

8. Send the tuple $\langle iv_p, enc_p \rangle$ back to the requesting sender over a secure communication channel.

3.3.4 -cLayerLocal

-cLayerLocal is applied to remove the initial local cLayer, added during +cLayerLocal, after a message is returned from the CaaS provider. It takes the CaaS provider's result $\langle iv_p, enc_p \rangle$ and iv_{u_1}, $kstr_{u_1}$ from +cLayerLocal as inputs. It calculates rts, the ciphertext ready to be sent to the SN provider, as follows:

1. Decrypt enc_p: $rts = enc_p \oplus kstr_{u_1}$.

2. The message $\langle rts, iv_p, dig_{u_1} \rangle$ is ready to be sent to all recipients R.

Figure 2 summarises the sequence to CaaS-encrypt Social Network messages. To recover CaaS-encrypted messages, a recipient's client software has to follow three steps: First, a cLayer is added to the received message by running the +cLayerLocal algorithm (see above) that sends the result to the CaaS provider. On the CaaS provider's side, the -cLayerRemote algorithm is executed and removes the CaaS's remote cLayer from the data before another call of

`-cLayerLocal` removes the final local layer of encryption. Figure 3 illustrates the sequence of operations that have to be executed after a message was received to decrypt a CaaS encrypted message.

3.3.5 -cLayerRemote

The `-cLayerRemote` procedure is executed after a CaaS user successfully authenticated. Its inputs are the credentials of a recipient $r \in R$ for authentication, the ciphertext enc_r received by r, the initialisation vector iv_p, and the list of participating users R including the sender. In case the authentication of r was successful, the CaaS provider runs the following steps to remove its cLayer from enc_r:

1. Sort the list R to obtain R'.

2. For all $r \in R'$ run $H_p(r_j) = H_p(H_p(r_{j-1}))$ for $j \in 1, \ldots, |R'|$ to obtain an iterative hash h_i of all participating users.

3. Calculate the symmetric secret encryption key $k_p = HKDF_p(h_i, X_p)$.

4. Calculate the decryption key stream $kstr_p = Sym^p_{stream}(iv_p, k_p)$.

5. Decrypt enc_r: $dec_p = enc_r \oplus kstr_p$.

6. Send dec_p back to the requesting client over a secure communication channel.

On reception of the CaaS provider's response, the message is still protected by the recipient's local cLayer. To remove this last protection layer, the recipient runs the `-cLayerLocal` procedure on dec_p. Now the recipient holds the cleartext $clear_r$ and can validate the message integrity using the message digest $digest_{u_1}$.

In case no adversary manipulated the data, $clear_r$ is the same as $clear_{u_1}$. For clarity, a short summary of the multiple encryption/decryption steps is given:

1. u_1 adds a cLayer: $enc_{u_1} = clear_{u_1} \oplus kstr_{u_1}$,

2. The provider adds a cLayer: $enc_p = enc_{u_1} \oplus kstr_p$,

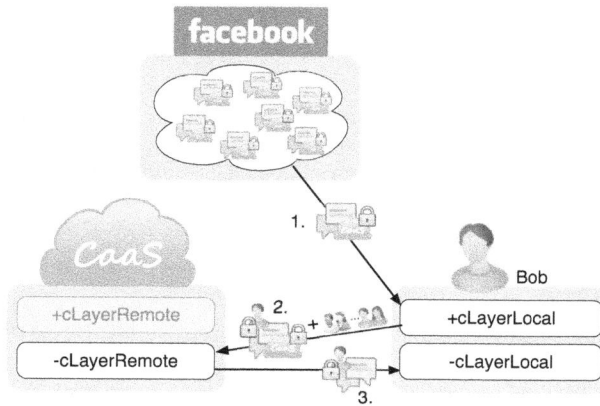

Figure 3: The post-receive sequence. First, Bob receives the CaaS encrypted message, then locally encrypts the data, sends it with the participants list to the CaaS service to remove the remote layer of encryption, finally removes his encryption layer and obtains the cleartext message.

3. u_1 removes his cLayer: $rts = enc_p \oplus kstr_{u_1}$,

4. rts is sent to (and stored at) the SN provider and received by r,

5. r adds a cLayer: $enc_r = rts \oplus kstr_r$,

6. The provider removes its cLayer: $dec_p = enc_r \oplus kstr_p$,

7. r removes his cLayer: $clear_r = dec_p \oplus kstr_r$.

$clear_{u_1}$ can hence be recovered from dec_p because XOR is commutative and self-inverse:

$$\begin{aligned} dec_p &= ((((((clear_{u_1} \oplus kstr_{u_1}) \oplus kstr_p) \oplus kstr_{u_1}) \oplus kstr_r) \\ &\quad \oplus kstr_p) \oplus kstr_r) \\ &= clear_{u_1} \oplus (kstr_{u_1} \oplus kstr_{u_1}) \oplus (kstr_p \oplus kstr_p) \\ &\quad \oplus (kstr_r \oplus kstr_r) \\ &= clear_{u_1} \oplus 0 \oplus 0 \oplus 0 \\ &= clear_{u_1} \end{aligned}$$

With a truly random key that is used only once, XOR encryption is called a One-Time Pad [23]. There are different symmetric encryption schemes, such as AES [20], that can be used in stream cipher mode, generating a key stream of arbitrary length. While a One-Time Pad encryption scheme is provably secure, the security of a stream cipher depends on the randomness characteristics of the Pseudo-Random Number Generator used to generate the key stream (cf. [19]).

4. SECURITY ANALYSIS

There are several possible attack vectors in the Confidentiality as a Service paradigm. These can be divided into internal and external attacks. An internal attack can be launched by any of the involved providers. For example, a malicious Social Network provider could try to decrypt data in the name of a CaaS user (mounting a CaaS identity impersonation attack). A second possible internal attack could be driven by a malicious CaaS provider that tries to request data from the Social Network provider in the name of a Social Network user (mounting a Social Network identity impersonation attack). An external attack could be mounted by a Social Network user that tries to illegally encrypt or decrypt a message and was originally not involved in the communication session. Subsequently these attacks are briefly discussed.

4.1 Malicious SN provider

The Social Network provider is responsible for storing the messages for its users and granting access to the messages to authorised users. To encrypt or decrypt a CaaS encrypted message in the name of a SN user, the SN provider would need to have access to the user's CaaS credentials. Since we require in **RegReq1** that the CaaS password must be different from the Social Network password, the SN provider is not able to encrypt or decrypt messages using the CaaS service in the name of a user by abusing password information.

In a second possible attack, a Social Network provider would register a CaaS account for one of its users. Upon detecting an encrypted message, the SN provider tries to impersonate one of the users involved in that conversation and register for a CaaS account, before that user can herself register with the CaaS provider. Therefore, we call this a pre-registration attack. As a result, the SN provider would be able to decrypt the message. Because the SN provider is responsible for authentication on its platform, it can make the CaaS provider believe that he is indeed authorised to access this user's account by faking the authentication response. In order to prevent this kind of attack, we implement the following countermeasure to minimise the threats of such a pre-registration attack.

When Alice intends to send a CaaS-encrypted message to Bob, the +cLayerCaaS algorithm (cf. Section 3.3.3) verifies the existence of a CaaS binding for Bob. If no such binding exists, the CaaS provider will deny the encryption. Thus, encrypted messages can only be sent, if the receiving SN users already have a CaaS account bound to their SN identities. Hence, the SN provider cannot register CaaS accounts for encrypted messages on-demand. The only remaining option for the SN provider is to preemptively pre-register CaaS accounts for all of its users (which can be easily detected, since none of them would be able to create a valid CaaS account). We believe that this measure has very little usability impact compared to the security benefit.

4.2 CaaS Provider

Messages presented to the CaaS provider are always protected by a cLayer added by a CaaS user. During encryption, message m_1 is encrypted with the user's keystream $kstr_{u_1}$. Hence, the CaaS provider only sees $enc_{u_1} = clear_{u_1} \oplus kstr_{u_1}$ and never gets in contact with $clear_{u_1}$. To decrypt the received message rts, a CaaS user u_2 adds another cLayer $enc_{u_2} = rts \oplus kstr_{u_2}$ and sends enc_{u_2} to the CaaS provider. In both situations, a malicious CaaS provider does not have enough information to obtain the message's cleartext because one commutative cLayer protects the message from being readable by the CaaS provider.

4.3 External User

An external user is one that cannot legitimately access the conversation, but may be in possession of a valid SN and CaaS account. First, as long as the SN access control mechanisms are working, this user should even not be able to access the encrypted data. Second, this user is also not capable of requesting decryption for the data at the CaaS provider, since his CaaS account is not part of the key for the data. To successfully mount an attack, an external user needs to get access to the ciphertext (i.e. break into the SN provider or steal a participant's SN account) and the decryption service (i.e. break into the CaaS provider or steal that participant's CaaS account).

5. IMPLEMENTATION

We provide both, a prototypical CaaS server implementation as well as a Greasemonkey user script, which integrates our CaaS approach into Facebook. We utilise the Advanced Encryption Standard (AES) in Counter Mode as stream cipher. AES is an industry standard symmetric cipher, that provides multiple stream cipher modes such as cipher feedback (CFB), output feedback (OFB) and counter mode (CTR). While all provide excellent security characteristics, CTR has significant efficiency advantages without weakening the security of the generated stream cipher (cf. [22]). In order to prevent key reuse attacks (cf. [19]), each encryption-decryption sequence includes the selection of a new random initialisation vector. XOR-based encryption additionally requires an out of band mechanism to check

message integrity, as used by the +cLayerUser and -cLayerUser algorithms. For that purpose, SHA-256 as a cryptographically secure hash function was selected.

We assume that most Facebook messages are short and typically not larger than about 8000 characters, which is more than three A4 pages of text without breaks. Consequently, we directly encrypt the messages. If larger pieces of data need to be protected, a bootstrapping scheme can be applied. In such a scheme, the client-side plugin only CaaS-encrypts a session key which is then prefixed to the message encrypted with that session key.

The server-side implementation is based on a Java REST webservice [8], using a relational database to store user accounts. Our webservice implementation can be run in any Java application container and hence is easily deployable without much effort. To ensure trusted communication between a client and the CaaS provider, TLS with a server-side certificate is used. The RESTful webservice is a comfortable interface for programmers to access the CaaS service API and simplifies the development of additional client applications.

As argued above, client-side usability is of utmost importance in order to gain the users' acceptance for privacy measures. Our intention was to implement a user registration interface that today's Internet users are accustomed to. Therefore, we provide an easy-to-use website to register for a new CaaS account and to bind existing Social Network accounts to. The CaaS account registration requires only an email address and a password. This credential set was chosen since these identification tokens are most frequently used and offer a good usability-to-security-ratio for this scenario. To bind a Facebook account to a CaaS account, the website utilises Facebook's Authentication API[5]. The user authenticates to Facebook and in return provides the CaaS provider with proof of authentication, his Facebook UID as well as the registered email address, as described in Section 3.3.1. After fetching both properties from Facebook – given the user's approval – these values are bound to the corresponding CaaS account.

At this point the binding is still inactive and requires the confirmation of the Email address given by Facebook. For that purpose, a confirmation link is sent to the email address which the user has to click on, in order to validate the binding. This is a standard procedure and proved to be easily accepted during our user study (cf. below).

After a successful binding of the Facebook identity, we use a Greasemonkey[6] script to be able to encrypt and decrypt messages within the regular Facebook UI. Greasemonkey is a Mozilla Firefox extension that allows end users to install third party JavaScript extensions, that can manipulate a displayed website.

The CaaS client currently supports the sending and receiving of CaaS encrypted messages through the regular Facebook user interface without requiring any understanding of cryptographic artefacts at the end-user's side. Figure 4 shows the modified message composer. When the user clicks the "New Message" button on the Facebook website, the CaaS script hooks into the message form. There is one listener that checks for new recipients and verifies if they are available for encrypted messaging (cf. Section 4.1). A

---

[5] https://developers.facebook.com/docs/authentication/

[6] http://www.greasespot.net/

second listener hooks into the "Send" button routine to run the required CaaS encryption sequence before sending the message through the Facebook messaging system to all recipients.

Figure 4: The modified Facebook message composer.

If a recipient was selected that already has an active Facebook-to-CaaS binding, its label is highlighted in green. In case the selected recipient does not have an active binding, its label is highlighted in red and a warning is displayed, that says that the message will be sent in clear and not CaaS-encrypted. This mechanism gives unambiguous feedback to the user and explains the current status of the message's security. If all recipients are valid recipients and the sender hits the "Send" button, the CaaS encryption sequence is triggered. In case no CaaS client session is active, a popup window is displayed that asks for the user's CaaS password. This password is cached for a configurable amount of time for the user's convenience. The added markers on the message box and the send button provide a concise visual indicator that this message will be protected.

Similar to sending a CaaS encrypted Facebook message, the script supports on-the-fly decryption and reading of cleartext messages. Therefore, the Facebook messages site is modified and parsed for CaaS encrypted messages. If such a message is found, the ciphertext is extracted and the CaaS decryption sequence transparently and automatically executed (cf. Section 3.1). On success, the client-side script locally removes the last cLayer and replaces the ciphertext with the recovered cleartext message in the site's DOM tree. Greasemonkey's sandbox environment prevents Facebook from inserting their own hooks into the DOM tree to eavesdrop on the messages after decryption. Figure 5 shows a comparison of the Facebook message site with and without CaaS-decryption.

If a CaaS-encrypted message was detected and successfully decrypted, a green border indicates that this message was protected using CaaS-encryption. Again, if no CaaS password was cached, a popup is displayed and asks the user to enter his password to decrypt the found messages.

To help users to intuitively understand that message protection is in place, protected content is annotated with visual indicators. Several studies (e. g. [29, 28]) found that visual privacy indicators outside of the actual website, such as little locks indicating a valid TLS session, are often overseen or ignored in the presence of a correct-looking web page content. Egelman et al. also found that the timing and placement of

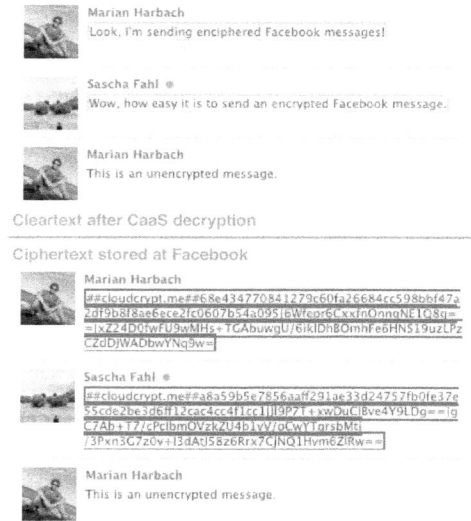

Figure 5: A comparison of the message with and without decryption.

privacy indicators plays a central role in the user's perception[10]. Users were ready to pay a higher price for a product while online-shopping, if a privacy indicator showed that a shop provided better privacy. However, this indicator only worked when placed immediately next to the offer.

Thus, in our prototype, a red border marks a piece of information that is potentially in need of protection or is unprotected, while a green border intuitively indicates successful protection. We believe that the visual indicators will also raise the user's awareness for private information in need of protection, and will therefore eventually increase the user's privacy perception and actual privacy.

Since our client-side prototype is written in Javascript, it is easily verifiable that the CaaS-client itself works as intended and does neither send any clear-text to the CaaS service nor does leak any other privacy related information.

Evaluation.

We conducted a user study with 20 undergrad students and found that registering for the CaaS service and binding a Facebook account took 3:08 minutes on average (ranging from 90 seconds to 6 minutes, all users could successfully finish the task). Additionally, we collected performance measurements to estimate the delay a user experiences when using CaaS-enhanced social networks. Our results indicate that there is only very little additional delay introduced to the regular Facebook webpage. In our experiments, it took between 5 to 6 seconds for the Facebook page to finish all relevant AJAX calls on the initial visit and about 1.5 seconds for subsequent interactions. On average, it took between 33ms and 154ms to CaaS-encrypt or -decrypt a message of 2 to 8000 characters (cf. Fig. 6), including network-based delays of a broadband cable provider (about 25ms round-trip time for an ICMP ping packet) and TLS session establishment. The tests were run on a 2.66 GHz Core2 Duo machine with 8 GB of RAM against a 3 GHz Pentium D dual core server having 4GB of RAM.

Using the proposed mechanism, encrypting a message upon

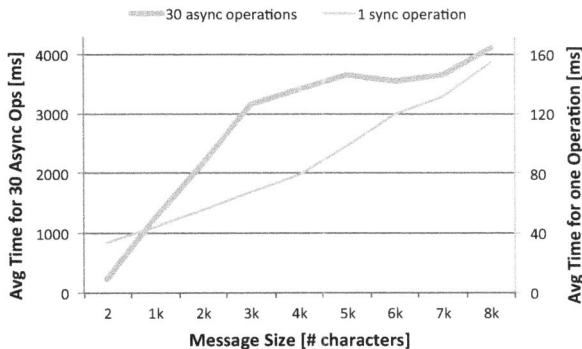

Figure 6: Response time for one CaaS operation (thin line) and 30 asynchronous decode operations (bold line) on variable message length.

sending or decrypting upon reception is only barely noticeable by the user. Asynchronously decrypting the entire message history (typically the past 30 messages) takes on average as long as it takes to load the page (between 222ms and 4101ms depending on the message size) and can begin while the rest of the page is still loading. We therefore believe that our confidentiality plugin does not disturb the normal Facebook experience.

A prototypical CaaS provider instance and the Facebook Greasemonkey plugin are available at `https://cloudcrypt.me` to practically evaluate the service and verify the results.

6. RELATED WORK

There are several recent approaches to secure content in social networks, especially Facebook. In 2008, Lucas et al. [18] proposed flyByNight, a prototype Facebook app that encrypts and decrypts messages using public key cryptography. The flyByNight server handles the key management and uses its own database to store the encrypted messages. By storing all encrypted messages in their database, flyByNight's resources need to scale as Facebook does, which can be very expensive. Additionally, by using Facebook's App API, all requests and all responses of the application travel through Facebook's severs, whereas in the CaaS approach, Facebook is not aware of any operations beyond regular message sending. Lucas et al. hinted at the necessity of usability, but did not show any usability features beyond stating that a privacy extension would need to be web-based, have good performance and require little technical knowledge. However, flyByNight requires the user to leave the regular Facebook UI experience and use another app for their messaging instead, which would lack all the convenience and usability features that Facebook provides.

Scramble! [4] is a PKI based Firefox plugin that stores encrypted social network content at a TinyLink server or stores it directly at the SN provider. However, key management is again complicated and relies on PGP mechanisms and must be dealt with explicitly by the user. Most notably, you need to be carrying your private key around in order to make this approach work on multiple devices.

Another approach was taken by Guha et al. [15], who use shared dictionaries to map different "atoms" of information to a similar, valid piece of information. For example, Alice's

address would be randomly replaced by Bob's, according to some mapping key. Their NOYB prototype can hide the fact that content is being protected but also necessitates key exchange using email. Additionally, reusing other users' information can have privacy implications of itself.

Baden et al. [3] present Persona, a privacy enhanced social network using public key cryptography and attribute-based encryption (ABE). They acknowledge the need to integrate their service with the popular networks and demonstrate a prototype that provides their services as a Facebook application. They argue that existing SN apps can be gradually migrated to use the Persona platform, at least for storage. Using the Facebook API, it is however not possible to access the messaging service, which might be considered to be one of the features with the most utility. The Persona platform also comes with the key management issues discussed before.

uprotect.it [21] also offers confidentiality services for Facebook. However, their service comes with several privacy problems. Because uprotect.it not only provides confidentiality but also stores the user content on their servers alongside the encryption keys, they are able to eavesdrop on the users' data, as stated in their Terms of Services[7].

encipher.it [11] provides a very lightweight approach, using a simple bookmarklet to apply symmetric AES encryption to arbitrary text. Sharing the key with whoever is supposed to decipher a message is entirely left to the user. Naturally, this approach does not integrate well with the normal user-experience of sending Facebook messages. There also is a possibility to use a Firefox GPG plugin with Facebook, so that inline ciphertext is automatically decrypted[8]. However, a valid public and private key pair is necessary and further key management issues are not addressed by this approach.

Anderson et al. [2] presented a concept to use rich-clients as a way to improve privacy. The SN provider is reduced to a mere content distribution server while the client handles cryptography and information semantics. Again, this approach would require a user to migrate to another SN and change the interaction patterns. In a similar fashion, a number of projects (e.g. [7, 9, 26]) proposed to distribute a Social Network across a peer-to-peer infrastructure, thereby removing the risks inherent to central service providers. However, these approaches struggle to gain broad acceptance and are often only used by privacy-aware or expert users. One of the central ideas of the CaaS approach is to protect existing and proprietary services transparently and therefore protect a large number of users that are already experiencing privacy problems.

None of the above approaches achieve the ease-of-use and non-intrusive integration into existing SN services offered by the CaaS paradigm.

7. CONCLUSION

In this paper, we presented a new paradigm for user-friendly, non-obtrusive confidential messaging for social networks. The key features of the paradigm are the separation of concerns, which protects the user from malicious SN and CaaS providers, and the usability concept, which eliminates all key-management issues for the user. We leverage the messaging workflow and the intuitive UI of existing social networks, which allows users to gain an intuitive awareness

---

[7] `https://uprotect.it/terms`
[8] `http://blog.fortinet.com/encrypting-facebook/`

of privacy as well as an ability to directly see which content is protected and which isn't. Since the CaaS provider does not need to store any keys or data, our paradigm has a very small resource footprint and hence has the potential to scale more easily to the sizes required by modern SN platforms. A user study showed that the CaaS enrolment procedure is quick and easy and requires no specialised knowledge. Our Facebook plugin demonstrates that privacy mechanisms can be transparently integrated into existing user interfaces without interruption of the user's regular workflow.

In future work, we will examine how multiple CaaS providers can be chained to increase the level of security. Furthermore, CaaS integration efforts for multiple other services, such as Twitter, Email and Dropbox, are underway.

8. REFERENCES

[1] A. Acquisti and R. Gross. Imagined Communities: Awareness, Information Sharing, and Privacy on the Facebook. In *Proceedings of the 11th International Conference on Privacy Enhancing Technologies*, pages 36–58. Springer, 2006.

[2] J. Anderson, C. Diaz, J. Bonneau, and F. Stajano. Privacy-enabling Social Networking over Untrusted Networks. In *Proceedings of the 2nd ACM Workshop on Online Social Networks*, pages 1–6, 2009.

[3] R. Baden, A. Bender, N. Spring, B. Bhattacharjee, and D. Starin. Persona: An Online Social Network With User-defined Privacy. In *Proceedings of the ACM SIGCOMM 2009 Conference on Data Communication*, pages 135–146, 2009.

[4] F. Beato, M. Kohlweiss, and K. Wouters. Scramble! Your Social Network Data. In *Proceedings of the 11th International Conference on Privacy Enhancing Technologies*, pages 211–225. Springer, 2011.

[5] D. Boyd. Facebooks Privacy Trainwreck: Exposure, Invasion, and Social Convergence. *Convergence: The International Journal of Research into New Media Technologies*, 14(1):13–20, 2008.

[6] D. Boyd. *Taken Out of Context: American Teen Sociality in Networked Publics*. PhD thesis, University of California-Berkeley, School of Information, 2008.

[7] S. Buchegger, D. Schiöberg, L.-H. Vu, and A. Datta. PeerSoN: P2P Social Networking: Early Experiences and Insights. In *Proceedings of the Second ACM EuroSys Workshop on Social Network Systems*, pages 46–52, 2009.

[8] B. Burke. *RESTful Java with Jax-RS*. O'Reilly Media, Inc., 1st edition, 2009.

[9] L. Cutillo, R. Molva, and T. Strufe. Safebook: A Privacy-preserving Online Social Network Leveraging on Real-life Trust. *Communications Magazine, IEEE*, 47(12):94 –101, dec. 2009.

[10] S. Egelman, J. Tsai, L. F. Cranor, and A. Acquisti. Timing is Everything?: The Effects of Timing and Placement of Online Privacy Indicators. In *Proceedings of the 27th ACM CHI'09*, pages 319–328. ACM, 2009.

[11] A. Ermak. encipher.it. http://encipher.it, 2011.

[12] L. Fang and K. LeFevre. Privacy Wizards for Social Networking Sites. In *Proceedings of WWW'10*, pages 351–360, 2010.

[13] S. Garfinkel. Email-based Identification and Authentication: An Alternative to PKI? *IEEE Security and Privacy*, 1(6):20–26, Nov. 2003.

[14] R. Gross and A. Acquisti. Information Revelation and Privacy in Online Social Networks. In *Proceedings of the 2005 ACM Workshop on Privacy in the Electronic Society*, pages 71–80, 2005.

[15] S. Guha, K. Tang, and P. Francis. NOYB: Privacy in Online Social Networks. In *Proceedings of the First Workshop on Online Social Networks*, pages 49–54. ACM, 2008.

[16] P. Gundecha, G. Barbier, and H. Liu. Exploiting Vulnerability to Secure User Privacy on a Social Networking Site. In *Proceedings of the 17th ACM SIGKDD Conference*, pages 511–519, 2011.

[17] Hush Communications Canada Inc. Hushmail - A Secure Web-based Free Email Service. http://www.hushmail.com/, last access: 14.10.11, 1999.

[18] M. M. Lucas and N. Borisov. FlyByNight: Mitigating the Privacy Risks of Social Networking. In *Proceedings of the 7th ACM Workshop on Privacy in the Electronic Society*, pages 1–8, 2008.

[19] A. J. Menezes, S. A. Vanstone, and P. C. V. Oorschot. *Handbook of Applied Cryptography*. CRC Press, Inc., Boca Raton, FL, USA, 1st edition, 1996.

[20] National Institute of Standards and Technology (NIST). Advanced Encryption Standard (AES) (FIPS PUB 197), October 2001.

[21] Reputation.com Inc. uProtect.it. http://uprotect.it, 2011.

[22] P. Rogaway and D. Wagner. Comments to NIST concerning AES Modes of Operations: CTR-Mode Encryption. National Institute of Standards and Technologies, 2000.

[23] C. Shannon. Communication Theory of Secrecy Systems. *Bell System Technical Journal*, 28:656–715, October 1949.

[24] R. Singel. Encrypted E-Mail Company Hushmail Spills to Feds. http://www.wired.com/threatlevel/2007/11/encrypted-e-mai/, last access: 14.10.11, Nov 2007.

[25] A. C. Squicciarini, M. Shehab, and F. Paci. Collective Privacy Management in Social Networks. In *Proceedings of WWW'09*, pages 521–530, 2009.

[26] The Diaspora Project. http://diasporafoundation.org/ – last access: 27.10.11, 2011.

[27] Z. Tufekci. Can You See Me Now? Audience and Disclosure Regulation in Online Social Network Sites. *Bulletin of Science, Technology & Society*, 28(1):20–36, 2008.

[28] T. Whalen and K. M. Inkpen. Gathering Evidence: Use of Visual Security Cues in Web Browsers. In *Proceedings of Graphics Interface 2005*, pages 137–144. Canadian Human-Computer Communications Society, 2005.

[29] M. Wu, R. C. Miller, and S. L. Garfinkel. Do Security Toolbars Actually Prevent Phishing Attacks? In *Proceedings of the 24th ACM CHI '06*, pages 601–610. ACM, 2006.

Maximizing Circle of Trust in Online Social Networks

Yilin Shen, Yu-Song Syu, Dung T. Nguyen, My T. Thai
Department of Computer and Information Science and Engineering
University of Florida, USA
{yshen, yssyu, dtnguyen, mythai}@cise.ufl.edu

ABSTRACT

As an imperative channel for fast information propagation, Online Social Networks(OSNs) also have their defects. One of them is the information leakage, i.e., information could be spread via OSNs to the users whom we are not willing to share with. Thus the problem of constructing a circle of trust to share information with as many friends as possible without further spreading it to unwanted targets has become a challenging research topic but still remained open.

Our work is the first attempt to study the *Maximum Circle of Trust* problem seeking to share the information with the maximum expected number of poster's friends such that the information spread to the unwanted targets is brought to its knees. First, we consider a special and more practical case with the two-hop information propagation and a single unwanted target. In this case, we show that this problem is NP-hard, which denies the existence of an exact polynomial-time algorithm. We thus propose a *Fully Polynomial-Time Approximation Scheme* (FPTAS), which can not only adjust any allowable performance error bound but also run in polynomial time with both the input size and allowed error. FPTAS is the best approximation solution one can ever wish for an NP-hard problem. We next consider the number of unwanted targets is bounded and prove that there does not exist an FPTAS in this case. Instead, we design a *Polynomial-Time Approximation Scheme* (PTAS) in which the allowable error can also be controlled. Finally, we consider a general case with many hops information propagation and further show its #P-hardness and propose an effective *Iterative Circle of Trust Detection* (ICTD) algorithm based on a novel greedy function. An extensive experiment on various real-word OSNs has validated the effectiveness of our proposed approximation and ICTD algorithms.

Categories and Subject Descriptors

G.2.2 [**Graph Theory**]: Network problems, Graph algorithms; G.2.1 [**Combinatorics**]: Counting problems

General Terms

Algorithms, Experimentation, Theory

Keywords

Online Social Networks, Circle of Trust, Computational Complexity, Approximation Algorithms

1. INTRODUCTION

The rapid growth of Online Social Networks (OSNs), such as Facebook, Twitter, and LinkedIn, has made them become one of the most important channels for fast information propagation and influence [4, 17]. Many individuals and companies use these popular media to share their messages with other users or advertise their products by leveraging the power of others' influences [4]. However, in spite of its benefits to information propagation, OSNs also have defects as media to leak information, that is, the information can be spread to the users whom we do not want to share with.

Let us consider the following simple example which highlights a basic need for any organizations or companies who use OSNs. Suppose that Bob wants to share with his friends some of his personal pictures and stories in Facebook, yet he is reluctant to let Chuck know about them. Being careful, Bob just shares to the list of his friends in Facebook where Chuck is not in that group with a belief that Chuck cannot see those pictures. Unfortunately, Alice, who is a friend of both Bob and Chuck, replied to the post, and thus Chuck will see the message from Alice and learn about Bob's sharing. Assume that Bob is extra careful by using the Custom Privacy function provided by Facebook to hide his sharing from Chuck. Unfortunately, this function only tracks and hide the message based on the message-ID, not on its propagation. Therefore, when Bob's friend Alice posts a new message *mentioning* Bob's pictures and stories, this new message cannot be hidden from Chuck anymore since its ID is no longer the same as the original message from Bob. Consequently, Chuck will still learn about Bob's pictures and stories. Thus it raises a practical question: Is there any mechanism for Bob to share his pictures and stories to as many friends as possible without reaching to Chuck?

What Bob really needs is that right before he is ready to share his stories, he should have an opportunity to construct on the fly a subset of his friends to share these stories with so that the probability of Chuck knowing them is very small. We refer to this subset as a circle of trust. As can be seen in Figure 1, right before he posts his message, a user can choose a Circle of Trust option in order to enter the list of unwanted targets and the leakage thresholds (the probability each unwanted target can see the message). After the input, a circle of trust will be automatically constructed on the fly and the user just simply posts to this circle. This circle of trust can be constructed for each of his post, depending on his needs.

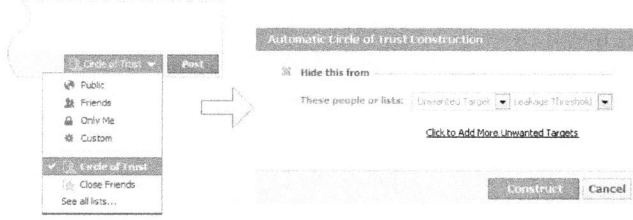

Figure 1: Constructing the Circle of Trust

In the meanwhile, since one of the main purposes of posting messages on OSNs is to share the information with as many friends as possible, we formulate a new optimization problem, called *Maximum Circle of Trust* (MCT), to construct a circle of trust with the maximum number of *visible friends* for a user s so that once s posts a message to this CT, the probability of such friends in this CT spreading the message to *unwanted targets* is under some certain threshold, where a friend of s is said to be visible to a message if the message appears on his wall, and the unwanted targets are referred to as those whom s does not want to share the information with.

In this paper, we study how to quickly construct the circle of trust by providing several algorithms and their hardness complexity, as follows:

- Since this is the first attempt to study the maximum circle of trust problem tackling the information leakage in online social networks, we first introduce the Independent Sharing-Mention propagation model tackling different information leakages in distinct OSNs.

- Since information can be propagated within a very limited number of hops (2 to 5) [6], we first focus our attention on the bounded-2-MCT problem, a special and more practical case of MCT problem with 2-hop information propagation and fixed number of unwanted targets. After proving its NP-hardness of a single unwanted target, we propose an FPTAS approximation algorithm based on the idea of scaling and dynamic programming. For multiple unwanted targets, we show that there is no FPTAS and thus design a PTAS algorithm, the best solution one can ever wish when the FPTAS does not exist. Note that, for NP-hard problems, the most desirable approximation algorithms are the full polynomial time approximation scheme (FPTAS) and polynomial time approximation scheme (PTAS) which can not only control any allowable errors but also run in polynomial time with the input size (also in polynomial time with error for F-PTAS). FPTAS and PTAS are the best one can hope for NP-hard problems, assuming P≠NP. Unfortunately, the design of such approximation schemes is very challenging and it may not exist for certain problems.

- For the general MCT problem, we prove its #P-hardness when the information can be propagated more than 2

hops. Due to its #P-hardness, we design an efficient ICTD algorithm based on a novel greedy function.

- The performance of our proposed approximation and ICTD algorithms are validated on Facebook, Twitter, Foursquare and Flickr datasets.

The rest of this paper is organized as follows. In Section 2, we introduce a novel ISM propagation model and the formal definition of the MCT problem. Section 3 includes the complexity results and approximation algorithms for the bounded-2-MCT problem. For general MCT problem, its #P-hardness and the ICTD algorithm are provided in Section 4. The experimental evaluation is illustrated in Section 5, and related work is presented in Section 6. Section 7 concludes the whole paper.

2. MODEL AND PROBLEM DEFINITION

In this section, we first introduce a novel information leakage propagation model, namely *Independent Sharing-Mention* (ISM) propagation model, in the context of different diffusion channels. Based on this model, we introduce the formal definition of our MCT problem.

2.1 ISM Propagation Model

In our model, we consider two types of information leakage propagations in OSNs between two friends u and v as illustrated in Figure 2:

- *Sharing*: u shares the message using functions provided by OSNs. For example, u can use "retweet" or "reply" to share on Twitter and "share", "comment" or "like" to share on Facebook. In this case, the message will appear on u's own wall and then be seen by v;

- *Mention*: u can also propagate the information to v by mentioning it with the same content (or retyping using his own words).

Correspondingly, between users u and v, we refer to the probability of a sharing and mention propagation (*Sharing Probability* and *Mention Probability*) as a_{uv} and p_{uv}.

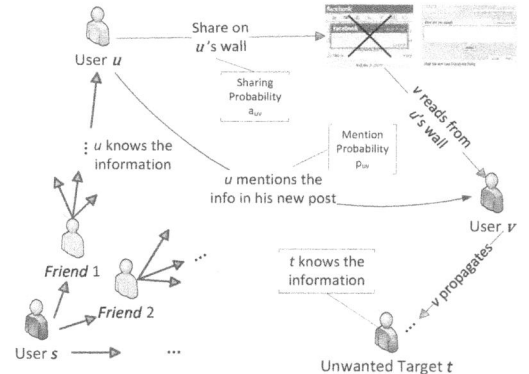

Figure 2: ISM Propagation Model

Therefore, each link (u, v) in OSNs has a two-tuple probabilities $\langle a_{uv}, p_{uv} \rangle$. Although a_{uv} and p_{uv} are not necessarily to be independent, our ISM model is independent in terms of the following two aspects: the independence between different links; the independence among the current propagation, the history propagation, and the future propagation.

As can be seen, this model can reflect the information propagation on a majority of existing OSNs by only choosing different parameters. For example, as Facebook provided a function in *Custom Privacy* to hide a certain information from specific users, which narrows down the sharing probability to 0 on Facebook if the source user blocks all his unwanted targets. Thus, the information propagation on Facebook only depends on mention probabilities. If we take Twitter as another example, the information propagations are dependent on both sharing probability and mention probability. That is, we can define p_{uv} as an alternative sharing-mention probability instead of mention probability for each link (u, v).

2.2 Problem Definition

In OSNs, when a user s posts some message m, his aim is usually to share it with as many friends as possible, i.e., to maximize the visibility of his message to his friends while preventing it from reaching to some *unwanted targets*. Considering that information can be spread at most δ hops, we study the following δ-*Hop-Propagation Maximum Circle Of Trust* (δ-MCT) problem, which constructs a circle of trust *to maximize the expected visible friends of s as well as to restrict the leakage probability of each unwanted target to a certain degree* so that s can safely post his message to this CT.

> PROBLEM 1 (δ-MCT PROBLEM). *Given a directed graph $G = (V, E)$ with $|V|$ users and $|E|$ edges underlying an OSN, where each edge (u, v) is associated with a tuple of sharing probability and mention probability $\langle a_{uv}, p_{uv} \rangle$. Let $T = \{t_1, \ldots, t_k\}$ be the set of $k = |T|$ unwanted targets and s be the source user with $|N(s) \setminus T| = S_n$ neighbors. The δ-MCT problem constructs a circle of trust (CT) with the maximum expected visible friends of s (Size of CT) such that the probability of each unwanted target t_i can see the message m posted by s after at most δ hops propagation is at most its leakage threshold τ_j, which lies in $[0, 1)$.*

In our paper, we assume that the source user s is *rational*. That is, he will neither tell the message to his unwanted targets nor share the message in online social networks with them. Then we immediately have the following lemma.

LEMMA 1. *When source user s is rational, all unwanted targets T must be at least two hops from s.*

3. BOUNDED-2-MCT PROBLEM

In this section, we consider the following two special and more practical factors in information propagations:

- The limited propagation hops: According to Cha *et al.* [6], majority of the messages are propagated within 2 hops in OSNs. Moreover, with recent new block functions of many OSNs, the chance of message being leaked by more than 2 hops is very limited.
- Once a user wants to post a message, the number of his unwanted targets is usually very small.

Motivated by these practical observations, we focus on the *Bounded-2-MCT* problem in which the message m can be spread at most 2 hops and the number of unwanted targets

is bounded by some constant κ. We further refer to this problem as *Single-2-MCT* when there is only a single unwanted target. In this section, we show the NP-hardness of Single-2-MCT and present an FPTAS approximation algorithm. For multiple unwanted targets $k \geq 2$, we further prove the non-existence of FPTAS algorithms and provide a PTAS approximation algorithm.

We note that FPTAS and PTAS are the most desirable solution for a NP-hard problem by trading accuracy for running time. That is, we can decide how to choose the error parameter based on the allowed time. For example, we can allow more errors when the time is limited and less errors otherwise. In particular, FPTAS is even better since it requires the algorithm to be polynomial in both the problem size and error parameter. Now we first show the following lemma, which can be obtained using contradiction method.

LEMMA 2. *For any user u except the unwanted targets, its propagation can lead to the information leakage if and only if it receives m directly from s when $\delta = 2$.*

3.1 NP-Completeness for Single-2-MCT

THEOREM 1. *Single-2-MCT is NP-complete.*

PROOF. In the proof, it is easy to see that the decision version of Single-2-MCT$\in$NP. To prove that Single-2-MCT is NP-hard, we reduce the known NP-hard subset sum problem to it, which asks if there exists a non-empty subset whose sum is Z given a set of integers $(z_1, z_2, \ldots, z_n)$ and an integer Z. Let I be an arbitrary instance of subset sum problem, our construction is as illustrated in Figure 3. We construct two terminal nodes s, t and n nodes N_i, $i = 1 \ldots n$ for each item in I. For each node N_i, we construct an edge from s to it with a sharing probability $a_{si} = \frac{z_i}{\sum_i z_i}$ and mention probability $p_{si} = 1 - e^{-\frac{z_i}{\sum_i z_i}}$; and another edge from N_i to t with mention probability $p_{it} = 1$. We set the leakage threshold $\tau = 1 - e^{-\frac{Z}{\sum_i z_i}}$ for the target t. We show that there is a subset sum of I iff our reduced instance has a Single-2-MCT with the expected visible users at least $\frac{Z}{\sum_i z_i}$.

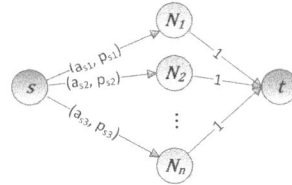

Figure 3: Single-2-MCT Reduction

First, suppose that R is a yes instance of I. Now let us consider a set $R' = \{N_i \mid i \in R\}$. If s posts his message m to R', then the leakage probability to t is exactly $1 - \prod_{i \in R} a_{si} p_{it} = \tau$ and the size of CT is $\sum_{i \in R} \frac{z_i}{\sum_i z_i} = \frac{Z}{\sum_i z_i}$, implying R' is a yes instance of Single-2-MCT.

Conversely, suppose that R' is a Single-2-MCT instance in G with respect to s and t with the leakage probability $\tau = 1 - \prod_{i \in R'} a_{si} p_{it}$, that is, $\sum_{i \in R'} \frac{z_i}{\sum_i z_i} \leq \frac{Z}{\sum_i z_i}$. Then $R = \{i \mid N_i \in R'\}$ is a subset sum of I. This is because the expected visible friends of R' is at least $\sum_{i \in R'} \frac{z_i}{\sum_i z_i} \geq \frac{Z}{\sum_i z_i}$. Thus, $\sum_{i \in R} \frac{z_i}{\sum_i z_i} = \frac{Z}{\sum_i z_i}$. □

3.2 FPTAS Algorithm for Single-2-MCT

Since the NP-hardness denies the existence of any polynomial algorithms for Single-2-MCT problem, we then focus on designing an effective Algorithm to solve it. The analysis shows that this algorithm is an FPTAS, which is the best approximation solution for an NP-hard problem.

According to Lemma 1, we only need to consider the case that t is two hops away from s in $G[E \setminus \{s, T\}]$ since t cannot see m if he is at least 3 hops away from s while $\delta = 2$. In this case, the probability that m will be leaked to t is $1 - \prod_{i \in N(s) \setminus \{t\}} (1 - a_{si} p_{it})^{x_i}$, which is implied by Lemma 2.

The basic idea of FPTAS algorithm with $k = 1$ has two main phases: (1) the scaling of sharing probability; (2) dynamic programming to find the minimum leakage probability w.r.t. the scaled sharing probabilities.

First, since all a_{si} are rational values, we can rewrite each of them with $\frac{an_{si}}{ad_{si}}$ where both an_{si} and ad_{si} are integers. We then define Ad be the least common multiple of all denominators ad_{si}. Thus, $a_{si} = \frac{an_{si} Ad / ad_{si}}{Ad}$, where the numerator is clearly an integer. Then, in the first phase, in order to avoid the case that $an_{si} Ad / ad_{si}$ is exponentially larger than S_n, we scale the sharing probability a_{si} for each s's neighbor by the factor $A = \frac{\varepsilon \max \left\{ \frac{an_{si} Ad}{ad_{si}} | a_{si} p_{it} \leq \tau \right\}}{S_n}$ and define its corresponding scaled sharing probability to be $a'_{si} = \lfloor \frac{an_{si}}{A} \rfloor$.

In the second step, we consider using dynamic programming to solve a complex problem by breaking the problem down into simpler subproblems in a recursive manner. That is, to solve the MCT problem w.r.t. the scaled sharing probabilities, we only need to define the recursion function as follows. Let $L_i(a)$ be the minimum leakage probability of a subset of s's first i friends with the total circle of trust having size equal to a. Thus, the recursion can be written as

$$L_i(a) = \begin{cases} L_{i-1}(a), & \text{if } a < a_i \\ \min \left\{ L_{i-1}(a), L_{i-1}(a - a'_{si}) + w_i \right\}, & \text{if } a \geq a_i \end{cases}$$
(1)

where $w_i = -\log(1 - a_{si} p_{it})$. The detail of FPTAS Algorithm is shown in Algorithm 1.

Input : Single-2-MCT instance
Output: visible friends Π_1^ε and size of CT π_1^ε

1   $a_{si} \leftarrow an_{si}/ad_{si}$ for each i;
2   $Ad \leftarrow$ the least common multiple of all denominators ad_{si};
   // Phase 1: Scaling
3   For some $\varepsilon > 0$, let $A \leftarrow \frac{\varepsilon \max \left\{ \frac{an_{si} Ad}{ad_{si}} | a_{si} p_{it} \leq \tau \right\}}{S_n}$;
4   For each neighbor $i \in N(s)$, define $a'_{si} = \lfloor \frac{an_{si}}{A} \rfloor$;
   // Phase 2: Dynamic Programming
5   $A_u \leftarrow \sum_{i \in N(s) \setminus \{t\}} a'_{si}$;
6   $L(a) = A_u + 1$ for all integers a less than A_u;
7   **for** $a \leftarrow 1$ to S_n **do**
8   Apply dynamic programming to find $L(a)$ using the recursion (1);
9   **end**
10   $\pi_1^\varepsilon \leftarrow \frac{1}{Ad} \max\{a | L(a) \leq \tau\}$;

Algorithm 1: FPTAS for Single-2-MCT

Now, we prove that Algorithm 1 is indeed an FPTAS algorithm, that is, we need to prove the approximation ratio $(1 - \varepsilon)$ and the time complexity is polynomial in both the input size and error parameter.

LEMMA 3. *Algorithm 1 is a $(1 - \varepsilon)$-approximation algorithm of Single-2-MCT.*

PROOF. Let Π^* be the optimal visible users, we have

$$\pi_1^\varepsilon = \sum_{i \in \Pi_1^\varepsilon} a_{si} \geq \frac{1}{Ad} \sum_{i \in \Pi_1^\varepsilon} A \left\lfloor \frac{an_{si}}{A} \right\rfloor \geq \frac{1}{Ad} \sum_{i \in \Pi^*} A \left\lfloor \frac{an_{si}}{A} \right\rfloor$$

$$\geq \frac{1}{Ad} \sum_{i \in \Pi^*} A \left(\frac{an_{si}}{A} - 1 \right) = \sum_{i \in \Pi^*} \left(a_{si} - \frac{A}{Ad} \right)$$

$$\geq \pi^* - \varepsilon \frac{|\Pi^*| \max\{a_{si} | a_{si} p_{it} \leq \tau\}}{S_n} \geq (1 - \varepsilon) \pi^*$$

where the last step holds since $\max\{a_{si} | a_{si} p_{it} \leq \tau\} \leq \pi^*$ and $|\Pi^*| \leq S_n$. □

LEMMA 4. *Algorithm 1 has the running time of $O(S_n^3 / \varepsilon)$.*

PROOF. The running time of Algorithm 1 is dependent on the second phase of dynamic programming, which has its running time $O(S_n A_u)$. That is,

$$S_n A_u \leq S_n \cdot S_n \frac{an_{si}}{A} \leq S_n^2 \frac{S_n}{\varepsilon} = \frac{S_n^3}{\varepsilon}$$

The proof is complete. □

The results of Lemma 3 and 4 imply the following theorem:

THEOREM 2. *Algorithm 1 is an FPTAS approximation algorithm for Single-2-MCT.*

3.3 No FPTAS for Any $k \geq 2$

As 2-MCT is NP-complete, one will question how tightly we can approximate the solution when $k \geq 2$. In this section, we further investigate that there is no FPTAS approximation algorithm of 2-MCT with any $k \geq 2$.

THEOREM 3. *There is no FPTAS for 2-MCT problem with any $k \geq 2$ unless P=NP.*

PROOF. We reduce the 2-MCT problem from EQUIPARTITION problem, which asks if there exists a subset of items R satisfying both $|R| = n/2$ and $\sum_{j \in R} \varpi_j = \sum_{j \notin R} \varpi_j$ given n items with integer weight ϖ_j for $j = 1, \ldots, n$ and even n. EQUIPARTITION problem has been proven to be NP-hard in [8]. Let a set of even number of n items with each integer weight ϖ_j be an arbitrary instance I of EQUIPARTITION. We must construct in polynomial time an instance of 2-MCT such that if we have a FPTAS to solve the 2-MCT on this instance, this algorithm can be applied to solve the EQUIPARTITION problem on I in polynomial time.

Our construction is as follows. Given n items, we construct $n + 3$ nodes for graph G: node u_i for each item; a source node s and 2 unwanted targets t_1 and t_2. The mention probability from s to each u_i is 1. For each u_i, the mention probability from him to t_1 and t_2 are $p_{i1} = 1 - e^{-\frac{\varpi_i}{\sum_i \varpi_i}}$ and $p_{i2} = 1 - e^{-\frac{\varpi_{\max} - \varpi_i}{n \varpi_{\max} - \sum_i \varpi_i}}$ respectively. Moreover, we set τ_1, τ_2 to be $1 - e^{-1/2}$ and all sharing probabilities $a_{sN(s)} = 1$. We first show that there is an EQUIPARTITION of I iff our reduced instance has 2-MCT of size at least $n/2$.

First, suppose that R is a yes instance of I. Clearly, $|R| = n/2$ and $\sum_{j \in R} \varpi_j = \sum_{j \notin R} \varpi_j$. Now let us consider a set $R' = \{N_i | i \in R\}$. If s posts his message m to R', then the leakage probability to t_1 and t_2 are

$$1 - \prod_{i \in R} (1 - p_{i1}) = 1 - \prod_{i \in R} e^{-\frac{\varpi_i}{\sum_i \varpi_i}} = 1 - e^{-1/2}$$

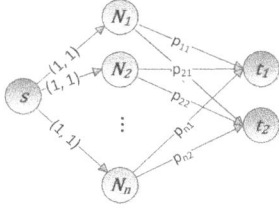

Figure 4: 2-MCT Reduction G from EQUIPARTITION (All edges from s to blue nodes have probability 1; an edge from N_i to t_1 and t_2 has probability $p_{i1} = 1 - e^{-\frac{\varpi_i}{\sum_i \varpi_i}}$ and $p_{i2} = 1 - e^{-\frac{\varpi_{\max} - \varpi_i}{n\varpi_{\max} - \sum_i \varpi_i}}$)

and

$$1 - \prod_{i \in R}\left(1 - p_{i2}\right) = 1 - \prod_{i \in R} e^{-\frac{\varpi_{\max} - \varpi_i}{n\varpi_{\max} - \sum_i \varpi_i}} = 1 - e^{-1/2}$$

which are no larger than τ_1 and τ_2. And the circle of trust has its size $n/2$, implying R' is a yes instance of 2-MCT.

Conversely, suppose that R' is a 2-MCT instance in G with respect to s and t. By satisfying

$$1 - \prod_{i \in R'} e^{-\frac{\varpi_i}{\sum_i \varpi_i}} \le 1 - e^{-1/2}$$

and

$$1 - \prod_{i \in R'} e^{-\frac{\varpi_{\max} - \varpi_i}{n\varpi_{\max} - \sum_i \varpi_i}} \le 1 - e^{-1/2}$$

we immediately have $\sum_{i \in R'} \varpi_i \le \frac{1}{2}\sum_{i \in N(s)} \varpi_i$ and $\sum_{i \in R'}\left(\varpi_{\max} - \varpi_i\right) \le \frac{1}{2}\left(n\varpi_{\max} - \sum_{i \in N(s)} \varpi_i\right)$. After summing these two inequalities up, we obtain $|R'| \le n/2$. Since the size of CT is at least $n/2$, i.e., $|R'| \ge n/2$, we obtain $|R'| = n/2$. Then, substituting $|R'| = n/2$ into the second above inequality, we have $\sum_{i \in R'} \varpi_i \ge \frac{1}{2}\sum_{i \in N(s)} \varpi_i$. Combining with the first one, $\sum_{i \in R'} \varpi_i = \frac{1}{2}\sum_{i \in N(s)} \varpi_i$. Thus, $R = \{i|N_i \in R'\}$ is a EQUIPARTITION of I.

Then, suppose that there is an FPTAS for 2-MCT, we show that this polynomial time algorithm can be applied to solve the NP-complete EQUIPARTITION problem, which leads to the contradiction. Let $\mathcal{A}$ be an FPTAS algorithm generating an $(1 - \varepsilon)$-approximation algorithm for 2-MCT for any $\varepsilon > 0$ in polynomial time with respect to both n and $1/\varepsilon$. When choosing $\varepsilon = \frac{1}{n+1}$, we have the following relations between the solution of $\pi^{\mathcal{A}}$ and optimal solution π^* as

$$\pi^{\mathcal{A}} \ge (1 - \varepsilon)\pi^* > \pi^* - \pi^*/n \ge \pi^* - 1$$

where the last step follows from a trivial observation that $\pi^* \le n$. Due to the equivalence between EQUIPARTITION and 2-MCT in our above reduction, we can obtain a solution $\pi^{\mathcal{A}} > \pi^* - 1$ for EQUIPARTITION. However, the integrality of solution to EQUIPARTITION implies that $\pi^* = \lceil \pi^{\mathcal{A}} \rceil$, which means that $\mathcal{A}$ can solve the EQUIPARTITION problem in polynomial time. This contradicts the fact that EQUIPARTITION is NP-hard. $\square$

3.4 PTAS Algorithm for Bounded-2-MCT

Because of the non-existence of FPTAS for the Bounded-2-MCT problem, we now focus our attention on designing a

PTAS solution, which is the best approximation solution we can expect. We first formulate the *Integer Linear Programming* (ILP) formulation for this problem and then propose the PTAS algorithm based on its relaxed LP formulation.

3.4.1 ILP Formulation

First, let us define an indicator variable x_i for each friend $i \in N(s)$ of s as $x_i = 1$ if i is visible to m, and 0 otherwise. Clearly, we have our objective to maximize the circle of trust, i.e., the expected number of visible friends of s. Thus, it can be written as the sum of sharing probabilities of s's friends except unwanted targets, that is, $\max \sum_{i \in N(s)\backslash T} a_i x_i$.

According to Lemma 2, which can be easily proven using contradiction method, the message will be leaked to t_j iff an s's neighbor i is informed with probability a_{si} and i further leaks to t_j with probability p_{it_j}. Therefore, the constraint w.r.t. each unwanted target t_j can be written as $1 - \prod_{i \in N(s)\backslash T}(1 - a_{si}p_{it_j})^{x_i} \le \tau_j$. After rearranging and choosing the logarithm of both sides in each constraint and relaxing $x_i \in \{0, 1\}$ to $x_i \ge 0$, we can obtain the following linear programming (LP):

$$
\begin{aligned}
\max \quad & \sum_{i \in N(s)\backslash T} a_i x_i \\
\text{s.t.} \quad & \sum_{i \in N(s)\backslash T} w_{ij} x_i \le c_j, \quad \forall j \in T \\
& x_i \ge 0
\end{aligned}
\tag{2}
$$

where $w_{ij} = -\log(1 - a_{si}p_{it_j})$ and $c_j = -\log(1 - \tau_j)$.

3.4.2 PTAS Algorithm for Bounded-2-MCT

Our PTAS algorithm for 2-MCT consists of two phases with respect to a threshold $\beta = \min\{\lceil \frac{k}{\varepsilon}\rceil - (k-1), |N(s)\backslash T|\}$ with k unwanted targets: (1) when the number of visible neighbors of s is less than β, we enumerate the solution and select a feasible solution π which induces a maximum visibility; (2) after initializing the current optimal solution as the one in the first phase, we check each combination of size β. For each combination Ω, we first use the LP rounding algorithm (as shown in Algorithm 3) to obtain a bounded solution π_Ω of the subproblem of 2-MCT in terms of the neighbor set $N(s)' = \{i|a_i \le \min i \in \Omega\}$ and $c'_j = c_j - \sum_{i \in \Omega} w_{ij}$. Then, we update the new optimal solution if $\sum_{i \in \Omega} a_i + \pi_\Omega > \pi$. The detail of PTAS algorithm is shown as Algorithm 2.

The subroutine of LP rounding algorithm, as shown in Algorithm 3, starts with a basic solution of LP (2) consisting of k fractional x_i^{LP}. Between the sum of a_{si} on integers x_i^{LP} and a_{sj} with the maximum fraction value x_j^{LP}, the algorithm returns the larger value as its solution.

Let π^k, π^{LP}, π^* be the solution of Algorithm 3, the optimal LP solution and the optimal solution of 2-MCT. We first show that Algorithm 3 has an $1/(k+1)$ approximation guarantee.

LEMMA 5. *Algorithm 3 is a $\frac{1}{k+1}$ approximation algorithm of Bounded-2-MCT.*

PROOF. According to Luenberger [11], each LP formulation with n variables and d constraints has a basic optimal solution with at most $\min\{d, n\}$ fractional values. We can obtain such a basic optimal solution x^* in the first step. Then

$$\pi^* \le \pi^{LP} \le \sum_{i \in I} a_i + kF_{\max} \le (k+1)\pi^k$$

```
        Input   : Bounded-2-MCT instance
        Output: visible friends $\Pi^\varepsilon$ and size of CT $\pi^\varepsilon$
 1   $\beta \leftarrow \min\{\lceil \frac{k}{\varepsilon} \rceil - (k+1), |N(s) \setminus T|\}$;
 2   $w_{ij} \leftarrow -\log(1 - p_{si}p_{it_j})$;
 3   $c_j \leftarrow -\log(1 - \tau_j)$;
 4   $\pi^\varepsilon \leftarrow 0$;
     // Phase 1
 5   foreach $\Lambda \subset N(s) \setminus T$ such that $|\Lambda| < \beta$ do
 6   |   if $\sum_{i \in \Lambda} w_{ij} x_i \le c_j$ for all $j \in T$ then
 7   |   |   if $\sum_{i \in \Lambda} a_i > \pi^\varepsilon$ then
 8   |   |   |   $\pi^\varepsilon \leftarrow \sum_{i \in \Lambda} a_i$;
 9   |   |   end
10   |   end
11   end
     // Phase 2
12   foreach $\Omega \subset N(s) \setminus T$ such that $|\Omega| = \beta$ do
13   |   if $\sum_{i \in \Omega} w_{ij} x_i \le c_j$ for all $j \in T$ then
14   |   |   Obtain the solution $\pi_\Omega^k$ of the subproblem
     |   |   with $N(s)'$ and $c_j'$ using LP rounding
     |   |   algorithm (Algorithm 3) ;
15   |   |   if $\sum_{i \in \Omega} a_i + \pi_\Omega^k > \pi^\varepsilon$ then
16   |   |   |   $\pi^\varepsilon \leftarrow \sum_{i \in \Omega} a_i + \pi_\Omega^k$;
17   |   |   end
18   |   end
19   end
```

Algorithm 2: PTAS for Bounded-2-MCT

```
        Input   : Bounded-2-MCT instance
        Output: visible friends $\Pi^k$ and size of CT $\pi^k$
 1   Obtain an optimal basic solution $x^{LP}$ by solving the
     LP (2) with $|\{i | 0 < x_i^{LP} < 1\}| \le k$;
 2   $I \leftarrow \{i | x_i^{LP} = 1\}$;
 3   $F \leftarrow \{i | 0 < x_i^{LP} < 1\}$;
 4   $\pi^k \leftarrow \max\{\sum_{i \in I} a_i, \max\{a_i | i \in F\}\}$;
```

Algorithm 3: LP Rounding Algorithm

where the last step follows from Algorithm 3. $\square$

Now, we prove that Algorithm 2 is indeed a PTAS algorithm, that is, we need to prove the approximation ratio $(1 - \varepsilon)$ and the time complexity is polynomial in the input size.

LEMMA 6. *Algorithm 2 is a $(1 - \varepsilon)$-approximation algorithm of Bounded-2-MCT.*

PROOF. If π^* has less than β items, we can obtain the optimal solution in the first phase by enumerating all possible combinations. This certainly leads to the optimal solution. When $\pi^* > \beta$, let $\Omega*$ be the β items having the maximum circle of trust in optimal solution, we consider two cases as follows:
Case 1: $\sum_{i \in \Omega^*} a_i \ge \frac{\beta}{\beta + k + 1} \pi^*$
From the last step and the condition of this case, we have

$$
\begin{aligned}
\pi^\varepsilon &\ge \sum_{i \in \Omega^*} a_i + \pi_\Omega^k \ge \sum_{i \in \Omega^*} a_i + \frac{1}{k+1}\pi_\Omega^* \text{ (Lemma 5)} \\
&\ge \sum_{i \in \Omega^*} a_i + \frac{1}{k+1}\left(\pi^* - \sum_{i \in \Omega^*} a_i\right) \text{(Definition of } \Omega^*) \\
&\ge \frac{1}{k+1}\pi^* + \frac{k}{k+1}\frac{\beta}{\beta+k+1}\pi^* = \frac{\beta+1}{\beta+k+1}\pi^*
\end{aligned}
$$

Case 2: $\sum_{i \in \Omega^*} a_i < \frac{\beta}{\beta+k+1} \pi^*$
First, among all these β neighbors of s, there is at least one having sharing probability less than $\frac{1}{\beta+k+1}\pi^*$. According

to the definition of Ω^*, i.e., all neighbors in Ω^* have higher sharing probability than others, all neighbors in π_Ω^k have $a_i \le \frac{1}{\beta+k+1}\pi^*$.

$$
\pi_\Omega^* \le \pi_\Omega^{LP} \le \pi_\Omega^k + \frac{k}{\beta+k+1}\pi_\Omega^*
$$

where the last step follows from the upper bound of all k fractional values according to Luenberger [11]. Therefore,

$$
\pi^* = \sum_{i \in \Omega^*} a_i + \pi_\Omega^* \le \pi^\varepsilon + \frac{k}{\beta+k+1}\pi_\Omega^*
$$

Then, we have

$$
\pi^\varepsilon \ge \frac{\beta+1}{\beta+k+1}\pi^* \ge \frac{\lceil \frac{k}{\varepsilon} \rceil - k}{\lceil \frac{k}{\varepsilon} \rceil}\pi^* \ge \frac{\frac{1}{\varepsilon} - 1}{\frac{1}{\varepsilon}}\pi^* = (1 - \varepsilon)\pi^*
$$

where the second step follows from the fact that $\frac{\beta+1}{\beta+k+1}$ is monotonously increasing with respect to β. $\square$

LEMMA 7. *Algorithm 2 has the running time of $O(S_n^{\lceil \kappa/\varepsilon \rceil})$, where constant κ is the upper bound of the number of unwanted targets k.*

PROOF. It is easy to see that the first phase has the running time at most $S_n^{\lceil \frac{k}{\varepsilon} \rceil - (k+1)}$. For the second phase, we need to solve LP (2) S_n^β times. According to Megiddo *et al.* [12], LP (2) S_n^β can be solved in $O(S_n)$ when k is upper bounded by some constant κ. Hence, the overall running time of Algorithm 3 is $O(S_n^{\lceil \kappa/\varepsilon \rceil})$. $\square$

The results of Lemma 6 and 7 imply the following theorem:

THEOREM 4. *Algorithm 2 is a PTAS approximation algorithm for Bounded-2-MCT.*

4. GENERAL δ-MCT PROBLEM

When the message can be propagated more than 2 hops, i.e., $\delta > 2$, one will be interested to see how hard a general MCT problem is and how to develop an efficient approach to solve it. In this section, we first prove that the MCT problem is #P-hard when $\delta > 2$. Due to its extreme challenge to design a fully polynomial-time randomized approximation scheme (FPRAS) for a #P-hard problem, we propose an effective ICTD algorithm based on a novel greedy function. The performance of our ICTD algorithm is further evaluated in the next section.

4.1 #P-Hardness when $\delta \ge 3$

THEOREM 5. *δ-MCT problem is #P-hard when $\delta \ge 3$.*

PROOF. We will show the reduction from 3-Conn$_2$ problem, which is defined in Definition 1 and proven to be #P-hard in Lemma 8. First of all, we notice that 3-Conn$_2$ problem can be polynomially solved if we can determine that 3-Conn$_2 \le r'/r$ in a graph G for any integer $r' \le r$. Since each $p(u,v)$ in G is a rational number which can be represented by a numerator and a denominator which are integers, we can define r to be the least common multiple of all the denominators such that a simple binary search from 1 to r can be finished within a polynomial time with respect to the input size.

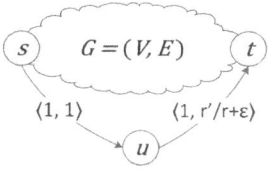

Figure 5: δ-MCT Reduction

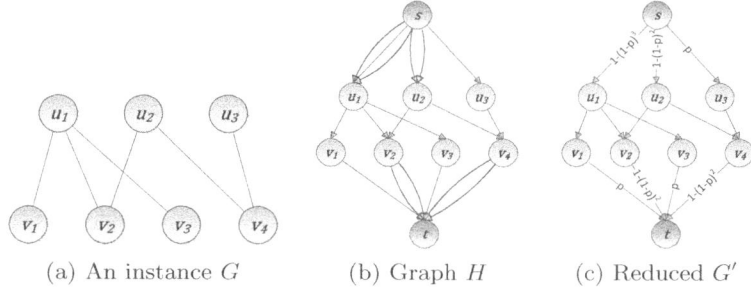

(a) An instance G (b) Graph H (c) Reduced G'

Figure 6: An Example of 3-Conn$_2$ Reduction

Therefore, let G, s and t be an arbitrary instance of 3-Conn$_2$, we must construct in a polynomial time a graph $G' = (V', E')$, a source user s and a set of unwanted targets T along with their leakage thresholds τ_j for each of them such that if we have a polynomial-time algorithm to solve the δ-MCT problem on our reduced instance, this algorithm can be applied to determine the upper bound of 3-Conn$_2$ problem on G.

As shown in Figure 5, our construction is as follows. First, we choose $s' = s$ and $T = \{t\}$. Then we set the sharing probability in each edge of G to be $1/|N(s)| + \epsilon_1$ where $0 < \epsilon_1 < \frac{1}{|N(s)|(|N(s)|-1)}$ and $|N(s)|$ is the number of neighbors of s. The mention probability is set to $p(i, j)$ in G for each edge. Then, we add a two-hop disjoint path between s and t onto the graph G with the intermediate node u. Both edges (s, u) and (u, t) have the sharing probability to be 1. And $p_{su} = 1$ and $p_{ut} = r' \le r + \epsilon_2$ for any integer $r' \le r$ and $\epsilon_2 < 1/r$. Besides, we set $T = \{t\}$ and its leakage threshold to $r'/r + \epsilon_2$.

Assume that $\mathcal{A}$ is a polynomial algorithm solving δ-MCT problem in our reduced instance. Let's consider two cases:

- If $\mathcal{A}$ returns the circle of trust with size larger than 1, we know all neighbors of s in G except u is visible to the message. That is, the 3-Conn$_2$ in G, s and t is less than or equal to r'/r;
- If $\mathcal{A}$ returns the circle of trust with size equal to 1, that is, $\mathcal{A}$ selected only one neighbor u of s, since the visibility $\left(\frac{1}{|N(s)|} + \epsilon_1 \right) (|N(s)| - 1) < 1$ when $\epsilon_1 < \frac{1}{|N(s)|(|N(s)|-1)}$ if only selecting $N - 1$ neighbors of s in G. Clearly, 3-Conn$_2$ in G, s and t is larger than r'/r.

Thus, $\mathcal{A}$ can be used to decide if 3-Conn$_2$ is less than r'/r, implying that our δ-MCT problem is at least as hard as 3-Conn$_2$. $\square$

DEFINITION 1 (3-CONN$_2$). *Given a directed graph G with $|V| = n$ nodes and a probability $p(u, v)$ for each pair of nodes denoting the probability of u being able to connect to v. Let s and t be two terminals in G. 3-Conn$_2$ asks for the probability that there is a path from source s to destination t in G and the path has its length no larger than 3 hops.*

LEMMA 8. *3-Conn$_2$ problem is #P-hard.*

PROOF. In this proof, we reduce the 3-Conn$_2$ problem from Counting Bipartite Independent Set (CBIS) problem, which asks for the total number of independent sets in a bipartite graph $G = (U, V; E)$. CBIS has been proven to be

#P-hard by Provan *et al.* [15]. Let a graph $G = (U, V; E)$ be an arbitrary instance of CBIS. We must construct in polynomial time a probabilistic graph G' and two terminals s, t such that if we have a polynomial-time algorithm to solve the 3-Conn$_2$ problem on the reduced instance, this algorithm can be applied to solve CBIS problem on G.

Our reduction is two phases: First, we construct the probabilistic graph H by adding two terminals s and t onto G. Between s and each $u \in U$, we add $\deg(u)$ number of edges where $\deg(u)$ is the degree of u in G. Similarly, between each $v \in U$ and t, we add $\deg(v)$ number of edges. And all edges in H have probability p with $0 < p < 1$. Secondly, we construct the probabilistic graph G' on H by replacing the multi-edges between each pair of nodes (u, v) with an edge of probability $1 - (1 - p)^\gamma$ where γ is the number of multi-edges between u and v. Note that the paths between s and t in G' are at most 3-hops. This reduction is depicted for an example in Figure 6.

Then we first show that CBIS in G is equivalent to counting the minimum cardinality $s - t$ cutsets in H. It is easy to see that the construction ensures that the $s - t$ cutsets contain at least $|E|$ edges. Also, it is clear that if there are $\deg(u) > 1$ edges between s and u, a minimum cutset includes either all or none of them. In addition, we note that (u, v) must not an edge of G if both (s, u) and (v, t) are included in a minimum cut since we can reduce the size of cutset by simply replacing the multi-edges in (s, u) and (v, t) with the edges incident to u and v in G, which contradicts that the cutset is minimum.

Therefore, suppose that $I_u \cup I_v$ is an independent set in G where $I_u \subseteq U$ and $I_v \subseteq V$, we have the cutset consisting of (s, u) for all $u \in I_u$, $(v, t) \in I_v$ for all $v \in I_v$ and all edges in E not incident to $I_u \cup I_v$. Conversely, suppose C is a minimum cutset in H, according to our above arguments, the endpoints (except s and t) incident to the edges in $C \setminus E$ forms an independent set in G.

Furthermore, it is easy to see that the probability that there is a path from s to t is the same in H and G' since only multi-edges in H are replaced in G' with simple edges with the same probability. According to Charles [7], if the 3-Conn$_2$ between s and t can be determined in G' (also H), this is suffices to obtain the $s - t$ pathset. Thus, the minimum $s - t$ cutsets can be further counted using the pathset, implying that 3-Conn$_2$ is at least as hard as CBIS. $\square$

4.2 ICTD Algorithm

As can be seen in the above proofs, the general MCT problem with $\delta \ge 3$ is related to a set of problems in network reliability [7], which is a long standing open problem.

Therefore, it is extremely challenging to design a FPRAS algorithm, which may not even exist. Instead, we propose an effective *Iterative Circle of Trust Detection* (ICTD) algorithm.

The idea of ICTD algorithm is to iteratively eliminate one of s's neighbors until each unwanted target t_j can see m with the leakage probability less than τ_j. Due to the objective of maximizing the circle of trust, we define the greedy function $f(v)$ to maximize

$$\frac{\sum_{t_j \in T, \tau_j(C) > \tau_j} |\tau_j(C) - \tau_j|}{a_{sv} + \sum_{i \in C_v} a_{si}} - \frac{\sum_{t_j \in T, \tau_j(C_v) > \tau_j} |\tau_j(C_v) - \tau_j|}{\sum_{i \in C_v} a_{si}}$$

where $\tau_j(C)$ is the expected probability that unwanted target t_j knows the information when s only chooses the subset C to share, and $C_v = C \setminus \{v\}$. Intuitively, we do not want to remove very close friends of s, whose sharing probabilities with s are relatively high. Therefore, the normalization factor is to ensure that the removed neighbor does not have a high sharing probability to s. In addition, it is not hard to see that this greedy function can reflect the impact on a user to the leakage by calculating the difference between before and after removing him from the circle of trust.

To calculate $\tau_j(C)$ in each iteration, we use the *Monte Carlo Sampling* method due to its #P-hardness according to Theorem 5. In the sampling subroutine, according to the ISM propagation model, the information is propagated via each edge (u, v) with mention probability p_{uv} on G until no newly informed users can be found or the message has been propagated δ hops. Then, in order to seek for the subset of unwanted targets in T knowing the information at the end propagation, we repeat the sampling 20,000 times and obtain average leaking probability for each unwanted target $t_j \in T$. The whole ICTD algorithm, shown as Algorithm 4, terminates until the average probability in sampling is less than τ_j for each unwanted target t_j. Clearly, our ICTD algorithm runs at most constant times of the multiply of the maximum sampling time and S_n^2.

Input : 2-MCT instance
Output: visible friends Π^h and size of CT π^h
1   $C \leftarrow N(s) \setminus T$;
2   **while** $\exists \tau_j(C) \geq \tau_j$ **do**
3 | Find $v \in C$ using Monte Carlo Sampling which maximizes $f(v)$;
4 | $C \leftarrow C \setminus \{v\}$;
5   **end**
6   $\Pi^h \leftarrow C$;
7   $\pi^h \leftarrow \sum_{i \in \Pi_h} a_{si}$;

Algorithm 4: ICTD Algorithm

5. EXPERIMENTAL EVALUATION

5.1 Dataset and Metrics

We examine the performance of our proposed algorithms on different real-world OSNs, including Facebook, Twitter, Foursquare, and Flickr, with different sizes and density as shown in Table 1. Here we omit the detailed descriptions of Facebook and Flickr datasets, which can be found in the provided references shown in Table 1. For Twitter, we used the unbiased sampling approach [9] to sample a portion of Twitter network from the complete Twitter network,

Table 1: Dataset

Dataset	Nodes	Edges	Density	Source
Facebook	63,731	905,565	4.46%	Ref [16]
Twitter	88,484	2,364,322	3.02%	Sampling in [5]
Foursquare	44,832	1,664,402	8.28%	Our data
Flickr	80,513	5,899,882	18.2%	DMML [2]

* Facebook and Flickr are undirected networks; Twitter and Foursquare are directed networks.

which is provided by Cha *et al.* [5]. And for Foursquare, we initially picked a seed set consisting of entrepreneurs and investors, from whom we used Foursquare API [1] to obtain the users and links within their two-hop neighbors.

For each dataset, we randomly assign sharing probability a_{uv} and propagation probability p_{uv} to each edge respectively, in which both of them lie in the interval $[0, 1]$. Then we evaluate the following metrics on these four datasets according to the application illustrated in Figure 1:

(1) *Size of CT*: defined as $\sum_{j \in CT} a_{sj}$. This is used to measure the expected visible neighbors of s;
(2) *Running Time*: the time a user needs to wait for the construction of CT before he posts a message. An effective solution should construct a CT within a second.

5.2 Performance of Proposed Algorithms

We compare our proposed PTAS algorithm and ICTD algorithm with the optimal solution in the above four datasets. Due to the impracticability to obtain optimal solution for an #P-hard problem, we select $\delta = 2$. In addition, since the leakage threshold is usually small, we set all of them to 0.1, i.e., $\tau_j = 0.1$ for any unwanted target t_j. The allowable error ε for PTAS algorithm is set to 0.01, that is, the result obtained from PTAS should be close to the optimal solution since the approximation ratio is close to 1. In our experiments, we test different numbers of unwanted targets and different leakage thresholds in each dataset. In each network, for a specific number of unwanted targets, we randomly choose a source and unwanted targets and perform the experiments 100 times. The size of CT is then averaged. To obtain the optimal solution, we solve the IP as in Section 3.4.1 using CPLEX optimization suite from ILOG [3].

As revealed in Figure 7, the solution of our PTAS algorithm is almost identical with the optimal solution when the allowable error is small. This empirical result once again claims that Algorithm 2 algorithm is PTAS. Also, in all four datasets, the expected size of CT obtained from our ICTD algorithm is at most 1% less than the optimal solution for different number of unwanted targets. It indicates that ICTD is very effective and our greedy function can actually reflect the influence of information leakage for each user in every iteration. When we fix the number of unwanted targets to be 5, Figure 8 reports the similar results in terms of different leakage thresholds τ_j from 0.05 to 0.3. In addition, as illustrated in Table 2, the running time of ICTD is very low, thus it is suitable for the design of this application. Even in Flickr, whose density is up to 20%, ICTD algorithm can finish detecting CT within 1 second when $\delta = 2$.

5.3 Findings using ICTD

With the effectiveness of ICTD observed through the above experiments, we confidently use ICTD to further analyze the

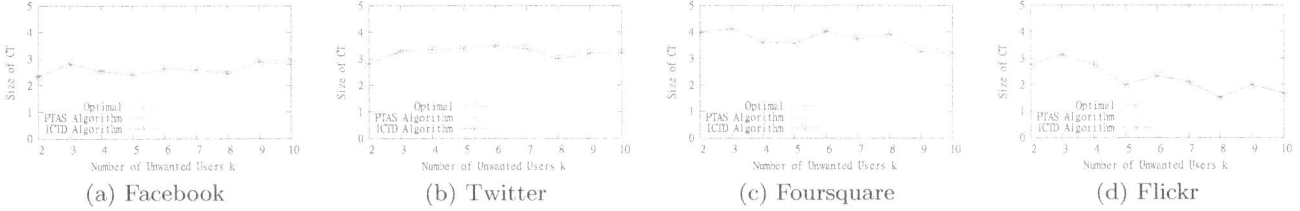

|(a) Facebook|(b) Twitter|(c) Foursquare|(d) Flickr|

Figure 7: Comparison Among Optimal Solution, PTAS Algorithm and ICTD on k when $\delta = 2$

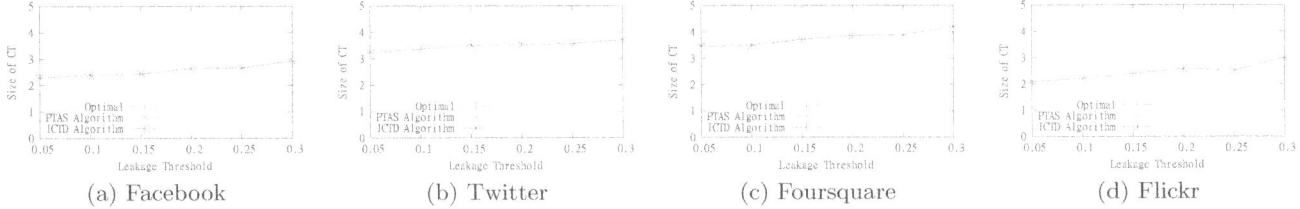

|(a) Facebook|(b) Twitter|(c) Foursquare|(d) Flickr|

Figure 8: Comparison Among Optimal Solution, PTAS Algorithm and ICTD on τ when $\delta = 2$

real-world traces and exploit some insight properties with respect to the securities in OSNs. In our experiments, we perform the following procedure on each dataset: We randomly select 40 source users. For each source user, we further randomly select 5 unwanted targets and deploy the ICTD algorithm to obtain the CT while δ is 2 and 3. We repeat this experiment 100 times and obtain the size of CT by taking the average value. Since the MCT problem is #P-hard when $\delta = 3$, calculating the leakage probability is time consuming. Therefore, we use a relatively larger leakage threshold $\tau_j = 0.15$ here to alleviate the running time of ICTD.

Propagation Hops and Size of CT: Our first observation, as revealed in Figure 9, shows that the higher δ is, the smaller the circle of trust we have. This intuitively agrees with what we expected since the information is more likely to leak to unwanted targets when it can propagate further. In our experiments, the sizes of CT in Facebook and Flickr are 20%-30% lower than the other two since they are undirected on which the information is easier to propagate than on directed networks Twitter and Foursquare. Again note that the size of CT refers to the expected visible friends who can see the message if posted to CT. When $\delta = 3$, the sizes of CT on Facebook and Flickr drop roughly 20%-30%, which is less than the decrease percentages on Twitter and Foursquare, i.e., more than 50%. This can again be explained due to their undirected properties. In addition, Facebook has its size of CT larger than Flickr since it has lower density. Therefore, it is not hard to see that the size of CT is quite sensitive to the information propagation hops.

Next, we take a look into the impact of information propagation hops on the running time of ICTD. As is shown in Table 2, although the running time for $\delta = 3$ is about from 20 to 30 times as large as that for $\delta = 2$, the detection of CT can still be finished around 1 second in Facebook, Twitter and Foursquare even when $\delta = 3$. In Flickr, our ICTD algorithm spends 25 seconds to construct a CT, which cannot be avoided due to its #P-hardness as proven in Theorem 5.

Popular Source Users and Their CTs: Consider popular source users (those who have a lot of friends) and other source users, we now are interested in finding relations

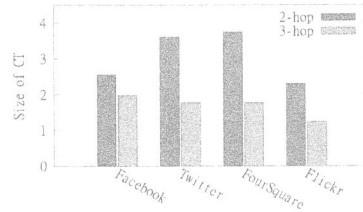

Figure 9: Propagation Hops and Size of CT

Table 2: Time (s) and Propagation Hops

Dataset/Hops	2-Hop	3-Hop	Increase Ratio
Facebook	0.03	0.94	30
Twitter	0.04	1.07	27
FourSquare	0.06	1.32	22
Flickr	0.8	25.2	30

between them and the size of their CTs. Intuitively, when a user is more popular, there is a higher chance that his friends will forward the information further. Thus, to avoid information leakage, the CT of popular sources possibly includes only a small fraction of their friends to CT.

To test our hypothesis, we select a set of source users with different degrees in each network. For each source, we choose ten random sets of five unwanted targets and compute the average size of CT. Figure 10 reports the relations between *Total Visible Friends* ($\sum_{j \in N(s) \setminus T} a_{sj}$) and *Visible Friends(%)* ($\frac{\sum_{j \in CT} a_{sj}}{\sum_{j \in N(s) \setminus T} a_{sj}}$). As we can see, the tested users are differentiated into two groups for each network. The red users have relatively smaller total friends and smaller percentage of CT. These users usually have fewer friends but some are gossipy. The elimination of each friends helps to reduce the leakage probability and size of CT as well. The other set of users, green users, usually have various kinds of friends such that their percentage of CT is always larger than 70% no matter whether or not they are popular.

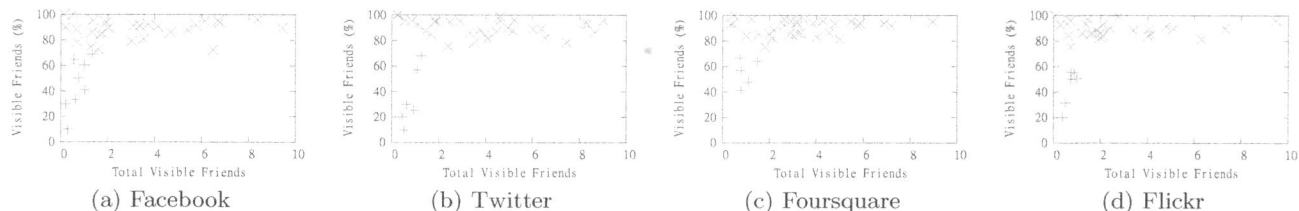

(a) Facebook   (b) Twitter   (c) Foursquare   (d) Flickr

Figure 10: Total Friends and Percentage of Visible Friends

6. RELATED WORK

This work is the first attempt to address the smartly sharing information in OSNs without leaking them to unwanted targets, thus there is not many related work. The most relevant works are the set of papers studied on the privacy issues in OSNs [10, 13, 14]. Lam *et al.* [10] showed that, in current OSNs, no matter how much efforts a user puts to protect his personal information, it cannot be prevented from being revealed by some malicious users by examining their "public" interactions with friends. Later on, for the sake of such unintentional information spreading, Ngoc *et al.* [13] then presented a new metric to quantify the privacy. Noting the potential risks by disclosing information to OSN companies, Nigusse *et al.* [14] proposed an *information flow model*, which made the existing privacy techniques more practical. However, these studies only focus on the users' personal profile, i.e., name, address, etc., but not on the information sharing and posting. In addition, they neglected the information leakage led by multi-hops diffusions.

7. CONCLUSION

In this paper, we study the optimization problem of constructing circle of trust to maximize the expected visible friends such that the probability of information leakage is reduced to some degree. In a special and more practical case of 2-hop information propagation and fixed number of unwanted targets, we prove the NP-hardness and design an FPTAS approximation algorithm for one unwanted target. Then we show the non-existence of FPTAS and design a PTAS approximation algorithm for multiple unwanted targets. In a general case, we further show its #P-hardness and provide the ICTD algorithm using a novel greedy function. The experiments on real-world datasets not only show the effectiveness of our proposed algorithms but also reveal the relations of information leakage with propagation hops and popular source users, which illustrates some crucial characteristics of OSNs that one may pay attention when investigating many security related problems in OSNs, especially the study of information leakage and tracing the misbehaving users.

8. REFERENCES

[1] https://developer.foursquare.com.
[2] http://socialcomputing.asu.edu/datasets/flickr.
[3] http://www-01.ibm.com/software/integration /optimization/cplex-optimizer/.
[4] http://www.marketingcharts.com.
[5] M. Cha, H. Haddadi, F. Benevenuto, and K. P. Gummadi. Measuring User Influence in Twitter: The Million Follower Fallacy. In *Proceedings of ICWSM '10*, May 2010.
[6] M. Cha, A. Mislove, and K. P. Gummadi. A measurement-driven analysis of information propagation in the flickr social network. In *Proceedings of WWW '09*, pages 721–730, New York, NY, USA, 2009. ACM.
[7] C. J. Colbourn. *The Combinatorics of Network Reliability*. Oxford University Press, Inc., New York, NY, USA, 1987.
[8] M. R. Garey and D. S. Johnson. *Computers and Intractability: A Guide to the Theory of NP-Completeness (Series of Books in the Mathematical Sciences)*. W. H. Freeman, first edition edition, Jan. 1979.
[9] M. Gjoka, M. Kurant, C. T. Butts, and A. Markopoulou. Walking in Facebook: A case study of unbiased sampling of OSNs. In *Proceedings of IEEE INFOCOM 2010*, pages 1–9. IEEE, Mar. 2010.
[10] I.-F. Lam, K.-T. Chen, and L.-J. Chen. Involuntary information leakage in social network services. In *Proceedings of IWSEC '08*, pages 167–183, Berlin, Heidelberg, 2008. Springer-Verlag.
[11] D. G. Luenberger. *Linear and Nonlinear Programming, Second Edition*. Springer, 2nd edition, Sept. 2003.
[12] N. Megiddo and A. Tamir. Linear time algorithms for some separable quadratic programming problems. *Operations Research Letters*, 13:203–211, 1993.
[13] T. H. Ngoc, I. Echizen, K. Komei, and H. Yoshiura. New approach to quantification of privacy on social network sites. In *Proceedings of AINA '10*, pages 556–564, Washington, DC, USA, 2010.
[14] G. Nigusse and B. D. Decker. Privacy codes of practice for the social web: The analysis of existing privacy codes and emerging social-centric privacy risks. In *AAAI Spring Symposium Series*, 2010.
[15] S. J. Provan and M. O. Ball. The Complexity of Counting Cuts and of Computing the Probability that a Graph is Connected. *SIAM Journal on Computing*, 12(4):777–788, 1983.
[16] B. Viswanath, A. Mislove, M. Cha, and K. P. Gummadi. On the Evolution of User Interaction in Facebook. In *Proceedings of WOSN'09*, Aug. 2009.
[17] S. T. Walters and C. Neighbors. Feedback interventions for college alcohol misuse: what, why and for whom? *Addict Behav*, 30(6):1168–82, 2005.

Cheap, Easy, and Massively Effective Viral Marketing in Social Networks: Truth or Fiction?

Thang N. Dinh, Dung T. Nguyen and My T. Thai
University of Florida
Gainesville, FL, 32603
{tdinh, dtnguyen, mythai}@cise.uf.edu

ABSTRACT

Online social networks (OSNs) have become one of the most effective channels for marketing and advertising. Since users are often influenced by their friends, "word-of-mouth" exchanges so-called viral marketing in social networks can be used to increases product adoption or widely spread content over the network. The common perception of viral marketing about being cheap, easy, and massively effective makes it an ideal replacement of traditional advertising. However, recent studies have revealed that the propagation often fades quickly within only few hops from the sources, counteracting the assumption on the self-perpetuating of influence considered in literature. With only limited influence propagation, is massively reaching customers via viral marketing still affordable? How to economically spend more resources to increase the spreading speed?

We investigate the cost-effective massive viral marketing problem, taking into the consideration the limited influence propagation. Both analytical analysis based on power-law network theory and numerical analysis demonstrate that the viral marketing might involve costly seeding. To minimize the seeding cost, we provide mathematical programming to find optimal seeding for medium-size networks and propose VirAds, an efficient algorithm, to tackle the problem on large-scale networks. VirAds guarantees a relative error bound of $O(1)$ from the optimal solutions in power-law networks and outperforms the greedy heuristics which realizes on the degree centrality. Moreover, we also show that, in general, approximating the optimal seeding within a ratio better than $O(\log n)$ is unlikely possible.

Categories and Subject Descriptors

G.2.2 [**Mathematics of Computing**]: Discrete Mathematics—*Graph theory*; I.1.2 [**Computing Methodologies**]: Algorithms—*Analysis of algorithms*

General Terms

Theory, Algorithm, Measurement

Keywords

Social media, influence propagation, power-law networks, approximation algorithm, hardness proof.

1. INTRODUCTION

Digitizing real world connections, online social networks (OSNs) such as Twitter, Facebook have been steadily growing. Two-third of everyone online is using social networks with 800 million active users using Facebook [2], 200 million twitters, 40 millions Google+ subscribers and so on. Social network sites such as Facebook and Youtube are often among top-ten visited websites on the Internet [1]. Much like real-world social networks, OSNs inherent the viral property in which information can spread and disseminate widely into networks via 'word-of-mouth' exchanges, creating an effective platform for marketing. OSNs quickly become one of the most attractive choices for brand awareness, encouraging discussion on improving products and for recruiting. Notable examples include the recent unrest in many Arab countries which are triggered by Facebook shared posts [23]; the customer outreach of Toyota on Twitter to repair its image after the massive safety recalls of its vehicles [22], and many others. Despite the huge economic and political impact, viral marketing in large scale OSNs is not well understood due to the extremely large numbers of users and complex structures of social links.

A major portion of viral marketing research has been devoted to the question of efficiently targeting a set of *influential nodes* in order to spread information widely into the network [16, 17, 11]. Two essential components to address the question are the diffusion models and the algorithms to select the initial set of nodes, called seeding. For a social network represented as a graph, a diffusion model defines the stochastic process that specifies how influence is propagated from the seeding to their neighbors, and further. In [16] Kempe et al. proposed two basic diffusion models, namely *independent cascade* model and *linear threshold* model. These two models and their extensions set the foundation to almost all existing algorithms to find seeding in social networks [16, 17, 11].

However, all mentioned models and algorithms ignore one important aspect of influence propagation in the real world. That is influence propagation often happens only within a close proximity of the seeding. For examples, study of Cha et. al. in Flickr network [9] reveals that the typical chain length is less than four; another study of Leskovec et. al. [18] suggests that social influence happens on the level of direct friends. Moreover, shared information in social networks such as Facebook, in most cases, can be seen only by friends or friends of friends i.e. the propagation is basically limited within two hops from the source. When the influence only propagates locally, is massively reaching customers via viral marketing still affordable? In addition, can we speed up the information spreading for time-critical applications such as political campaigns?

We formulate a new optimization problem, called *the cost-effective, fast, and massive viral marketing* (CFM) problem. The problem seeks for a minimal cost seeding, measured as the number of nodes, to massively and quickly spread the influence to the whole network (or a large segment of the network). The new aspect in our model is that the influence is limited to the nodes that are within d hops from the seeding for some constant $d \geq 1$. In other words, the influence is forced to spread to the whole networks within d propagation rounds. Hence, adjusting d gives us an important ability to control how fast the spread of influence within a network. Unfortunately, the huge magnitude of OSN users and data available on OSNs poses a substantial challenge to control how information can quickly spread out to the whole network.

In this paper, we develop solutions to the CFM problem and address the above two questions. More specifically, our contributions are summarized as follows:

- Our first finding shows that the seeding for fast and massive spreading must contain a non-trivial fraction of nodes in the networks, which is cost-prohibitive for large social networks. This is confirmed by both our theoretical analysis based on the power-law model in [4] and our extensive experiments.

- We propose VirAds, a scalable algorithm to find a set of minimal seeding to expeditiously propagate the influence to the whole network. VirAds outperforms the greedy heuristics based on well-known degree centrality and scales up to networks of hundred of million links. We prove that the algorithm guarantees a relative error bound of $O(1)$, assuming that the network is power-law.

- We show how hard to obtain a near optimal solution for CFM by proving the impossibility to approximate the optimal solution within a ratio better than $O(\log n)$.

Related Work. Viral marketing can be thought of as a diffusion of information about the product and its adoption over the network. Kempe et al. [16, 17] formulated the influence maximization problem as an optimization problem. They showed the problem to be NP-complete and devised an $(1 - 1/e - \epsilon)$ approximation algorithm. A major drawback of their algorithm is that the accuracy ϵ, and efficiency depends on the number of times running Monte-Carlo simulation of the propagation model. Later, Leskovec et al. [19] study the influence propagation in a different perspective in which they aim to find a set of nodes in networks to detect the spread of virus as soon as possible. They improve the simple greedy method to run faster. The greedy algorithm

is furthered improved by Chen et al. [10] by using an influence estimation. However, the proposed algorithm might only perform well for small values of propagation probabilities. In addition, the algorithm time complexity should be $O((m + k) \log n)$ instead of the claimed $O(k \log m + m)$.

Influence propagation with limited number of hops is first considered in Wang *et al.* [26] in which the proposed heuristic has high time complexity. Feng et al. [27] show NP-completeness for the problem. We note that none of the mentioned approaches handled large-scale social networks of million of nodes as we shall study in Section 6.

Organization. We introduce the limited hop influence model and the cost-effective, massive and fast propagation problem (CFM) in Section 2. In Section 3, we answer the question on the seeding cost by analyzing the propagation process on power-law networks. We present VirAds, a scalable algorithm to find a minimal seeding for the CFM problem in Section 4. The hardness of finding a cost-effective seeding is addressed in Section 5. Finally, we perform extensive experiments on large social networks such as Facebook and Orkut to confirm the efficiency of our proposed algorithm and analyze the results to give new observations to information diffusion process in networks.

2. PROBLEM DEFINITIONS

We are given a *social network* modeled as an undirected graph $G = (V, E)$ where the vertices in V represent users in the network and the edges in E represent social links between users. We use n and m to denote the number of vertices and edges, respectively. The set of neighbors of a vertex $v \in V$ is denoted by $N(v)$ and we denote by $d(v) = |N(v)|$ the degree of node v.

We continue with specifying the diffusion model that governs the process of influence propagation. Existing diffusion models can be categorized into two main groups [16]:

- *Threshold model.* Each node v in the network has a threshold $t_v \in [0, 1]$, typically drawn from some probability distribution. Each connection (u, v) between nodes u and v is assigned a weight $w(u, v)$. For a node v, let $F(v)$ be the set of neighbors of v that are already influenced. Then v is influenced if $t_v \leq \sum_{u \in F(v)} w(u, v)$.

- *Cascade model.* Whenever a node u is influenced, it is given a single chance to activate each of its neighbor v with a given probability $p(u, v)$.

Most viral marketing papers assume that the probabilities $p(u, v)$ or weights $w(u, v)$ and thresholds t_v are given as a part of the input. However, they are generally not available and inferring those probabilities and thresholds has remained a non trivial problem [15]. Therefore, in addition to the bounded propagation hop, we use a simplified variation of the linear threshold model in which a vertex is activated if a fraction ρ of its neighbors are active as follows.

Locally Bounded Diffusion Model. Let $R_0 \subset V$ be the subset of vertices selected to initiate the influence propagation, which we call the *seeding*. We also call a vertex $v \in R_0$ a seed. The propagation process happens in round, with all vertices in R_0 are influenced (thus active in adopting the behavior) at round $t = 0$. At a particular round $t \geq 0$, each vertex is either active (adopted the behavior) or inactive and each vertex's tendency to become active increases when more of its neighbors become active. If an inactive vertex u has more than $\lceil \rho \, d(u) \rceil$ active neighbors at round t, then it becomes active at round $t+1$, where ρ is the *influence factor* as discussed later. The process goes on for a maximum number of d rounds and a vertex once becomes active will remain active until the end. We say an initial set R_0 of vertices to be a *d-seeding* if R_0 can make all vertices in the networks active within at most d rounds.

The influence factor $0 < \rho < 1$ is a constant that decides how widely and quickly the influence propagates through the network. Influence factor ρ reflects real-world factors such as how easy to share the content with others, or some intrinsic benefit for those who initially adopt the behavior. In case $\rho = 1/2$ the model is also known as the *majority* model that has many application in distributed computing, voting system [21], etc.

Problem Definition. Given the diffusion model, the *Cost-effective, Fast, and Massive viral marketing (CFM)* problem is defined as follows

DEFINITION 1 (CFM PROBLEM). *Given an undirected graph $G = (V, E)$ modeling a social network and an influence factor $0 < \rho < 1$, find in V a minimum size d-seeding i.e. a subset of vertices that can activate all vertices in the network within at most d rounds.*

Generalization. The diffusion model can be generalized in several ways. For example, the model can be extended naturally to cover directed networks or specify different influence factor ρ_v for each node $v \in V$. For simplicity we stick with the current model to avoid setting parameters during the experiments. Nevertheless, major results such as the approximation ratio of the VirAds algorithm in Section 4 or the hardness of approximation result in Section 5 still hold for the generalized models.

3. COST OF MASSIVE MARKETING

In this section, we give a negative answer for the first question in the introduction about the initial seeding cost. We exploit the power-law topology found in most social networks [7, 8, 12] to demonstrate that when the propagation hop is limited, a large number of seeding nodes is needed to spread the influence throughout the network. The size of seeding is proved to be a constant fraction of the number of vertices n, which is prohibitive for large social networks of millions of nodes. We first summarize the well-known power-law model in [3]; then we use the model to prove the prohibitive seeding cost for the CFM problem.

3.1 Power-law Network Model.

Many complex systems of interest including OSNs are found to have the degree distributions approximately follows the power laws [7, 8, 12]. That is the fraction of nodes in the network having k connections to other nodes is proportional to $k^{-\gamma}$, where γ is a parameter whose value is typically in the range $2 < \gamma < 3$. Those networks have been used in studying different aspects of the scale-free networks [3, 5, 14]. We follow the $P(\alpha, \gamma)$ power-law model in [3] in which the number of vertices of degree k is $\lfloor \frac{e^\alpha}{k^\gamma} \rfloor$ where e^α is the normalization factor. For convenience, we shall refer to such a network as a $P(\alpha, \gamma)$ network.

We can deduce that the maximum degree in a $P(\alpha, \gamma)$ network is $e^{\frac{\alpha}{\gamma}}$ (since for $k > e^{\frac{\alpha}{\gamma}}$, the number of edges will

be less than 1). The number of vertices and edges are

$$n = \sum_{k=1}^{e^{\frac{\alpha}{\gamma}}} \frac{e^\alpha}{k^\gamma} \approx \begin{cases} \zeta(\gamma)e^\alpha & \text{if } \gamma > 1 \\ \alpha e^\alpha & \text{if } \gamma = 1 \\ \frac{e^{\frac{\alpha}{\gamma}}}{1-\gamma} & \text{if } \gamma < 1 \end{cases},$$

$$m = \frac{1}{2}\sum_{k=1}^{e^{\frac{\alpha}{\gamma}}} k\frac{e^\alpha}{k^\gamma} \approx \begin{cases} \frac{1}{2}\zeta(\gamma-1)e^\alpha & \text{if } \gamma > 2 \\ \frac{1}{4}\alpha e^\alpha & \text{if } \gamma = 2 \\ \frac{1}{2}\frac{e^{\frac{2\alpha}{\gamma}}}{2-\gamma} & \text{if } \gamma < 2 \end{cases} \quad (3.1)$$

where $\zeta(\gamma) = \sum_{i=1}^\infty \frac{1}{i^\gamma}$ is the Riemann Zeta function [3] which converges for $\gamma > 1$ and diverges for all $\gamma \leq 1$. Without affecting the conclusion, we will simply use real numbers instead of rounding down to integers. The error terms are sufficiently small and can be bounded in our proofs.

While the scale of the network depends on α, the parameter γ decides the connection pattern and many other important characterizations of the network. For instance, the larger γ, the sparser and the more "power-law" the network is. Hence, the parameter γ is often regarded as the characteristic constant for scale-free networks.

3.2 Prohibitive Seeding Costs

We prove that the seeding must contain at least $\Omega(n)$ vertices if the propagation is locally bounded. The result is stated in the following theorem.

THEOREM 1. *Given a power-law network $G \in P(\alpha, \gamma)$, with $\gamma > 2$ and constant $0 < \rho < 1$, any d-seeding is of size at least $\Omega(n)$.*

PROOF. The proof consists of two parts. In the first part, we show that the volume i.e. the total degree of vertices, of any d-seeding must be $\Omega(m)$. In the second part, we prove that any subset of vertices $S \subset V$ with volume $\text{vol}(S) = \Omega(m)$ in a power-law network with power-law exponent $\gamma > 2$, will imply that $|S| = \Omega(n)$. Thus, the theorem follows.

In the first part, we consider two separate cases

Case $\rho > \frac{1}{2}$: Let $S = R_0$ be the optimal solution for the CFM problem on $G = (V, E)$, and $S = R_0, R_1, R_2, \ldots, R_d$ are vertices that become active at round $0, 1, 2, \ldots, d$, respectively (see Fig. 3). Notice that $\{R_i\}_{i=0}^d$ form a partition of V. Moreover, for each $1 \leq t \leq d$ the following inequality holds.

$$|\phi(R_t, \bigcup_{i=0}^{t-1} R_i)| \geq \frac{\rho}{1-\rho}\left(|\phi(R_t, \bigcup_{j=t+1}^d R_j)| + 2|\phi(R_t, R_t)|\right) \tag{3.2}$$

where $\phi(A, B)$ denotes the set of edges connecting one vertex in A to one vertex in B. The inequality means that at least a fraction $\frac{\rho}{1-\rho}$ among edges incident with the vertices activated in round t must be incident with active vertices in the previous rounds.

Sum up all inequalities in (3.2) for $t = 1..d$, we have

$$\sum_{t=1}^d |\phi(R_t, \bigcup_{i=0}^{t-1} R_i)| \geq \frac{\rho}{1-\rho}\sum_{t=1}^d \left(|\phi(R_t, \bigcup_{j=t+1}^d R_j)| + 2|\phi(R_t, R_t)|\right)$$

Eliminate the common factors in both sides, we have

$$\sum_{i=0}^{d-1} |\phi(R_i, \bigcup_{t=i+1}^{d} R_t)|$$

$$\geq \frac{\rho}{1-\rho} \sum_{j=1}^{d-1} |\phi(R_j, \bigcup_{t=j+1}^{d} R_t)| + 2\sum_{t=1}^{d-1} |\phi(R_t, R_t)|$$

After some algebra, we obtain

$$\text{vol}(R_0) \geq |\phi(R_0, \bigcup_{t=1}^{d} R_t)|$$

$$\geq \frac{2\rho-1}{1-\rho} \sum_{j=1}^{d-1} |\phi(R_i, \bigcup_{t=j+1}^{d} R_t)| + 2\sum_{t=1}^{d} |\phi(R_t, R_t)|$$

$$\Leftrightarrow \frac{\rho}{1-\rho} |\phi(R_0, V)| - |\phi(R_0, R_0)|$$

$$\geq \frac{2\rho-1}{1-\rho} |E| + \frac{3-4\rho}{1-\rho} \sum_{t=1}^{d} |\phi(R_t, R_t)| \qquad (3.3)$$

Hence, when $\rho > 1/2$, $\text{vol}(R_0) \geq \frac{2\rho-1}{1-\rho} |E| = \Omega(m)$ for any d-seeding R_0.

Case $\rho \leq \frac{1}{2}$: We say that an edge is active if it is incident to at least one active vertex. At round $t = 0$, there are at most $\text{vol}(R_0)$ active edges, those who are incident to R_0. Eq. 3.2 implies that the number of active edges in each round increases at most ρ^{-1} times. After d rounds, the number of active edges will be bounded by $\text{vol}(R_0) \times \rho^{-d}$. Since, all edges are active at the end we have the inequality:

$$\text{vol}(R_0) \geq \rho^{-d} |E|.$$

In the second part of the proof, we show that if a subset $S \subset V$ has $\text{vol}(S) = \Omega(m)$, then $|S| = \Omega(n)$ whenever the power-law exponent $\gamma > 2$. Assume that $\text{vol}(S) \geq cm$, for some positive constant c. The size of S is minimum when S contains only the highest degree vertices of V. Let k_0 be the minimum degree of vertices in S in that extreme case, by Eq. 3.1 we have

$$cm = \frac{c}{2} \sum_{k=1}^{e^{\frac{\alpha}{\gamma}}} k \frac{e^\alpha}{k^\gamma} \leq \text{vol}(S) \leq \frac{1}{2} \sum_{k=k_0}^{e^{\frac{\alpha}{\gamma}}} k \frac{e^\alpha}{k^\gamma}$$

Simplify two sides, we have

$$\sum_{k=1}^{k_0-1} \frac{1}{k^{\gamma-1}} \leq (1-c) \sum_{k=1}^{e^{\frac{\alpha}{\gamma}}} \frac{1}{k^{\gamma-1}} = (1-c)\zeta(\gamma-1)$$

Since, the zeta function $\zeta(\gamma-1)$ converges for $\gamma > 2$, there exists a constant $k_{\rho,\gamma}$ that depends only on ρ and γ that satisfies

$$\sum_{k=1}^{k_{\rho,\gamma}} \frac{1}{k^{\gamma-1}} > (1-c)\zeta(\gamma-1)$$

Obviously, we have $k_0 \leq k_{\rho,\gamma}$. Thus, the number of vertices that are in S is at least

$$\sum_{k=k_{\rho,\gamma}}^{e^{\frac{\alpha}{\gamma}}} \frac{e^\alpha}{k^\gamma} = (1 - \sum_{k=1}^{k_{\rho,\gamma}} \frac{1}{k^\gamma})n = \Omega(n)$$

We have the last step because the sum $\sum_{k=1}^{k_{\rho,\gamma}} \frac{1}{k^\gamma}$ is bounded by a constant since $k_{\rho,\gamma}$ is a constant. □

In both cases $\rho > 1/2$ and $\rho \leq 1/2$, the size of a d-seeding set is at least $\Omega(n)$. However, we can see a clear difference in the propagation speed with respect to d between two cases. When $\rho < 1/2$, the number of active edges can increase exponentially (but is still bounded if d is a constant) and, it is likely that the number of active vertices also exponentially increases. In contrast, when $\rho > 1/2$, exploding in the number of active edges (and hence active vertices) is impossible as the volume of the d-seeding is tied to the number of edges m by a fixed constant $\frac{2\rho-1}{1-\rho}$, regardless of the value of d.

4. COST-EFFECTIVE & EXPEDITIOUS SOCIAL MARKETING ALGORITHM

In order to understand the influence propagation when the number of propagation hops is bounded, we propose VirAds, an efficient algorithm for the CFM problem. With the huge magnitude of OSN users and data available on OSNs, scalability becomes the major problem in designing algorithm for CFM. VirAds is scalable to network of hundred of millions links and provides high quality solutions in our experiments.

Before presenting VirAds, we consider a natural greedy for the CFM problem in which the vertex that can activate the most number of inactive vertices within d hops is selected in each step. This greedy is unlikely to perform well on practice for following two reasons. First, at early steps, when not many vertices are selected, every vertex is likely to activate only itself after being chosen as a seed. Thus, the algorithm cannot distinguish between good and bad seeds. Second, the algorithm suffers serious scalability problems. To select a vertex, the algorithm has to evaluate for each vertex v how many vertices will be activated after adding v to the seeding, e.g. by invoking an $O(m+n)$ Breadth-First Search procedure rooted at v. In the worst-case when $O(n)$ vertices are needed to evaluate, this alone can take $O(n(m + n))$. Moreover, as shown in the previous section, the seeding size can be easily $\Omega(n)$; thus, the worst-case running time of the naive greedy algorithm is $O(n^2(m+n))$, which is prohibitive for large-scale networks.

As shown in Algorithm 1, our VirAds algorithm overcomes the mentioned problems in the naive greedy by favoring the vertex which can activate the most number of *edges* (indeed, it also considers the number of active neighbor around each vertex). This avoids the first problem of the naive greedy algorithm. At early steps, the algorithm behaves similar to the degree-based heuristics that favors vertices with high degree. However, when a certain number of vertices are selected, VirAds will make the selection based on the information within d-hop neighbor around the considered vertices rather than only one-hop neighbor as in the degree-based heuristic.

The scalability problem is tackled in VirAds by efficiently keeping track of the following measures for each vertex v.

- $\mathbf{r_v}$: the round in which v is activated

- $\mathbf{n_v^{(e)}}$: The number of new active edges after adding v into the seeding

- $\mathbf{n_v^{(a)}}$: The number of extra active neighbors v needs in order to activate v

Algorithm 1: VirAds - Viral Advertising in OSNs

Input: Graph $G = (V, E)$, $0 < \rho < 1$, $d \in \mathbb{N}^+$
Output: A small d-seeding

$n_v^{(e)} \leftarrow d(v), n_v^{(a)} \leftarrow \rho \cdot d(v), r_v \leftarrow d+1, v \in V$;
$r_v^{(i)} = 0, i = 0..d, P \leftarrow \emptyset$;
while *there exist inactive vertices* **do**
  repeat
    $u \leftarrow \operatorname{argmax}_{v \notin P} \{n_v^{(e)} + n_v^{(a)}\}$;
    Recompute $n_v^{(e)}$ as the number of new active edges after adding u.
  until $u = \operatorname{argmax}_{v \notin P} \{n_v^{(e)} + n_v^{(a)}\}$;
  $P \leftarrow P \cup \{u\}$;
  Initialize a queue: $Q \leftarrow \{(u, r_v)\}$;
  $r_u \leftarrow 0$;
  foreach $x \in N(u)$ **do**
    $n_x^{(a)} \leftarrow \max\{n_x^{(a)} - 1, 0\}$;
  while $Q \neq \emptyset$ **do**
    $(t, \tilde{r}_t) \leftarrow Q.pop()$;
    foreach $w \in N(t)$ **do**
      foreach $i = r_t$ to $\min\{\tilde{r}_t - 1, r_w - 2\}$ **do**
        $r_w^{(i)} = r_w^{(i)} + 1$;
        if $(r_w^{(i)} \geq \rho \cdot d_w) \wedge (r_w \geq d) \wedge (i+1 < d)$
        then
          foreach $x \in N(w)$ **do**
            $n_x^{(a)} \leftarrow \max\{n_x^{(a)} - 1, 0\}$;
          $r_w = i + 1$;
          if $w \notin Q$ **then**
            $Q.push((w, r_w))$;
Output P;

- $\mathbf{r_v^{(i)}}$: The number of activated neighbors of v up to round i where $i = 1..d$.

Given those measures, VirAds selects in each step the vertex u with the highest *effectiveness* which is defined as $n_u^{(e)} + n_u^{(a)}$. After that, the algorithm needs to update the measures for all the remaining vertices.

Except for $n_v^{(e)}$, we show that all other measures can be effectively kept track of in only $O((m+n)d)$ during the whole algorithm. When a vertex u is selected, it causes a chain-reaction and activate a sequence of vertices or lower the rounds in which vertices are activated. New activated vertices together with their active rounds are successively pushed into the queue Q for further updating much like what happens in the Bellman-Ford shortest-paths algorithm. Everytime we pop a vertex v from Q, if r_v, the current active round of v, is different from $\tilde{r}_v$, the active round of v when v is pushed into Q, we update for each neighbor w of v the values of r_w and $r_w^{(i)}$. If any neighbor w of v changes its active round and w is not in Q, we push w into Q for further update. The update process stops when Q is empty. Note that for each node $u \in V$, changing of r_u can cause at most d update for $r_w^{(.)}$ where w is a neighbor of u. For all neighbors of u, the total number of update is, hence, $O(d \cdot d(u))$. Thus, the total time for updating $r_w^{(.)}$ $\forall w \in V$ in VirAds will be at most $O((m+n) \cdot d)$.

To maintain $n_v^{(e)}$, the easiest approach is to recompute all $n_v^{(e)}$. This approach, called *Exhaustive Update*, is extremely time-consuming as discussed in the naive greedy. Instead, we only update $n_v^{(e)}$ when "necessary". In details, vertices are stored in a max priority queue in which the priority is their *effectiveness*. In each step, the vertex u with the highest effectiveness is extracted and $n_u^{(e)}$ is recomputed. If after updating, u still has the highest effectiveness, u is then selected. Otherwise, u is pushed back to the priority queue, and the new vertex with the highest effectiveness is considered, and so on.

Approximation Ratio for Power-law Networks.
The CFM problem can be easily shown to be NP-hard by a reduction from the set cover problem. Thus, we are left with two choices: designing heuristics which have no worst-case performance guarantees or designing approximation algorithms which can guarantee the produced solutions are within a certain factor from the optimal. Formally, a β- approximation algorithm for a minimization (maximization) problem always returns solutions that are at most β times larger (smaller) than an optimal solution.

Unfortunately, there is unlikely an approximation algorithm with factor less than $O(\log n)$ as shown in next section. However, if we assume the network is power-law, our VirAds is an approximation algorithm for CFM with a constant factor.

THEOREM 2. *In power-law networks, VirAds is an $O(1)$ approximation algorithm for the CFM problem for bounded value of d.*

The theorem follows directly from the result in previous section that the optimal solution has size at least $\Omega(n)$ in power-law networks. Thus, the ratio between the VirAds's solution and the optimal solution is bounded by a constant.

5. HARDNESS OF IDENTIFYING SEEDING WITH GUARANTEES

This section provides the hardness of approximating the optimal solutions of the CFM problem, the impossibility of finding near-optimal solutions in polynomial time. In previous Section, we can obtain $O(1)$ approximation algorithms for CFM when the network is power-law. However, without the power-law assumption, there is no algorithm that can approximate the problem within a factor less than $O(\log n)$. We first prove the hardness for the case when $d = 1$, which is an essential step in proving the hardness for the general case $d \geq 1$.

5.1 One-hop CFM

We prove that the CFM problem cannot be approximated within a factor $\ln \Delta - O(\ln \ln \Delta)$ in graphs of maximum degree Δ, unless P=NP. The proof uses a gap-reduction from an instance of the *Bounded Set Cover* problem (SC_B) to an instance of CFM problem whose degrees are bounded by $B' = B$ poly log B. For background on hardness of approximation and gap-reduction we refer to reference [6].

DEFINITION 2 (BOUNDED SET COVER). *Given a set system $(\mathcal{U}, \mathcal{S})$, where $\mathcal{U} = \{e_1, e_2, \ldots, e_{n_s}\}$ is a universe and $\mathcal{S}$ is a collection of subsets of $\mathcal{U}$. Each subset in $\mathcal{S}$ has at most B elements and each element belongs to at most B subsets, for a predefined constant $B > 0$. A cover is a subfamily*

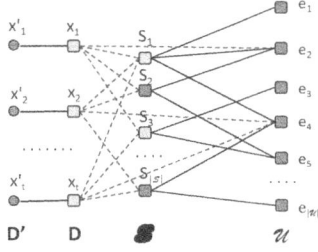

Figure 1: Reduction from SC_B to CFM when $d = 1$

$\mathcal{C} \subseteq \mathcal{S}$ of sets whose union is $\mathcal{U}$. Find a cover which uses the minimum number of subsets.

We state the tight inapproximability result for the bounded set cover by Trevisan [24] in the following lemma.

LEMMA 1. *There exist constants $B_0, c_0 > 0$ such that for every $B \geq B_0$ it is NP-hard to approximate the SC_B problem within a factor of $\ln B - c_0 \ln \ln B$.*

The proof in [24] reduces an instance of $GAP - SAT_{1,\gamma}$ of size n_S to an instance $\mathcal{F} = (\mathcal{U}, \mathcal{S})$ of SC_B by settings parameters l, m in Feige's construction [13] to be $\theta(\ln \ln B)$ and $\frac{B}{poly \log(B)}$, respectively. Denote by Δ_S the maximum cardinality of sets, and by f the maximum frequency of elements in $\mathcal{U}$, we have

- $|\mathcal{U}| = mn_S^l \text{ poly } \log B, |\mathcal{S}| = n_S^l \text{ poly } \log B$
- $\Delta_S \leq B, f \leq \text{ poly } \log B$ for sufficient large B.

SC_B-CFM reduction. For each instance $\mathcal{F} = (\mathcal{U}, \mathcal{S})$ of SC_B, we construct a graph $\mathcal{H} = (V, E)$ as follows (Fig. 1):

- Construct a bipartite graph with the vertex set $\mathcal{U} \cup \mathcal{S}$ and edges between S and all elements $e_i \in S$, for each $S \in \mathcal{S}$.

- Add a set D consisting of t vertices and a set D' with same number of vertices, say $D = \{x_1, x_2, \ldots, x_t\}$ and $D' = \{x_1', x_2', \ldots, x_t'\}$, where $t = \frac{|\mathcal{U}|}{B \ln^2 B}$.

- Connect x_i to $x_i', \forall i = 1 \ldots t$. This enforces the selection of x_i in the optimal CFM.

- Connect each vertex $e_j \in \mathcal{U}$ to $\lceil \frac{\rho}{1-\rho} f(e_j) \rceil - 1$ and each vertex $S_k \in \mathcal{S}$ to $\lceil \frac{\rho}{1-\rho} |S_k| \rceil$ vertices in D, where $f(e_j)$ is the frequency of element e_j. During the connection, we balance the degrees of vertices in D.

We can assume w.l.o.g. that optimal solutions of CFM contains all vertices in D but not ones in D'. Then, all vertices in $\mathcal{S}$ will be activated after the first round, and the a vertex in $\mathcal{U}$ is activated if and only if one of its neighbors in $\mathcal{S}$ is selected into the solution. Thus, the following lemma holds.

LEMMA 2. *The size difference between the optimal CFM of $\mathcal{H}$ and the optimal SC_B of $\mathcal{F}$ is exactly the cardinality of D, i.e., $OPT_{CFM}(\mathcal{H}) = OPT_{SC}(\mathcal{F}) + t$.*

The key to preserve the hardness ratio is to keep the degree of vertices in $\mathcal{H}$ bounded and the gap between the optimal solutions' sizes small.

LEMMA 3. *If $t = \frac{|\mathcal{U}|}{B \ln^2 B}$, then the maximum degree of vertices in $\mathcal{H}$ will be $B' = \Delta(\mathcal{H}) = O(B \text{ poly } \log B)$.*

PROOF. We can verify that vertices in $\mathcal{S}$ and $\mathcal{U}$ have degree $O(B)$. Vertices in D have degrees at most $\frac{\text{vol}(D)}{t} + 1$, where $\text{vol}(D)$ is the total degree of vertices in D. Define $\phi(X, Y)$ as the set of edges crossing between two vertex subsets X and Y. We have

$$\text{vol}(D) = |\phi(D, D')| + |\phi(D, \mathcal{U})| + |\phi(D, \mathcal{S})|$$
$$= |D| + \sum_{S_k \in \mathcal{S}} \lceil \frac{\rho}{1-\rho} |S_k| \rceil + \sum_{e_j \in \mathcal{U}} \lceil \frac{\rho}{1-\rho} f(e_j) - 1 \rceil$$
$$\leq \frac{2\rho}{1-\rho} |\mathcal{S}| B + |\mathcal{S}| + t = \left(\frac{2\rho}{1-\rho} B + 1 \right) |\mathcal{S}| + t \quad (5.1)$$

We have used the facts that $\sum_{S_k \in \mathcal{S}} |S_k| = \sum_{e_j \in \mathcal{U}} f(e_j)$ and $|S_k| \leq B, \forall S_k \in \mathcal{S}$.

Thus,

$$B' \leq \frac{1}{t} \left(\left(\frac{2\rho}{1-\rho} B + 1 \right) |\mathcal{S}| + t \right) + 1$$
$$\leq \left(\frac{2\rho}{1-\rho} B + 1 \right) \frac{B \ln^2 B \, n_S^l \text{ poly } \log B}{mn^l \text{ poly } \log B}$$
$$\leq O(B \text{ poly } \log B) \quad (5.2)$$

This completes the proof. $\square$

THEOREM 3. *When $d = 1$, it is NP-hard to approximate the CFM problem in graphs with degrees bounded by B' within a factor of $\ln B' - c_1 \ln \ln B'$, for some constant $c_1 > 0$.*

PROOF. We prove by contradiction. Assume there exists algorithm $\mathcal{A}$ to find in graph with degrees bounded by B' and $d = 1$ a CFM of size at most $(\ln B' - c_1 \ln \ln B') OPT_{CFM}$, where OPT_{CFM} is the size of an optimal CFM. Let $\mathcal{F} = (\mathcal{U}, \mathcal{S})$ be an instance of SC_B with the optimal solution of size OPT_{SC}. Construct an instance $\mathcal{H}$ of CFM problem using the reduction SC_B-CFM as shown above. From (5.2), there exists constant $\beta > 0$ so that $B' \leq B \ln^\beta B$. Using algorithm $\mathcal{A}$ on $\mathcal{H}$, we obtain a solution of size at most $(\ln B' - c_1 \ln \ln B') OPT_{CFM}$. We can then convert that to a solution of SC_B by excluding vertices in D (see Lemma 2) and obtain a set cover of size at most

$$(\ln B' - c_1 \ln \ln B')(OPT_{SC} + t) - t \quad (5.3)$$

Since each set in $\mathcal{S}$ can cover at most B elements, we have $OPT_{SC} \geq \frac{|\mathcal{U}|}{B} = \frac{tB \ln^2 B}{B}$, thus $t \leq \frac{OPT_{SC}}{\ln^2 B}$. If we select $c_1 = c_0 + \beta + 1$, the solution of SC_B is then, after some algebra, at most $(\ln B - c_0 \ln \ln B) OPT_{SC}$ that contradicts the Lemma 1. $\square$

Similarly, with appropriate setting in Feige's construction [13], we obtain the following hardness result regarding the network size n (the proof detail can be found in the technical report on our website).

THEOREM 4. *For any $\epsilon > 0$, the CFM problem, when $d = 1$, cannot be approximated within a factor $(\frac{1}{2} - \epsilon) \ln n$, unless $NP \subset DTIME(n^{O(\log \log n)})$.*

Note that Theorems 3 and 4 are incomparable in general. Let Δ be the maximum degree, Theorem 3 implies the hardness of approximation with factor $(1 - \epsilon) \ln \Delta$, which is larger than $(\frac{1}{2} - n)\ln n$ if $\Delta \approx n$, but smaller when $\Delta < \sqrt{n}$, for example in power-law graphs with the exponent $\gamma > 2$. In addition, the Theorem 4 uses a stronger assumption than that in Theorem 3.

5.2 Multiple-hop CFM

We now present a gap reduction from the CFM problem to the one-hop CFM problem with $d \geq 2$. The hardness result follows immediately by the Theorem 3 in the previous section.

Given a graph $G = (V, E)$ as an instance of the CFM problem. We will construct an instance $G' = (V', E')$ of the CFM problem as follows (and as illustrated in Fig. 3). We

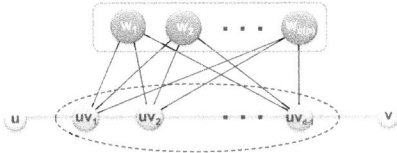

Figure 2: The transmitter gadget.

add $c(\rho)$ vertices $w_1, w_2, \ldots, w_{c(\rho)}$, called flashpoints, where $c(\rho) = \min\{t \in \mathbb{N} \mid \frac{t-1}{t+1} \leq \rho < \frac{t}{t+1}\}$. These vertices will be selected at the beginning to kick off the activation of other nodes. Furthermore, each "flashpoint" w_p is connected to a dummy vertex z_p.

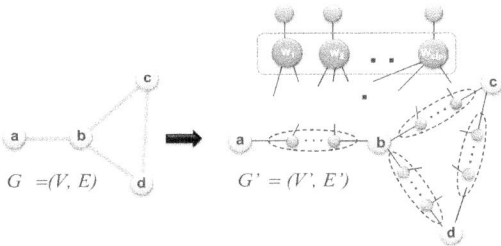

Figure 3: Gap-reduction from one-hop CFM to d-hop CFM.

Replace each edge $(u, v) \in E$ by a gadget called transmitter. The transmitter connecting vertex u and v is a chain of $d - 1$ path, named uv_1 to uv_{d-1}. The vertex u is connected to uv_1, uv_1 is connected to uv_2 and so on, vertex uv_{d-1} is connected to v. Each vertex uv_i, $i = 1..d - 1$ is connected to all flashpoints. An example for transmitter is shown in Fig. 2. The transmitter is designed so that if all flashpoints and vertex u are selected at the beginning, then vertex uv_{d-1} will be activated after $d-1$ rounds. Hence, the number of activated neighbors of v after $d - 1$ rounds will equal the number of selected neighbors of v in the original graph.

Finally, we replace each edge (w_p, z_p) by a transmitter. In order to activate all dummy vertices z_p after d rounds, we can assume, w.l.o.g., that all flashpoints must be selected in an optimal solution. The following lemma follows directly from the construction.

LEMMA 4. *Every solution of size k for the one-hop ($d = 1$) CFM problem in G induces a solution of size $k + c(\rho)$ for the d-hop CFM problem in G'.*

On another direction, we also have the following lemma.

LEMMA 5. *An optimal solution of size k' for the d-hop CFM problem induces a size $k' - c(\rho)$ solution for the one-hop CFM problem in G.*

PROOF. For a transmitter connecting u to v, if the solution of the d-hop CFM problem contains any of the intermediate vertices $uv_1, \ldots, uv_{d-1}$, we can replace that vertex in the solution with either u or v to obtain a new solution of same size (or less). Hence, we can assume, w.l.o.g., that none of the intermediate vertices are selected. Therefore, all flashpoints must be selected in order to activate the dummy vertices. It is easy to see that the solution of d-hop CFM excluding the flashpoints will be a solution of one-hop CFM in G with size $k' - c(\rho)$. $\square$

Note that the number of vertices in G' is upper-bounded by dn^2 i.e. $\ln|V'| < 2ln|V| + lnd$. Thus, using the same arguments used in the proof of Theorem 4, we can show that a $(\frac{1}{4} - \epsilon)\ln n$ approximation algorithm algorithm lead to a $(\frac{1}{2} - \epsilon)\ln n$ approximation algorithm for the one-hop CFM problem (contradicts Theorem 4).

THEOREM 5. *The CFM problem cannot be approximated within $(\frac{1}{4} - \epsilon)\log n$ for $d \geq 1$, unless $NP \subset DTIME(n^{O(\log \log n)})$*

6. EMPIRICAL STUDY

In this section we perform experiments on OSNs to show the efficiency of our algorithms in comparison with simple degree centrality heuristic and study the trade-off between the number of times the information is allowed to propagate in the network and the seeding size.

6.1 Comparing to Optimal Seeding

One advantage of our discrete diffusion model over probabilistic ones [16, 17] is that the exact solution can be found using mathematical programming. This enables us to study the exact behavior of the seeding size when the number of propagation hop varies.

We formulate the CFM problem as an $0 - 1$ Integer Linear Programming (ILP) problem below.

$$\text{minimize} \sum_{v \in V} x_v^0 \qquad (6.1)$$

$$\text{subject to} \sum_{v \in V} x_v^d \geq |V| \qquad (6.2)$$

$$\sum_{w \in N(v)} x_w^{i-1} + \lceil \rho \cdot d(v) \rceil x_v^{i-1} \geq \lceil \rho \cdot d(v) \rceil x_v^i$$

$$\forall v \in V, i = 1..d \qquad (6.3)$$

$$x_v^i \geq x_v^{i-1} \qquad \forall v \in V, i = 1..d \qquad (6.4)$$

$$x_v^i \in \{0, 1\} \qquad \forall v \in V, i = 0..d \qquad (6.5)$$

where $x_v^i = \begin{cases} 0 & \text{if v is inactive at round } i \\ 1 & \text{otherwise} \end{cases}$.

The objective of the ILP is to select a minimum number of seeds at the beginning. The constraint (2) guarantees all nodes are activated at the end, while (3) deals with propagation condition; the constraint (4) is simply to keep vertices active once they are activated.

We solve the ILP problem on Erdos collaboration networks, the social network of famous mathematician, [8]. The network consists of 6100 vertices and 15030 edges. The ILP

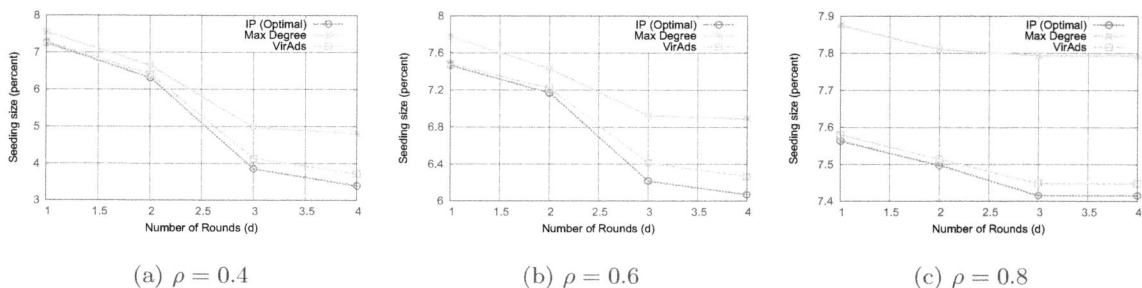

(a) $\rho = 0.4$	(b) $\rho = 0.6$	(c) $\rho = 0.8$

Figure 4: Seeding size (in percent) on Erdos's Collaboration network. VirAds produces close to the optimal seeding in only fractions of a second (in comparison to 2 days running time of the IP(optimal))

is solved with the optimization package GUROBI 4.5 on Intel Xeon 2.93 Ghz PC and setting the time limit for the solver to be 2 days. The running time of the IP solver increases significantly when d increases. For $d = 1, 2$, and 3, the solver return the optimal solutions. However, for $d = 4$, the solver cannot find the optimal solutions within the time limit and returns sub-optimal solutions with relative errors at most 15%.

The optimal (or sub-optimal) seeding sizes are shown in Figs. 4a, 4b, and 4c for $\rho = 0.4, 0.6$ and 0.8, respectively. VirAds provides close-to-optimal solutions and performs much better Max Degree. Especially, when $\rho = 0.8$ the VirAds's seeding is only different with the optimal solutions by one or two nodes. In addition, VirAds only takes fractions of a second to generate the solutions.

As proven in Section 3, the seeding takes a constant fraction of nodes in the network. For Erdos Colloboration Network, the seeding consists of 3.8% to 7% the number of nodes in the networks. Further, the seeding can consist as high as 20% to 40% nodes in the network for larger social networks in next section.

Although the mathematical approach can provide accurate measurement on the optimal seeding size, it cannot be applied for larger networks. The rest of our experiments measures the quality and scalability of our proposed algorithm VirAds on a collection of large networks.

6.2 Large Social Networks

We select networks of various sizes including Coauthors network in Physics sections of the e-print arXiv[16], Facebook[25] and Orkut[20], a social networking run by Google. Links in all three networks are undirected and unweighted. The sizes of the networks are presented in Table 1.

Table 1: Sizes of the investigated networks

	Physics	Facebook	Orkut
Vertices	37,154	90,269	3,072,441
Edges	231,584	3,646,662	223,534,301
Avg. Degree	12.5	80.8	145.5

Physics: We shall refer the physics coauthors network as Physics network or simply Physics. Each node in the network represents an author and there is an edge between two authors if they coauthor one or more papers. *Facebook* dataset consists 52% of the users in the New Orleans [25].

Orkut dataset is collected by performing crawling in last 2006 [20]. It contains about 11.3% of Orkut's users.

6.3 Solution Quality in Large Social Networks

We compare our VirAds algorithm with the following heuristics *Random* method in which vertices are picked up randomly until forming a d-seeding and *Max Degree* method in which vertices with highest degree are selected until forming a d-hop seeding. Finally, we compare VirAds with its naive implementation, called *Exhaustive Update*, in which after selecting a vertex into the seeding, the effectiveness of all the remaining vertices are recalculated. With more accurate estimation on vertex effectiveness, Exhaustive Search is expected to produce higher quality solutions than those of VirAds.

The seeding size with different number of propagation hop d when $\rho = 0.3$ are shown in Fig. 5. To our surprise, VirAds even performs equal or better than *Exhaustive Update* despite that it uses significantly less effort to update vertex effectiveness. VirAds has smaller seeding in Physics than *Exhaustive Update*; both of them give similar results for Faceboook; while *Exhaustive Update* cannot finish on Orkut after 48 hours and was forced to terminate. Sparingly update the vertices' effectiveness turns out to be efficient enough since the influence propagation is locally bounded. In addition, the seeds produced by VirAds are almost two times smaller than those of *Random*.

The gap between VirAds and Max Degree is narrowed when the number of maximum hops increases. Hence, selecting nodes with high degrees as seeding is a good long-term strategy, but might not be efficient for fast propagation when the number of hops is limited. In Facebook and Orkut, when $d = 1$, *Max Degree* has 60% to 70% more vertices in the seeding than *VirAds*. In Physics, the gap between VirAds and the *Max Degree* is less impressive. Nevertheless, VirAds consistently produces the best solutions in all networks.

6.4 Scalability

The running time of all methods at different propagation hop d are presented in Fig 6. The time is measured in second and presented in the log scale. The running times increase slightly together with the number of propagation rounds d, and are proportional to the size of the network. The *Exhaustive Update* has the worst running time, taking up to 15 minutes for Physics, 20 minutes for Facebook. For Orkut, the algorithm cannot finish within 2 days, as mentioned. The three remaining algorithms *VirAds*, *Max Degree*, and *Ran-*

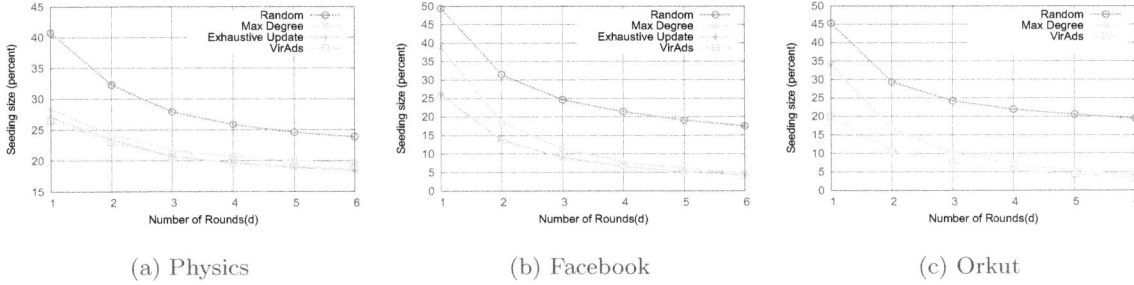

(a) Physics   (b) Facebook   (c) Orkut

Figure 5: Seeding size when the number of propagation hop d varies ($\rho = 0.3$). VirAds consistently has the best performance.

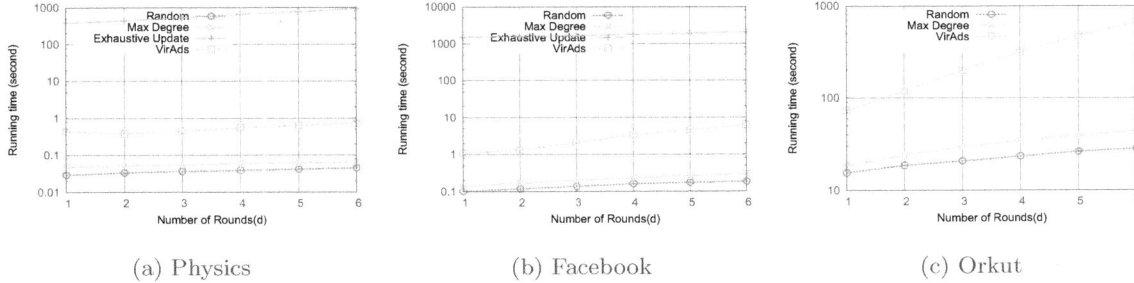

(a) Physics   (b) Facebook   (c) Orkut

Figure 6: Running time when the number of propagation hop d varies ($\rho = 0.3$). Even for the largest network of 110 million edges, VirAds takes less than 12 minutes.

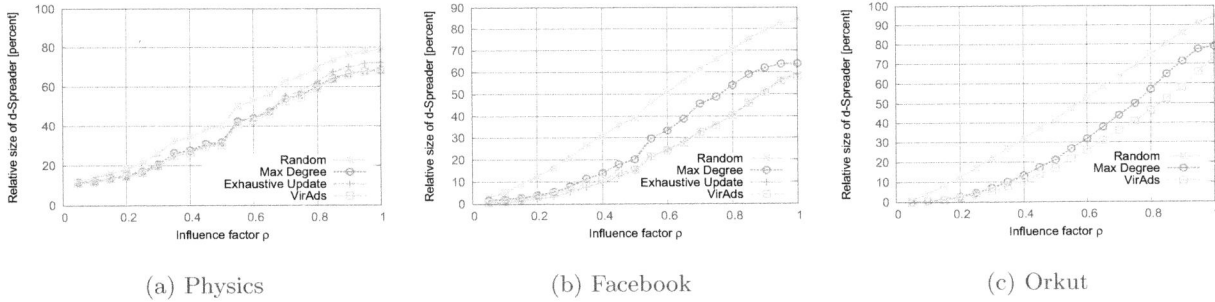

(a) Physics   (b) Facebook   (c) Orkut

Figure 7: Seeding size at different influence factors ρ (the maximum number of propagation hops is $d = 4$).

dom take less than one second for Physics, and less than 10 seconds for Facebook. Even on the largest network Orkut with more than 220 million edges, VirAds requires less than 12 minutes to complete.

6.5 Influence factor

We study the performance of VirAds and the other method at different influence factor ρ. The number of propagation rounds d is fixed to 4. The size of d-seeding sets are shown in Figures 7. VirAds is clearly still the best performer. The seeding sizes of VirAds are up to 5 times smaller than those of Max Degree for small ρ (although it's hard to see this on the charts due to small seeding sizes).

Since all tested networks are social networks with small diameter, the seeding sizes go to zero when ρ is close to zero. The exception is the Physics, in which the seeding sizes do not go below 10% the number of vertices in the networks

even when $\rho = 0.05$. A closer look into the Physics network reveals that the network contain many isolated cliques of small sizes (2, 3, 4, and so on) which correspond to authors that appear in only one paper. In each clique, regardless of the threshold ρ, at least one vertex must be selected, thus the seeding size cannot get below the number of isolated cliques in the networks. To eliminate the effect of isolated cliques, a possible approach is to restrict the problem to the largest component in the network.

7. CONCLUSIONS

We present the first work that explores the time aspect of influence propagation in social networks. We demonstrate that massively advertising involves costly seeding when imposing the limit on the propagation. Because of the power-law degree distribution observed in social networks, the seeding might involve a constant fraction of nodes in the networks, which is prohibitive for large networks. The old strategy for viral marketing that targets nodes with high degree in the network might be no longer suitable when we need the influence to propagate quickly throughout the network. Instead, an optimization-based solution such as VirAds is more suitable to discover a low-cost set of influential users.

8. ACKNOWLEDGEMENT

This work is partially supported by the DTRA YIP grant number HDTRA1-09-1-0061 and the NSF CAREER Award number 0953284.

9. REFERENCES

[1] Alexa 2010. http://www.alexa.com/topsites.

[2] Facebook statistics 2010. http://www.facebook.com/press/info.php?statistics.

[3] W. Aiello, F. Chung, and L. Lu. A random graph model for massive graphs. In *STOC '00*, New York, NY, USA, 2000. ACM.

[4] W. Aiello, F. Chung, and L. Lu. A random graph model for power law graphs. *Experimental Math*, 10:53–66, 2000.

[5] W. Aiello, F. Chung, and L. Lu. Random evolution in massive graphs. In *In Handbook of Massive Data Sets*. Kluwer Academic Publishers, 2001.

[6] S. Arora and B. Barak. *Computational complexity: a modern approach*. Cambridge University Press, 2009.

[7] A. Barabasi, R. Albert, and H. Jeong. Scale-free characteristics of random networks: the topology of the world-wide web. *Physica A*, 281, 2000.

[8] A. Barabasi, H. Jeong, Z. Neda, E. Ravasz, A. Schubert, and T. Vicsek. Evolution of the social network of scientific collaborations. *Physica A: Statistical Mechanics and its Applications*, 311(3-4):590–614, 2002.

[9] M. Cha, A. Mislove, and K. P. Gummadi. A measurement-driven analysis of information propagation in the flickr social network. In *WWW '09*, pages 721–730, New York, NY, USA, 2009. ACM.

[10] N. Chen. On the approximability of influence in social networks. *SIAM Journal of Discrete Mathematics*, 23(3):1400–1415, 2009.

[11] W. Chen, Y. Wang, and S. Yang. Efficient influence maximization in social networks. In *KDD '09*, pages 199–208, New York, NY, USA, 2009. ACM.

[12] A. Clauset, C. R. Shalizi, and M. E. J. Newman. Power-law distributions in empirical data. *SIAM Reviews*, 2007.

[13] U. Feige. A threshold of ln n for approximating set cover. *Journal of ACM*, 45(4):634–652, 1998.

[14] A. Ferrante. Hardness and approximation algorithms of some graph problems, 2006.

[15] A. Goyal, F. Bonchi, and L. V. S. Lakshmanan. Learning influence probabilities in social networks. *WSDM '10*, pages 241–250, 2010.

[16] D. Kempe, J. Kleinberg, and É. Tardos. Maximizing the spread of influence through a social network. In *KDD'03*, pages 137–146. ACM New York, NY, USA, 2003.

[17] D. Kempe, J. Kleinberg, and E. Tardos. Influential nodes in a diffusion model for social networks. In *ICALP '05*, pages 1127–1138, 2005.

[18] J. Leskovec, L. A. Adamic, and B. A. Huberman. The dynamics of viral marketing. *ACM Trans. Web*, 1, 2007.

[19] J. Leskovec, A. Krause, C. Guestrin, C. Faloutsos, J. VanBriesen, and N. Glance. Cost-effective outbreak detection in networks. In *ACM KDD '07*, pages 420–429, New York, NY, USA, 2007. ACM.

[20] A. Mislove, M. Marcon, K. P. Gummadi, P. Druschel, and B. Bhattacharjee. Measurement and Analysis of Online Social Networks. In *IMC'07*, San Diego, CA, October 2007.

[21] D. Peleg. Local majority voting, small coalitions and controlling monopolies in graphs: A review. In *SIROCCO'96*, pages 152–169, 1996.

[22] L. Rao. Toyota Turns To Twitter To Repair Its Image. http://techcrunch.com/2010/03/02/toyota-turns-to-twitter-to-repair-its-image/, Mar. 2010.

[23] C. Shirky. The Political Power of Social Media: Technology, the Public Sphere, and Political Change, 2011.

[24] L. Trevisan. Non-approximability results for optimization problems on bounded degree instances. In *ACM STOC '01*, pages 453–461, New York, NY, USA, 2001. ACM.

[25] B. Viswanath, A. Mislove, M. Cha, and K. P. Gummadi. On the evolution of user interaction in facebook. In *WOSN'09*, August 2009.

[26] F. Wang, E. Camacho, and K. Xu. Positive influence dominating set in online social networks. In *COCOA '09*, pages 313–321, Berlin, Heidelberg, 2009. Springer-Verlag.

[27] F. Zou, Z. Zhang, and W. Wu. Latency-bounded minimum influential node selection in social networks. In B. Liu, A. Bestavros, D.-Z. Du, and J. Wang, editors, *WASA*, LNCS, pages 519–526, 2009.

Graph Data Partition Models for Online Social Networks

Prima Chairunnanda, Simon Forsyth, Khuzaima Daudjee
David R. Cheriton School of Computer Science
University of Waterloo
Waterloo, Ontario, Canada
{pchairun, swforsyt, kdaudjee}@uwaterloo.ca

ABSTRACT

Online social networks have become important vehicles for connecting people for work and leisure. As these networks grow, data that are stored over these networks also grow, and management of these data becomes a challenge. Graph data models are a natural fit for representing online social networks but need to support distribution to allow the associated graph databases to scale while offering acceptable performance. We provide scalability by considering methods for partitioning graph databases and implement one within the Neo4j architecture based on distributing the vertices of the graph. We evaluate its performance in several simple scenarios and demonstrate that it is possible to partition a graph database without incurring significant overhead other than that required by network delays. We identify and discuss several methods to reduce the observed network delays in our prototype.

Categories and Subject Descriptors

H.2.4 [**Systems**]: Distributed Databases; E.2 [**Data Structures**]: Graphs and networks

General Terms

Design, Performance, Experimentation

Keywords

Distributed graph database, Graph representation

1. INTRODUCTION

During the last decade, online social networks (OSNs) have emerged to the forefront of the Internet. Based on a recent Internet traffic analysis [1], three of the ten most frequently visited websites are OSNs. In an OSN, users are connected to each other via edges. Edges can be undirected (e.g. "Friends" in Facebook) or directed (e.g. "Follows" in Twitter).

How to store this information is central to any OSN, and is an active research area. Key-value storage systems and Relational Database Management Systems (RDBMS) appear favoured choices,

as is evident from Facebook using Cassandra [6] and MySQL, and MySpace using Microsoft SqlServer. However, a graph can naturally represent many OSN constructs, with users and objects as vertices connected via edges. Furthermore, many services offered by an OSN are equivalent to traversing this graph. Listing a tweet's followers is traversing all "Follows" edges in the reverse direction. Viewing a friend's photo album can be seen as traversing all "UploadPhoto" and "TaggedIn" edges.

Models that fit the data they represent are often easier to understand and are potentially more efficient. For example, a graph database can ensure that well-connected sub-graphs remain in the same partition on the assumption that they will be frequently accessed together. A graph database is therefore able to naturally provide bounds on the number of servers needed to provide a complete answer to many queries. There have been a lot of studies revolving around distributed RDBMS, key-value stores, and column store databases, but graph DBMSs have received little attention.

Among the current graph DBMSs, there are variations in how a graph is viewed. At the simplest level, a graph consists of vertices connected via edges. Clearly this does not suffice for real-life applications, as there needs to be labels on the nodes and edges themselves. Neo4j adds the notion of *edge type* and *properties* to further describe nodes and edges. Relaxing the restriction on edges, HypergraphDB [5] allows a single edge to connect more than two vertices to express more complex semantics. Resource Description Framework (RDF) is yet another alternative, where information is encoded in triplets (*subject, predicate, object*). In essence, each triplet represents a directed edge between the *subject* and *object*. How to store the triplets again varies among RDF databases, where some storing as graphs (e.g. AllegroGraph), some as tuples in an underlying relational databases (e.g. Virtuoso [4]), and a number of others using proprietary formats.

Regardless of the underlying physical representation of the data, employing a single centralized graph DBMS will quickly become a bottleneck. OSNs deal with huge amount of data, potentially consisting of trillions of vertices and edges. Thus, methods to effectively scale graph DBMSs are needed to improve their utility to an OSN.

One popular approach to overcome the bottleneck is to use multiple instances of a DBMS, each holding a shard of the database. Averbuch and Neumann [2] explored the problem of partitioning in Neo4j graph database, but their experiments used an emulator relying on graph colouring. We demonstrate that there exist partition models that can be implemented with minimal computation overhead and remove physical limits from the size of the graph. Moreover, such models provide potential for load-balancing and increased parallelism for queries that do not require access to the entire graph. Our implementation, called PNeo4j, extends the

Neo4j graph database to support partitioning. Pregel [7] introduces a computational model for distributed graph traversal, but does not specifically address the challenges of partitioning the graph in the first place.

This paper is organized as follows: we first visit important design decisions we made for PNeo4j in Section 2, followed by our specific implementation details in Section 3. We then present our experimental results in Section 4, and finally we conclude in Section 5.

2. DESIGN

2.1 System Architecture

We use the following system model assumptions as a basis for evaluating partitioning techniques. We are not interested in fault-tolerance for the initial implementation but are interested in achieving efficiency. Therefore, we attempt to minimize the amount of information sharing in the design. Clients and their queries are assumed to run in the context of a single server. The client will not start a transaction on one partition and complete it on another, instead the first server contacted as part of a transaction will be responsible for all queries that make up the transaction. We assume that a method exists for the client to find the initial server.

The servers hosting the partitions can have knowledge of all other servers. We do not require all servers to be available to function, but do require the server hosting an object to be available when that object is accessed.

2.2 Partition Model

We consider three methods for partitioning a graph database: across vertices, across edges, and among the properties associated with the edges and/or vertices in the graph.

2.2.1 Vertex Partitioning

The most studied method [2][7][8] for splitting a graph is cutting the graph. That is, the graph is partitioned into subgraphs, where each vertex belongs to exactly one subgraph. The subgraphs then become shards of the original graph.

2.2.2 Edge Partitioning

Another possibility is to split the graph into subgraphs by their edges. Each partition contains a subset of the edges from the original graph, with the total graph being reconstructed from all the partitions. In some applications, edges may have types to give more semantics to the relationship. To give a concrete example, in Facebook, two friends are connected by a "Friend" edge, while a user and an event are connected by an "Attending" edge. For these graphs, it is also reasonable to partition the graph into subgraphs, each containing the edges and vertices for a unique set of edge types.

2.2.3 Property Partitioning

The last possibility has been considered by Neo Technologies for version 2 of Neo4j [10]. Vertices and edges require relatively little storage space, but properties have arbitrary length and so may require significantly more space, limiting the maximum graph size. By storing the properties in a separate key-value store and entering the much shorter keys into the graph database, a single server may store a bigger graph. However, as the entire graph and the property keys must still fit onto a single server, the number of vertices and edges is still limited by the storage capacity of a single server.

2.2.4 Discussion

As the goal is to create a scalable shared-nothing database, we examined each method in terms of perceived scalability and amount of data that must be shared. For the case of vertex partitioning, there is no physical limit on graph size. However, since an edge that crosses a shard boundary must be accessible from both sides, at the minimum it must be duplicated on the two partitions hosting the endpoint vertices. For edge partitioning, the maximum size is limited by the largest overlay graph consisting of one edge type. Edge partitioning also duplicates vertices that have edges not located on the same server. Finally, property partitioning requires the entire graph to be contained within a single machine, limiting graph size. Partitioning the properties does allow for the least amount of required duplication.

These options are not mutually exclusive and all of them may be used within the context of a single graph, though with an increase in complexity for database design and development.

We chose to implement partitioning across vertices so as to remove restrictions on the physical limit on graph size for all graphs. However, we note that edge partitioning has a potentially useful property. The partitions generated from edge partitioning may naturally be load-balanced because vertices will likely be present in multiple partitions. As a consequence, queries involving that vertex can be answered by any of those partitions, potentially speeding up traversals since the initial vertex is likely to be on the originating server. When queries mainly involve only one edge type, partitioning by edge-type might look attractive as cross-partition traversals can be avoided. However, the server hosting that edge type could become hotspot.

When seen from an OSN perspective, vertex partitioning also has an additional advantage. The types of queries operating on an OSN are usually a form of traversal from a particular starting vertex, i.e. they exhibit spatial locality. After a particular vertex is visited, each of its neighbouring vertices will have an increased chance to be accessed next. It is, therefore, beneficial to have neighbours hosted in the same machine. Several systems, such as SPAR[11], exploit this behaviour in their replication design for OSNs.

The requirement of spatial locality becomes much more important when more OSN entities are represented as nodes in the graph. For instance, the school a user goes to can either be stored as a property of the user, or as a node with inward edges of type "AttendSchool" coming from the students of the school. The latter representation has the advantage that the graph is more complete and can be interpreted on its own, as edges explicitly indicate a connection, while the interpretation of property values are application dependent. This has direct consequence on the length of traversal path. Let us consider the query to find the school attended by the most number of a user's friends. When school is represented by property and friendship by an edge, the query involves traversing an edge, then querying a node's property. The query will instead traverse two edges if both are represented as edges.

If there is an edge connecting two vertices and the vertices are located in different subgraphs, the edge is a *crossing-edge*. We assume assignment of vertices to partitions should be chosen to minimize network traffic and it is therefore beneficial to minimize the number of crossing-edges. As the number of crossing-edges increases, the probability that a traversal must cross a partition boundary increases, incurring additional network costs.

There have been studies on using graph min-cut algorithms to minimize the number of crossing-edges, e.g. [2][3]. However, we are specifically interested in the behaviour at partition boundaries, and so manually cut the graphs to ensure our traversals cross par-

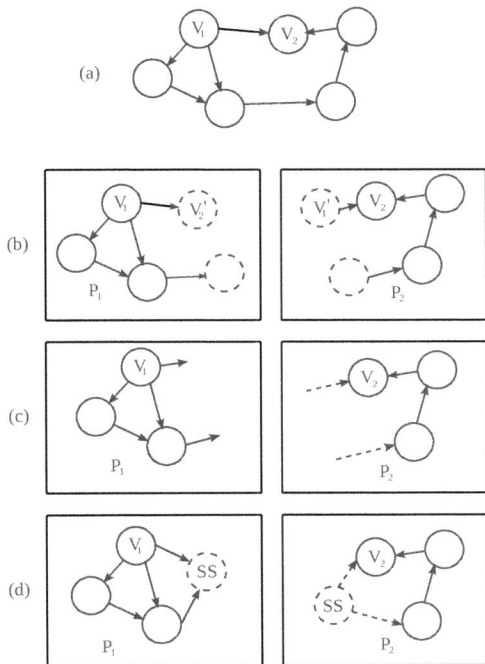

Figure 1: Visualization of crossing-edge representations. (a) shows the original graph, while (b), (c), and (d) show the graph partitioned over P1 and P2, for the Ghost Vertex, Dangling Edge, and Super Source/Sink models respectively. Dotted lines indicate ghost objects. In (d), the vertex marked "SS" is the Super Source/Sink.

titions. We defer the study of different min-cut algorithms for our system to other work.

2.3 Crossing-Edge Representation

We consider three different kinds of representations to model a crossing-edge in our system. We discuss the advantages and disadvantages of each model as well as the additional cost imposed by the model.

All examples in this subsection assume a crossing-edge connecting two vertices V_1 and V_2 located in partition P_1 and P_2, respectively. The original graph is shown in Figure 1(a). Without loss of generality, we assume the edge is directed from V_1 to V_2.

2.3.1 Ghost Vertex Model

In the Ghost Vertex model, we create a ghost vertex in P_1 to represent V_2, as depicted in Figure 1(b). A ghost vertex is a vertex with a single property containing the location of the real vertex. The edge connecting the two vertices is duplicated across both partitions. In essence, V_1 is now connected to the ghost of V_2 (denoted as V_2'). On the P_2 side, another ghost vertex to represent V_1 and an edge from V_1' to V_2 is created.

A major advantage of this model is that all partitions contain valid graphs. This model can thus be implemented as middleware on top of any single machine graph database without modifying the underlying system. When a client arrives at a ghost vertex, the middleware will return a proxy which will contact the remote partition for any requests related to that vertex. However, a middleware approach is typically slower than a more intrusive one because the middleware needs to do additional processing on top of the regular database access.

Identifying a ghost vertex is also a challenge. For example, consider the situation of V_1 connected to V_2 as above. Later, say, a new edge is to be created between another vertex V_3 owned by P_2 to vertex V_1. In this case, P_2 can either create a new ghost vertex or reuse its existing ghost for V_1. The first option increases the required storage and makes avoiding duplicate vertices during traversal more difficult, while reuse complicates edge creation since a check must be made to see if the vertex already exists, costing additional time or space.

2.3.2 Dangling Edge Model

Instead of materializing ghost vertices, we can leave one end of the crossing-edge unconnected (Figure 1(c)). To achieve this, we require a method to identify vertices that are not part of the current partition. A simple method is to incorporate an identifier for the partition each vertex is assigned to as part of the vertex ID and then use that ID to identify if the vertex is local. A separate lookup table could be used, in which case, since most vertices are expected to be internal to the partition, a flag should be set within the edge to avoid making many failed lookups.

To avoid duplication of data, one of the two dangling edges is demoted to a ghost edge. Like a ghost vertex, a ghost edge stores only the location and ID of the actual edge, and all requests are forwarded to the remote partition. In PNeo4j, we always choose the incoming dangling edge to be the ghost edge. Due to this characteristic, it might be more beneficial to choose the semantic of the edge so that it mimics the natural order of traversal between the vertices, avoiding traversal of the ghost edges. For instance, supposing the query is to find all events created by a particular user, having the edges point outward from the user to the events (denoting a "Creates" semantic) might yield some performance benefit compared to the edges pointing inward (denoting a "Created by" semantic).

By removing the ghost vertices, we eliminate the storage cost of a crossing-edge to one extra edge. More importantly, we never have to synchronize vertices between partitions since they are not shared. By not storing properties at the ghost edge, we restrict synchronization to edge deletion.

2.3.3 Super Source/Sink Model

The Dangling Edge model has the problem that a partitioned graph is not actually a graph on any of the servers, as some endpoint vertices are missing. One possible solution to this is to materialize a single vertex that is used as a marker for all crossing-edges, as shown in Figure 1(d). Borrowing from flow network terminology, we call this a Super Source/Sink (SuperSS) vertex, because it consumes all incoming and outgoing flows to/from crossing-edges. The additional cost to represent a crossing-edge is thus only one extra edge since only one SuperSS is created regardless of the number of crossing-edges in the partition.

This solution has a serious pitfall. To modify an edge, both vertices must be locked to ensure that a vertex is not deleted and to prevent the addition of two edges causing one to not be associated with the vertex. The SuperSS vertex are connected with all edges that have one end in a remote partition. It follows that any changes to any crossing-edge in the partition would require locking the SuperSS vertex, greatly reducing the concurrency of the system and increasing the potential for deadlock for transactions that cross partitions. Therefore, such an option is not advisable for a graph database.

3. IMPLEMENTATION

3.1 Neo4j

Neo4j[1] is an open source graph DBMS specialized for high-speed graph traversal. It supports ACID transactions at a read-committed isolation level and provides for manual locking to allow the user to achieve higher levels of isolation. Transactions are logged to ensure durability and the system provides some consistency guarantees, such as preventing connections to non-existing vertices. In addition, it supports a High-Availability mode [9], in which the database is fully replicated across several systems. One system is designated as the master. The other systems are slaves and may have stale copies of the data. Writes are supported on slaves, but they synchronize with the master using the two-phase commit protocol on every write. Still, such replication does not completely address the scaling out of the database, because the total amount of data is limited by the storage capacity of the smallest server.

3.2 Vertex/Edge Identifier

In Neo4j, each object is uniquely identified by an identifier (ID) generated by the system. Once assigned, an object's ID will not change, but if the object is deleted, its ID may be reassigned to a new object.

As of version 1.3, Neo4j supports 2^{34} vertices and 2^{35} edges. Neo4j uses the *long* Java data type for an ID, theoretically allowing 2^{64} unique objects. The upper bits of the vertex ID space are unused and always 0. Our implementation uses the most significant 16 bits of an ID to record the partition that owns a vertex.

Each partition in PNeo4j is assigned a unique 16-bit *partition identifier* (PID). When the PID is present in the object's ID, the ID is a *global identifier* (GID), and it ensures the object is uniquely identifiable across all partitions. The PID value of 0 is reserved to preserve compatibility with Neo4j. The PID is not persisted to disk. Instead, when an object is loaded, PNeo4j adds the PID to create the GID of the object.

Internally, Neo4j assigns an ID to properties attached to objects. As this ID is not exposed to clients, we do not need to modify Neo4j's handling of property IDs.

3.3 Partition Policy

In the interest of avoiding extra complexity, all vertices are created in the partition that receives the request. If a user wants to create a vertex in a specific partition, that partition must be contacted. This is sufficient to let us create partitioned graphs to test partition traversals.

Because we include the partition identifier as part of the ID, an automatic repartitioning scheme could generate errors for missing vertices, as its ID could change after a read since the only isolation level we support is read committed. This problem can be avoided by implementing additional isolation levels (a read lock is required to ensure that a vertex does not move during a transaction).

3.4 Transactions

A single transaction may require operations across multiple partitions. Our implementation generates a global transaction ID for a transaction the first time a partition contacts another partition. This ID is then used in all further communication related to that transaction. Two-phase commit protocol is employed to provide consistency across partitions.

We assume that all operations related to a transaction will originate from the partition that created the transaction. That is, all

---

Table 1: Time to traverse one edge 1,000,000 times (ms)

Database	Intrapartition	Interpartition		
		Local source	Local dest	Fully remote
Neo4j	1130	-	-	-
PNeo4j	1157	31068	77646	166189

---

partitions involved in a transaction after the first will not contact any other partition with respect to that transaction. Because the global transaction IDs are hidden from the client and because none of the functions in our current design create recursive calls between partitions, this assumption is valid for our implementation. As a concrete example, when we are traversing a crossing edge from a remote partition P_2 to another remote partition P_3, the originating partition P_1 will first get information about the edge from P_2, determine it is crossing on to another partition P_3, then contact P_3 to continue the traversal. Consequently, the originating server will act as the coordinator for the two-phase commit. Note that it means PNeo4j does not impose any additional connectivity requirement on top of that required for two-phase commit, which is that participants are not necessarily contactable from other participants other than the coordinator. While our implementation does not handle failure of the originating server, additional logging on the remote partitions would address this issue.

4. PERFORMANCE EVALUATION

4.1 Test Environment

All experiments were performed on a single computer running Linux hosting each partition on a different network port. All tests were run on the same machine. Latency averaged 0.01ms between partitions. The baseline Neo4j system used for comparison is version 1.3M03, and our modifications were made to the slightly newer 1.3M04 milestone, released two weeks later.

4.2 Cross-Partition Traversal

Averbuch and Neumann [2] performed one test on their implementation of a partitioned graph database: traverse one edge in a two vertex database 1,000,000 times. They used an emulator that used a single partition with a colouring property to indicate virtual partitions for their remaining experiments. As part of our motivation was to see if the performance problem they observed was surmountable, we repeated their experiment with our implementation.

We test all possible arrangements of the source and destination vertices. Both the source vertex and the destination vertex can be either local to the partition that initiates the transaction, or remote from it. Since a remote source in our design implies that the edge is also remote, they are ordered in the table by increasing remoteness.

Each trial was run with a five second warm-up period and each case presents the mean of five runs. We also show the results of the same test with an unmodified copy of Neo4j (with both vertices local by definition).

The results in Table 1 show that increasing the quantity of remote information increases the time required for the traversal. Indeed, as desired, the costs reflect the number of network messages that need to be sent for each case: zero for fully local, one for a remote destination (to access the remote vertex), and two for a remote source (one to access the remote vertex and one to access the remote edge). Importantly, the overhead in the purely local case is minimal. This is in contrast to results in [2], which showed a significant perfor-

---

[1] http://neo4j.org

mance penalty even for fully local traversals, attributed partly to the increased software stack in their implementation.

5. CONCLUSIONS

We examined three methods for partitioning a database and identified vertex-based partitioning as the only one that does not impose a storage limit on scalability. Of the three methods presented for implementing vertex-based partitioning, the dangling edge model would have the least overhead associated with edge modification.

We implemented the dangling-edge scheme in a graph database. Our tests show that performance within a single partition is maintained, and performance is affected by the network overhead associated with communication between partitions. For scenarios where spatial locality is observed, such as traversals within a close group of friends in OSNs or route-finding in a road network on the assumption that most desired routes are local, traversals are unlikely to cross multiple partitions, and thus PNeo4j incurs only minimal performance penalty. Optimizations such as in [8] may be possible to reduce cross-partition performance hit due to network communication.

Our current implementation does not ship traversal processing to servers other than the one contacted by the client, generating network traffic proportional to the number of vertices not present in that server. Methods to ship processing of the traversal to each remote server are expected to improve performance.

6. REFERENCES

[1] Alexa. Alexa top 500 global sites. http://www.alexa.com/topsites.

[2] A. Averbuch and M. Neumann. Partitioning graph databases. Technical report, 2010.

[3] C. Curino, E. Jones, Y. Zhang, and S. Madden. Schism: a workload-driven approach to database replication and partitioning. *Proc. VLDB Endow.*, September 2010.

[4] O. Erling and I. Mikhailov. Rdf support in the virtuoso dbms. In T. Pellegrini, S. Auer, K. Tochtermann, and S. Schaffert, editors, *Networked Knowledge - Networked Media*, volume 221 of *Studies in Computational Intelligence*, pages 7–24. Springer Berlin / Heidelberg, 2009.

[5] B. Iordanov. Hypergraphdb: a generalized graph database. In *Proceedings of the 2010 international conference on Web-age information management*, WAIM'10, pages 25–36, Berlin, Heidelberg, 2010. Springer-Verlag.

[6] A. Lakshman and P. Malik. Cassandra: a decentralized structured storage system. *SIGOPS Oper. Syst. Rev.*, April 2010.

[7] G. Malewicz, M. H. Austern, A. J. Bik, J. C. Dehnert, I. Horn, N. Leiser, and G. Czajkowski. Pregel: a system for large-scale graph processing. SIGMOD '10, 2010.

[8] V. Muntés-Mulero, N. Martínez-Bazán, J.-L. Larriba-Pey, E. Pacitti, and P. Valduriez. Graph partitioning strategies for efficient bfs in shared-nothing parallel systems. WAIM'10, 2010.

[9] Neo Technology. 7.1 architecture. http://docs.neo4j.org/chunked/stable/ha-architecture.html.

[10] Neo Technology. Roadmap. http://wiki.neo4j.org/content/Roadmap.

[11] J. M. Pujol, V. Erramilli, G. Siganos, X. Yang, N. Laoutaris, P. Chhabra, and P. Rodriguez. The little engine(s) that could: scaling online social networks. In *Proceedings of the ACM SIGCOMM 2010 conference*, SIGCOMM '10, pages 375–386, New York, NY, USA, 2010. ACM.

Exploring (the Poetics of) Strange (and Fractal) Hypertexts

Charlie Hargood, David E. Millard
Matt R. Taylor
School of Electronics and Computer Science,
University of Southampton, UK
{cah07r, dem, mrt}@ecs.soton.ac.uk

Rosamund Davies
Samuel Brooker
School of Humanities and Social Sciences,
University of Greenwich, UK
{R.Davies, S.Brooker}@greenwich.ac.uk

ABSTRACT

The ACM Hypertext conference has a rich history of challenging the node-link hegemony of the web. At Hypertext 2011 Pisarski [12] suggested that to refocus on nodes in hypertext might unlock a new poetics, and at Hypertext 2001 Bernstein [3] lamented the lack of strange hypertexts: playful tools that experiment with hypertext structure and form. As part of the emerging Strange Hypertexts community project we have been exploring a number of exotic hypertext tools, and in this paper we set out an early experiment with media and creative writing undergraduates to see what effect one particular form – *Fractal Narratives*, a hypertext where readers drill down into text in a reoccurring pattern – would have on their writing. In this particular trial, we found that most students did not engage in the structure from a storytelling point of view, although they did find value from a planning point of view. Participants conceptually saw the value in non-linear storytelling but few exploited the fractal structure to actually do this. Participant feedback leads us to conclude that while new poetics do emerge from strange hypertexts, this should be viewed as an ongoing process that can be reinforced and encouraged by designing tools that highlight and support those emerging poetics in a series of feedback loops, and by providing writing contexts where they can be highlighted and collaboratively explored.

Categories and Subject Descriptors

H5.4 [Hypertext/Hypermedia]: Theory.

General Terms

Design, Human Factors

Keywords

Strange Hypertext, Fractal Narratives, Hypertext Poetics.

1. INTRODUCTION

Concern over the preeminence of the node-link model in hypertext is a recurrent theme in the hypertext community. At Hypertext 2011 Pisarski [12] explored and advocated the possibilities of new approaches to hypertext: moving away from the topographical paradigm, or even spatial hypertext, to other forms that would prioritize the node as much as the link. Such forms, he speculated, would unlock a new poetics of hypertext.

Ten years previously, in Hypertext 2001, Bernstein noted a dearth of *strange hypertext*, and presented two exotic tools for hypertext – Card Shark, based on a card playing metaphor and Thespis, a kind of virtual play. Ten years previously to that, in 1991, Halasz delivered a keynote calling for an end to the 'Tyranny of the Link' [6], a theme revisited a few years later by Hall et al. when they identified the button as something that could be replaced with a more dynamic open model [7].

We are currently engaged in an ongoing effort to establish a community of writers and technologists who wish to explore strange hypertexts[1]. In this paper we set out an early experiment we have conducted to explore what effect an exotic hypertext structure has on writing: would writers engage with the structure and incorporate it into their stories, and might it result in the emergence of new poetics as predicted by Pisarski?

The vehicle for our work was a small hypertext engine that runs *Fractal Narratives*. These are hypertexts where the reader drills down into the text in a reoccurring pattern, rather than navigating between texts using links. The interface is one of fluid links [14], with the text appearing in-line as the reader navigates. The tool was introduced through a number of structured sessions to media and creative writing undergraduates, and the experience evaluated afterwards through focus groups and qualitative and quantitative analysis of their work.

2. BACKGROUND

In her recent book *The Possible Worlds of Hypertext Fiction*, Bell [2] echoes the words of many commentators, when she states that hypertext fiction 'might not constitute a radically new literary genre... but rather that it adds new dimensions to fictional self-reflexivity', already associated with postmodernist print fiction.

Since this association was established in the late 1980s and early 1990s, postmodernist aesthetics have become commonplace in mainstream culture, from the networked identities of Facebook [3] to the fragmented, non-linear and self-reflexive storytelling of film directors such as Tarantino (*Pulp Fiction* 1994 US), Nolan (*Memento* 2000 US) and Iñárritu, (*Amores Perros* 2000 Mexico, *21 grams* 2003 US, *Babel* 2006 US). However, hypertext fiction itself does not seem as yet to have hit the mainstream. Bernstein [4] has suggested that it is, in fact, precisely hypertext fiction's early association with a particular moment of literary postmodernism, which now risks historicising it as a genre and limiting its potential to develop as a contemporary form, to expand its audience, its cannon and its range of storytelling [5].

Bernstein's suggestion is that more efforts should be concentrated on exploring where hypertext fiction should go next. There are many potential avenues for exploration and innovation. These include the platforms and the tools available, as well as potential

---

[1] www.strangehypertexts.org

narrative poetics, forms and techniques. Pisarski suggests one potential avenue when, in contrast to a more usual focus on the link, he advocates a 'poetics of a hypertext node' as an approach to both analyzing and potentially inventing 'hypertext-friendly plots' [12].

Bernstein coined the phrase Strange Hypertext in 2001 to describe hypertexts that pushed beyond the standard node-link model [3]. Although non-node-link hypertext systems did exist, notably the spatial hypertext pioneered in systems like VIKI and VKB [10], Bernstein's argument was that modern Rapid Application Development (RAD) techniques made it possible to explore more playful forms much more easily than ever before. As an example he presented Card Shark, a story that is read by playing story cards in a sequence, and Thespis, a scripted play unfolding in a virtual space that the reader can explore at will. The ideas around Card Shark were later extended and the form described as *Sculptural Hypertext* [13] - because in practice all links (cards) are originally available, before being carved away according to the rules of the cards already in play.

Despite the acceleration of the RAD techniques highlighted by Bernstein, and the ubiquity of the web as a platform, strange hypertexts have still not really been the subject of any significant analysis in the hypertext community. The Strange Hypertext community was formed out of the Narrative and Hypertext Workshop at Hypertext 2011[2]. Its ambition is to explore exotic hypertext tools, and to find, promote and create new and unusual hypertext forms.

3. FRACTAL NARRATIVES

Fractal Narratives are based around the principle that any two consecutive text nodes in a story can be extended by adding a third optional text node between them. By applying this principle recursively, inserting further text nodes between the new element and the originals, an author can subdivide nodes with potentially infinite level-of-detail. Assuming that the transitions between each text node are seamless, the story can then be arbitrarily scaled without significantly affecting the flow or cohesion of the narrative as a whole. Since individual sections of the narrative can be extended independently, the reader maintains complete control over the level-of-detail of all aspects of the story. The idea was to explore a different aesthetic to that of node-link narratives. Aarseth has characterized the reader experience of the latter as 'the jump' - the sudden displacement of the user's position in the text.' [1] *Fractal Narratives* remove this experience of displacement, focusing instead on the effects of the contextual regulation of connectivity and autonomy between nodes [12], such as both disorientation and amplification.

Treating the static start/end nodes (see fig 1) as necessarily privileged frame elements (that still form part of the text), the rest of a fractal narrative comprises a binary tree stored as an XML document. A key motivation when creating the authoring tool was to conceal the underlying complexity of the system from the (non-technical) users and present a simpler interface that conformed more to their expectations of a writing tool. The user is able to extend the story by clicking on placeholders, which indicate areas of the narrative where new text nodes can be inserted. This in turn brings up a text entry box, allowing the user to write and edit the story content in place. JavaScript is utilized to handle the insertion and deletion of text nodes and placeholders without requiring the

[2] http://nht.ecs.soton.ac.uk/2011

[3] http://www.ryman-novel.com/

page to reload and thus interrupt the authoring process. Since the whole structure remains in view throughout the authoring process there is no bias towards depth or breadth, and authors are free to create symmetric or non-symmetric trees as they prefer.

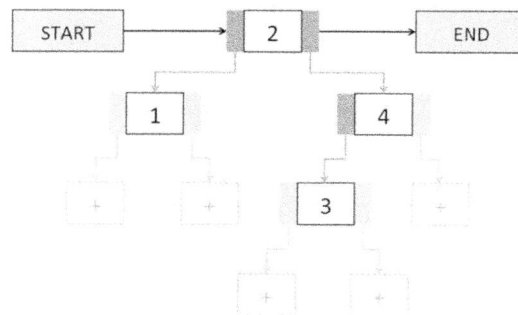

Figure 1: Example Fractal Narrative Structure; in expanded form the nodes are read in the order START, 1, 2, 3, 4, END

3.1 Experiment Aims and Methodology

In order to test its ease of use and appeal to a general user, and avoid preconceptions about hypertext style and form, it was decided to give the *Fractal Narratives* tool to writers who had experience of both creative writing and consumer digital platforms, but no established assumptions about the kind of storytelling suitable to hypertext.

The tool was given to media and creative writing undergraduates as a 3 week section of a module, *Writing the Digital Self,* which formed part of the second year of a 3 year UK BA (Hons) Degree, comprised of four modules of study a year. The participants had been introduced to the hypertext novel *253* [3] as part of this module. However they had no other experience as readers or writers of hypertext fiction. Depending on the individual, their prior writing experience was in some or all of: prose; poetry; journalism; stage and screen writing. The tool was explained to them through a short verbal presentation, with visual projection of the site. They were asked to read through the information on the site, to begin with the two initial nodes, add an initial 'middle' node in the first week and then to develop the story over the next two weeks. This activity formed part of a log book of weekly assignments for the module. The participants gave feedback in the form of both written questionnaires and a group discussion, which was transcribed.

3.2 Experiment Findings

Having completed the experiment there are both some quantitative and qualitative observations we can make.

3.2.1 System Usage

We are able to make some observations about the way the students used the system. In total 43 users signed up, of which 41 created a story, and of those 36 created a story that went beyond the mandatory 2 initial nodes and actually included some 'fractal nodes' (nodes not a start or end). Of those participants that utilized the fractal nature of the system we have compiled some basic average usage statistics, as displayed in Table 1.

Table 1. Average statistics for stories of more than 2 nodes.

No. Nodes	Max Node Depth	Average Node Depth	Average Node Length
5.4	2.9	1.2	97.4

Table 1 shows us that the users generally created mostly very short stories (averaging less than six nodes per story), and that individual nodes were also quite short (averaging less than 98 characters). It also shows an average maximum depth (maximum levels below the initial beginning and end nodes) of 2.9 and an average overall depth of all nodes in the story of 1.2.

We can further explore this by examining the features of nodes at different depths within the story to understand how the users had utilized the fractal nature of the system. This is displayed in Table 2, with data for each level of depth covering frequency and length (in characters). It is to be noted that this table excludes stories that didn't use that fractal nature of the system and only comprised of the mandatory start and end nodes.

Table 2. System Usage: statistics for nodes of different depths.

Depth	Frequency of Nodes	Average Node Length	Node Length Min	Node Length Max
0	72	78.3	3	466
1	36	96.3	23	337
2	48	115	18	507
3	24	97.5	19	457
4	8	122.9	32	444
5	2	98.5	41	156
6	2	117.5	75	160
7	1	170	170	170

From this data we find that over a third of the nodes are made up of the start and end nodes (depth 0). We also find that these nodes are on average the shortest, with users going into greater levels of detail within fractal nodes than start/end nodes. Excluding the depth 0 nodes the most common 'fractal node' depth is 2 which also represents a depth with a rise in length. It is possible that users use the first two depths (0 and 1) to write short plot structural milestones for beginning, middle, and end, rather than going in to any detail. This would explain why these nodes are generally shorter than the mean length for nodes overall.

3.2.2 Resulting Works

Since the narratives were all quite short, only a few of them really explored the notion of detail and depth as originally envisaged. One example is provided by *Triple Indemnity* (Figure 2), which, riffing on a noir theme, begins with a pregnant moment: 'It was a rainy night. It was time to make my move' and then expands it. First greater detail is provided on the setting: 'Every droplet of water that cascaded down the windows was rattling their panes.' Then it is possible for the reader to open up the story at different points, both to expand the thoughts of the narrator and to connect to different time frames (see Figure 2). Another narrative, *Can't Stop*, generated depth through the exploration of multiple perspectives on a situation. Such narrative strategies are not dissimilar to those of node-link hypertext fiction, which also frequently brings together different and discontinuous time frames and perspectives. Those participants' narratives which focused on a chronological unfolding of continuous time, on the other hand, functioned less well as fractal narratives, since the opening up of nodes served rather to fill in gaps in the story, than to drill down into it and expand it in depth.

It was evident, in fact, that some of the narratives were not operating according to fractal logic at all, but according to other organizing principles. Many of the narratives in fact had a linear structure. The reader was not offered any choice as to what node to click, but, having read the initial two nodes and opened the third node, was then directed on a path through a linear story. In several of the narratives this progression was structured so as to provide successive revelations and reversals and/or to put a new spin on the ending, which the reader had already read. Other narratives experimented with different approaches to non-linear storytelling, sending the reader on a path which moved backwards and forwards through the events of the story.

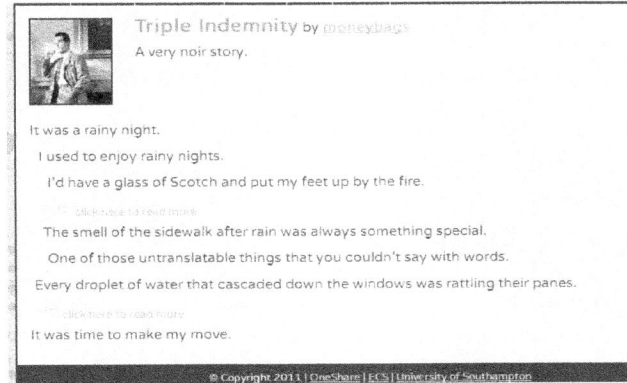

Figure 2: The Fractal Narrative Tool showing expansions on the story 'Triple Indemnity'

Rather than exploiting the storytelling potential of fractals or depth, both the linear and nonlinear storytelling examples described above thus pick up instead on the potential for 'hooking' a reader with the beginning and end of a story and gradually unfolding to him how the former led to the latter. This focus on the how and the why, rather than the what is a feature of many contemporary cinematic narratives, in which non-linear and multiple perspective storytelling techniques are employed to unfold what is ultimately a closed and linear text. Such cinematic narratives were indeed explicitly referenced by the participants in their discussion of their own stories. This will be expanded on in the next section.

An important effect of the *Fractal Narratives* structure then is that, having opened up all the nodes, the reader is presented with a complete and unified text, in a linear arrangement, which she is able to compare with the non-linear, fragmented and possibly confusing or tortuous ways in which she has read it. This may also then encourage her to return to an earlier, unexplored node after uncovering a clue in a subsequent one. Thus, although the narrative strategies that appeared most successfully to explore depth in the fractal narratives discussed above, such as different time frames and points of view, are familiar from existing hypertext fiction, *Fractal Narratives* nevertheless provide a very different reader experience to that of node-link hypertext fiction. However, we would argue, it is still potentially a multilinear one.

Although Aarseth [1] states that a narrative, which describes a sequence of events non-sequentially, but in a linear arrangement of text, cannot be called a non-linear text [5][9], we would argue that, since *Fractal Narratives* make it possible to offer readers a choice of how to read the story, their poetics complies with Ensslin's statement that 'hypertexts defy the macrostructural monolinearity and hierarchies of the majority of literary print media, as the order and selection of text units varies from reader to reader and from reading to reading' [5]. The characteristic hypertext fiction reader's experience of only having a glancing view, of never having the complete story [8], [11] is also conceivable in a large scale fractal narrative, (although the narratives involved in this particular experiment were all quite short, meaning that all the nodes could quite quickly be opened by a reader in one sitting, even though the order of opening would still vary each time).

We would suggest therefore that *Fractal Narratives* are nonlinear or multilinear texts, but, while their poetics is multilinear, it is not one of discontinuity or 'the jump'. The idea is rather that a fractal narrative offers the potential of expanding (and potentially contracting) a narrative in the same way that one might zoom in on an image to reveal further detail and more dimensions, while nevertheless continuing to view the same image. This seems to us to be a valid and potentially productive addition to hypertextual techniques and aesthetics.

3.2.3 Participant Responses

The Poetics of Fractal Narratives

The majority of the participants did not however seem to be particularly inspired by the potential of fractals as a poetic device, despite the fact that this was explained to them on the website and that some said they did understand the concept. In discussing their experience of writing and reading the *Fractal Narratives*, participants put more emphasis on the possibilities offered by the way that the narratives hook the reader with both beginning and end of the story and then allow him to explore how the one led to the other. They cited *Pulp Fiction* (Tarantino 1994), *Memento* (Nolan 2000) and *Eternal Sunshine of the Spotless Mind* (Gondry 2004) among others, as examples of narratives, which worked in similar ways. This emphasis suggests that the majority of the participants were in fact writing and reading the *Fractal Narratives* as linear texts, which employed non-linear storytelling techniques, like the cinematic narratives they cited, narratives which, as discussed above, Aarseth [1] rules out from being non-linear or multilinear texts. The participants' interpretation of the tools thus corresponded to the kinds of narratives and modes of narration that the participants were already familiar with, rather than to the intentions of the tool's designers. Thus, although they were enthusiastic about non-linear storytelling and their writings and readings opened up some unexpected insights, the participants' unfamiliarity with non-linear texts also limited their ability to exploit the potential of *Fractal Narratives*. It was nevertheless clear that participants' experimentation had developed their understanding and piqued their interest, introducing them to new ideas, such as the importance of the kind of 'contextual regulation' of nodes identified by Pisarski [12]. The latter's discussion of the tension between connectivity and autonomy in the content of nodes and how this functions as a hypertextual narrative device finds its counterpart in the participants' similarly themed discussion of the need to keep the content of the nodes 'open ended':

Participant A: '...you kind of had to have it a bit open ended in a way because then you might want to add a line between the middle and the first line. So it had a narrative, but it had to be a bit vague...it was interesting'

However participants also said that the one line text entry boxes of the display made them conceive of their stories in one line sentences. Many seemed paradoxically to understand *Fractal Narratives* as exercises in simplicity and conciseness, rather than in exploring detail and depth.

It is also possible that the representational conventions of the *Fractal Narratives* authoring tool encouraged the participants' tendency to follow linear narrative strategies, since the nodes in the authoring interface were organized in a linear visual display, rather than represented in a branching structure.

Reading/Writing

As Landow [8] and Aarseth [1] point out, the poststructuralist elision of the boundary between writing and reading is an unavoidable reality of hypertext fiction. Critics of hypertext, have to acknowledge their own investment in and construction of the narrative in very concrete ways, and also the fact that they can achieve only a partial rather than an exhaustive reading. The text is thus both unstable and inexhaustible.

In the *Fractal Narratives* experiment, participants recounted feelings of both pleasure and anxiety in their acknowledgement of this instability and the particular dynamic between writer and reader. One recurring trope of discussion was around their desire to receive feedback on what they had written. For one participant, this needed to be in the form of collective authoring.

Participant L: '...people should be able to add to your story to see how it could evolve...That would definitely have been more fun. Because you'd be checking up on it. You'd be seeing 'oh what's happened...''

Her view was shared by others. Some said they wanted to have the option to write both single author and collective narratives or to be able to keep intact both an original core text and its expanded collective version. Others simply wanted readers to be able to post comments. Overall, there was a strong sense expressed by the group, in line with the practices and conventions of social media, that online writing necessitated a rapid and explicit feedback loop between writer and reader, in way that print based writing did not. They expressed disappointment that this was not forthcoming on the *Fractal Narratives* site. One participant, drawing on the traditional paradigm of the writer as sole author, expressed concern about losing control of his text if the distinction between reader and writer was elided. Other participants, however, were more concerned about their lack of control as writers in relation to the technology. They felt that the *Fractal Narratives* authoring tool to some extent dictated the way that they wrote, which led to feelings of anxiety and frustration.

Participant G: 'I just found myself less in control of what the story was, because I was trying to fit it onto what the previous or the next sentence was going to be, which I didn't like because I like to be in control and I didn't feel I was.'

A sense of rising panic for the writer stemmed from the fact that, each time he or she created a new node in the authoring tool, two more empty nodes would open up in a never ending process of empty boxes to be filled. Thus what became the chief source of pleasure for the reader was a major source of stress for the writer. Several participants said the reason that they confined their stories to short sentences was that they felt that this would make the contextual regulation of the nodes easier.

Narrative and Structure

Conversely some participants said they thought the authoring tool would work well as a more general planning tool for writers, because, by encouraging the writer to start with beginning and end and expand the middle, it put more overt emphasis on structure than they were used to when writing short stories.

Participant H; '... if you don't use it for...well, as its original purpose... it would actually be a good way of writing a story and *you could just take out paragraphs without having to delete them and you could just see how your story works.'*

This emphasis on structure is in fact the standard approach in screenwriting practice, where writers tend to comprehensively plan a story, beginning to end, scene by scene, before starting to write a script. In screenwriting, where words metamorphose into images on screen, structure is treated as the essential storytelling material. In prose narrative, on the other hand, great emphasis is laid on the choice and arrangement of words themselves. Those students who did not study screenwriting said they were not used to planning their stories structurally, but to a more spontaneous (and linear) development:

Participant H: *'Normally you just write stories as you're going along, rather than think about the beginning and then jump straight to the end.'*

Both hypertext and screenwriting are modes of writing where meaning is created through structure, to the extent that narrative development by the writer requires detailed and formal structural planning. This would seem to explain both why participants looked to cinematic narrative for models in their work and why they had problems with the fractal narrative tool. Participants' difficulties with the tool and sense of being out of control appeared to be down in part to the fact they did not attempt to map out a structure first, but tried instantly to arrive at the exact and final formulation of words in each text box as they went along. A more fruitful approach might have been to first plan the movement and dimensions of the story, node by node, then go back and decide on the final choice of words. Participants expressed the view that, while taxing, this approach could potentially bring beneficial rigor and clarity to their writing.

4. CONCLUSIONS

Our experiment with *Fractal Narratives* developed an innovative hypertext tool, using fluid links [14], which non-technical users could manipulate through a simple interface and which they found easy to use to create and instantly publish narratives. However, at the same time, by concealing the underlying structure of the hypertext, the interface also appears to have limited writers' control and understanding of the tool. This problem was exacerbated by the fact that most of the writers were unused to thinking structurally about their writing in the first place.

Here is one point at which the blurred distinction between hypertextual reading and writing comes into focus. The multilinear or antilinear [5] structure of hypertext fiction has often been contrasted with the necessarily linear nature of the reader's journey through it [5] [9]. To come at this logic from the other direction, reading a hypertext may be a linear journey, but writing it cannot be. Taking into account the fact that writers need to grasp the non-linear structure they are working with, in its next iteration our authoring/publishing tool needs to identify more fully the points of overlap and divergence between how one might write a fractal narrative and how one might read it. Our study also raises the question of the role that an authoring tool might and should play in helping writers to acquire the particular skillset necessary to a particular genre of writing; skillsets traditionally required through reading relevant work by other writers.

This is therefore both an authorial and technical challenge. In terms of authoring, our experiences have given us ideas about how to guide and workshop with writers new to hypertext fiction in order to help them understand and explore the potential of *Strange Hypertexts*. In the context of *Fractal Narratives,* we would aim to explore with them first the notion of depth and detail

as narrative devices and as part of different narrative aesthetics, considering models from both print and digital fiction, as well as some specific fractal examples and giving more time for experimentation and opportunities for collaboration and feedback between writers and readers. While, on the technical side, the authoring tools need to interpret these emerging poetics into layout and vocabulary that encourages authors to think about structure before they begin writing: emphasizing depth visually, showing levels and symmetry more clearly, or creating workflow that separates structural construction from actual writing.

In our work we set out to investigate strange hypertexts and analyze the emergent poetics of *Fractal Narratives*. Our early experiment has shown that while poetics do start to emerge, this is an ongoing cycle and must be reinforced with tool/interface development and appropriate learning contexts. By being aware of and understanding these poetics as they emerge from real use we believe we can begin to tutor new writers more successfully, and design authoring tools that encourage authors to build on the strengths of strange forms.

REFERENCES

[1] Aarseth, E. J. in *Hyper/text/theory* (ed. George Landow) Baltimore: John Hopkins University Press, 1994,.

[2] Bell, A, *The Possible Worlds of Hypertext Fiction*, Basingstoke: Palgrave Macmillan 2010

[3] Bernstein M. 2001 Card shark and thespis: exotic tools for hypertext narrative. In Proceedings of the 12th ACM conference on Hypertext and Hypermedia ACM, New York, NY, USA, 41-50.

[4] Bernstein M. 2011. Wandering Monsters! on the problem of coherent hypertext narrative. In Proceedings of the Narrative and Hypertext Workshop at ACM Hypertext 2011.

[5] Ensslin, A, *Canonizing Hypertext*, London: Continuum 2007

[6] Halasz, F. G. 1991. "Seven issues": Revisited. Closing plenary address. In *Proceedings of ACM Hyper- text '91 Conference,* San Antonio, Texas, December 18, 1991.

[7] Hall, W. 1994 Ending the Tyranny of the Button. IEEE Multimedia, 1 (1). pp. 60-68.

[8] Landow, G. P. 'What's a Critic to Do?: Critical Theory in the Age of Hypertext' in *Hyper/text/theory* (ed. George Landow) Baltimore: John Hopkins University Press, 1994.

[9] Liestøl, Gunnar, Wittgenstein, Genette and the Reader's Narrative in Hypertext in *Hyper/text/theory* (ed. George Landow) Baltimore: John Hopkins University Press, 1994.

[10] Marshall, C. C., Shipman III, F.M. & Coombs, J.C., 1994. VIKI: spatial hypertext supporting emergent structure. In Proceedings of the 1994 ACM European conference on Hypermedia technology ECHT 1994. ACM Press, pp. 13-23.

[11] Murray, J, *Hamlet on the Holodeck*, Cambridge, Mass.: MIT Press 1997

[12] Pisarski, M, 'New Plots for Hypertext? Towards Poetics of a Hypertext Node'. Hypertext 2011

[13] Weal, M. J., Bernstein, M. and Millard, D. E. 2002 On Writing Sculptural Hypertext. In: The Thirteenth ACM Conference on Hypertext and Hypermedia, June, Maryland, USA. pp. 65

[14] Zellweger, P., Chang, B., Mackinlay, J.D. 1998. Fluid Links for Informed and Incremental Link Transitions. ACM Hypertext 1998: pg 50-57

Content vs. Context for Sentiment Analysis: a Comparative Analysis over Microblogs

Fotis Aisopos[$], George Papadakis[$,◇], Konstantinos Tserpes[$], Theodora Varvarigou[$]

◇ L3S Research Center, Germany   papadakis@L3S.de

[$] ICCS, National Technical University of Athens, Greece   {fotais, gpapadis, tserpes, dora}@mail.ntua.gr

ABSTRACT

Microblog content poses serious challenges to the applicability of traditional sentiment analysis and classification methods, due to its inherent characteristics. To tackle them, we introduce a method that relies on two orthogonal, but complementary sources of evidence: content-based features captured by n-gram graphs and context-based ones captured by polarity ratio. Both are language-neutral and noise-tolerant, guaranteeing high effectiveness and robustness in the settings we are considering. To ensure our approach can be integrated into practical applications with large volumes of data, we also aim at enhancing its time efficiency: we propose alternative sets of features with low extraction cost, explore dimensionality reduction and discretization techniques and experiment with multiple classification algorithms. We then evaluate our methods over a large, real-world data set extracted from Twitter, with the outcomes indicating significant improvements over the traditional techniques.

Categories and Subject Descriptors

H.3.3 [**Information Storage and Retrieval**]: Information Search and Retrieval—Information filtering

Keywords

Sentiment Analysis, N-gram Graphs, Social Context

1. INTRODUCTION

The advent of the Web 2.0 and Social Media platforms led to an unprecedented increase in the volume of the user-generated content that is available on the Web [24]. One of the most popular services is microblogging, with Twitter[1] constituting the most successful application of this kind: it encompasses around 180 million users that post more than 1 billion messages per week[2]. A large portion of this content - if not its majority - is subjective, containing opinions and sentiments on various topics of interest [21]. Thus it includes valuable information for a number of tasks that range

---

[1]http://twitter.com
[2]http://blog.kissmetrics.com/twitter-statistics/

from product marketing to politics and policy making. To leverage this bulk of subjective information, automatic techniques are required for processing it; this need recently gave rise to *Sentiment Analysis* (**SA**), also known as *Opinion Mining* in the IR community [30]. The popularity of this field is reflected in the high number of on-line services offering sentiment extraction from Twitter messages, such as Twendz[3] and TweetFeel[4].

Existing SA systems typically aim at extracting sentiment-expressive textual patterns from unstructured documents. To this end, they employ either discriminative (series of) words [5] or dictionaries that assess the meaning and the lexical category of specific words and phrases (e.g., SentiWordNet[5]) [14, 21, 31]. Although these approaches are sufficiently effective in the context of specific settings (e.g., large curated documents), they are built on the assumption that the input documents are written in the particular language their methods are crafted for, not including noisy content and misspelled words. However, these fundamental assumptions are broken by the inherent characteristics of microblog content, which call for a *language-agnostic* SA approach that is tolerant to high levels of noise:

(**i**) *Sparsity.* Microblog posts solely comprise free-form text that is rather short in length (e.g., maximum 140 characters in Twitter). Due to their limited size, they typically consist of a few words, thus involving little extra information that can be used as evidence for identifying their polarity.

(**ii**) *Non-standard vocabulary.* Microblog posts are informal, as they are mainly exchanged between fellows who indulge in using slang words and non-standard expressions (e.g., "koo" instead of "cool") [6]. Also, the limited size of messages urges authors to shorten words into new forms that bear little similarity to the original one. For instance, "great" is replaced by "gr8" and "congratulations" by "congratz".

(**iii**) *Noise.* The real-time nature of microblogging encourages users to post their messages without verifying their correctness with respect to grammar or syntactic rules. In case a message (or part of it) is incomprehensible, the author can simply replace it with a new one. As a result, the user-generated, microblog content abounds in misspelled words and incorrect phrases, thus entailing high levels of noise.

(**iv**) *Multilinguality.* Although the majority of users stems from English-speaking countries, microblogging platforms are popular world-wide [13]; their user base encompasses

---

[3]http://twendz.waggeneredstrom.com
[4]http://www.tweetfeel.com
[5]http://sentiwordnet.isti.cnr.it

people talking in various languages and dialects, thus rendering inapplicable the language-specific SA methods.

In this paper, we introduce a novel approach for SA that relies on two *orthogonal*, yet *complementary* sources of evidence, both being language-neutral and robust to noise. The first one extracts reliable content-based features using the n-gram graphs document representation model. The second one considers the contextual information of individual messages in order to infer their sentiment without considering their content. It relies on social graph connections to capture the general mood expressed in the *social context* of each message: its author, her friends as well as the users closer to her (i.e., those friends that share higher levels of homophily with her). It also considers the general mood related to the resources contained in each message: its topic(s), the users it mentions as well as the media items it points to, information that is excluded from the content features. We thus compare between two distinct sources of evidence and analytically examine how they perform in conjunction.

In addition to effectiveness, we also pay attention to improving efficiency. We actually aim at identifying those classification settings that offer the best balance between effectiveness and efficiency. To this end, we investigate four possibilities: first, we propose alternative features with low extraction cost for both sources of evidence. Second, we experiment with attribute filtering approaches in order to reduce the feature space to its minimal subset that maintains the original levels of accuracy at a significantly lower processing time. Third, we propose discretization techniques that turn our numeric features into nominal ones, which involve higher classification efficiency [16]. Last but not least, we examine several classification algorithms of varying time complexity. We analytically examine the actual performance of all these classification settings, applying them on a large-scale, real-world data set of Twitter data.

On the whole, the main contributions of our paper can be summarized as follows:

- We distinguish between two orthogonal, yet complementary categories of SA features: the content-based and context-based ones. The former detects novel textual patterns in microblog messages, while the latter encapsulate the aggregate polarity of their social context.

- We examine the n-gram graphs performance in the context of SA over microblog content. We explain how their features can be discretized and compare their numeric and their nominal form with the traditional representation models. We also compare it with the alternative of exclusively considering specific punctuation features.

- We introduce Polarity Ratio as a novel metric encapsulating the aggregate sentiment of a document collection and explain how it can form the basis for context-based features. We apply it on several aspects of a document's social context and present an approach for discretizing its value. Also, we compare it with the efficient alternative of considering several direct contextual features.

- We apply our features to several state-of-the-art classification algorithms and evaluate their performance over a large, real-world data collection comprising 3 million Twitter messages.

The rest of the paper is structured as follows: Section 2 formally defines the problem we are tackling, while Section 3 presents the main characteristics of Twitter. We present our approach in Section 4 and in Section 5 we evaluate its performance over a thorough experimental study. Related work is discussed in Section 6, followed by our conclusions and future directions in Section 7.

2. PROBLEM FORMULATION

Sentiment Analysis is distinguished in three tasks [18]:

(i) *Document-level SA* assumes each document to express a single opinion about a particular topic or object,

(ii) *Sentence-level SA* splits each document into sentences, hypothesizing that they express individual opinions, and

(iii) *Feature-level SA* splits each document and sentence into polarized phrases that correspond to a particular feature of the discussed object or topic.

In this work, we exclusively focus on document-level SA in the context of microblog posts. In particular, we aim at detecting the polarity of individual Twitter messages, which typically consist of few sentences. Given their limited length, though, the problem we are tackling is very close to the Sentence-level SA, as well.

In practice, the task of document-level SA is typically cast as a binary classification problem, where the goal is to identify whether a document expresses a negative or a positive opinion [18]. Formally, it is defined as follows:

Problem 1 (BINARY POLARITY CLASSIFICATION).
Given a collection of documents $\mathcal{D}$ and the set of binary polarization classes $\mathcal{P}_\mathcal{B} = \{negative, positive\}$, the goal is to approximate *the unknown target function $\Phi_\mathcal{B} : \mathcal{D} \to \mathcal{P}_\mathcal{B}$, which describes the documents' polarization according to a golden standard, by means of a function $\Phi'_\mathcal{B} : \mathcal{T} \to \mathcal{P}_\mathcal{B}$ that is called the **binary polarity classifier**.*

This formulation simplifies the task of SA, as it is based on the assumption that each document is subjective (i.e., it expresses a single, polarized opinion). In practice, however, a document can be neutral, as well, containing objective (i.e., factual) information. For this reason, we additionally consider the following, more general problem of document-level SA:

Problem 2 (GENERAL POLARITY CLASSIFICATION).
*Given a collection of documents $\mathcal{D}$ and the set of all polarization classes $\mathcal{P}_\mathcal{G} = \{negative, neutral, positive\}$, the goal is to approximate the unknown target function $\Phi_\mathcal{G} : \mathcal{D} \to \mathcal{P}_\mathcal{G}$, which describes the polarization of documents according to a golden standard, by means of a function $\Phi'_\mathcal{G} : \mathcal{T} \to \mathcal{P}_\mathcal{G}$ that is called the **general polarity classifier**.*

Note that both problems are modeled as *single-label classification* tasks (i.e., each document belongs to a single polarity class). Note also that some works address them in a slightly different manner [18]: given a set of documents, its elements are first categorized into a binary scale of objective (i.e., neutral) and subjective (i.e., polarized) ones; in a second stage, they further categorize the subjective documents into negative and positive ones. In this work, we consider the multiclass version of Problem 2 so as to compare its performance with that of Problem 1 on an equal basis (i.e., applying both of them on the same data). In this way, we provide a holistic overview of SA in real settings, and analytically examine the effect of extending Problem 1 with the class of objective documents.

3. PRELIMINARIES

Among all microblogging platforms, we selected Twitter for developing and testing our approach, due to the following advantages it conveys:

(i) *Strict interaction.* Twitter defines a single, strict way of interaction, allowing users to post only short messages of up to 140 characters - called *tweets.* To draw the attention of other users, tweets typically contain original, self-contained content that requires the minimum attention from readers. Thus, user sentiments are exclusively encapsulated in tweets, unlike other platforms that offer diverse ways for expressing them (e.g., the "Like" and the "+1" buttons in Facebook[6] and Google+[7], respectively).

(ii) *Social graph.* The morphology of Twitter's social graph captures the relationships between its users in an unequivocal way. More specifically, users can register to any account that is of particular interest to them in order to receive notification for its latest posts; the subscriber is called *follower*, the content provider is the *followee*, and their connection is modeled by a directed edge that points from the former to the latter. This allows for a particular category of interpersonal connections, namely the **reciprocal friends**; these are followers that are followed back by their followees, thus indicating a particularly close relationship between them (i.e., each one finds the other of particular interest). Their strong connection is typically interpreted as a sign of high levels of homophily, in the sense that they share a highly similar background, such as common age, sex or education [32].

(iii) *Public content.* The vast majority of Twitter's content is public and accessible, enabling us to harvest an adequate volume of content for experimentation.

(iv) *Timed activity.* Tweets are timestamped, thus indicating their sequence of appearance. As we explain below, this is critical for deriving past contextual evidence from the activity relevant to individual tweets.

In the following, we analyze the intrinsic characteristics of Twitter that lie at the core of our methods:

(i) *Hashtags.* Users typically categorize their tweets in topics that can be freely defined by any user. This is simply done by adding a topic tag - called *hashtag* - usually at the end of the tweet. To distinguish it from the rest of the message, a hashtag starts with the symbol #, which is then followed by one or more concatenated words or alphanumerics (e.g., #fb). This notation enables the efficient and effective identification of tweets pertaining to a specific topic (i.e., **topic tweets**). Note, though, that a single tweet can be associated with multiple hashtags.

(ii) *Mentions.* Twitter often serves as a platform for discussions among its members (i.e., chat). To facilitate this functionality, a user can address another person simply by adding a *mention* to her username. This is a special notation formed by concatenating the symbol @ at the beginning of the corresponding username (e.g., *@erwtokritos*). In this way, it is easy to identify and aggregate all the tweets pertaining to a particular user (i.e., **mention tweets**).

(iii) *External Pointers.* A common practice in Twitter is to inform one's followers about interesting Web resources (e.g., on-line videos), by posting the corresponding link. Given that URLs spread unchanged even among users that speak different languages, it is easy to track the messages pertaining to a specific resource (i.e., **URL tweets**).

(iv) *Emoticons.* Subjective tweets usually denote the opinion of their author with the help of standard "smileys": posi-

tive sentiments are usually marked with one of the following annotations: ":)", "(:", ":-)", "(-:", ":)", "(:", ":D" or "=)", whereas the negative ones are typically annotated by the following emoticons: ":(", "):", ":-(", ")-:", ": (" or ") :" [1, 5, 22]. We call **positive tweets** the messages annotated with at least one from the former group of emoticons, and **negative tweets** those annotated with at least one from the latter [1, 5, 22]; messages that belong to either of these categories are collectively called **polarized tweets**. **Neutral tweets**, on the other hand, are those lacking any polarity indicators. Tweets containing both positive and negative emoticons are entirely excluded from our analysis; the reason is that they are not suitable for the task of single-label, document-level SA we are considering, but rather for the feature-level one, which is out of the scope of this work.

(v) *Retweets.* Users typically share with their followers interesting tweets that have been posted by other users. To distinguish these messages from their own tweets, they mark them as *retweets*, adding the special annotation "*RT @X*" usually at their beginning. In this way, they give credit to the original author (i.e., the user *X*) and enable us to distinguish genuine tweets from the reproduced ones.

Of the above features, the first four offer valuable contextual information for individual tweets. Retweets are excluded from our analysis, as they do not provide any novel information.

4. APPROACH

In this section, we elaborate on the main techniques that provide the textual and contextual features of our approach. We accompany them with discretization techniques for enhancing their efficiency and consider alternative sets of features with a lower extraction cost, as well.

4.1 Content-based Models

Textual patterns are typically captured through language-specific representation models that detect frequent sequences of words (i.e., word n-grams) [5]. The settings we are considering in this work, however, pose significant obstacles to the applicability of term-based techniques, urging us to consider character-based models instead. Several reasons advocate this choice: first, character n-grams have been verified to outperform word n-grams in various applications, ranging from spam filtering [15] to authorship attribution [7] and utterance recognition [33]. Second, there is no standard tokenization approach for multilingual documents; words are typically identified through the whitespace that delimit them, but there are languages, such as Chinese, where different words can be concatenated in a single token.

Most importantly, though, term-based models depend on dictionary-based and language-specific techniques, such as *stemming* and *lemmatization*, to tackle *synonymy*; that is, words with the same meaning, but different syntactic form (e.g., quickly and rapidly), which are considered as distinct features, unless sophisticated methods for matching them are employed. Such techniques are inapplicable to the user-generated, multilingual microblog content, whose inherent noise (i.e., spelling mistakes) and neologisms further aggravate synonymy. As a result, both the effectiveness and the efficiency of term-based models is significantly degraded in our settings; the former is restricted due to missed patterns, stemming from semantically equivalent features that are treated as different, whereas the latter suffers from the *curse of dimensionality*; the diversity of the vocabulary leads

---

[6]http://www.facebook.com/
[7]http://plus.google.com

to a feature space with excessively high complexity and high computational cost.

For these reasons, we focus in the following on character-based representation models, namely the character n-grams and the character n-gram graphs. We also consider the term vector model - free from any optimizations - in order to illustrate the shortcomings of language-dependent methods in our settings. For each model, we explain how it represents individual tweets as well as a collection of tweets sharing the same polarity.

4.1.1 Term Vector Model

Given a collection of tweets T, this model aggregates the set of distinct words (i.e., tokens) $\mathcal{W}$ that are contained in it. Each tweet $t_i \in T$ is then represented as a vector $\vec{v}_{t_i} = (v_1, v_2, \ldots, v_{|\mathcal{W}|})$ of size $|\mathcal{W}|$, whose j-th dimension v_j corresponds to the TF-IDF weight of the j-th token $w_j \in \mathcal{W}$; that is, its value is defined as the product of its *Term Frequency* TF_i (i.e., the number of times w_j occurs in t_i) and its *Inverse Document Frequency* IDF_i (i.e., the cross-document frequency of w_j) [19]. The latter is defined as $DF_i = \log |T|/|\{t : w_i \in t \wedge t \in T\}|$, where the numerator stands for the size of the input tweets collection, and the denominator expresses the number of tweets that contain the word w_i. Similar to individual tweets, each polarity class T_p is modeled as a term vector $\vec{v}_{T_p}$ that comprises all tokens of the tweets t_i corresponding to it (i.e., $t_i \in T_p$).

4.1.2 Character N-grams Model

The set of *character n-grams* of a tweet comprises all substrings of length n of its text. The most common sizes for n are 2 (*bigrams*), 3 (*trigrams*) and 4 (*four-grams*). For example, the trigrams representation of the phrase "home_phone" is the following: { hom, ome, me_, _ph, pho, hon, one }. According to this model, each tweet t_i is represented by a vector v_{t_i} whose i-th dimension corresponds to the Term Frequency of the i-th n-gram [19]. Similarly, a polarity class T_p is modeled as a vector v_{T_p} that comprises all the n-grams contained in its tweets.

The main advantages of this model over the previous one are its language neutrality and its tolerance to noise and spelling mistakes: by considering substrings instead of entire words, their impact on the identified patterns is significantly reduced.

4.1.3 Character N-gram Graphs Model

The main drawback of the previous model is that it converts a tweet into a bag of n-grams, thus disregarding the valuable information that is encapsulated in the sequence of the n-grams of the original text. To overcome this problem, the *character n-gram graphs* method associates all neighboring character n-grams with edges that denote their (average) co-occurrence rate inside an individual tweet or a collection of tweets [9]. That is, it forms a graph whose nodes correspond to distinct n-grams, while its edges are weighted proportionally to the average distance - in terms of n-grams - between the adjacent nodes. To illustrate this structure, Figure 1 depicts the n-gram graph derived from the phrase "home_phone". Apparently, it conveys more information than the trigram representation of the same phrase in Section 4.1.2.

Formally, a character n-gram graph is defined as [9]:

Definition 1 (N-GRAM GRAPH). *An n-gram graph is a graph $G = \{V^G, E^G, W\}$, where V^G is the set of vertices*

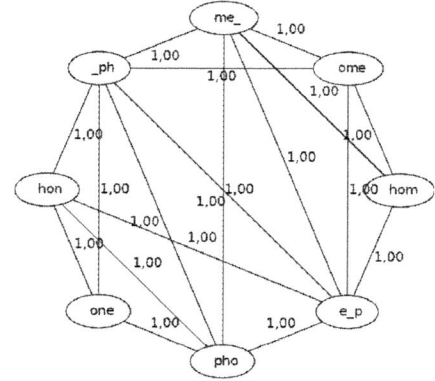

Figure 1: An example of a tri-gram graph that represents the phrase "home_phone".

(labeled by the corresponding character n-gram), E^G is the set of undirected edges (labeled by the concatenation of the labels of their adjacent vertices in alphabetical order), and W is a function assigning a weight to every edge.

According to this model, each tweet t_i is represented by a character n-gram graph G_{t_i} - called **tweet graph** - that is constructed by running a window of size n over it. During this process, the tweet is analyzed into overlapping character n-grams, recording information about the neighboring ones (i.e., those placed within the same window). Thus, an edge $e^{G_{t_i}} \in E^{G_{t_i}}$ connecting a pair of n-grams indicates proximity of these character sequences in the original text within the predefined window of size n [9]. The actual weight of the edges is estimated by measuring the percentage of co-occurrences of the corresponding vertices n-grams within the specified window.

A polarity class T_p is modeled by a single graph G_{T_p} that uniformly represents the tweets comprising it. This **class graph** is formed with the help of the *update functionality* [10][8]: given a set of tweets of the same polarity T_p, it builds an initially empty graph G_{T_p}. The i-th tweet $t_i \in T_p$ is transformed into the tweet graph G_{t_i} that is then merged with G_{T_p} to form a new graph G_u consisting of the union of the nodes and edges of the individual graphs; their weights are set equal to the average value of the weights of the individual graphs. More formally, G_u has the following properties: $G_u = (E^u, V^u, W^{u_i})$, where $E^u = E^{G_{T_p}} \cup E^{G_{t_i}}$, $V^u = V^{G_{T_p}} \cup V^{G_{t_i}}$ and $W^{u_i}(e) = W^{G_{T_p}}(e) + (W^{G_{t_i}}(e) - W^{G_{T_p}}(e)) \times 1/i$. Note that the division by i ensures that the aggregated weight converges to the mean value of the corresponding edge among all individual tweet graphs, thus turning the update functionality independent of the order by which tweets are merged [10]. After merging all individual tweet graphs into the class graph G_{T_p}, its edges $E^{G_{T_p}}$ encapsulate the most characteristic patterns contained in the class' content, such as recurring and neighboring character sequences, special characters, and digits.

To estimate the similarity between a tweet graph G_{t_i} and a class graph G_{T_p}, we employ one of the established n-gram graph similarity metrics [9]:

---

[8]An alternative approach would simply extract the class graph from the single tweet formed by the concatenation of all individual tweets. This practice, though, inserts noise in the form of edges between the last and the first n-gram of two consecutive, but actually independent tweets. In this way, it also depends on the order of concatenation.

(i) *Containment Similarity* (**CS**), which expresses the proportion of edges of graph G_{t_i} that are shared with graph G_{T_p}. Assuming that G is an n-gram graph, e is an n-gram graph edge and that for the function $\mu(e, G)$ it stands that $\mu(e, G) = 1$, if and only if $e \in G$, and 0 otherwise, then:

$$\mathrm{CS}(G_{t_i}, G_{T_p}) = \sum_{e \in G_{t_i}} \mu(e, G_{T_p}) / \min(|G_{t_i}|, |G_{T_p}|),$$

where $|G|$ denotes the *size of the n-gram graph* G (i.e., the number of edges it contains).

(ii) *Value Similarity* (**VS**), which indicates how many of the edges contained in graph G_{t_i} are shared with graph G_{T_p}, considering also their weights. In more detail, every common edge e having weights $w^{t_i}(e)$ and $w^{T_p}(e)$ in G_{t_i} and G_{T_p}, respectively, contributes $\mathrm{VR}(e) / \max(|G_{t_i}|, |G_{T_p}|)$ to the VS, where the *ValueRatio (VR)* is a symmetric, scaling factor that is defined as: $\mathrm{VR}(e) = \frac{\min(w^{t_i}(e), w^{T_p}(e))}{\max(w^{t_i}(e), w^{T_p}(e))}$. It takes values in the interval $[0, 1]$, with non-matching edges having no contribution to it (i.e., for an edge $e \notin G_{t_i}$ we have $\mathrm{VR}(e) = 0$). The full equation for *VS* now is:

$$\mathrm{VS}(G_{t_i}, G_{T_p}) = \frac{\sum_{e \in G_{t_i}} \frac{\min(w^{t_i}(e), w^{T_p}(e))}{\max(w^{t_i}(e), w^{T_p}(e))}}{\max(|G_{t_i}|, |G_{T_p}|)}.$$

This measure converges to 1 for graphs that share both the edges and weights, with a value of VS = 1 indicating perfect match between the compared graphs.

(iii) *Normalized Value Similarity* (**NVS**), which decouples value similarity from the effect of the largest graph's size. Its value is derived from the combination of VS with SS (i.e., the *size similarity* of two graphs) as follows:

$$\mathrm{NVS}(G_{t_i}, G_{T_p}) = \mathrm{VS}(G_{t_i}, G_{T_p}) / \mathrm{SS}(G_{t_i}, G_{T_p}),$$

where $\mathrm{SS}(G_{t_i}, G_{T_p}) = \min(|G_{t_i}|, |G_{T_p}|) / \max(|G_{t_i}|, |G_{T_p}|)$.

On the whole, the n-gram graphs representation model captures the common textual patterns between a tweet t_i and a polarity class T_p through their CS, VS and the NVS similarities. These measures are substantially different from the cosine similarity of the n-grams model: the latter operates on the level of individual n-grams, whereas CS considers pairs of neighboring n-grams. VS goes one step further considering pairs of neighboring n-grams that have the same co-occurrence rate (i.e., edge weight), while NVS further enhances this approach by removing the effect of the relative size of the compared graphs.

The exact process for classifying a tweet t_i with the help of the n-gram graphs in the case of Problem 2 is presented in Figure 2: the tweet graph G_{t_i} is compared with each class graph (i.e., $G_{T_{neg}}$, $G_{T_{neu}}$, $G_{T_{pos}}$) to estimate its closeness to the corresponding polarity class. This is encapsulated in the values of three similarity metrics per class (i.e., CS, NVS and VS), which collectively form the feature vector that is given as input to a trained classifier. Based on the 9 - in total - features, the classifier decides for the most likely class label of tweet t_i. The same process is followed in case of Problem 1 with the only difference that there is no comparison with the neutral class graph $G_{T_{neu}}$ (i.e., the feature vector comprises just 6 features). This makes clear that the feature space of the n-gram graphs model depends on the number of considered classes and does not suffer from the dimensionality curse of the aforementioned representation models; the number of features the latter entail depends on the diversity of the vocabulary of the input document collection, typically amounting to several thousands of them (see Section 5 for more details).

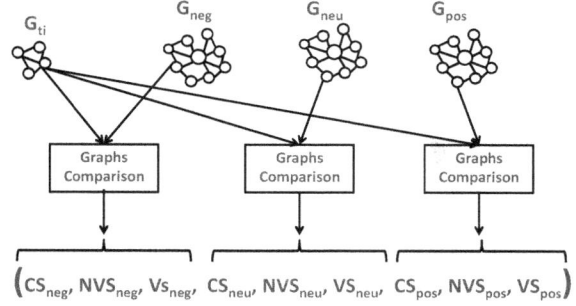

Figure 2: Deriving the feature vector from the n-gram graphs model for Problem 2.

Discretized N-Gram Graph Model. To enhance the classification efficiency of the n-gram graphs model, we propose an intuitive method for discretizing its similarity values. It employs pair-wise comparisons between the values of the same metric for different polarity classes, producing a nominal label according to the following discretization function:

$$dsim(sim_{pol_1}, sim_{pol_2}) = \begin{cases} pol_2, & \text{if } sim_{pol_1} < sim_{pol_2} \\ equal, & \text{if } sim_{pol_1} = sim_{pol_2} \\ pol_1, & \text{if } sim_{pol_1} < sim_{pol_2}, \end{cases}$$

where sim is the similarity metric (i.e., $sim \in \{CS, VS,$ or $NVS\}$) and pol_1 and pol_2 are the involved polarity classes (i.e., $pol_1, pol_2 \in \{neg, neu, pos\}$).

Thus, a tweet is classified in the Binary Polarity Problem according to 3 nominal features: $dsim(CS_{neg}, CS_{pos})$, $dsim(NVS_{neg}, NVS_{pos})$, and $dsim(VS_{neg}, VS_{pos})$. In the case of Problem 2, the following 6 additional features are derived from the comparisons of the neutral class similarities with the corresponding ones of the negative and the positive class: $dsim(CS_{neg}, CS_{neu})$, $dsim(NVS_{neg}, NVS_{neu})$, $dsim(VS_{neg}, VS_{neu})$, $dsim(CS_{neu}, CS_{pos})$, $dsim(NVS_{neu}, NVS_{pos})$, and $dsim(VS_{neu}, VS_{pos})$.

4.1.4 Punctuation Model

An alternative, language-agnostic method for detecting textual patterns has been proposed in [5]. It exclusively takes into account the punctuation and special characters that are contained in a tweet, thus being robust to spelling mistakes and neologisms. Its main advantage, though, is its minimal cost for extracting its features: they can be derived from a simple inspection of the characters of individual messages. In the following, we present its features, illustrating the rationale behind them through their average value for each polarity class, as it was estimated over the data set of 3 million tweets (1 million of randomly selected tweets per class) that is presented in Section 5.

(i) *Number of Special Characters.* It denotes the number of characters in a tweet that are neither alphanumerics nor white space. The higher their number is, the more likely is the corresponding message to be subjective. For example, it is common to add punctuation characters to stress a feeling and to replace abusive words with a series of incomprehensible symbols. Indeed, neutral tweets contain - on average - just 6.05 characters of this kind, whereas the positive and negative ones contain 6.44 and 7.76 characters, respectively.

(ii) *Number of "!".* Exclamation marks constitute a typical annotation for positive sentiments; the higher their number is, the more intense the positive feeling of a message is. Thus, positive messages contain 0.65 such characters on average, whereas the negative and the neutral ones contain 0.40 and 0.45 exclamation marks, respectively.

(iii) *Number of Quotes.* Quoted sentences are more likely to be found in objective tweets, whose authors cite other people's statements. Indeed, neutral messages contain 0.15 quotes on average, whereas subjective ones contain almost half as much: 0.08 for negative and 0.09 for positive tweets.

(iv) *Number of "?".* The higher the number of question marks in a message is, the more likely it is to be subjective, usually expressing a negative feeling. On average, tweets of this polarity contain 0.19 question marks in comparison to 0.16 and 0.14 for positive and neutral ones, respectively.

(v) *Number of Capitalized Tokens.* With the exception of abbreviations, capitalized tokens offer a strong indication for subjectivity; the higher their number is, the more intense the expressed feeling is. On average, negative and positive tweets contain 2.31 and 2.17 capitalized tokens, respectively, whereas objective tweets involve just 1.58 tokens of this kind.

(vi) *Tweet Length in Characters.* Negative tweets were found to consist - on average - of 95.05 characters, thus being larger than those of the other two polarity classes. They are followed by the the neutral ones that comprise 90.64 characters and the positive ones with just 88.92 characters.

4.2 Context-based Models

In addition to the textual patterns, another reliable source of evidence for detecting a tweet's sentiment is its **social context**. As such, we define any indication that associates it - directly or indirectly - with other messages (i.e., hashtags and URLs) or with members of the underlying social network (i.e., the author of the message, her friends as well as the users mentioned in it). In a similar vein to the spread of happiness that was suggested in [4], we argue that the overall polarity of the associated entities is critical for the polarity of individual messages; for example, the more positive tweets a user's friends have posted in the past, the more likely is her next tweet to be positive, as well. Note that this idea lies at the core of [27], as well, but it is employed in the context of *user-level sentiment analysis* (i.e., identifying the sentiment of a specific user with respect to a particular topic).

To quantify the effect of social context, we introduce a metric that estimates the aggregate sentiment of a set of tweets: the Polarity Ratio. We explain how it can be applied to the social context of individual tweets and present an intuitive way of discretizing its values. To verify its utility, we also examine an alternative approach of minimal extraction cost that relies on the raw form of the same contextual features (i.e., without taking the Polarity Ratio into account).

4.2.1 Social Polarity Model

The aggregate sentiment of a set of tweets is determined by the dominant polarity class: if the positive messages significantly outnumber the negative ones, the overall sentiment is considered positive and vice versa. This notion can be quantified through the following measure:

Definition 2 (POLARITY RATIO). *Given a collection of tweets T, their **polarity ratio** $r_p(T)$ is defined as follows:*

$$r_p(T) = \begin{cases} \frac{|PT|+1}{|NT|+1} - 1, & if\ |NT| < |PT| \\[2ex] -\frac{|NT|+1}{|PT|+1} + 1, & if\ |PT| \leq |NT| \end{cases}$$

where $NT \subseteq T$ and $PT \subseteq T$ stand for the sets of negative tweets and positive tweets, respectively, with $|NT|$ and $|PT|$ representing their cardinality.

Polarity Ratio (**PR**) is defined in the interval $(-\infty, +\infty)$, with positive values suggesting the prevalence of positive

tweets, and vice versa. More specifically, a positive value n suggests that the positive tweets are $n + 1$ times more than the negative ones. Values very close to 0 corresponds to neutral aggregate polarity, denoting the absence of polarized tweets or the relatively equal portion of positive and negative tweets (i.e., $NT \approx PT$).

PR can be applied to all components of a tweet's social context, provided that they are represented by the set of messages pertaining to them. For example, the polarity ratio of the author's friends is calculated from the entire set of polarized messages they have already posted. Note that a critical point in this procedure is the temporal aspect of the tweets: we can only consider all the messages posted before the message in question. This is because we can only employ evidence from a tweet's past in order to predict its polarity.

In this work, we consider the following features:

(i) *Author Polarity Ratio.* It denotes the aggregate polarity of all messages posted by the same author prior to the given tweet t. Its value expresses her overall mood in the past, which is decisive for the sentiment of the subsequently published tweets. The more positive (negative) tweets she has already published, the more likely it is for t to be positive (negative), as well.

(ii) *Author's Followees Polarity Ratio.* Users pay particular attention to the messages posted by the users they subscribe to. They are expected, therefore, to be influenced by their opinions and sentiments. The higher (lower) the polarity ratio of their posts is, the more probable it is for t to be positive (negative) as well. To quantify this notion, this feature captures the aggregate sentiment of all messages posted by the author's followees prior to tweet t.

(iii) *Author's Reciprocal Friends Polarity Ratio.* It expresses the aggregate sentiment of the tweets posted by the author's reciprocal friends before she posted tweet t. These friends are expected to share a higher degree of homophily with the author [32] and, thus, the higher (lower) the polarity ratio of their posts is, the more probable it is for t to be positive (negative), as well.

(iv) *Topic(s) Polarity Ratio.* This feature is only valid for tweets containing at least one hashtag. It denotes the overall sentiment of all tweets that - regardless of their author - pertain to the same topic and have been posted prior to the given tweet t. In case a tweet contains more than one hashtag, this feature considers the entire set of tweets that is derived from the union of the individual sets of topic tweets. The higher the portion of positive (negative) tweets in the resulting set, the more likely it is for t to be positive (negative), as well.

(v) *Mention(s) Polarity Ratio.* This feature applies only to tweets containing at least one mention to a Twitter user. It represents the overall sentiment of all tweets that - regardless of their author - mention the same user and have been posted prior to the given tweet t. In case of multiple mentions, this feature considers the union of the individual sets of mention tweets. The more positive (negative) tweets mention a particular user, the more likely it is for t to be positive (negative), as well.

(vi) *URL(s) Polarity Ratio.* This feature is only applicable to tweets that contain at least one URL. It expresses the aggregate polarity of all tweets with the same URL that have been posted prior to the given tweet t, regardless of their author. In case a single tweet contains multiple URLs, this feature considers the union of the individual URL tweets. The more positive (negative) tweets are associated with the referenced URL(s), the more likely it is for t to be positive (negative), as well.

Note that the first half of these features are based on social graph information, while the second half is exclusively derived from the related resources.

Discretized Social Polarity Model. Polarity Ratio produces numeric values, but their actual magnitude might be less significant than their polarity sign (i.e., positive or negative). If this is true, the processing of the corresponding nominal attributes will be significantly more efficient [16]. To validate these premises, we developed a novel method for discretizing the polarity ratio that depends on the polarity classification problem at hand. For its general version (i.e., Problem 2), the discretized polarity ratio $dr_p^{\mathcal{G}}(T)$ over a collection of tweets T takes as value one of the three polarity classes, based on the numeric value of $r_p(T)$, as follows:

$$dr_p^{\mathcal{G}}(T) = \begin{cases} negative, & \text{if } r_p(T) \leq -1 \\ neutral, & \text{if } -1 < r_p(T) < 1 \\ positive, & \text{if } 1 \leq r_p(T). \end{cases}$$

For its binary version (i.e., Problem 1), the discretized polarity ratio $dr_p^{\mathcal{B}}(T)$ is defined as follows:

$$dr_p^{\mathcal{B}}(T) = \begin{cases} negative, & \text{if } r_p(T) < 0 \\ equal, & \text{if } r_p(T) = 0 \\ positive, & \text{if } r_p(T) > 0. \end{cases}$$

4.2.2   Social Context Model

To reduce the feature extraction cost of the above model, we also consider an alternative set of context-based features that can be directly derived from a user's account and the characteristics of her messages. To illustrate their functionality, we present their average value for each polarity class, as it was derived from the data set of 3 million tweets (1 million tweets per class) that is presented in Section 5.

(i) *Number of Author's Tweets.* It represents the number of tweets the author of the given tweet t had published, prior to posting t. The authors of neutral tweets are more prolific, posting 387 messages on average, whereas the authors of negative and positive ones post 356 and 298 tweets, respectively.

(ii) *Number of Author's Followees.* It denotes the number of users the author of the input tweet t had subscribed to, prior to publishing t. Authors of neutral tweets were found to have the most subscriptions (351 followees on average), followed by the authors of the positive (281 followees) and the negative ones (271 followees).

(iii) *Number of Author's Reciprocal Friends.* It stands for the number of reciprocal friends the author of the given tweet had, before publishing it. Authors of neutral tweets were found to have substantially more reciprocal friends (244 on average), followed by the authors of positive (195) and negative ones (181).

(iv) *Number of Topics.* It denotes the number of hashtags contained in the given tweet. Objective messages are typically related to a larger number of topics (0.14 hashtags on average), while subjective tweets contain almost half as much (0.08 hashtags), independently of their polarity.

(v) *Number of Mentions.* It expresses the number of users mentioned in the input tweet. Positive tweets were found to contain the highest amount of mentions (0.75 on average),

whereas negative and neutral ones merely refer to 0.51 and 0.54 users, respectively.

(vi) *Number of URLs.* It denotes the number of URLs that the given tweet contains. The higher their number is, the more likely the author is to provide her subscribers with objective information; indeed, neutral tweets contain the highest number of links (0.43 on average), whereas the positive ones contain half as much (0.21). Negative ones lie in the middle of these two extremes, with 0.36 URLs on average.

Basically, these features rely on the same evidence with the Polarity Ratio model, but do not take into account the aggregate polarity of the underlying instances. Thus, they are directly comparable with it, illustrating the contribution of Polarity Ratio to the accuracy of context-based models.

5.   EVALUATION

In this section, we analytically present our thorough experimental study that aims at identifying the optimal *classification settings* for Sentiment Analysis over microblogs; that is, the combination of a classification algorithm and a set of features that offers the best balance between effectiveness and efficiency.

Data Set. To examine the performance of our models in practical settings, we conducted a thorough experimental study on a large-scale multilingual collection of real Twitter messages. It is the same data set that was employed in [35], comprising 476 million tweets posted in a period of 7 months - from June 2009 until December 2009. Among them, we identified 6.12 million negative and 14.12 million positive tweets following the common practice in the literature, which employs emoticons as a golden standard [5, 1, 22][9]. We randomly selected 1 million tweets from both polarity classes to form the data set for Problem 1, called D_{binary}. We additionally selected a random sample of neutral tweets to create the data set for Problem 2, called $D_{general}$. Both of them are among the largest data sets employed so far in the context of Sentiment Analysis over microblogs. Note also that our sampling did not restrict the selected tweets to specific language, so as to ensure the multilinguality of our data sets.

To derive the social context of individual tweets, we employed the snapshot of the entire Twitter social graph that was used in [17], which dates from August 2009. This time period coincides with that of the recorded messages, but does not depict the actual evolution of the underlying social network during that period. Its static information allows only for a mere approximation of the actual performance of the context-based models. To estimate the actual value of the polarity ratios they involve, we relied again on the positive and negative emoticons.

Metrics. To measure the effectiveness of the classification models, we considered the established metric of **classification accuracy** α. It expresses the portion of the correctly classified tweets and is formally defined as follows: $\alpha = \frac{TP}{TP+FP}$, where TP stands for true positives (i.e., the number of tweets that were assigned to the correct polarity class) and FP denotes false positives (i.e., the number of incorrectly classified tweets).

Evaluation Method. To evaluate the performance of

---

[9]Assuming that a positive (negative) emoticon always corresponds to a positive (negative) sentiment is a simplification hypothesis. Nevertheless, it is the only method employed in the literature for large-scale experimental studies.

	Prob. 1	Prob. 2
Term Vector	67.38%	50.68%
2-grams	61.99%	50.11%
3-grams	68.72%	53.15%
4-grams	70.62%	53.41%
2-gram Graphs	64.38%	45.86%
3-gram Graphs	79.95%	65.28%
4-gram Graphs	**91.51%**	**83.80%**
Discr. 2-gram Graphs	65.58%	48.01%
Discr. 3-gram Graphs	89.71%	78.52%
Discr. 4-gram Graphs	**97.12%**	**93.43%**

Table 1: Accuracy of Naive Bayes Multinomial.

	Prob. 1	Prob. 2
Term Vector	70.66%	52.65%
2-grams	69.80%	57.36%
3-grams	72.89%	57.86%
4-grams	71.76%	54.63%
2-gram Graphs	68.70%	57.11%
3-gram Graphs	74.02%	63.12%
4-gram Graphs	**86.10%**	**79.18%**
Discr. 2-gram Graphs	64.35%	52.67%
Discr. 3-gram Graphs	71.69%	60.89%
Discr. 4-gram Graphs	**84.57%**	**78.82%**

Table 2: Accuracy of Support Vector Machines.

	Prob. 1	Prob. 2
Term Vector	1,245	1,221
2-grams	1,796	1,848
3-grams	6,255	6,358
4-grams	10,888	11,045
2-gram Graphs	6	9
3-gram Graphs	6	9
4-gram Graphs	6	9
Discr. 2-gram Graphs	3	9
Discr. 3-gram Graphs	3	9
Discr. 4-gram Graphs	3	9

Table 3: Number of features per representation model.

our models, we employ the 10-fold cross-validation approach. For the evaluation of the n-gram graphs model, we followed a special procedure: first, we randomly selected half of the training set of each polarity class to build the corresponding class graph. Then, the tweet graphs of all training instances are compared with all polarity graphs and the classification algorithm is trained over the resulting similarities values. Finally, the tweet graphs of the testing instances are compared with all class graphs and the trained algorithm decides for their label according to the derived similarity features. It should be stressed at this point that the emoticons were removed from all training and testing tweets, when building any of their representation models.

Classification Algorithms. To thoroughly evaluate the performance of our models, we consider several state-of-the-art classification algorithms of varying time and space complexity. For the comparative analysis of the document representation models, we employed the Naive Bayes Multinomial (**NBM**) and the Support Vector Machines (**SVM**), two established algorithms for text-categorization, with the former being substantially more efficient than the latter [34]. For the rest of the models, we employed three of the most popular and established classification algorithms: Naive Bayes (**NB**), C4.5 and the SVM. They comprise a quite representative set of classification methods with respect not only to their internal functionality (i.e., probabilistic learning, decision trees and statistical learning, respectively), but also to their efficiency (they appear in ascending order of time complexity). For a detailed description of these algorithms, see [34].

Setup. All models and experiments were fully implemented in Java, version 1.6. For the functionality of the n-gram graphs, we employed the open source library of JInsect[10]. For the implementation of the classification algorithms, we used the Weka open source library[11], version 3.6 [34]. The only exception was the use of the LIBLINEAR optimization technique [8], which was employed for scaling the SVM to the high dimensionality of the term vector and the n-grams models. Given that LIBLINEAR also employs linear kernels for training the SVM, it is directly comparable with the Weka's default SVM configuration, which was applied to the other models. In every case, we employed the default configuration of the algorithms, without fine-tuning any of the parameters. All experiments were performed on a desktop machine with 8 cores of Intel i7, 16GB of RAM memory, running Linux (kernel version 2.6.38).

Comparison of Content-based Models. To identify the most appropriate representation model for the sparse, noisy, multilingual, user-generated content of microblogs, we applied all models of Sections 4.1.1 to 4.1.3 to the data sets

D_{binary} and $D_{general}$. For the term vector and character n-grams model, we did not employ any preprocessing technique, due to the multilingual content we are considering. To limit the feature space, we merely employed a threshold of minimum frequency, setting it equal to 0.01% of the size of the input tweets collection. Thus, words or n-grams that appear in less than 200 (300) of the tweets of D_{binary} ($D_{general}$) were not taken into account for Problem 1 (Problem 2). The outcomes of our experiments are presented in Tables 1 to 3.

Table 1 reveals the following interesting pattern in the performance of NBM over both polarity classification problems: the accuracy of the n-grams model increases with the increase in n, exceeding that of the term vector model for $n > 2$ (i.e., for trigrams and four-grams). As expected, the n-gram graphs follow the same pattern: the higher the value of n, the higher the classification accuracy. Most importantly, though, they outperform both the term vector and the corresponding n-grams model in all cases, but for $n > 2$. It is remarkable, though, that the discretization of the graph similarities conveys a significant increase to the performance of the n-gram graphs, which exceed 10% in most cases. On the whole, the highest accuracy is achieved by the four-gram graphs with discretized similarity values.

Similar patterns are depicted in the performance of SVM: the term vector model exhibits the lowest effectiveness, followed by the n-grams model, whose accuracy increases with the increase of n. The n-gram graphs outperform all other models, with their accuracy increasing proportionally to n. Note, though, that their discretized values induce no improvement in accuracy, probably because SVM are crafted for numeric attributes. It is also worth noting that, in several cases, the SVM exhibits a lower performance than NBM; the reason is that we skipped the time-consuming process of configuring SVM parameters (e.g., kernel functions) to their optimal values.

The low efficiency of the traditional representation models is reflected in Table 3: the n-grams involve the most complex feature space among all representation models, with their dimensionality increasing significantly with the increase of n. They are followed by the term vector model, which employs around 30% less features than bigrams; this is because n-grams are more frequent than entire tokens, thus resulting in a higher number of features that exceed the frequency threshold. In complete contrast, the n-gram graphs involve three orders of magnitude less features, as their dimensionality depends on the number of classes rather than the diversity of the vocabulary of the given tweets.

On the whole, the four-gram graphs achieve the highest accuracy across all representation models and classification algorithms - especially after discretizing their values - even when they are combined with a highly efficient, but simple

---

[10]http://sourceforge.net/projects/jinsect
[11]http://www.cs.waikato.ac.nz/ml/weka

	Problem 1						Problem 2					
	4-gram Graphs	Discr. Graphs	Punct.	Polarity	Discr. Polarity	Social Context	4-gram Graphs	Discr. Graphs	Punct.	Polarity	Discr. Polarity	Social Context
NB	91.51%	96.36%	56.64%	53.40%	74.61%	51.05%	75.82%	93.43%	44.69%	37.40%	60.02%	34.33%
C4.5	**98.76%**	97.17%	60.98%	80.08%	72.89%	60.44%	**96.85%**	94.98%	46.00%	66.55%	61.47%	46.38%
SVM	86.10%	84.57%	50.12%	73.19%	72.89%	56.93%	79.18%	78.82%	39.02%	52.86%	57.27%	36.68%

Table 4: Accuracy of all combinations between models and classification algorithms over both polarity problems.

algorithm like NBM. This means that they are more suitable for tackling the inherent characteristics of microblog content (cf. Section 1) and, thus, we exclusively employ this content-based model in the following.

Content-based vs. Context-based Models The performance of all models of Sections 4.1.3 to 4.2.2 is illustrated in Table 4. Note that the lowest meaningful accuracy (i.e., the performance of the random classifier) is 50% for Problem 1 and 33.33% for Problem 2.

We can notice the following patterns: first, the four-gram graphs model outperforms Social Polarity by (around) 20% in the case of Problem 1 and 30% for Problem 2. Given, though, that the latter does not consider textual patterns at all, its performance is remarkable, as its accuracy is comparable or even better than that of the traditional document representation models (i.e., term vector and n-grams model).

Second, the features with low extraction cost (i.e., Punctuation and Social Context Model) have a performance very close to that of the random classifier, unless they are combined with C4.5. Even in that case, though, their accuracy is significantly lower than that of the n-gram graphs and the Social Polarity model, respectively. For context-based models, this apparently means that plain context features capture rather poor information, thus turning PR indispensable for high effectiveness.

Third, the discretization methods have a rather small impact on the effectiveness of all models across both polarity problems: they degrade accuracy just by 6% for Social Polarity and less than 3% for 4-gram Graphs. For NB, though, they consistently boost accuracy by more than 10%.

Fourth, the additional, third polarity class in Problem 2 has a significant impact on the less effective approaches, reducing their accuracy by 10% in most cases. However, considering the highest performance in each problem, we can see that the effect of the additional class is minimal, lowering accuracy just by 2%.

Fifth, and most important, the C4.5 algorithm achieves the highest performance across most models and problems, taking values very close to absolute correctness. However, there is no clear winner between NB and SVM, probably because of the absence of configuration for the parameters of the latter. Nevertheless, the performance of NB is very close to that of C4.5 when applied on discretized features. In fact, the combination of NB with discretized features provides the best balance between effectiveness and efficiency: it is by far the most efficient combination, while its effectiveness is just 2% lower than the maximum one in both problems.

It is worth noting at this point that we also examined the combination of context-based models with content-based ones, but do not present the exact outcomes due to lack of space. It suffices to say that it was significantly lower than that of the four-gram graphs across all algorithms and problems. For instance, the accuracy of C4.5 was 93.09% and 89.75% for Problem 1 and Problem 2, respectively; for the other algorithms, though, the performance was around the average accuracy of the individual values. This means that

Model	Problem 1	Problem 2
4-gram Graphs	CS_{neg}, CS_{pos}	$CS_{neg}, CS_{neu}, CS_{pos}$
Discr. Graphs	$dsim(CS_{neg}, CS_{pos})$	$dsim(CS_{neg}, CS_{neu})$ $dsim(CS_{neg}, CS_{pos})$ $dsim(CS_{neu}, CS_{pos})$

Table 5: The selected features of the 4-gram graphs model for both polarity classification problems.

	Problem 1		Problem 2	
	4-gram Graphs	Discr. Graphs	4-gram Graphs	Discr. Graphs
NB	82.87%	97.12%	76.41%	94.92%
C4.5	97.42%	97.12%	95.40%	94.92%
SVM	84.53%	97.12%	80.43%	94.82%

Table 6: Accuracy of the *filtered* features of the four-gram graphs model.

their combination inserts noise in the classification procedure, thus indicating that the four-gram graphs model alone provides the optimal approach to SA over microblog content.

Attribute Filtering over 4-gram Graphs. To further enhance the efficiency of the four-gram graphs model, we applied on its features the correlation-based feature subset selection method [12] combined with the best-first search algorithm. The selected features for both problems are depicted in Table 5. Basically, the features that rely on the containment similarity were chosen, indicating that CS captures the most reliable textual patterns. Their performance over D_{binary} and $D_{general}$ is presented in Table 6.

We can easily notice that there is a negligible decrease in accuracy by around 1% for the numeric features. In the case of the nominal features, however, the reduction is even lower, being - in fact - statistically insignificant. Most importantly, though, the discretized features exhibit exactly the same accuracy across all algorithms. This means that all useful information is encapsulated in the selected features, enabling the use of simple, highly efficient classification algorithms without any impact on effectiveness.

6. RELATED WORK

Several surveys have recently reviewed the most prominent works on Sentiment Analysis [23, 28, 30]. Among them, though, only [30] discusses the new trend of mining sentiments in the streaming, user-generated content of microblogs. Similar to our work, the majority of relevant papers examines SA on the level of individual documents. Depending on the specific sub-problem they are tackling, they can be grouped in the following categories:

Predictive Sentiment Analysis. The aim of these works is to discover strong correlations between the aggregate sentiment of a collection of tweets and the traditional measures for polling public opinion (e.g., political elections). For example, [21] employed a large corpus of Twitter messages and verified that its aggregate mood provides a good estimation of the *evolution* of consumer confidence and the approval of presidential work in the USA. In a similar vein, [31] analyzed a large collection of tweets and found out that the relative frequency of mentions to political parties was strongly correlated with the actual outcomes of Germany's presidential elections in 2009. Equally strong is also the correlation of Twitter's aggregate mood with the evolution of stock markets and the value of the Dow Jones Industrial Average, in particular [2].

Fine-grained Sentiment Analysis. The goal of these works is to identify the correct feeling among a larger set of possible sentiments. For example, [3] considers the six distinct emotional states, collectively called POMS (i.e., Tension, Depression, Anger, Vigour, Fatigue and Confusion), whereas [29] considers the eight primary emotions (i.e., acceptance, fear, anger, joy, anticipation, sadness, disgust and surprise). At a finer sentiment granularity, [5] defines 51 different sentiments extracted from hashtags along with 16 ones extracted from smileys, introducing a classification scheme that applies k-NN on top of context-based features.

Target-dependent Sentiment Analysis. The works of this category apply SA techniques on the results of keyword queries, categorizing them into positive, negative and (rarely) neutral. This task has already been explored in the context of Web pages and news articles [20] as well as for customer reviews [25]. In the field of microblogs, it is primarily explored by on-line services that offer SA over Twitter, such as Twendz and TweetFeel. Furthermore, works in [11] and [26] attempted binary Sentiment Classification in Twitter using content as well as context features in the second case, reaching accuracies up to 84.7% in the best case. The main drawback of those solutions is that they are language-dependent, with the exception of [11], and they are also based on target-independent algorithms. [14] improves on them with a novel, three-step approach that is target-dependent and context-aware.

7. CONCLUSIONS

In this paper, we examined several content-based techniques for capturing textual patterns for SA over microblog content and verified that traditional models are inadequate for tackling the intricacies it involves. For higher effectiveness, we proposed contextual features as well as the n-gram graphs model and several techniques for enhancing their efficiency: discretization, attribute filtering and naive classification algorithms. Our experimental evaluation validated that high levels of accuracy and efficiency can be achieved simply by assigning each tweet to the polarity class that shares the maximum number of neighboring pairs of 4-grams with it.

In the future, we intend to further improve the performance of contextual features, as they are particularly useful in real-world integrated SA applications: they involve a minimal extraction cost (merely requiring some counters) and are capable of handling the intricacies of microblog content. Our plan is to enhance PR by taking time into account, so that it considers only the latest posts of a message's context. We also plan to examine how the update functionality of n-gram graphs adapts to new patterns, supporting the evolution of sentiments over time.

Acknowledgement

This work has been partly funded by the FP7 EU Project SocIoS (Contract No. 257774).

References

[1] L. Barbosa and J. Feng. Robust sentiment detection on twitter from biased and noisy data. In *COLING*, pages 36–44, 2010.

[2] J. Bollen, H. Mao, and X. Zeng. Twitter mood predicts the stock market. *Journal of Computational Science*, 2011.

[3] J. Bollen, A. Pepe, and H. Mao. Modeling public mood and emotion: Twitter sentiment and socio-economic phenomena. In *ICWSM*, 2011.

[4] N. Christakis and J. Fowler. *Connected: The surprising power of our social networks and how they shape our lives*. Little, Brown and Company, 2009.

[5] D. Davidov, O. Tsur, and A. Rappoport. Enhanced sentiment learning using twitter hashtags and smileys. In *COLING*, 2010.

[6] J. Eisenstein, B. O'Connor, N. A. Smith, and E. P. Xing. A latent variable model for geographic lexical variation. In *EMNLP*, pages 1277–1287, 2010.

[7] H. Escalante, T. Solorio, and M. Montes-y Gómez. Local histograms of character n-grams for authorship attribution. In *ACL*, pages 288–298, 2011.

[8] R. Fan, K. Chang, C. Hsieh, X. Wang, and C. Lin. Liblinear: A library for large linear classification. *JMLR*, 9:1871–1874, 2008.

[9] G. Giannakopoulos, V. Karkaletsis, G. A. Vouros, and P. Stamatopoulos. Summarization system evaluation revisited: N-gram graphs. *TSLP*, 5(3), 2008.

[10] G. Giannakopoulos and T. Palpanas. Content and type as orthogonal modeling features. *International Journal of Advances on Networks and Services*, 3(2), 2010.

[11] A. Go, R. Bhayani, and L. Huang. Twitter sentiment classification using distant supervision. *Processing*, pages 1–6, 2009.

[12] M. Hall. *Correlation-based feature selection for machine learning*. PhD thesis, University of Waikato, 1999.

[13] M. Hurst, M. Siegler, and N. Glance. On estimating the geographic distribution of social media. In *ICWSM*, 2007.

[14] L. Jiang, M. Yu, M. Zhou, X. Liu, and T. Zhao. Target-dependent Twitter sentiment classification. In *COLING*, 2011.

[15] I. Kanaris, K. Kanaris, I. Houvardas, and E. Stamatatos. Words versus character n-grams for anti-spam filtering. *IJAIT*, 16(6):1047, 2007.

[16] L. Kurgan and K. Cios. Caim discretization algorithm. *IEEE TKDE*, pages 145–153, 2004.

[17] H. Kwak, C. Lee, H. Park, and S. Moon. What is Twitter, a social network or a news media? In *WWW*, 2010.

[18] B. Liu. *Web data mining*. Springer, 2007.

[19] C. Manning, P. Raghavan, and H. Schütze. *Introduction to information retrieval*. Cambridge University Press, 2008.

[20] T. Nasukawa and J. Yi. Sentiment analysis: capturing favorability using natural language processing. In *K-CAP*, 2003.

[21] B. O'Connor, R. Balasubramanyan, B. R. Routledge, and N. A. Smith. From tweets to polls: Linking text sentiment to public opinion time series. In *ICWSM*, 2010.

[22] A. Pak and P. Paroubek. Twitter as a corpus for sentiment analysis and opinion mining. In *LREC*, 2010.

[23] B. Pang and L. Lee. Opinion mining and sentiment analysis. *Foundations and Trends in Information Retrieval*, 2008.

[24] G. Shao. Understanding the appeal of user-generated media: a uses and gratification perspective. *Internet Research*, 2009.

[25] G. Somprasertsri, P. Lalitrojwong, and P. Lalitrojwong. Mining feature-opinion in online customer reviews for opinion summarization. *Journal of Univ. Comp. Science*, 2010.

[26] M. Speriosu, N. Sudan, S. Upadhyay, and J. Baldridge. Twitter polarity classification with label propagation over lexical links and the follower graph. In *EMNLP*, pages 53–63, 2011.

[27] C. Tan, L. Lee, J. Tang, L. Jiang, M. Zhou, and P. Li. User-level sentiment analysis incorporating social networks. In *KDD*, 2011.

[28] H. Tang, S. Tan, and X. Cheng. A survey on sentiment detection of reviews. *Expert Systems with Applications*, 2009.

[29] K. Tsagkalidou, V. Koutsonikola, A. Vakali, and K. Kafetsios. Emotional aware clustering on micro-blogging sources. In *ACII*, 2011.

[30] M. Tsytsarau and T. Palpanas. Survey on mining subjective data on the web. *Data Mining and Knowledge Discovery Journal*, 2011.

[31] A. Tumasjan, T. O. Sprenger, P. G. Sandner, and I. M. Welpe. Predicting elections with twitter: What 140 characters reveal about political sentiment. In *ICWSM*, 2010.

[32] J. Weng, E.-P. Lim, J. Jiang, and Q. He. Twitterrank: finding topic-sensitive influential twitterers. In *WSDM*, 2010.

[33] T. Wilson and S. Raaijmakers. Comparing word, character, and phoneme n-grams for subjective utterance recognition. In *INTERSPEECH*, 2008.

[34] I. Witten and E. Frank. *Data Mining: Practical machine learning tools and techniques*. Morgan Kaufmann, 2005.

[35] J. Yang and J. Leskovec. Patterns of temporal variation in online media. In *WSDM*, pages 177–186, 2011.

Evaluation of a Domain-Aware Approach to User Model Interoperability

Eddie Walsh
Knowledge and Data
Engineering Group
Trinity College Dublin
Dublin 2, Ireland
Eddie.Walsh@scss.tcd.ie

Alexander O'Connor
Knowledge and Data
Engineering Group
Trinity College Dublin
Dublin 2, Ireland
Alex.OConnor
@scss.tcd.ie

Vincent Wade
Knowledge and Data
Engineering Group
Trinity College Dublin
Dublin 2, Ireland
Vincent.Wade@scss.tcd.ie

ABSTRACT

It is becoming increasingly important to facilitate the integrated management of user information. Exchanging user information across heterogeneous systems has many benefits, particularly in enhancing the quality and quantity of user information available for personalization. One common approach to user model interoperability is the use of mapping tools to manually build rich executable mappings between user models. A key problem with existing approaches is that the mapping tools are often too generic for these specialized tasks and do not provide any support to an administrator mapping in a specific domain such as user models. This paper presents a novel approach to user model interoperability which lowers the complexity and provides support to administrators in completing user model mappings. The domain-aware approach to user model interoperability incorporates interchangeable domain knowledge directly into the integration tools. This approach was implemented in a system called FUMES which is a mapping creation and execution environment that includes two domain-aware mechanisms; a canonical user model and user model mapping types. FUMES was deployed in an integration of existing user models and the domain-aware approach was then evaluated in a user study. The evaluation consisted of a direct comparison with a generic approach to user model interoperability which was applied using the commercial mapping tool, Altova Mapforce. The results of this evaluation demonstrate improvements in mapping accuracy and usability when using the domain-aware approach compared to the generic mapping approach.

Categories and Subject Descriptors

D.2.12 [**Software Engineering**]: Interoperability—*Data mapping*; D.2.11 [**Software Engineering**]: Software Architectures—*Domain-specific architectures*; H.5.4 [**Information Interfaces and Presentation**]: Hypertext/Hypermedia

General Terms

Design, Experimentation, Human Factors

Keywords

User Modeling, Integration, eLearning, Personalization

1. INTRODUCTION

A vast amount of information about users is now being accumulated within organizations and on the open web [13]. Within organizations such as those in the corporate, academic, medical or governmental domains, extensive user information is a central component of many systems. For example, in recent surveys 90% of responding companies use administration systems to manage human resources [24] and 79% have used or plan to use a learning management system to manage employee educational profiles [21]. Similarly, on the open web, users provide and manage their own information through the many services they use. For example, popular social networking websites such as Facebook and LinkedIn allow users to maintain extensive personal and professional profiles. In many cases, these various online systems and services are gathering information about the same user; however, this information is rarely connected and shared due to many organizational and technological boundaries [13]. Federating user information from multiple sources can potentially bring many benefits to enhance the user experience in software applications [3]. Richer and more dynamic models of the user can be constructed [20]. Sharing user information in this way can increase the knowledge of the user available to each system thereby allowing improved user-centric functionality, while at the same time reducing repetitive user interactions [29]. Potentially, the main benefit of user model federation is in the area of personalization. In this case, richer user models allow for more tailoring of content and services to the specific needs of each individual user.

As with all interoperability scenarios, there are major challenges in sharing user information effectively. Even if the user information is accessible, the heterogeneity of the various systems and their representations of user information can be significant at the structural, syntactical and semantic levels. Manual mapping techniques have often been adopted when attempting to overcome this heterogeneity [28]. Manual mapping consists of one or more mapping administrators [19] identifying and mapping equivalent attributes between data models often using custom-made translation scripts or one of the many generic mapping tools available such as Altova Mapforce [2].

However, as user models begin to exchange more expansive and detailed types of user information, the mappings that are required also become more specialized. For example, education-based user models could exchange information such as a user's identification details, social connections, learning preferences, course assessments and current competencies. This expansive user information increases the complexity of the manual mapping task requiring mapping administrators that possess increasingly specialized domain knowledge. Current generic mapping approaches and tools offer little support for domain-specific mapping tasks.

In this paper, the development and evaluation of a novel domain-aware approach to user model interoperability is presented. Domain-awareness is defined as the incorporation of domain-specific knowledge into generic tools and processes to support complex tasks in a particular domain. In this case, domain-awareness is the application of knowledge of the user domain to support the mapping of user models. The domain-aware approach is applied in the creation and execution of mappings in the form of two domain-aware mechanisms, a canonical user model and user model mapping types, which tailor the process to the user domain. The canonical user model is a consistent shared user model that all mappings are created to and the user model mapping types are mapping components specifically for creating mappings between user models. The application of the domain-aware approach in a mapping-based exchange system called FUMES is presented. Finally, a user-based evaluation of the domain-aware approach is presented which demonstrates improvements in mapping accuracy and usability when compared to a generic mapping approach.

2. RELATED WORK

A variety of approaches to provide user model interoperability have been attempted. These approaches have examined a number of key issues in this area such as the management of multiple user model exchange scenarios and the syntactic and semantic heterogeneity of user models.

The management of user model exchange between systems is generally performed using a centralized or distributed approach. In early systems, the completely centralized approach was the most common implementation in the form of the user model server [11] [23]. However, its inability to support self-contained systems led to variations on these designs that were more flexible [12] [20] [17]. Some designs for totally distributed approaches have been put forward but implementations are less common due to the complexity involved in the process [30]. Currently, the most common implementations are hybrid approaches that take aspects of both the distributed and centralized methods to create solutions that are less difficult to develop and can support independent, heterogeneous systems [28] [8] [14] [6].

When executing the exchange of user models, some of the approaches identified use a pre-runtime, administrator-initialized process [17]. Other approaches can perform the exchange in a runtime, on-demand process [28] [12] [20] [30]. In many of the approaches the exchange is performed using complete user models, however, some implement more complex exchange using user model fragments [20] [30] [17].

Most approaches provide support for multiple user models interoperability scenarios. An important aspect of this is the resolution of inconsistencies such as overlap and incompleteness of user information [3] [17]. Only a few of the approaches provide details on how they reconcile these inconsistencies [28] [8]. Some solutions include the removal of repeated and conflicting information through intelligent mappings [28]. These mappings can eliminate overlapping information based on dates or precedence. For the problem of incompleteness, no solutions were provided by these approaches. Some suggested that the exchange would sometimes result in partial user models, which few existing systems are capable of utilizing [28].

To provide syntactic interoperability of user models, the adoption of a common user model format and exchange protocol is the typical solution. Some of the research approaches use semantic web technologies such as RDF or OWL to represent the user model information [1] [28] [17] [8]. These languages provide more explicit semantics and can be used for additional benefits such as reasoning. However, the most common format to represent and extract user information from existing applications is XML [11] [16] [25]. For the transfer protocol, the most popular method is certainly the common adoption of web service technologies such as REST and SOAP [12] [8] [14].

To overcome semantic heterogeneity, standardization or mapping techniques are often used. Most of the approaches have adopted some form of a canonical model but these have been designed for different purposes. Several approaches use the canonical model as the standard to which every application should conform to provide interoperability [12] [20] [17]. This bypasses many of the semantic interoperability problems. However, many of these approaches have developed different canonical models limiting wider interoperability. Some approaches have used the canonical model as a basis to perform semantic mappings from the individual systems to a common location [28] [8]. In this way it is a means to reduce heterogeneity between different systems and control the number of mappings required [28]. This approach provides much greater potential for widespread interoperability between truly heterogeneous applications. Many approaches have developed canonical model ontologies that are based upon the main user model specifications such as IMS LIP [17], or else use GUMO [28] [20]. This, combined with the adoption of RDF or OWL as the user model format, has led to some of these approaches using ontology matching and mapping techniques.

However, few of the approaches that acknowledged the need for semantic mapping provide custom tools to aid the process. Semantic integration is generally provided by either manually writing custom integration scripts or by employing one of the current generic schema or ontology mapping tools available such as Altova Mapforce [2], COMA++ [4] and PROMPT [26]. Surveys of users of these tools have found them to be often too general and built without domain-specific mechanisms, lacking visual displays or easy to use tools, and not allowing for expressive enough mappings [18]. Some of the approaches mention that these tools provide semi-automation of the mapping process [28]. However, for the more heterogeneous user models this will likely provide limited benefits and a complex manual mapping stage will still be required [7].

Overall, these approaches are representative of the current level of progress in the field of user model interoperability.

One of the key issues that emerged was the lack of domain-specific tools to support the resolution of heterogeneity in the user models. Current mapping tools are not easy to use for this complex task and significant improvements in user model interoperability can be made by improving the integration tools and making them more suitable for domain-specific tasks.

3. DOMAIN-AWARE USER MODEL INTEROPERABILITY

The domain-aware approach incorporates domain-specific knowledge into generic tools and processes to support complex tasks in a particular domain. To apply this approach to user model interoperability, knowledge of the user domain is leveraged to support the mapping of the user models. The domain-aware approach is applied in the creation and execution of mappings in the form of two domain-aware mechanisms. These mechanisms, a canonical user model and user model mapping types, tailor the process to the user domain. The canonical user model is a shared user model representation that all mappings are created to and the user model mapping types are mapping components that are specifically designed for mapping user information and facilitating reuse. Both of these mechanisms were selected as they allow the addition of domain-awareness in key areas of the mapping process but do not significantly restrict the tool to a single domain; allowing rapid interchangeability to reuse the tools in other domains.

Some examples of other potential domain-aware mechanisms include a mapping visualization designed specifically for user model information or a specialized user model matching algorithm that derives suggestions for mappings between user models. However, in contrast with the two chosen mechanisms, these mechanisms would restrict the tool to the user model domain and require significant development effort to apply the tool in other domains. In the following sections, both of the chosen domain-aware mechanisms are described in more detail.

3.1 Canonical User Model

As a single user model standard has yet to gain widespread adoption, much research has been conducted into other methods to overcome heterogeneity. One approach that is common in other areas, such as the federation of database systems, is the provision of mappings. Mapping consists of creating direct associations between equivalent elements of individual data models. Figure 1 shows the direct mapping approach using four user models as an example. In this case, mappings are created from user model 1 to user model 2, 3 and 4 directly. Similarly, the remaining user models are all mapped to each other in this approach. For data translation, these mappings can be executed to transform the relevant data between different user model representations.

A variation of this approach takes aspects of both standardization and mapping to provide canonical model mapping. In this form, mappings are created from each user model solely to a canonical model, which provides a common representation of user model concepts. This approach is also shown in Figure 1. For data translation, the mappings can be executed to transform data into a canonical representation before transforming into the chosen target user model representation.

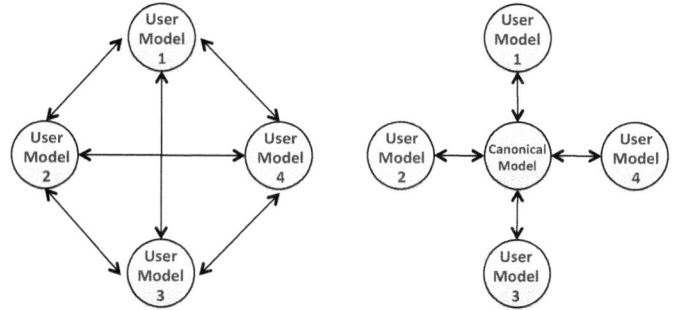

Figure 1: Direct and canonical mapping approaches

There are advantages and disadvantages to both approaches. One of the key issues is the quantity of mappings required by each approach. In the direct mapping approach, each user model is directly mapped to every other. Each time a new system is added to an interoperability scenario the number of bi-directional mappings sets required will correspond to the number of previously mapped systems. Thus, the total number of mapping sets required will increase every time a new system is added. The canonical model mapping approach results in the number of mapping sets being controlled. Each time a new application is added it only requires one bi-directional mapping to the canonical model. It is then, as a result of previous mappings to the canonical model, mapped to every other application automatically.

The quantity of mappings required raises a number of related issues. If the mappings are manually created the workload for an administrator is less when using a canonical model mapping approach rather than a direct mapping approach. The maintenance of the mappings is also affected. If the source user models are edited, the number of mappings to be changed is less in the canonical model mapping approach than in the direct mapping approach. The performance of the execution of the mappings can also be impacted upon by the quantity of mappings. As a result, the direct mapping approach is potentially slower than the canonical model approach to execute mappings for data exchange purposes.

However, the canonical model mapping approach produces new issues not present in the direct mapping approach. As a complete user model representation is infeasible, the canonical model must be editable and extensible to support a wide variety of user information. This raises the issues of evolution and management of the canonical model over time. Changes to the structure of the canonical model could potentially require changes to multiple existing mappings. This requirement for extensibility could also be a benefit of the canonical model approach as it provides more flexibility and is not as constrained as a standardized user model such as the IMS Learner Information Package (LIP) [22].

This research is focused on the application of domain-aware mechanisms to the creation and execution of mappings for the purpose of user model interoperability. As a result, the canonical model approach has been adopted for a number of key reasons.

In the creation of mappings, the canonical model approach can be used within a manual mapping tool. Using a canonical model provides consistency across multiple mapping creation scenarios and as a result can allow the visualization to be clearer and easier to navigate. This can potentially improve the manual mapping process for the administrator.

In the execution of mappings, the use of a canonical model also provides benefits in the automatic exchange of user models. The canonical model provides control of the number of mappings required in multi-system interoperability scenarios. It potentially makes the integration of a new user model much easier as a single mapping set to the canonical model is required. The lower number of mappings could also improve the overall performance of the user model interoperability.

3.2 User Model Mapping Types

Many generic mapping types have been developed to overcome heterogeneity issues and are commonly used in many mapping tools [2]. However to date, no mapping types have been developed that focus on common mapping problems in a specific domain such as user models. The development of user model mapping types is another method where domain-awareness can be applied to a commonly generic process.

From examining sample user information from a variety of educational web systems such as Sakai [27], Moodle [25], AHA! [16], CUMULATE [11] and APeLS [15] a set of common user model mapping types in the educational domain have been derived. These user model mapping types consist of core generic mapping types, which are equivalent to those in many other generic integration tools such as Mapforce, but they are combined with domain-specific information to provide an administrator with a selection of mappings that are specifically for heterogeneous user models. In the following sections, some of the most common generic mapping types are explained and in Table 1 examples of how they can be used to form user model mapping types are given.

Schema mappings are the most basic form of generic mapping and are created between the equivalent schema elements of two user models. Instance mappings allow more complex mapping of specific instance data from user model elements. Functional mappings allow generic manipulation of instance data in an exchange between user model schema elements. Types include numeric mappings which allow mathematical manipulation of numerical data, format conversions which allow manipulation of data types such as dates, and interval mappings which allow manipulation of data that contains numeric intervals.

These mapping types can also represent many-to-one, one-to-many or many-to-many relationships. For example, the schema mapping can be joined, where multiple schema elements from one user model are equivalent to one schema element in another user model, and separated, where one schema element is equivalent to multiple schema elements. Multiple instance values can also be defined as equivalent within a single mapping.

Similarly to existing integration tools, these generic mapping types can be used to construct mappings between user models. The administrator must construct the entire mapping from the start each time, identifying every required value and have a complete understanding of how it should function. However, the generic mapping types can be combined and stored with domain-specific information to create user model mapping types that are more specialized for mapping between different categories of user information. In a web-based system, these user model mapping types can be reused by the administrator or shared with other administrators to build a large collection of relevant mappings in the domain of interest.

A basic example of a user model mapping, as can be seen in Table 1, would be the conversion of a numeric grade to a text-based grade between user models where 11-20 = Pass and 0-10 = Fail. If this mapping does not already exist, it could be created using the generic interval mapping and saved as a user model mapping type, called for example "Convert grades from 0-20 to Pass/Fail". This domain-specific mapping would then be available to be reused any time this conversion was required in a user model. The administrator does not have to construct the entire mapping and can just search and select it from a list of relevant user model mappings.

Overall, the domain-aware approach to mapping has many benefits. Potentially, there would be a large amount of domain-specific mappings created in an area such as user models. In a web-based system, there is significant potential for mapping reuse, collaborative mapping and improving automatic matching based on the analysis of existing approved mappings. These domain-aware mapping types should be more relevant and easier to find and implement by an administrator who is not an expert in mapping techniques.

The generic mapping types and subsequent user model mapping types were identified using an evidence-based approach where existing education-based user models were analyzed for potentially shareable information. The selected systems are a representative sample of typical educational web systems and use many common user modeling techniques, such as the overlay approach in adaptive systems [10], that would potentially be present in other systems' user models. More mapping types are likely to be included as the analysis is expanded to other types of user data.

4. FEDERATED USER MODEL EXCHANGE SERVICE (FUMES)

Providing a means to analyze the domain-aware approach has led to the development of an interoperability system called the Federated User Model Exchange Service (FUMES) [31], shown in Figure 2. FUMES combines an administrator-led mapping creation stage with an automatic mapping execution stage to provide a comprehensive user model interoperability process. To support both stages FUMES includes two key components, the Mapping Tool and the Translation Service. Both of these components incorporate the two domain-aware mechanisms, the canonical user model and the user model mapping types, to provide greater support in the complex task of mapping heterogeneous user models.

The Mapping Tool is a graphical tool for the manual creation of mappings between user models and is shown in Figure 3. The administrator can use this tool to perform a number of tasks such as the graphical creation and testing of user model mappings. Both domain-aware mechanisms are supported within the Mapping Tool. The canonical model is used in the visual creation of the mappings. This is fundamentally different to the majority of existing mapping tools as it provides a clearer and more consistent visualization, allowing the administrator to continually map to the same user model structure. The canonical user model is based on the IMS Learner Information Package (LIP) specification

Table 1: Mapping Type Examples

Generic Mapping Type	Example
Schema equivalence	value1 = valueA
Schema join	value1 + value2 = valueA
Schema split	value1 = valueA + valueB + valueC
Instance multiple	value1[value2, value3] = valueA[valueB,valueC]
Instance join	value1[value2] + value3[value4] = valueA[valueB]
Instance split	value1[value2] = valueA[valueB] + valueC[valueD]
Numeric	value1[value2] * 100 = valueA[valueB]
Interval	value1(value2-value3) = valueA[valueB]

User Model Mapping Type	Example
Basic name equivalence	firstname = forename
Join first name & last name	firstname + lastname = fullname
Split address into sections	address = street + city + country
Convert user ids	userid[jsmith, rjones] = userid[06125,00242]
Join SQL concepts	concept[SQL1] + concept[SQL2] = concept[SQLA]
Split SQL concepts	concept[SQL1] = concept[SQLA] + concept[SQLB]
Multiply grade by 100	score[0.8] * 100 = result[80]
Convert grades from 0-20 to Pass/Fail	score[11-20,0-10] = grade[Pass,Fail]

[22]. The user model mapping types are also used in the visual creation of mappings, allowing the administrator to generate and reuse specialized user model mappings more quickly. The mappings created by the Mapping Tool are stored in the FUMES database for later use in exchanging user models between systems. The mappings are saved as XQuery, a powerful query and translation language, which allows for the easy execution of mappings to exchange between XML-based user models.

When the administrator-led mapping creation stage has been completed for a number of systems, FUMES can perform a mapping execution stage to automatically exchange user information between those systems. The central point for exchange is the Translation Service. This service handles the management of the user model interchange and translates between the various user model representations. The Translation Service uses the web service approaches REST and SOAP to allow access to heterogeneous user models and provides a means to transfer them between different systems using common technological standards. Currently, the Translation Service supports user models represented

in XML; the most commonly used format in existing web systems. In the future, case study integrations will be conducted with user models represented using semantic web technologies such as RDF and OWL. The two domain-aware mechanisms are also supported in the Translation Service. The heterogeneous user models are translated into the common canonical user model representation during exchange scenarios allowing greater control of the mapping execution. The user model mappings also allow for easier maintenance and potential performance gains, as fewer mappings are required compared to traditional mapping systems.

To date, all of the main aspects of FUMES have been developed and deployed successfully in integration scenarios with existing systems. Future work will address some key challenges in the provision of long-term user model interoperability using the domain-aware approach, specifically focusing on sharing, reuse and collaboration within the system. One of the key challenges of applying the domain-aware approach is that the required mechanisms, such as the canonical model, may not be available for new domains and will need to be developed prior to using domain-aware

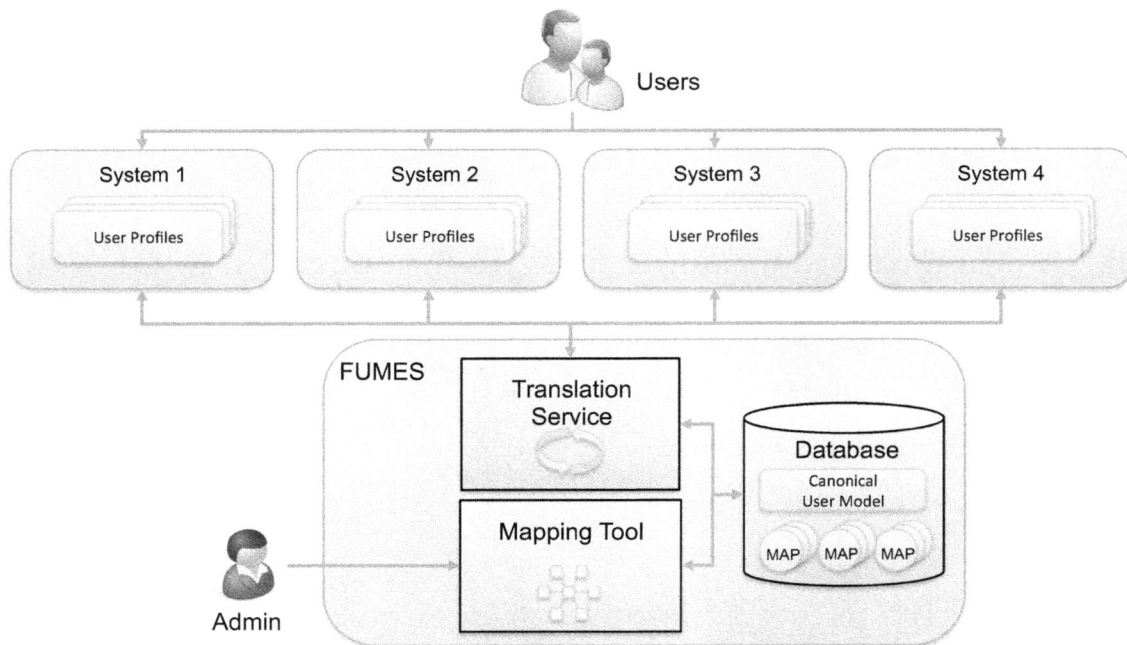

Figure 2: FUMES Architecture

integration tools. Making this process quicker and easier for administrators will be a key focus of future development of the tool, however, the adoption of web-based technologies allows administrators to easily share and reuse different canonical models. Similarly, the user model mappings can be reused by the administrator or shared with other administrators to build a large collection of relevant mappings in the domain of interest. Also, as mentioned in Section 3.1, editing and extending the canonical model is important in the integration of multiple heterogeneous user models and greater support for this will be provided in future versions of the tools, including the automatic editing of related existing mappings.

5. EVALUATION OF DOMAIN-AWARE USER MODEL INTEROPERABILITY

In the following section, a user-based evaluation of the domain-aware approach to user model interoperability is presented, consisting of the experimental setup used and results.

5.1 Experimental Setup

The evaluation of the domain-aware approach to user model interoperability consisted of a comparison of FUMES, which contains the domain-aware mechanisms, and the commercial mapping tool Altova Mapforce, in which a typical generic mapping approach was applied. Experiment participants were required to perform the mapping administrator role and complete four mapping tasks using both FUMES and Mapforce. The participants conducted the experiment individually and the order in which they used the tools was alternated to account for any learning of the tasks during the experiment. The evaluation was conducted initially with 12 participants who were all technically proficient and had limited experience in user models and mapping techniques. The overall experiment duration was two hours, one hour for the participant to use each tool. This included 20 minutes basic training in the tool using example mappings, 30 minutes completing the mapping tasks, and 10 minutes completing the feedback questionnaires.

The mapping tasks were chosen to represent typical mappings between multiple heterogeneous systems. The mapping tasks and user models were derived from existing systems and focus on general identification, assessment and competency information in the area of SQL. The four user models were retrieved from Sakai [27] and Moodle [25] which are the two most popular open source Learning Management Systems (LMS), an adaptive SQL web course based on the APeLS system [15], and a web-based user modeling system, CUMULATE [11]. The mapping tasks increase in difficulty with the third and fourth tasks being more complex and requiring more domain-specific knowledge than the first and second tasks. In order to manage the total duration of the experiment it was necessary to have a time limit associated with each task. The first and second tasks were limited to five minutes (300 seconds) and the third and fourth tasks were limited to ten minutes (600 seconds). When the time limit was reached the participants were asked to continue to the next task. The mapping tasks are described in the following sections.

Task 1 *Map forename in UM1 to its equivalent in UM4.*

This mapping task was the most basic and consisted of a direct equivalence mapping between two equal elements.

Task 2 *Map the country from address in UM3 to its equivalent in UM4.*

This mapping task was a more difficult mapping that required the tokenization of an address string and extraction of the country segment.

202

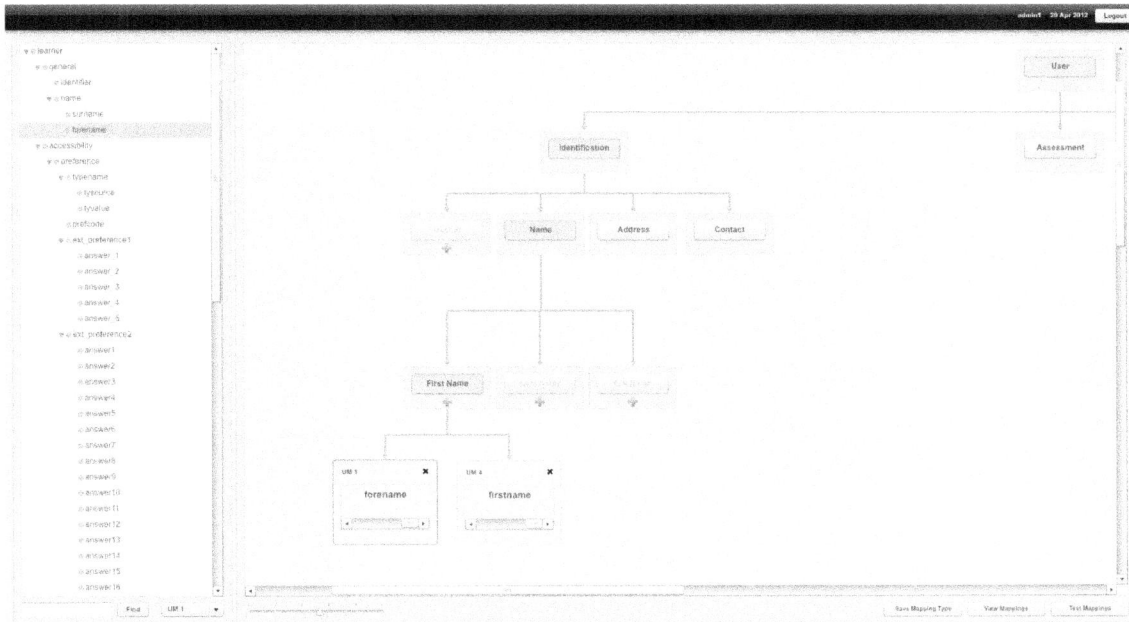

Figure 3: FUMES Mapping Tool

Task 3 *Map the finalscore for "Final Exam" in "Advanced Database Systems" in UM3 to its equivalent in UM4. Use the following to convert the finalscore: 11-20 = Pass, 0-10 = Fail.*

This mapping task was significantly more complex and involved the identification of a numeric grade within a course and its conversion to an equivalent text-based course grade.

Task 4 *Map the concept "db.tables.populate.insert" in UM1 to its equivalent numeric knowledge value in UM2. Use the following to convert the concept: concept exists = 0, concept does not exist = 1.*

This mapping task was the most complex and involved checking for the existence of a text-based competency and its conversion to a numeric knowledge value.

The mapping tasks represented the identification, creation and verification of executable mappings between existing systems that could be used in a real user model exchange scenario. Each of these tasks required the participants to examine the user models, identify the appropriate section of the source and target user models, select the appropriate mapping type, and construct and test the mapping.

When using FUMES the participants used the domain-aware approach represented by the domain-aware mechanisms, the canonical user model and user model mapping types. The canonical model in the experiment is based on the IMS LIP specification [22] and represents general identification, assessment and competency information in the area of SQL. To complete the tasks, 25 user model mapping types were provided in FUMES which represented typical mappings in user models in the area of identification, assessment and competencies. In Mapforce, the participants used a generic approach and mapped directly between the user models using a selection of 10 relevant generic mapping types to construct the mapping tasks.

5.2 Results

In the following section, the results from the experiment are presented and analyzed. This includes an analysis of the accuracy and duration of the mapping tasks and an analysis of the overall usability of the mapping tool.

5.2.1 Mapping Accuracy and Duration

In this section the results of the mapping tasks in both FUMES and Mapforce are compared for accuracy and duration.

To analyze the accuracy a gold standard for each mapping task was created. The gold standard consisted of the various stages involved in successfully completing the mappings in both tools. For each stage of each task an accuracy score was given; 0 for incomplete or major errors, 0.5 for minor errors or 1 for completed stages. The overall mean of these stages was then used to calculate a percentage accuracy score for each individual task and for the tasks overall.

As can been seen in Figure 4, task 1 had 100% accuracy in both tools. This demonstrates that users can perform basic equivalence mappings in both tools equally well. For task 2, there is a difference in accuracy of 33%, in task 3 it is 30% and in task 4 it is 20%. The decline in the difference could indicate that it takes longer to learn how to map accurately using the generic approach in Mapforce.

There was an overall difference in accuracy across all tasks of 29%. Paired t-tests were carried out on the accuracy results and showed there is a statistically significant difference in accuracy ($p<0.001$) between the domain-aware approach in FUMES and the generic approach using Mapforce. These results represent the mapping task accuracy within the specified time limits. It is possible that higher levels of accuracy would be achievable in these tools if there were no time limits applied.

To analyze the duration of the mapping tasks, the average time taken in both FUMES and Mapforce to perform each of

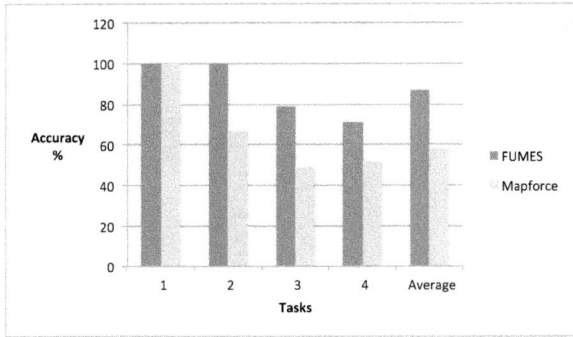

Figure 4: Task Accuracy Results

the mapping tasks was recorded. Each task had a time limit to control the overall duration of the experiment. The first and second tasks were limited to five minutes (300 seconds) and the third and fourth tasks were limited to ten minutes (600 seconds).

As can be seen in Figure 5, the first task is completed much faster in Mapforce (47% of the allotted time in FUMES vs 26% in Mapforce). The likely reason for this is because, in Mapforce, no complex mapping components were required for this task and the mapping could be created using a simple line connector between the equivalent parts of the user model. FUMES uses the canonical model mapping approach which, in these tasks, requires two mappings to the canonical model for every one direct mapping in generic approach. Task 2 is completed faster in FUMES (68% of the allotted time in FUMES vs 96% in Mapforce). This indicates that participants took longer to learn how to use the generic mapping types in Mapforce. Durations for task 3 (90% of the allotted time in FUMES vs 89% in Mapforce) and task 4 (81% of the allotted time in FUMES vs 90% in Mapforce) are much closer indicating that the most complex mappings were difficult to fully complete in both tools.

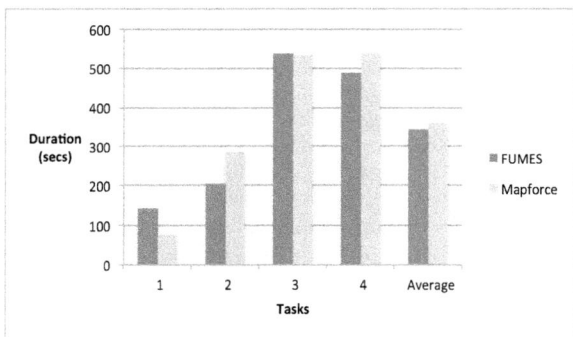

Figure 5: Task Duration Results

The average time spent on all the mapping tasks in FUMES is 76% of the maximum allotted time compared to 80% in Mapforce. Paired t-tests show that this is not a statistically significant difference ($p > 0.05$) so we can not conclude that mapping is faster using the domain-aware approach. However, a similar amount of time is required to perform the mapping task in both tools. This result is important because, as described in Section 3.1, the canonical model approach requires more mappings than the direct approach

initially. However, as the number of systems increases, the canonical approach will require less mappings than the direct approach. Therefore the canonical model approach would almost certainly be faster than the direct approach when creating larger numbers of mappings between user models.

5.2.2 Mapping Tool Usability

Following the analysis of the accuracy and duration of the mapping tasks, the overall usability of both tools was analyzed. This was a questionnaire-based analysis consisting of a System Usability Scale (SUS) [9] study followed by a series of custom task and tool related questions.

SUS is a widely used and reliable questionnaire tool for measuring the usability of a variety of products and services. It generates a single value that can be used to determine the usability of an individual system and to compare the usability of multiple systems. To determine the relative value of the SUS score an adjective rating scale can be applied [5]. FUMES obtained a SUS score of 72 that indicates a "good" level of usability and Mapforce obtained a score of 50 that indicates "ok" usability.

Following the SUS study, the participants were asked a number of custom task and tool related questions. The responses are summarized in Figure 6. For all of these questions a more positive response was recorded when using FUMES compared to Mapforce. The participants stated that it was easier to complete the tasks in FUMES and that they found FUMES more helpful. They also found it easier to navigate the user models, and to identify, create and test mappings using FUMES.

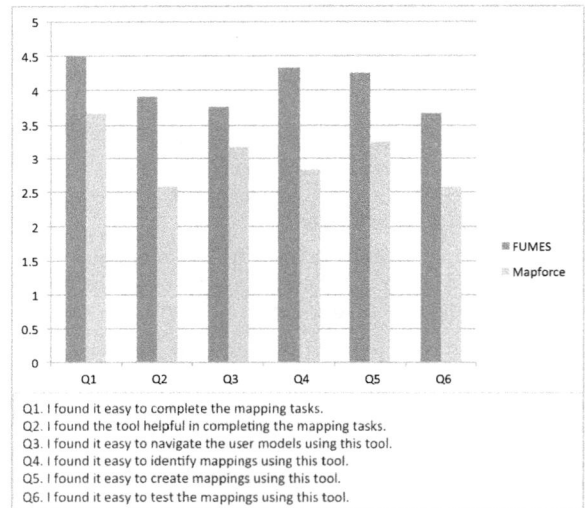

Q1. I found it easy to complete the mapping tasks.
Q2. I found the tool helpful in completing the mapping tasks.
Q3. I found it easy to navigate the user models using this tool.
Q4. I found it easy to identify mappings using this tool.
Q5. I found it easy to create mappings using this tool.
Q6. I found it easy to test the mappings using this tool.

Figure 6: Task Related Results

To gain further understanding of how the participants viewed both tools a number of open questions were also presented to the participants. The participants were asked which aspects of the tools they liked. For FUMES the most common responses were the general ease-of-use of the user interface and the ability to use user model mapping types. For Mapforce, the most common responses were the navigation and drag and drop functionality and the ability to create and link mapping types.

The participants were also asked what aspects of the tools

they disliked. In this case, the most common responses for FUMES were related to the layout, buttons and xml viewing in the testing area. For Mapforce, the most common responses were selecting mapping types and creating mappings and the cluttered user interface when there are multiple mappings between user models.

Finally, participants were asked to directly compare the mapping approaches (i.e. direct mapping or canonical model mapping) and mapping creation (i.e. generic mapping types or user model mapping types) of the two tools. 67% of participants stated that they found the FUMES mapping approach easier to use. The most common comments were that it was easier to create mappings in the user model domain using the canonical model. However, some noted the domain-specific nature of the user interface and questioned its applicability to other domains. 33% of participants also stated that they preferred the direct mapping approach with most comments stating that they found that approach more intuitive. 100% of participants stated that they found it easier to create mappings in FUMES. The most common comments were that the user model mappings were more relevant and easier to use.

6. DISCUSSION

The results provided by the user study have generated a number of interesting insights into the impact of the domain-aware approach to user model interoperability.

Mapforce was chosen to deploy a generic mapping approach in this experiment as it was one of the best mapping tools available and one of the few tools which could create and execute the required complex mappings. Its graphical interface was also more independent of any translation language and did not require the administrator to have specific skills to start mapping. Mapforce is a large commercial tool and contains many more features than were used in this experiment. However, the results of the experiment demonstrate that for mapping tasks in a restricted domain, the domain-aware approach in FUMES performs better than the generic approach when using Mapforce.

The domain-aware approach in FUMES provides a significant increase in accuracy and has similar mapping duration except in the case of the most basic equivalence mappings. Many of these basic equivalence mappings could also potentially be completed through the introduction of an automatic matching tool which will be incorporated into FUMES in the future. Across the tasks, there is a decrease in the accuracy difference between tools indicating that Mapforce may take longer to learn how to use. There is a significant increase in duration of mappings from more simple mappings to more complex mappings. The more complex mappings took approximately three times longer than the more basic mappings. This suggests that mapping tools should provide more support in the completion of complex mappings.

The domain-aware approach in FUMES also provides better usability than the generic approach in Mapforce. This was demonstrated using both the SUS questionnaire and the tool and task related questions. It is possible that some of the recorded improvement in usability was as a result of the general layout and appearance of the user interface. However, this is likely to be negligible as the most significant differences in the design of FUMES when compared to Mapforce result from the use of the domain-aware mechanisms.

While the mapping accuracy and duration analysis was focused on assessing the overall impact of the domain-aware approach on user model mapping, the usability study also gave some insights into the impact of the individual domain-aware mechanisms. The answers and comments from the participants clearly state that the user model mapping types were preferred to the generic mapping types although some users preferred the flexibility of linking different mapping types in Mapforce. The use of the canonical model mapping approach was also preferred but not as conclusively. One third of users preferred the direct mapping approach used in Mapforce which suggests that further analysis may be required in order to determine if the canonical model approach is suitable for all users in all interoperability scenarios.

Overall, the evaluation has provided interesting insights into many aspects of the domain-aware approach. However, there are also other areas where experimentation could be performed in the future to examine the approach in further detail. These include examining the performance of users with varying skill sets, investigating the evolution of the domain-aware mechanisms over time with a small group of long-term users, and examining use in other domains.

7. CONCLUSIONS

This paper has described the development and evaluation of a novel approach to user model interoperability called the domain-aware approach. This approach differs from existing generic approaches by incorporating domain knowledge in tools and processes to support complex mapping tasks in specific domains. For user model interoperability, this approach is encapsulated in a system called FUMES. FUMES supports the creation of mappings between heterogeneous user models and the execution of those mappings to exchange user models between multiple systems. The domain-aware approach is provided in FUMES through two mechanisms: a canonical user model and user model mapping types. Both of these components provide domain knowledge that can support an administrator in the complex task of mapping user models.

The evaluation of the domain-aware approach in FUMES consisted of a direct comparison with a generic approach to user model mapping using an existing commercial mapping tool, Altova Mapforce. This evaluation took the form of a user study which examined both tools for mapping accuracy, duration and overall usability. The results of the evaluation were presented and they demonstrated that the domain-aware approach provides significant improvements in accuracy and usability while maintaining the speed of the majority of the mapping process. Overall, the results demonstrate that incorporating domain knowledge within the tools and processes allows administrators to perform better in what is typically the very complex and difficult task of mapping user models.

8. ACKNOWLEDGMENTS

This work is conducted within the AMAS (Adaptive Media and Services for Dynamic Personalization) research project which is funded by Science Foundation Ireland via grant 08/IN.1/I2103. The goal of AMAS is to research and develop innovative techniques and technologies to support dynamic, integrated adaptivity and personalization of web media and services to enable rich repurposing of existing content and web services.

9. REFERENCES

[1] F. Abel, N. Henze, E. Herder, and D. Krause. Interweaving public user profiles on the web. In P. D. Bra, A. Kobsa, and D. N. Chin, editors, *User Modeling, Adaptation and Personalization*, volume 6075 of *Lecture Notes in Computer Science*, pages 16–27. Leibnitz University, Springer, 2010.

[2] Altova. Mapforce. http://www.altova.com/mapforce.html, 2011.

[3] L. Aroyo, P. Dolog, A. Naeve, M. Nilsson, and F. Wild. Interoperability in Personalized Adaptive Learning. *Educational Technology & Society*, 9(2):4–18, 2006.

[4] D. Aumueller, H.-H. Do, S. Massmann, and E. Rahm. Schema and ontology matching with COMA++. In *Proceedings of the 2005 ACM SIGMOD international conference on Management of data - SIGMOD '05*, page 906, New York, USA, 2005. ACM Press.

[5] A. Bangor, T. Staff, P. Kortum, and J. Miller. Determining What Individual SUS Scores Mean : Adding an Adjective Rating Scale. *Journal of Usability Studies*, 4(3):114–123, 2009.

[6] S. Berkovsky, T. Kuflik, and F. Ricci. Mediation of user models for enhanced personalization in recommender systems. *User Modeling and User-Adapted Interaction*, 18(3):245–286, Nov. 2007.

[7] P. A. Bernstein and S. Melnik. Model management 2.0: Manipulating Richer Mappings. In *Proceedings of the 2007 ACM SIGMOD international conference on Management of data - SIGMOD '07*, page 1, New York, New York, USA, 2007. ACM Press.

[8] M. Bielikova and J. Kuruc. Sharing user models for adaptive hypermedia applications. *5th International Conference on Intelligent Systems Design and Applications (ISDA'05)*, pages 506–511, 2005.

[9] J. Brooke. SUS-A quick and dirty usability scale. *Usability evaluation in industry*, Sept. 1996.

[10] P. Brusilovsky and E. Millán. User models for adaptive hypermedia and adaptive educational systems. *The adaptive web*, pages 3–53, 2007.

[11] P. Brusilovsky, S. Sosnovsky, and O. Shcherbinina. User modeling in a distributed e-learning architecture. *User Modeling 2005*, (0310576):387–391, 2005.

[12] P. Brusilovsky, S. Sosnovsky, and M. Yudelson. Ontology-based framework for user model interoperability in distributed learning environments. In *World Conference on E-Learning, E-Learn*, pages 2851–2855, 2005.

[13] F. Carmagnola, F. Cena, and C. Gena. User model interoperability: a survey. *User Modeling and User-Adapted Interaction*, 21(3):285–331, Feb. 2011.

[14] F. Cena and R. Furnari. A soa-based framework to support user model interoperability. In *Adaptive Hypermedia and Adaptive Web-Based Systems*, pages 284–287. Springer, 2008.

[15] O. Conlan and V. Wade. Evaluation of APeLS - An Adaptive eLearning Service Based on the Multi-Model, Metadata-Driven Approach. In P. De Bra and W. Nejdl, editors, *Third International Conference on Adaptive Hypermedia and Adaptive Web-Based Systems (AH2004)*, pages 291–295. Springer Berlin / Heidelberg, 2004.

[16] P. De Bra, A. Aerts, B. Berden, B. De Lange, B. Rousseau, T. Santic, D. Smits, and N. Stash. AHA! The adaptive hypermedia architecture. *Proceedings of the fourteenth ACM conference on Hypertext and hypermedia HYPERTEXT 03*, 4(1):81–84, 2003.

[17] P. Dolog and M. Schäfer. Learner modeling on the semantic web. In *Proceedings of Personalisation on the Semantic Web Workshop (PerSWeb) at the 10th International Conference on User Modelling 2005*, volume 5, Edinburgh, Scotland, 2005.

[18] S. Falconer, N. Noy, and M.-a. Storey. Ontology mapping-a user survey. In *Proceedings of the Workshop on Ontology Matching (OM2007) at ISWC/ASWC2007, Busan, South Korea*, 2007.

[19] B. Haslhofer. A Comparative Study of Mapping Solutions for Enabling Metadata Interoperability, 2008.

[20] D. Heckmann, T. Schwartz, B. Brandherm, and A. Kröner. Decentralized user modeling with UserML and GUMO. In *Decentralized, Agent Based and Social Approaches to User Modeling, Workshop DASUM-05 at 9th International Conference on User Modelling, UM2005*, pages 61–66. Citeseer, 2005.

[21] IMC (UK) Learning Ltd. Learning Management Systems - are organisations making the most of them? Technical report, IMC (UK) Learning Ltd, 2010.

[22] IMS Global Learning Consortium. IMS Learner Information Package Specification. http://www.imsglobal.org/profiles/, 2011.

[23] J. Kay and B. Kummerfeld. Personis: a server for user models. In *Adaptive Hypermedia and Adaptive Web-Based Systems*, pages 203–212, 2002.

[24] L. Martin. CedarCrestone 2010-2011 HR Systems Survey Highlights. Technical report, 2011.

[25] Moodle. Moodle. http://moodle.org/, 2011.

[26] N. F. Noy and M. A. Musen. The PROMPT suite: interactive tools for ontology merging and mapping. *International Journal of Human-Computer Studies*, 59(6):983–1024, Dec. 2003.

[27] Sakai. Sakai. http://sakaiproject.org/, 2011.

[28] K. Van Der Sluijs and G.-j. Houben. A generic component for exchanging user models between web-based systems. *International Journal of Continuing Education and Lifelong Learning*, 16:64–76, 2006.

[29] J. Vassileva. Distributed user modelling for universal information access. *International Journal of Human-Computer Interaction*, pages 122–126, 2001.

[30] J. Vassileva, G. McCalla, and J. Greer. Multi-agent multi-user modeling in I-Help. *User Modeling and User-Adapted Interaction*, 13(1):179–210, 2002.

[31] E. Walsh, A. O'Connor, and V. Wade. Supporting Learner Model Exchange in Educational Web Systems. *7th International Conference on Web Information Systems and Technologies*, 2011.

Learning User Characteristics from Social Tagging Behavior

Karin Schöfegger
Knowledge Management
Institute
Graz University of Technology
Graz, Austria
k.schoefegger@gmail.com

Christian Körner
Knowledge Management
Institute
Graz University of Technology
Graz, Austria
christian.koerner@tugraz.at

Philipp Singer
Knowledge Management
Institute
Graz University of Technology
Graz, Austria
philipp.singer@tugraz.at

Michael Granitzer
Chair of Media Informatics
University of Passau
Passau, Germany
Michael.Granitzer@uni-passau.de

ABSTRACT

In social tagging systems the tagging activities of users leave a huge amount of implicit information about them. The users choose tags for the resources they annotate based on their interests, background knowledge, personal opinion and other criteria. Whilst existing research in mining social tagging data mostly focused on gaining a deeper understanding of the user's interests and the emerging structures in those systems, little work has yet been done to use the rich implicit information in tagging activities to unveil to what degree users' tags convey information about their background. The automatic inference of user background information can be used to complete user profiles which in turn supports various recommendation mechanisms. This work illustrates the application of supervised learning mechanisms to analyze a large online corpus of tagged academic literature for extraction of user characteristics from tagging behavior. As a representative example of background characteristics we mine the user's research discipline. Our results show that tags convey rich information that can help designers of those systems to better understand and support their prolific users - users that tag actively - beyond their interests.

Categories and Subject Descriptors

H.1.2 [**User/Machine Systems**]: Human Factors; H.1.2 [**Information Systems**]: Models and Principles—*Human information processing*; H.4 [**Information Systems Applications**]: Miscellaneous

General Terms

Algorithms, Human Factors

Keywords

tagging, user background, social software

1. INTRODUCTION

Tagging provides an easy and intuitive way for users to annotate, organize and re-find resources. For this reason a huge number of systems have added tagging functionality. To give some examples: *Delicious* is a social bookmarking platform that enables users to apply tags in order to organize their websites, *YouTube* allows content creators to assign tags such that their videos can be found more easily later on and *Mendeley* a platform were users can annotate their papers by using tags. While in recent years a lot of research investigated social tagging systems and the resulting folksonomic structure or mined the user's interests to support personalization in those systems, there still exists little information about how users' background (e.g., research discipline, gender, location, ...) becomes manifested in their used tags. This is mainly due to a lack of profile information in social tagging datasets (see the call for social tagging datasets by Körner et al. [4] for details). Subsequently little is known about how users' background information is reflected in the tags used.

In this work we explore to what degree users' tags convey information about their characteristics in the setting of social tagging systems for academic publications. According to Brusilovsky et al. [2] or Webb et al. [11], one of the most popular user characteristics modeled in adaptive hypermedia as well as web personalization besides user interest and knowledge is *personal information* (or user background). This user background is usually defined as rather static information such as demographics (e.g., name, age, gender, location) or information about the user's profession, area of work, job responsibilities etc. This background information is usually provided explicitly by the user.

In the academic setting, a user's research discipline is an important piece of background information to improve e.g., recommendations and information retrieval, which is why we chose this as a representative example to illustrate the automatic inference based on tagging data. To investigate how information about the user's background can be deducted from tagging data, we use a snapshot of the Mendeley[1] system. We train a classifier to detect a user's discipline based on his/her previous tagging activities. In our experiments we generated various classification settings and showed that we can achieve reasonable results by using a Naive Bayes classifier. Nevertheless, there are still some obstacles - such as overlapping tag representations of disciplines - that limit the performance of the classification task and leave room for future improvements.

Our work is relevant for designers, data analysts and researchers who are interested in the analysis of user behavior in social tagging systems as well as researchers who want to gather further information about the user-base of these systems.

2. RELATED WORK

Whilst inferring interest form tagging behavior to create and maintain a user model has already been tackled in various works by e.g. Yeung et al. [13], Stoynachvich et al. [10] or Michlmayr and Cayzer [6], mining other user characteristics has yet to be taken up by the research community. The work of Popescu et al. [8] is to the best of our knowledge the only publication that deals with inferring user characteristics from tags. In this work, a large dataset of Flickr[2] was analyzed to unveil personal information such as gender or home location of a user.

The majority of existing approaches that mine user characteristics is based on data such as search queries or web server logs. In information retrieval it is well researched that search keywords can be used to infer background information of users (see e.g. Baeza-Yates [1]). Weber et al. [12] present approaches to infer demographic background information such as gender, income, or race. The authors provide a demographic description of a large sample of search engine users in the US and show that it agrees well with the distribution of the US population. This work also highlights differences in search behavior of specific user classes. Jansen et al. [3] present approaches to identify a user's location, geographical interest, topic and level of interest or commercial intent.

A closely related research area is the automated categorization (or classification) of texts into predefined categories where texts are usually represented as a bag of (extracted) keywords. Sebastiani [9] for example provides a concise review of machine learning approaches for text classification, approaches applying social tags for text classification are presented e.g. in Zubiaga et al. [15] or in Noll and Meinel [7]. The work of Yin et al. [14] tackles the more general case of classifying web objects which do not necessarily need to contain any textual content.

3. TERMINOLOGY

Social Tagging refers to the act of assigning keywords (so called "tags") to resources. The corresponding tripartite

structure (user, tags and resources) that emerges over time is commonly known as *folksonomy*. A restriction of a folksonomy to one single user is known as a *personomy*. Usually, U refers to the set of users, R to the set of resources and T to the set of distinct tags in a folksonomy. The set of tags in a folksonomy (or personomy) is called collaborative (or personal) tag space. The set of resources a user annotated is named his/her user library. In this context, the following definitions are used throughout this work:

A *User model $UM(u)$* is a machine readable representation of a personomy. We define a user model $UM(u_i)$ of user $u \in U$ as a set of weighted tags (the tags he/she used to annotate publications):

$$UM(u_j) = (t_1, w(t_1, u_j)), (t_2, w(t_2, u_j)), \\ ..., (t_n^d, w(t_n, u_j)) \tag{1}$$

where the weight $w(t_i, u_j)$ of a tag t_i with respect to the user u_j is given by a certain weighting function w and T and U denote the set of tags and users respectively. Often, the weight is given by the frequency how often the user has used this tag, but we also test in addition to that binary values indication whether or not the user has used this tag. For our experiments we test values of a parameter k, which means that the users of our dataset need to contain at least k tags. Correspondingly, the datasets are named $_k$ throughout this work where k varies between $1, 5, 10, 15, 20, 25$.

A *Discipline representation $DR(d)$* is defined as a set of tags, which are identified through the tag assignments of users who explicitly self-assigned themselves into a specific discipline. As thus the number of tags representing a discipline grows rather large, we limited for some of our experiments the tag space in the following way: We constructed for each discipline a tag ranking and limited this list to the top-dr tags. The tag rankings we tested were (a) *POP*: tag popularity as measured by tag frequency for documents within a research discipline and (b) *TfIdf* value of a tag (in analogy to TfIdf value for tags assigned to a document). Formally, a discipline $d_j \in D$ is represented by a set of weighted tags:

$$DR(d_j) = (t_1, w(t_1, d_j)), (t_2, w(t_2, d_j)), \\ ..., (t_n^d, w(t_n, d_j)) \tag{2}$$

4. LEARNING USER CHARACTERISTICS FROM TAGGING BEHAVIOR

Our aim is to illustrate the automatic inference of user background information from tagging activities. This can be seen as a supervised learning setting: Given a user's tag annotations as an input, we want to train a classifier to correctly identify the user's research discipline. More formally, given a list of user models as input samples $I = \{UM(u_1), UM(u_2), ...UM(u_n)\}$, we want to learn the function

$$g_D : T \to D \tag{3}$$

which maps each user model $UM(u_i)$ correctly to a corresponding research discipline $d_i(u_i) \in D$, where D denotes the set of possible research disciplines D=$\{d_1, ...d_d\}$.

In machine learning, a wide range of possible supervised learning algorithms are available, each with its strength and weaknesses. As we have a similar approach as text classification, our intuition was that a *Naive Bayes* classifier (see

[1] http://www.mendeley.com
[2] http://www.flickr.com

section 4.2) should perform well, because this is an established method for such problems. To find the best performing classifier for our datasets at hand, we have tested and compared Naive Bayes to other supervised machine learning techniques such as *Support Vector Machines* (SVM), *Logistic Regression* and *Stochastic Gradient Descent*. To find the best parameters for each classification model we performed grid search with nested cross validation tuning the classification for the best weighted average F1-score over all available classes (each class represents a research disciplines). We show our best model estimation and results in section 5 and our final model has been analyzed using a stratified 2-fold cross validation.

4.1 Datasets

We used a tagging snapshot of the reference management software and social academic network Mendeley for our experiments. The data set is a large scale subset from data available in their data repository, which was anonymized to avoid privacy issues. It consists of $24,388,545$ tag assignments by $75,204$ users of the system (each user in our dataset has explicitly added information about his/her research discipline) with $2,272,530$ distinct tags for $4,639,558$ resources. The only pre-processing step applied to the dataset was to lower case the tags to merge similar tags such as 'book' and 'Book'.

Ground Truth for Supervised Learning. In Mendeley, users have to sign up in order to be able to use all available functionalities of the system. During this process, they are encouraged to add their background information such as research discipline, institution, position, location or gender. In this work, we focus on research discipline as a prime example for users' background information. Having access to this explicitly added information about a user's background in addition to his/her tagging activities provides us with unique and large-scale ground truth data. Table 1 lists the main research disciplines currently found in the Mendeley system as well as the number of users per discipline in our snapshot.

4.2 Naive Bayes

At the core of each classification task is a learning algorithm that trains the classifier. As mentioned, we tested several algorithms and for our dataset, Naive Bayes outperformed each of the other approaches on our datasets (see section 5). A Naive Bayes algorithm has the "naive" assumption that every feature pair of a class is independent, even though that is not always the case in a real world scenario. More formally, the probability of a feature vector $x_1, ..., x_n$ belonging to class y can now be stated as follows (cf. [5]):

$$P(y|x_1, ..., x_n) \propto P(y) \prod_{i=1}^{n} P(x_i|y) \qquad (4)$$

In our case, for each training sample, the feature vector $x_1, ..., x_n$ represents the user model $UM(u)$ and class y is the user's research discipline. $P(y|x_1, ..., x_n)$ can be seen as a measure of how much evidence $x_1, ..., x_n$ contributes that y is the correct discipline [5]. There are two basic ways we can use Naive Bayes classifiers in text classification that differ in the assumption they take regarding the distribution of $P(y|x_1, ..., x_n)$. The first one is the *Multinomial Naive Bayes* that works best with tag frequency counts and TfIdf

Table 1: Overview of Mendeley disciplines and their occurrences in our dataset

Nr.	Discipline	Users
1	Arts and Literature	1,306
2	Astronomy/Astrophysics/Space Science	614
3	Biological Sciences	13,879
4	Business Administration	2,183
5	Chemistry	2,724
6	Computer and Information Science	12,710
7	Earth Sciences	1,596
8	Economics	1,734
9	Education	2,726
10	Electrical and Electronic Engineering	2,549
11	Engineering	4,898
12	Environmental Sciences	2,317
13	Humanities	1,827
14	Law	562
15	Linguistics	645
16	Management Science/Operations Research	938
17	Materials Science	1,118
18	Mathematics	990
19	Medicine	5,603
20	Philosophy	696
21	Physics	4,028
22	Psychology	3,408
23	Social Sciences	5,353
24	Sports and Recreation	210
25	Design	581

values (see our description of discipline representations in section 3). On the other hand the *Multivariate Bernoulli Naive Bayes* works with binary feature values - i.e., stating if the tag does or does not occur in the user model.

Table 2: Number of samples of each complete discipline dataset and results of the discipline classification experiment for the test set using our best performing Naive Bayes classifier.

Data	Samples	Features	Prec	Recall	F1	Baseline F1
min25	21,857	1,109,051	0.59	0.60	0.59	0.07
min20	24,777	1,114,364	0.58	0.59	0.58	0.07
min15	28,632	1,121,893	0.58	0.59	0.58	0.07
min10	34,674	1,170,320	0.57	0.58	0.56	0.06
min5	46,212	1,139,839	0.54	0.55	0.54	0.06
all	75,195	1,191,013	0.47	0.47	0.45	0.06

5. EXPERIMENT

The research question we want to answer is the following: Given the user model of a user in form of a tag vector, is it possible to automatically infer the user's research discipline? For training and testing, the ground truth for the supervised learning algorithm is the self-assigned Mendeley discipline category (see table 1).

We applied Naive Bayes on several possible datasets: (a) In the basic setting we use the complete user model, thus all tags used by the users create the feature space for our supervised learning mechanism. (b) We limit the user models in the dataset to users with a minimum amount of tags as a 'richer' user model improves the amount of information available to classify a user into a discipline, thus results of the classification task should increase. (c) In a large scale setting this can be computationally intensive, thus we tried several discipline representations as described in section 3 which limits the user models and tag space to the tags available in the discipline representations.

All these datasets (b) (c) are variations of our basic dataset in (a) to find the best performing setting.

In our performed experiment to learn the user's discipline our first intuition that Naive Bayes should perform the best has been approved (data not shown as our main intention was to show that it is possible to successfully train a classifier to automatically infer the user's discipline), thus the observations described in the following refer to this setting. The results show that the best way to represent the feature space is to use TfIdf feature values instead of using just the tag occurrence or - as a further refinement - binarize our feature values. Interestingly it is not useful to limit our datasets based on different discipline representations or restrict the user models to contain at least k tags from the tags used for the discipline representations. This shows us that the classification task is performing well for small datasets but even very large representations and user models are very useful and it is not necessary to restrict them. However restriction of the discipline representations can be useful in order to improve your classifier results. It is always necessary to try out different restrictions and find a good balance between dataset size and classification results. In order to verify that many features do not falsify our classification task we applied a χ^2 feature selection method to our datasets, but this also did not provide any better results than taking the complete feature and user space. The best model for both of our dataset at hand is the Multinomial Naive Bayes classifier. In the rest of this section the results of the experiment will be explained.

Table 2 lists our applied datasets and the corresponding precision, recall and weighted f1-score for our final Naive Bayes classifier. For comparison of the performance of our classification model, we also show the baseline weighted f1-score when classifying every sample to the most frequent discipline. We chose not to limit our datasets any further because of removing even more users. The results show that it is necessary to apply some sort of activity restriction to the dataset to achieve useful results. Activity restriction refers to remove non-active taggers, leaving only the prolific users in the dataset. This becomes obvious when comparing the result from the dataset without an activity restriction (named 'all' dataset in the table) to the ones with an activity level. The rest of this section will focus on the dataset with a minimum restriction of 25 used tags per user (min25), because we could achieve the best results while we still have a good amount of users for the training and test set (approximately 11,000 each).

Figure 1 illustrates the confusion matrix for the test set applied to our trained classifier. The confusion matrix shows the percentage of each true class (represented in rows and stating the real chosen research discipline of a user) to be classified as a corresponding predicted discipline in a column. The disciplines stated in table 1 are represented by their IDs. As one can see the majority of users get classified into their correct class. However, the problem is that there is often the case that disciplines - especially ones that just have a few user samples - get classified wrongly into disciplines with ID 3, 6 and 23. These classes are the ones that are the most frequent in our dataset and this is a result of the high skewness in our data. A more equally distributed dataset would most likely lead to better results (see Table 1); we did not do that as this would have reduced the number of samples in our data significantly.

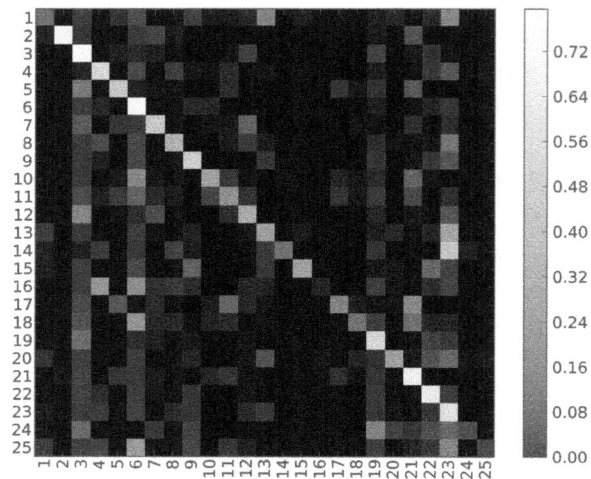

Figure 1: Confusion matrix for discipline classification - Percentage of true class in rows

In some cases it is possible that two classes share a similar tag vocabulary (the discipline representations overlap to a large extent) and therefore the classifier cannot differentiate samples of those classes correctly. To give an example: Figure 1 shows that disciplineID 16 (Management Science/Operations Research) often gets identified as class 4 (Business Administration). The classifier results indicate that similar tags are the most indicative for both disciplines and these two disciplines are also similar in a real environment. Table 3 shows the top 10 discriminative tags for the five most common disciplines obtained by our classifier in the min25 dataset.

6. CONCLUSION AND FUTURE WORK

This paper gives insight into the first endeavor of classifying users into research disciplines based on their tagging vocabulary. For this purpose we tested several regarding learning algorithms, minimal length of a user model, different research discipline representations and various activity restrictions. Naive Bayes classification outperformed other supervised machine learning algorithms for our discipline classification task. While these experiments still have some issues such as overlapping disciplines (i.e., disciplines which are thematically very close and are thus described by a relatively large overlapping set of tags), the overall performance shows well that it is possible to extract background information from a user's personomy. A potential method to improve the process of identification of user properties might be to cluster tags in order to segregate overlapping classes.

Another observation we made was that the limitation of the dataset to tags from discipline representation instead of the complete set of tags as features for the learning algorithm does not influence the results significantly. Thus when dealing with large data, it is reasonable to work with representations (e.g. top 100 tags of a research discipline) instead of the complete set of features available.

We performed our experiments on a Mendeley snapshot which includes researchers, librarians and people generally interested in research articles. While we believe that our approach generalizes on other datasets, the results of the

Table 3: Top-10 tags determined by our Naive Bayes classifier for the five most used disciplines in our test set of the min25 dataset.

Discipline	#Users	Top-10 Tags
Biological Sciences	2,258	genome, dna, mutation, mice, cancer, humans, phylogeny, animals, evolution, review
Computer and Information Science	1,629	semantic web, visualization, machine learning, web, evaluation, security, ontology, design, clustering, survey
Social Sciences	890	africa, politics, education, culture, policy, globalization, democracy, history, identity, gender
Medicine	833	review, prognosis, adolescent, risk factors, aged, middle aged, humans, female, adult, male
Engineering	626	thesis, heat transfer, cfd, model, modelling, control, optimization, modeling, review, simulation

application of this method on more broad themed tagging systems is a topic of future work. We furthermore plan to tune the algorithm to perform better as well as to further investigate the identification of other profile properties (such as gender, country of origin, profession etc.). We applied the approach described in this work for research disciplines straightforward also to identify gender and profession but as those results were not satisfying, additional features other than the list of used tags will be necessary.

Potential applications of this research are recommendation engines that lack user background information, the discovery of user communities based on implicit user background. With this work we hope to have created a good starting point to investigate the extraction of user background information from tagging behavior.

7. ACKNOWLEDGMENTS

This work has been funded by the European Commission as part of the FP7 Marie Curie IAPP project TEAM (grant no. 251514) and FP7 ICT project IntelLEO, by the OEFG (Austrian Science Foundation) under MOEL grant no. 490 and by the FWF Austrian Science Fund Grant I677. The dataset used in this work was kindly provided by Mendeley Ltd.

8. REFERENCES

[1] R. A. Baeza-Yates. Applications of Web Query Mining. In D. E. Losada and J. M. Fernandez-Luna, editors, *Advances in Information Retrieval ECIR 2005*, volume 3408, pages 7–22. Springer, 2005.

[2] P. Brusilovsky and E. Millán. User Models for Adaptive Hypermedia and Adaptive Educational Systems. In P. Brusilovsky, A. Kobsa, and W. Nejdl, editors, *The Adaptive Web*, volume 4321 of *Lecture Notes in Computer Science*. Springer, 2007.

[3] B. Jansen, M. Zhang, D. Booth, D. Park, Y. Zhang, A. Kathuria, and P. Bonner. To what degree can log data profile a web searcher? *Proceedings of the American Society for Information Science and Technology*, 46(1):1–19, Nov. 2009.

[4] C. Körner and M. Strohmaier. A call for social tagging datasets, 2010.

[5] C. D. Manning, P. Raghavan, and H. Schtze. *Introduction to Information Retrieval.* Cambridge University Press, New York, NY, USA, 2008.

[6] E. Michlmayr and S. Cayzer. Learning user profiles from tagging data and leveraging them for personal(ized) information access. In *Proceedings of the Workshop on Tagging and Metadata for Social Information Organization, 16th International World Wide Web Conference*, 2007.

[7] M. G. Noll and C. Meinel. Exploring social annotations for web document classification. *Proceedings of the 2008 ACM symposium on Applied computing - SAC '08*, page 2315, 2008.

[8] A. Popescu and G. Grefenstette. Mining user home location and gender from flickr tags. In *ICWSM*. The AAAI Press, 2010.

[9] F. Sebastiani. Machine Learning in Automated Text Categorization. *ACM Computing Surveys*, 34(1):1–47, 2001.

[10] J. Stoyanovich, S. Amer-Yahia, C. Marlow, and C. Yu. Leveraging tagging to model user interests in del.icio.us. In *AAAI'08: Proceedings of the 2008 AAAI Social Information Spring Symposium*, 2008.

[11] G. I. Webb, M. J. Pazzani, and D. Billsus. Machine learning for user modeling. *User Modeling and UserAdapted Interaction*, 11(1):19–29, 2001.

[12] I. Weber and C. Castillo. The demographics of web search categories and subject descriptors. In *Proceedings of SIGIR'10*, Geneva, Switzerland, 2010.

[13] C.-m. A. Yeung, N. Gibbins, and N. Shadbolt. Discovering and Modelling Multiple Interests of Users in Collaborative Tagging Systems. *2008 IEEE/WIC/ACM International Conference on Web Intelligence and Intelligent Agent Technology*, pages 115–118, Dec. 2008.

[14] Z. Yin, R. Li, Q. Mei, and J. Han. Exploring social tagging graph for web object classification. *Proceedings of the 15th ACM International Conference on Knowledge Discovery and Data Mining*, 2009.

[15] A. Zubiaga, R. Martínez, and V. Fresno. Getting the most out of social annotations for web page classification. *Proceedings of the 9th ACM symposium on Document engineering*, page 74, 2009.

Detecting Overlapping Communities in Folksonomies

Abhijnan Chakraborty   Saptarshi Ghosh   Niloy Ganguly
Department of Computer Science and Engineering
Indian Institute of Technology Kharagpur, Kharagpur – 721302, India

ABSTRACT

Folksonomies like Delicious and LastFm are modelled as tripartite (user-resource-tag) hypergraphs for studying their network properties. Detecting communities of similar nodes from such networks is a challenging problem. Most existing algorithms for community detection in folksonomies assign unique communities to nodes, whereas in reality, users have multiple topical interests and the same resource is often tagged with semantically different tags. The few attempts to detect overlapping communities work on *projections* of the hypergraph, which results in significant loss of information contained in the original tripartite structure. We propose the first algorithm to detect overlapping communities in folksonomies using the complete hypergraph structure. Our algorithm converts a hypergraph into its corresponding line-graph, using measures of hyperedge similarity, whereby any community detection algorithm on unipartite graphs can be used to produce overlapping communities in the folksonomy. Through extensive experiments on synthetic as well as real folksonomy data, we demonstrate that the proposed algorithm can detect better community structures as compared to existing state-of-the-art algorithms for folksonomies.

Categories and Subject Desriptors: E.1 [**Data Structures**]: Graphs and Networks; G.2.2 [**Graph Theory**]: Hypergraphs

Keywords: Folksonomy, tripartite hypergraph, overlapping community, link clustering

1. INTRODUCTION

Some of the most popular sites in the Web today are social tagging sites or folksonomies (e.g., Flickr, Delicious, LastFm) where users share various types of resources (e.g., photos, URLs, music files) and collaboratively annotate the resources with descriptive keywords (tags) in order to facilitate efficient search and retrieval of interesting resources. Some folksonomies also allow users to create a social network by connecting with other users having similar interests.

With their growing popularity, a huge amount of resources is being shared on these folksonomies; consequently it has become practically impossible for a user to discover on her own, interesting resources and people having common interests. Hence it is important to develop algorithms for search as well as recommendation of resources and potential friends to the users. One approach to these tasks is to group the various entities (resources, tags, users) into communities or clusters, which are typically thought of as groups of entities having more / better interactions among themselves than with entities outside the group.

Folksonomies are modelled as *tripartite hypergraphs* having user, resource and tag nodes, where a hyperedge (u, t, r) indicates that user u has annotated resource r with tag t. Several algorithms have been proposed for detecting communities in hypergraphs, using techniques such as modularity maximization [10–12], identifying maximally connected sub-hypergraphs [2], and so on. But, almost all of the prior approaches do not consider an important aspect of the problem – they assign a single community to each node, whereas in reality, nodes in folksonomies frequently belong to *multiple overlapping communities*. For instance, users have multiple topics of interest, and thus link to resources and tags of many different semantic categories. Similarly, the same resource is frequently associated with semantically different tags by users who appreciate different aspects of the resource.

To the best of our knowledge, only two studies have addressed the problem of identifying overlapping communities in folksonomies. (i) Wang *et al.* [15] proposed an algorithm to detect overlapping communities of *users* in folksonomies considering only the user-tag relationships (i.e. the user-tag bipartite projection of the hypergraph), and (ii) Papadopoulos *et al.* [13] detected overlapping *tag* communities by taking a projection of the hypergraph onto the set of tags. Taking projections (as used by both these approaches) results in loss of some of the information contained in the original tripartite network and it is known that qualities of the communities obtained from projected networks are not as good as those obtained from the original network [6]. Also, none of these algorithms consider the resource nodes in the hypergraph. However, it is necessary to detect overlapping communities of users, resources and tags simultaneously for personalized recommendation of resources and tags to users. Thus the goal of this paper is to propose such an algorithm that utilizes the complete tripartite structure to detect overlapping communities.

Though a node in a network can be associated to multiple semantic topics, a *link* is usually associated with only one semantics [1] – for instance, a user can have multiple topical interests, but each link created by the user is likely to be associated with exactly one of his interests. Link clustering algorithms utilize this notion to detect overlapping communities, by clustering links instead of the more conventional approach of clustering nodes – though each link is placed in exactly one link cluster, this automatically associates multiple overlapping communities with the nodes since a node inherits membership of all the communities into which its links are placed. Link clustering algorithms have recently been proposed for unipartite networks [1, 4] and bipartite networks [15]; however, to our knowledge, this is the first attempt to cluster links in tripartite hypergraphs.

Thus, the present work takes the first important step towards detecting overlapping communities in folksonomies considering the complete hypergraph structure. The algorithm is detailed in Section 2 (a rudimentary version of the algorithm was presented in the poster [5]). Experiments on synthetically generated hypergraphs show that the proposed algorithm out-performs both the existing algorithms [13,15] which use projections of the triparite network to detect overlapping communities (Section 3). Further, using data from three popular real folksonomies – Delicious, MovieLens and LastFm – we also show that the proposed algorithm can successfully identify better overlapping community structures in real folksonomies (Section 4). Section 5 concludes the paper.

2. PROPOSED ALGORITHM – OHC

In this section, we present the proposed link-clustering algorithm for detecting overlapping communities in tripartite hypergraphs, which we name as 'Overlapping Hypergraph Clustering' algorithm (abbreviated to 'OHC'). As discussed earlier, a folksonomy is modelled as a tripartite hypergraph $G = (V, E)$ where the vertex set V consists of 3 partite sets V^X, V^Y and V^Z. Each hyperedge in hyperedge set E connects a triple of nodes (a, b, c) where $a \in V^X, b \in V^Y$ and $c \in V^Z$.

For a given hypergraph G, we compute the *weighted line graph* G' which is a *unipartite graph* in which the hyperedges in G are *nodes*, and two nodes e_1 and e_2 in G' are connected by an edge if e_1 and e_2 are *adjacent* in G (i.e. the two hyperedges have at least one common node in G). The weight of the edge (e_1, e_2) in G' represents the similarity α between the two hyperedges e_1 and e_2 in the hypergraph G, which is computed as follows.

Let $N^X(i)$, $N^Y(i)$ and $N^Z(i)$ denote the set of neighbours of node i of type V^X, V^Y and V^Z respectively (if $i \in V^X$, then $N^X(i) = \phi$ since nodes in the same partite set are not linked). Similarity between two *adjacent* hyperedges $e_1 = (a, b, c)$ and $e_2 = (p, q, r)$ (where $a, p \in V^X$; $b, q \in V^Y$; $c, r \in V^Z$ and assumed $a = p$) is measured by the relative overlap among the neighbours of the non-common nodes of the same type:

$$\alpha(e_1, e_2) = \frac{|S \bigcap S'| + |N^Y(c) \bigcap N^Y(r)| + |N^Z(b) \bigcap N^Z(q)|}{|S \bigcup S'| + |N^Y(c) \bigcup N^Y(r)| + |N^Z(b) \bigcup N^Z(q)|}$$

where $S = N^X(b) \bigcup N^X(c)$ and $S' = N^X(q) \bigcup N^X(r)$. Non-adjacent hyperedges are considered to have zero similarity.

It can be noted that the similarity for hyperedges can be computed in various other ways like expressing hyperedges as feature vectors and measuring cosine similarity or Pear-

son correlation among these feature vectors. We selected the above definition since it can be computed locally for a pair of hyperedges and can thus be computed efficiently for large real folksonomies. Further, a similar metric was found to perform well in detecting overlapping communities in unipartite graphs [1].

Once the *weighted line graph* G' is constructed from the given tripartite hypergraph G, *any* non-overlapping community detection algorithm for unipartite graphs can be used to cluster the nodes in G' (i.e. the hyperedges in G). We used the Infomap algorithm [14] which is known to be a relaible method for identifying communities [7]. Further, as Infomap has low computational complexity, it can be used efficiently on *weighted line graphs* of large real folksonomies. As we get the node communities in G', each hyperedge in G gets placed into a single link-community. This automatically assigns multiple overlapping communities to nodes in G, since a node inherits membership of all those communities into which the hyperedges connected with this node are placed.

Time Complexity: Let the number of nodes in the hypergraph be n and average node-degree be d, which implies that the number of hyperedges will be $\frac{n \cdot d}{3}$. Each hyperedge will, on average, be adjacent to $3(d-1)$ other hyperedges. So, the *line graph* will have $\frac{n \cdot d}{3}$ nodes and $\frac{n \cdot d}{3} \times 3(d-1) = O(n \cdot d^2)$ edges. Since time complexity of Infomap algorithm is linear in the size of the graph [7] and similarity calculation in the hypergraph also takes $O(n \cdot d^2)$ time; the time complexity of OHC is $O(n \cdot d^2)$. It is to be noted that real-world folksonomies are known to be sparse, having small average degree d. So, essentially the complexity of our algorithm becomes $O(n)$ which makes this algorithm scalable for work in large real world folksonomy.

3. EXPERIMENTS ON SYNTHETIC HYPERGRAPHS

In this section, we evaluate the performance of our proposed OHC algorithm by comparing with the existing algorithms by Wang *et al.* [15] and Papadopoulos *et al.* [13], which are henceforth referred to as 'CL' (abbreviation of 'Correlational Learning') and 'HGC' (as referred by the respective authors) respectively [1].

Since evaluation of clustering is difficult without the knowledge of 'ground truth' regarding the community memberships of nodes, we have used synthetically generated hypergraphs with a known community structure for evaluation of the algorithms. We discuss the generation of synthetic hypergraphs and the metric used to evaluate the algorithms, followed by the results of experiments on synthetic hypergraphs.

3.1 Generation of Synthetic Hypergraphs

Synthetic hypergraphs are generated using a modified version of the method used in [15]. The generator algorithm takes the following as input: (i) Number of nodes in a partite set (all 3 partite sets V^X, V^Y and V^Z are assumed to contain equal number of nodes), (ii) Number of communities C, (iii) Fraction γ of nodes which belong to multiple communities and (iv) Hyperedge density β (i.e. fraction of total number of hyperedges possible in the hypergraph).

---

[1] We acknowledge the authors of [13,15] for providing us with the implementations of their algorithms.

Initially, the nodes in each partite set are evenly distributed among each community under consideration (e.g. $|V^X|/C$ nodes in set V^X are assigned to each of the C communities). Subsequently, γ fraction of nodes are selected at random from each of V^X, V^Y and V^Z, and each selected node is assigned to some randomly chosen communities apart from the one it already has been assigned to. Nodes assigned to the same community are then randomly selected, one from each partite set, and interconnected with hyperedges. The number of hyperedges is decided based on the specified density β.

The above assignment of communities to nodes constitutes the 'ground truth'. After a hypergraph is generated, information about the communities is hidden, and then communities are detected from the hypergraph by different community detection algorithms. The community structure detected by each algorithm is compared with the ground truth using the metric Normalized Mutual Information.

Normalized Mutual Information (NMI): NMI is an information-theoretic measure of similarity between two partitioning of a set of elements, which can be used to compare two community structures for the same graph (as identified by different algorithms). The traditional definition of NMI does *not* consider the case of a node being present in multiple communities; hence we use an alternative definition of NMI considering overlapping communities, as proposed in [8]. The NMI value is in the range $[0, 1]$; higher the NMI value, the more similar are the two community structures (refer to [8] for details).

3.2 Results of Experiments

The CL and HGC algorithms produce only user and tag communities respectively. Hence, while calculating the NMI value for these algorithms, we have used the community memberships of only the user (respectively, tag) nodes according to the ground truth. On the other hand, the proposed OHC algorithm gives composite communities containing all three types of nodes. Hence, while evaluate OHC, we considered the community memberships of all three types of nodes.

For all the following experiments, $|V^X| = |V^Y| = |V^Z| = 200$ and number of communities $C = 20$. For each result, random hypergraphs were generated 50 times using the same set of parameter values and the average performances over all 50 runs are reported.

Performance w.r.t. number of hyperedges: To study how the number of hyperedges affects the performance of the clustering algorithms, we generated synthetic hypergraphs having various hyperedge densities $\beta = 0.1, 0.2, \ldots, 1.0$. In each of these hypergraphs, 10% of nodes in each partite set belonged to multiple communities (i.e., $\gamma = 0.1$). The NMI values for the three algorithms are shown in Figure 1(a). It can be clearly seen that, across all hyperedge densities, OHC performs significantly better than HGC and CL algorithms. A possible explanation for this is that, as stated earlier, the proposed OHC algorithm utilizes the complete tripartite structure of the hypergraph, whereas both CL and HGC algorithms work on unweighted projections which is known to result in significant loss of information [6].

Also note that even for very low hyperedge densities, when detecting community structures is difficult, the

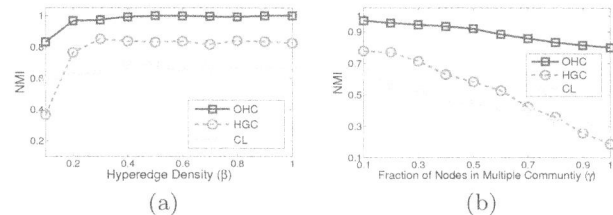

(a)   (b)

Figure 1: Comparison of proposed OHC algorithm with CL and HGC algorithms – variation of NMI values (a) with varying hyperedge density when 10% nodes belong to multiple communities and (b) with varying fraction of nodes in multiple communities, keeping hyperedge density constant at 0.2

proposed OHC algorithm performs very well resulting in NMI scores above 0.8. This makes OHC suitable for real world folksonomies where hyperedge density is typically low.

Performance w.r.t. fraction of nodes in multiple communities: A node belonging to multiple communities creates hyperedges to nodes in all those communities; hence, from the perspective of a particular community, the hyperedges created by this member node to nodes in other communities reduces the exclusivity of this particular community. As the number of nodes in multiple overlapping communities increases, the fraction of inter-community hyperedges increases making the community structure more difficult to identify.

We generated synthetic hypergraphs by varying the fraction of nodes in multiple communities (γ) while keeping hyperedge density (β) constant at 0.2. This low value of hyperedge density was chosen to measure the effectiveness of the algorithms in sparse environment (as in real-world foksnomies). Figure 1(b) shows that OHC performs consistently better than HGC and CL algorithms in this case as well. Further, as the community structure becomes more and more complex, the information loss as a result of projections becomes increasingly more crucial, hence the performance of the HGC and CL algorithms degrade sharply with increase in γ. On the other hand, the performance of our OHC algorithm shows relatively much greater stability.

The above experiments clearly validate our motivation and show that considering the complete tripartite structure of hypergraphs can result in better identification of community structure, as compared to considering projections (as done in prior algorithms).

4. EXPERIMENTS ON REAL FOLK-SONOMIES

Now we apply the proposed OHC algorithm to gain insights into the community structures prevalent in real folksonomies. For this, we use the publicly available datasets [3] of the folksonomies Delicious (www.delicious.com), LastFm (www.last.fm) and MovieLens (movielens.umn.edu). The statistics of these data sets are summarized in Table 1.

4.1 Results

For all three datasets, OHC algorithm successfully groups semantically related resources and tags and the users tag-

Dataset	users	resources	tags	hyperedges
Delicious	1,867	69,226	53,388	437,593
LastFm	1,892	17,632	11,946	186,479
MovieLens	2,113	10,197	13,222	47,957

Table 1: Statistics of real folksonomy datasets

ging these resources. As an illustration, Table 2 shows the resources and tags placed in some example communities for each of the three datasets. It is evident that the resources and tags that are placed in the same community are often related to a common semantic theme. A closer look at Table 2 reveals that the algorithm also correctly identifies nodes that are related to multiple overlapping communities (themes). For instance, the band 'Van Halen' is placed in two different communities detected from LastFm. The Wikipedia article about 'Van Halen' justifies this placement, stating their genre as both 'Hard Rock' and 'Heavy Metal'.

There are substantial amounts of overlap detected by OHC algorithm in all three datasets. Figure 2 shows the cumulative distribution of the fraction of communities which overlap with a given number of other communities, for LastFm and MovieLens. A similar pattern was detected in Delicious, which we omit due to lack of space.

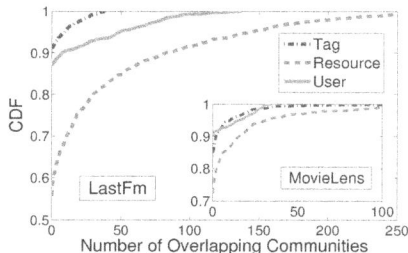

Figure 2: Distribution of the fraction of communities which overlap with a given number of other communities, for LastFm and MovieLens (inset)

4.2 Evaluation of Communities Detected

The principal difficulty in evaluating the communities detected in real folksonomies is the absence of 'ground truth' regarding the community memberships of nodes, since their huge size makes it impossible for human experts to evaluate the quality of identified communities. Hence, we use the following two methods for evaluation.

First, we use the graph-based metric **Conductance**, which has been shown to correctly conform with the intuitive notion of communities and is extensively used for evaluating quality of communities in OSNs (see [9] for details). As conductance is defined only for unipartite networks, we compare tag communities detected by HGC with the tag nodes in the communities identified by our OHC algorithm.

Second, in case of the folksonomies which allow users to form a social network among themselves, we can assume that users having similar interests are likely to be linked in the social network, or to have a common social neighbourhood (a property known as *homophily*). We utilize this notion to evaluate the user communities detected by CL algorithm and the user nodes in the communities identified by OHC algorithm.

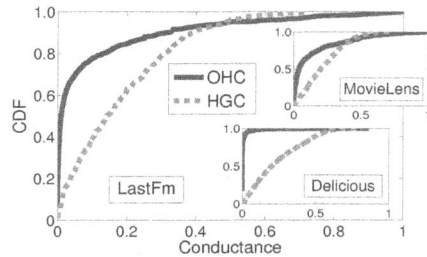

Figure 3: Distribution of conductance values of tag communities identified by OHC and HGC algorithms, for LastFm (main plot), Delicious and MovieLens (both inset)

Comparison of conductance values: The conductance value ranges from 0 to 1 where a *lower* value signifies *better* community structure [9]. Figure 3 shows the cumulative distribution of conductance values of detected tag communities by the two algorithms. Across all three datasets, OHC produces more communities having lower conductance values, which implies that OHC can find communities of better quality than obtained by HGC algorithm. The reason for this superior performance is that OHC groups semantically related nodes into relatively smaller cohesive communities instead of creating a few number of generalized large communities. For examples of semantically related communities, refer to Table 2.

Comparing detected user communities with social network: In case of folksonomies which allow users to form a social network, there can be two types of relationships among users – explicit social connections in the social network, and implicit connections through their tagging behaviour (e.g. tagging the same resource) in the hypergraph. A community detection algorithm for hypergraphs utilizes the implicit relationships to identify the community structure, and we propose to evaluate the detected community structure using the explicit connections that the users themselves create (in the social network). For instance, if a large fraction of the users who are socially linked (or share a common social neighbourhood in the social network) are placed in the same community (by the algorithm), the detected community structure can be said to group together users having common interests.

Hence, to compare the community structure identified by two algorithms, we consider the user-pairs who are within a certain distance from each other in the social network (where distance 1 implies friends, i.e. two users who are directly linked), and compute the fraction of such user-pairs who have been placed in a common community by the algorithm. Figure 4(a) shows the results for the proposed OHC algorithm and the CL algorithm, for the LastFm dataset. Across all distances, OHC places a larger number of user-pairs who share a common social neighborhood, in a common community than the CL algorithm. Also, as the distance between two users in the social network increases, both algorithms put a smaller fraction of such user-pairs in the same community.

We can also investigate the reverse question – among the users who are placed in a common community (by a community detection algorithm), what fraction of these users are

Community	Theme	Examples of member nodes
LastFm Artists (resources)	Hard Rock	*Van Halen, Deep Purple, Aerosmith,* Alice Cooper, Guns N' Roses, Scorpions, Bon Jovi
	Heavy Metal	*Van Halen, Deep Purple, Aerosmith,* Iron Maiden, Motorhead, Metallica
LastFm Tags	Metal	*blues rock, psychedelic rock, rap metal, nu metal,* metal, symphonic metal, doom metal
	Rock	*blues rock, psychedelic rock, rap metal, nu metal,* progressive rock, art rock, soft rock
MovieLens Movies (resources)	Superhero	*The Incredibles, Shrek, Shrek 2, Incredible Hulk,* Batman Begins, Spider-Man, Superman
	Animation	*The Incredibles, Shrek, Shrek 2, Incredible Hulk,* Kung fu Panda, Toy Story
MovieLens Tags	Criticism	*violent, brutal,* waste of celluloid, disturbing, junk, tragically stupid, lousy script
	Violence	*violent, brutal,* murder, fatality, civil war, great villain, dark, serial killer, war film
Delicious Tags	Web 2.0	socialnetworking, socialmedia, php, drupal, xml, webdesign, twitter, skype, ruby

Table 2: **Examples of communities detected by OHC algorithm. Nodes related to a common theme are successfully clustered. Nodes related to multiple themes (italicized) are placed in overlapping communities.**

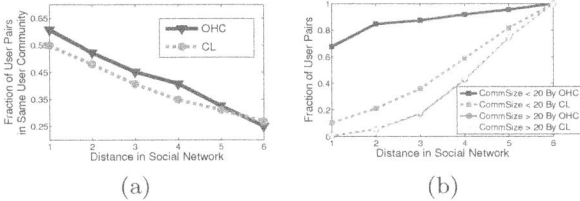

(a)   (b)

Figure 4: **Community structure detected by the proposed OHC algorithm and the CL algorithm with the social network in (a) LastFm and (b) Delicious**

actually connected in the social network (or share a common social neighbourhood)? It is meaningful to answer this question taking the community sizes into consideration, since 'quality' of large communities is known to be lower than that for smaller communities [9]; Figure 4(b) shows the fraction of users who are placed in a common community by the OHC and CL algorithms, that are within a certain distance in the social network (where distance 1 implies friends), for the Delicious dataset. For detected user-communities of size lesser than 20, more than 70% of the users who are placed in a common community by OHC are actually connected (friends) in the social network, whereas the corresponding value for the CL algorithm is much lesser. However, for larger detected communities (> 20 users), the fraction of user-pairs who share a common social neighbourhood is much lower and almost identical for both algorithms.

The above results show that for real folksonomies as well, the proposed OHC algorithm can detect much better community structure as compared to CL and HGC algorithms.

5. CONCLUSION

In this paper, we proposed the first algorithm to detect overlapping communities considering the full tripartite hypergraph structure of folksonomies. Through extensive experiments on synthetic as well as real folksonomy networks, we showed that the proposed algorithm out-performs existing algorithms that consider projections of hypergaphs. The proposed algorithm can be effectively used in recommending interesting resources and friends to users. Our future work will be to build such a recommendation system utilizing the proposed algorithm.

Acknowledgment We thank the anonymous reviewers for their constructive suggestions. This research was supported in part by a grant from the Indo-German Max Planck Centre for Computer Science (IMPECS).

6. REFERENCES

[1] Y.-Y. Ahn, J. P. Bagrow, and S. Lehmann. Link communities reveal multiscale complexity in networks. *Nature*, 466(7307):761–764, August 2010.

[2] M. Brinkmeier, J. Werner, and S. Recknagel. Communities in graphs and hypergraphs. In *Proc. ACM International Conference on Information and Knowledge Management (CIKM)*, 2007.

[3] I. Cantador, P. Brusilovsky, and T. Kuflik. Workshop on Information Heterogeneity and Fusion in Recommender Systems (with ACM RecSys), 2011.

[4] T. S. Evans and R. Lambiotte. Line graphs, link partitions, and overlapping communities. *Phys. Rev. E*, 80:016105, 2009.

[5] S. Ghosh, P. Kane, and N. Ganguly. Identifying overlapping communities in folksonomies or tripartite hypergraphs. In *Proc. ACM International Conference on World Wide Web (WWW) companion volume*, 2011.

[6] R. Guimerà, M. Sales-Pardo, and L. A. N. Amaral. Module identification in bipartite and directed networks. *Phys. Rev. E*, 76:036102, Sep 2007.

[7] A. Lancichinetti and S. Fortunato. Community detection algorithms: a comparative analysis. *Phys. Rev. E*, 80:056117, Sep 2009.

[8] A. Lancichinetti, S. Fortunato, and J. Kertesz. Detecting the overlapping and hierarchical community structure in complex networks. *New Journal of Physics*, 11:033015, 2009.

[9] J. Leskovec, K. J. Lang, A. Dasgupta, and M. W. Mahoney. Statistical properties of community structure in large social and information networks. In *Proc. ACM International Conference on World Wide Web (WWW)*, 2008.

[10] T. Murata. Modularity for heterogeneous networks. In *Proc. ACM International Conference on Hypertext and Hypermedia*, 2010.

[11] T. Murata. Detecting communities from social tagging networks based on tripartite modularity. In *Proc. Workshop on Link Analysis in Heterogeneous Information Networks*, 2011.

[12] N. Neubauer and K. Obermayer. Towards community detection in k-partite k-uniform hypergraphs. In *Proc. Workshop on Analyzing Networks and Learning with Graphs*, 2009.

[13] S. Papadopoulos, Y. Kompatsiaris, and A. Vakali. A graph-based clustering scheme for identifying related tags in folksonomies. In *Proc. Data Warehousing and Knowledge Discovery Conference*, 2010.

[14] M. Rosvall and C. T. Bergstrom. Maps of random walks on complex networks reveal community structure. *PNAS*, 105:1118–1123, Jan 2008.

[15] X. Wang, L. Tang, H. Gao, and H. Liu. Discovering Overlapping Groups in Social Media. In *Proc. IEEE International Conference on Data Mining (ICDM)*, 2010.

Predicting Semantic Annotations on the Real-Time Web*

Elham Khabiri
Texas A&M University
College Station, TX
khabiri@cse.tamu.edu

James Caverlee
Texas A&M University
College Station, TX 77843
caverlee@cse.tamu.edu

Krishna Y. Kamath
Texas A&M University
College Station, TX 77843
kykamath@cse.tamu.edu

ABSTRACT

The explosion of the real-time web has spurred a growing need for new methods to organize, monitor, and distill relevant information from these large-scale social streams. One especially encouraging development is the self-curation of the real-time web via *user-driven linking*, in which users annotate their own status updates with lightweight semantic annotations – or *hashtags*. Unfortunately, there is evidence that hashtag growth is not keeping pace with the growth of the overall real-time web. In a random sample of 3 million tweets, we find that only 10.2% contain at least one hashtag. Hence, in this paper we explore the possibility of predicting hashtags for un-annotated status updates. Toward this end, we propose and evaluate a graph-based prediction framework. Three of the unique features of the approach are: (i) a path aggregation technique for scoring the closeness of terms and hashtags in the graph; (ii) pivot term selection, for identifying high value terms in status updates; and (iii) a dynamic sliding window for recommending hashtags reflecting the current status of the real-time web. Experimentally we find encouraging results in comparison with Bayesian and data mining-based approaches.

Categories and Subject Descriptors

H.4 [**Information Systems Applications**]: Miscellaneous

Keywords

social media, hashtag prediction

1. INTRODUCTION

The real-time web has grown at an astonishing rate in the past several years. As one example, Twitter has rapidly

*This work was supported in part by DARPA grant N66001-10-1-4044 and by a Google Research Award. Any opinions, findings and conclusions or recommendations expressed in this material are the author(s) and do not necessarily reflect those of the sponsors.

Figure 1: Two sample tweets annotated with the hashtag #health.

grown from handling 5,000 tweets per day in 2007 to 50 million tweets per day in 2010 to 140 million per tweets per day in 2011. At an order of magnitude higher, Facebook reported in 2009 that it was handling around 1 billion chat messages per day,[1] and there is widespread evidence of massive growth in web-based commenting systems (like on Reddit, Digg, and NYTimes) and other real-time "social awareness streams" [17].

Coupled with this explosion in content reflecting the real-time interests of web users is the need for new methods to organize, monitor, and distill relevant information from these large-scale social streams. Along this line, there have been a number of recent efforts aimed at providing a search and analytics tools over the real-time web for making sense of the aggregate activities of millions of users [2, 3, 12, 24]. One especially encouraging development is the self-curation of the real-time web via *user-driven linking*, in which users annotate their own status updates with lightweight semantic annotations – or *hashtags*. On Twitter, for example, these hashtags are inserted into tweets by users and serve many functions. For example, some reflect categorical information about the tweet as in Figure 1, where both have been annotated with the hashtag #health. Some hashtags reflect events related to a tweet (e.g., #ht2012) and many others reflect the sentiment of the tweet (e.g., #Iloveapple, #sucks). And of course, as user-generated descriptors, some are nonsensical or of interest only to the user posting the hashtag.

By linking status updates to hashtag-like semantic descriptors, users provide a potentially scalable mechanism to organize the real-time web as it continues to grow. As users continue to post status updates with hashtags, there will always be additional semantic cues for organizing these updates. For example, as new issues become associated

---

[1] http://www.facebook.com/note.php?note_id=91351698919

with the "Health" concept, we would expect to see new updates using the #health hashtag. In this way, the user-driven semantic annotation of the real-time web could provide an evolving framework for improving information navigation in these systems (by linking similar updates according to common hashtags), by inducing concept hierarchies over these status updates (so that #cancer-related updates are organized under the umbrella of #health), for supporting serendipitous exploration of the real-time web, improving the recall of search operators (by returning both #apple and #mac related updates for queries about the company), and so on. Indeed, a recent study of Twitter search shows that hashtags are popular as queries, and that these queries are often repeated so that users may monitor search results [25]. By linking untagged updates with hashtag-like semantic descriptors, such searches could have expanded coverage.

Unfortunately, there is evidence that hashtag growth is not keeping pace with the growth of the overall real-time web. In a random sample of 3 million tweets, we find that only 10.2% contain at least one hashtag, meaning that 89.8% are un-labeled and would be left out of any hashtag-oriented search or monitoring application. In addition, there is mounting evidence that many hashtags may convey little semantic information or are being used as tools of spammers and other polluters of these systems [10, 13, 14]. Hence, in this paper we explore the possibility of predicting hashtags for un-annotated status updates. Can we determine the appropriate semantic label for an update?

Toward this end, we propose and evaluate a graph-based prediction framework in which terms in status updates are linked to hashtags based on their co-occurrence. Since many relevant hashtags may not co-occur with all possible terms, we develop a path aggregation technique for scoring the closeness of terms and hashtags in the graph. In this way, high-value hashtags may be associated with status updates, even if no terms in the update have ever co-occurred with the hashtag. Additionally, we augment the baseline method with a pivot term selection approach for identifying high value terms in status updates, and a dynamic sliding window for recommending hashtags reflecting the current status of the real-time web. Experimentally we find encouraging results in comparison with Bayesian and data mining-based approaches.

The organization of the rest of the paper is as follows. Section 2 gives a brief overview of the related work. In Section 3 we provide the formal definition of the problem of predicting semantic annotations for the real-time web and present the step-by-step development of the proposed graph-based hashtag prediction framework. Section 4 details the Twitter-based dataset, introduces several alternative approaches that we compare the proposed model with, and presents the results of a comparative evaluation of the proposed approach. Finally in Section 5 we conclude with a summary and some final thoughts.

2. RELATED WORK

User-driven tagging is one of the organizing principles of most social media services – including image tagging (e.g., on Flickr), video tagging (e.g., on YouTube), and web page tagging (e.g., using Del.ico.us), among many others. And in these contexts, there has been considerable work in recommending tags. In one direction, researchers have sought methods to aggregate the collective knowledge of web users

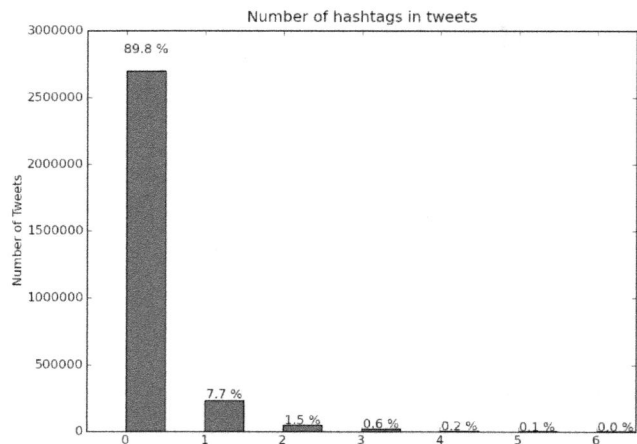

Figure 2: Most tweets are annotated with no hashtags. In a random sample of 3 million tweets, we find that 7.7% contain exactly one hashtag, and 2.5% contain more than one hashtag.

to expand the small set of tags applied to a resource with other user-contributed tags [20, 6]. In a different direction, other studies have recommended personalized tags for each user based on the user's history, bookmarks, and other personal documents [5, 18]. In collaborative filtering based approaches [20, 22, 27, 7, 16], the number and frequency of tag co-occurrence builds the core model of tag recommendation. Given a set of tags already input by the user for a new resource such as a picture, URL, or a blog post, these algorithms suggest new tags based on the number of co-occurrences of such input tags with the previous annotations. There are many studies on the usage of data mining approaches (like association rules) to predict the appropriate tags for content-rich resources such as webpages [8][26]. Several efforts have focused on graph-based approaches, in which the relationships among tags, resources and users are modeled as a tri-partite [11] graph. In such settings, important "power" tags, users, and resources may be identified through the application of a PageRank-like iterative algorithm. Similarly a tag-document bipartite graph has been used as the basis to cluster tags and documents, as discussed in [21]. In addition to these efforts, there have been many other approaches for tag recommendation [15, 9, 4, 28, 30].

Compared to these efforts, predicting semantic annotations for the real-time web differs in three fundamental ways. First, in traditional social media tag prediction, the tagged resource itself (e.g., the video, the image) is typically made available for collaborative tagging. That is, an image on Flickr may attract dozens or hundreds of contributors who provide their own tagging perspective on what the image is, providing a rich source of tagged information for a single image. In comparison, a status update on the real-time web is annotated by just one user and typically with only one hashtag, meaning there is not a rich collection of collaboratively shared hashtags available to describe a single status update. Second, for the purposes of hashtag prediction, the status update itself is a sparsely described object.

Most status updates are short (as on Twitter, where there is a 140 character limit) and so there is little evidence in the status update itself; in contrast, web pages and other social media often contain richly available descriptive evidence (e.g., in the text of the page itself) to augment tag prediction. Third, the real-time web is necessarily a rapidly evolving medium, with millions of updates per day and highly-dynamic tagging behavior, meaning that the tags themselves may rapidly evolve and change in use and purpose (as compared to a Flickr photo of a well-known landmark, in which the tags associated with the landmark are typically much longer-lived and less dynamic). Hence, it is important to develop a new approach for predicting semantic annotations on the real-time web.

3. PREDICTING SEMANTIC ANNOTATIONS

In this section, we formalize the problem of predicting semantic annotations for the real-time web and introduce a hashtag graph-based prediction framework.

3.1 Problem Statement

Let $T = \{T_1, T_2, ..., T_n\}$ be the set of status updates (i.e., tweets), and $T_i = \{u_1, u_2, ..., u_m\}$ be a set of unigram terms, and $H = \{h_1, h_2, ..., h_m\}$ be the set of hashtags. Our goal is for an unlabeled status update T_i to predict a hashtag h_j that "correctly" annotates the update. Of course, it is challenging to determine what is the "correct" choice of hashtag. In one direction, the evaluation of hashtag prediction can be based on a user study in which human subjects are asked to evaluate the quality of predicted hashtags for each of the testing tweets. A recent study [6] argues that human evaluation of tags may lead to errors in assessment due to multi-lingual tags, missing context, differences of level of details, and the interdependence of tags. Alternatively, we can adopt a purely machine-based evaluation framework in which the prediction model is built over a training set and then used to predict the hashtags for a test set. In this case, the hashtags themselves are removed from the test set and then the quality of the prediction is in identifying the actual hashtag that had been used. Such an approach, while providing less flexibility (e.g., by not accepting #nba as a reasonable tag for a sports-related tweet actually annotated with #basketball), does provide for fast evaluation and comparison across multiple methods. Hence, in this paper, we adopt this second approach.

Concretely, we adopt an evaluation framework in which a portion of the data is used as a training set for learning the prediction model, and a separate testing set is used for evaluation. The model is used to predict the hashtags of test tweets in which all the hashtags are removed. The predicted k tags are denoted t_{pred}. The actual tags applied to the tweet are denoted t_{real}. For varying values of k, we can evaluate the quality of hashtag prediction using precision:

$$prec = \frac{|t_{real} \cap t_{pred}|}{|t_{pred}|}$$

where predicting only hashtags that are actually used results in a precision of 1, whereas predicting none of the correct tags actually used results in a precision of 0. We additionally evaluate the quality of hashtag prediction using recall:

$$rec = \frac{|t_{real} \cap t_{pred}|}{|t_{real}|}$$

Figure 3: Although "senate" and "#deathcare" have not appeared together in any tweets, the two are related, as revealed by the short path (2 hops) in the semantic graph.

where identifying all of the correct hashtags results in a recall of 1. Finally, we also consider the combined F-measure:

$$f = \frac{2 \times prec \times rec}{prec + rec}$$

We measure the overall precision, recall and F-measure by averaging over all testing tweets.

3.2 Hashtag Graph-Based Prediction

Given the overall goal, we propose in this section a graph-based prediction approach. The core idea is to identify implicit relationships among the hashtags and terms used in tweets to build a semantic graph that may then be used to connect the terms in unlabeled tweets to the appropriate hashtags. The baseline assumption is that terms and hashtags that are used together are related and hence close in terms of meaning. For example, Figure 3 shows a subgraph built over a large Twitter dataset (described more fully in the experimental evaluation) in which a term like "senate" is linked to "reform" due to the use of both terms in many tweets. Similarly, "senate" and the hashtag "#obama" are linked due to their co-occurrence. However, strictly considering co-occurrence alone will miss the implicit connection between "senate" and "#deathcare". Returning to Figure 1 we find that terms like "sick" and "patient" are close in the semantic graph to the hashtag "#health". By identifying these implicit connections across all of the terms used in an unlabeled tweet, the proposed approach seeks to find hashtags that are close in terms of this semantic graph. Hence, for a tweet T, we can estimate the appropriateness of a hashtag h as an aggregation operation over all of the terms occurring in T:

$$score(T, h) = \sum_{t_i \in T} p\text{-}score(t_i, h) \qquad (1)$$

where $p\text{-}score(t_i, h)$ is an estimate of $p(h|t_i)$ – the conditional probability of the hashtag being used, when t_i is observed.

However, naive application of such an approach will face several challenges. First, how should evidence from different terms from a single tweet be aggregated to find the consensus of the tweet? In other words, a tweet containing terms like "senate" and "healthcare" may be closely linked to many candidate hashtags. In what ways can we distill the most

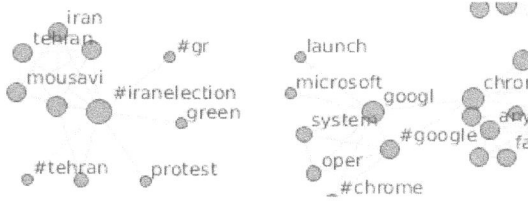

Figure 4: Relationship among hashtag and terms. The left side shows terms and hashtags related to the Iran election; the right side is technology-centric.

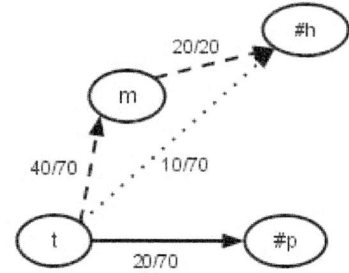

Figure 5: The score of hash #h related to term t is calculated by the summation of all the path scores between these two nodes.

likely hashtags from a long list of candidates? Second, aggregating the evidence across all terms in a tweet may lead to topic drift, in which particular terms are closely linked to hashtags that are not at all relevant to the overall tweet. For example, the term "state'" in the first tweet shown in Figure 1 may be linked to hashtags associated with mental states, states like Texas and Oregon, and other concepts not at all linked to the hashtag "#health". Third, the probability of a hashtag given a term may change over time. For example, the term "obama" will be closely linked with different terms and different hashtags based on the political debate of the day, whether the election is upcoming, and so on. Hence, careful determination of the temporal relationships between terms and hashtags is important.

With these challenges in mind, we now detail three specific steps toward hashtag graph-based prediction: (i) a path aggregation technique for scoring the closeness of terms and hashtags in the graph; (ii) pivot term selection, for identifying high value terms in status updates; and (iii) a dynamic sliding window for recommending hashtags reflecting the current status of the real-time web.

3.2.1 Linking Terms and Hashtags

First, we build a semantic graph and propose a path aggregation technique for scoring the closeness of terms and hashtags in the graph. We build a graph $G = (N, E)$ with nodes $N = \{n_1, n_2, ..., n_m\}$ in which n_i is either a term or a hashtag and edges $E = \{e_1, e_2, ..., e_r\}$ in which e_j is the weighted edge between two nodes. To avoid noise and to keep our graph less polluted we only create an edge between two nodes when the number of co-occurrences is greater than a threshold. The co-occurrence is measured by considering all tweets in the training set and counting the number of times two elements (either terms or hashtags) occur together in the same tweet. In this way, we may filter out non-important edges that have happened by chance. A sample graph is illustrated in Figure 4, which shows the relationship between terms and hashtags.

But what is the appropriate weighting function for edges between nodes? This weighting function can be used to identify the relative "closeness" of terms and hashtags that are directly connected. In one direction, the co-occurrence count itself may be used. Consider the case that terms A and B have co-occurred 10 times together, and both A and B occur across all tweets exactly 10 times each. So, A and B always co-occur together and never apart. Now suppose A appears 100 times, but only in 10 cases did it co-occur with B. In this case, the "closeness" of A and B is less than in the first case. Hence, we normalize the co-occurrence value by

the number of the times a term has appeared in the whole corpus which is equal to the number of outlinks of that node. This *normalized weight score*, $NW_{(n,n+1)}$, is the normalized weight of the edge between node n and node $n + 1$:

$$NW_{(n,n+1)} = \frac{W_{(n,n+1)}}{\sum_{p \in Outlink(n)} W(n,p)} \quad (2)$$

where $W_{(n,n+1)}$ is the co-occurrence count of the two elements n and $n + 1$ (terms or hashtags). By this normalization we consider the amount of the node devotion to the relationship with another node. Therefore an edge to a more general term will receive smaller weight in comparison with an edge to a more specific term. Now the question is how to measure the "closeness" of nodes that are more than one hop away? What will happen if the relevant hashtag was found two or three hops away? Shall we penalize the score of the hashtags that are located farther from a particular term? And to what degree?

To formalize the problem we say that the hashtag h is reachable from term t_i in radius m as $t_i \leadsto^m h$. For a single path from a term to a hashtag, we propose to consider the product of all the edge weights in the path, where the edge weights themselves are decayed by a factor β. The decay factor is to penalize the nodes that are far from the source node, so that we still consider them as candidate hashtags but with lower significance than ones that are directly connected in the graph. The score for a path is then:

$$score\_path(t_i \leadsto^m h) = \prod_{n=0}^{m-1} NW_{(n,n+1)} * \beta^n \quad (3)$$

where the normalized edge weights between nodes are decayed, and so the farther a hashtag is from a term source node, the less score it gets.

To find the overall score of a hashtag h from term t_i we measure aggregation scores of all of the paths existing between them. So that if a hashtag is reachable by more than one path it shows more relevance to the term in comparison with the case that it is only reachable by one path. Hence, this aggregated path score is:

$$p\text{-}score(t_i, h) = \sum_{m=1}^{M} score\text{-}path(t_i \leadsto^m h) \quad (4)$$

where we consider all paths from a term to a hashtag. For example in Figure 5 hashtag h is reachable from a term t

once in 1 hop (the dotted path,) and the other time through 2 hops (the dashed path). In this way, we link terms to hashtags.

3.2.2 Selecting Pivot Terms

Given the semantic graph and the method for linking terms to hashtags, the aggregation method described in Equation 1 can be applied immediately. However, by considering all terms in a tweet for finding appropriate hashtags may introduce noise in the case of spurious term-hashtag connections caused by considering isolated linkages between terms and hashtags without regard for the overall tweet content. For example for the tweet "So there is actually a python module called pyjamas", many of the terms are not significant for predicting an appropriate semantic annotation; "so", "there", "is", and so on are relatively common terms and they convey little information about the tweet. In contrast, "python", "module", and "pyjamas" are all strong cues.

Hence, we propose to select a subset of terms from each tweet based on their high information content. This *pivot term selection* results in keeping the model small and eliminating terms that are ineffective for tag prediction. While there are a number of ways to select pivot terms, we consider two approaches – by inverse document frequency and by entropy.

To select pivot terms by inverse document frequency measure (IDF), we consider the number of times a term was used in all the tweets – df_t – within the training set.

$$IDF(t) = log\frac{N}{df_t} \qquad (5)$$

where N is the total number of tweets in the training set. Hence we identify the terms with high IDF and eliminate the more general terms with low value.

For entropy-based pivot term selection, we identify terms with low entropy (which tend to be more specific) and eliminate terms with high entropy (which tend to be more general non-informative terms). The entropy of term t is measured as:

$$Entropy(t) = - \sum_{h_i \in H} p(h_i|t) \times log(p(h_i|t)) \qquad (6)$$

where H is the set of all hashtags that co-occur with term t. By selecting as pivot terms those terms that are low in entropy, the goal is to find good predictors of hashtags. To illustrate, Table 1 shows a sample of terms with high entropy versus those with low entropy in a large collection of tweets (described in the following section). The terms with lower entropy are more specific and terms with higher entropy are more general terms.

3.2.3 Sliding Windows

Finally, since the real-time web is constantly changing, we augment the baseline hashtag prediction approach with a *sliding window*. The intuition is that the recency of hashtags is a strong indicator of their appropriateness for annotating tweets. For example, events such as Gaddafi's death or the Super Bowl, shifting user interests, or announcements of new products will drive a changing portfolio of hashtags in use by users of the real-time web. Thus, a higher importance can be assigned to more recent hashtags than those introduced a long time ago.

Concretely, we propose to build the semantic graph based on the past Δ time, rather than considering the entire his-

Low Entropy	High Entropy
twade sherlock	win house
vancouver perception	save chance
tweekly intriguing	post prize
wesson legend	good top
naraku equivalent	american person
crunchy irm	end night
tempting tub	tip group
jumper drinking	stop hot
chilli whistle	week nice

Table 1: Sample of terms with high/low entropy.

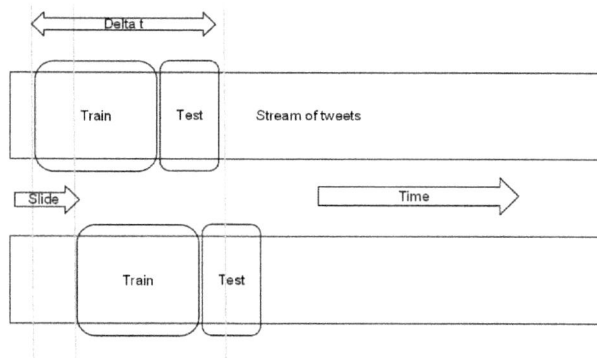

Figure 6: From the stream of tweets we construct a time-window of Δ and split the data into 80-20 train-test sets within each window. We repeat the experiments for all sliding windows.

tory. The sliding window could be an hour, day, week, or month. In this way, the predicted hashtags can be based on this sliding window as illustrated in Figure 6, reflecting the current composition of hashtags.

Additionally, the model may be smoothed by considering a mixture of both the most recent window and the global history. For example if we build the model based on the past day, could we improve it by considering the information from the past week? Therefore we suggest a smoothing process that takes into account both the recent history and the complete history:

$$smooth\text{-}score(t_i, h) = 0.9 * p\text{-}score(t_i, h) + 0.1 * G(h|t_i) \qquad (7)$$

where $G(h|t_i)$ is the global probability of hashtag h given term t_i. Also note that the global model can be calculated offline, so that it can be efficiently incorporated into the sliding window approach.

4. EVALUATION

In this section, we present an experimental study of hashtag recommendation. We describe the dataset, metrics used, introduce several alternative adaptations of tag prediction in social media to the problem of hashtag prediction, and present the results of a comparative study.

4.1 Dataset

For the experimental evaluation, we adopt the Stanford Twitter dataset containing 344 million Twitter posts from 20 million users covering a 6 month period from 06/01/2009 to 11/31/2009 [29]. This dataset contains about 20-30% of all public tweets published on Twitter during this time frame. After removing tweets with empty text, we arrive at a dataset described in Table 2. Eliminating terms and hashtags with length less than 2 and those that were used fewer than 10 times in tweets, we arrive at nearly 500K unique terms and 100K unique hashtags in the dataset. We randomly split the data into an 80/20 mix, so that 80% of the tweets with hashtags are used as training and 20% of tweets with hashtags are for testing.

Total number of tweets	344,139,347
Total tweets with hash	36,558,421
Size of term dictionary	502,684
Size of hash dictionary	134,522

Table 2: Statistics of Twitter dataset.

4.2 Alternative Methods

As we discussed in the related work section, there have been a number of studies of tag recommendation over traditional social media. We now describe adaptations of several of these alternative approaches, in which we customize the techniques for hashtag prediction.

4.2.1 Adapting Flickr-Based Tag Recommendation

The first approach was developed in the context of tag recommendation for photos on Flickr [20]. In this context, it is assumed that each photo has already been tagged by some set of users. Based on the co-occurrences of these tags with tags associated with other photos, the method can recommend additional tags for the baseline photo. The authors propose two aggregation methods for scoring and ranking candidate tags in order of their appropriateness – by voting and by summation. The *voting-based method* considers the number of times that a candidate tag was seen. As an example consider A and B as the two input tags for a photo. Suppose A co-occurs with $\{M, N\}$ and B co-occurs with $\{M, P\}$. The votes will be $\{M : 2, N : 1, P : 1\}$, meaning that M will be the most highly-rated new tag to be recommended. The *summation-based method* additionally uses the co-occurrence value of the tags. Suppose for the same example that the co-occurrence values are: $A \rightarrow \{M : 1, N : 9\}$ and $B \rightarrow \{M : 2, P : 10\}$. Then the summation-based method will score the three tags as: $\{M : 3, N : 10, P : 10\}$, where now M is the lowest-score tag. Translating from Flickr tag recommendation to our context, we can consider each term as an object and then consider all of the hashtags that were used with this term across all tweets. Therefore we have each tweet made of p terms: $T_i = \{t_1, t_2, ..., t_p\}$. Hence, the voting-based method becomes:

$$vote(h, T) = \sum_{t_i \in T} vote(h, t_i)$$

where

$$vote(h, t_i) = \begin{cases} 1 & \text{if } h, t_i \text{ co-occur} \\ 0 & \text{otherwise} \end{cases}$$

in which we consider all of the hashtags that have co-occurred with each of the terms in tweet T and count the number of times a hash has co-occurred with each of the t_i in T. For the summation-based method we can consider the number of co-occurrences of hashtag h and the terms in a tweet T.

$$sum(h, T) = \sum_{t_i \in T} count(h, t_i)$$

where $count(h, t_i)$ denotes the number of co-occurrences of hashtag h and the terms in a tweet T. In both methods the scores are additionally normalized with a promotion score in which the stability of the term, descriptiveness of hashtag and the rank of hashtag in the co-occurrence list of the terms is considered. For more explanation we refer the interested reader to [20].

4.2.2 Bayesian Prediction

The second approach is based on Bayesian principles and also originates in image-based tag prediction [27]. Adapting this method, we can consider the co-occurrence of hashtags and terms along with the user tag history. Here, the probability of suggesting a hashtag h to a user u for the resource t_i is defined as:

$$p(h|u, t_i) = \frac{p(u, t_i|h) * p(h)}{p(u, t_i)} = \frac{p(u|h) * p(t_i|h) * p(h)}{p(u, t_i)} \quad (8)$$

where $p(h|u, t_i)$ is the probability that user u uses hashtag h to annotate resource t_i, $p(u, t_i|h)$ is the posterior probability of user u and resource t_i given a hashtag h, and $p(h)$ is the prior probability of hashtag h. Having the score of a hashtag h for each of the terms t_i we can find the total score of a hashtag for the whole tweet T as:

$$p(h|u, T) = \sum_{t_i \in T} p(h|u, t_i) \quad (9)$$

In this method since the user tagging history is taken into account, the score measured for each hashtag is a personalized score.

4.2.3 Association Rule Mining

The third approach is based on market-basket data mining principles for predicting tags [8][26]. In the market-basket model we have a large set of items and a large set of baskets containing a subset of items [1]. We are interested to identify the items that are purchased together frequently in a basket. This model generates the association rule of the form $\{I_1, I_2, .., I_n\} \Rightarrow \{h\}$ meaning that finding $I = \{I_1, I_2, .., I_n\}$ in a basket, there is a good chance of finding h in it. In particular, the popular association rule mining approach can be used to identify interesting relationships among terms and hashtags based on the probability of occurrence of the terms with their related hashtags. Adapting the market-basket model to the hashtag prediction problem, the baskets are the tweets, and the items are the terms and hashtags appearing in a tweet. The goal is to find the most probable hashtags when a set of terms I has been observed in a tweet. In this model we care about the term-hashtag pairs that appear frequently together and are considered to have high *support*. Another metric called *confidence* implies the probability of finding h knowing that I has occurred. The rules with high confidence and support construct the useful association rules. Here we define $supp(I)$ as the number of tweets in which I has appeared and $conf(I \Rightarrow h)$ as the probability of using hashtag h when I is observed in a tweet as a set of terms:

$$conf(I \Rightarrow h) = P(h|I) = \frac{supp(I, h)}{supp(I)} \qquad (10)$$

which is the number of times the terms I and hashtag h appear together divided by the number of times that the terms I appeared in the training dataset. In this way, association rules are used to find interesting term-hashtag relationships. The length of association rule can vary. In practice, the most interesting rules have a length of less than 3 for short text dataset. Hence, we first extract all possible association rules from the training set, keep only those of length 3 or less. To predict the hashtags for a new tweet, the rules with the same input terms and high confidence and support are used. As an example for the tweet "Freedom for journalism in Iran", we can consider the rules with support more than a threshold (30 in this case), resulting in the following high confidence rules: $\{freedom, iran\} \rightarrow \#iran$, $\{iran, journal\} \rightarrow \#iranelection$. Therefore the suggested hashtags will be $\{\#iran, \#iranelection\}$.

4.3 Experimental Results

We now evaluate the performance of the proposed graph-based approach to predict annotations. To do this we use the metrics described in Section 3.1 and the Twitter dataset described in Section 4.1. In particular, we perform three set of experiments: (i) to estimate the parameters and pivot selection methods used in the graph based approach; (ii) to compare the performance of our approach with the alternate approaches described earlier in this section; and (iii) to analyze the graph-based prediction approach.

4.3.1 Parameter Estimation

We estimate three parameters used by the graph-based approach: (i) the number of hops to consider from a pivot term; (ii) the decay factor (β) for penalizing nodes far from the pivot term; and (iii) the length of the sliding window (Δ). In addition to these parameters, we also compare the two pivot term selection methods – by entropy and by inverse document frequency.

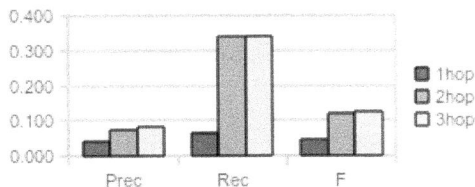

Figure 7: Increasing the number of hops identifies more relevant hashtags in the semantic graph.

Number of Hops: In this experiment we estimate the maximum number of hops to take from a pivot term to determine candidate hashtags for annotation. For example, while a value of one hop will consider only the immediate neighbors of a term, a choice of hops greater than 1 will consider hashtags that do not directly co-occur with the pivot term but are related to it. Hence in this experiment, we tried different number of hops after setting $\beta = 0.80$ and $\Delta = 1$ week. The result of this experiment is shown in Figure 7. We observe a

large improvement in recall as the number of hops increases to 2, suggesting that these nearby hashtags are good candidates (even if they have not co-occurred directly with the terms in a particular status update). We also note that the recall and F-measure are nearly the same comparing hops 2 and 3, meaning that additional exploration of the semantic graph identifies few additional significant hashtags. Since this larger exploration comes at a larger computational cost, we set the number of hops to 2 for the remainder of the experiments.

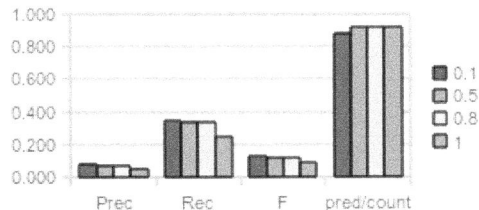

Figure 8: A smaller decay factor results in better performance but fewer overall predictions.

Decay Factor (β): To determine the choice of decay factor β, we set β to values ranging 0.0 to 1.0 and observe the performance of the approach. In addition to β, we set the number of hops to 2 and $\Delta = 1$ week. The result of this experiment is shown in Figure 8. Here we also show the rate of $pc = \frac{pred}{count}$ which measures the proportion of times that the semantic graph-based approach could predict at least one hashtag for the tweets in the test set. We see that a smaller decay factor results in a better performance but fewer overall predictions. Hence, to balance these two factors, we set $\beta = 0.8$.

Δ T	Precision	Recall	F-measure
hourly	0.041	0.042	0.041
hourly4	0.038	0.040	0.039
daily	0.109	0.107	0.107
weekly	**0.174**	**0.261**	**0.203**
monthly	0.132	0.201	0.152

Table 3: Comparing AR predictions with different ΔT. The weekly sliding window builds a better prediction model.

Length of Sliding Window (Δ): We additionally repeated the experiments by varying the length Δ to different values. We set the number of hops to 2 and parameter $\beta = 0.8$. The result of this experiment is shown in Table 3. We see 1 week of sliding window gives the best performance. In comparison, we see that the hourly, 4 hours and daily windows are sparse resulting in poor performance, while a month data tends to recommend outdated hashtags which also results in poor performance.

Approach to Select Pivot Terms: As described in Section 3.2.2, an important problem in the graph-based prediction framework is to select correct pivot terms. We now evaluate the performance of our approach using the two methods – entropy and document frequency. The results are shown in

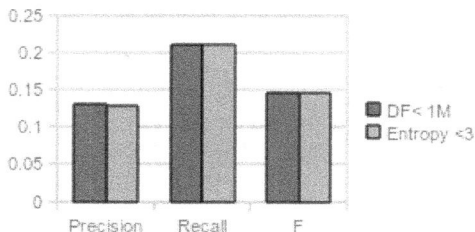

Figure 9: DF and Entropy pivot selection perform nearly equally well.

Method	Precision	Recall	F-measure
promo-vote	0.008	0.025	0.011
promo-sum	0.004	0.014	0.006
bayes	0.023	0.039	0.027
assoc-rule	**0.167**	**0.218**	**0.189**

Table 4: Comparing alternative approaches over 1000 test tweets.

Figure 9. Interestingly, we observe little difference between the performance of these two approaches. Since document frequency is simpler to maintain for all terms, we select it for the remainder of the experiments.

4.3.2 Comparison of Annotation Prediction Methods

We next evaluate the effectiveness of the several alternative methods for predicting hashtags. We then present the results of comparing our graph-based approach in detail against the best of these alternative methods.

Comparison of Alternate Methods: The comparison between annotating approaches in [20], [27], and [8], described earlier in this section, is shown in Table 4. For association rules, we report results for $conf = 0.1$ and $sup = 30$; we additionally varied the support threshold between 10 and 100 but found little change in results. We see that the association rule approach results in the best precision, recall, and F-measure (it also is relatively more efficient than the alternate approaches). Intuitively, the association rule approach is effective at weeding out large numbers of weak term-hashtag pairs (via the confidence and support thresholds), resulting in the best relative performance.

Graph-based vs Association Rule: Since association rule mining approach performs the best among the alternate approaches, we now compare it with our graph-based proposed method. Figure 10 compares the association rule based model and the graph-based approach for windows of different lengths. We observe that the association rule approach gives good performance when the length of the sliding windows is large (since it has access to a larger training set to identify term-hashtag relationships). However the graph-based model has a higher recall in all cases and better precision for the shorter sliding windows. These results suggest that the graph-based approach can identify implicit relationships among terms and hashtags by linking terms and hashtags that may have never occurred together.

Combining AR and Graph-Based Approaches: A pos-

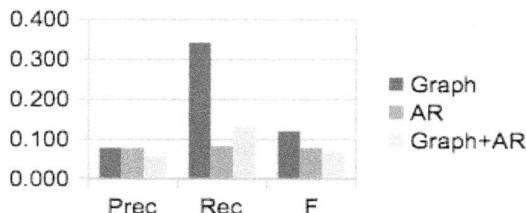

Figure 11: Combining AR with the semantic graph improves recall but not precision.

sible extension of the association rule based model is to combine it with the graph-based annotation prediction method. In this way we could take advantage of the properties of the graph-based model for revealing implicit relationships. Hence, we augmented the term-hashtag association rules discovered by association rule mining by additionally scoring related hashtags using the graph-based approach. In this way, additional hashtags may be identified, offering the possibility of increased recall. We evaluated the performance of this extended version and report the results in Figure 11. While we do observe that the recall of the combined approach is higher than the baseline association rule approach, it is still less than the pure graph-based approach. And disappointingly, the precision of the combined approach is worse than either alternative, suggesting the need for careful future study of the combination of these two approaches.

4.3.3 Analysis of Graph-Based Approach

Finally, we turn our attention to analyzing several properties of the graph-based prediction approach and describe a technique to extend its performance using tweet and hashtag categorization.

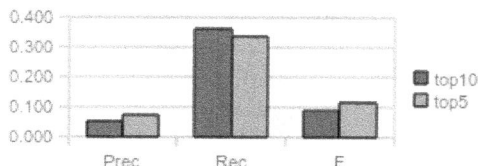

Figure 12: Increasing the number of selected hashtags (topK) lowers precision and increases recall.

Impact of Number of Hashtags: Based on the scores for hashtags generated by our system we select the first top-K hashtags. We observe that when top-K is small, we have higher precision and when it is larger we have higher recall. We consider top-$K = 5$ for the experiments since it gives us a good balance of precision and recall.

Impact of Smoothing: In Section 3, we described a smoothing model considering a mixture of both the most recent window and the global history in terms of hashtag-term linkages in the semantic graph. Performance of this smoothed model with others is shown in Figure 13. We observe a small increase in precision, but almost no improvement in

(a) hourly

(b) hourly4

(c) daily

(d) weekly

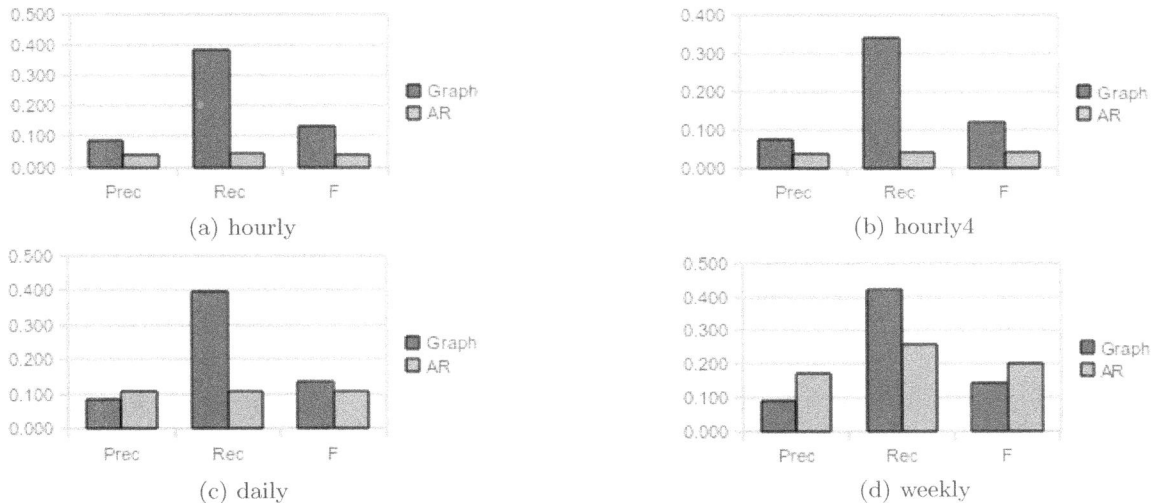

Figure 10: Comparing the graph-based and Association Rule based models for different sliding windows. The graph-based approach achieves high recall in all cases and better precision for the shorter sliding windows. The AR approach works well over the longest time horizon, when the training set is the largest.

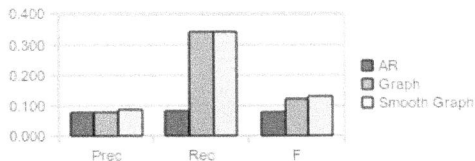

Figure 13: Smoothing increases precision by incorporating longer-term term-hashtag relationships.

recall. Additionally, since we are dealing with more data in the smoothed approach, the time taken to build model is greater, which may be infeasible for real-time annotation as status updates are inserted into the system.

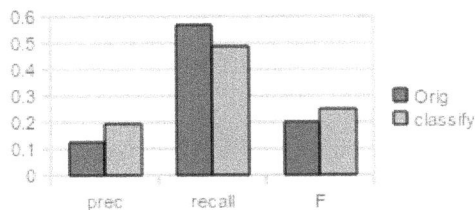

Figure 14: Classification of tweets increases the performance of the baseline approach.

Extending the Approach with Categorical Information: So far, we have studied semantic annotation of status updates using only the content of the updates themselves, without access to additional meta-information about the updates. It may be reasonable to expect that incorporating the category of the update into the prediction framework could increase its performance. Hence, we explore the possibility of improving the predictor by filtering out all suggested hashtags that belong to categories other than the category of the status update itself. Towards this goal, we assume there exists a tweet classifier similar to what is proposed in [19, 23] that can categorize both tweets and hashtags. Here we use the top-500 frequent hashtags that are already labeled by [19] into 8 categories: *Celebrities, Game, Political, Idioms, Music, Movies, Sports, Technology*. Then we consider only the tweets that contain at least one of these labeled hashtags (resulting in 12 million tweets in the dataset). Figure 14 compares this categorical extension with the baseline graph-based model. As expected, we see an increase in precision for the categorical extension, but a decrease in recall. This suggests the potential for incorporating more refined categorical (and perhaps sentiment-based) information into the hashtag prediction framework.

5. CONCLUSION

In this paper, we proposed a graph-based prediction framework for increasing the coverage of semantic annotations in real-time web status updates. We saw how the path aggregation technique for scoring the closeness of terms and hashtags in the graph, pivot term selection, and the dynamic sliding window led to encouraging results in comparison with alternative methods. As systems like Twitter and Facebook continue to grow, the proposed approach could be used to extend the small fraction of self-curated messages to organize the vast majority of messages that have not been annotated. In this way, the feedback between small-scale curation and automated methods may provide an evolving framework for ongoing organization of real-time web content. In our future work, we are interested to augment the baseline model presented here with information from each user's social network, so that hashtags adopted by a user's community may provide a more personalized set of hashtag recommendations. We are also interested to study the impact of increasing spam and low-quality hashtags on the performance of hashtag prediction.

6. REFERENCES

[1] R. Agrawal, T. Imieliński, and A. Swami. Mining association rules between sets of items in large databases. *SIGMOD Rec.*, 22:207–216, June 1993.

[2] D. M. Best, S. Bohn, D. Love, A. Wynne, and W. A. Pike. Real-time visualization of network behaviors for situational awareness. In *Proceedings of the Seventh International Symposium on Visualization for Cyber Security*, VizSec '10, 2010.

[3] A. Bifet and E. Frank. Sentiment knowledge discovery in twitter streaming data. In *Proceedings of the 13th international conference on Discovery science*, DS'10, pages 1–15, Berlin, Heidelberg, 2010. Springer-Verlag.

[4] A. Byde, H. Wan, and S. Cayzer. Personalized tag recommendations via tagging and content-based similarity metrics. In *Proceedings of the International Conference on Weblogs and Social Media*, March 2007.

[5] P. A. Chirita, S. Costache, S. Handschuh, and W. Nejdl. PTAG: Large Scale Automatic Generation of Personalized Annotation TAGs for the Web. May 2007.

[6] N. Garg and I. Weber. Personalized, interactive tag recommendation for flickr. In *Proceedings of the 2008 ACM conference on Recommender systems*, RecSys '08, 2008.

[7] S. Golder and B. A. Huberman. The structure of collaborative tagging systems. *Journal of Information Science*, 32:198–208, 2006.

[8] P. Heymann, D. Ramage, and H. Garcia-Molina. Social tag prediction. In *SIGIR '08: Proceedings of the 31st annual international ACM SIGIR conference on Research and development in information retrieval*, 2008.

[9] J. Illig, A. Hotho, R. Jäschke, and G. Stumme. A comparison of content-based tag recommendations in folksonomy systems. In *Proceedings of the First international conference on Knowledge processing and data analysis*, KONT'07/KPP'07.

[10] D. Irani, S. Webb, C. Pu, and K. Li. Study of Trend-Stuffing on Twitter through Text Classification. 2010.

[11] R. Jäschke, L. Marinho, A. Hotho, S.-T. Lars, and S. Gerd. Tag recommendations in social bookmarking systems. *AI Commun.*, 21, 2008.

[12] K. Y. Kamath and J. Caverlee. Transient crowd discovery on the real-time social web. In *Proceedings of the fourth ACM international conference on Web search and data mining*, WSDM '11, pages 585–594, New York, NY, USA, 2011. ACM.

[13] G. Koutrika, F. A. Effendi, Z. Gyöngyi, P. Heymann, and H. Garcia-Molina. Combating spam in tagging systems: An evaluation. *ACM Trans. Web.*

[14] K. Lee, J. Caverlee, K. Y. Kamath, and Z. Cheng. Detecting collective attention spam. In *Proceedings of the 2nd Joint WICOW/AIRWeb Workshop on Web Quality*, WebQuality '12, 2012.

[15] P. Mika. Ontologies are us: A unified model of social networks and semantics. Lecture Notes in Computer Science, pages 522–536. Springer, 2005.

[16] G. Mishne. In *Proceedings of the 15th international conference on World Wide Web*, New York, NY, USA.

[17] M. Naaman, J. Boase, and C.-H. Lai. Is it really about me?: message content in social awareness streams. In *Proceedings of the 2010 ACM conference on Computer supported cooperative work*, CSCW '10, 2010.

[18] A. Rae, B. Sigurbjörnsson, and R. van Zwol. Improving tag recommendation using social networks. In *Adaptivity, Personalization and Fusion of Heterogeneous Information*, RIAO '10, 2010.

[19] D. M. Romero, B. Meeder, and J. Kleinberg. Differences in the mechanics of information diffusion across topics: idioms, political hashtags, and complex contagion on twitter. WWW '11, 2011.

[20] B. Sigurbjörnsson and R. van Zwol. Flickr tag recommendation based on collective knowledge. In *WWW '08: Proceeding of the 17th international conference on World Wide Web*, 2008.

[21] Y. Song, Z. Zhuang, H. Li, Q. Zhao, J. Li, W.-C. Lee, and C. L. Giles. Real-time automatic tag recommendation. In *Proceedings of the 31st annual international ACM SIGIR conference on Research and development in information retrieval*, SIGIR '08, 2008.

[22] S. C. Sood and K. J. Hammond. Tagassist: Automatic tag suggestion for blog posts. In *In International Conference on Weblogs and Social*, 2007.

[23] B. Sriram, D. Fuhry, E. Demir, H. Ferhatosmanoglu, and M. Demirbas. Short text classification in twitter to improve information filtering. SIGIR '10.

[24] J. Sun, C. Faloutsos, S. Papadimitriou, and P. S. Yu. Graphscope: parameter-free mining of large time-evolving graphs. In *Proceedings of the 13th ACM SIGKDD International Conference on Knowledge Discovery and Data Mining*, 2007.

[25] J. Teevan, D. Ramage, and M. R. Morris. #twittersearch: a comparison of microblog search and web search. WSDM '11, 2011.

[26] J. Wang, L. Hong, and B. D. Davison. Rsdc'09: Tag recommendation using keywords and association rules.

[27] Z. Wang and Z. Deng. Tag recommendation based on bayesian principle. In *Proceedings of the 6th international conference on Advanced data mining and applications*.

[28] Z. Xu, Y. Fu, J. Mao, and D. Su. Towards the semantic web: Collaborative tag suggestions. In *Proceedings of Collaborative Web Tagging Workshop at 15th International World Wide Web Conference*, 2006.

[29] J. Yang and J. Leskovec. Patterns of temporal variation in online media. In *WSDM*, pages 177–186, 2011.

[30] Z.-K. Zhang, T. Zhou, and Y.-C. Zhang. Personalized recommendation via integrated diffusion on user-item-tag tripartite graphs. 2009.

Understanding and Leveraging Tag-based Relations in On-line Social Networks

Marek Lipczak[*]
Faculty of Computer Science
Dalhousie University
Halifax, Canada, B3H 1W5
lipczak@cs.dal.ca

Börkur Sigurbjörnsson[†]
brandcrumb
Barcelona, Spain
borkur@acm.org

Alejandro Jaimes
Yahoo! Research
Barcelona, Spain
ajaimes@yahoo-inc.com

ABSTRACT

In most social networks, measuring similarity between users is crucial for providing new functionalities, understanding the dynamics of such networks, and growing them (e.g., people you may know recommendations depend on similarity, as does link prediction). In this paper, we study a large sample of Flickr user actions and compare tags across different explicit and implicit network relations. In particular, we compare tag similarities in explicit networks (based on contact, friend, and family links), and implicit networks (created by actions such as comments and selecting favorite photos). We perform an in-depth analysis of these five types of links specifically focusing on tagging, and compare different tag similarity metrics. Our motivation is that understanding the differences in such networks, as well as how different similarity metrics perform, can be useful in similarity-based recommendation applications (e.g., collaborative filtering), and in traditional social network analysis problems (e.g., link prediction). We specifically show that different types of relationships require different similarity metrics. Our findings could lead to the construction of better user models, among others.

Categories and Subject Descriptors

H.3.4 [**Information Storage and Retrieval**]: Systems and Software—*information networks*; H.3.5 [**Information Storage and Retrieval**]: Online Information Services — *data sharing, web-based services*

Keywords

explicit social networks, implicit social networks, social tagging, user modeling, user similarity

---

[*]Research conducted on an internship at Yahoo! Research Barcelona.
[†]Research conducted while with Yahoo! Research.

1. INTRODUCTION

Flickr and other social media sites have – by design – a strong social component. Flickr users can interact with each other in various ways, both by explicitly adding other users to their social network and by interacting with the photos of other users – inside or outside their social network. From these various types of interaction possibilities we can derive different social links. In this paper we examine several social link types derived from Flickr interaction. We look at explicit social networks where users have identified other Flickr users as *contacts*, *friends* or *family*. We also look at implicitly derived social networks where we define a connection from one user to another if they *comment* on the other's photo or indicate it as one of their *favorites*. Our goal is to identify the characteristics of the connections within each network and how they differ across networks. More specifically, we are interested in information sharing patterns among the users connected by various social links. For this purpose we use the tagging feature available in Flickr. The tags assigned to users' photos allow us to gain deeper understanding about the scope and specificity of relations between users and the common topics of interest.

To determine the practical implications of differences in tag-sharing patterns, we analyze the similarity of connected users in terms of the tags assigned to their photos. We evaluate several tag-based user similarity metrics, for each link type, in a network reconstruction task. That is, we look at how well the similarity metrics can be used to differentiate connected and unconnected users. As we are able to distinguish the most important features of each metric (e.g., frequency of tag use or specificity of shared tags), comparison of the performance of the metrics gives us new insights about the characteristics of each link type. We show that the accuracy of a similarity metric depends on the type of link. Strong social links, such as family links, are best reconstructed using similarity metrics that rely on the specificity of the tags shared between users. Weaker social links, such as comments, are best reconstructed using the number of common shared tags. In addition, various similarity metrics can be used to specify sub-types of links within a single link type (e.g., differentiate between typical family links and family links utilized by close communities of interest). The comparison of similarity metrics in the network reconstruction task shows that cosine similarity, which is often the default option in measuring tag-based similarity between users, is outperformed by other much simpler metrics for all types of links. We also show that a state-of-the-art metric – Maximal Information Path can be reduced to a much simpler form that takes into consideration only the most specific tag shared between two users.

The main contribution of our work can be summarized as follows: (1) we provide a large-scale analysis of user behavior in various social networks within a single social system (2) we define the key characteristics of tag-based similarity metrics and show their performance is dependent on the types of links that they represent (3) we show that the comparison between the results of various similarity metrics can be useful to determine the character of ties between pairs of users. Although we focus our analysis on Flickr, the results are likely to be generalizable to other social systems with social network structure. More specifically, for social networks with a single link type our analysis can be useful in differentiating between types of social ties, for example separating links based on acquaintance and shared interests.

2. RELATED WORK

We examine related work in three groups: (1) social network analysis (implicit and explicit links); (2) tag-based similarity; and (3) Flickr.

Access to massive on-line data sets opened the possibility of characterizing and modeling large-scale social networks (explicit [10, 12] and implicit [11, 19]). For example, Grabowicz et al. [7] utilized various types of implicit links in Twitter (mentions and retweets) to better determine the character of explicit connections between Twitter users. In a preliminary study, Mitzlaff et al. [15] compared implicit and explicit networks generated by the users of BibSonomy, a social tagging system. The study revealed differences in graph characteristics between the two types of networks; however, according to the authors the differences were likely to be caused by the character of relations represented by specific types of links, not by its explicit or implicit nature. We found a similar pattern while examining Flickr's data set, in which the characteristics of the networks were likely to be caused by the on-line or off-line character of relations. In a broader perspective, our work relates to a well-studied problem of strong and weak social ties [8]. As we demonstrate, the representation of strong real-life ties in on-line social networks (e.g., family links) is scattered and incomplete, therefore these relations cannot be discovered based on graph characteristics. Our experiments suggest that this task can be achieved using various types of tags and tag-based similarity metrics.

One of the main problems with understanding large scale social relations is the limited access to information about human behavior [22]. A useful source of such information can be human-generated tags attached to on-line content. The tags can serve as the description of the content as well as the perception of the content by users. It has been shown that within the same social tagging system, users connected by various types of social links are more likely to use the same tags [3, 20, 21]. More specifically, users connected by explicit links tend to have higher similarity than users connected by implicit links [15]. Schifanella et al. [21] showed that the predictive power of tags in terms of discovering social relations can be improved by utilizing tag-specific similarity metrics (e.g., Maximal Information Path). We show that this metric does not generalize to implicit social relations.

Flickr, thanks to its large and vivid community of users is an interesting object of study in on-line social behavior. Flickr's social network has been used in studies on informa-

tion propagation [4], link prediction [9, 21] and community detection [5], among others. The information sharing patterns and their impact on user similarity metrics revealed in our work are potentially useful in any of these areas. Our results are aligned with the work on tagging motivation [1, 16, 17]. These studies point out three main reasons for picture tagging: self-organization, communication with family and friends, and communication with broader audience. Our work shows that some of these differences are reflected by the nature of shared tags between different link types.

3. DATA DESCRIPTION

We obtained a Flickr sample of activity of a subset of users up to May 2008. In particular, we collected social links, comment, favorite and tagging actions for the users in the sample. All data was anonymized. The dataset contained over 6.5 million users who were linked by the five link types described below. The specific statistics for each link type can be found in Table 1. The table also contains the abbreviations used for the link types throughout the paper. In the following sub-sections we describe different aspects of the dataset in further detail.

3.1 Explicit and Implicit Networks

Flickr allows its users to choose three types of explicit social connections. A user can declare another user as a *contact*, *friend* or *family* member. The links are not reciprocal by default and do not need confirmation from the "connected" user, who can remain unconnected with the author of the relation or establish a connection of a different type. To generate the explicit social networks we used the set of contact relations between users (Flickr's social network) creating a directed, unweighted graph $G_{contact} = (V, E)$ in which each node v represents a single user and each edge e represents a directed connection between two users. Flickr allows each contact link to be specified as *friend* or *family*. The user can leave these fields blank or choose one or two options. If such choice was made we moved the edge from the contact graph to one of two graphs representing *friend* and *family* connections.

We focused on two types of user actions to build implicit networks: commenting on photos of other users and marking photos as favorites. Using the information about comment actions we generated an implicit social network between Flickr users, which is a directed, unweighted graph $G_{comment} = (V, E)$ in which each node v represents a single user and each edge e represents a directed connection between a user u_a and any other user u_b, on whose photo u_a made a comment action. An analogous implicit social network was constructed based on the favorite actions. Although it is possible to weight the links based on the number of comments or favorites, we decided to keep the links unweighted. Although we lose some information about the strength of the connection, which can be expressed with the number of comments (or favorites), the connection strength is also unknown for the explicit links. Therefore, by keeping the implicit links unweighted, we unify the format and available information for all types of links.

3.2 Tagging

Tags are free-form keywords that are assigned to a resource. In general, the most common purpose of tags is describing the content of the resource; however, users have

Table 1: Statistics for social link types; *max in-deg.* **and** *max out-deg.* **columns present the maximal and minimal out-degree of a node in a user graph;** *user % in wcc* **is the ratio of users in the giant weakly connected component;** *comp.* **is the total number of components;** *max p* **is the maximal non-empty p-core;** *max p 2 comp.* **is the maximal p-core with at least two distinct components;** *avg #tags sh. per pair* **is the average number of tags shared by a pair of users (see Section 4 and Section 5.1 for detailed description).**

	links	users	max in-deg.	max out-deg.	user % in wcc	comp.	max p	max p 2 comp.	links with shared tag	total unique shared tags	avg #tags sh. per pair
Family (Fml)	7M	2.6M	3K	8K	0.26	560K	75	55	716K(10%)	276K(2.07%)	18.65
Friend (Frn)	36M	4.3M	10K	18K	0.75	335K	256	23	8.4M(23%)	677K(0.28%)	28.56
Contact (Cnt)	32M	2.5M	25K	19K	0.80	199K	335	13	16M(50%)	708K(0.09%)	46.97
Favorite (Fav)	43M	2.1M	34K	20K	0.97	31K	204	3	29M(67%)	898K(0.05%)	58.23
Comment (Cmt)	63M	3.4M	16K	19K	0.89	244K	559	14	45M(71%)	1015K(0.04%)	61.09

extended their functionality to other purposes [6]. In most social systems, the vocabulary of tags is unconstrained and unknown to the user while tagging. Therefore users may create ad-hoc tags that in their opinion match the posted resource. Tagging is a popular form of photo description among Flickr users. From 6.5 million users in our sample, 3.2 million (49%) have at least one tag assigned to their photos. In our sample, over 99% of tag to photo assignments are done by the photo's owner. Although it is unlikely that users would tag photos they do not own, the Flickr community has developed a tag suggestion mechanism. The suggestions are made using the photo comments feature (e.g., "You may tag your photo as *flickrdiamond*"). Often these tags act as an invitation of a photo to a specific Flickr group (e.g., *NaturesFinest*). We refer to these tags as "appreciation tags", because in most cases they represent the appreciation of the commenting user for the work of the photographer. As we discuss in section 7.2.3, appreciation has a great impact on the similarity score calculated for Flickr users.

Tags assigned to users' content are a valuable source of information for modeling user interests and behavior [20, 23]. To build a tag-based profile for each user u in the sample we took the set of their public photos and extracted tags that were assigned to the photos. The user profile is represented by a set of distinct tags – V_u assigned to the photos together with a score which represents the number of such assignments.

4. SOCIAL BEHAVIOR

In this section we provide general graph characteristics of the five investigated social link types. The characteristics are later used to better understand the tag sharing patterns and relations between similarity scores calculated based on the tag profiles of users. For each link type we discuss the basic statistics, i.e., number of users, number of links, maximal in- and out-degree. In addition, we look at the component structure of the graphs observing the number of the users in the giant weakly connected component and the peripheral components including the number of disconnected pairs – components built of only two users. To gain more insights about the structure of the giant component we extracted p-cores of each graph (a p-core of level p contains only nodes with out-degree at least p). For these we report the maximal p for which the p-core is not empty and maximal value of p for which the graph contains at least two disjoint components. The statistics are presented in Table 1.

4.1 Explicit Networks

Family and friend links have much higher maximal out-degree than in-degree which suggests a hub structure. The hubs are users who are diligently adding to the system all their relations. The highest out-degree for the family links is roughly 8,000, which poses a question about the character of these links. Likely, these are not traditionally understood family connections but a community of users who utilize these links to represent their closeness of interests. Later, we confirm this hypothesis observing sets of tags shared between users (see Section 5.3). Conversely, the contact links have higher maximal in-degree than out-degree. Contact links often represent the connections made within the system. Therefore these links are more likely to point to authorities, which in the case of Flickr are semi-professional photographers publishing high-quality pictures. Looking at the component structure of the explicit networks we observe that a large number of links lies outside the giant weakly connected component. It is especially visible for the family links. Only 26% of the users in this network are part of the giant weakly connected component (i.e., there is a path between each pair of them while we disregard the direction of the links). This network has also over $250K$ pairs of users completely disconnected from the rest of the network. It suggests that, despite the occurrence of high-degree users, the majority of these links represent real off-line family relations. This representation is, however, incomplete and scattered. Comparing to the family links, friend and contact links create much more connected graphs, but still their connectivity is lower than in the case of implicit networks. Finally, the results of the p-cores experiments reveal low connectivity and high modularity of the giant component for the family links. Low connectivity results in relatively low value of maximal not empty $p-core$. The high value of $p = 55$, for which we can still observe two disjoint components shows that there is no single core of the graph. Other disjoint components vanish at p equal to 26 and 20. These components are likely to gather the communities of close interests which use the family links to represent their bounds.

4.2 Implicit Networks

The favorite links create an authority structure (much higher maximal in-degree than out-degree). This feature makes it similar to the contact links. The favorite graph has a very high ratio of links in the giant component and relatively low maximal p-core and low maximal p-core with more than two components. All these features confirm the star-based structure of the network. The in- and out-degree structure of comment graph is much more balanced with the in/out degree correlation reaching 0.77 (comparing to 0.43 for favorite links). The non-empty p-core for the comment graph reaches 559 which suggests a large and dense community of users that are likely to comment each-others pictures (compare to non-empty p-core reaching 68 for MSN network with 240 million users [11]).

As in any social system the types of relations between users blend together within a single social network producing complex graph characteristics for each examined network. Nevertheless, comparison of a few explicit and implicit social graphs allow us to distinguish two factors which seem to have the highest impact on the observed characteristics. We can notice the scattered and incomplete representation of off-line social links and the authority-based organization of a dense community of users formed on-line within the social system. The former is mostly visible for the family links and the latter for favorite links.

5. TAGGING BEHAVIOR

In this section we discuss the characteristics of social links based on the tags shared between users connected by each of the five social link types. In our experiments we looked at the overlap between tag profiles of users. In addition, we used the document frequency (or DF) score as the proxy of tag specificity. Given our problem, the document frequency is understood as the number of users with a given tag.

5.1 Tagging Activity of Users

First, we look at the general patterns in tag usage by users of various link types. Users connected by family links have the least amount of tags assigned to their pictures. Only 21% of users with at least one family link have one or more tags assigned to their photos. This percentage grows for the users of friend and contact links and is even higher for the favorite and comment links. A similar pattern was found by Nov et al. [17] while comparing tag vocabularies of users motivated to tag for family and for a broader audience. We have also noticed a weak correlation between the number of out-going links and the number of tags in the profile which is the largest for comment links – Pearson correlation coefficient equal to 0.29. The coefficient decreases to 0.04 for family links. One of the reasons could be the use of private photos which were not considered in our study. Another reason is likely the general activity pattern, which suggests that users who often comment on or favorite photos are also more likely to post and tag a large number of photos.

Independently of their origin, these differences affect the total number of links between users that share at least one tag. For example, only 10% of family links is made between users that have at least one tag in common, but this number grows to 71% for comment links (Table 1). The same trend is observed for the average number of tags shared by a pair of users connected by each link type. Conversely, for family and friend links we can observe the highest percentage of distinct tags (Table 1). These are all distinct tags that were shared by at least one pair of users linked in a network divided by the total number of shared tags.

5.2 Categories of Shared Tags

To reveal the types of tags that are most and least useful in discriminating links between the users of various link types

we utilized the classification scheme proposed by Overell et al. [18]. The authors used information extracted from Word-Net and Wikipedia to classify over 200,000 Flickr tags into main semantic categories of WordNet (Fig. 1). The authors used a two-step approach. The Wikipedia articles are first classified into WordNet semantic categories. In the next step tags are mapped to Wikipedia articles using the anchor text of Wikipedia links. A preliminary observation of the list of most discriminative tags suggested that many of them are appreciation tags (defined in Section 3.2). Therefore, we decided to extend the classification scheme with this type of tags. To automatically extract the appreciation tags from the database we used simple heuristics based on two basic characteristics of these tags – the fact that they are directly assigned or suggested by a user that is not the owner of the photo, some time after the photo is uploaded to the system. We selected two sets of tags – tags that were frequently assigned to photos not by their owners and a set of tags that were frequently assigned to the photo at least ten hours after its upload. We selected only tags that matched at least one of these criteria in at least 80% of user profiles. The combined set of appreciation tags contained over 20 thousand unique tags. In 99% of cases these tags were not captured in any of the WordNet classes. The fact that a classification mechanism based on information extracted from WordNet and Wikipedia was not able to cover appreciation tags is caused by the way these tags are designed. Appreciation tags are usually complex phrases meant to be easily distinguishable from other tags (e.g., *goldenphotographeraward*).

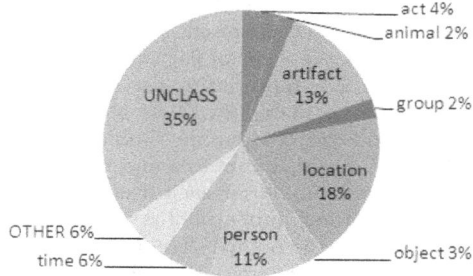

Figure 1: The coverage of eight largest categories from Overell et al. tag classification in our data.

In order to compare the importance of a tag category between types of social links we examined the position of tags from the category in Chi-square based tag ranking for each social link type. We used only tags that could be found in more than 100 user profiles ($DF > 100$) to ensure the data is sufficient for statistical analysis, the most specific tags are addressed separately in the next section. Chi-square [14] is widely used in supervised feature selection tasks to determine if a feature is a good predictor of a class. In our problem, chi-square statistic ranks tags shared between users showing how well they predict the occurrence of a social link between users. Therefore, if tags from a given category are in general good predictors of a link, they should be high in the ranking. We have experimented with three IR measures that can be used in such tasks: normalized discounted cumulative gain, average precision and median position. All of them agree on the relative importance of tag categories for various link types. Therefore, we report only the results of the median position as they are easy to be intuitively in-

Table 2: The ranking of discriminative value of tags from various categories for five link types.

	adverb	adjective	attribute	state	person	location	artifact	animal	plant	appreciation
Fml	**0.91**	**0.79**	**0.79**	**0.67**	**0.52**	**0.58**	0.47	0.51	0.48	0.88
Frn	0.69	0.59	0.60	0.56	0.47	0.52	0.51	0.55	0.57	0.94
Cnt	0.47	0.47	0.49	0.47	0.43	0.53	0.56	0.66	0.68	0.96
Fav	0.54	0.56	0.56	0.51	0.44	0.49	**0.59**	0.72	0.76	0.96
Cmt	0.50	0.54	0.54	0.50	0.41	0.52	0.57	**0.76**	**0.79**	**0.98**

terpreted. Median position is defined for a set of tags from a given category as the position of the median tag from the category among all the tags in the ranking. The position is normalized so the first tag in the ranking has position 1.0 and the last one 0.0. If the majority of the tags from the category can be found in the first half of the ranking the median position score for the category will be over 0.5.

The comparison of the median position of tags from various categories confirms the relations between link types revealed in previous experiments (Table 2). For all categories two extremes are family or friendship links and comment or favorite links. Whenever one category gets high positions in the ranking of one type of links it gets the low positions in the other. Observing the specific categories of tags we can notice that users connected by family and friend links are strongly bound by tags classified as *adverbs* (e.g., sometimes, slowly) and *adjectives* (e.g., strange, comfortable). Even when we look at noun categories we see that categories important for these types of links are *attribute* (e.g., red, modesty) and *state* (e.g., despair, fascination). It demonstrates that users connected by family and friendship links share the ways they characterize photos and objects captured on them including their emotions and opinions towards photographed objects. Considering the largest categories of tags we see that family and friends share tags from categories *person* and *location*. In the first category we can notice the importance of names used as tags (e.g., amanda, chris). The second is dominated by geographical locations which suggests that users connected by these links live in close proximity. The last large category – *artifact* (e.g., street, leica) is the domain of comment and favorite links. Another two categories that are highly ranked for these types of links are *animal* and *plant*. Both of them are a frequent object of photographic interests. Therefore, users bound by these links share the description of their interests. Nevertheless, these users are still most strongly bound by the opinions about the pictures. However, unlike users connected by family links who use adverbs and adjectives to describe their opinions, comment and favorite users adapted the community-driven set of appreciation tags. These tags completely dominate the top of the ranking of discriminative tags for comment and favorite links. The appreciation tags are also high in the ranking of other link types, which shows that there is no complete separation between two types of links. We discuss this problem in more details in Section 7.2.2.

5.3 Specificity of Shared Tags

One of the factors that characterize the relation of a pair of users is the most specific tag shared between them (i.e., the tag with the lowest document frequency score among all the tags shared between users). To examine the specificity of information shared between users, we extracted the most specific tag that is shared between each pair of linked

users that share at least one tag. We sorted the links by the document frequency of the most specific tag and plotted a cumulative distribution of the links given the most specific tag they share. The ratio of family links which are bound by a very specific tag is higher than the ratio for comment links (Fig. 2(a)). However, as the document frequency of the most specific tag grows the difference becomes smaller and at DF equal to 350 the pattern breaks. Unexpectedly, there is a large number of family and friend links that share only relatively general tags (compared to other link types). The explanation of this fact is the larger number of tags that are generally present in profiles (and shared) between the users connected by comment, favorite and contact links. As the number is higher than in case of family links it is more likely to find a specific tag shared by users, purely by chance. To control the impact of this factor we limited the set of observed users only to users with at least 100 distinct tags in their profiles. In this case the higher specificity of tags shared between family and friends is clearly visible (Fig. 2(b)).

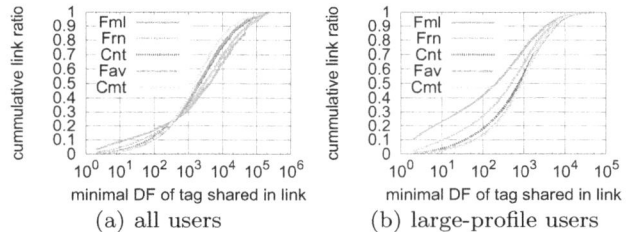

(a) all users   (b) large-profile users

Figure 2: The cumulative ratio of user pairs against the value of document frequency (DF) of the most specific tag they share.

As the most specific shared tags are difficult to capture by any classification scheme we decided to examine the set of these tags manually. We focused on two sub-sets of tags: the most specific tags that are shared between less than ten users in total and specific tags that are shared by large number of users. Among the most specific tags for family and friend links we found tags that are likely to fall under three distinct categories: location (i.e., specific names of geographical locations), event (i.e., names or acronyms of social events), names (i.e., specific variations of names and nick-names). Sharing of these tags may reflect real-life relationships between users. Among the most specific tags shared between large number of family linked users we can find tags that well describe communities of interest (e.g., a community of users interested in taking pictures of doll figurines). It suggests that these communities choose to use the family links as a strong representation of their interest bounds. For comment, favorite and contact links both groups of tags seems to be dominated by appreciation tags.

6. USER SIMILARITY AS NETWORK RECONSTRUCTION

In order to study the tag-based relations between users, we examined a practical problem of content-based network reconstruction. Its objective is to reveal the links between pairs of objects through their pair-wise similarity. In our case the similarity is calculated based on the tag profiles of users. The network reconstruction task is often referred as content-based link prediction task [9, 21].

6.1 Tag-based Similarity Metrics

We compared a range of similarity metrics based on different features – frequency of tags in users' profiles (e.g., cosine similarity), number of tags shared between users (e.g., Dice coefficient) and specificity of shared tags (e.g., maximal information path). All metrics are symmetrical. We use the following notation: u_1, u_2 – users for which the similarity is calculated; V_u – set of tags from the profile of user u; $tf_u(t)$ number of times tag t was used by user u (term frequency); $df(t)$ – number of users with tag t (document frequency); U – set of all users.

Cosine similarity.

Cosine similarity is a metric adapted from the vector space model used to represent textual documents. In the model each document is represented by a vector of terms with weights that mark the number of occurrences of a term in a document. By analogy, we consider a user as a document and a set of user's tags as terms. The similarity between two users is calculated as the cosine between two user vectors (Eq. 1). In the textual domain it is reasonable to decrease the weight of terms that are shared between a large number of documents extending the term frequency factor tf by an inverse document frequency factor idf (Eq. 2). In our experiments, we tested both approaches, considering each user profile as a single document.

$$cos(u_1, u_2) = \frac{\sum_{t \in V_1 \cap V_2} tfidf_1(t) \cdot tfidf_2(t)}{\sqrt{\sum_{t \in V_1} tfidf_1(t)^2} \sqrt{\sum_{t \in V_2} tfidf_2(t)^2}} \quad (1)$$

$$tfidf_u(t) = tf_u(t) \cdot log\frac{|U|}{df(t)} \quad (2)$$

Dice coefficient.

When used as tag-based similarity metric, the Dice coefficient is the size of an intersection of two user profiles normalized by the sum of profile sizes (Eq. 3).

$$dice(u_1, u_2) = \frac{2|V_1 \cap V_2|}{|V_1| + |V_2|} \quad (3)$$

Tag overlap.

Tag overlap is a simplification of the Dice coefficient, without the normalization factor (Eq. 4).

$$overlap(u_1, u_2) = |V_1 \cap V_2| \quad (4)$$

Table 3: Similarity factors included in the metrics.

factor	cosine similarity	tag overlap	dice coefficient	min. common DF	MIP
tag frequency	+				
vocabulary overlap	+	+	+		
tag specificity	+			+	+
profile based norm	+		+		+

Maximal Information Path (MIP).

The Maximal Information Path is a metric proposed by Schifanella et al. [21] specifically to calculate the similarity of user profiles. It is an adaptation of the Lin similarity [13] used to calculate semantic relatedness of terms in a concept hierarchy. Lin based his similarity on the probability of occurrence of the terms in textual corpora, which determines the specificity of a term. The score is proportional to the specificity of the lowest common ancestor of two terms and inversely proportional to the terms' specificity. MIP is a generalization of the score in which the lowest common ancestor is replaced by the specificity of tag shared between two users and the users are represented by the most specific tags in their profiles (Eq. 5). The specificity of the tag is expressed as the ratio of user profiles which contain the tag.

$$mip(u_1, u_2) = \frac{2log(\min_{t \in V_1 \cap V_2} \frac{df(t)}{|U|})}{log(\min_{t \in V_1} \frac{df(t)}{|U|}) + log(\min_{t \in V_2} \frac{df(t)}{|U|})} \quad (5)$$

Minimal common DF.

The Minimal common DF is a simplification of the maximal information path metric in which we consider only the specificity of the most specific shared tag (Eq. 6).

$$minDF(u_1, u_2) = \frac{2}{\min_{t \in V_1 \cap V_2} df(t)} \quad (6)$$

6.2 Metrics Characteristics

The introduced tag-based similarity metrics are based on four main similarity factors: *tag frequency*, *vocabulary overlap*, *tag specificity* and *profile based norm* (Table 3). Tag frequency represents the personal importance of a tag and is considered as one of the most important features in tag-based user models [2]. Vocabulary overlap is the number of tags that are shared between two users. This factor is driven by frequent tags shared between a large group of users. Conversely, tag specificity utilizes the discriminative power of tags shared between a small number of users. Finally, profile based norm attempts to equalize the impact of undesired factors (e.g., different level of user activity) to make the scores calculated for different user pairs comparable.

6.2.1 Cosine Similarity and Tag Popularity

At first sight, among all the tested metrics only cosine similarity uses all similarity factors. Other metrics focus on a single factor – vocabulary overlap or tag specificity, which in case of the Dice coefficient and maximal information path is normalized by a profile based norm. However, the characteristics of the metrics change when we consider the specific application of similarity based on tag-based user profiles. Tag profiles of users are characterized by heavy tailed frequency distributions [23] – a user is likely to use a small group of tags much more often than other tags. The construction of cosine similarity, which multiplies or squares frequencies of tags makes it very sensitive to these tags. If the frequently used tags of two users match, it completely dominates the outcome of cosine similarity. This fact can be illustrated with an example of two Flickr users with profiles of more than 50 unique tags that are completely disjoint with one exception of a tag that is used very frequently by both of them – *canon*. The cosine similarity between the users is equal to 0.87, which signifies almost a perfect match between the profiles (compare to 0.024 which is the average similarity between a pair of users). Therefore, despite the fact that cosine similarity utilizes all similarity factors, its result is driven mostly by the most frequently used tags. Unlike textual documents, where it is not likely to find the same term in all sentences (with the exception of stop-words), user profiles can be strongly biased by frequently used tags. Some tags (e.g., *canon*) are likely to be used in a great majority of user's posts. In the text mining domain, the importance of the most frequent term can be to some extent reduced by the use of the IDF factor. The terms that are frequently used in a textual document are likely to be used in many documents. However, in tag-based user profiles the most frequently used tags strongly depend on the tagging habits of users. For example, the tag *canon*, which (when used) is very often the most frequent tag in a user profile, in our sample, can be found in the second hundred of tags ranked by the DF score. As a result, the IDF factor has little or no impact on the performance of the cosine similarity metric. We confirmed this observation by comparing the results of both versions of the metric (detailed results omitted due to space constraints).

6.2.2 *Maximal Information Path and Tag Specificity*

Another aspect of tag-based user profiles that influences the characteristics of maximal information path similarity is the long tail of user profile distribution, which contains a large number of infrequently used tags. As it is relatively easy to find specific tags among them, all users are likely to have very specific tags in their profiles. This fact puts under consideration the analogy with the Lin similarity. The normalization factor in MIP depends on the most specific tag in the user's profile, hence its variability is low. As a result, the MIP score could, in practice, be equal to the minimal document frequency of the common tags.

7. EXPERIMENTS

To test the discriminative power of each similarity metric we calculated the similarity between each pair of users in our sample. This way we obtained a ranking of user pairs with respect to their similarity. Each similarity metric is able to produce a non-zero score if there is at least one tag shared between two users. The ranking was later matched with the social links of each type. We decided to follow the evaluation technique proposed in previous work [9, 21] and present the results in the form of ROC curves. Therefore, we gradually extended the set of the evaluated pairs following

the decreasing values of the similarity metrics. At each step we calculated the *true positive rate*, which is the ratio of linked user pairs in the evaluated sample among all linked pairs and *false positive rate*, which is the ratio of non linked pairs in the sample among all non linked pairs. Plotting both rates for the increasing size of evaluated sample allows us to picture the discriminative power of the ranking function, which is, in our case, any of the similarity metrics. The observation of receiver operating characteristics shows that despite their simplicity all metrics act as a proper ranking function (Fig 3). For all types of social links they achieve the highest accuracy for the most highly ranked connections (steep curve close to the origin).

Our Flickr sample contains over 6.5 million users. Therefore, even though we considered only scalable tag-based similarity metrics the computation of pair-wise similarity scores between all users is not feasible. In order to limit the computational cost of the experiments based on tag similarity, we sampled the user set. Two sampling approaches were used. The *random sample* contained 100 thousand users randomly chosen from the pool of users that had at least one link of any type. No constraints on their tag profiles was made, so it was possible that the sampled user had no tags. In the second sample we focused only on users with *rich tag profiles*. We selected 104, 003 users who had at least 100 unique tags in their profiles, each of the tags being used at least three times. We put no constraints on the minimal document frequency of tags.

7.1 Comparison of Sampling Approaches

In the random sampling approach we did not take into account the general activity of the users in the system. Hence, it is likely that we picked a substantial amount of inactive users, that used the system for a short time and left. Therefore we can assume that this method underestimates the typical activity of Flickr users. This fact mostly affects the implicit networks where a large number of links are established by a small group of active users. On the other hand, the sampling based on tag use overestimates the typical activity which affects the explicit networks (e.g., family links), because users of these links are generally less active. The main difference in the results of the two sampling methods is the performance of the metrics for comment and favorite links (Table 4). Since for these link types the sampling method based on the size of tag profiles is more representative, we decided to focus on this sample in further discussion of the results. We also use this sample in the additional experiments presented in this section.

7.2 Social Link Types

A comparison of the performance of similarity metrics for various types of social links reveals interesting differences. Starting with the family links which represent the strongest social ties, we see that the most accurate ranking is created by the maximal information path (MIP) and minimal common document frequency (min. common DF) (Table 4, Fig. 3(a)). Both metrics are based on the specificity of shared tags, which suggest that family linked users are distinguishable by the most specific tags they use. The worst ranking is produced by the metrics based on the number of shared tags – tag overlap and Dice coefficient. While we move towards links representing weaker social connections the number of common tags shared becomes more discrim-

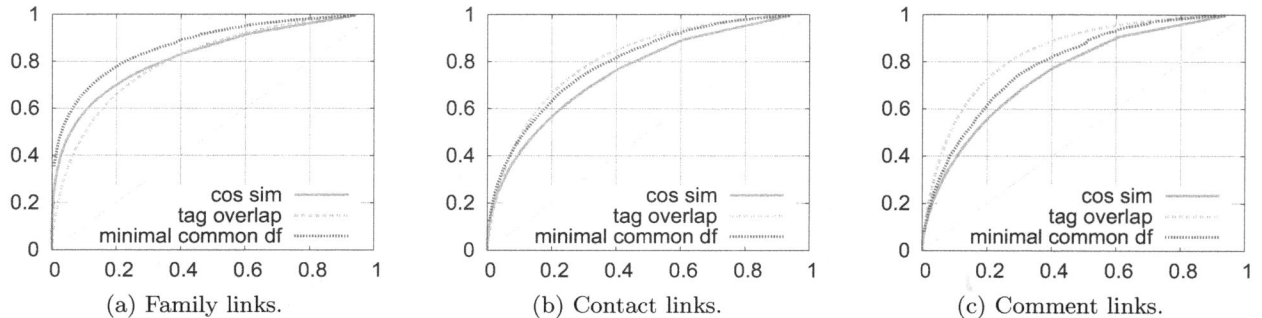

(a) Family links. (b) Contact links. (c) Comment links.

Figure 3: ROC curve of three similarity metrics (rich tag profile sample). Friend and favorite links are omitted as they show similar characteristics as family and comment links respectively.

Table 4: Area under the ROC curve for two sampling approaches.

	Fml	Frn	Cnt	Fav	Cmt
rich tag profiles sample					
cos sim	0.81	0.78	0.74	0.73	0.74
dice coefficient	0.78	0.78	0.78	0.79	0.81
tag overlap	0.80	0.79	**0.80**	**0.82**	**0.83**
MIP	**0.87**	**0.82**	0.79	0.78	0.78
min. common DF	**0.87**	**0.82**	0.79	0.78	0.78
random sample					
cos sim	0.72	0.75	0.75	0.73	0.76
dice coefficient	0.69	0.70	0.75	0.76	0.80
tag overlap	0.66	0.73	0.85	**0.89**	**0.91**
MIP	**0.82**	**0.84**	0.85	0.87	0.89
min. common DF	0.81	**0.84**	**0.88**	0.89	**0.91**

inative for linked users. For contact links tag overlap is as accurate as tag specificity based metrics and they are both more accurate than cosine similarity (Fig. 3(b)). For the implicit social links, tag overlap becomes more accurate than metrics based on tag specificity. It suggests that implicitly connected users share a large number of general tags. Surprisingly, cosine similarity, which is the most complex similarity metric tested, performed the worst (Fig. 3(c)). It is followed by the Dice coefficient. Both of them include a normalization factor based on the size of the user profile. One of its objectives is to mitigate the advantage of users with large tag profiles; however, it seems to be the wrong strategy. Another drawback of cosine similarity is the focus on the most frequently used tag, whereas for implicit networks the broad overlap of vocabulary seems to be more important. Considering the results for all link types, the accuracy of the MIP metric was always nearly identical to minimal common document frequency and the value of Dice coefficient was always between cosine similarity and tag overlap. Therefore, for clarity we do not present the results of these metrics in the figures.

7.2.1 Types of Links or Types of Users?

One of the potential explanations for the difference in the performance of similarity metrics for various link types is that each of them is used by a specific group of users with links of a single type only. Such distinction between two types of users was suggested by Negoescu et al. [16]. In such case, the characteristics of users' personal behavior could influence the characteristics of the link type. To study this problem we compared the similarity between users and their neighbors connected by friend and favorite links. For each user we collected the neighbors for both link types and separated them into three groups: friends, whose photo was added to favorites (Frn ∩ Fav), friends with no favorited photos (Frn \ Fav) and users with favorited photos, but no friendship relation (Fav \ Frn). In the rich profile sample 63% of users contain both at least one friend and favorite link. It shows that Flickr users tend to have relations of different type. 33% of users have a neighbor in the three sets. To simplify the presentation of results we focused only on these users. We calculated the average similarity between a user and their neighbors in any of the sets using cosine similarity, tag overlap and min. common DF metrics. For all metrics the highest similarity was observed for Frn ∩ Fav neighbors. Futher, comparing Fav \ Frn and Frn \ Fav relations we see that the former has higher tag overlap similarity and the latter higher minimal common DF and cosine similarity. All pair-wise differences are statistically significant. The results show that Flickr users tend to have diverse relations and the similarity between them and their neighbors should be expressed with a metric that is tailored to specific characteristics of a link type that connects them. This fact has a direct implication on the link recommendation task – while searching for similar users the notion of similarity is dependent on the type of links that we are aiming to predict.

Table 5: Average similarity between users and the set of their neighbors of favorite and/or friend links

	Fav ∩ Frn	Fav \ Frn	Frn \ Fav
cos sim	**0.062**	0.023	**0.043**
tag overlap	**36.72**	30.84	27.20
min. common DF	**0.162**	0.032	**0.088**

7.2.2 Link Sub-Types within a Single Network

The difference between various similarity metrics can be utilized in another interesting practical problem – disambiguation of various link types within a single social network. As discussed in Section 4, the family links are likely to be a mix between commonly understood family connections and close communities that share common interests. We can assume that the former can mostly be found among the disconnected pairs of users, whereas the latter are mostly present in the giant connected component. We used this assumption to evaluate the ability of similarity metrics in discriminating the two types of relations. For each metric we sorted the family links in decreasing order of their similarity and following the order we observed how many of the links can be found within the giant component (in a sliding window of 5000 links). The comparison of the results for the metrics shows that tag overlap promotes the links within the component, whereas cosine similarity and minimal common DF promotes links outside the component (Fig. 4). Revealing the true character of a social link can be used in content dissemination tasks, for example to avoid automatic notification of contacts based on shared interests, when a user submitted a set of family photos.

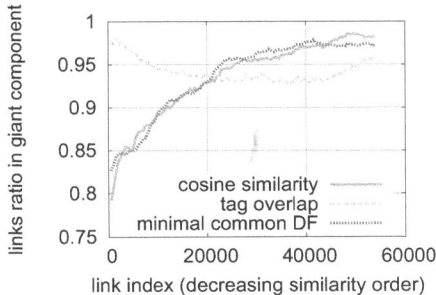

Figure 4: User similarity within and outside the giant weakly connected component for the family links.

7.2.3 Tag Categories

Finally, we turn our attention to different types of tags that can be used to calculate the similarity between users. To test the discriminative power of tags of specific category, we re-ran the experiments limiting the tags in the user profile to a single category. The accuracy of the similarity metrics agrees with the outcome of Chi-square based analysis (Section 5.2). For each category, the distribution of the network reconstruction accuracy follows the the Chi-square ranks for the link types. Because of space constraints, we present the results for appreciation and person categories (Fig. 5). In general, limiting the tag vocabulary to a single category decreases the accuracy of network reconstruction. It is expected as users are likely to be related through tags of many categories. The only exception from this rule are appreciation tags. These tags are very precise in distinguishing the linked user pairs. Despite the fact that appreciation tags are shared by less than 2% of user pairs in total (Fig. 5(a)), they are shared in 54% of comment links (this value drops to 25% for family links). This confirms the special social character of appreciation tags.

8. CONCLUSIONS AND FUTURE WORK

In this paper we compared the characteristics of five social links that represent the various types of relations between Flickr users. Our main goal was to characterize the relations based on the tags shared between users. To achieve it, we examined the performance of a wide-range of tag-based similarity metrics in a content-based network reconstruction

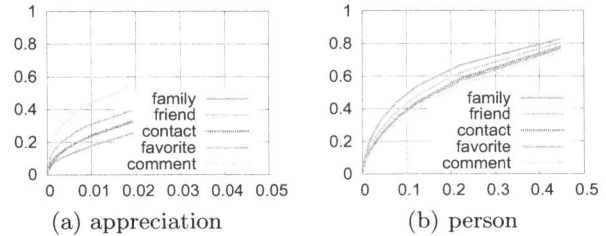

Figure 5: ROC curve for tag overlap similarity for five types of social links.

task. We found that different types of networks can be best reconstructed with different similarity metrics. The explanation of this fact can be found in a specific set of tags and general tag classes that are most important in the process of differentiating linked and not linked users.

Our experiments demonstrate the dual character of social relations in Flickr: relations based on acquaintance and common interests. The first type of relation is characterized by very specific tags. These tags are mostly used to describe people, locations and events which may play a role in linked users' real off-line life. On the other hand, the relations between users that share common interests are mostly based on tags used to express the appreciation of other's work. These are general tags that are used by communities of users. To a lesser degree, these relations can be also characterized by tags that describe the general photographic interests of users. The acquaintance type of relation is mostly expressed in explicit social networks (i.e., family and friend links), and the interest type of relations in implicit networks (i.e., comment and favorite links). Therefore, both types of networks are best reconstructed with different similarity metrics (minimal common DF for explicit networks and tag overlap for implicit networks). As Flickr users are free to use the explicit links to represent any type of relations we should expect that interest relations are also represented in the acquaintance networks (e.g., family network). The graph properties of the family links seem to confirm this: we demonstrated that different similarity metrics can be used to distinguish two types of relations within a single network. Comparing the links from friend and favorite networks, we also showed that the same users are likely to keep both types of relations and within the relations of a single user we can also find differences in the character of shared tags.

In the future we would like to extend our analysis to microbloging services with a single explicit network and multiple forms of implicit networks that capture various forms of interaction (e.g., mentions, re-tweets, replies in Twitter). We would also like to work on practical applications which can utilize the results of the analysis presented (link prediction and tag categorization). A link prediction task should explicitly distinguish the types of relations based on acquaintance and interests. Our experiments confirmed the practical usability of the tag classification scheme based on WordNet categories. For both explicit and implicit networks the most accurate results were obtained using tags not classified by the method proposed by Overell et al., suggesting that this classification should be extended by problem-specific categories that can be mined by utilizing the information about tag usage patterns.

9. ACKNOWLEDGMENTS

This research is partially supported by European Community's Seventh Framework Programme FP7/2007-2013 under the ARCOMEM and Social Media projects, and by the Spanish Centre for the Development of Industrial Technology under the CENIT program, project CEN-20101037 (www.cenitsocialmedia.es), "Social Media."

10. REFERENCES

[1] M. Ames and M. Naaman. Why we tag: motivations for annotation in mobile and online media. In *Proceedings of the SIGCHI conference on Human factors in computing systems*, CHI '07, pages 971–980, New York, NY, USA, 2007. ACM.

[2] Y. Cai and Q. Li. Personalized search by tag-based user profile and resource profile in collaborative tagging systems. In *Proceedings of the 19th ACM international conference on Information and knowledge management*, CIKM '10, pages 969–978, New York, NY, USA, 2010. ACM.

[3] A. Capocci, A. Baldassarri, V. D. P. Servedio, and V. Loreto. Friendship, collaboration and semantics in flickr: from social interaction to semantic similarity. In *Proceedings of the International Workshop on Modeling Social Media*, MSM '10, pages 8:1–8:4, New York, NY, USA, 2010. ACM.

[4] M. Cha, A. Mislove, and K. P. Gummadi. A measurement-driven analysis of information propagation in the flickr social network. In *Proceedings of the 18th international conference on World wide web*, WWW '09, pages 721–730, New York, NY, USA, 2009. ACM.

[5] R. Ghosh and K. Lerman. Community detection using a measure of global influence. In L. Giles, M. Smith, J. Yen, and H. Zhang, editors, *Advances in Social Network Mining and Analysis*, volume 5498 of *Lecture Notes in Computer Science*, pages 20–35. Springer Berlin / Heidelberg, 2010.

[6] S. A. Golder and B. A. Huberman. Usage patterns of collaborative tagging systems. *J. Inf. Sci.*, 32(2):198–208, 2006.

[7] P. A. Grabowicz, J. J. Ramasco, E. Moro, J. Pujol, and V. M. Eguiluz. Social features of online networks: the strength of weak ties in online social media. 2011.

[8] M. Granovetter. The strength of weak ties: A network theory revisited. *Sociological Theory*, 1(1983):201–233, 1983.

[9] V. Leroy, B. B. Cambazoglu, and F. Bonchi. Cold start link prediction. In *Proceedings of the 16th ACM SIGKDD international conference on Knowledge discovery and data mining*, KDD '10, pages 393–402, New York, NY, USA, 2010. ACM.

[10] J. Leskovec, L. Backstrom, R. Kumar, and A. Tomkins. Microscopic evolution of social networks. In *KDD '08: Proceeding of the 14th ACM SIGKDD international conference on Knowledge discovery and data mining*, pages 462–470, New York, NY, USA, 2008. ACM.

[11] J. Leskovec and E. Horvitz. Worldwide buzz: Planetary-scale views on an instant-messaging network. Technical report, Microsoft Research, 2007.

[12] J. Leskovec, K. J. Lang, A. Dasgupta, and M. W. Mahoney. Statistical properties of community structure in large social and information networks. In *WWW '08: Proceeding of the 17th international conference on World Wide Web*, pages 695–704, New York, NY, USA, 2008. ACM.

[13] D. Lin. An information-theoretic definition of similarity. In *Proceedings of the Fifteenth International Conference on Machine Learning*, ICML '98, pages 296–304, San Francisco, CA, USA, 1998. Morgan Kaufmann Publishers Inc.

[14] H. Liu and R. Setiono. Chi2: Feature selection and discretization of numeric attributes. In *International Conference on Tools with Artificial Intelligence*, 1995.

[15] F. Mitzlaff, D. Benz, S. Gerd, and A. Hotho. Visit click be my friend: an analysis of evidence networks of user relationships in bibsonomy. In *Proceedings of the 21st ACM conference on Hypertext and hypermedia*, HT '10, pages 265–270, New York, NY, USA, 2010. ACM.

[16] R. A. Negoescu, A. C. Loui, and D. Gatica-Perez. Kodak moments and flickr diamonds: how users shape large-scale media. In *Proceedings of the international conference on Multimedia*, MM '10, pages 1027–1030, New York, NY, USA, 2010. ACM.

[17] O. Nov, M. Naaman, and C. Ye. What drives content tagging: the case of photos on Flickr. In *CHI '08: Proceeding of the twenty-sixth annual SIGCHI conference on Human factors in computing systems*, pages 1097–1100, New York, NY, USA, 2008. ACM.

[18] S. Overell, B. Sigurbjörnsson, and R. van Zwol. Classifying tags using open content resources. In *Proceedings of the Second ACM International Conference on Web Search and Data Mining*, WSDM '09, pages 64–73, New York, NY, USA, 2009. ACM.

[19] M. Roth, A. Ben-David, D. Deutscher, G. Flysher, I. Horn, A. Leichtberg, N. Leiser, Y. Matias, and R. Merom. Suggesting friends using the implicit social graph. In *Proceedings of the 16th ACM SIGKDD international conference on Knowledge discovery and data mining*, KDD '10, pages 233–242, New York, NY, USA, 2010. ACM.

[20] E. Santos-Neto, D. Condon, N. Andrade, A. Iamnitchi, and M. Ripeanu. Individual and social behavior in tagging systems. In *Proceedings of the 20th ACM conference on Hypertext and hypermedia*, HT '09, pages 183–192, New York, NY, USA, 2009. ACM.

[21] R. Schifanella, A. Barrat, C. Cattuto, B. Markines, and F. Menczer. Folks in folksonomies: social link prediction from shared metadata. In *Proceedings of the third ACM international conference on Web search and data mining*, WSDM '10, pages 271–280, New York, NY, USA, 2010. ACM.

[22] A. Vespignani. Predicting the behavior of Techno-Social systems. *Science*, 325(5939):425–428, July 2009.

[23] R. Wetzker, C. Zimmermann, C. Bauckhage, and S. Albayrak. I tag, you tag: translating tags for advanced user models. In *Proceedings of the third ACM international conference on Web search and data mining*, WSDM '10, pages 71–80, New York, NY, USA, 2010. ACM.

Using the Overlapping Community Structure of a Network of Tags to Improve Text Clustering

Nuno Cravino
nuno.cravino@dcc.fc.up.pt

José Devezas
jld@dcc.fc.up.pt

Álvaro Figueira
arf@dcc.fc.up.pt

CRACS/INESC TEC, Faculdade de Ciências, Universidade do Porto
Rua do Campo Alegre, 1021/1055, 4169-007 Porto, Portugal

ABSTRACT

Breadcrumbs is a folksonomy of news clips, where users can aggregate fragments of text taken from online news. Besides the textual content, each news clip contains a set of metadata fields associated with it. User-defined tags are one of the most important of those information fields. Based on a small data set of news clips, we build a network of co-occurrence of tags in news clips, and use it to improve text clustering. We do this by defining a weighted cosine similarity proximity measure that takes into account both the clip vectors and the tag vectors. The tag weight is computed using the related tags that are present in the discovered community. We then use the resulting vectors together with the new distance metric, which allows us to identify socially biased document clusters. Our study indicates that using the structural features of the network of tags leads to a positive impact in the clustering process.

Categories and Subject Descriptors

G.2.2 [**Discrete Mathematics**]: Graph Theory—*graph algorithms, network problems*; H.3.3 [**Information Storage and Retrieval**]: Information Search and Retrieval—*Clustering*; I.5.3 [**Pattern Recognition**]: Clustering—*algorithms, similarity measures*

General Terms

Algorithms, Experimentation

Keywords

Text clustering, user-defined tags, network of co-occurrence of tags, overlapping community structure, news clips

1. INTRODUCTION

Tagging is a frequent behavior of people consuming online information. Many well-known online systems take advantage of tags in order to improve the organization of the

stored content, or to enhance the accuracy of search results from user queries. Collaborative tagging systems [4] such as Delicious and Flickr (to name a few) have had great popularity recently. These systems allow their users to tag web pages, or photos, eventually in a collaborative way. This folksonomic [4] way of creating tags, while associating them to web content, is helping systems to automatically enhance the existing clustering processes and grouping techniques. We believe our new classification technique has potential to produce even better results by making it closer to a human-only classification, while being performed automatically.

While collaborative tagging offers many advantages over the use of controlled vocabularies [11], they also suffer from several limitations at the same time due to the unrestricted nature of tagging [4]. The fact that many tags are ambiguous has limited the effectiveness of collaborative tagging systems in document description and retrieval. Unlike keywords, hierarchies or even taxonomies, tags usually lack any form of explicit organization and normalization.

The Breadcrumbs system [1] helps users to collect and store text clips from online sources, usually from news sites, in a Personal Digital Library. The clips can then be tagged or commented by users. Our system performs an automatic text mining and clustering organization of this personal clipping collection by grouping clips with similar semantic value and taking the tags as a positive bias in the classification of content. We also provide to each user a means to dynamically change the intensity on the use of tags on the clustering process.

Unlike many other approaches [2, 7, 12], we take the view that tags may stand outside of the clustering process of the documents and form on their own a, eventually overlapping, community structure. Therefore, the discovery of this community structure of tags would be the first step in order to enhance text clustering. In this article we report an experiment where we define a distance metric based on a weighted cosine similarity, that combines the textual features with the community structure of a network of tags in order to improve the clustering of documents, in a socially biased way.

2. RELATED WORK

Using social features to improve text clustering is a subject that has recently been explored by Ares et al. [2]. They used a constrained clustering algorithm [13] to take advantage of the social tags associated with a set of bookmarked web pages in Delicious, by turning them into constraints between these documents. Simpson et al. [10] applied clustering to a tag co-occurrence graph in order to find related

Table 1: Average clustering coefficient and average shortest path length of the tag network and a random network with the same number of edges and nodes.

Network	Clustering Coefficient	Path Length
Random	0.04623016	3.8594669
Tags	0.85450065	3.4942602

tags and to establish a hierarchy of tags from a flat tag list. They experimented with divisive clustering and betweenness centrality clustering, concluding that the betweenness method performed poorly on a graph of densely interconnected tags, resulting in a large dominant cluster. Han et al. [5] proposed the k-nearest neighbor classification algorithm that assigns a degree of relevance to attributes and uses them in a weighted cosine similarity measure. Yeung et al. [3] took advantage of a folksonomy to create a disambiguation system based on the clustering of social tags. Using the clusters of the network of tags, they obtained the different groups of tags or documents associated with the distinct meanings of an ambiguous tag. Wartena et al. [14] studied the usage of tag co-occurrence for recommendation, introducing second order co-occurrence as a stable measure for tag similarities, where distances can be computed equally between users, items and tags.

We use a different approach to improve text clustering, based on the network of co-occurrence of tags. In 2008, Wu has analyzed a set of tags as a social network, revealing that it shared the traditional features of regular social networks, including the short average path length, a high clustering coefficient and a power law distribution of the node degrees [15]. They concluded that this type of networks had small world and scale-free characteristics. Based on Wu's conclusions, we apply overlapping community detection methodologies to our network of tags and use this information to determine related tags and to improve text clustering. We use the Speaker-listener Label Propagation Algorithm (SLPA) proposed by Xie et al. [16] to identify the cover (the overlapping community structure) of our network of tags.

3. A FOLKSONOMY OF NEWS CLIPS

Our data set is composed of 121 user-defined clips of news, from online sources, that were further associated with user-defined tags, having an average text length of 118.6 ± 135.5 words, and an average of 2.6 ± 0.9 tags per clip. The clips were collected in a single session by five users of the Breadcrumbs system, with a focus on five topics: the Libyan revolution, the US tax plan to tackle debt, the world debt crisis, Greek debt related events and Italy rating downgrade. Based on this data set, we construct a weighted network with tags as nodes, where each edge represents the co-occurrence count of tags in the same document. The resulting network has 111 nodes and 189 edges, a density of 0.03096 and a diameter of 19. This network displays a higher average clustering coefficient than a random network with the same node set, and low average shortest path as shown in Table 1. Also the node degree distribution follows an heavy tailed distribution as shown in Figure 1. These structural characteristics

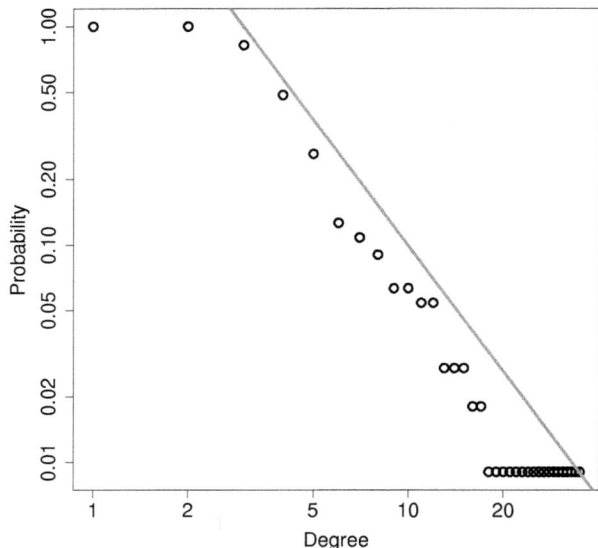

Figure 1: Degree distribution with best fit power law line.

show that the graph displays community structure, making it a suitable choice for community detection.

4. NEWS CLIPS CLUSTERING

Given the community structure yielded by the structural features of the network we are able to execute an overlapping community detection algorithm over the graph to find tag communities. We use the social information yielded by the detection to improve the existing text clustering technique as part of the Breadcrumbs system. In the next sections, we describe the text clustering process and the tag clustering process, and we explain how this information is combined.

4.1 Text Clustering

The Breadcrumbs system performs text clustering of user owned collections of clips using k-means clustering with the word vectors of each documents as data points. This clustering technique classifies the collection into k different clusters of clips with related context.

The current technique makes sole use of the clip's text, which leaves out any social information that can be obtained from the clip's metadata. We integrate the folksonomy information with the current clustering technique to yield a socially improved clustering method.

4.2 Tag Clustering

Tags can have related meanings in different social contexts. Given this intrinsic property we perform overlapping cluster/community detection over the network of tags. The resulting communities represent the communities of related tags, which are sets of tags with related social context and semantics, that are used to improve the text clustering technique.

We use the overlapping community detection algorithm SLPA mainly due to its near linear complexity in sparse graphs. In principle any other algorithm capable of performing overlapping cluster/community detection should be able to perform the task in its stead. This algorithm works by propagating labels throughout each node of the network that are repeatedly stored in memory for every node. It has two parameters, a threshold r of probability, used in post-processing, and the number of iterations T. After an initialization step, SLPA starts by taking each node in a role as listener and receives one random label from each of its neighbors (speakers) and stores it in a temporary list. The listener then chooses a label from this list and adds it to its own memory according to a function based on the label occurrence count. The previous process is iterated a number of times according to the parameter, and the node memories are post-processed. The post-processing step consists of the computation of the occurrence probability for all labels and the removal from node memory of all labels with an occurrence probability below the threshold. The sets of nodes that share a certain label in its memory are constructed yielding the communities of related tags.

We introduced modifications to this algorithm to make it work with a weighted network using a modified labels list to store the sum of weights connecting to the speakers from where the label came from. The listener rule was also modified to return the label with the maximum value for the product of the sum of its weights with its occurrence count. Running the tag clustering algorithm results in nine overlapping communities, with sizes ranging from 4 to 33 nodes, where communities of 5 nodes are the most frequently identified.

4.3 Socially Biased Document Clustering

The socially biased clustering is performed by executing the modified SLPA over the network of tags with $T = 200$ iterations in the evolution step, and $r = 0.02$ for the threshold in the post-processing step. Using the community information produced, we construct the word vector for each clip according to the tf-idf score, and the tag vector for each clip using the following tag weighting function:

$$w(t, d) = (1 - SS) \times tfidf(t, d) + SS \times \frac{1}{|C_t|} \sum_{tr \in C_t} tfidf(tr, d)$$

where SS is the Social Slider, a real number between 0 and 1, with 0 disabling any biasing and 1 discarding all information but that contained in the tag clusters. This value controls the level of integration of social information derived from the tag communities in the text clustering, being used to impart the tag weight function and the subsequent clustering with a quantitative social bias. C_t is the union of all overlapping communities of tags related with a tag t.

We construct the k-means data point vectors by concatenating the two vectors with a unique ID and each data point is pre-processed according to the equation:

$$v'_i = \begin{cases} v_i \times (1 - SS) & i < j \\ v_i \times SS & i \geq j \end{cases}$$

where j is the vector index of the first tag component, v the original data point, and v' the resulting data point. The Social Slider(SS) value is also used here to control the integration of social information. We then use the pre-processed data points to run k-means using a distance given by the cosine similarity proximity measure:

$$Cos_{dist}(a, b) = 1 - \left(\frac{\sum_{i=1}^{n} (a_i \times b_i)}{\sqrt{\sum_{i=1}^{n} (a_i)^2} \times \sqrt{\sum_{i=1}^{n} (b_i)^2}} \right)$$

where n is the length of the vectors a and b.

The complexity added over that of k-means is for the SLPA step $O(K|T|)$ where K is the number of iterations and T the set of tags. For the tag vector calculation, the complexity is $O(|C||T|I)$, where C is the set of clips and I the implementation-dependent complexity of tf-idf. The pre-processing step has a complexity of $O(|C||S|)$ where $|S|$ is the size of each data point.

5. EVALUATION OF CLUSTERING

We manually annotate the news clips collection, classifying each clip into one of the following six classes: Libya, US Tax, World Debt Crisis, Italy Downgrading, Greece, and Other. We use this clustering partition as our "ground truth", to which we compare the partitions resulting from the text clustering and from the combination of the text clustering with the tag clustering. In Table 2 we present the confusion matrix analysis for each of the methods, where "class" refers to our manual annotation of the clips and "cluster" refers to the partitions identified by the tested methods — Text clustering in Table 2a and Text+Tags clustering in Table 2b. The true positive rate (TPR) for the text-based method is 32.15% and the false positive rate (FPR) is 26.32%. Even though the TPR for the combined text and tags method takes a lower value of 29.70%, the FPR also decreases to 23.55%, which means that the text-based method achieves a higher number of correctly classified documents, but also a higher number of incorrectly classified documents. Since these metrics do not provide the grounds for a conclusion, we use the Rand index [9] to measure the similarity of the resulting partitions with the ground truth, i.e. the percentage of correct decisions, and the F-score to calculate the accuracy of the two methods, first using $\beta = 1$ and then using $\beta = 0.5$ and $\beta = 2$ to penalize the false negatives less and more strongly, respectively, than the false positives. Table 3 depicts the evaluation of the identified partitions using a null weight (Text), as well as a 50% weight (Text+Tags) for the social aspect. That is, for the Text clustering, we set the social slider to zero ($SS = 0$), while for the Text+Tags clustering we set the social slider to 0.5 ($SS = 0.5$), in our weighted cosine similarity proximity measure.

As we can see in Table 3b, we obtain a higher Rand index when using the social structure of the network of tags in the clustering process. On the other hand, by looking at the F-score for either method in Table 3a, we verify that using the community structure of the co-occurrence of tags in news clips slightly decreases the accuracy of the clustering method, except when given a higher weight to the precision ($\beta < 1$), being consistent with the changes in the values of Precision and Recall elicited by the choice of clustering method shown in Table 3c. Since the F-score values for the two clustering methods are very close together and the Rand index isn't by itself conclusive, we further investigate by calculating the adjusted Rand index according to Hubert & Arabie [6] and Morey & Agresti [8]. These adjusted for chance metrics are depicted in Table 3b. The resulting values are in agreement with the previously calculated Rand index, indicating that the higher Rand index for the Text+Tags clustering represented in fact a significant result.

Table 2: Confusion matrix for the resulting partitions.

(a) Text clustering.

	Same cluster	Different clusters	Total
Same class	TP = 460	FN = 971	1431
Different classes	FP = 1534	TN = 4295	5829
Total	1994	5266	7260

(b) Text+Tags clustering.

	Same cluster	Different clusters	Total
Same class	TP = 425	FN = 1006	1431
Different classes	FP = 1373	TN = 4456	5829
Total	1798	5462	7260

Table 3: Evaluation of the clustering methods.

(a) F-score for $\beta = 0.5$, $\beta = 1$ and $\beta = 2$.

Clustering	$F_{0.5}$	F_1	F_2
Text	0.2444988	**0.2686131**	**0.2980047**
Text+Tags	**0.246434**	0.2632394	0.2825047

(b) Rand index and adjusted Rand indices according to Hubert & Arabie and Morey & Agresti.

Clustering	Rand index	HA ARI	MA ARI
Text	0.65495868	0.05075362	0.07524322
Text+Tags	**0.67231405**	**0.05602792**	**0.08241934**

(c) Precision and Recall

Clustering	Precision	Recall
Text	0.230692	**0.321454**
Text+Tags	**0.236374**	0.296995

6. CONCLUSIONS

We have proposed a weighted cosine similarity proximity measure that takes into account the social information present in the underlying network of tags in a folksonomy. We used this metric as the distance function of the k-means algorithm, in order to cluster news clips together. The proposed clustering method is based on the usage of what we call a social slider, where the user can set the degree to which the social aspect of the news clipping process influences the grouping of news clips in his/her own Personal Digital Library, or across the whole system. The data points we use not only include information about the textual content and the tags of the news clips, but also about the related tags, which are identified based on the overlapping community structure of the global network of tags. We performed an evaluation of the identified partitions, comparing them to our manually annotated partition. The socially biased document clustering method that we've introduced here was able to produce an improved clustering partition, by taking advantage of the social features in our documents. Identifying the overlapping community structure of the network of tags

associated with the Breadcrumbs folksonomy seems to improve regular text clustering, resulting in a better grouping division of our news clips collection. We hypothesize that, as the network of tags grows and its community structure becomes stronger, groups of tags will become more cohesive and continuously result in improved socially biased clusters.

7. FUTURE WORK

As future work, we would like to replicate this experiment at a larger scale, after the data set of news clips has been increased. We believe this would reflect on the improvement of the social structure in the network of tags and therefore result in better clusters for higher values of the social slider. Additionally, we would like to test the complexity of our methodology and work on the problems that a large-scale environment introduces.

8. ACKNOWLEDGMENTS

This work is financed by the ERDF - European Regional Development Fund through the COMPETE Programme (operational programme for competitiveness) and by National Funds througg the FCT - Fundação para a Ciência e a Tecnologia(Portuguese Foundation for Science and Technology) within project UTA-Est/MAI/0007/2009.

9. REFERENCES

[1] Álvaro Figueira et al. Breadcrumbs: A social network based on the relations established by collections of fragments taken from online news. *Retrieved January 19, 2012, from http://breadcrumbs.up.pt*.

[2] M. Ares, J. Parapar, and A. Barreiro. Improving Text Clustering with Social Tagging. In *Proceedings of the Fifth International Conference on Weblogs and Social Media (ICWSM 2011)*, pages 430–433, Barcelona, Spain, 2011.

[3] C. M. Au Yeung, N. Gibbins, and N. Shadbolt. Contextualising tags in collaborative tagging systems. In *Proceedings of the 20th ACM conference on Hypertext and hypermedia*, pages 251–260. ACM, 2009.

[4] S. Golder and B. Huberman. Usage patterns of collaborative tagging systems. *Journal of Information Science*, 32(2):198–208, 2006.

[5] E. Han, G. Karypis, and V. Kumar. Text categorization using weight adjusted k-nearest neighbor classification. *Advances in Knowledge Discovery and Data Mining*, pages 53–65, 2001.

[6] L. Hubert and P. Arabie. Comparing partitions. *Journal of Classification*, 2(1):193–218, 1985.

[7] X. Ji, W. Xu, and S. Zhu. Document clustering with prior knowledge. In *Proceedings of the 29th annual international ACM SIGIR conference on Research and development in information retrieval*, pages 405–412, 2006.

[8] L. Morey and A. Agresti. The measurement of classification agreement: an adjustment to the Rand statistic for chance agreement. *Educational and Psychological Measurement*, 44(1):33–37, 1984.

[9] W. M. Rand. Objective Criteria for the Evaluation of Methods Clustering. *Journal of the American Statistical Association*, 66(336):846–850, 1971.

[10] E. Simpson. Clustering tags in enterprise and web folksonomies. *HP Labs Techincal Reports*, 2008.

[11] F. Suchanek, M. Vojnovic, and D. Gunawardena. Social tags: meaning and suggestions. In *Proceeding of the 17th ACM conference on Information and knowledge management*, pages 223–232. ACM, 2008.

[12] J. Tang. Improved K-means Clustering Algorithm Based on User Tag. *Journal of Convergence Information Technology*, 5(10):124–130, 2010.

[13] K. Wagstaff, C. Cardie, S. Rogers, and S. Schrödl. Constrained k-means clustering with background knowledge. In *Proceedings of the Eighteenth International Conference on Machine Learning*, pages 577–584, 2001.

[14] C. Wartena, R. Brussee, and M. Wibbels. Using tag co-occurrence for recommendation. In *Ninth International Conference on Intelligent Systems Design and Applications (ISDA 2009)*, pages 273–278. IEEE, 2009.

[15] C. Wu. Analysis of Tags as a Social Network. In *International Conference on Computer Science and Software Engineering (ICCSSE 2008)*, volume 4, pages 651–654. IEEE, 2008.

[16] J. Xie, B. Szymanski, and X. Liu. SLPA: Uncovering overlapping communities in social networks via a speaker-listener interaction dynamic process. *Arxiv preprint arXiv:1109.5720*, 2011.

Anatomy of a Conference

Bjoern-Elmar Macek *   Christoph Scholz *   Martin Atzmueller   Gerd Stumme

Knowledge and Data Engineering Group, University of Kassel
Wilhelmshöher Allee 73, D-34121 Kassel, Germany
{macek,scholz,atzmueller,stumme}@cs.uni-kassel.de

ABSTRACT

This paper presents an anatomy of Hypertext 2011 – focusing on the dynamic and static behavior of the participants. We consider data collected by the CONFERATOR system at the conference, and provide statistics concerning participants, presenters, session chairs, different communities, and according roles. Additionally, we perform an in-depth analysis of these actors during the conference concerning their communication and track visiting behavior.

Categories and Subject Descriptors

J.4 [**Computer Applications**]: Social and Behavioral Science

General Terms

Human Factors, Measurements

Keywords

social network analysis, rfid, proximity, contact network, conference

1. INTRODUCTION

In business and science, conferences provide important interactions: They foster the exchange of knowledge and enable face-to-face contacts between their participants for personal networking, e. g., in order to start interesting discussions, to form and strengthen cooperations (and business relations), and to initiate new projects. Understanding the mechanisms in such contexts is important to increase the efficiency and effectiveness of individual networking. Therefore, the analysis of conferences provides an interesting research field. However, such an analysis is not easy if conventional tools like questionnaires are used, since then mostly *static* analyses of the behavior and processes can be performed, while the *dynamic* nature of conference interactions is not accounted for.

In this paper, we present an in-depth analysis of the static and dynamic nature of a conference (Hypertext 2011). We collected data

---

*Both authors contributed equally to this work.

using the CONFERATOR system:[1] It employs active RFID technology provided by the SocioPatterns consortium.[2] CONFERATOR is a personalized conference management system for organizing social contacts and the conference program. Using the system, RFID data capturing the contacts and locations of the conference participants were collected at Hypertext 2011. To this end, we used a new generation of resource-aware active RFID tags, called proximity tags. The technical innovation of these proximity tags is the ability to detect other proximity tags within a range of up to 1.5 meters.

One of the first experiments using this kind of RFID tags at conferences was performed by Cattuto and colleagues, cf. [1, 9, 18]. We extend their findings with a number of (un-)expected results for homophily and session attendance of the participants. To the best of our knowledge, this paper proposes the first comprehensive analysis of the track attendance of the participants, their communication behavior and an analysis concerning their submitted papers. By investigating different correlations between the selected features in the data we find insights into the anatomy of the Hypertext conference 2011. We also describe an analysis of the data along several dimensions: First, we provide an overview of the collected data, discuss the overall structure, and analyze general effects concerning different groups (e.g., presenters, chairs, track participants, etc.). Furthermore, we consider different communities, e.g., concerning the individual tracks and sessions, but also automatically mined communities. We show an analysis of different roles in these contexts by characterizing the different participating subjects and groups at the conference and by mining role profiles.

The rest of the paper is structured as follows: Section 2 discusses related work. After that, Section 3 introduces the RFID-Setup and explains the CONFERATOR system in more detail. Next, Section 4 describes the collected dataset. Section 5 starts the analysis: We discuss the community structure and the static and dynamic analysis of the behavior of conference participants. Furthermore, we analyze different roles and derive role profiles using pattern mining. Finally, Section 6 concludes the paper with a short summary.

2. RELATED WORK

Homophily and mixing patterns in social networks have been investigated, e.g., by McPherson et al. [13] from a sociological point of view. They observed, that it is far more likely for people to connect to each other if they have something in common. We extend those findings by showing that in some contexts people are more interested in talking to people with different fields of interest. Cattuto and colleagues presented several important results by analyzing social dynamics in various environments using RFID technol-

---

[1] http://www.conferator.org
[2] http://www.sociopatterns.org

Figure 1: Proximity tag (left) and RFID reader (right)

ogy: In [9], the authors compare the social activity of conference attendees with their research seniority and their activity in social web platforms like Facebook, Twitter and others. They also extend their focus to schools [17] and hospitals [11]. They present aggregations of contact measures between different groups of users. In contrast to their work, we focus on correlating the conversation profiles and the participants' track attendance with features like the track communities, the organizational roles within the conference such as session chairs and speakers, and their submitted papers. The characterization of nodes in a social network is an interesting and challenging task. Several works like [10] and [16] present methods to cluster nodes of a social network into different roles. In this work, we focus on the method proposed in [16], because this method allows us to consider a given community structure.

Subgroup discovery [20, 7] aims at identifying exceptional patterns with respect to a given target property of interest according to a specific quality measure. We apply subgroup discovery for the characterization of different roles. Similar work has been done, for example, in characterizing spammers [6], and in identifying profiles for the maturity of tags in social bookmarking systems [3].

3. CONFERATOR – A SOCIAL CONFERENCE MANAGEMENT SYSTEM

In the following section we first outline the active RFID technology used in the CONFERATOR system. Next we introduce the CONFERATOR and its functionality.

3.1 RFID Setup

One of the key components of CONFERATOR is a new generation of so-called proximity tags (see Figure 1), developed by the SocioPatterns project. The most important feature of these tags is the possibility to detect other proximity tags within a range of up to 1.5 meters, which allows the identification of face-to-face contacts.

The RFID setup at a conference requires the installation of RFID-Readers at fixed positions in the conference area. The RFID readers (see Figure 1) receive the signals from the tags that are worn by the participants and forward them to a central server. This makes it possible to determine the location of each tag and therefore the location of a conference participant at room-level basis. For obtaining the location of participants there are several options [15], including a simple algorithm proposed in [14]: Here, the participant is assigned to the room whose RFID readers received most packages with the weakest signal strength. For more details on the proximity tags, we refer to Barrat et al. [8] and the OpenBeacon website.[3]

3.2 Conferator

The CONFERATOR-system [2] is a social and ubiquitous conference guiding system. CONFERATOR consists of two parts: The TalkRadar[4] of the University of Pittsburgh. TalkRadar is based on Pittsburgh's Conference Navigator [19]. and the PeerRadar.

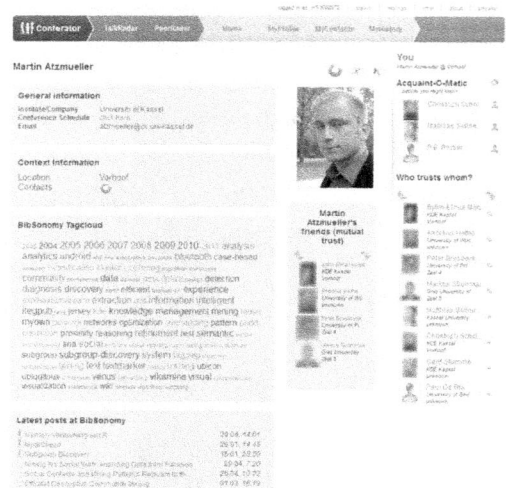

Figure 2: Screenshot of the CONFERATOR's PeerRadar showing a user profile page. The page shows information about latest BibSonomy posts, trust circles, context information (e.g. current position), social tags and general information (e.g. institute or email address).

TalkRadar allows conference participants to manage their conference schedule, PeerRadar is like an online business card, that supports the social interaction at a conference. In PeerRadar, for example, it is possible for conference participants to see their own contacts or to browse through other conference attendees' user profiles (see Figure 2). CONFERATOR has successfully been deployed at several events, e.g., the LWA 2010[5] and LWA 2011[6] conferences, the Hypertext 2011[7] conference, and a technology day of the VENUS[8] project. In this paper, we focus on data collected with the PeerRadar component of CONFERATOR at Hypertext 2011.

4. DATA SET

In the following section we first describe our dataset collected at the Hypertext 2011 conference in Eindhoven, before presenting some overview statistics of the collected data.

4.1 RFID Data

At the Hypertext 2011 conference, we asked each conference participant to wear an active RFID tag. All in all 75 of 95 participants took part in our experiment which started June 6, 2011 at 14:00 and ended June 9, 2011 at 14:00. In the four days of the conference we recorded 2620 face-to-face contacts between participants. As in [18], a face-to-face contact is recorded when the duration of the contact is at least 20 seconds. A contact ends when the two corresponding proximity tags do not detect each other for more than 60 seconds. Obviously the length of a contact plays an important role in defining a contact. In Figure 3, we see the distribution of the corresponding contact durations of all conference face-to-face contacts. Here, the x-axis represents the minimum duration of a contact in seconds, while the y-axis shows the probability of a contact having at least this duration. The axes are scaled logarithmically. As already observed, e.g., in [12] and [4], we see that

---

[3]http://www.openbeacon.org
[4]Since June 2011, CONFERATOR is jointly developed with the Personalized Adaptive Web Systems Lab (http://www2.sis.pitt.edu/~paws/)

[5]http://www.kde.cs.uni-kassel.de/conf/lwa10/
[6]http://lwa2011.cs.uni-magdeburg.de/
[7]http://www.ht2011.org/
[8]www.iteg.uni-kassel.de/

most of the contacts are less than one minute and that the durations show a long-tailed distribution. The average path length (APL) is also similar to the findings in [12] and [4].

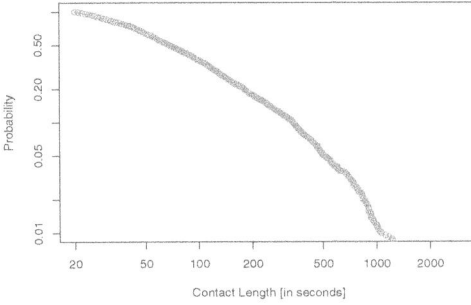

Figure 3: Cumulated contact length distribution of all face-to-face contacts between participants of the hypertext conference.

In the following, we introduce the notation for the contact graph $G_\Sigma(i)$. An edge $\{u, v\}$ is contained in $G_\Sigma(i)$, iff the sum of all contact durations between participants u and v is at least i seconds. In Table 1 we present some standard statistics of the contact graph $G_\Sigma(i)$. The diameter of the contact graph $G_\Sigma(i)$ shows similar values to those already presented results in [12][4].

The high average degree of the contact graph $G_\Sigma(20)$ indicates that those taking part in the experiment (at least briefly) came into contact with the majority ($\frac{41}{75} = 55\%$) of the other participants. For longer conversations this average degree decreases very quickly. Here, for example, in average each participant only has contact with approximately $\frac{10}{75} = 13\%$ of the other participants taking into account conversations longer than 10 minutes.

Table 1: General statistics for several contact graphs with different thresholds (in seconds). Here d is the diameter, APL the average path length and LCN the largest clique number in $G_\Sigma(i)$

Network	$|V|$	$|E|$	d	Avg.Deg.	APL	LCN
$G_\Sigma(20)$	68	698	4	41	1.76	14
$G_\Sigma(60)$	66	498	4	30	1.91	11
$G_\Sigma(300)$	60	246	5	16	2.36	8
$G_\Sigma(600)$	58	142	7	10	3.01	5
$G_\Sigma(900)$	53	98	8	7	7.39	4

In this paper, we focus on the different community structures, i.e. partitionings, induced by country of origin, academic status, affiliation with the Hypertext conference series, and affiliation with one of the four conference tracks. In Table 2, we present some statistics about the different community stuctures. We classify participants as highly affiliated with the Hypertext conference series if they presented a paper more than three times at Hypertext conferences in different years. The affiliation of a participant is low when he or she has never presented a paper or presented a paper at Hypertext 2011 for the first time. All other participants are classified with a medium affiliation. For every author and coauthor of a paper we define his or her track membership by the track the paper was submitted to. The session and track chairs are also assigned to their respective tracks. For attendees who could not be assigned to a track, this information is not available (n/a).

Table 2: Partitions of the set of participants into communities according to country, academic status, affiliation with HT and track. For each community, its number of participants is listed.

Country	
Australia	3
Austria	3
Belgium	2
Canada	2
Denmark	2
Finland	1
France	1
Germany	11
Ireland	2
Italy	5
Japan	6
Netherlands	9
Poland	1
Slovakia	1
Spain	3
United Kingdom	10
USA	10
n/a	3

Academic Status	
Professor	14
PhD-candidate	34
PhD	20
Other	7

Affiliation with HT	
high	12
medium	17
low	46

Track	
DynHyp	12
SocialMedia	19
StoryTelling	6
UbiquHyp	5
n/a	33

As already mentioned we placed several RFID readers at fixed positions in the conference area. To identify the track attendance of all participants we particularly fixed one RFID reader in each lecture room. Figure 4 gives an overview about how many track members attended their own and the other tracks, respectively.

In the Social Media pie chart we see for example, that 60% of all participants who visited the Social Media track are also members of the Social Media track. 5% are members of the Interaction, Narrative and Story Telling track, 11% are members of the Emerging Structures and Ubiquitous Hypermedia track and 24% are members of the Dynamic and Computed Hypermedia track. A more detailed analysis of the track attendance and the behaviour of the participants is described in Section 5.2.

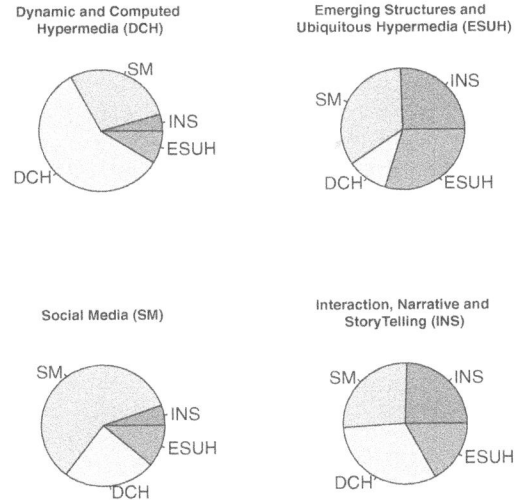

Figure 4: Overview of the track attendance for the different tracks. Each pie chart visualizes the distribution of track attendance by members of the different tracks.

5. ANALYSIS

In this section, we investigate the correlation between the given community structures and their contact patterns, followed by an in-depth analysis of the conversation behavior of participants and their visited tracks and sessions. We conclude the analysis by extracting several roles from contact graphs in order to reveal additional information on how the participants are embedded within the social network of this conference. For this purpose, we mine descriptive (subgroup) patterns characterizing prominent roles, and include a detailed time-based analysis.

5.1 Community Structure

In the following, we analyze the connection between the link structure of the contact graph and the four partitionings in communities listed in Figure 2. To analyze the compatibility of the link structure and a community structure, we use the alignment measure proposed in [16]. For this measure we recall from [16] the definitions of *complete node pairs* and *pure node pairs*. A *complete node pair* is a pair (u, v) of nodes where both nodes u and v are linked and belong to the same community. A *pure node pair* is a pair (u, v) where u and v are not linked and do not belong to the same community. As in [16], we define the parameters p and q as

$$p = \frac{\text{\# complete node pairs}}{\text{\# total linked node pairs}}$$
$$q = \frac{\text{\# pure node pairs}}{\text{\# total non-linked node pairs}} \quad (1)$$

Here we note, that high values for p and q indicate that the community structure fits the link structure well. In our experiments we use the p- and q-values to analyze how the four different community partitionings induced by track, country, academic status and affiliation are aligned to the link structure of the hypertext contact graph. We focus in particular on the change of alignment when only longer contacts are considered. This means that we calculate and compare the p- and q-values for the contact graphs $G_\Sigma(60)$, $G_\Sigma(120)$, $G_\Sigma(180)$, ...

The results are shown in Figure 5 (p-value) and in Figure 6 (q-value). In these figures, for example, looking at contacts with contact lengths of more than 1 minute, we observe that the probability of being in contact within the same track-community is 39.3%. If there is no contact between two persons the probability of them being in different communities is 82.1%. In general, we see that the p-value fluctuation of the community structures, affiliation, country and academic status over the different time thresholds is rather low. Only the p value for country increases from 18.2% to 41.1% between time threshold 1 and 26.

Looking at the p-value for the community structure track we see an interesting development. The greater the length of a conversation the higher the probability of having a contact within the same track-community. Here, the increase is from 39.3% to 83%. A possible reason for this might be that some tracks are filtered out, because of the increasing time threshold. For example, when only participants of one track are available the p-value is clearly one. In this paper, we show that the probability to have a contact within the same community is dependent on the contact length. We validate our conclusion by calculating the p-values for the community structure track over different permutations of the participants' track attendance. Here, we repeat the experiment 100 times and average the p-value results. The result is shown in Figure 7. We see that the p-values of the real community structure increase much faster than the p-values of the random community structure. In Figure 6, we see that the q-value for all community structures track, country and affiliation and academic status is monotonically increasing. This is

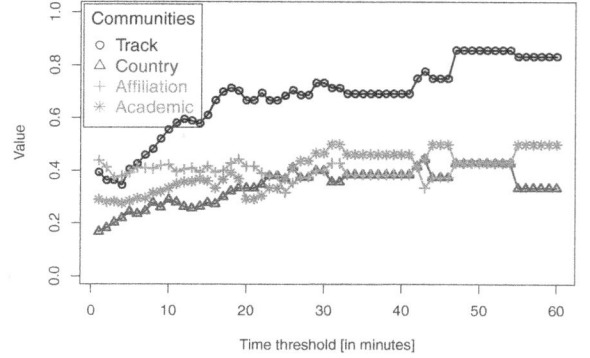

Figure 5: Overview of the p value results for the community structures track, country, affiliation and academic status.

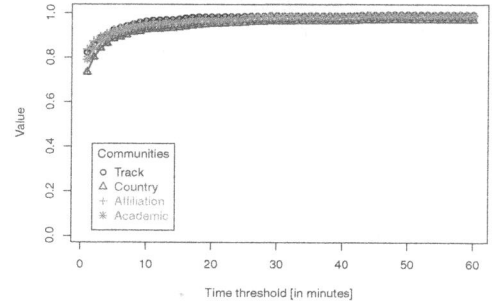

Figure 6: Overview of the q value results for the community structures track, country, affiliation and academic status.

not surprising since the increase (from time threshold t to $t + 1$) of the number of *total non-linked node pairs* must be at least the increase of the number of *pure node pairs*.

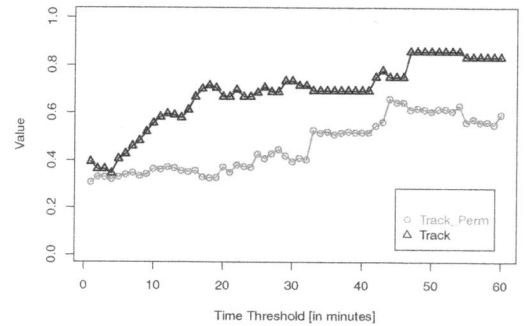

Figure 7: Overview of the p value results for the community structure track and the average p values of the community structure over 100 permutations of the participants' track-membership.

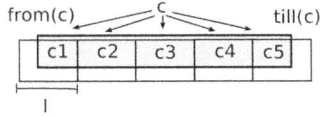

Figure 8: Example of a contact c sliced into five different parts with a maximum length of l seconds.

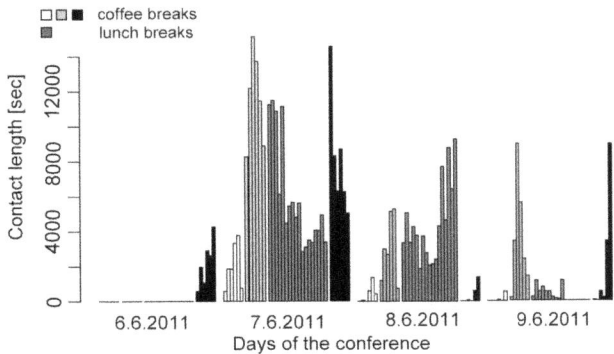

Figure 9: Time slices containing contact durations for the complete conference except for the sessions. The start times of the coffee breaks were as follows: 8:30, 10:30, 15:30 and 16:00. Their duration was always 30 minutes. The start and duration of lunch breaks varied. Except for the last day all started at 12:30 and took at least one hour. Each bar represents a 5 minute slice; adjacent bars belong to the same break.

5.2 Communication and Tracks

In this section, we analyze how the participants and different tracks connect with each other. Furthermore, we indirectly consider their current research topics using contacts and session attendances as proxies. We discriminate between several relevant groups of time intervals in the conference's schedule, namely the poster session, the sessions (where the speakers present their work), the coffee break, and the lunch breaks after the sessions. Since there are almost no conversations during the lectures, we also take the breaks and the poster session into account when analyzing the contacts.

We interpret the contact lengths as a measure for social activity. In order to capture the change of social dynamics over time we divide the contacts into intervals of a fixed length $l = 5$ minutes, as depicted in Figure 8.

5.2.1 Contacts on a Global Scale

In order to get a general overview of the social activity, we present a complete overview of all the breaks of the four day conference in Figure 9. Since the setup of the CONFERATOR system started in the middle of the first day, all previous time slices are empty. As expected, there were a lot of interactions between participants which decreased over time as the conference progressed. This can partly be explained by leaving participants who were returning their RFID tags. The short peaks at the last two coffee breaks are also an exception and might be explained by the conference attendees saying goodbye to each other.

5.2.2 Social Activity of Communities

Hypertext 2011 addressed a variety of research fields. It started in 1987 as a group of researchers and companies with the main focus on hypertext and the internet and first widened its interest to *Interaction, Narrative, and Storytelling* (INS). Afterwards it broad-

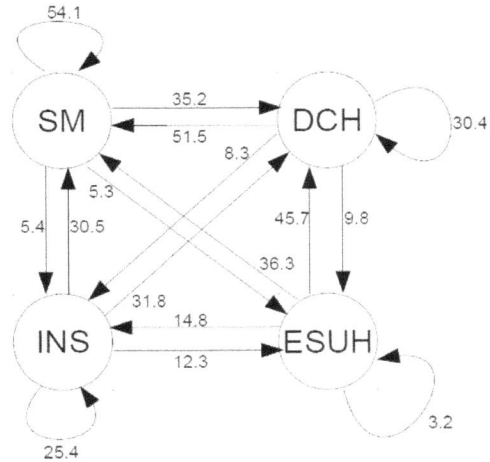

Figure 10: The contact length distribution (in percent) for conversations between all combinations of tracks. Here, for example a directed edge from track SM to track INS with weight 5.4 indicates, that the fraction of all cumulated contacts between the SM track and the INS track relative to all cumulated contacts of SM is 5.4 percent.

ened its scope towards the social and semantic web and finally to ubiquitous topics. This is reflected in the the four tracks in 2011.

Since the benefits of greater creativity in a broader and more diverse environment only appear if conversations and exchange of ideas is going on beyond the tracks' bounds, we investigate the links between the tracks. A complete overview of the social activity for these communities is given in Figure 10. Obviously all tracks are linked very well - which indicates good opportunities for inspiring conversations. Nevertheless, there are some differences: While the older tracks are focused on talking with their own members and the biggest communities, namely *Dynamic and Computed Hypermedia* (DCH) and *Social Media* (SM), *Emerging Structures and Ubiquitous Hypermedia* (ESUH) as the youngest addition to this conference concentrated primarily on communication with the two larger tracks and less with their direct research colleagues.

Figure 12 shows the communication structure between professors, post docs and research assistants. It is noticeable that conversations between professors and research assistants are significantly shorter than conversations between members of other groups such as for instance professors and post docs. These two groups actually had the three longest conversations among them during the experiment.

5.2.3 Individual Social Activity

A closer look at the communication structure reveals that, as expected, participants can get alot of attention by holding a talk. What might be unexpected is the people who will be attracted. For our analysis we do not consider two keynote lectures for which the presenters did not wear RFID tags. Furthermore, the session directly before the poster session is also excluded, since we assume that the attention easily shifted away from the recent speakers of the last session. The final series of lectures is also removed due to the low number of participants. In Figure 13, we plot the distribution of contact lengths between all tracks, highlighting the two that just ended their parallel session. The average contact lengths per track member depicted in this figure reveal that the majority of participants talked to members of those tracks that just presented their

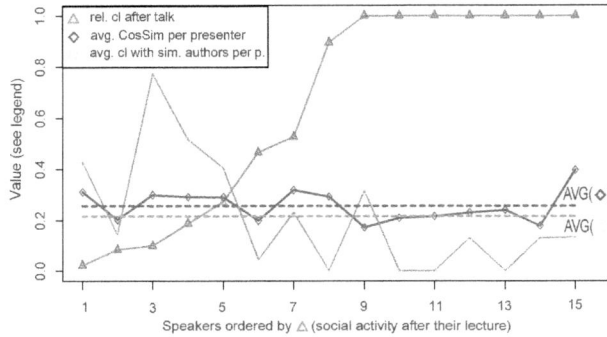

Figure 11: The triangles denote the normalized contact lengths (cl): dur_u, while the averaged similarities $CosSim^u$ of the paper of u to the other research results in the proceedings are represented by the diamonds. The percentage of the duration of contacts, that u had with the top 10 similar speakers based upon $CosSim$: $t_{\mathrm{rel}}(u)$ are represented by the squares.

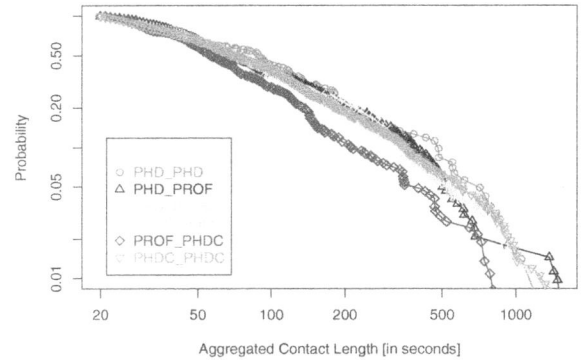

Figure 12: The cumulative contact length distribution for conversations between professors(PROF), post docs(PHD) and research assistants(PHDC). The two communities are seperated with an underscore within the legend.

work. We examplarily plot the data for only one session. However, the same observation holds for five of the six considered coffee breaks. So being a member of a track that recently gave a lecture in a session seems to attrack conversation partners.

It seems self-evident that the social attention is directed towards the speakers of the recent session, but this is only partially true. In the following, we examine the hypothesis that a speaker is socially more active in the break after the session in which he presented his work: We calculate the duration of all contacts in this interval for each speaker; $C_{u_2}^{u_1}[t_{\mathrm{from}}, t_{\mathrm{till}}]$ represents all contacts between users u_1 and u_2 from t_{from} to t_{till}. The sub- and superscripts of C and the denoted timestamps are interpreted as a filter for the contained contacts. Following this semantic, '*' will be used as a wildcard symbol. The sum of all contact lengths in seconds for a given set of conversations C is given by $\mathrm{dur}(C)$. We aim to keep the values comparable despite the different social nature of users u – some tend to talk more in general than others. Furtermore, coffee breaks are significantly shorter than lunch breaks. Therefore, we divide the durations by $\max_{\mathrm{dur}_u}$: This equals the maximum of the sum of all contact durations during each break of the same category for user u. Let t_{from} denote the start and t_{till} the end of the respective break, then

$$\mathrm{dur}_u = \frac{\mathrm{dur}(C_*^u[t_{\mathrm{from}}, t_{\mathrm{till}}])}{\max_{\mathrm{dur}_u}}$$

is a value in the interval [0, 1]. The higher the value, the more socially active was the user during this time. For $\mathrm{dur}_u = 1$, the break after the presentation was indeed the most active one.

As discussed above, we removed all speakers for our analysis that either did not wear an RFID tag or had their talk directly before the poster session, since the it has its own social dynamics. The values for all speakers are plotted in Figure 11. The speakers are ordered on the x-axis by increasing dur_u. It is easy to see, that seven (46%) of the observable speakers were most active after their lecture.

Then, a natural question is, whether there are any features that connect these seven speakers. An intuitive hypothesis claims, that presenters whose papers are related to the work of a large number of other presenters get more attention. However, in the data we cannot confirm this. In order to analyze, if increased social activity is related to the content of the presented work, we analyze the documents contained in the Hypertext proceedings: For every pair of speakers $u_1, u_2 \in S$, $CosSim(u_1, u_2)$ measures the cosine sim-

ilarity of the stemmed bag of words representation of their papers with all stop words removed. In order to capture the overall relatedness of one paper to the others, we calculated the average value of all paper similarities with all other speakers' work for each presenter $u \in S$:

$$CosSim^u = \sum_{u' \in S, u \neq u'} \frac{CosSim(u, u')}{|S|}$$

The values were also plotted in Figure 11, marked with a diamond. Obviously, the hypothesis, that a higher $CosSim^u$, the more people might be interested in the work and also in speaking with the author does not hold. There is no direct correlation between both values. Nevertheless, it is worth mentioning that for five of the seven presenters who did not have an increased social activity ($\mathrm{dur}_u < 0, 8$), the paper similarity measure is above average, while for six of out the seven presenters who were most active after their session, the value is below. This is the exact opposite of what might be expected. Since the differences between high and low values are too insignificant, we cannot draw strong conclusions. A reason for this might be that some information is lost by averaging the similarity values; the existence of speakers u' with very high values $CosSim(u, u')$ is not reflected.

Instead, we now focus on the contact lengths of speaker u to those 10 other speakers S_u whose work is most similar to their own. We plotted the following values and their average in the Figure 11:

$$t_{\mathrm{rel}}(u) = \sum_{u' \in S_u} \frac{\mathrm{dur}(C_{u'}^u[*, *])}{\mathrm{dur}(C_*^u[*, *])}$$

We obtain a similar result as before, but observe a much stronger inverse correlation with the normalized contact lengths. This seems to justify the hypothesis, that speakers get a lot of attention mostly from those participants who did not present very similar research results. In the context of [13] and most of the assumptions in the state of the art of social network analysis, this result is surprising, since it is not only "similarity that breeds connection" but also differences.

Furthermore, not only the breaks after a session are of special interest, since the breaks before a session provide the possibility for session chairs and speakers to coordinate their presentation or clar-

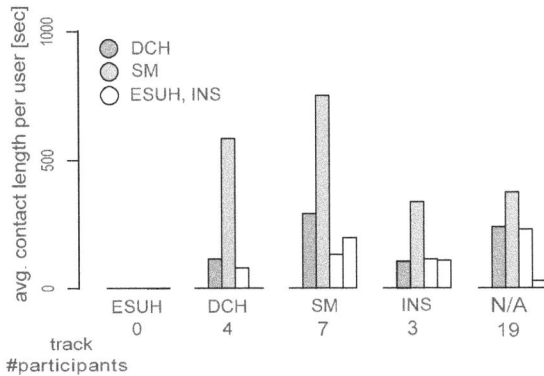

Figure 13: Normalized contact lengths for conversations between the participants of the different tracks after parallels session of the SM and the DCH track. Attendees without track assignment are denoted by category N/A.

ify final questions, e.g., the technical setup of the speaker's desk. Therefore, we tested the hypothesis that the structure of a conference organization may be reflected in the contact data. Despite the fact that there was only a small number of session chairs at the conference and some of them did not wear an RFID tag, there were no significant contacts between speakers and session chairs of the same track directly before the presentations.

5.2.4 Session Attendance of Communities

In the following, we examine the session attendance of the participants. We measure the attention and popularity of the given tracks by interpreting the session attendance as a decision process in which the members of the audience had to choose between two tracks to follow (see Figure 14).

The most obvious observation is that all tracks focused on their own community. Also a phenomenon that correlates with the observations above is that the new community ESUH played a special role at the Hypertext 2011 as it got a lot of attention from other tracks. This might reflect the mutual interest in one another and the beginning of an integration process of the communities. The big picture shows that SM was the most popular track and had even more attendance than the DCH track in 2011.

5.2.5 Session Attendance of Individuals

Based upon the hypothesis that people who focus on attending sessions of a favored track also have the most contacts to its members, we calculate the following two vectors for each user: One contains the number of presentations visited for each track and the other contains the length of contacts with its members. The cosine similarities between those two vectors are plotted in Figure 15.

For all tracks the values span the full range from low to very high correlation. The core, however, has a significantly higher average than the small communities. This is not surprising, while INS like all of the older tracks is mainly focused on exchanging ideas with their colleagues they might already know from a Hypertext in previous years. They had only a small number of lectures compared to the rest. This leads to other tracks being visited more often than their own. For ESUH it is very similar. While the number of lectures is comparable to the tracks from the core giving them the opportunity to focus on their own presentations, they tend to socialize more with the core - maybe due to the integration process.

The core itself has far better opportunities to only listen to top-

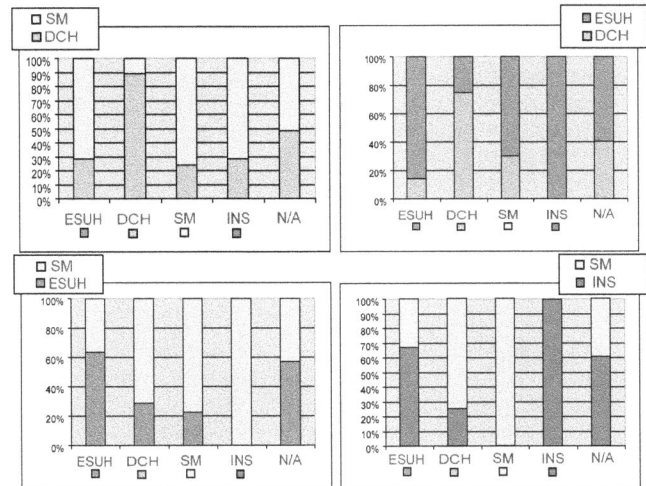

Figure 14: In five sessions, the four pairs of tracks were held in parallel (the combination of DCH/SM occurred twice). Each bar shows which percentage of the members of the respective track were spent in either of the two parallel sessions.

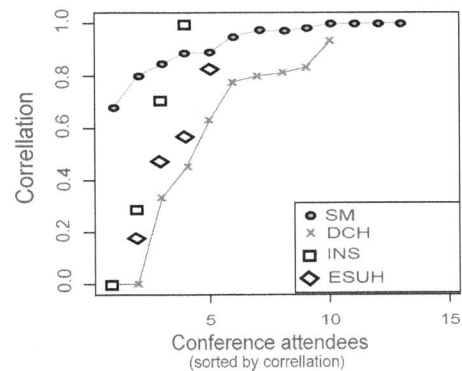

Figure 15: Correlation for the attendances of tracks and contacts to track members.

ics and also talk to members of their own tracks which is directly reflected in Figure 15.

5.3 Roles

The characterization of nodes in a social network is a very challenging task. In this section we focus on exploring the connection between academic jobs and influential and authoritarian persons of the Hypertext conference. First, we discuss the concepts for determining roles. After that, we present a detailed time-based analysis of role patterns. Finally, we use subgroup discovery to find more interesting patterns.

5.3.1 Determination of Roles

For this purpose we use a technique proposed in [16], which devides all nodes (conference participants) into four roles: Ambassador, Bridge, Loner and Big Fish. Intuitively, Ambassadors are nodes with contacts to many diverse communities, whereas Big Fishes only have a lot of contacts within one or at least less communities. Bridges are similar to Ambassadors, but with less contacts. A Loner is a role with less connections to different communities and less contacts.

251

In the following, we define these four roles more formally. Here, we use the definition given in [16]. To identify one of the four roles [16] used the relative degree of a node and a community metric. Whereas the relative degree of a node is simply the degree of the node divided by the maximum degree of all nodes, it is much harder to calculate the community metric. Here [16] present the new community metric $rawComm$ that estimates the number of communities a node is connected to. The community metric $rawComm$ for a node u is defined as

$$rawComm(u) = \sum_{j \in N(u)} r_u(v), \qquad (2)$$

where $N(i)$ is the neighborhood of node u. The function $r_u(v)$ is the community membership contribution from node v to node u. In [16] the function $r_u(v)$ is defined on unweighted graphs. We extend the definition of [16] for weighted graphs, taking into account the observation of section 5.1 that the probability of conversations to be in the same commnunity is dependent on the conversation length. We define the community membership contribution $r_u(v)$ from node v to node u as

$$r_u(v) = \frac{1}{1 + \sum_{k \in n_1} p_k + |n_2|(1-q)}, \qquad (3)$$

where n_1 is a set of nodes in $N(u)$ that is linked to u. n_2 is a set of nodes in $N(u)$ that is not linked to u and p_k is the probability that a link of node k to v with weight w exists within the same community. The probability q is defined in equation 1.

Now we can define the four roles Ambassador, Bridge, Big Fish and Loner for node u. The role of node u is defined as

$$role(u) = \begin{cases} \text{Ambassador} & rdeg(u) \geq s, rawComm(u) \geq t \\ \text{Bridge} & rdeg(u) < s, rawComm(u) \geq t \\ \text{Big Fish} & rdeg(u) \geq s, rawComm(u) < t \\ \text{Loner} & rdeg(u) < s, rawComm(u) < t \end{cases},$$

where $s, t \in [0, 1]$ are appropriate thresholds.

As described in Section 5.1, concerning all analyzed community structures, the track community fits best to the link structure of the social network. For this reason we decided to use the track community structure to analyze the function of all nodes in the network. One question that could arise here is why we do not simply count the number of communities a node is connected to. Unfortunately, as described below we do not know the tracks of all conference participants. For this reason we use the afore mentioned probabilistic model to determine the roles of the whole graph with the rawComm metric. We will compare our results to a similar analysis of another conference that was performed in [4].

5.3.2 Time-based Analysis

In our experiments we tested a lot of threshold parameters s and t. It turned out that the parameter setting $s, t = 0.4$ is a good choice to find an adequate number of Ambassadors and Bridges. In Figure 16 we see the results for the Ambassador analysis. As expected for conservations of two minutes or longer, most of the professors, session chairs and oldies function as Ambassadors. Here for conversations of one/two minute(s) or longer 75% of the professors are Ambassadors, 17% are Bridges and 8% are Loners.

As shown in Figure 17 for conversations longer than five minutes professors, oldies and session chairs become Bridges, and retain that status for conversations of greater lengths. A possible explanation of this is that for instance professors entering a conference venue generally know quite a number of people there. Thus they

briefly greet and get into contact with many people and thereby function as Ambassadors. These conversations, however, will not take more than five minutes in most cases. Then, professors will possibly start having longer conversations with few people they know best. This is how they might lose their status as Ambassadors.

The observation that professors lose their status as Ambassadors is different to the observation in [4]. Here professors retain their status as Ambassadors over the whole time. An interesting observation is that similar to the result in [4] the number of Big Fishes is very small. In Figure 18 we see that the fraction of professors, oldies and session chairs who are Loners is significantly smaller than that of phd-candidates, phds and presenters.

The differences to [4] concerning the results of the role analysis might be explained by the different kind of conference: The respective conference (LWA, of the german computer science society GI), is only held in Germany, and is regularly visited by a rather stable community. This offers the opportunity for more familiar relationships between researchers, which potentially results in longer conversations in general.

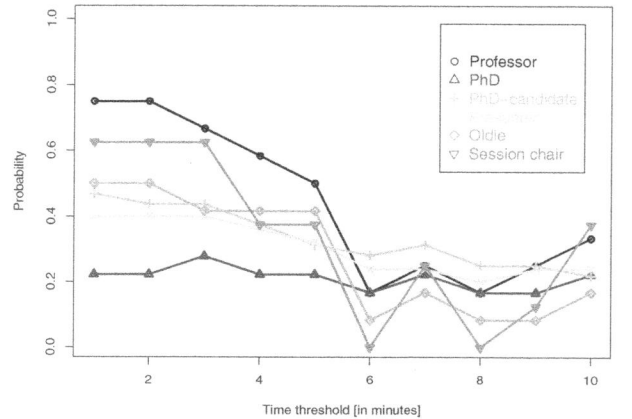

Figure 16: Fraction of professors, session chairs, etc. that belongs to the Ambassador role.

5.3.3 Mining Role Patterns

To characterize the different roles of the participants, we applied subgroup discovery techniques for mining role patterns. Subgroup discovery (cf. [5, 7]) aims at identifying interesting patterns with respect to a given target property according to a specific interestingness measure. Pattern mining using subgroup discovery is especially suited for identifying local patterns in the data, that is, *nuggets* that hold for specific subsets.

In our context, the target properties of interest are given by the different roles of participants in the contact graph. We aim at describing a subgroup (set of participants) with a specific role as closely as possible using a set of descriptive features, e.g., their country of origin, title, role as session chair, invited speaker, or presenter of a conference paper. We computed the roles according to different minimal conversation lengths (60, 180, 300 seconds). For subgroup discovery, we applied then the according role distributions. In the following, we discuss several examplary results. For an overview of the distribution of roles in the different episodes we refer to Table 3.

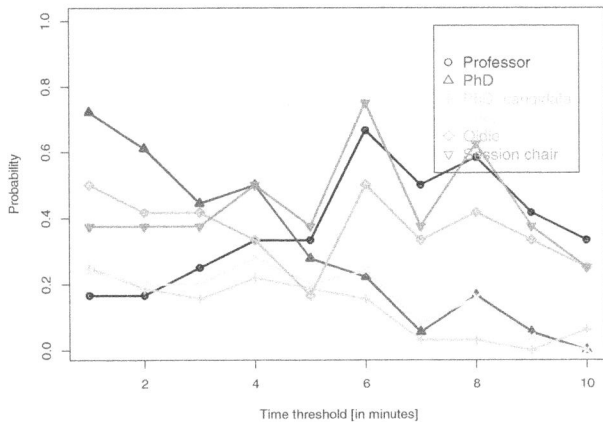

Figure 17: Fraction of professors, session chairs, etc. that belongs to the Bridge role.

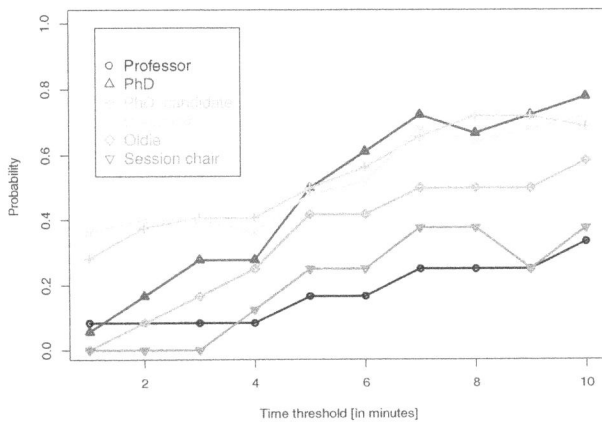

Figure 18: Fraction of professors, session chairs, ... that belongs to the Loner role.

Concerning the minimal conversation length of 60 seconds (Table 4), it is easy to see that the session chairs serve as Ambassadors during the confernce (the remaining session chairs are Bridges). Furthermore a *strong* affiliation to Hypertext plays an important role for being an Ambassador for the conference. The feature *Affil-*

Table 3: Overview on role shares (absolute/relative frequency) of the 66 conference participants wearing RFID-tags considering their (conversation) contact graphs: The table shows the statistics for three minimal conversation length thresholds (60, 180, 300 seconds).

sec	#Ambassador (%)	#Bridge (%)	#Loner (%)
60	29 (0.44)	26 (0.40)	11 (0.17)
180	28 (0.42)	18 (0.27)	20 (0.30)
300	21 (0.32)	16 (0.24)	28 (0.42)

iation denotes the familiarity with Hypertext, such that authors of at most one Hypertext paper published in 2011 get a *low* affiliation score, authors who published one or two papers before Hypertext 2011 get a *medium* affiliation score, and authors with at least 3 papers before Hypertext 2011 get a *strong* affiliation score. Considering the 60 seconds threshold, it is also evident that the participants from the Netherlands (including in particular the organizers) are typical bridges, as expected. This is especially visible in subgroup #3 of Table 4 with a target share of 100%.

Table 4: Subgroup results for a minimal conversation length of 60 seconds. The table shows the target variable, the lift (relative target increase w.r.t. the default), the share of the target in the subgroup, the size of the subgroup, and the subgroup pattern.

Min. Contact Length: 60 sec				
#	Target	Lift	Share	Size	Pattern
1	Ambassador	1.42	0.63	8	SessionChair=true
2	Ambassador	1.14	0.50	12	Affiliation=strong
3	Bridge	2.54	1.0	6	Country=Netherlands AND Presenter=No
4	Bridge	2.18	0.86	7	Country=Netherlands
5	Bridge	0.95	0.37	8	SessionChair=true

Considering the minimal conversation length of 180 seconds (Table 5) the overall picture changes a little. While the session chairs are stable in their roles, it seems, that the strengths of the Ambassador and Bridge associations is decreased.

Table 5: Subgroup results for a minimal conversation length of 180 seconds. The table shows the target variable, the lift (relative target increase w.r.t. the default), the share of the target in the subgroup, the size of the subgroup, and the pattern.

Min. Contact Length: 180 sec				
#	Target	Lift	Share	Size	Pattern
1	Ambassador	1.47	0.63	8	SessionChair=true
2	Ambassador	0.98	0.42	12	Affiliation=strong
3	Bridge	1.05	0.29	7	Country=Netherlands
4	Bridge	1.83	0.50	6	SessionChair=true AND Affiliation=strong
5	Bridge	1.53	0.42	12	Affiliation=strong
6	Bridge	1.38	0.37	8	SessionChair=true

The 300 seconds minimal conversation length (which usually excludes smalltalk) continues the trend regarding the organizers, cf. Table 6. For the session chairs, their bridge role stabilizes. This is especially interesting concerning the session chairs who are not track chairs. The role of Ambassador is only more pronounced for those session chairs that also have a strong affiliation with the Hypertext conference.

6. CONCLUSIONS

In this paper, we described the anatomy of a conference – focusing on the dynamic and static behavior of the participants at Hypertext 2011. For the analysis, we applied data collected by the Conferator system. We presented basic overview statistics concerning the participants, the presenters, the session chairs, and different communities. Additionally, we performed an in-depth analysis of these actors during the conference concerning their communication behavior, their session and track attendence, and the influence of the according communities. We also analyzed the roles of the conference participants in a time-based analysis and a pattern mining approach for the characterization of roles.

Table 6: Subgroup results for a minimal conversation length of 300 seconds. The table shows the target variable, the lift (relative target increase w.r.t. the default), the share of the target in the subgroup, the size of the subgroup, and the pattern.

#	Target	Lift	Share	Size	Pattern
	Min. Contact Length: 300 sec				
1	Ambassador	1.57	0.50	6	SessionChair=true AND Affiliation=strong
2	Ambassador	1.31	0.42	12	Affiliation=strong
3	Ambassador	1.18	0.37	8	SessionChair=true
4	Bridge	2.48	0.60	5	SessionChair=true AND TrackChair=false
5	Bridge	1.55	0.37	8	SessionChair=true

In summary, we found that longer conversations are more probable, if the dialogue partners are both members of the same track. In contrast to intuition, an analysis of the presenters showed, that these were more involved in talks with participants presenting rather dissimilar work based on the content of their papers. Finally, using a combined approach of applying role mining and subgroup discovery, we found that the strenght of the affiliation is one of the strongest features in patterns (as would be expected) that determines the ability to connect between different communities. Overall, our analyses span a wide range and should enable the reader to obtain a good impression of conference interactions – most specifically for the Hypertext conference.

7. ACKNOWLEDGEMENTS

This work has been performed in the VENUS research cluster at the interdisciplinary Research Center for Information System Design (ITeG) at the University of Kassel. VENUS is supported by the government of Hesse as part of the program for excellence in research and development (LOEWE). CONFERATOR applies active RFID technology which was developed within the SocioPatterns project, whose generous support we kindly acknowledge.

8. REFERENCES

[1] H. Alani, M. Szomszor, C. Cattuto, W. V. den Broeck, G. Correndo, and A. Barrat. Live Social Semantics. In *Intl. Semantic Web Conference*, pages 698–714, 2009.

[2] M. Atzmueller, D. Benz, S. Doerfel, A. Hotho, R. Jäschke, B. E. Macek, F. Mitzlaff, C. Scholz, and G. Stumme. Enhancing Social Interactions at Conferences. *it+ti*, 3:1–6, 2011.

[3] M. Atzmueller, D. Benz, A. Hotho, and G. Stumme. Towards Mining Semantic Maturity in Social Bookmarking Systems. In *Proc. Workshop Social Data on the Web, 10th Intl. Semantic Web Conference*, 2011.

[4] M. Atzmueller, S. Doerfel, A. Hotho, F. Mitzlaff, and G. Stumme. Face-to-Face Contacts during a Conference: Communities, Roles, and Key Players. In *Proc. Workshop on Mining Ubiquitous and Social Environments (MUSE 2011) at ECML/PKDD 2011*, 2011.

[5] M. Atzmueller and F. Lemmerich. Fast Subgroup Discovery for Continuous Target Concepts. In *Proc. 18th Intl. Symposium on Methodologies for Intelligent Systems (ISMIS 2009)*, volume 5722 of *LNCS*, pages 1–15, 2009.

[6] M. Atzmueller, F. Lemmerich, B. Krause, and A. Hotho. Who are the Spammers? Understandable Local Patterns for Concept Description. In *Proc. 7th Conference on Computer Methods and Systems*, 2009.

[7] M. Atzmueller, F. Puppe, and H.-P. Buscher. Exploiting Background Knowledge for Knowledge-Intensive Subgroup Discovery. In *Proc. 19th Intl. Joint Conference on Artificial Intelligence (IJCAI-05)*, pages 647–652, 2005.

[8] A. Barrat, C. Cattuto, V. Colizza, J.-F. Pinton, W. V. den Broeck, and A. Vespignani. High Resolution Dynamical Mapping of Social Interactions with Active RFID. *CoRR*, abs/0811.4170, 2008.

[9] A. Barrat, C. Cattuto, M. Szomszor, W. V. den Broeck, and H. Alani. Social Dynamics in Conferences: Analyses of Data from the Live Social Semantics Application. In *Proceedings Intl. Semantic Web Conference*, volume 6497 of *Lecture Notes in Computer Science*, pages 17–33, 2010.

[10] B.-H. Chou and E. Suzuki. Discovering Community-Oriented Roles of Nodes in a Social Network. In *DaWak*, pages 52–64, 2010.

[11] L. Isella, M. Romano, A. Barrat, C. Cattuto, V. Colizza, W. V. den Broeck, F. Gesualdo, E. Pandolfi, L. Rava, C. Rizzo, and A. E. Tozzi. Close encounters in a pediatric ward: measuring face-to-face proximity and mixing patterns with wearable sensors. *CoRR*, abs/1104.2515, 2011.

[12] L. Isella, J. Stehlé, A. Barrat, C. Cattuto, J.-F. Pinton, and W. V. den Broeck. What's in a crowd? Analysis of face-to-face behavioral networks. *CoRR*, abs/1006.1260, 2010.

[13] M. McPherson, L. Smith-Lovin, and J. M. Cook. Birds of a Feather: Homophily in Social Networks. *Annu. Rev. Sociol.*, 27(1):415–444, 2001.

[14] M. Meriac, A. Fiedler, A. Hohendorf, J. Reinhardt, M. Starostik, and J. Mohnke. Localization Techniques for a Mobile Museum Information System. In *Proceedings of WCI (Wireless Communication and Information)*, 2007.

[15] C. Scholz, S. Doerfel, M. Atzmueller, A. Hotho, and G. Stumme. Resource-Aware On-Line RFID Localization Using Proximity Data. In *Proc. ECML/PKDD 2011*, pages 129–144, 2011.

[16] J. Scripps, P.-N. Tan, and A.-H. Esfahanian. Exploration of Link Structure and Community-Based Node Roles in Network Analysis. In *ICDM*, pages 649–654, 2007.

[17] J. Stehle, N. Voirin, A. Barrat, C. Cattuto, L. Isella, J.-F. Pinton, M. Quaggiotto, W. V. den Broeck, C. Regis, B. Lina, and P. Vanhems. High-Resolution Measurements of Face-to-Face Contact Patterns in a Primary School. *CoRR*, abs/1109.1015, 2011.

[18] M. Szomszor, C. Cattuto, W. V. den Broeck, A. Barrat, and H. Alani. Semantics, Sensors, and the Social Web: The Live Social Semantics Experiments. In *Proc. ESWC*, pages 196–210, 2010.

[19] C. Wongchokprasitti, P. Brusilovsky, and D. Para. Conference Navigator 2.0: Community-Based Recommendation for Academic Conferences. In *Proc. SRS*, 2010.

[20] S. Wrobel. An Algorithm for Multi-Relational Discovery of Subgroups. In *Proc. 1st Europ. Symp. Principles of Data Mining and Knowledge Discovery (PKDD-97)*, pages 78–87, 1997.

Diversity Dynamics in Online Networks

Jérôme Kunegis[1], Sergej Sizov[1], Felix Schwagereit[1], Damien Fay[2]
[1] Institute for Web Science and Technologies, University of Koblenz–Landau, Germany
[2] Dept. of Computer Science, University College Cork, Ireland
{kunegis,sizov,schwagereit}@uni-koblenz.de, d.fay@4c.ucc.ie

ABSTRACT

Diversity is an important characterization aspect for online social networks that usually denotes the homogeneity of a network's content and structure. This paper addresses the fundamental question of diversity evolution in large-scale online communities over time. In doing so, we study different established notions of network diversity, based on paths in the network, degree distributions, eigenvalues, cycle distributions, and control models. This leads to five appropriate characteristic network statistics that capture corresponding aspects of network diversity: effective diameter, Gini coefficient, fractional network rank, weighted spectral distribution, and number of driver nodes of a network. Consequently, we present and discuss comprehensive experiments with a broad range of directed, undirected, and bipartite networks from several different network categories – including hyperlink, interaction, and social networks. An important general observation is that network diversity shrinks over time. From the conceptual perspective, our work generalizes previous work on shrinking network diameters, putting it in the context of network diversity. We explain our observations by means of established network models and introduce the novel notion of eigenvalue centrality preferential attachment.

Categories and Subject Descriptors

H.4 [**Information Systems Applications**]: Miscellaneous; H.4.0 [**Information Systems Applications**]: General

General Terms

Algorithms, Experimentation

Keywords

Social networks, diversity, network evolution, Gini coefficient, controllability, matrix rank, entropy

1. INTRODUCTION

Networks provide an adequate and established model to study a broad range of complex structures and processes in online environments. Common examples include web pages (connected by hyperlinks), online users (e.g., connected through friendship lists on social networking sites), relationships between users and content items (e.g., authorship, comments, like buttons, etc.), and online communication (e.g., responses in online discussions, retweets and citations in microblogs).

The diversity of a network is a generic concept that encompasses several specific network characteristics. On a general level, diversity denotes collections of objects which are different from each other. In a network, the term *diversity* can refer to several concepts, each implementing the notion of diversity using different features of the network. These characteristics are dynamic and change in parallel with network evolution.

This paper is devoted to questions of measuring and understanding diversity dynamics in evolving networks. Our presentation is organized as follows:

1. We sketch a definition of diversity aspects, based on paths in the network, degree distribution, eigenvalues, cycle distributions, and control models (Section 2).

2. We introduce appropriate network statistics that capture corresponding aspects of network diversity: effective diameter, Gini coefficient, fractional network rank, weighted spectral distribution, and number of driver nodes of a network (Section 3).

3. We show and discuss results of a systematic empirical evaluation on a comprehensive collection of 20 real-world network datasets (Section 4.1).

4. We give theoretical explanations for the systematically observed diversity shrinking, considering this as a feature of the general diversity concept. In particular, we introduce the preferential attachment model for eigenvector centralities, which plausibly explains the shrinking of the fractional network rank (Section 4.2).

5. We discuss related work and point out its relationships to our investigations in Section 5.

2. WHAT IS NETWORK DIVERSITY?

Diversity is generally defined as the quality of a collection of things containing many *different* or *unlike* objects. In

Table 1: The measures of diversity we study. The first column gives the aspect of a network that is covered by the measure. The second column describes in what case a network can be called diverse under that aspect. The third column gives our proposed measures of diversity.

	Aspect	A network is diverse when	Diversity measure
3.1	Paths between nodes	Paths are long	Effective diameter
3.2	Degrees of nodes	Degrees are equal	Gini coefficient of the degree distribution
3.3	Communities	Communities have similar sizes	Fractional rank of the adjacency matrix
3.4	Random walks	Random walks have high probability of return	Weighted spectral distribution
3.5	Control of nodes	Nodes are hard to control	Number of driver nodes

the context of social media, the diversity of a system can be understood as the diversity of opinions, topics and communities. For instance, in a movie recommender system, we understand that the community has more diversity when the movies being watched and rated are different from one user to another. On the other hand, a community in which most people watch the same fixed set of movies is not diverse. In particular, this notion of diversity is independent of the notion of size: A movie recommender community may have many users and include many movies, and still lack diversity, because most users have seen the exact same movies. Thus, diversity does not denote the size but the distinctness of the content. In the context of a network such as the user–movie graph, diversity is thus achieved when many users have seen *different* sets of movies. Equivalently, we can require that individual movies have been seen by different sets of users.

The notion of diversity thus defined can be applied to other types of networks. For instance, diversity in a hyperlink network means that not all websites link to the same websites, but have a large variety in their link targets; in a trust network, diversity means that not everyone trusts the same set of people.

To give an exact numerical definition of diversity, we may look at various features of a graph. For instance in a user–movie network, we can look at the distribution of users that have seen each movie: If a small number of movies has been seen by a large number of people, and a large number of movies has been seen by only few people, then we may call the user–movie network not diverse. In this case, we have in fact looked at the *degree* of movie vertices in the network, and how they are distributed. Thus, a measure of network diversity can be defined using the degree distribution. Based on this, a possible measure of diversity is the Gini coefficient of the degree distribution – one of the five measures of diversity we will study.

Beyond the degree distribution, the measures of diversity we inspect will be based on paths in the network, communities, random walks, and a model of network control. Table 1 gives an overview.

2.1 Evolution of Diversity Measures

During the lifetime of a network, a given network measure will be subject to nontrivial fluctuations. For instance, the network density (i.e., the mean degree of nodes) has been shown to first grow very fast, then decline, and then end up growing slowly for the rest of a network's lifetime [14]. Therefore, any long-term meaningful pattern of change in a network measure can typically only be observed in one specific phase of a network's existence. As another example, a well-known result states that the density of networks grows over time [17]. Our tests on actual network datasets how-

ever show that the growth of the density is only present in networks in the later phases of their evolution. For these reasons, we will be interested here in the evolution of diversity measures only in mature networks.

Studying the evolution of network measures only on mature networks may seem self-defeating: By using mature networks, it would seem that by definition the diversity measure must be shrinking. However, this is wrong. First, we will not use network measures themselves as the definition of maturity. Instead, we will use, as a structural property, the giant connected component, which appears over time in all large networks we studied. We will use this giant connected component as a sign of maturity of a network. In all networks, the largest connected component contains more than 95% of all nodes when 70% of all edges (by time) are present. Thus, to make the evaluation equal over all networks, we will use this value of 70% for all networks: Order all edges by arrival times, and inspect the evolution of the network measures across the arrival of the remaining 30% of edges. Here, the value of 30% is arbitrary, but was chosen to be as big as possible without restricting the amount of nodes that are not covered by our analysis, not being in the giant connected component.

Another way to look at this is to consider the derivative of network measures. Ideally, a network measure would grow smoothly in function of time, and we would use its derivative to show a trend in the network, for instance to prove that the diversity is shrinking. Since however the arrival of edges is discrete and the growth of networks contains noise, the actual evolution of network measures is not smooth, and has to be computed over a longer time period. The choice of 30% can then be seen as a compromise between looking at only the derivative at the end of the timeline, and computing the evolution of a network measure over a long enough time interval such that random fluctuations in the value are factored out.

3. MEASURING NETWORK DIVERSITY

Let $G = (V, E)$ be a graph, in which V is the set of vertices and E is the set of edges. Edges will be denoted as $\{i, j\} \in E$, with $i, j \in V$. The graphs we consider are all undirected. The degree $d(i)$ of a vertex i is the number of neighbors of i. In other words,

$$d(i) = |\{j \mid \{i, j\} \in E\}|.$$

Basic statistics of G are based on the number of vertices $|V|$ and the number of edges $|E|$. For instance, we can define the density of a graph as the average number of neighbors of a node, i.e. $2|E|/|V|$. The density increases with time generally, as observed in [17]. This result is expected, as most statistics that measure the *size* of the graph in some way are expected to grow. For constructing more powerful statistics, we employ methods of spectral graph theory, i.e. we represent graphs as matrices, and look at their specific decompositions.

Let $\mathbf{A} \in \mathbb{R}^{|V| \times |V|}$ be the adjacency matrix of G defined as $\mathbf{A}_{ij} = 1$ when $\{i, j\} \in E$ and $\mathbf{A}_{ij} = 0$ otherwise. This matrix plays a fundamental role in spectral graph theory, and other matrices can be defined based on $\mathbf{A}$. We also will consider the diagonal degree matrix $\mathbf{D} \in \mathbb{R}^{|V| \times |V|}$ defined by $\mathbf{D}_{ii} = d(i)$.

Bipartite networks.

In some cases, the vertex set V can be partitioned into two sets V_1 and V_2, such that all edges connect a vertex in V_1 with a vertex in V_2. This structure has consequences on some network measures; for instance it makes the clustering coefficient always zero. Other measures are however unaffected.

Multiple edges.

In some networks, multiple edges can connect the same node pair. In that case, E is a multiset, and the adjacency matrix does not contain only the values 0 and 1, but allows any nonnegative integer. In networks with multiple edges, the degree $d(i)$ is defined to take into account multiple edges, i.e. it equals the number of incident edges, not the number of adjacent vertices.

We will now review the five measures of network diversity we use. Each of these measures is based on a single aspect of a network, as summarized in Table 1. In each case, there are alternative measures based on the same aspect, and we will explain for each measure why we chose it specifically and not another one.

3.1 Diameter

The first measure of diversity we look at is the network diameter. The diameter is a very common network measure that equals the longest shortest path in the network. It is typically used to describe a network as a *small world* [22]. A small-world network is one in which the diameter is small, and the clustering coefficient is high. The intuition between pairing these two measures is to combine a measure of local coherence, the clustering coefficient, with a measure of the overall coherence, the diameter. The given reference shows that the diameter places each network on a continuum between two extremes. On one hand, a lattice graph has a high local coherence, and thus a high clustering coefficient, but a low global coherence, and thus a large diameter. It could be said that the lattice has a high diversity, since its parts are very far from each other, as measured by the typical distance of nodes. On the other hand, a random graph has a low clustering coefficient and a low diameter, denoting low diversity, due to the fact that every node is reachable in few hops from every node. This is consistent with the interpretation of the random graph as having low diversity, since all nodes are near to each other, and thus any local structure is lost. Therefore, the diameter of a network can be considered a measure of the network diversity.

To be precise, the diameter measures the largest distance between two nodes of a network. The distance between two nodes in a network is defined as the minimal number of edges needed to go from one node to the other. In practice,

the diameter is susceptible to long branches connected to the rest of the network on just one end. Therefore, a common variant is the 90-percentile effective diameter, defined as the number of steps needed to reach 90% of all nodes, counted over all nodes [17]. We refer to this graph property as $\delta_{0.9}(G)$, and will use it in the rest of this paper.

Another related network measure is the radius, i.e. the shortest eccentricity of all nodes, where the eccentricity of a node is defined as the longest distance from that node to any other node. Like the diameter, the radius is skewed by the presence of long branches.

In [17], the diameter is observed to shrink over time, implying that the diversity of the network is becoming less over time. Due to the high runtime complexity of computing the exact effective diameter, we estimate it by sampling vertices, and computing their distance to all other vertices.

3.2 Gini Coefficient

The Gini coefficient is a measure of the inequality of a distribution. As a new diversity measure for networks, we apply it to the edge distribution. A measure of inequality can be interpreted to denote the opposite of diversity, since a network in which the distribution of edges is equal can be understood as having more diversity. As mentioned in the last section, the example of the user–movie network illustrates the Gini coefficient. When all movies have been seen by the same number of people, the diversity of the network is higher. If instead a small number of movies have been seen by many people and most movies have been seen by only few people, then the network is not very diverse. Thus, network diversity can be measured by inspecting how far the distribution of edges to nodes is away from an equitable distribution.

The Gini coefficient is defined using the Lorenz curve, a curve that can be drawn from a given distribution, and that is intended to visualize how far the distribution deviates from an equal distribution. An example is shown in Figure 1, for the Internet topology network. In the context of networks, the Lorenz curve describes the distribution of edges. In an undirected network, each edge is attached to two nodes. We can therefore consider each edge to belong to the two nodes that the edge connects. Thus, a network can be viewed as a distribution of edges over vertices. The number of edges owned by a vertex is then equal to the number of neighbors of that vertex, i.e. the degree. The sum of all degrees in the network thus equals twice the number of edges in the network.

The Lorenz curve connects the points $(0, 0)$ and $(1, 1)$. A point (x, y) is part of the curve when the share x of *poorest* nodes own the share y of all edges. Here *poorest* is meant as having the least degree. If the edges are equally distributed between all nodes, the share x of the poorest nodes own exactly a share $y = x$ of all edges, and therefore the Lorenz curve follows the diagonal of the plot. If the distribution of edges is less equal, the Lorenz curve is situated below the diagonal. In the extreme case of one node owning all edges[1], the Lorenz curve tends to the two line segments connecting the three points $(0, 0)$, $(1, 0)$ and $(1, 1)$.

To assess the degree to which the distribution of edges is equitable, we can look at the area between the main diagonal and the Lorenz curve. This area is zero when the distribution is equitable, and $1/2$ if it is completely unequitable.

---

[1]This is only possible if all edges were loops.

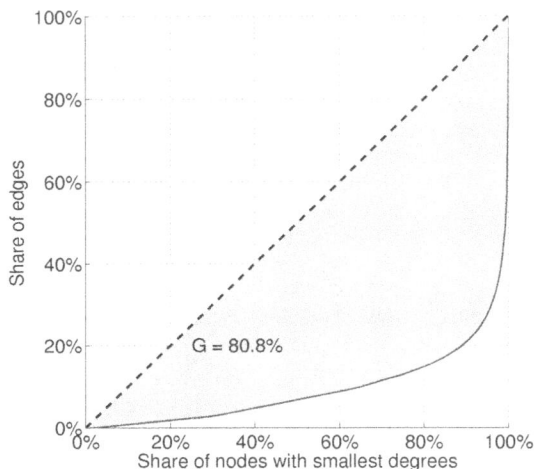

Figure 1: The Lorenz curve (in blue) of the Internet topology network's degree distribution. The Gini coefficient G is twice the gray area.

Multiplied by two, this area equals the Gini coefficient G, which is thus a value between 0 and 1, denoting a fair distribution for $G = 0$ and an unfair distribution for $G = 1$.

Other measures exist to denote the inequality of a distribution, for instance the Hoover index [7], which is also based on the Lorenz curve and correlates highly with the Gini coefficient, but also with the entropy of the distribution. The entropy of a distribution is however dependent on the number of nodes present: Its maximal value is the logarithm of the number of variables, and it would therefore have to be normalized. The Gini coefficient instead is independent of the network size by construction.

3.3 Fractional Rank

Another way to look at the diversity of a network is to consider the number of clusters of well-connected nodes it contains. If a network contains a large number of such clusters, we can rightly call it diverse. If we now simply define a cluster as a set of nodes being tightly connected, this leads to the problem that whatever method for identifying clusters we used, we arrive at the situation in which individual badly connected nodes form their own clusters. Thus, the total number of clusters would reach high values in any network. Even if we only restrict the definition to connected networks, individual clusters may be much larger than others, and a network with a very large dominating cluster and many small clusters should result in a small diversity according to our definition. Thus, we need to weight clusters by their size.

There are many ways to define clustering of networks, and to define the weight of a cluster. However, most of these algorithms are not scalable to large graphs, sometimes without any known polynomial-time algorithm. Therefore, we chose the eigenvalue decomposition as a clustering, in the sense that it decomposes network into a sum of rank-1 matrices, each of which can be interpreted as one cluster whose weight is the corresponding eigenvalue. The idea we follow here is to introduce a fractional extension of the rank of a matrix. Consider the eigenvalue decomposition of the adjacency matrix $\mathbf{A}$

$$\mathbf{A} = \mathbf{U}\mathbf{\Lambda}\mathbf{U}^{\mathrm{T}} = \sum_k \lambda_k \mathbf{u}_k \mathbf{u}_k^{\mathrm{T}},$$

where (λ_k) and $(\mathbf{u}_k)$ are the eigenvalues and eigenvectors of $\mathbf{A}$, for $1 \leq k \leq n$. Each rank-one matrix $\lambda_k \mathbf{u}_k \mathbf{u}_k^{\mathrm{T}}$ can be interpreted as the adjacency matrix of a subcommunity of the network, in which the eigenvalue λ_k determines the weight of the subcommunity. The rank of $\mathbf{A}$ can then be written as

$$\mathrm{rank}(\mathbf{A}) = \sum_k [\lambda_k],$$

in which $[\lambda] = 1$ when $\lambda \neq 0$ and $[\lambda] = 0$ otherwise. We thus see that the rank counts the number of clusters with nonzero weight. This is clearly a measure of the diversity of the network, but not a very good one, because very small eigenvalues contribute a value of one, although their corresponding cluster is very small.

Therefore, we propose to compute a *fractional rank* in which each eigenvalue is counted in proportion to its size. We start with the largest eigenvalue λ_1 and define its weight to be one. Then, each subsequent eigenvalue λ_k is weighted as $(\lambda_k/\lambda_1)^2$. The sum of these values then gives the network rank:

$$\mathrm{rank_F}(\mathbf{G}) = \sum_k \left(\frac{\lambda_k}{\lambda_1}\right)^2$$

We can rewrite this as the ratio of the Frobenius norm $\|\mathbf{A}\|_{\mathrm{F}}$ and the spectral norm $\|\mathbf{A}\|_2$ of $\mathbf{A}$:

$$\mathrm{rank_F}(\mathbf{G}) = \left(\sum_k \lambda_k^2\right)/\lambda_1^2 = \frac{\|\mathbf{A}\|_{\mathrm{F}}^2}{\|\mathbf{A}\|_2^2}$$

This is true because the spectral norm equals the largest absolute eigenvalue $|\lambda_1|$, and the Frobenius norm equals the square root the the sum of squared eigenvalues of $\mathbf{A}$. We will call this number the fractional rank of G. Note that because the square Frobenius norm $\|\mathbf{A}\|_{\mathrm{F}}^2$ equals the sum of squared eigenvalues, we have $\mathrm{rank_F}(\mathbf{A}) \geq 1$. The fractional rank can be easily computed using the number of edges in the graph and the spectral norm, because $\|\mathbf{A}\|_{\mathrm{F}}^2 = \sum_{i,j} \mathbf{A}_{ij}^2 = 2|E|$. The spectral norm $\|\mathbf{A}\|_2$ equals the largest absolute value and can be computed by power iteration.

As an alternative, using the sum of absolute eigenvalues instead of squared eigenvalues gives a slightly different measure, which in tests gave very similar results as the variant presented here. Using the square however has the advantage of making it possible to express the fractional rank as the quotient of the Frobenius norm and the spectral norm, which can both be efficiently computed. Using the absolute value would make it necessary to compute the nuclear norm, which is much more expensive to compute in general. Alternative measures of diversity based on clustering can be found by taking any method of clustering the nodes of a graph and defining weights for individual clusters. We chose the eigenvalue decomposition because it is fast to compute, and because it automatically gives weights for the clusters in form of absolute eigenvalues.

3.4 Weighted Spectral Distribution

Another motivation for the diversity in a network is to consider random walks. A random walk is a process starting at a given node i and proceeding along edges in a random manner. At each node, the random walk chooses one of the neighbors of that node uniformly at random; i.e. with probability equal to $1/d(i)$. Random walks can be used to measure how well connected a network is. For instance, one can consider the probability of return to the starting node i after k steps. If it is low, then the network possesses low locality, which we interpret as a low diversity. If the probability to return to the initial node is high, then we interpret that as a sign of diversity.

Another way to consider the return probability is as mixing rates. Imagine that a network starts out with a different label (or *opinion*) on each node, and that at each step, we diffuse the labels along the edges. Let $L(i)$ be the label initially present at node i. Then, after k steps of diffusion, the amount of label $L(i)$ at node i will equal the return probability for a random walk starting at node i. The rate with which the labels of the network converge to a uniform distribution over all vertices is called the mixing rate. Thus, a network with high return probability will have low mixing rate, and thus labels will propagate slower in it. Since the diffusion process can be understood as a dilution of the labeling, a low mixing rate thus indicates a high network diversity.

The weighted spectral distribution (WSD) was introduced in [9] as a metric for comparing two graphs. Random walk cycles are central to the metric and the weighted spectral distribution sums the probabilities of all such cycles by noting that they are related to the eigenvalues (λ_k) of the normalized adjacency matrix $\mathbf{Z} = \mathbf{I} - \mathbf{D}^{-1/2}\mathbf{A}\mathbf{D}^{-1/2}$ as

$$\vartheta(G, n) = \sum_k (1 - \lambda_k)^n = \sum_C \frac{1}{d(u_1)d(u_2)\ldots d(u_n)}, \quad (1)$$

where $\vartheta(G, n)$ is the weighted spectral distribution of the graph[2] G, C is the set of all cycles of size n in the graph and $d(u_i)$ is the degree of the ith node in a cycle.

To compute the weighted spectral distribution $\vartheta(G, n)$, we thus need to compute all eigenvalues, or alternatively to enumerate all n-cycles. Both operations are very expensive, and cannot be achieved in practice on large datasets. Therefore, we will use, as a proxy, a simplified variant. Instead of considering the sum over *all* eigenvalues of the matrix $\mathbf{Z}$, we will consider the sum over the r dominant ones:

$$\vartheta_r(G, n) = \sum_{k=1}^r (1 - \lambda_k)^n, \quad (2)$$

where the dominant eigenvalues of $\mathbf{Z}$ are defined as those with the greatest distance to $\lambda = 1$. This is not an approximation to $\vartheta(G, n)$. Instead, it is a value that is constructed to vary in conjunction with it, both reproducing shifts in the overall distribution of eigenvalues in the range $[0, 2]$.

As a network evolves, a falling weighted spectral distribution shows that this sum is falling and so the probability of taking a random walk of length n and returning to the source node is in general falling in the network. Another way of expressing this is that the number of *escape routes or noncycles* has increased. This in turn occurs when the community structure of networks becomes more blurred; random walks are more likely to jump away from the community

where they started. Thus the lower the weighted spectral distribution, the lower the diversity of a network.

There is also an interesting link between the weighted spectral distribution and pseudo-random graphs which we shall briefly comment on. For a general graph a measure called the *deviation from pseudo-randomness*[3] has been defined by Fan Chung [5] in terms of λ_k as:

$$\text{dev}(G) = \sum_k (1 - \lambda_k)^4 + 20\sqrt{\text{Irr}(G)} \quad (3)$$

where $\text{Irr}(G)$ is the irregularity of the graph [5][4]. Note that the first term on the right hand side is the weighted spectral distribution with $n = 4$. As $\text{Irr}(G) > 0$, the weighted spectral distribution forms a lower bound on the deviation of the graph from pseudo-randomness. In a pseudo-random graph all nodes are essentially equal and so it has minimal diversity; i.e. there are no communities. This provides a different interpretation for the link between a lower weighted spectral distribution and lower diversity.

3.5 Controllability

A less-known way to assess the structure of a network consists in measuring how well it can be controlled. For instance, assume that we want to influence opinions in a social network, but are only able to directly influence k persons in the network. Assuming that opinions will spread through the network, how big has k to be in order for us to be able to influence all nodes in a network, in a way that any arbitrary opinion can be given to any node? A solution to this problem is given in [18], in which such *driver nodes* are identified and, surprisingly, they are not necessarily the nodes with highest degree. In fact, the authors of that article state that driver nodes tend to *avoid the hubs* of the network.

The resulting computational model uses differential equations to model diffusion and can be reduced to finding a maximal matching in the bipartite double cover of the network [18]. The maximal matching in a bipartite graph can be computed efficiently because of König's theorem. It states that perfect matchings and minimal vertex covers have equal size in bipartite graphs, and thus the corresponding integer program formulations are equivalent to their relaxations.

The number of driver nodes N_D needed to control a graph $G = (V, E)$ equals $|V|$ minus the size of the maximum matching in the bipartite cover of the network, which equals the maximal directed 2-matching in the network. The bipartite double cover of a network $G = (V, E)$ is constructed by mapping each vertex $u \in V$ to two vertices $(u, 1)$ and $(u, 2)$, and mapping each edge $\{u, v\}$ to the edges $\{(u, 1), (v, 2)\}$ and $\{(u, 2), (v, 1)\}$. Equivalently this corresponds to the size of the maximal directed 2-matching. A 2-matching is a set of edges such that each vertex is incident to at most two edges. A directed 2-matching is a set of directed edges, such that each vertex is incident to at most one ingoing and one outgoing edge. Here, we interpret an undirected graph as a directed graph where each edge corresponds to two directed

---

[2] The authors in [9] recommend a value of $n = 4$ as is used in this paper.

[3] A pseudo-random graph is one for which an equivalence class of properties of random graphs hold; an initial list of these properties can be found in [6].

[4] The irregularity of a graph is difficult to estimate and is not used in this paper.

Table 2: The list of network datasets used in this study. Flags: U = Unipartite, B = Bipartite, M = Multiple edges.

	Network	Flags	$|V|$	$|E|$
[23] ben	Wikibooks, English	B	167,525	1,164,576
[23] bfr	Wikibooks, French	B	30,997	201,727
[4] DG	Digg	U M	30,398	87,627
[23] el	Wikipedia, Greek	B	149,904	1,837,141
[16] EL	Wikipedia elections	U M	8,297	107,071
[13] EN	Enron	U M	87,273	1,148,072
[19] EP	Epinions	U M	131,828	841,372
[20] Fc	Filmtipset	B	75,360	1,266,753
[3] HA	Haggle	U	274	28,244
[23] lv	Wikipedia, Latvian	B	111,515	946,173
[12] M2	MovieLens 1M	B	9,746	1,000,209
[23] nen	Wikinews, English	B	173,772	901,416
[23] nfr	Wikinews, French	B	26,546	193,618
[21] Ol	Facebook friendships	U	63,731	1,545,686
[21] Ow	Facebook wall posts	U M	63,891	876,993
[8] RM	Reality Mining	U	96	1,086,404
[23] sk	Wikipedia, Slovak	B	278,982	2,812,157
[23] sr	Wikipedia, Serbian	B	400,624	3,243,236
[26] TO	Internet topology	U	34,761	171,403
[23] vi	Wikipedia, Vietnamese	B	471,433	2,756,694

edges:

$$|V| - N_D(G) = \max_{M \subseteq V^2} |M|$$

$$\text{s.t.} \quad |\{(i,j) \in M \mid i = u, \{i,j\} \in E\}| \leq 1 \quad \text{for all } u \in V,$$

$$|\{(i,j) \in M \mid j = u, \{i,j\} \in E\}| \leq 1 \quad \text{for all } u \in V.$$

The result is the number $N_D(G)$ of vertices needed to control a given network. We conjecture that a network that is hard to control (i.e., has a high value N_D), is more diverse. Thus, we expect N_D to be a measure of the diversity of a network. A maximal matching in a bipartite graph can be found in runtime $O(|V|^{1/2}|E|)$ [18], and thus can be computed efficiently even for large networks.

There are no equivalent alternatives to using the number of driver nodes of a network known to the authors, in particular that are easy to compute.

4. EVALUATION

We compute the diversity measures defined in the previous section in function of time using a collection of networks in which edge arrival times are known, and thus a snapshot of the network at any time in the past can be obtained. We use a collection of 20 network datasets, summarized in Table 2. The networks are taken from the Koblenz Network Collection (KONECT)[5], an online collection of network datasets. First, we describe the key observations, and then review interpretations of the results.

4.1 Observations

Figure 2 shows, as a characteristic example, the evolution of all diversity measures for the Internet topology network. A systematic overview of similar results for all discussed networks is given in the Appendix.

---

[5]http://konect.uni-koblenz.de/

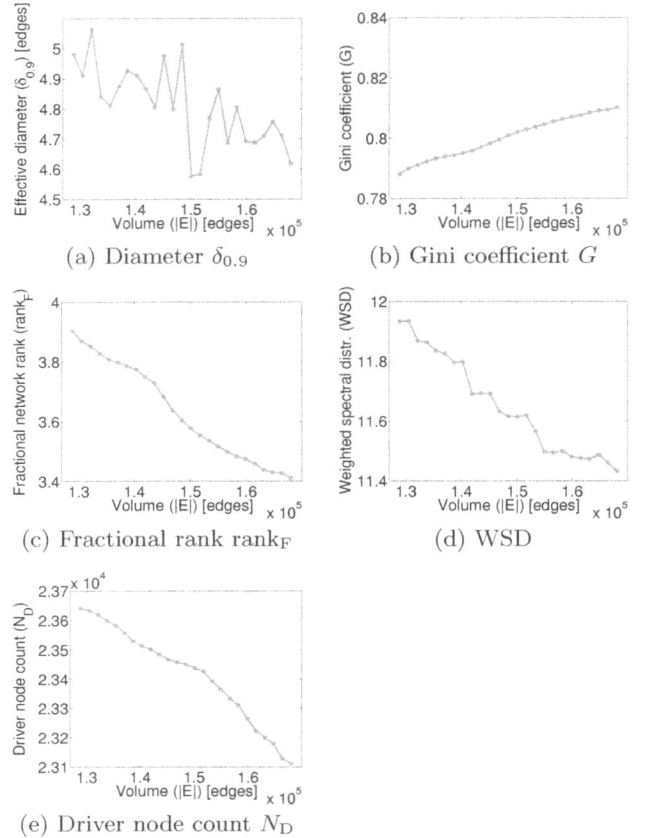

(a) Diameter $\delta_{0.9}$ (b) Gini coefficient G

(c) Fractional rank rank_F (d) WSD

(e) Driver node count N_D

Figure 2: The five measures of diversity plotted over time for the Internet topology network.

Each individual plot shows the evolution for one diversity measure and for one network, over the period that begins at 70% of present edges and finishes with the full network. For the weighted spectral distribution, the number of eigenvalues computed is a constant per network, varying between 10 and 50.

As a general observation, all measures except the diameter evolve in a way that is consistent with a *shrinking* diversity. Furthermore, we make the following observations.

Diameter.

The diameter is decreasing in general. We observe that the diameter varies from one timepoint to the other more than its overall trend. This is an indication that the diameter is not a robust measure. This is in opposition to reference [17], where a consistently shrinking effective diameter is reported for multiple networks.

Gini coefficient.

The Gini coefficient increases monotonously in slightly over half of all networks. Thus, the degree distribution of these networks becomes more heavy-tailed over time, and the diversity of the network decreases. In a few networks, the Gini coefficient decreases monotonously. These are the two Facebook networks, the Filmtipset comment network and the Wikipedia election network. Of these, three are online social networks.

Fractional rank.

The fractional rank is decreasing for the majority of networks, but by far not for all networks. A decreasing fractional rank indicates, as we discussed in the previous section, a decreasing diversity in terms of communities. Thus, we can interpret a shrinking fractional rank as a faster relative growth of larger communities than of smaller communities.

Weighted spectral distribution.

The normalized rank is consistently decreasing in most datasets. The change is however very small. This implies that the weighted spectral distribution shifts towards zero over time. We will inspect this in detail in Section 4.2.

Controllability.

The number of driver nodes N_D is decreasing for almost all networks. This pattern is the more consistent than for the other four measures. A decreasing number of driver nodes means that less and less vertices are necessary to be controlled in order to control the whole network. Thus, the diversity of the network is going down. The exceptions are the two interaction networks Haggle and Reality Mining. Both of these networks consist of persons connected by real-life interaction, collected using portable devices. The fact that both real-life interaction networks are exceptions to the rule of the shrinking number of driver nodes is interesting; it suggests that real-life networks behave differently than online social networks.

4.2 Interpretation

To explain the falling of the various measures of diversity, we propose explanations based on known network models, as well as one new model, preferential attachment applied to eigenvector centrality.

4.2.1 Preferential Attachment on Degrees

Preferential attachment is a general principle of network growth which states that new edges will connect to a vertex with a probability that is proportional to the importance of that vertex [1]. Preferential attachment can be used both to explain an increasing Gini coefficient, as well as a shrinking fractional network rank.

The fact that the Gini coefficient increases means that the degree of nodes with high degree grows faster than that of nodes with lower degree. This is explained by the preferential attachment model applied to the degree of nodes: If new edges are created with a probability that is proportional to the degree of nodes, then the degree of nodes will grow faster for nodes with high degree, and thus the distribution of edges over nodes will be more and more skewed towards a few nodes with very high degree, and many other nodes with small degree. This will result in an increasing Gini coefficient, as observed.

4.2.2 Preferential Attachment on Eigenvectors

A shrinking fractional rank can also be explained by a new variant of the preferential attachment model: The eigenvector centrality preferential attachment, which states that the probability that an edge attaches to a vertex is proportional to that node's eigenvector centrality. The eigenvector centrality is a centrality measure for nodes in a network, based on the eigenvalue decomposition of the network's adjacency matrix. It is defined as the vertex's entry in the adjacency

matrix's dominant eigenvector. This value is always nonnegative due to the Perron–Frobenius theorem.

When an unconnected node is added to a network, the fractional rank does not change. This follows directly from the fact that adding a zero row and column to a matrix will add an eigenvalue of zero to the spectrum. When an edge is added, the situation is more complex. In the case the fractional rank $\text{rank}_F(G)$ we can make the following derivation. Remember that the fractional rank can be written as

$$\text{rank}_F(G) = \frac{2|E|}{\lambda_1^2},$$

where $|E|$ is the number of edges and λ_1 is the eigenvalue of $\mathbf{A}$ with largest absolute value. Let $\tilde{G} = (V, E \cup \{i,j\})$ be the graph G to which the edge $\{i,j\}$ has been added. Also, let $\tilde{\mathbf{A}}$ be its adjacency matrix. Then, the new largest eigenvalue $\tilde{\lambda}_1$ can be estimated in the following way [2]. Let $\mathbf{e}_i \in \mathbb{R}^{|V|}$ be the vertex vector defined by $(\mathbf{e}_i)_j = 1$ when $i = j$ and $(\mathbf{e}_i)_j = 0$ otherwise. Also, let $\mathbf{A} = \mathbf{U}\mathbf{\Lambda}\mathbf{U}^T$ be the eigenvalue decomposition of $\mathbf{A}$. Then, the new adjacency matrix $\tilde{\mathbf{A}}$ can be written as

$$\tilde{\mathbf{A}} = \mathbf{A} + \mathbf{e}_i\mathbf{e}_j^T + \mathbf{e}_j\mathbf{e}_i^T.$$

Now, assuming we want to write the new adjacency matrix as $\tilde{\mathbf{A}}$ as $\tilde{\mathbf{A}} = \mathbf{U}\tilde{\mathbf{\Lambda}}\mathbf{U}^T$, we get

$$\tilde{\mathbf{\Lambda}} = \mathbf{\Lambda} + \mathbf{U}^T(\mathbf{e}_i\mathbf{e}_j^T + \mathbf{e}_j\mathbf{e}_i^T)\mathbf{U}.$$

The matrix $\tilde{\mathbf{\Lambda}}$ defined in this way is not diagonal. However, in practice it is usually almost diagonal, and its largest diagonal value can be estimated as

$$\tilde{\lambda}_1 = \lambda_1 + \mathbf{U}_{i1}\mathbf{U}_{j1} + \mathbf{U}_{j1}\mathbf{U}_{i1}$$

The meaning of this expression is that approximately, by adding the edge $\{i,j\}$, the dominant eigenvalue of the adjacency matrix $\mathbf{A}$ will grow by the double of the product of the entries i and j of the dominant eigenvector of $\mathbf{A}$. Plugging this result into the definition of the fractional rank, it follows that $\text{rank}_F(G)$ shrinks when

$$\frac{2|E|}{\lambda_1} > \frac{2(|E|+1)}{\lambda_1 + 2\mathbf{U}_{i1}\mathbf{U}_{j1}},$$

or equivalently when

$$\mathbf{U}_{i1}\mathbf{U}_{j1} > \frac{\lambda_1}{2|E|}.$$

In other words, the fractional rank shrinks when the values $\mathbf{U}_{i1}$ and $\mathbf{U}_{j1}$ are large enough. Remember that the dominant eigenvector $\mathbf{U}_{\bullet 1}$ of $\mathbf{A}$ is nonnegative and can be interpreted as the eigenvector centrality of nodes in G. Thus, the fractional rank shrinks when the product of the eigenvector centralities of the connected vertices are large enough. This can be understood as a form of preferential attachment: When new edges connect to central nodes, the fractional rank shrinks. The difference with the preferential attachment model is in the choice of the eigenvector centrality instead of the degree centrality.

4.2.3 Spectral Growth

Another way to analyse the evolution of the fractional network rank is to look at models predicting the evolution of the largest eigenvalue λ_1. It follows from the definition of $\text{rank}_F(G)$ that the fractional network rank shrinks when the

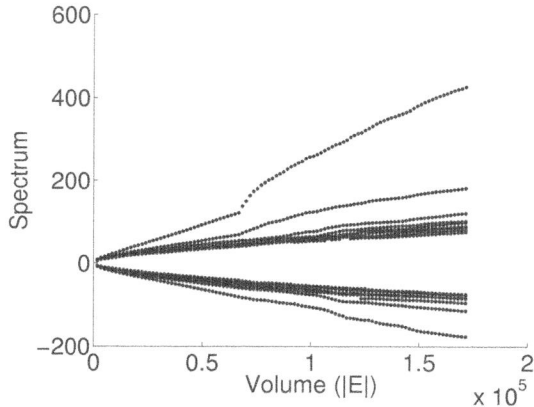

Figure 3: The evolution of the largest absolute eigenvalues of the adjacency matrix A in the Internet topology network. A linear extrapolation of the growth of these eigenvalues leads to shrinking values for both the absolute and fractional network rank.

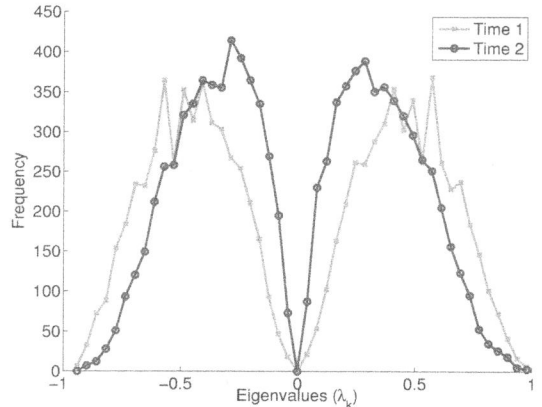

Figure 4: The evolution of the weighted spectral distribution in the Internet topology network. This shows the distribution of the absolute eigenvalues of the normalized adjacency matrix N, which is shifting towards zero over time.

largest eigenvalue λ_1 grows faster than the square root of the number of edges $|E|$. A corresponding model is given in [11], where the largest eigenvalue λ_1 grows as $|V|^{1/4}$. According to [17], the number of edges $|E|$ grows super-linearly in the number of vertices $|V|$, i.e. there is a constant $c > 1$ such that $|E| \sim |V|^c$. Plugging this into the definition of the fractional network rank, we get

$$\text{rank}_F(G) = \frac{2|E|}{\lambda_1^2} \sim \frac{|V|^c}{\lambda_1^2} \sim \frac{|V|^c}{(|V|^{1/4})^2} = |V|^{c-1/2}.$$

Thus, the fractional network rank will shrink when $c < 3/2$. Interestingly, the constant c has been reported to vary between 1.1 and 1.7 in [17]. This explains why in our experiments, the fractional rank does not *always* shrink, but only in most cases.

4.2.4 Spectral Evolution Model

The spectral evolution model from [15] implies that the fractional rank decreases. In this model, it is assumed that over time, only the eigenvalues of the adjacency matrix **A** grow, and that the eigenvectors of **A** stay constant. Specifically, it predicts that the evolution of each eigenvalue is linear. An example of spectral growth is shown in Figure 3 for the Internet topology network.

If spectral growth is extrapolated linearly into the future, the eigenvalue with the largest growth rate will overtake all others, and the network rank will decrease until is reaches the number of eigenvalues that have the same maximal growth rate. This explains a shrinking fractional rank in many networks, as a single eigenvalue becomes dominant.

4.2.5 Weighted Spectral Distribution

Because we used a low-rank replacement for the weighted spectral distribution, we need to verify the behavior of the actual weighted spectral distribution, to check whether the replacement measure is justified.

An example of the actual weighted spectral distribution is shown in Figure 4 using the example of the Internet topology network. The plots shows the spectral distribution at the beginning and end of our test phase adding 30% of all

edges. As the figure shows, the distribution of eigenvalues is shifted towards zero over time smoothly, justifying the usage of the largest absolute eigenvalues of the normalized adjacency matrix instead of the full spectral distribution.

5. RELATED WORK

Other network measures exist which also, when interpreted in the right way, may seem to implement a notion of diversity: the entropy and the connectivity.

The entropy is a measure used in thermodynamics to characterize the *disorder* of a physical system. In information theory, the entropy is a measure of the quantity of information. Given a random variable, its entropy can be used to describe its *randomness*, with an entropy of zero denoting complete certainty about the distribution, and an entropy of $\ln(n)$ denoting a completely uniform distribution over n states. This definition can be directly applied to various distributions in a network, in particular to the degree distribution. This leads to a known network measure, which is called the *entropy of degree sequence* (EDS) in [25]. In experiments, we found that it correlates highly with the network size, and that a normalized variant must be used instead. If this is done, the resulting measure correlates well with the Gini coefficient, and therefore we do not include it here.

The connectivity of a network can also be used as a measure denoting the lack of diversity. The two common measures of connectivity are however not suited to this: The classical connectivity defined as the size of the minimal nontrivial cut has the value one in virtually all real-world network due to the presence of vertices with degree one. The algebraic connectivity on the other hand is sensible as a number. It is defined as the smallest nonzero eigenvalue of the Laplacian matrix $\mathbf{D} - \mathbf{A}$. However, it can be shown that it is nondecreasing under the addition of edges, and is its evolution is thus monotonous, as long as no edges are removed from a network [10]. This follows from the fact that adding an edge to a network will add a positive-semidefinite matrix to the Laplacian, which can only increase but not decrease eigenvalues [24, p. 97].

6. CONCLUSION

In this paper, we introduced multiple measures of diversity in large networks, and systematically studied their temporal evolution using multiple real datasets. We found that for all measures of diversity except the diameter, the evaluation of these measures on mature networks indicate that the diversity is shrinking, a result that can be interpreted as a consolidation of the network structure. The fact that the diameter does not shrink consistently must be contrasted to a previous result observing the diameter of networks to be shrinking over time [17], a result that we interpret as an indication that the diameter is not well-suited as a measure of diversity in the general case.

To explain the shrinking of the various measures, we provided multiple models, based on existing models such as preferential attachment and spectral growth, but also a new interpretation of preferential attachment based on eigenvector centralities. We conclude from these observations that a different choice of preferential attachment variant leads to the shrinking of a corresponding measure of diversity, an indication that the preferential attachment model is valid for several aspects of networks, making it fundamental to models of network growth, whatever the specific feature they consider.

ACKNOWLEDGMENTS

The research leading to these results has received funding from the European Community's Seventh Frame Programme under grant agreement n° 257859, ROBUST.

APPENDIX:
NETWORK DIVERSITY RESULTS

Figure 5 shows the evolution of all five network diversity measures applied to our collection of network datasets.

7. REFERENCES

[1] A.-L. Barabási and R. Albert. Emergence of scaling in random networks. *Science*, 286(5439):509–512, 1999.

[2] J. Bunch, C. Nielsen, and D. Sorensen. Rank-one modification of the symmetric eigenproblem. *Numerische Math.*, 31(1):31–48, 1978.

[3] A. Chaintreau, P. Hui, J. Crowcroft, C. Diot, R. Gass, and J. Scott. Impact of human mobility on opportunistic forwarding algorithms. *IEEE Trans. on Mobile Computing*, 6(6):606–620, 2007.

[4] M. D. Choudhury, H. Sundaram, A. John, and D. D. Seligmann. Social synchrony: Predicting mimicry of user actions in online social media. In *Proc. Int. Conf. on Computational Science and Engineering*, pages 151–158, 2009.

[5] F. Chung. *Spectral Graph Theory*. American Math. Society, 1997.

[6] F. Chung and R. Graham. Quasi-random graphs with given degree sequences. *Random Struct. Algorithms*, 32(1):1–19, 2008.

[7] P. B. Coulter. *Measuring Inequality: A Methodological Handbook*. Westview Press, 1989.

[8] N. Eagle and A. (Sandy) Pentland. Reality Mining: Sensing complex social systems. *Personal Ubiquitous Computing*, 10(4):255–268, 2006.

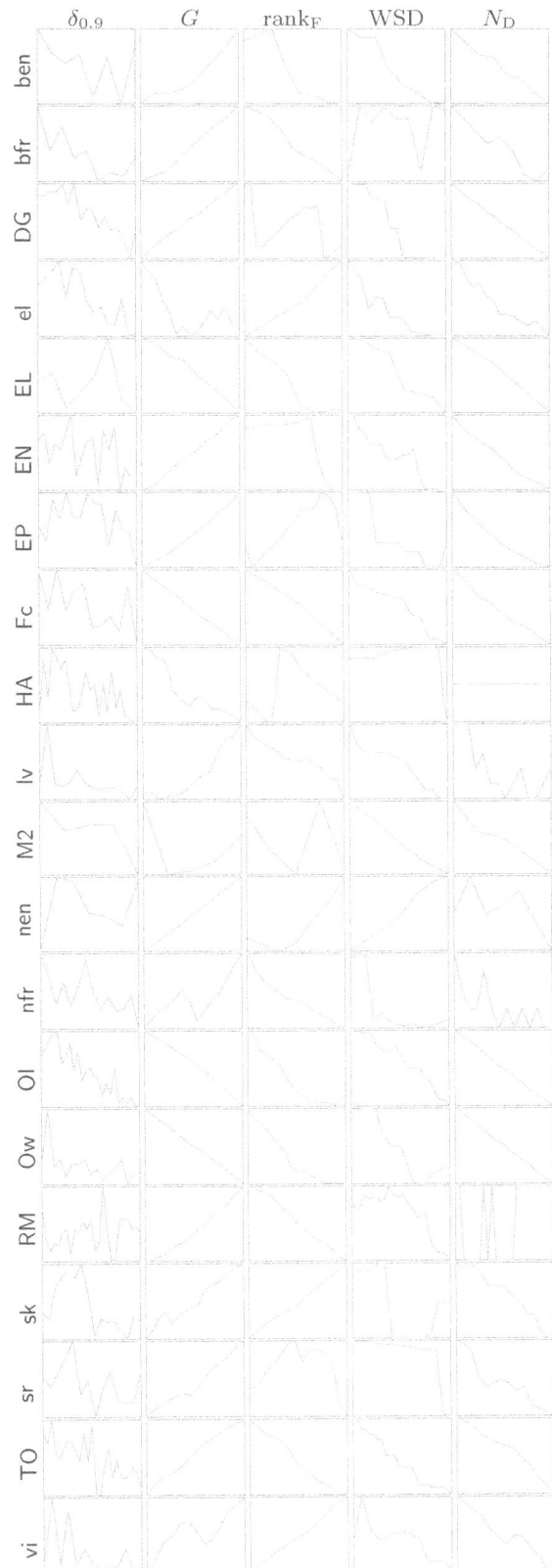

Figure 5: Full overview of diversity dynamics for all evaluated network datasets (cf. Table 2)

[9] D. Fay, H. Haddadi, A. Thomason, A. W. Moore, R. Mortier, A. Jamakovic, S. Uhlig, and M. Rio. Weighted spectral distribution for Internet topology analysis: Theory and applications. *IEEE Trans. on Networking*, 18(1):164–176, 2010.

[10] M. Fiedler. Algebraic connectivity of graphs. *Czechoslovak Math. J.*, 23(98):298–305, 1973.

[11] K.-I. Goh, B. Kahng, and D. Kim. Spectra and eigenvectors of scale-free networks. *Phys. Rev. E*, 64(5):051903, 2001.

[12] GroupLens Research. MovieLens data sets. http://www.grouplens.org/node/73, October 2006.

[13] B. Klimt and Y. Yang. The Enron corpus: A new dataset for email classification research. In *Proc. European Conf. on Machine Learning*, pages 217–226, 2004.

[14] R. Kumar, J. Novak, and A. Tomkins. Structure and evolution of online social networks. In *Proc. Int. Conf. on Knowledge Discovery and Data Mining*, pages 611–617, 2006.

[15] J. Kunegis, D. Fay, and C. Bauckhage. Network growth and the spectral evolution model. In *Proc. Int. Conf. on Information and Knowledge Management*, pages 739–748, 2010.

[16] J. Leskovec, D. Huttenlocher, and J. Kleinberg. Governance in social media: A case study of the Wikipedia promotion process. In *Proc. Int. Conf. on Weblogs and Social Media*, 2010.

[17] J. Leskovec, J. Kleinberg, and C. Faloutsos. Graph evolution: Densification and shrinking diameters. *ACM Trans. Knowledge Discovery from Data*, 1(1):1–40, 2007.

[18] Y.-Y. Liu, J.-J. Slotine, and A.-L. Barabási. Controllability of complex networks. *Nature*, 473:167–173, May 2011.

[19] P. Massa and P. Avesani. Controversial users demand local trust metrics: an experimental study on epinions.com community. In *Proc. American Association for Artificial Intelligence Conf.*, pages 121–126, 2005.

[20] A. Said, E. W. De Luca, and S. Albayrak. How social relationships affect user similarities. In *Proc. IUI Workshop on Social Recommender Systems*, 2010.

[21] B. Viswanath, A. Mislove, M. Cha, and K. P. Gummadi. On the evolution of user interaction in Facebook. In *Proc. Workshop on Online Social Networks*, pages 37–42, 2009.

[22] D. J. Watts and S. H. Strogatz. Collective dynamics of 'small-world' networks. *Nature*, 393(6684):440–442, June 1998.

[23] Wikimedia Foundation. Wikimedia downloads. http://download.wikimedia.org/, January 2010.

[24] J. H. Wilkinson. *The Algebraic Eigenvalue Problem*. Oxford University Press, 1965.

[25] J. Wu, Y.-J. Tan, H.-Z. Deng, and D.-Z. Zhu. A new measure of heterogeneity of complex networks based on degree sequence. In *Unifying Themes in Complex Systems*, pages 66–73. 2010.

[26] B. Zhang, R. Liu, D. Massey, and L. Zhang. Collecting the Internet AS-level topology. *SIGCOMM Computer Commun. Rev.*, 35(1):53–61, 2005.

An Evaluation of Tailored Web Materials for Public Administration

Nathalie Colineau & Cécile Paris
CSIRO – ICT Centre
cnr. Vimiera and Pembroke Roads
Marsfield, NSW 2122, Australia
(+61) 2 9372 4222

{nathalie.colineau,cecile.paris}@csiro.au

Keith Vander Linden
Department of Computer Science
Calvin College
Grand Rapids, MI, 49546, USA
(+1) 616 526 7111

kvlinden@calvin.edu

ABSTRACT

Public Administration organizations generally write their citizen-focused, informational materials for generic audiences because they don't have the resources to produce personalized materials for everyone. The goal of this project is to replace these generic materials, which must include careful discussions of the conditions distinguishing the various constituencies within the generic audience, with tailored materials, which can be automatically personalized to focus on the information relevant to an individual reader. Two key questions must be addressed. First, are the automatically produced, tailored forms more effective than the generic forms they replace, and second, is the time the reader spends specifying the demographic information on which the tailoring is based too costly to be worth the effort. This paper describes an adaptive hypermedia application that produces tailored materials for students exploring government educational entitlement programs, and focuses in particular on the effectiveness of the generated tailored material.

Categories and Subject Descriptors

H.5 [**Information Interfaces and Presentation**]: General; I.2.7; [**Natural Language Processing**]: Language Generation.

General Terms

Documentation, Human Factors.

Keywords

Tailored Information Delivery, Natural Language Generation, Public Administration.

1. INTRODUCTION

Citizen-focused materials in Public Administration (PA) must describe public programs and present the conditions under which individuals or organizations are eligible for them. Because PA constituencies are diverse, these conditions and associated informational materials are notoriously complicated. While PA organizations could assign a personal case worker to each citizen who would, like a personal physician, communicate directly with that citizen, cost and resource constraints generally force the organizations to communicate with their constituency en masse using generic materials. Unfortunately, generic materials tend to

be longer and harder to understand than materials tailored for particular readers.

This paper describes an application that automatically produces tailored informational materials. The application represents and reasons about conditions and concepts using semantic web technologies and generates tailored materials using discourse planning technologies. This application has been developed in collaboration with Centrelink, the Australian service-delivery organization for Human Services, and focuses on materials for students exploring educational entitlement programs.

As an example of the sort of PA materials addressed in this work, consider the website that Centrelink publishes for its Youth Allowance (YA) program, an entitlement program that helps Australian students with the cost of studying [4]. This website is targeted at a generic audience. Figure 1(a) shows an excerpt that details the eligibility conditions for the program (i.e., "You may be eligible for Youth Allowance if..."). In order to cover all possible student readers, this webpage includes a rather complex set of conditions with overlapping age ranges (i.e., 18-24, 16-24, 16-20, 16-17 and 15) and carefully-worded logical explanatory texts corresponding to each condition. Compare this with the excerpt from the tailored website generated by the prototype application described in this paper; see Figure 1(b). Here, the tailored text covers the same basic conditions but has been tailored for a reader who has indicated that she is a 19-year-old Australian resident planning to attend university full time. Given the context of this reader, the prototype has replaced the rather complex eligibility text with a one-paragraph summary of the eligibility conditions the reader is known to satisfy ("You've told us that you meet the following criteria: ..."). A similar simplification occurs later in the document in the materials related to the reader's likely payment rates. While the generic site for Youth Allowance must list all eleven possible payment rates, the tailored site needs only to list the one rate relevant for the given reader.

There are two key questions with respect to tailoring applications such as the one described here. First, will the tailored version of the material be sufficiently clear to enable readers to comprehend the content more accurately than they currently do with the generic versions? Second, will the extra time that the reader must spend specifying the demographic information on which the tailoring is based slow them down in comparison to the generic website, which requires no such information? This paper addresses these questions by reviewing relevant work, describing an application that produces tailored materials with a particular emphasis on the forms of tailoring it produces, and presenting the results of a pair of studies designed to evaluate the relative

Eligibility

You may be eligible for **Youth Allowance** if you are:

> 18*-24 years old and studying full-time.
> 16-24 years old and undertaking a full-time Australian Apprenticeship.
> 16-20 years old and looking for full-time work or undertaking a combination of approved activities, or have a temporary exemption from the participation and activity test requirements. If you do not have a Year 12 certificate or an equivalent qualification (Certificate level II or above) you will generally be expected to undertake study or training to meet the activity test.

*You may be eligible for Youth Allowance if you are 16-17 years old and studying full time (or 15 in certain circumstances) if you:

> need to live away from home to study, or
> are considered independent for Youth Allowance.

Other payments

If you are 21 and over and looking for work you may be eligible for Newstart Allowance.

If you are 25 and over and studying you may be eligible for Austudy.

More information

> Approved activities for jobseekers
> Independence test for Youth Allowance
> Participation and activity test requirements
> Youth Allowance section

(a)

Am I Eligible?

You've told us that you meet the following criteria:

> You are under 25 years of age.
> You are an Australian citizen, permanent visa holder or resident. (details)
> You are undertaking an approved course or Australian Apprenticeship. (details)

so you should be eligible for this program.

(b)

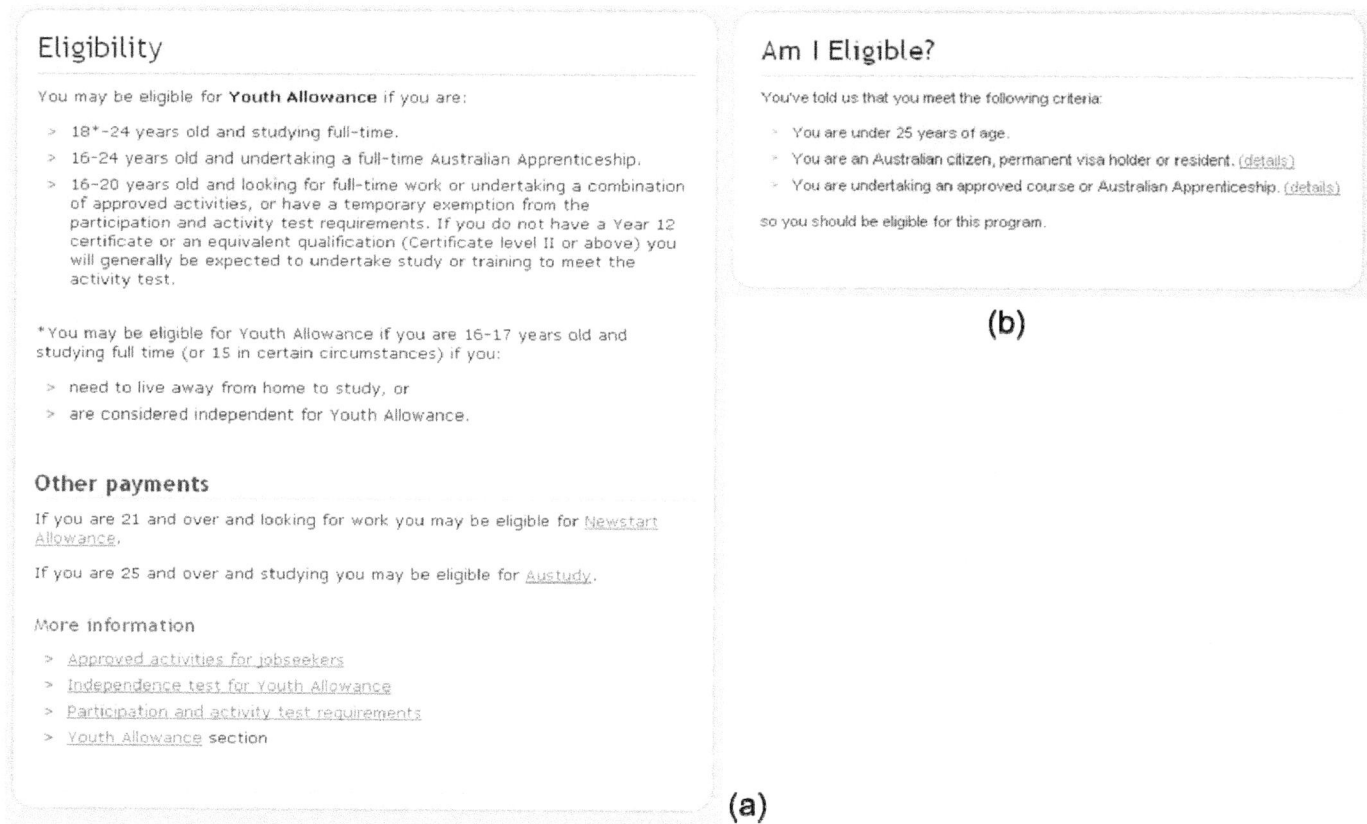

Figure 1. (a) an excerpt from the current website; (b) a corresponding excerpt from the tailored website.

comprehensibility and efficiency of the generic and the tailored websites.

2. RELATED WORK

The Adaptive Hypermedia (AH) prototype application described in this paper is based on technologies from Document Automation (DA), Natural Language Generation (NLG) and Ontology Verbalization (OV). The types of tailoring it generates are inspired by tailoring research in eHealth.

2.1 Tailoring in DA and NLG

This work draws on the practice of current DA systems (e.g., HotDocs, Exari, and Arbortext)[1] and on the theory and techniques developed in NLG [14] [13].

DA tools have been used in the legal profession to automate the production of custom-built legal documents (e.g., deeds of sale, standardized agreements, etc.) and in the technical documentation field to produce model-specific product documentation. These tools provide mail-merge-like features extended with conditional inclusion/exclusion of coarse-grained text units generally on the order of sections, paragraphs or perhaps sentences. The work reported in this paper can be seen as part of the broader field of DA but, as will be shown, deploys more sophisticated ontological representations [6] and planning and generation techniques [7].

Tailoring systems have been studied extensively in NLG. For example, the STOP system developed by Reiter *et al.* (2003) produced tailored smoking cessation letters using a combination of tailoring techniques, though Reiter and his colleagues were unable to demonstrate the effectiveness of the tailored letters in a large field study within their target audience [15]. DiMarco and her colleagues developed HealthDoc, which generates tailored health-education documents from a master document [8]. In the domain of corporate communication, the SciFly system developed by Colineau and Paris produced tailored informational brochures and succeeded in demonstrating effectiveness in its evaluation [5]. The work presented in this paper manages more coarse-grained text units than do STOP and HealthDoc and thus addresses fewer issues in sentence-level generation. The work follows more directly from SciFly in that it is based on the same implementation platform [13], a platform whose architecture is built around a hierarchical text planner [11].

2.2 Adaptive Hypermedia (AH)

A variety of techniques, including those from DA and NLG, have been applied to the adaptive presentation of hypermedia content. Using the terms and categories defined by Kobsa *et al.* (2001) in their survey of AH [10], the application described here collects user-supplied demographic data using an on-line questionnaire, which is commonly done in fielded systems, and then tailors the bulk of its content using a fragment-variant approach, which selects and assembles pre-authored fragments of text. This approach works well for the carefully-worded, legal content commonly found in citizen-focused PA texts, where generating

---

[1] See http://www.hotdocs.com/, http://www.exari.com/ and http://www.ptc.com/products/arbortext/.

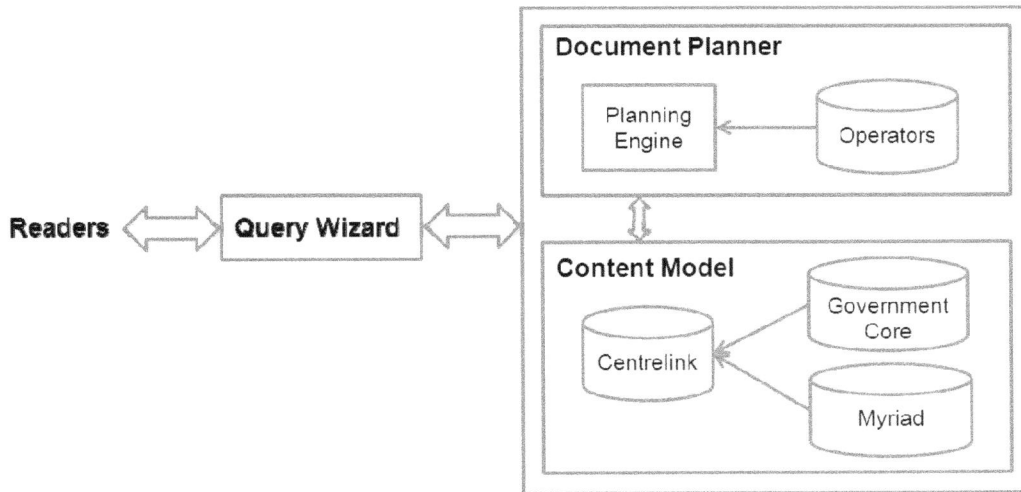

Figure 2. The system architecture

sentences on-the-fly from first principles is not possible given that all material has to be legally approved before release.

The application represents and reasons about its users and its content using a knowledge base implemented with semantic web technologies [16], which can be seen as what Bunt *et al.* would categorize as domain-dependent, abstract information [2]. Of particular concern in citizen-focused PA texts is the notion of eligibility. The application uses OWL-DL [12] to represent and reason about eligibility conditions in order to determine both whether a user is eligible for a particular program and what content to include.

2.3 Ontology Verbalization (OV)

The application's use of OWL-based representations of eligibility conditions makes it possible to use OV techniques, which take logical expressions written in an ontology language and generate corresponding textual descriptions [17]. This approach tends to implement structural mappings from all possible ontological expressions to simple textual forms that are accurate but perhaps not as fluent as might be desired.

The work described here implements OV for the subset of OWL expressions most commonly used in citizen-focused PA documents. To improve the fluency of the output, it also provides a mechanism for authors to override the automated expression when logical expressions become too complex to produce sufficiently fluent texts or when the texts must be more carefully crafted for legal purposes. This tool, which is not addressed in this paper, is a frame-based authoring tool (cf. [1]) that allows authors to specify domain content, including conditions and text. More details on this tool can be found elsewhere [7].

2.4 Tailoring in E-Health

While there is surprisingly little work on tailored communication in PA applications, work on tailoring has been a common theme in eHealth applications [3]. In a recent meta-study of tailored health documents [9], Hawkins *et al.* report that tailoring in eHealth has generally proven to be effective, particularly when there is a relatively large variation in the readers. The PA domain serves a similarly diverse constituency that varies on a number of scales, including age, race, domicile, family status, etc.

Hawkins *et al.* identified the following three forms of tailoring as being commonly effective in eHealth applications:

- **Personalization** – A document should identify itself to its reader as a tailored document, for example, by saying things like "this document has been produced for you…"

- **Feedback** – A document should refer to information provided by the reader, for example, by saying things like "You've told us that …".

- **Content matching** – A document should include the most appropriate content for a particular reader, for example, by choosing information units based on the reader's personal information. This comprises a variety of content selection techniques.

The prototype adaptive hypermedia application described here deploys all three forms of tailoring.

Given that these forms were developed in eHealth rather than PA, it was not clear that they would be equally effective in PA. One difference between typical eHealth applications and the PA application discussed in this paper is that eHealth readers must be convinced to change their lifestyle, say to stop smoking or eat more vegetables, which can be difficult. In contrast, PA readers are looking for government financial assistance and are highly motivated to sort out eligibility conditions.

3. APPLICATION

The prototype application, whose architecture is shown in Figure 2, comprises a web-based query wizard, which collects demographic information about the reader, the Document Planner, which uses this information to select and structure web materials that are tailored for the reader, and a Content Model, which represents and reasons over the information content.

3.1 Query Wizard

The query wizard, shown on the left of Figure 2, uses a simple JQuery-based questionnaire to collect demographic information from the reader, including their age, citizenship, race, school plans, and living arrangements, see Figure 3. It includes all the user information required to make eligibility and tailoring decisions throughout the website.

The wizard stores the user information in the Content Model and then asks the Document Planner to select and present a suitably tailored presentation of the material relevant to the context. If the reader provides no information, then the planner returns a full,

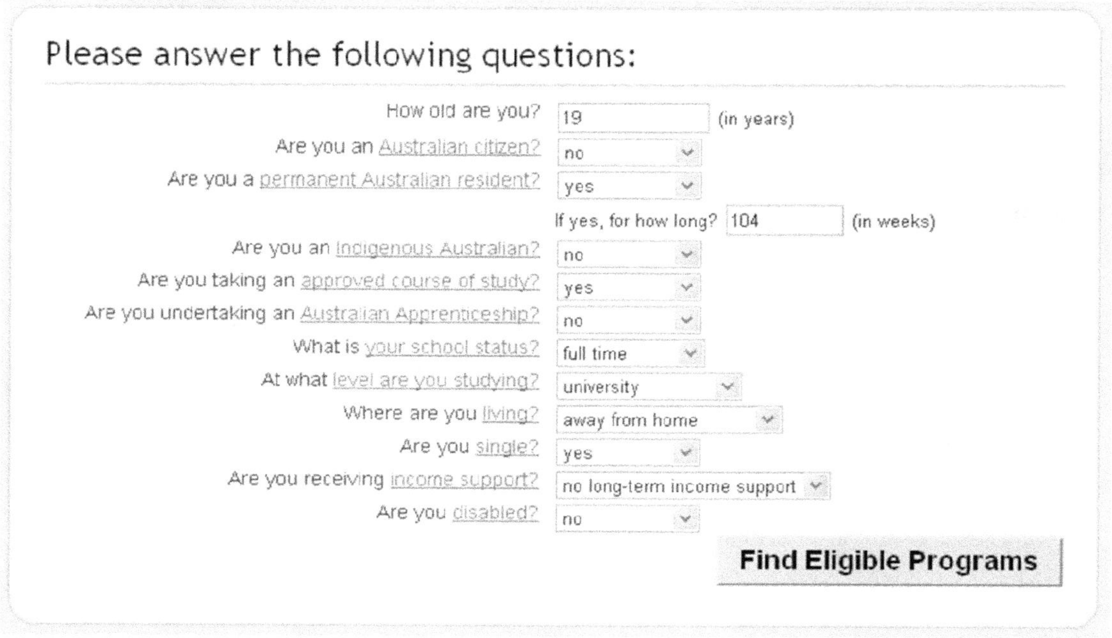

Please answer the following questions:

How old are you? `19` (in years)

Are you an Australian citizen? `no`

Are you a permanent Australian resident? `yes`

If yes, for how long? `104` (in weeks)

Are you an Indigenous Australian? `no`

Are you taking an approved course of study? `yes`

Are you undertaking an Australian Apprenticeship? `no`

What is your school status? `full time`

At what level are you studying? `university`

Where are you living? `away from home`

Are you single? `yes`

Are you receiving income support? `no long-term income support`

Are you disabled? `no`

Find Eligible Programs

Figure 3. The query wizard

generic presentation of the materials. The more information the reader provides, the more feedback and content matching the planner delivers.

In the early phases of development, it was unclear how much information readers would be willing to provide through the query wizard. So a preliminary study, described below, evaluated the relative desirability of a short query wizard, with a minimal set of four questions, and a longer query wizard, with more questions but resulting in more highly tailored material. As detailed below, readers preferred the longer wizard. The question then became whether or not the cost of filling out the longer query wizard would be outweighed by the value of the resulting tailored material. This was the focus of the second study described here.

The application has the ability to automatically plan wizard questions using OV techniques, but the system tested in this study used the hand-authored, JQuery wizard shown in Figure 3. Details on the OV query mechanism can be found elsewhere [7].

3.2 Document Planner

The Document Planner, shown in the upper-right of Figure 2, plans the document structure and content using a text planning engine driven by declarative plan operators. The plan operators are designed to build hierarchical text structures with conditionally included constituents. This technology is well-known in NLG [14], and its use in the Myriad platform, the platform underlying the application, is documented elsewhere [13].

The prototype exhibits one key departure from traditional approaches to building NLG applications in that it is a hybrid system that works with both coarse-grained information units on the order of sections, paragraphs and sentences, termed fragment variants in the AH community [10], and the fine-grained information units on the order of words as is more common in NLG systems. Traditional NLG applications include tactical generation components that work exclusively with units at the lexical and sentence levels. This application structures the output

by combining hand-written text fragments where available and using finer-grained OV where necessary.

This hybrid approach to NLG implements the three forms of tailoring discussed above as follows.

Personalization is simple enough that it requires only basic information on how to address the reader. For example, the tailored output for the YA program webpage opens with the following statement:

"This web material has been produced for you on 19/Jan/2012 10:29AM based on the information you have provided."

This basic form of tailoring has proven to be effective as the material is more likely to be read, remembered, and considered as interesting if people believe it has been produced for them. The planner uses a simple template-filling mechanism to produce this text, and places it on the webpage that links to the one shown in Figure 1(b).

Feedback is more involved, requiring finer-grained content and more detailed generation techniques. For example, the portion of the Youth Allowance brochure tailored for a reader known to be a 21-year-old Australian citizen working as an apprentice includes the text shown in Figure 1(b). The planner uses simple templates to produce the opening and closing texts in this example (i.e., "You've told us that…" and "so you should be eligible…") and OV to produce the declarative conditional expressions listed in the bullets. It uses the reasoning capabilities of the content model (see the next section) to determine the eligibility conditions the reader is known to satisfy, in this case age, residency and study conditions, and then constructs the feedback paragraph for the reader as appropriate. Had the reader's circumstances on any of these conditions been unknown, the planner would have included full descriptions of the unknown conditions in the tailored output. For example, Figure 4 shows the eligibility page tailored for a reader who is known to be an 18 year-old Australian citizen but whose course of study is unknown. The age and citizenship

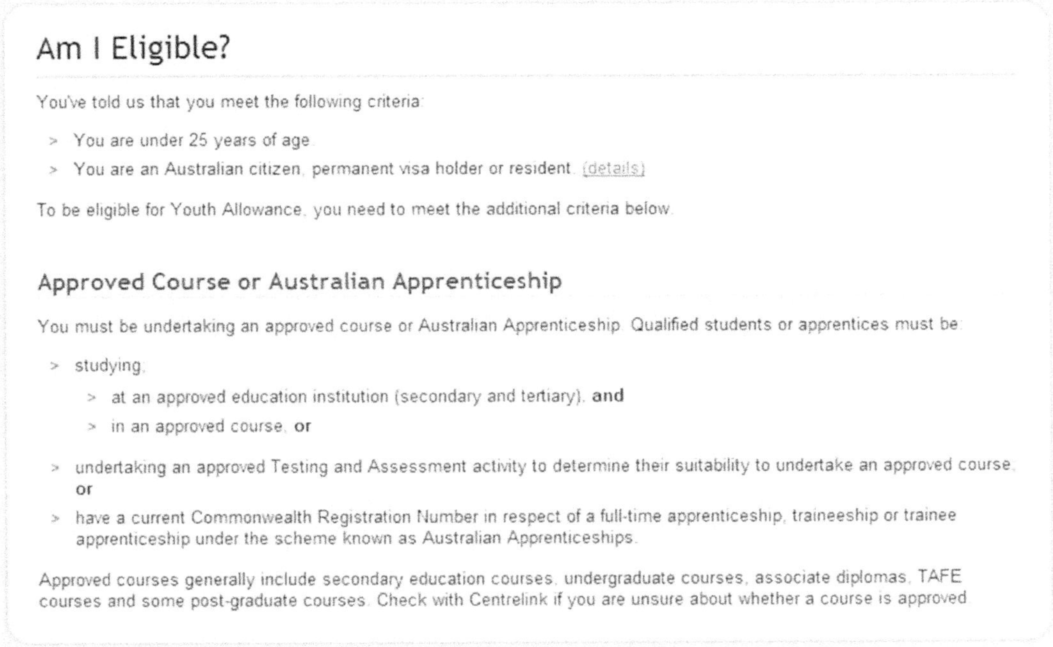

Am I Eligible?

You've told us that you meet the following criteria:

> You are under 25 years of age.
> You are an Australian citizen, permanent visa holder or resident. (details)

To be eligible for Youth Allowance, you need to meet the additional criteria below.

Approved Course or Australian Apprenticeship

You must be undertaking an approved course or Australian Apprenticeship. Qualified students or apprentices must be:

> studying:
>> at an approved education institution (secondary and tertiary), **and**
>> in an approved course, **or**

> undertaking an approved Testing and Assessment activity to determine their suitability to undertake an approved course, **or**
> have a current Commonwealth Registration Number in respect of a full-time apprenticeship, traineeship or trainee apprenticeship under the scheme known as Australian Apprenticeships.

Approved courses generally include secondary education courses, undergraduate courses, associate diplomas, TAFE courses and some post-graduate courses. Check with Centrelink if you are unsure about whether a course is approved.

Figure 4. A feedback page in which age and citizenship are known but school status is not known

conditions are mentioned only briefly, while the full explanation of the course requirements is given. The assumption is that if readers do not specify a condition, they will need a full description of that condition.

Content matching in the prototype application is based on eligibility. The Content Model can represent and reason about eligibility conditions on any content element at any level of abstraction, which allows the document planner to include only those content elements that are relevant to the current reader. For example, the 21-year-old, Australian university student addressed by the text in Figure 1(b) is not eligible for the ABSTUDY program because she is not an indigenous Australian nor for the Austudy program, because she is too young. So the application does not include any discussion of either of these programs. It focuses instead on the one program for which the reader is eligible, Youth Allowance. The hope was that this would help readers determine their eligibility more accurately.

Similarly, the planner can match the appropriate payment rate to a given reader, a computation that requires choosing among potentially many possible rates based on the reader's circumstances. In the case of Youth Allowance, there are eight rates from which to choose. With the information about the reader collected by the Query Wizard, the prototype can select one rate to present. The hope was that this would help readers determine their potential payments more accurately.

After the reader completes the wizard, the planner produces a list of student programs for which the reader may potentially be eligible based on the information they have provided. If the reader provides no information, then the list includes all the programs, as shown in Figure 5. Here, all three programs are listed: Youth Allowance (YA), Austudy and ABSTUDY, each with a short hand-authored description fragment and a list of conditions for which the reader's information is unknown (i.e., "Note: The following criteria, for which we don't know..."). The Content Model includes both short and long versions of the program

descriptions which the Document Planner deploys as appropriate (cf. Kobsa *et al.*'s notion of fragment variants [**10**]). The Content Model also includes OWL-DL representations of each of the listed conditions and an optional hand-authored text for the description. The Document Planner chooses the hand-authored version when available and otherwise reverts to OV for the condition. For example, Figure 4 shows two conditional expressions produced with OV (i.e., "You are under 25..." and "You are an Australian citizen...") and one hand-authored condition expression (i.e., "You must be undertaking an approved course or Australian Apprenticeship."). The OV expressions are relatively simple to produce automatically. Conjunctions and disjunctions, however, such as the one shown in this hand-authored text, are a well-known problem area for NLG systems, and while the prototype application can use OV to generate the course condition (i.e., "You must be undertaking an approved course and you must be..."), the hand-authored version is easier to read. This is the motivation for adopting a hybrid solution to NLG in the prototype application.

Note also that the OV mechanism is capable of producing both declarative forms (e.g., "you are under 25...") and obligative forms (i.e., "you must be under 25..."). The discourse planner chooses the appropriate form based on whether the reader's circumstances are known or unknown.

3.3 Content Model

The Content Model, shown on the lower-right of Figure 2, represents the conceptual structure of the domain, the user model and the text fragments for all the entities being expressed. It is implemented using OWL-DL [**16**] and supports the reasoning required for tailoring discussed above using HermiT [**12**].

To support reuse of the various elements of this model by other administrative organizations or by other tailored delivery applications, the model is divided into the three separate but integrated ontologies:

Program list

Based on the information you have provided, you may be eligible for one or more of the following programs:

> **Youth Allowance**
> Youth Allowance provides assistance for young people who are studying full-time, undertaking a full-time Australian Apprenticeship or training and/or looking for work. It may also provide assistance for young people who are ill or temporarily incapacitated.
>
> **Note:** The following criteria, for which we don't know your current status, are required for Youth Allowance:
>
> > - You must be under 25 years of age.
> > - You must be an Australian citizen, permanent visa holder or resident. (details)
> > - You must be undertaking an approved course or Australian Apprenticeship. (details)

> **Austudy**
> Austudy provides support for student and Australian Apprentices 25 years of age or over.
>
> **Note:** The following criteria, for which we don't know your current status, are required for Austudy:
>
> > - You must be 25 years of age or older.
> > - You must be an Australian citizen, permanent visa holder or resident. (details)
> > - You must be undertaking an approved course or Australian Apprenticeship. (details)
> > - You must be studying full time. (details)

> **ABSTUDY**
> ABSTUDY is the Aboriginal and Torres Strait Islander Study Benefit Scheme. ABSTUDY is paid to assist Aboriginal and Torres Strait Islander people to stay at school or go on to further studies.
>
> **Note:** The following criteria, for which we don't know your current status, are required for ABSTUDY:
>
> > - You must be an Indigenous Australian. (details)
> > - You must be an Australian citizen. (details)
> > - You must be undertaking an approved course or Australian Apprenticeship. (details)

Figure 5. The list of programs the user may be eligible

- The **Myriad** ontology represents those entities and relationships required for the document planner, e.g., the *Person* entity and the *hasAge* relationship.

- The **Government core** ontology represents general PA elements, e.g., *Program* and *hasCondition*.

- The **Centrelink** ontology represents those elements specific to the particular organization being models, e.g., Centrelink's Youth Allowance program.

More details on this structure can be found elsewhere [6].

These three ontologies work together to support the full context of communication. This includes: (1) a user model, which represents the demographic information provided by the reader through the Query Wizard; and (2) a domain model, which represents the content fragments, domain entities and eligibility constraints. The user and domain models are not explicitly shown in Figure 2. The Content Model also supports the representation of a device context, the discourse history and the task context, but these are not deployed in this application [13]. This structure is designed to minimize the effort required to port the knowledge base to new domains, but the true cost of this in the general case is unclear; a preliminary study of this issue is reported elsewhere [13].

The prototype supports the eligibility reasoning required for tailoring decisions using categorical reasoning as implemented by HermiT [12], a reasoner for OWL ontologies. For each reader, the prototype asserts an individual of class Person and sets the properties for that individual as appropriate, e.g., race, age, etc. It then uses HermiT's classification to determine if the individual's properties satisfy the properties required for any of the programs

or other content elements. The results of this reasoning are provided to the Document Planner for use as described above.

The text shown in Figure 5 also includes hyperlinks to definitions of the more complex conditions (i.e., through the hypertext link on "(details)"). For example, the definition of indigenous Australian includes the following text:

> *An Indigenous Australian is someone who:*
> - *is of Australian Aboriginal or Torres Strait Islander descent*
> - *identifies as an Australian Aboriginal or Torres Strait Islander person, and*
> - *is accepted as such by the community in which they live, or have lived.*
>
> *You may be asked to provide evidence to prove you meet all three parts of this definition.*

This important legal text is socially and politically sensitive and must, therefore, be carefully worded. This is the primary motivation for including hand-authored text fragments in the Content Model and for using hybrid technologies for text planning and generation.

Details on the nature of this model and the reasoning it supports, particularly with respect to PA and information sharing, can be found elsewhere [6] [7].

4. EVALUATION

Two evaluations of this application have been conducted: first, a qualitative evaluation and second a more quantitative study. This section details both.

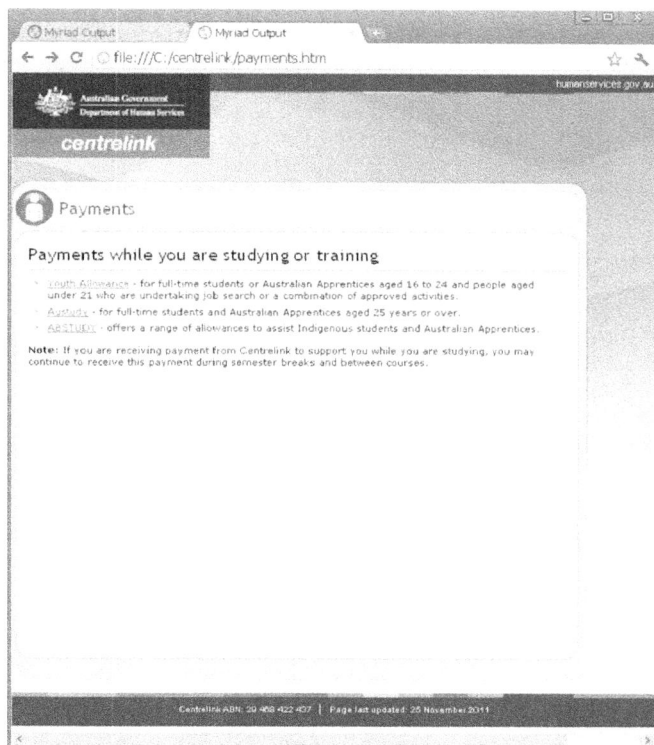

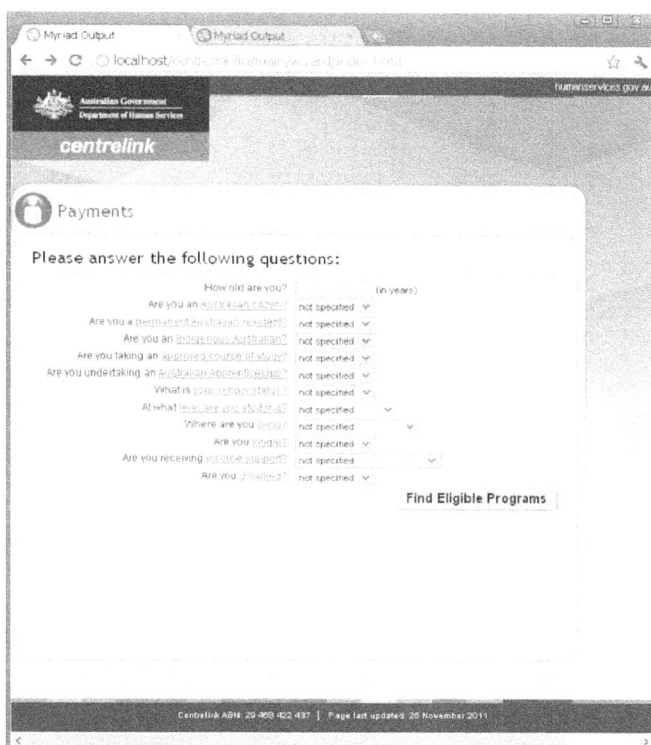

(a)

(b)

Figure 6. (a) First page of the generic website; (b) first page of the tailored website

4.1 A Qualitative Study of User Impressions

Centrelink's Concept Lab, an independent evaluation team within Centrelink, ran a qualitative evaluation of the first version of this application in May 2011. The goal was to evaluate the desirability of the tailored forms and their presentation in a brochure format, and to assess whether citizens would be willing to provide the personal information required to receive tailored information. There was particular interest in ascertaining how detailed a questionnaire the readers would be willing to answer, so both a short and a long form were provided. The short form included only four questions; the long form included twelve. These original forms differed slightly from the current form of the questionnaire shown in Figure 3. The test website also provided both web-formatted and paper-formatted output, all presented electronically.

4.1.1 Method

The evaluation included 15 participants, all of whom were of an age appropriate for Youth Allowance (YA) and of whom 14 were currently in receipt of YA payments. The materials included information on the YA, ABSTUDY and Austudy programs.

During 30-minute sessions, the participants explored the prototype, which included both the short and long forms of the query wizard and produced the program list as well as both the web and paper versions of the program materials. The free flowing nature of the subjects' exploration was not conducive to asking a structured set of questions. Instead, all participants were encouraged throughout the sessions to provide their preferences and feedback as to which wizard they preferred and if they were in favor of the concept of tailoring. The feedback was consistent throughout all 15 sessions.

4.1.2 Results

During the sessions the participants explored the prototype and tested the two different pathways: the "quick" wizard and the "detailed" wizard. Those who chose first the quick wizard thought it would be the fastest way to collect relevant information but later realized that the detailed wizard, through a more comprehensive question set, was providing them with more relevant content. All participants were able to answer the questions of the query wizard with ease, and all indicated that their structure was clear, concise and easy to follow.

All the participants expressed a preference for the tailored version of the brochure over the automatically-generated untailored version, with a preference for the longer more detailed form of the wizard. They even asked for a greater number of questions provided that it would lead to a greater level of tailoring.

Some suggested that we rephrase some of the questions, e.g., 'are you intending on studying', so that they could also use the tool to run different scenarios and understand under which conditions they could potentially qualify for Centrelink student payments.

The participants also expressed preferences for each of the three forms of tailoring deployed in the materials when they noticed them. All participants who noticed and commented on the personalization (e.g., "The following content sections have each been produced for you.") liked it. All participants noticed the feedback in the tailored eligibility section and immediately indicated that they liked it. Finally, all participants preferred the shorter materials made possible by tailored content elision (e.g., the elision of the full definition of race in the eligibility section).

The results of this study generally supported the desirability of tailoring in this domain, its value, the acceptability of the query wizard approach and provided some helpful feedback on expression forms and structure.

4.2 A Quantitative Performance Comparison

Given the favorable reception of the application's brochure output in the first evaluation, the prototype application was upgraded based on the subjects' comments, and a second evaluation was conducted. The objective of this second study was to evaluate whether providing tailored PA web materials helps readers find the information they need more accurately and efficiently. Where the first study included both web and paper-brochure-formatted output forms, the second study focused on web output and conducted a direct comparison between the prototype's automatically tailored website and Centrelink's existing website. The study was conducted from November 29th through December 8th, 2011 at Calvin College (USA).

4.2.1 Method

We compared two sets of webpages: 1) a set of generic pages corresponding to an extract of the current Centrelink website about student payment programs, and 2) a tailored version of the generic pages. The first page of each of these websites is shown in Figure 6. With the current generic version, see Figure 6(a), readers have to choose a particular student program, then sift through the eligibility conditions to determine whether they are eligible or not for this program, and then the payment conditions to determine the amount they may get if any. With the tailored version, see Figure 6(b), readers have to answer a short questionnaire, as described above in Section 3.1, to inform the system about their situation, and, based on this information, the system tells them the program(s) they may be eligible for and the amount they may be paid under each program. The format of both test websites is consistent and based on the current government website with extraneous links and information removed for the purpose of testing.

We tested these two online versions with a group of 28 students aged 18-20 from the introductory programming course at Calvin College. These students were very much like the recipients of Youth Allowance demographically, except that they were US and Canadian citizens rather than Australian residents (e.g., similar age, currently going to school full-time at an accredited university or college, single with no children). They received course credit for being part of the study and knew nothing of Myriad (the underlying system tested), Centrelink (the Australian government agency providing these student programs), Youth Allowance or the project in advance. The students were presented with scenarios: they were to imagine they were Australian and had been Australian residents for more than two years (i.e., >104 weeks), not looking for full-time work, and living in the dorms (i.e., away from home), as many of these students were. The students had to perform two tasks with slight variations of this scenario (e.g., age difference).

The students were split into two groups of 14, so that we could test each student for both versions and account for order effects. To counterbalance the effect of the order in which the systems were tested, we had group 1 evaluate first the tailored version and then the generic version, while group 2 started first with the generic version and then moved to the tailored version.

When testing each version, we asked students to determine: (1) whether they were eligible for any of the student payment programs; and (2) how much payment they may receive. We measured the accuracy of their answers and recorded the time it took them to answer each question. Then, we asked students to rate how confident they were about their answers, using a 6 point-scale from 0 (completely unconfident) to 5 (completely confident). To analyze the results, we conducted an analysis of variance using a mixed model with two fixed effects (i.e., group and tailoring) and one random effect of subjects. In all the results described below, group 1 (G1) refers to the group that saw the tailored version first, and group 2 (G2) to the group that saw the existing generic website first.

4.2.2 Results

Determining eligibility – The first question asked to students was to determine whether they were eligible for any of the student programs. We recorded their answers encoding them as 1 for correct and 0 for incorrect. As shown in Figure 7, both groups performed better with the tailored material. We noted that the difference in performance is more noticeable for group 1 who made almost twice as many mistakes with the non-tailored version. The results of the ANOVA confirmed that the difference between the generic and the tailored versions was statistically significant ($F(1, 26) = 6.56$; $p < 0.025$).

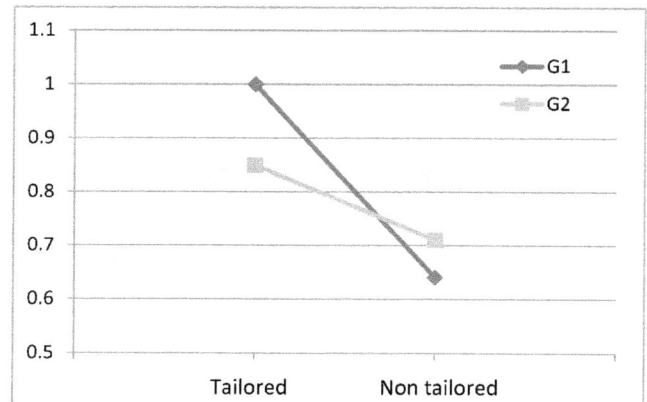

Figure 7. Plot of the correctness of answers' mean against the tailoring effect

We recorded the time (in seconds) the students needed to determine their eligibility. The difference in task performance varies widely from one student to another ranging from 12 to 268 seconds. We also observed that the task performance varies a lot in the generic version from the first trial to the second with a group mean ranging from 106 to 51 seconds. Comparing the performance between the two trials (see Figure 8), we noticed that regardless of the version tested, students seemed to be faster when performing the task a second time (i.e., in the second trial).

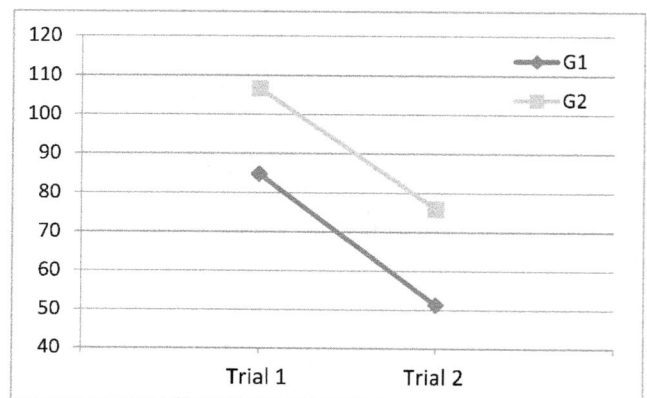

Figure 8. Plot of the time mean against the trial effect

We conducted an ANOVA which confirmed that there was a statistically significant effect of order ($F_{(1, 26)} = 5.93$; $p < 0.025$). The familiarity with the task may have played a role here, although as seen previously, this did not have any effect on the accuracy of their responses.

Determining the payment rate – The second question asked to students was to determine the fortnightly rate they may receive. (Note, being eligible to a student payment program did not guarantee students would be paid anything, as this depends on their income or that of their family). As shown in Figure 9, we observed here a larger difference in scores between the tailored and the non-tailored version with students making on average twice as many mistakes with the non-tailored version. The ANOVA results confirmed that the difference observed was statistically significant ($F_{(1, 26)} = 7.55$; $p < 0.02$).

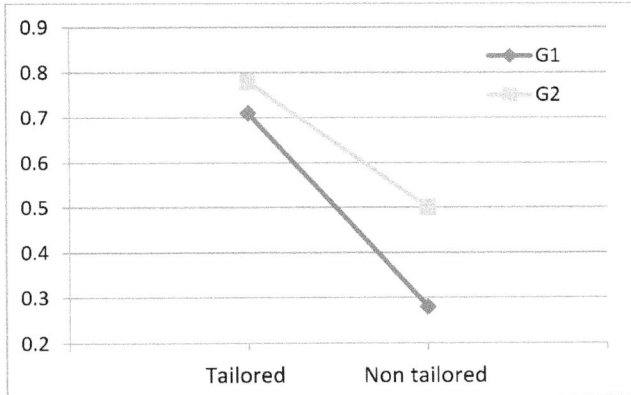

Figure 9. Plot of the correctness of answers' mean against the tailoring effect

We recorded the time students needed to answer the second question. As previously observed, we noted differences in task performance between students, ranging from 9 to 266 seconds, with an overall average of 79.5 seconds. As shown in Figure 10, students tended to be faster when performing the task the second time regardless of the version tested. This difference is statistically significant ($F_{(1, 26)} = 4.74$; $p < 0.05$), demonstrating an effect of order.

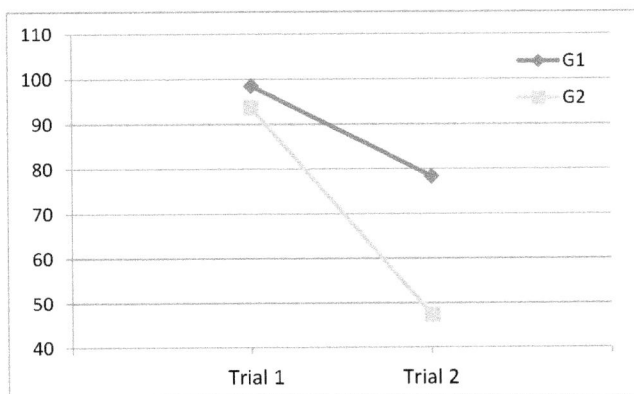

Figure 10. Plot of the time mean against the trial effect

Level of Confidence – Finally, comparing how confident students were in relation to their answers, we did not find any effect of tailoring ($F_{(1, 26)} = 1.95$; $p > 0.05$). Although G2 seemed to be more confident with the tailored version, participants in G1 were almost as confident with both versions. We noticed however that

both groups seemed to be more confident when performing the task the second time, as shown in Figure 11. This difference, although quite large for G2, was not significant ($F_{(1, 26)} = 3.83$; $p > 0.05$). Therefore, regardless of the time spent and mistakes made, students were reasonably confident about their answers.

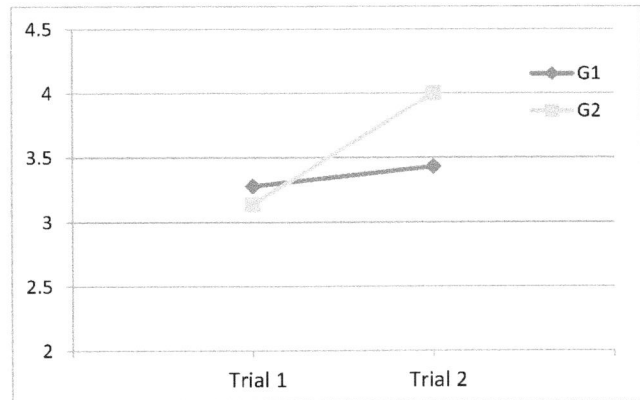

Figure 11. Plot of the confidence level mean against the time effect

Preferences – At the end of the test the subjects were asked reflective questions on which website they preferred and which made their job easier ("Did you prefer one version of the system over the other?"; "Which system made the tasks easier to do?" and "How useful was the questionnaire (wizard) in guiding you through the process?"). The participants overwhelmingly preferred the tailored website, and found that it made the task easier (see Figure 12). When asked about the usefulness of the tailored website's wizard, using a 4 point-scale from 0 (not useful) to 3 (very useful), the average response was useful (2.0).

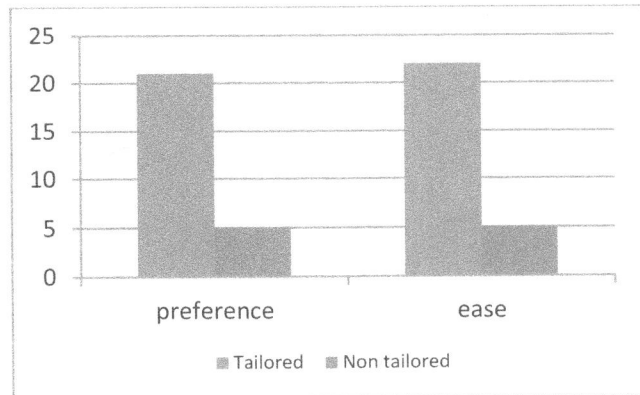

Figure 12. Answers to the reflective questions

4.2.3 Discussion

This study shows that tailoring the information presented to students helped them determine with more accuracy whether they were eligible to a particular student assistance program and how much they may receive. The tailored version of the system did not help student find the information more efficiently, but considering that students had to complete the Query Wizard for the information to be tailored to their circumstances, it is sufficient to know that it did not penalize them either. The students preferred the tailored web site and found it easier to use.

5. CONCLUSIONS

This paper describes an adaptive hypermedia prototype that produces a tailored informational website for applications in a Public Administration domain and its evaluation. It has reviewed the architecture of the application, detailed the forms of the tailoring used and the motivation for using them, and has concluded with a description of two usability studies of the application, the first qualitative and the second quantitative. The qualitative study suggested the desirability of tailored brochures and the acceptability of the use of a query wizard. The quantitative study demonstrated that readers made significantly fewer mistakes with the tailored website and that the use of a detailed query wizard did not slow them down, nor did it affect their confidence in their answers.

The next steps for this work are to pursue more detailed evaluations of the effectiveness of tailored information, including the automatically generated query wizard, and to continue work on the authoring tool to enable a public servant to enter the required information appropriately in the prototype.

6. ACKNOWLEDGEMENTS

This research has been funded by the CSIRO-Centrelink Human Services Delivery Research Alliance (HSDRA) and by Calvin College. The authors would like to thank Carol Taylor and Liz Mclachlan from the Centrelink Student Communication Team, Matt Barden from the Centrelink Student Payments Team and Susie Hardy and Rowena Alder who ran the study in the Centrelink Concept Lab. Thanks also go to Adam Strickland, who built significant portions of the prototype, to all the students who participated in the experiment and to the anonymous reviewers.

7. REFERENCES

[1] Peter Brusilovsky, "Developing adaptive educational hypermedia systems: From design models to authoring tools," in *Authoring Tools for Advanced Technology Learning Environment*, T. Murray, S. Blessing, and S. Ainsworth, Eds. Dordrecht: Kluwer Academic Publishers, 2003, pp. 377-409.

[2] Andrea Bunt, Giuseppe Carenini, and Chistina Conati, "Adaptive Content Presentation for the Web," in *The Adaptive Web: Methods and Strategies of Web Personalization*. Berlin: Springer-Verlag, 2007, ch. 13, pp. 409-432.

[3] Alison Cawsey, Floriana Grasso, and Cecile Paris, "Adaptive Information for Consumers of Healthcare," in *The Adaptive Web: Methods and Strategies of Web Personalization*. Berlin: Springer-Verlag, 2007, pp. 465-484.

[4] Centrelink. Youth Allowance. [Online]. http://www.centrelink.gov.au/internet/internet.nsf/publicati ons/st002.htm

[5] Nathalie Colineau and Cecile Paris, "Does Tailoring Help People Find the Information They Need?," *The New Review of Hypermedia and Multimedia*, vol. 15, no. 3, pp. 267-286, 2009.

[6] Nathalie Colineau, Cécile Paris, and Keith Vander Linden, "Automatically Generating Citizen-Focused Brochures for Public Administration," in *Proceedings of the 12th Annual International Conference on Digital Government Research*, College Park, MD, 2011, June 12-15, 2011.

[7] Nathalie Colineau, Cécile Paris, and Keith Vander Linden, "Expressing Conditions in Tailored Brochures for Public Administration," in *Proceedings of the 11th ACM Symposium on Document Engineering*, Mountain View, CA, 2011, pp. 209-218.

[8] Chyrsanne DiMarco et al., "Authoring and Generation of Individualised Patient Education Materials," *Journal on Information Technology in Healthcare*, vol. 6, no. 1, pp. 63-71, 2008.

[9] Robert P. Hawkins, Matthew Kreuter, Kenneth Resnicow, Martin Fishbein, and Arie Dijkstra, "Understanding tailoring in communicating about health," *Health Education Research*, vol. 23, no. 3, pp. 454-466, 2008.

[10] Albred Kobsa, Jurgen Koenemann, and Wolfgang Pohl, "Personalised hypermedia presentation techniques for improving online customer relationships," *Knowledge Engineering Review*, vol. 16, no. 2, pp. 111-155, 2001.

[11] Johanna D. Moore and Cecile L. Paris, "Planning text for advisory dialogues: Capturing intentional and rhetorical information," *Computational Linguistics*, vol. 19, no. 4, pp. 651-694, 1993.

[12] Boris Motik, Rob Shearer, and Ian Horrocks, "Hypertableau Reasoning for Description Logics," *Journal of Artificial Intelligence Research*, vol. 36, pp. 165-228, 2009.

[13] Cécile L Paris, Nathalie Colineau, Andrew Lampert, and Keith Vander Linden, "Discourse Planning for Information Composition and Delivery: A Reusable Platform," *Natural Language Engineering*, vol. 16, no. 1, pp. 61-98, 2010.

[14] Ehud Reiter and Robert Dale, *Building Natural Language Generation Systems*.: Cambridge University Press, 2000.

[15] Ehud Reiter, Roma Robertson, and Liesl M. Osman, "Lessons from a Failure: Generating Tailored Smoking Cessation Letters," *Artificial Intelligence*, vol. 144, no. 1, pp. 41-58, 2003.

[16] Michael K. Smith, Chris Welty, and Deborah L. McGuinness. OWL Web Ontology Language Guide. [Online]. http://www.w3.org/TR/owl-guide/

[17] Allan Third, Sandra Williams, and Richard Power, "OWL to English: a tool for generating organised easily-navigated hypertexts from ontologies," in *Proceedings of the 10th International Semantic Web Conference*, Bonn, Germany, 2011.

Early Detection of Buzzwords
Based on Large-scale Time-Series Analysis of Blog Entries

Shinsuke Nakajima
Faculty of Computer Science
and Engineering
Kyoto Sangyo University
Kyoto, Japan
nakajima@cse.kyoto-
su.ac.jp

Jianwei Zhang
Faculty of Computer Science
and Engineering
Kyoto Sangyo University
Kyoto, Japan
zjw@cc.kyoto-su.ac.jp

Yoichi Inagaki
kizasi Company,Inc.
Tokyo, Japan
inagaki@kizasi.jp

Reyn Nakamoto
kizasi Company,Inc.
Tokyo, Japan
reyn@kizasi.jp

ABSTRACT

In this paper, we discuss a method for early detection of "gradual buzzwords" by analyzing time-series data of blog entries. We observe the process in which certain topics grow to become major buzzwords and determine the key indicators that are necessary for their early detection. From the analysis results based on 81,922,977 blog entries from 3,776,154 blog websites posted in the past two years, we find that as topics grow to become major buzzwords, the percentages of blog entries from the blogger communities closely related to the target buzzword decrease gradually, and the percentages of blog entries from the weakly related blogger communities increase gradually. We then describe a method for early detection of these buzzwords, which is dependent on identifying the blogger communities which are closely related to these buzzwords. Moreover, we verify the effectiveness of the proposed method through experimentation that compares the rankings of several buzzword candidates with a real-life idol group popularity competition.

Categories and Subject Descriptors

H.3.3 [**Information Search and Retrieval**]: Information filtering; H.5.4 [**Hypertext/Hypermedia**]: Navigation

General Terms

Algorithms, Measurement, Experimentation

Keywords

Buzzword detection, Time-series analysis, Blogger community

1. INTRODUCTION

Buzzwords are terms or phrases describing topics that have become popular to general population. They represent the latest trends happening around the world–what people are talking about and what people are currently interested in. This information is very valuable, especially to businesses and marketers; and as such, it would be quite useful if we could detect it at an early stage. However, it is difficult to detect which topics will become the new buzzwords.

Most people become familiar with buzzwords as they are introduced by TV, news or magazines after they have become popular. However, there is often a core set of enthusiasts who talk about these buzzwords before they become popular to the masses. By focusing on this core set of people, we can find potential buzzword candidates.

We categorize buzzwords into two types by their growth patterns: "bursty buzzwords" and "gradual buzzwords." Bursty buzzwords attract people's attention suddenly and become known simultaneously throughout multiple communities, probably because they are featured on TV, news or magazines. Gradual buzzwords begin from a restricted community, spread little by little to other communities, and finally become widely known to most people.

Figure 1 shows the curve variation of blogger numbers for these two types of buzzwords. Some researchers have aimed at extracting bursty buzzwords [3, 16, 13, 14, 11, 2, 1]. However, in this paper we focus on early detection of gradual buzzwords.

In our research, we focus on blogs for the medium of buzzword analysis. Different from the mass media, blogs are an information source in which users can express their ideas, interests, and feelings in real time. Since blogs reflect the people's concern and public opinions, they are a significant source of current trend data. For example, many companies analyze blog entries to determine the opinions of their products. We argue that blog analysis can help detect the forerunners of buzzwords before they become widely known in the world. We use blog data consisting of 81,922,977 blog entries from 3,776,154 blog websites in the past two years provided by the company kizasi.jp [1].

---

[1] http://kizasi.jp/

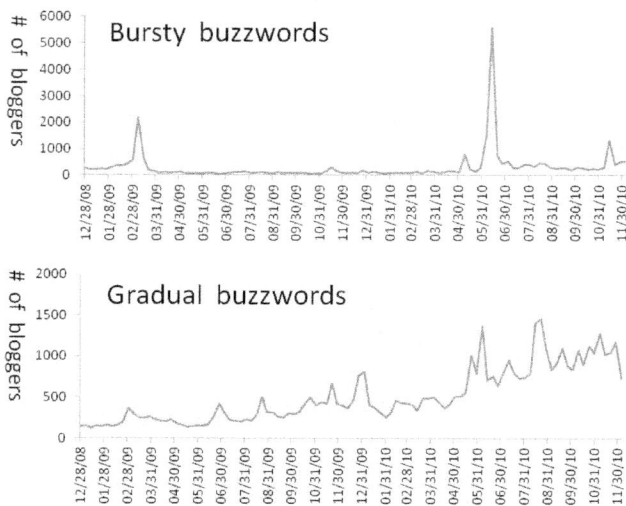

Figure 1: Comparison of curve shapes between bursty buzzwords and gradual buzzwords

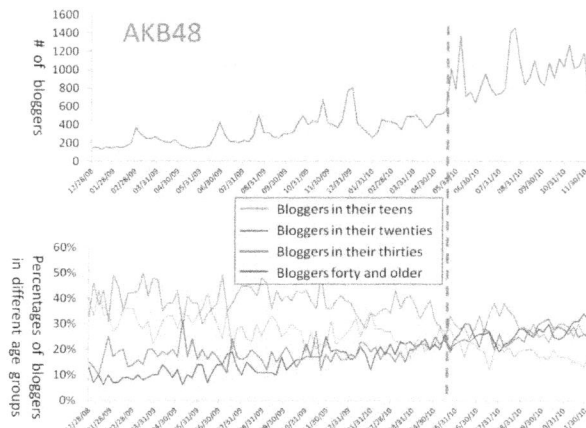

Figure 2: Numbers of bloggers and percentages of bloggers in different age groups (Topic: AKB48)

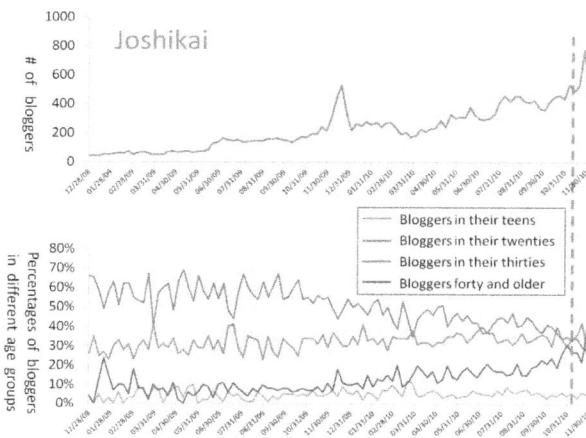

Figure 3: Numbers of bloggers and percentages of bloggers in different age groups (Topic: Joshikai)

We judge whether a topic can grow to become a major buzzword by analyzing the time-series variation of blog entries related to the topic. We focus on two particular features: (1) the increase in the number of bloggers mentioning a topic, and (2) the growth of the topic's popularity between different blogger communities, particularly from restricted blogger communities to general blogger communities. Our previous research [12] extracted 122 blogger communities based on bloggers' interests. These blogger communities are used for the analysis of the growth of topic popularity between communities.

In order to establish the analysis method for early detection of buzzwords, we pick up several major buzzwords from "Words of the Year [2]," observe how they spread throughout the world, and point out what is necessary for a practical application system.

The remainder of this paper is organized as follows. Section 2 presents the feature of the gradual buzzwords. Section 3 describes the formation of blogger communities. Section 4 analyzes the buzzword growth between blogger communities. Section 5 summarizes the necessary functions of a practical system that can detect buzzwords at an early stage. Section 6 reports an experimental result based on the rankings of buzzword candidates. Section 7 reviews related work. Finally, we conclude the paper in Section 8.

2. FEATURE ANALYSIS OF BUZZWORDS

In this paper, we focus on gradual buzzwords–topics that are initially only talked about in a restricted community and gradually spread to other communities. We are not considering bursty buzzwords, which are topics that suddenly become notable in most communities and only last for a short period. For the gradual buzzwords, two features are observed: (1) the increase in the number of bloggers mentioning a topic and (2) the growth of the scope of blog-

gers. In this section, we describe these two features using two examples of topics that have become buzzwords.

2.1 Increase in the number of bloggers

When detecting a new buzzword, the increase in the number of bloggers who mention a topic is the first feature we observe. By definition, a buzzword must be well known, and thus we observe if there is an increase in the number of bloggers who mention the topic. Figure 2 shows the variation of the numbers of bloggers and the percentages of bloggers in different age groups who have talked about the topic "AKB48 [3]" during the period from December 28, 2008 to November 30, 2010. Figure 3 shows the variation for the topic "Joshikai [4]" during the same period. In the

---

[2] "Words of the Year" is an annual event in Japan that elects some words reflecting the social trends in that year.

[3] "AKB48" is a Japanese female idol group consisting of 48 young members.

[4] "Joshikai" is a Japanese term with the meaning of a girls-only party or event.

upper graphs of two figures, the horizontal axis represents the dates and the vertical axis represents the numbers of bloggers who posted blog entries including the topic keywords. Both "AKB48" and "Joshikai" are the topics that became well known by 2010. From the graphs, it can be observed that these two topics were not talked about by many bloggers in the beginning (December 2008) and after that the numbers of bloggers who talk about them increased gradually.

A potential method for extracting buzzwords is to detect the gradual increase in the number of bloggers. However, although the numbers of bloggers increase on the whole, we also observe that there are repeated cycles of small increases and decreases during this process. Therefore, it is difficult to extract gradual buzzwords at an early stage by only focusing on the increase in blogger numbers. Moreover, even if the numbers of bloggers who talk about a topic (e.g., "AKB48") increase, it is unknown whether the topic has become a major buzzword which can be recognized by most people, or if it just restricted to a specific community (e.g, idol fans). Therefore, we also analyze the growth of popularity between different blogger communities in the next section.

2.2 Growth of the scope of bloggers

As described in Section 2.1, it is not easy to detect gradual buzzwords only focusing on the increase in the number of bloggers. Therefore, we also observe whether a topic has been recognized by multiple communities. The communities can be blogger groups of different sexes, different ages, different regions, or blogger groups in which bloggers have same interests (e.g., politics, diet, soccer, stock, etc.). The topical feature of a gradual buzzword is that although initially, it is talked about only in a restricted community, it gradually spreads to most communities. Analyzing the growth of a topic to multiple communities is important for detecting the forerunners of gradual buzzwords.

In the lower graphs of Figure 2 and Figure 3, bloggers are divided into four groups by their ages: people between ten and twenty years of age (for simplicity's sake, we will refer to them as "teens"), people in their twenties, people in their thirties, people forty and older. The horizontal axis represents the dates and the vertical axis represents the percentages of bloggers in each different age group who have talked about the topic. On each date, the sum of the percentages of bloggers in different age groups is 100%.

From the lower graph of Figure 2, we can observe that "AKB48" was mainly talked about by teen bloggers in 2008 and 2009. Actually, "AKB48" is an idol group that is originally popular only within the younger generation. However, by May 2010, the percentages of bloggers in their twenties, thirties and forties have caught up with that of the teen bloggers. The lower graph of Figure 2 reveals that "AKB48" has gradually become known to other age groups. From the lower graph of Figure 3, we can observe that "Joshikai" was familiar only to the bloggers in their twenties in 2008 and 2009. By October 2010, the percentages of bloggers in their thirties and forties age groups have caught up with that of the twenties age group. This indicates that "Joshikai" was initially talked about by the twenties age group and then had gradually become known to other age groups. "Joshikai" often includes drinking alcoholic beverages, and thus, it is less talked about by teen bloggers.

These two figures show that the topics that are originally

dominant in a specific age group, then spread to other age groups gradually. It is the typical feature of gradual buzzwords that they are recognized from a restricted community to other general communities. As shown in Figure 2 and Figure 3, May 2010 for "AKB48" and October 2010 for "Joshikai" are the turning points where they expand from a buzzword candidate to a major buzzword. It can be also observed that the numbers of bloggers who talk about these two buzzwords continue increasing even after the turning points.

As mentioned above, it is a key point for early detection of gradual buzzwords to identify the process in which a topic popular only in a specific community grows to become a common topic known to most communities. However, for the growth of buzzwords between communities, it is insufficient to only consider the groups of bloggers of different ages. In the next section, we describe the formation of blogger communities based on bloggers' potential interests.

3. BLOGGER COMMUNITY FORMATION

Many SNS services require users to register their communities. The users select the communities that they want to take part in according to their own subjective judgment. However, it is possible that a person registers only in the "politics" community, but actually he also has an interest in "artist."

We extract some popular topics daily discussed in the blog as the names of potential communities, and automatically categorize bloggers into their appropriate potential communities. A potential community in our research is a group of bloggers who take interest in a topic. For example, the "politics" community is the group of bloggers who have an interest in "politics." Potential communities of bloggers are objectively identified by analyzing bloggers' entries that they posted. Even if one does not declare his interest in a topic explicitly, if he has posted many blog entries related to the topic, our method can categorize him into the appropriate community automatically.

Next, we briefly describe the formation of bloggers' potential communities. The details of the method can be found in our previous paper [12].

3.1 Extraction of potential communities' names and construction of their co-occurrence dictionaries

The names of potential communities are the topics that are often talked about in blogs. The keywords matching the patterns such as "expert in *" and "fan of *" are first extracted from the Web. Then, they are filtered by their occurrence frequency and finally the most appropriate are selected manually. We end up with a list of potential communities (e.g., politics, artist, etc.), and a list of bloggers who have an interest in these topics (e.g., a group of bloggers familiar with politics, or a group of bloggers always paying attention to certain artists, etc.). As of October 2011, 122 potential communities are used as the analysis targets.

For each potential community, a co-occurrence dictionary is automatically constructed. For each keyword representing the community, we extract the top n words that have high co-occurrence frequency with it. Specifically, n is 400 in our current implementation. Figure 4 is an example of the co-occurrence dictionary. For example, the community "politics" has its domain-specific words, such as "pre-

Communities		Co-occurrence words						
i	c_i	$j = 1$		2		...	400	
1	politics	premier	$y_{1,1}$	party	$y_{1,2}$	... ...	bill	$y_{1,400}$
2	artist	entertainment	$y_{2,1}$	concert	$y_{2,2}$	... ...	album	$y_{2,400}$
3	computer	windows	$y_{3,1}$	desktop	$y_{3,2}$	... ...	hardware	$y_{3,400}$
⋮	⋮	⋮	⋮	⋮	⋮	⋮ ⋮	⋮	⋮
122	...	...	...	...	...	... ...	...	...

Figure 4: Example of co-occurrence dictionary

mier," "party" and "bill," and the community "artist" has its domain-specific words, such as "entertainment," "concert" and "album." The column c_i shows the names of potential communities, and each row shows their co-occurrence words and corresponding co-occurrence frequency y_{ij}.

3.2 Calculation of bloggers' degrees of interests in community topics

A blogger's score representing the degree of interest in a community topic is calculated by considering how often as well as how in-depth he has posted blog entries related to the community topic. If a blogger has an extensive use of co-occurrence words of a community, a high score is attached to him.

We first calculate $score_{c_i}(e_k)$, the score of a blog entry e_k with regard to the community c_i, as follows:

$$score_{c_i}(e_k) = \sum_{j=1}^{n} x_{ij} \cdot y_{ij} \cdot z_{ij} \qquad (1)$$

where $n = 400$ is the number of the co-occurrence words, $x_{ij} = (n - j + 1)/n$ is the weight of the jth co-occurrence word that decreases as j increases, y_{ij} is the co-occurrence frequency of the jth co-occurrence word, and z_{ij} is a binary value that indicates whether the entry e_k contains the jth co-occurrence word or not.

We next calculate $score_{c_i}(b)$, the score of a blogger b with regard to the community c_i, as follows:

$$score_{c_i}(b) = \frac{1}{n} \cdot \frac{\log(m)}{m} \cdot \sum_{k=1}^{m} score_{c_i}(e_k) \qquad (2)$$

where e_k is an entry that the blogger b posted, m is the number of entries that the blogger b has posted during a given period, $n = 400$ is the number of the co-occurrence words and l is the number of the co-occurrence words that occurred in all the entries posted by the blogger b. l/n indicates the coverage ratio of the co-occurrence words that the blogger b has used. $\log(m)/m$ reduces the effect that a blogger frequently posts a large amount of entries, but most of them are the entries unrelated to the target community.

A blogger is categorized into a potential community if his score is larger than a given threshold. In addition, a blogger may be categorized into two or more communities and thus may have two or more scores. For example, if a blogger belongs to both the "politics" community and the "artist" community, he has a score representing his degree of interest in "politics" and another score representing his degree of interest in "artist."

4. ANALYSIS OF BUZZWORD POPULARITY GROWTH BETWEEN COMMUNITIES

4.1 Observation on percentage variation of blog entries from different communities

We pick up six major buzzwords that were elected to "Words of the Year" in Japan, and observe how these topics spread through blogosphere. These six major buzzwords are "AKB48," "Joshikai," "Smartphone," "Android," "Facebook," and "K-POP." Figure 5 shows their variation curves. For each buzzword, the upper graph shows the variation of the total numbers of blog entries in which the buzzword is mentioned. The observation period is two years from August 2009 to July 2011 and the numbers of blog entries are counted on a weekly span. As shown in the upper graphs, for all of the six buzzwords, the total numbers of blog entries continue increasing on the whole, which meets the first feature of gradual buzzwords described in Section 2.1.

The lower graph in Figure 5 shows the percentages of blog entries from four manually selected different communities. These four communities are manually extracted from the 122 potential communities identified in Section 3 based on our visual examination of communities with the remarkable upward tendencies or downward tendencies. It should also be noted that since a blogger may belong to two or more communities, the sum of the percentages of the four communities in every week may exceed 1. Among the four communities, there exist the communities closely related to the target buzzword. They are marked as follows:

AKB48: "Female star" and "Artist"

Joshikai: "Love/Marriage" and "Smiley"

Smartphone: "Internet" and "Cellphone"

Android: "Cellphone" and "Computer"

Facebook: "School life" and "World region"

K-POP: "Artist" and "Korean star"

It can be observed that the percentages of blog entries from the communities closely related to the target buzzword decrease from a high value to a low one, whereas the percentages from the communities weakly related to the target buzzword increase gradually. The observation results reveal the second feature described in Section 2.2: Before a topic becomes a major buzzword, a large fraction of blog entries are posted from restricted blogger communities that are closely related to the target topic. But as the target topic

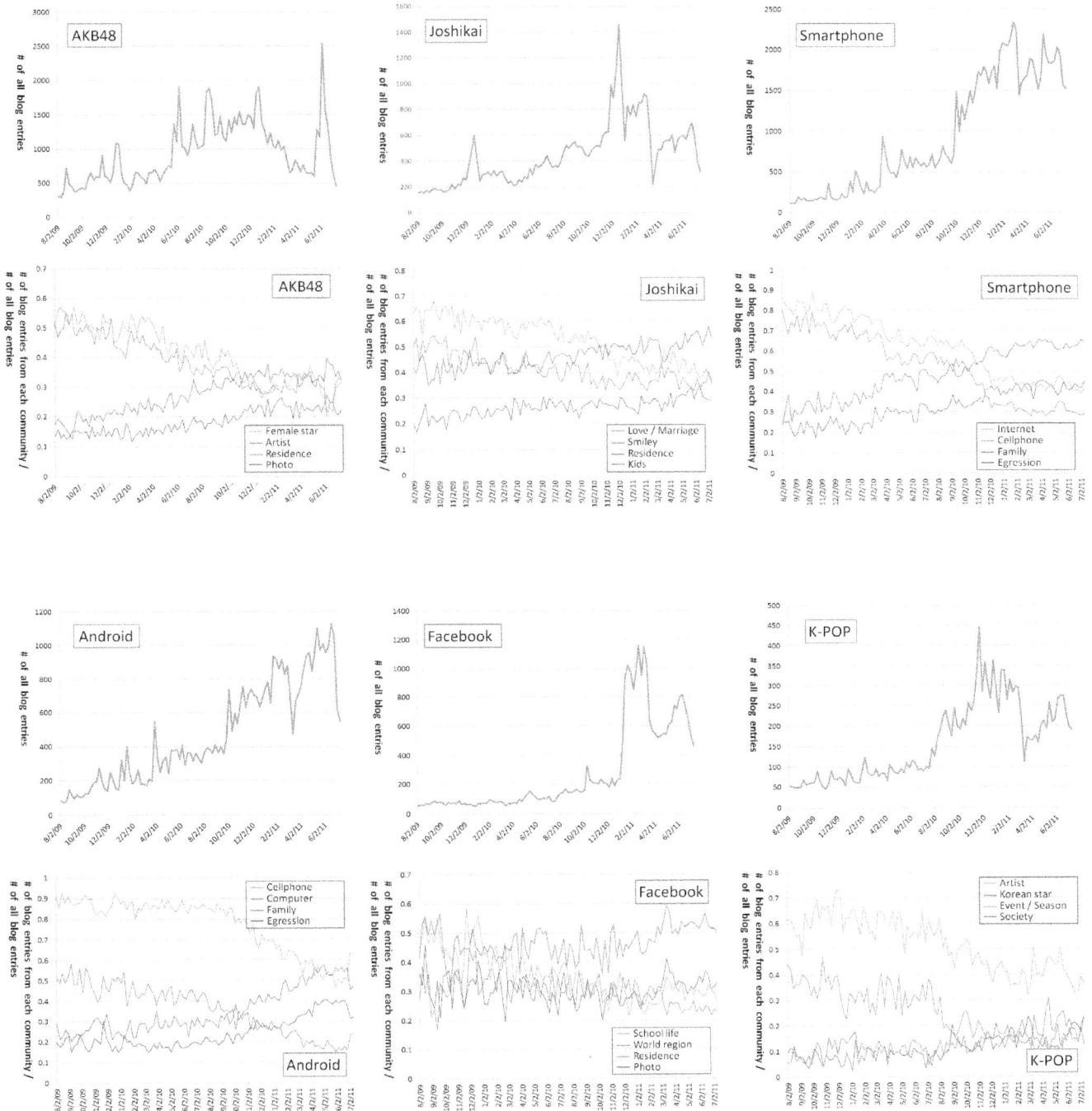

Figure 5: Numbers of blog entries including a buzzword and percentages of blog entries from different communities

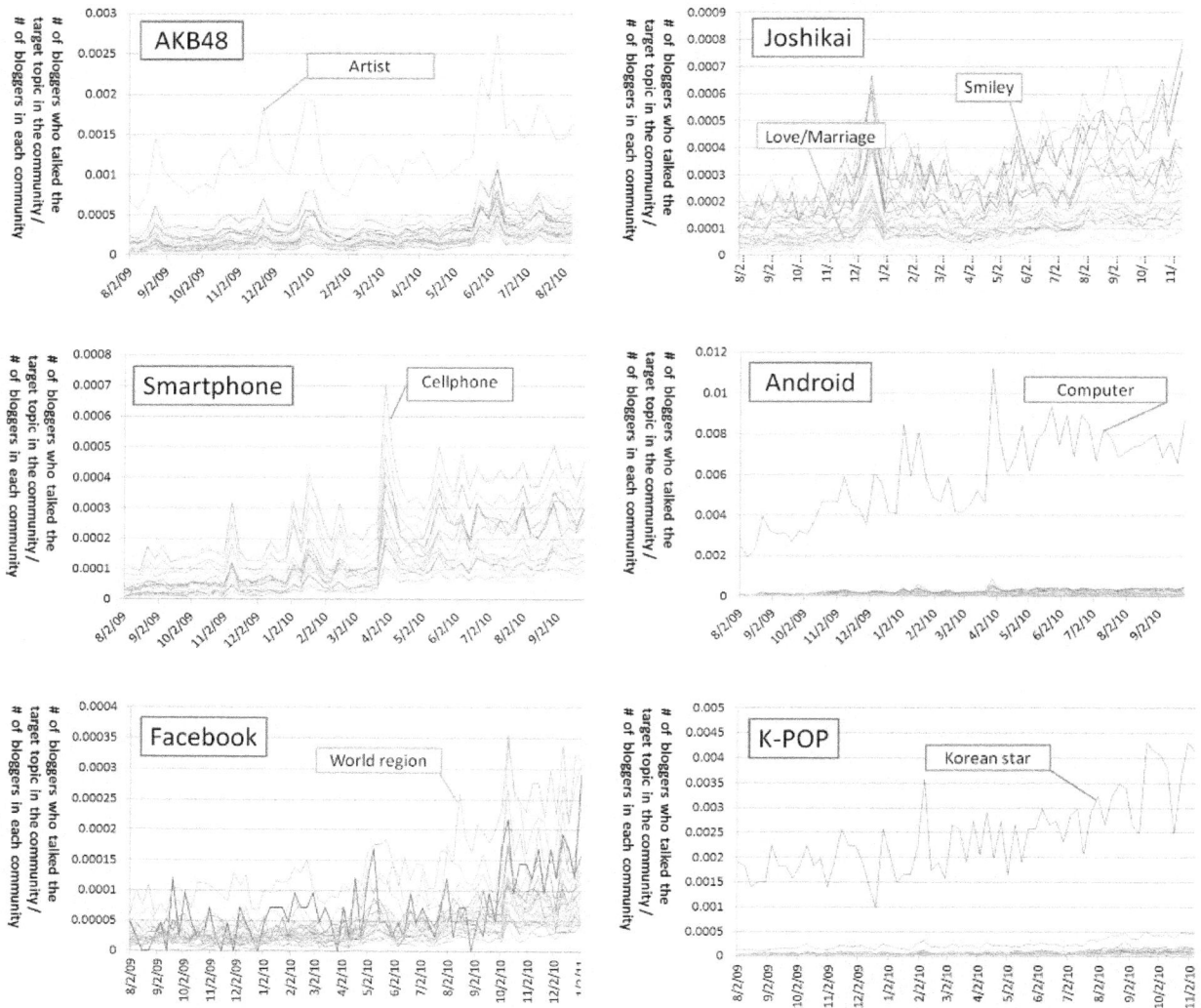

Figure 6: Ratios of bloggers in a community who talked about the target topic to all the bloggers in the community

approaches becoming a major buzzword, it extends pass the original community and is recognized by other communities. This indicates that we can detect a topic's growth process from a buzzword candidate to a major buzzword by analyzing the percentage variation of blog entries from different blog communities.

In the aforementioned examples, "Photo," "Residence" and "Family" appear repeatedly. These are communities which are weakly related to the target buzzwords. They are general groups which are indicative of the general population popularity. They also can be easily identified in advance. On the other hand, we have the communities that are more closely related to a target topic, and are more difficult to identify in advance. For the aforementioned examples, the closely related communities are manually selected. However, automatically extracting them is necessary for implementing a practical system that can early detect buzzwords. We describe a method for automatically identifying the communities closely related to a target topic in the next section.

4.2 Identification of communities closely related to target topics

The percentage of bloggers within a community who have talked about a target topic can be used to identify communities that are closely related. This is the ratio of bloggers who have talked about a target topic to the total number of bloggers within the same community A community can be judged to be related to a target topic if this ratio is large.

We also considered using the percentage of blog entries from each community, as shown in Section 4.1. However, the sizes of various communities vary widely, which means that larger communities with more entries would naturally have a larger percentage without normalization.

Figure 6 shows the ratio of bloggers who have talked about each topic in a community to the total numbers of bloggers in the community. Thirty communities with the largest numbers of blog entries including each topic are compared. In these graphs, the top community is "Artist" for the "AKB48" topic, "Cellphone" for the "Smartphone" topic,

"Computer" for the "Android" topic, "World region" for the "Facebook" topic, and "Korean star" for the "K-POP" topic. These are closely related to the corresponding topics as indicated by having a much higher percentages than other communities.

Although this method can not necessarily identify all the communities closely related to target topics (e.g., for the "Joshikai" topic), most of successful examples indicate that it is effective for identifying them. We also plan to further improve this method by integrating with other techniques, for example, analyzing the overlap of co-occurrence words between a target topic and each community name.

In order to detect whether a topic has grown up a major buzzword, it is necessary to identify the communities closely related to the target topic and observe the decrease of the percentages of blog entries from these communities. In the next section, we further analyze how the curves of percentage variation of blog entries from closely related communities change.

4.3 Slope analysis of percentage variation of blog entries

In this section, we analyze the percentage variation of blog entries from different communities during the process in which that a topic grows to become a major buzzword. We then discuss what kind of conditions can indicate the high probability that it will become a major buzzword.

Figure 7 shows the variation for all the six buzzwords. The upper graphs show the increase in the total numbers of blog entries including each buzzword. Especially, the vertical bars mark the time just before the numbers of blog entries increase suddenly. It is before this point that the system must identify the buzzwords to be effective. Therefore, for the six topics, we further analyze the decline in percentage of blog entries from closely related communities up until time marked in the upper graphs. The lower graphs show the percentage decrease of blog entries from the closely related communities. The curves show the actual variation and the straight lines are their approximation based on the least-squares method [6]. The slopes of the straight lines are marked in the lower graphs. As we can see, among the twelve communities (two communities/each topic * six topics), the slopes of ten communities are less than or equal to -0.0003. Only two slopes (-0.00004 for the "Cellphone" community for the "Android" topic, and -0.000005 for the "World region" community for the "Facebook" topic) are larger than -0.0003. Although the further investigation should be done, this value may be considered a rough threshold. Moreover, the period and the scale of percentage decrease should also be further analyzed.

The similar method can be applied to the analysis of percentage increase in the numbers of blog entries from weakly related communities. It will also be further discussed in our future work.

5. MOVING TOWARDS THE IMPLEMENTATION OF THE SYSTEM FOR EARLY DETECTION OF BUZZWORDS

The ultimate goal of our research is to implement a practical system that can detect buzzwords at an early stage. It can be used to the following two applications:

1. When a user specifies a buzzword candidate, the system analyzes whether it will become a major buzzword.

2. When a user specifies a category (e.g., car or digital camera, etc.), the system provides a ranking list of the items included in the category (e.g, various car models or various camera models, etc.) based on the probabilities that they will become major buzzwords.

We summarize the necessary functions for implementing such systems as follows:

1. Automatic identification of communities closely related and weakly related to the target topics.

2. Analysis of percentage variation of blog entries from closely related communities and weakly related communities, including slope coefficients, increase/decrease periods, increase/decrease scales, etc.

3. Calculation of scores for the target topics that indicate the probability that they will become major buzzwords.

For the first function, we have demonstrated the possibility of automatic identification of closely related and weakly related communities in Section 4.2. For the second function, we have analyzed the slopes of approximate straight lines in Section 4.3 and plan to further discuss the increase/decrease periods and scales in the future. The third function is also a task for our future work as well.

6. EXPERIMENTAL EVALUATION WITH RANKING OF BUZZWORD CANDIDATES

As described in Section 5, ranking the items (buzzword candidates) in a category is a useful application, which can sort based on which one is more likely to become a major buzzword. In this section, we report an experimental result of ranking the items to a real-life idol group popularity competition.

In this idol group election, the members were selected based on fans' votes once every year during 2009 - 2011. The members with the most votes from fans were selected. We considered the three elections which were held on July 8, 2009, June 9, 2010, and June 9, 2011. We focused on the top ten people in the final third election. The actual results of the real election were as follows:

Member (1st ranking -> 2nd ranking -> 3rd ranking)

A (1 -> 2 -> 1),   B (2 -> 1 -> 2),   C (9 -> <u>8 -> 3</u>),

D (3 -> 3 -> 4),   E (4 -> 5 -> 5),   F (6 -> 7 -> 6),

G (5 -> 6 -> 7),   H (<u>7 -> 4</u> -> 8),   I (27 -> <u>19 -> 9</u>),

J (<u>out of range -> 11</u> -> 10)

We see if our method of ranking the members matched the elections results. For each member, we did perform the slope analysis as described in Section 4.3. The graph line for ratio of number of blog entries from a closely related community to total number of blog entries was approximated to a straight line. Then, the members were ranked based on the approximate straight lines' slopes. The member with

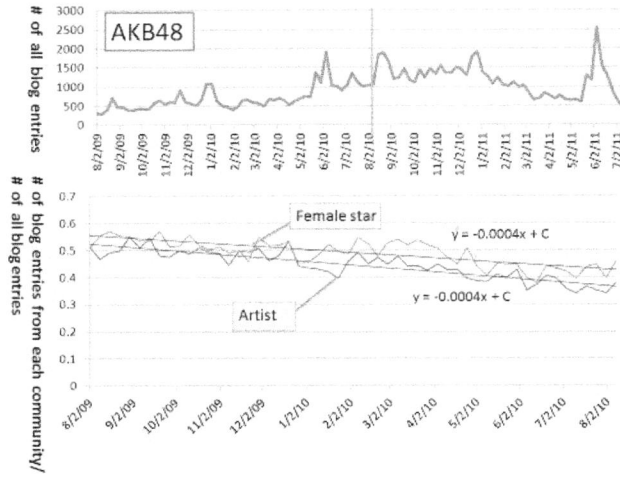

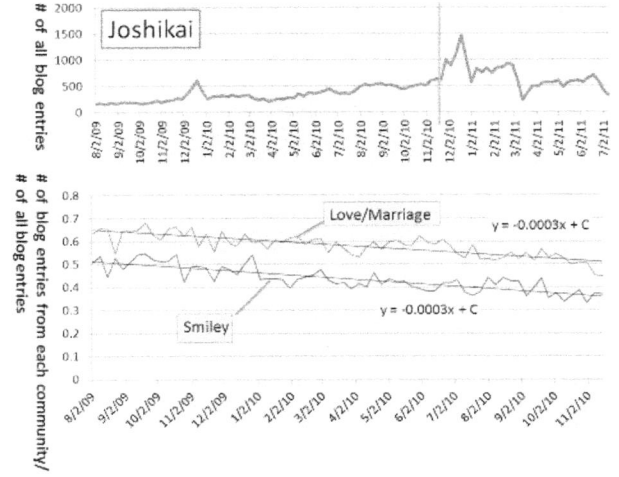

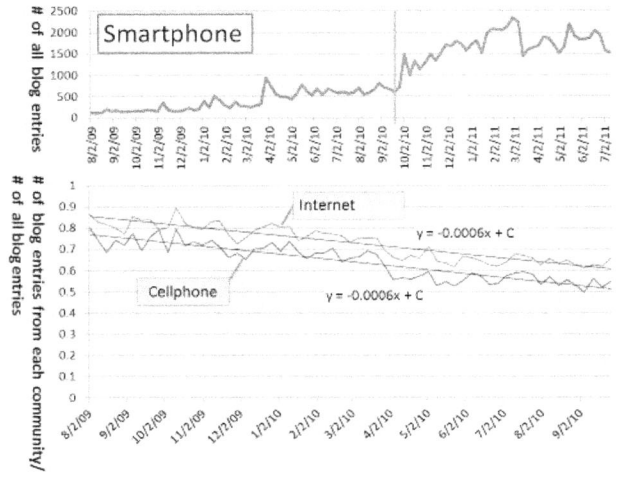

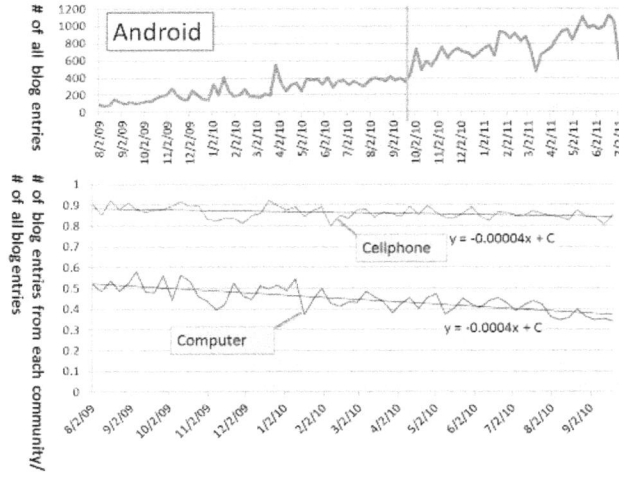

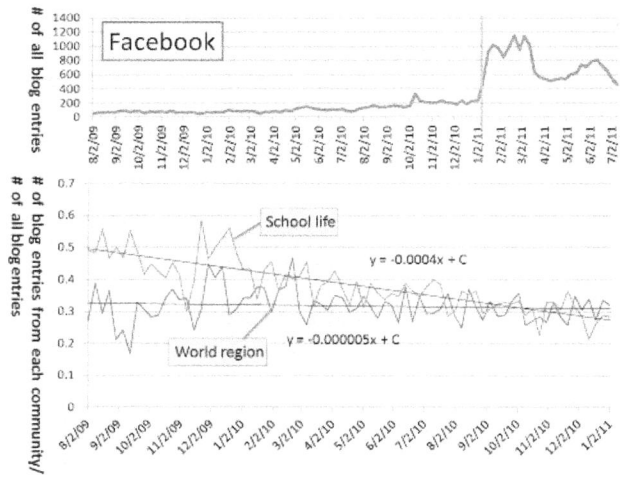

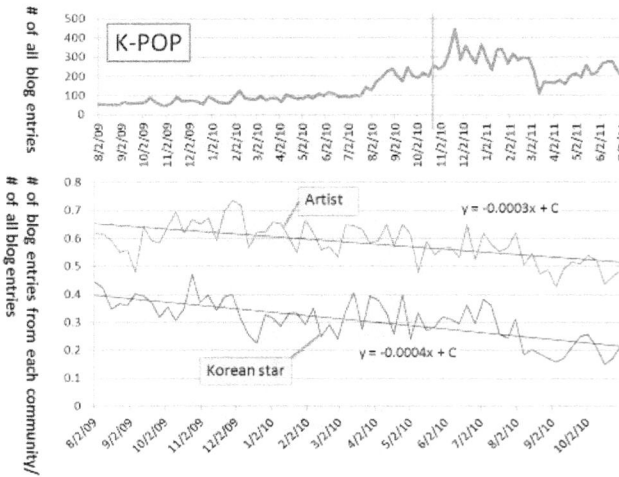

Figure 7: Approximate straight lines of percentage decrease of blog entries from closely related communities

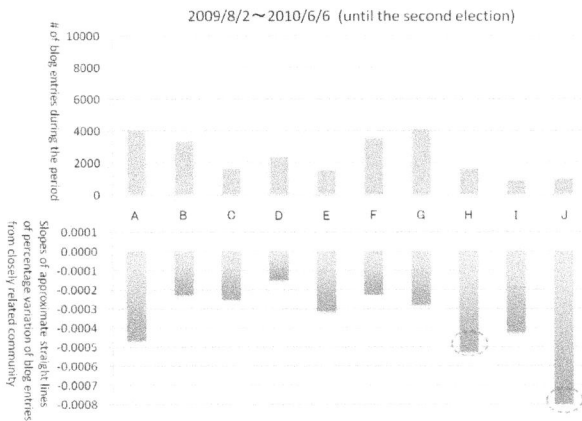

Figure 8: Slope comparison of approximate straight lines of percentage variation of blog entries from a closely related community (until the second election)

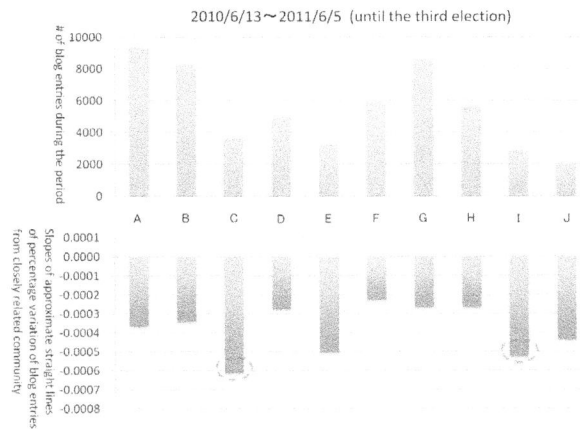

Figure 9: Slope comparison of approximate straight lines of percentage variation of blog entries from a closely related community (until the third election)

a smaller slope is more likely to become a major buzzword. For example, the slope of "-0.0008" means a steeper decrease than "-0.0002," and the member with the slope of "-0.0008" is more likely to become a major buzzword than that with "-0.0002."

This analysis of blog entries was conducted for two periods: one is after the first election and before the second election (August 2, 2009 - June 6, 2010), the other is after the second election and before the third election (June 23, 2010 - June 5, 2011). Figure 8 and Figure 9 show the analysis results for the period until the second election and for the period until the third election respectively. The upper graphs show the total numbers of blog entries in which the name of each "AKB48" member (each buzzword candidate) was mentioned, and the lower graphs show each member's slopes of percentage decrease of blog entries from the closely related community "Artist." By our method, the members with the smaller slopes are considered to be more likely to become a major buzzword. Figure 8 shows J̲ and H̲ were two members with the smallest slopes. In the real second election, their rankings rose sharply: out of range -> 11 and 7 -> 4. Figure 9 shows C̲ and I̲ had the smallest slopes. In the real third election, their rankings also rose sharply: 8 -> 3 and 19 -> 9. The results support our argument in this paper.

The upper graphs in Figure 8 and Figure 9 also show it was difficult to detect the remarkable growth of members only focusing on the increase in the total numbers of blog entries. Only analyzing the total numbers of blog entries can not discriminate whether a topic becomes popular only in a restricted community or has extended to other communities.

7. RELATED WORK

Buzzword detection is closely related to the concept of burstiness. Kleinberg [8] modeled "burst of activity" using an infinite-state automaton in which bursts appeared naturally at state transitions. By assigning costs to state transitions, the model can prevent short bursts and identify the lasting periods of bursts. Yi [16] adopted Kleinberg's

model and further proposed an algorithm that detected buzzwords considering their momentum and relative duration. Araujo et al. [2] studied alternative cost functions to the one proposed by Kleinberg and investigated the best distribution of states. Parikh et al. [13] described how to detect bursts in user queries in a large-scale eCommerce system. Lappas et al. [10] built a parameter-free and linear-time approach to identify the time intervals of maximum burstiness for a given term and utilized burstiness information to enhance the search process. There also exist some practical or demonstration systems for detecting buzzwords or trends, such as Yahoo! Buzz Index [1], BlogPulse [3], Buzz of the Day [14], TwitterMonitor [11]. Yahoo! Buzz Index [1] calculates a subject's buzz score based on the percentage of Yahoo! users searching for that subject on a given day, and identifies "leaders" (subjects with the highest buzz scores) and " movers" (subjects with the highest percentage increase in buzz scores from one day to the next). BlogPulse [3] extracted key phrases and key people from blog entries by calculating the ratio of the frequency of occurrence of a phrase or a person name to its average frequency over the past two weeks. TwitterMonitor [11] performed trend detection over the Twitter system by detecting bursty keywords, grouping them as a trend and depicting the evolution of its popularity. These mainly seek to detect bursty buzzwords, the first type categorized in Section 1, by analyzing term frequency, user popularity or time varying patterns, etc. Our research aims to extract gradual buzzwords, the second type categorized in Section 1, by analyzing the growth of topics between communities.

Kumar et al. [9] extracted bursts of activity within blog communities. Gruhl et al. [4] studied the dynamics of information propagation from individual to individual within blog communities. Different from the information propagation between bloggers within a blog community in their research, we focus on the topic growth from restricted communities to other general communities. Also, the communities in their research were identified by links between blogs, whereas the communities extracted in our research are based on bloggers' interests in topics. Based on a document clustering method considering similarity and novelty [7], Ishikawa et al. developed a system to visualize the transition of topics extracted from news articles [5]. Takamura et al. [15] proposed a method for document stream summarization, solving the problems that (1) similar documents can mention different events if they are temporally distant and (2) documents on a single topic can be posted with some temporal delay. Their idea will help us identify the documents related to target topics so as to improve the accuracy of our system.

8. CONCLUSIONS

In this paper, we discussed what is necessary for early detection of buzzwords by analyzing large-scale time-series data of blog entries. More specifically, we analyzed how some topics that had become major buzzwords spread based on 81,922,977 blog entries from 3,776,154 blog websites posted in the last two years. As a result, we found that during the process in which a buzzword candidate becomes a major buzzword, the percentages of blog entries from the communities closely related to the target topic decreased gradually, whereas the percentages of blog entries from the weakly related communities increased gradually. Based on the observation and analysis results, we discussed the necessary functions of the system for early detection of buzzwords. Moreover, the experimental results of ranking comparison between ten buzzword candidates verified the feasibility of our proposition.

In the future, we will further establish the methods for automatically extracting closely related and weakly related communities, and an equation for calculating the probability that a buzzword candidate will become a major buzzword. Also, more evaluation experiments will be conducted for other categories. Finally, we will implement a practical system that can extract buzzwords at an early stage.

9. ACKNOWLEDGMENTS

This work was supported in part by the MEXT Grant-in-Aid for Scientific Research(C) (#23500140).

10. REFERENCES

[1] Yahoo! Buzz Index. http://buzzlog.yahoo.com/overall/

[2] L. Araujo and J. J. M. Guervos, "Automatic Detection of Trends in Time-stamped Sequences: An Evolutionary Approach," *Soft Computing*, Vol. 14, No. 3, pp. 211–227, 2010.

[3] N. S. Glance, M. Hurst and T. Tomokiyo, "BlogPulse: Automated Trend Discovery for Weblogs," In *WWW 2004 workshop*.

[4] D. Gruhl, R. Guha, D. L-Nowell, A. Tomkins, "Information Diffusion Through Blogspace," In *WWW 2004*.

[5] Y. Ishikawa and M. Hasegawa, "T-Scroll: Visualizing Trends in a Time-Series of Documents for Interactive User Exploration," In *ECDL 2007*.

[6] T. Kariya and H. Kurata, "*Generalized Least Squares*," Wiley, 2004.

[7] S. Khy, Y. Ishikawa and H. Kitagawa, "A Novelty-based Clustering Method for On-line Documents," In *World Wide Web Journal*, Vol. 11, No. 1, pp. 1–37, 2008.

[8] J. M. Kleinberg, "Bursty and Hierarchical Structure in Streams," In *SIGKDD 2002*.

[9] R. Kumar, J. Novak, P. Raghavan and A. Tomkins, "On the Bursty Evolution of Blogspace," In *WWW 2003*.

[10] T. Lappas, B. Arai, M. Platakis, D. Kotsakos and D. Gunopulos, "On Burstiness-aware Search for Document Sequences," In *SIGKDD 2009*.

[11] M. Mathioudakis and N. Koudas, "TwitterMonitor: Trend Detection over the Twitter Stream," In *SIGMOD 2010*.

[12] S. Nakajima, J. Zhang, Y. Inagaki, T. Kusano and R. Nakamoto, "Blog Ranking Based on Bloggers' Knowledge Level for Providing Credible Information," In *WISE 2009*.

[13] N. Parikh and N. Sundaresan, "Scalable and Near Real-Time Burst Detection from eCommerce Queries," In *KDD 2008*.

[14] N. Parikh and N. Sundaresan, "Buzz-Based Recommender System," In *WWW 2009*.

[15] H. Takamura, H. Yokono and M. Okumura, "Summarizing a Document Stream," In *ECIR 2011*.

[16] J. Yi, "Detecting Buzz from Time-Sequenced Document Streams," In *EEE 2005*.

Semantics + Filtering + Search = Twitcident Exploring Information in Social Web Streams

Fabian Abel, Claudia Hauff,
Geert-Jan Houben, Ke Tao
Web Information Systems, TU Delft
PO Box 5031, 2600 GA Delft, the Netherlands
{f.abel,c.hauff,g.j.p.m.houben,
k.tao}@tudelft.nl

Richard Stronkman
Twitcident.com
Koningin Wilheminaplein 400, 1062 KS
Amsterdam, the Netherlands
richard@twitcident.com

ABSTRACT

Automatically filtering relevant information about a real-world incident from Social Web streams and making the information accessible and findable in the given context of the incident are non-trivial scientific challenges. In this paper, we engineer and evaluate solutions that analyze the semantics of Social Web data streams to solve these challenges. We introduce Twitcident, a framework and Web-based system for filtering, searching and analyzing information about real-world incidents or crises. Given an incident, our framework automatically starts tracking and filtering information that is relevant for the incident from Social Web streams and Twitter particularly. It enriches the semantics of streamed messages to profile incidents and to continuously improve and adapt the information filtering to the current temporal context. Faceted search and analytical tools allow people and emergency services to retrieve particular information fragments and overview and analyze the current situation as reported on the Social Web.

We put our Twitcident system into practice by connecting it to emergency broadcasting services in the Netherlands to allow for the retrieval of relevant information from Twitter streams for any incident that is reported by those services. We conduct large-scale experiments in which we evaluate (i) strategies for filtering relevant information for a given incident and (ii) search strategies for finding particular information pieces. Our results prove that the semantic enrichment offered by our framework leads to major and significant improvements of both the filtering and the search performance. A demonstration is available via: http://wis.ewi.tudelft.nl/twitcident/.

Categories and Subject Descriptors

H.3.3 [**Information Systems**]: Information Search and Retrieval—*Information filtering*

General Terms

Algorithms, Design, Experimentation

Keywords

Semantic Enrichment, Social Web Streams, Filtering

1. INTRODUCTION

During crisis situations such as large fires, storms or other types of incidents, people nowadays report and discuss about their observations, experiences and opinions in their Social Web streams. Therefore, valuable information that is of use for both emergency services and the general public is available online. Recent studies show that data from the Social Web and particularly Twitter helps to detect incidents and topics [15, 19, 23] or to analyze afterwards the information streams that people generated about a topic [7, 13, 18]. However, (i) automatically filtering relevant information about an incident from Social Web streams and (ii) making the information accessible and findable for people who are demanding information about an incident are two fundamental challenges that have not been answered sufficiently by literature yet.

In this paper, we tackle these two challenges and present Twitcident, a framework for filtering, searching and analyzing Twitter information streams during incidents. Here, filtering refers to an automatic process while search involves a user who is issuing a query. We showcase our framework and present the Twitcident system[1] which monitors emergency broadcasting services and automatically collects and filters Twitter messages whenever an incident occurs. Incidents are thus primarily events that typically require actions of emergency services. Twitter messages (tweets) as well as other types of Social Web status messages are typically very short—e.g. tweets are limited to 140 characters—which makes it difficult to identify relevant tweets. Initiatives such as the TREC task on filtering micro-blogging data[2] illustrate that there is currently a high demand in solving these filtering and search problems.

We approach these problems by enriching the semantics of short messages which includes named entity recognition, tweet classification as well as linkage to related external Web resources. Semantic enrichment also builds the basis for the search and analytics functionality that is provided by our Twitcident framework. Given the semantically enriched Social Web content about an incident, we allow users to explore information along different types of information needs (e.g. damage, casualties). Therefore, we inte-

---

[1] http://twitcident.com
[2] http://sites.google.com/site/trecmicroblogtrack/

grate faceted search strategies [1] that go beyond traditional keyword search as offered by Twitter[3] or topic-based browsing as proposed by Bernstein et al. [2]. Moreover, users can overview information by exploiting Twitcident realtime analytics that allow users to get an understanding of how different types of information are posted over time. The main contributions of this paper can be summarized as follows.

- We introduce a framework for incident-driven information filtering and search on Social Web streams. Our framework features automated incident profiling, aggregation, semantic enrichment and filtering functionality. Furthermore, it provides advanced search and analytics functionality that allows users to find and understand relevant information. (Section 3)
- We propose and evaluate strategies for solving two fundamental research challenges: (1) information filtering and (2) search on Social Web streams.

  1. We compare different stream filtering strategies on a large Twitter corpus and prove that the semantic filtering strategies of our Twitcident framework lead to major improvements compared to keyword-based filtering. (Section 4)
  2. We employ faceted search strategies that enable users to find relevant information in Social Web streams. Our evaluation confirms that the semantic faceted search strategies, which are applied on top of the filtered streams, enhance keyword-based search significantly. Contextualization (adapting to the temporal context of a search activity) and personalization (adapting to the interests of the user who performs the activity) gains further improvements. (Section 5)

- We apply our Twitcident system to incidents that happen during everyday life (mainly targeted towards the Netherlands) and discuss experiences and insights we gained from running Twitcident in practice. (Section 6)

2. RELATED WORK

In the last decade, Social Web platforms such as Twitter gained huge popularity and researchers started to investigate the motivation for using these systems [8], user behavior [12, 17], emerging network structures [10, 16], information propagation principles [10, 13, 18] and event detection based on Social Web streams [19, 23]. Yet, supporting users in finding information in Twitter streams has not been studied extensively yet. Chen et al. proposed strategies for recommending entire conversations on Twitter [4] as well as URLs that are posted in tweets [5]. Dong et al. [6] exploited Twitter data to improve the ranking of fresh URLs in search engines [6].

However, yet there exists little research on engineering search and retrieval of relevant information from Social Web streams. Marcus et al. [14] studied how to visualize Twitter streams. Bernstein et al. [2] proposed a topic-based browsing interface for Twitter in which a user can navigate through her personal Twitter stream by means of tag clouds. So far, there is a lack of research on how messages posted in Social Web streams can satisfy information needs of individual users. In fact, Teevan et al. [22] confirm studies that emphasize Twitter's role as news source [10, 20] and reveal that there are significant differences in the search behavior on Twitter compared to traditional Web search: Twitter users are specifically interested in information related

[3] http://twitter.com/search

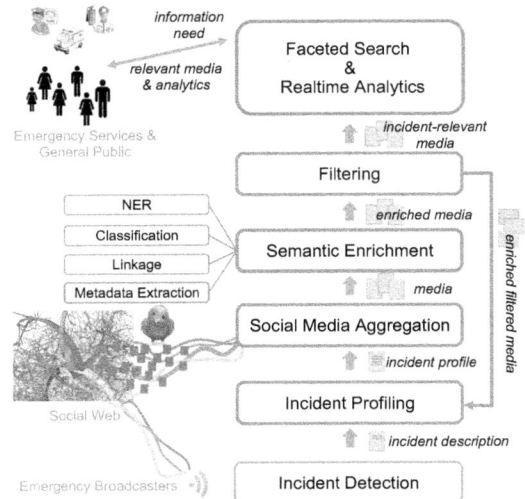

Figure 1: Twitcident architecture: (i) *incident profiling* and *filtering* of social media that is relevant to an incident (green boxes) and (ii) provide *faceted search* and *realtime analytics* functionality to explore and overview the media (blue box). Both types of components benefit from the *semantic enrichment*.

to events and often use the rudimental search functionality of Twitter to monitor search results. With Twitcident, we introduce a framework that automates the process of monitoring relevant information published in Social Web streams and therefore reduces the efforts that users need to invest to satisfy their information needs. On top of the automatically filtered streams, Twitcident provides faceted search functionality as introduced in previous work [1].

3. TWITCIDENT

In this section, we will overview the architecture of the Twitcident framework and detail its key components that allow for filtering, searching and analyzing information available in Social Web streams. The Web-based front-end of the Twitcident system is depicted in Figure 2 and allows users to explore and analyze information from Social Web streams during incidents such as natural disasters, fires or other types of emergency events.

3.1 Architecture

The Twitcident framework architecture is summarized in Figure 1. The core framework functionality is triggered by an incident detection module that senses for incidents being broadcasted by emergency services. Whenever an incident is detected, Twitcident starts a new thread for profiling the incident and aggregating social media and Twitter messages from the Web. The collected messages are further processed by the semantic enrichment module which features named entity recognition (NER), classification of messages, linkage of messages to external Web resources and further metadata extraction. The semantic enrichment is one of the key enabling components of the Twitcident framework as it (i) supports semantic filtering of Twitter messages to identify those tweets that are relevant for a given incident, (ii) allows for faceted search on the filtered media and (iii) gives means for summarizing information about incidents and providing realtime analytics.

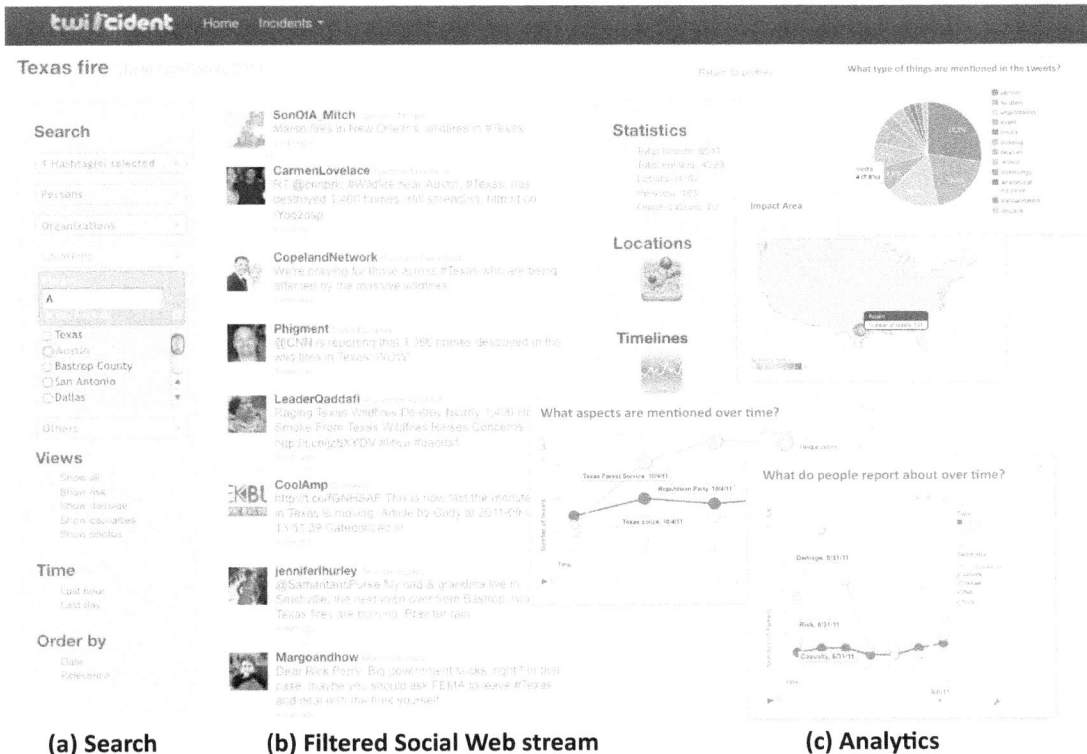

(a) Search　　**(b) Filtered Social Web stream**　　**(c) Analytics**

Figure 2: Screenshot of the Twitcident system: (a) search and filtering functionality to explore and retrieve particular Twitter messages, (b) messages that are related to the given incident (here: fires in Texas) and match the given query of the user and (c) realtime analytics of the matching messages.

In the Twitcident system, both faceted search and realtime analytics are made available to client users via a graphical user interface that is displayed in Figure 2. The search functionality allows end-users to further filter messages about an incident while analytics deliver diagrams and gadgets that enable users to analyze and overview how people report about the incident on the Social Web. We now discuss each of the components of our architecture in detail.

3.2 Incident Detection

For detecting incidents, the Twitcident system relies on emergency broadcasting services. In the Netherlands, incidents which require the police, fire department or other public emergency services to take an action and which are moreover of interest to the general public, are immediately published via the P2000 communication network and describe what type of incident has happened, where and when it happened and also what scale the incident is classified as. Figure 3(a) shows an example P2000 message informing about a large fire incident that happened in the city of Moerdijk, the Netherlands[4]. The figure visualizes the automatic workflow that is triggered whenever a new incident is reported. For a given incident it may happen that several different P2000 messages are broadcasted which requires Twitcident to first perform duplicate detection before starting a new incident monitoring thread. Therefore, the incident detection component compares the location, starting time and type of the newly reported incident with the incidents that are already monitored by Twitcident. If a new

incident is detected then the Twitcident framework translates the broadcasted message into an initial incident profile that is applied as query to collect relevant messages from the Social Web and Twitter in particular. All incidents that are monitored by the Twitcident system are listed on the dashboard that is depicted in Figure 3(b).

3.3 Incident Profiling and Filtering

While monitoring an incident, Twitcident continuously adapts the incident profiling to improve the filtering of messages. This process is realized via the following components (see Figure 1): (i) incident profiling, (ii) social media aggregation, (iii) semantic enrichment and (iv) filtering.

3.3.1 Incident Profiling

Based on the initial incident description and the collected, enriched Social Web messages, the incident profiling module generates an incident profile that is used to refine the media aggregation and the filtering. An incident profile is a set of weighted facet-value pairs that describe the characteristics of the incident:

Definition 1. An *incident profile* of an incident $i \in I$ is a set of tuples $((f, v), w(i, (f, v)))$ where (f, v) is a facet-value pair that describes a certain characteristic f of the incident and $w(i, (f, v))$ specifies the importance of the facet-value pair for the incident that is computed by a weighting function w:

$$P(i) = \{((f,v), w(i,(f,v))) | (f,v) \in FVPs, i \in I, \quad (1)$$
$$w(i,(f,v))) \in [0..1]\}$$

Here, $FVPs$ and I denote the set of facet-value pairs and incidents respectively. A facet-value pair characterizes a cer-

---

[4]http://nl.wikipedia.org/wiki/Brand_Moerdijk_5_januari_2011

287

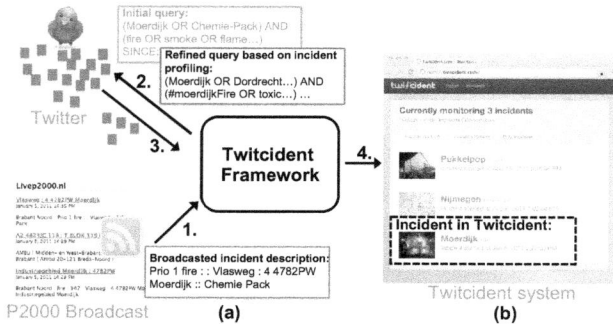

Figure 3: Incident detection: (1) as soon as an incident is broadcasted via the P2000 network, the Twitcident framework (2) transforms the encoded P2000 message into an initial incident query to (3) collect Twitter messages that are possibly relevant for the incident so that (4) information about the incident can be accessed via the Twitcident system. Over time, the incident profiling effects refinements of the queries that are used to collect tweets. The screenshot shows the dashboard of popular incidents that are (and have been) monitored by Twitcident.

tain attribute (facet) of an incident with a certain value. Twitcident allows for various types of facets including locations, persons, incident classes or keywords. Therefore, the aforementioned fire that happened in Moerdijk may have the following incident profile: $P(i_{moerdijk}) = \{((location, Moerdijk), 1.0), ((location, Dordrecht), 0.73), ((type, Fire), 1.0), \ldots\}$. The weight that is associated with each facet-value pair ranges between 0 and 1: the higher the weight, the more important the facet-value pair for the incident. We apply the relative occurrence frequency as basic weighting strategy, i.e. the fraction of messages about the incident that mention the given facet-value pair. Incident profiles are continuously updated to adapt to topic changes that arise within an incident. To prevent topic drift, we combine the current profile with the initial incident profile following a classical mixture approach: $P(i) = \lambda P_{initial}(i) + (1 - \lambda)P_{current}(i)$ where we experimented with $\lambda \in [0..1]$ ranging between 0.25 and 0.5.

3.3.2 Social Media Aggregation

Based on the incident profiling, the Twitcident system exploits the social media aggregation component to collect Twitter messages as well as related pictures and videos that are posted on platforms such as Twitpic or Twitvid[5] respectively. Twitcident utilizes both the REST API and the Streaming API of Twitter[6] to collect messages. The REST API allows for querying Twitter messages that have been published within the last seven days and therefore enables Twitcident to collect those incident-related tweets that have been posted before Twitcident detected the incident. The Streaming API does not allow for querying previously published tweets but allows Twitcident to continuously listen for current tweets that mention keywords related to an incident.

3.3.3 Semantic Enrichment

The aggregated Social Web content (Twitter messages) is processed by the semantic enrichment component of Twitcident which features the following functionality.

[5] http://twitpic.com and http://twitvid.com
[6] http://dev.twitter.com/docs

NER. The named entity recognition (NER) module assembles four different services for detecting entities such as persons, locations or organizations that are mentioned in tweets: DBpedia spotlight, Alchemy, OpenCalais and Zemanta[7]. As those entity recognition services only function for English texts, Twitcident translates non-English tweets to English[8]. The extracted entities are mapped to concepts in DBpedia [3], the RDF representation of Wikipedia, and the type of an entity is utilized to specify the facet of the corresponding facet-value pair. For example, given a Twitter message such as *"#txfire is approaching Austin, 50 houses destroyed already http://bit.ly/3r6fgt"*, the NER module allows for detecting the facet-value pair *"(location, dbpedia:Austin_Texas)"*[9].

Classification. Twitcident classifies the content of Twitter messages into reports about casualties, damages or risks and also categorizes the type of experience that is reported in a tweet, e.g. whether the publisher of a tweet is seeing, feeling, hearing or smelling something. The classification is done by means of hand-crafted rules (e.g. *if a tweet mentions $(X_1 \text{ AND } X_2 \ldots) \text{ OR} \ldots \text{ then classify as } Y$*) that operate on both the facet-value pairs and the plain words that are mentioned in a tweet.

Linkage. By following links that are posted within messages, Twitcident further contextualizes the semantics of a message. Therefore, the semantic enrichment module extracts the main content of the Web resource that is referenced from a tweet using Boilerpipe[10] and processes it via the NER module to further enrich the Twitter message with facet-value pairs that describe its content. For the aforementioned tweet which lists *"http://bit.ly/3r6fgt"*, one may extract additional facet-value pairs such as *"(location, dbpedia:Bastrop_Texas)"* or *"(organization, dbpedia:Texas_Forrest_Service)"*.

Metadata extraction. Twitcident also collects and infers additional metadata about Twitter messages such as pictures referenced from the tweet or background information about the publisher of a tweet; for example, the profile picture, number of followers, number of tweets published during the incident or the location of the user when publishing her tweets. Such provenance data is important for end-users to assess the trustworthiness of a tweet and is moreover exploited by the Twitcident system when tweets that match the current query are sorted according to their relevance (see the search in Figure 2(a)).

Enriched Twitter messages can therefore also be represented by means of a set of weighted facet-value pairs. In line with Definition 1, the profile $P(t)$ of a Twitter message $t \in T$ can therefore specified as: $P(t) = \{((f,v), w(t,(f,v)))| (f,v) \in FVPs, t \in T, w(t,(f,v))) \in [0..1]\}$.

3.3.4 Filtering

The goal of the filtering step is to automatically identify those tweets that are relevant to an incident. Therefore, the Twitcident filtering component first detects the

[7] http://dbpedia.org/spotlight, http://alchemyapi.com, http://opencalais.com, http://zemanta.com
[8] Language detection:
http://code.google.com/p/language-detection/
Translation: http://code.google.com/apis/language/translate/overview.html
[9] The namespace abbreviation "dbpedia" points to:
http://dbpedia.org/resource/
[10] http://code.google.com/p/boilerpipe/

language of a Twitter message and filters out all tweets that do not match the target language(s). In the deployed Twitcident system, we only consider Dutch or English tweets as relevant and discard Twitter messages for which we detect another language. Based on this pre-processing, the Twitcident framework features two core filtering strategies: (i) semantic filtering and (ii) semantic filtering with news contextualization.

3.3.4.1 Semantic Filtering.

Given the current incident profile $P(i)$ and the set of semantically enriched Twitter messages $P(t)$, the core challenge is to decide whether a tweet t is relevant for an incident i. The semantic filtering strategy therefore exploits the set of alternative labels of a DBpedia URI v that is mentioned in the facet-value pairs (f, v) of $P(i)$. If an alternative label is mentioned in the content of a Twitter message t then the corresponding facet-value pair (f, v) is added to the tweet profile. Given the further enriched tweet profile—denoted as $\bar{P}(t)$—and $P(i)@k$, the top k weighted facet-value pairs of the incident profile $P(i)$, the semantic filtering strategy computes the similarity between $P(i)@k$ and $\bar{P}(t)$ and considers a tweet t relevant to an incident i if $filter_{sem}(P(i), P(t)) = 1$:

$$filter_{sem}(P(i), P(t)) = \begin{cases} 1 & \text{if } sim(P(i)@k, \bar{P}(t)) > \delta \\ 0 & \text{otherwise} \end{cases} \quad (2)$$

In our experiments in Section 4, we use $P(i)@20$, apply the Jaccard similarity coefficient to compute $sim(P(i), \bar{P}(t))$ and set $\delta = 0$ as threshold. A Twitter message t is thus relevant if at least one facet-value pair of $P(i)@k$ also occurs in $\bar{P}(t)$.

3.3.4.2 Semantic Filtering with News Context.

As Twitter users might be influenced by public news media, Twitcident also monitors popular news agencies. The semantic filtering with news contextualization therefore extends the semantic filtering by enriching the incident profile $P(i)$ with information from mainstream news media before generating $\bar{P}(t)$. In particular, $P(i)$ is complemented with facet-value pairs that are extracted from related news articles. A news article is considered to be related to an incident if it matches the initial incident profile $P(i)$. The expanded incident profile $\bar{P}(i)$ is then used to perform the semantic filtering as described above. A tweet t is considered to be relevant to an incident i if $sim(\bar{P}(i)@k, \bar{P}(t)) > \delta$.

3.4 Faceted Search and Analytics

Incident detection, incident profiling, media aggregation, semantic enrichment and filtering are automatic processes that deliver information about an incident as reported by people on the Social Web. However, in order to find information in the filtered Social Web streams, appropriate functionality for search and analysis has to be engineered as well. The Twitcident framework approaches the challenge of retrieving relevant information from Social Web streams by means of faceted search as proposed in [1]. In this section, we re-visit the different faceted search strategies provided by the Twitcident framework and detail Twitcident analytics.

3.4.1 Faceted Search Strategies

The faceted search functionality allows users to further filter incident-related messages by selecting facet-value pairs that should be featured by the retrieved messages. A faceted query q thus may consist of several facet-value pairs. Only those tweets that match all the facet-value constraints will be returned to the user. The ranking of the tweets that match a query is a research problem of its own and is, in the context of micro-blogging systems, usually solved by ranking according to recency [22]. Twitcident ranks the matching tweets according to their (i) creation time or (ii) relevance. The relevance is computed by exploiting various features including provenance information such as the authority score of the user who published a tweet [21].

A key challenge in engineering a faceted search interface is to support the facet-value selection as good as possible. Hence, the facet-value pairs that are presented in the faceted search interface (see Figure 1(a)) have to be ranked so that users can quickly narrow down the search result lists until they find the tweets that fulfill their information needs. The Twitcident framework provides different strategies that allow for ranking facet-value pairs and therefore generating query recommendations.

3.4.1.1 Frequency-based Faceted Search.

A straightforward approach is to rank the facet-value pairs $(f, v) \in FVPs$ based on their occurrence frequency in the current hit list H of Twitter messages that match the current query $q = \{(f, v) | (f, v) \in FVPs \text{ selected as filter}\}$, i.e. messages that contain all facet-value pairs in q:

$$rank_{frequency}((f, v), H) = |H_{(f,v)}| \quad (3)$$

$|H_{(f,v)}|$ is the number of (remaining) messages that contain the facet-value pair (f, v) which can be applied to further filter the given hit list H. By ranking those facet values high that appear in most of the messages, $rank_{frequency}$ minimizes the risk of ranking relevant facet values too low. However, it might increase the effort that a user has to invest to narrow down search results: by selecting facet values which occur in most of the remaining tweets the size of the hit list is reduced slowly.

3.4.1.2 Time-sensitive Faceted Search.

Topics that are reported and discussed on the Social Web about an incident may change over time [10, 13]. Hence, also the information demands of users who are seeking relevant details about an incident are likely to shift. The time-sensitive faceted search strategy adapts to this behavior and promotes those trending facet-value pairs that are often mentioned in recent Social Web messages:

$$rank_{time}((f, v), H) =$$
$$max(\{age(m) | m \in H\}) - \frac{\sum_{m \in H_{(f,v)}} age(m)}{|\{m \in H_{(f,v)}\}|} \quad (4)$$

Here, $age(m)$ is the age of a message $m \in H$ (and $m \in H_{(f,v)}$) with respect to the current time when the query is issued. $rank_{time}((f, v), H)$ thus calculates the temporal distance between the oldest message in the hit list and the average age of messages that contain the given facet-value pair (f, v). The younger the average age of messages that mention (f, v), the higher the ranking score.

3.4.1.3 Personalized Faceted Search.

Individual users may have different information needs that are reflected by their personal interests. To adapt the faceted search to the individual demands of a user, the Twitcident framework infers a user's interests from her Twitter activities, i.e. from the tweets a user published herself. The interest profile $P(u)$ of a user $u \in U$ can therefore be represented in the same way as incident or tweet profiles (cf. Definition 1), hence as a set of weighted facet-value pairs.

$$P(u) = \{((f,v), w(u, (f,v)))|$$

$$(f,v) \in \bigcup_{t \in T_u} P(t), u \in U, w(u, (f,v))) \in [0..1]\} \quad (5)$$

Twitcident analyzes the entire Twitter timeline of a user to construct a profile. It thus considers all the profiles $P(t)$ of tweets that the user published and weighs the facet-value pairs according to their occurrence frequency in the tweets. Given a facet-value pair (f,v), the personalized facet ranking strategy utilizes the weight $w(u, (f,v))$ in $P(u)$ to determine the ranking score:

$$rank_{pers}((f,v), P(u)) = \begin{cases} w(u, (f,v)) & \text{if } (f,v) \in P(u) \\ 0 & \text{otherwise} \end{cases} \quad (6)$$

The Twitcident framework moreover allows to combine different faceted search strategies using their normalized ranking score so that $rank((f,v), H) \in [0..1]$. In our experiments in Section 5, we combine the personalized and time-sensitive ranking strategy with the frequency-based strategy and set $\lambda = 0.5$, for example: $rank_{combine}((f,v), H) = \lambda rank_{frequency}((f,v), H) + (1-\lambda)rank_{personalized}((f,v), H)$.

3.4.2 Realtime Analytics

Based on the semantic enrichment, the Twitcident framework provides functionality to analyze the current Social Web stream about an incident. Figure 2 shows some of the graphical gadgets that are delivered to the users such as the evolution of topics over time or the geographical impact area of an incident. Twitcident exploits the incident and tweet profiles to generate these diagrams. For example, the impact area of an incident is deduced from the geographical location of Twitter messages that report about experiences of users, e.g. in which people state that they see, hear or smell something. The analytical tools adapt furthermore to the current context of a user: if a user further filters the Social Web stream by means of faceted search then the diagrams summarize and visualize only that fraction of the information that matches the filter.

Having introduced the core functionalities of the Twitcident framework, we will, in the next sections, evaluate the two fundamental research challenges that we approach with the Twitcident framework: the automated filtering of relevant information from Social Web streams (see Section 4) and search within Social Web streams (see Section 5).

4. EVALUATION OF TWEET FILTERING

On Twitter, people publish around 200 million messages per day[11]. Automatically retrieving and filtering information about particular incidents from Twitter streams is thus a non-trivial problem. In this section, we evaluate and compare the different strategies that Twitcident provides in order to solve this challenge and investigate the following research questions:

1. Which filtering strategy performs best in retrieving messages that are relevant for a given incident? How do semantic filtering strategies perform in comparison to keyword-based approaches?

2. How are the filtering strategies affected by the characteristics of the (initial) incident description?

---

[11]http://blog.twitter.com/2011/06/200-million-tweets-per-day.html

Corpus	#Elements
Crawled Twitter TREC 2011 Corpus	14,958,450
English Twitter Corpus	4,766,901
RSS News Feeds	62
News Articles	13,959
Entities extracted from English tweets	6,193,060
Entities extracted from News Articles	357,559

Table 1: Statistics of the Twitter corpus, the external news sources and the extracted named entities.

4.1 Experimental Setup

We evaluate the filtering strategies in context of the TREC microblog benchmarking task that was published this year, for the first time, at TREC[12]. The task is defined as retrieving the *interesting* and relevant Twitter messages for a given topic and a given time frame. As data, a corpus of sixteen million Twitter message IDs was released (which were posted on Twitter over a period of 2 weeks, from January 24, 2011 to February 8, 2011) together with 50 topics such as *Mexico drug war* or *Protests in Jordan*. In our experiments, we interpret these topics as incidents and consider the label of the topic (e.g. *Protests in Jordan*) as the initial incident description which the Twitcident framework exploits to perform incident profiling and tweet filtering (see Figure 1). The TREC topics are of different scale and most topics relate to a geographic location. Therefore, they have similar properties like the incidents that are monitored by Twitcident in practice.

For the top tweets returned by each filtering strategy for each topic, TREC provided relevance judgements indicating whether a tweet is considered to be relevant for a topic. On average, 58.35 tweets per topic were considered as relevant. Given these relevance judgments, we measure the performance via the mean average precision (MAP), precision within the top k returned items (P@k) and recall.

4.1.1 Dataset Characteristics

Table 1 gives an overview of the crawled dataset. Since over time, less tweets are available for public access, we were only able to crawl approximately fifteen million tweets (crawled in June/July), of which nearly five million tweets were detected to be written in English. Employing NER on the English tweets resulted in a total over six million named entities among which we find approximately 0.14 million distinct entities. The external news corpus was derived by extracting articles from 62 RSS feeds of prominent news media such as BBC, CNN or New York Times in the same time period as the Twitter posts.

4.1.2 Baseline: Keyword Filtering

We compare the semantic filtering strategies provided by the Twitcident framework with a keyword-based filtering baseline that interprets the label of a topic as a keyword query. The baseline evaluates a query and generates a ranking of tweets using language modeling with relevance model RM2 [11]. Apart from filtering out non-English tweets, the baseline also filters out re-tweets, tweets with less than 100 characters and tweets with words that contain a single letter three or more times in sequence (e.g., "ooooooooooh"). It thereby aims to remove chatter from a stream of tweets.

---

[12]Text REtrieval Conference: http://trec.nist.gov/

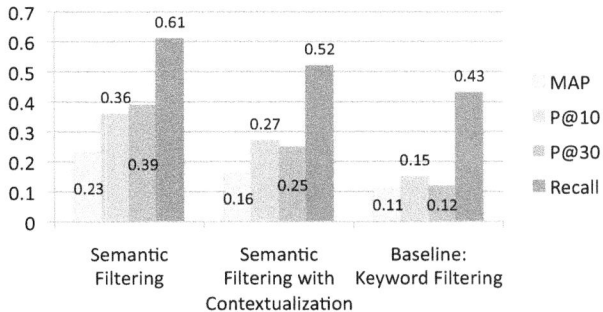

Figure 4: Result overview on the filtering strategies. Reported are the mean average precision (MAP), precision at k (P@10, P@30) and recall.

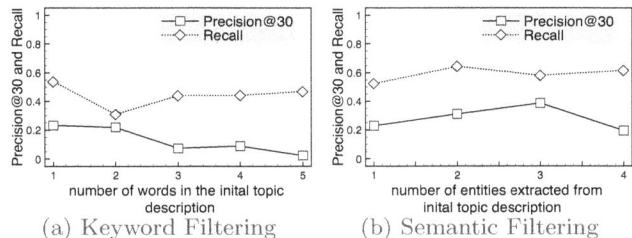

(a) Keyword Filtering   (b) Semantic Filtering

Figure 5: Robustness of (a) keyword-based filtering and (b) semantic filtering: correlation between the number of (a) words and (b) semantic concepts that can be extracted from the initial topic description and the filtering performance (P@30 and Recall).

4.2 Experimental Results

Figure 4 summarizes the results of our filtering evaluation and demonstrates that the semantic strategies of the Twitcident framework clearly outperform the keyword-based filtering regarding all metrics[13]. For example, the semantic filtering performs—with respect to MAP, P@10 and P@30—more than twice as good as the baseline and regarding recall it improves the filtering performance by 41.8%. News-based contextualization also leads to major improvements in comparison to the keyword-based baseline. However, it performs worse than the semantic filtering which does incident profiling solely on tweets. This indicates that facet-value pairs that are extracted from news articles, which report about the same incident/topic, seem to include noise in the incident profiling and filtering process.

Figure 5 illustrates the impact of the initial topic description on the filtering. The x-axis specifies the number of (a) words and (b) facet-value pairs that are extracted from the initial description while the y-axis marks precision@30 and recall. For keyword filtering, we observe that the precision almost gradually drops the more keywords are listed in the initial topic description so that for topics that feature six keywords, the average precision is just 0.03. In contrast, the semantic filtering, which does not consider all keywords from the topic description but considers only named entities for the topic profiling, is more robust and also achieves in the worst case a considerably higher average precision of 0.2. For both strategies, the recall increases slightly the more concepts are extracted from the initial topic description. Again, the semantic filtering performs better than the keyword-based filtering and features a more stable behavior when characteristics of the topic description vary.

4.3 Synopsis

In conclusion, we can therefore answer the research questions raised at the beginning of this section as follows.

1. Semantic filtering allows for the best filtering performance. It clearly outperforms the keyword-based strategy and more than doubles the mean average precision.
2. The complexity of a topic, measured by the number of concepts that can be extracted from the initial topic description, impacts the precision of the keyword-based strategy negatively: the higher the complexity the lower the precision. The semantic filtering strategy is more robust and also achieves high precisions for complex topics.

---

[13]The keyword-based baseline deployed by the TREC microblog organizers features with 0.14 and 0.11 regarding MAP and P@30 respectively a similar performance as our keyword-based strategy.

5. EVALUATION OF FACETED SEARCH

Based on the automatic filtering of Social Web streams for detecting messages that are relevant for a given incident, the Twitcident framework provides faceted search functionality that allows users to further filter the messages and retrieve information they are interested in. In line with the evaluations done in [1], we now evaluate also the quality of the faceted search strategies on top of the automatic filtering process and study the following research questions:

1. How well does faceted search supported by the Twitcident framework perform in comparison to keyword search?
2. What faceted search strategy supports users best in finding relevant Twitter messages?
3. What factors influence the performance of the faceted search strategies?

5.1 Experimental Setup

In order to answer the above research questions and evaluate the faceted search strategies (see Section 3.4.1), we applied an evaluation methodology introduced by Koren et al. [9] that simulates the clicking behavior of users in the context of faceted search interfaces. In a faceted search interface, a user can select a facet-value pair to refine the query and drill down the search result list until she finds a relevant document. We model the user's facet-value pair selection behavior by means of a *first-match user* that selects the first matching facet-value pair and continues to refine the query until no more appropriate facet-value pairs can be selected.

To evaluate the performance, we used again the TREC microblog dataset described in Section 4.1.1 and generated search settings by randomly selecting, for each of the 50 topics, 50 re-tweets which mention at least one hashtag—thus resulting in 2500 settings. Each search setting consists of (i) a target tweet (= the tweet that was re-tweeted), (ii) a user that is searching for the tweet (= the user who re-tweeted the tweet) and (iii) the timestamp of the search activity (= the time when the user re-tweeted the message). The set of candidate items is given by all those tweets which have been published before the search activity and are considered to be relevant to the corresponding topic based on the semantic filtering strategy of the Twitcident framework. We thus test—except for the incident detection—the entire pipeline of the Twitcident framework as depicted in Figure 1. The filtering delivered, on average, more than 5000 candidates per search setting while there is only exactly one Twitter message that is considered to be relevant, namely the Twitter message that was actually re-tweeted by the user.

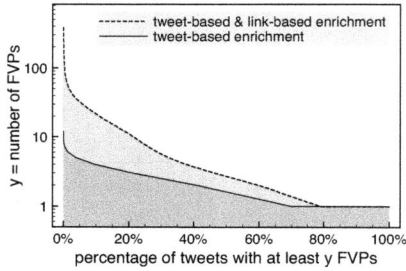

Figure 6: Impact of link-based semantic enrichment: the histogram shows the fraction of Twitter messages that feature at least y facet-value pairs (FVPs) for (i) semantic enrichment solely on tweets (tweet-based) and (ii) the link-based strategy that follows links which are posted in Twitter messages.

For measuring the performance of the search strategies, we use the mean reciprocal rank (MRR) of the target item in the search result ranking[14] when the user selects it. Furthermore, we utilize MRR of the first relevant facet-value pair and success at rank k (S@k) which is the probability that a relevant facet-value pair, that the user selects to narrow down the search result list, appears within the top k of the facet-value pair ranking. Both metrics are direct indicators for the effort a user needs to spend using the search interface: the higher MRR and S@k, the faster the user will find a relevant facet-value pair when scanning the facet-value pair ranking.

5.1.1 Dataset Characteristics

In the faceted search evaluation, we moreover experiment with the link-based semantic enrichment that is provided by the Twitcident framework (see Section 3.3.3). As depicted in Figure 6, we observe that the extraction of facet-value pairs from Web resources that are linked from a Twitter message allows to further extend the profile of the corresponding tweet. It therefore reduces the level of sparsity. For example, for the semantic enrichment, which is solely based on tweets, 41.2% of the messages feature at least two facet-value pairs while the additional link-based enrichment allows for representing 60.1% of the tweets with at least two facet-value pairs.

5.1.2 Baseline Strategies

We compare the faceted search strategies of the Twitcident framework (see Section 3.4.1) with two baseline strategies that exploit hashtags:

Hashtag-based Keyword Search. For this baseline strategy, the user randomly selects one of the hashtags that is mentioned in the Twitter message the user is searching for[15]. Given the messages that match this keyword query, the user starts scanning the result list.

Hashtag-based Faceted Search This strategy interprets hashtags as facet values and therefore ranks the hashtag-based facet-value pairs in the same way as the frequency-based faceted search strategy (see Section 3.4.1), i.e. according to their occurrence frequency in the current search result list. The selection of hashtag-based facet-value pairs is simulated according to the aforementioned procedure.

---

[14]Tweets are ranked according to their creation time so that the latest tweets appear at the top of the ranking.

[15]To not discriminate the hashtag-based search strategies, we selected the search settings so that each target tweet contains at least one hashtag.

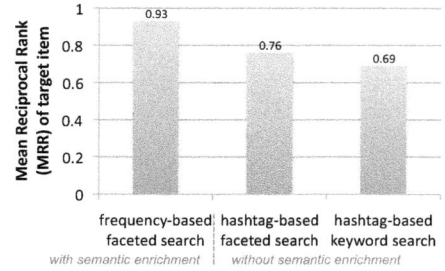

Figure 7: Result overview of search strategies: comparison of hashtag-based and semantic search.

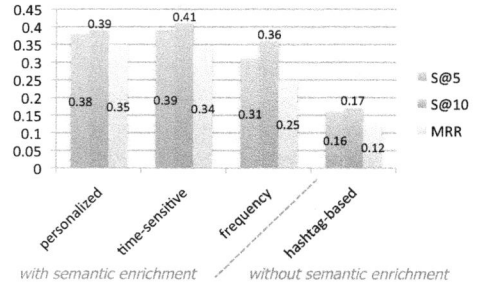

Figure 8: Result overview of the faceted search strategies. Reported are the mean reciprocal rank (MRR) of the first relevant facet-value pair (FVP) and success at k (S@5, S@10), i.e. the probability that a relevant FVP appears within the top k.

5.2 Experimental Results

Figure 7 compares the frequency-based faceted search strategy featured by the Twitcident framework with the hashtag-based search strategies. The comparison of the MRR scores reveals that the semantic faceted search strategy improves the search performance significantly by 34.8% and 22.4% over the hashtag-based keyword search and the hashtag-based faceted search strategy[16]. Interpreting hashtags as facet values leads to an improvement over the single keyword query as well. However, the semantic enrichment provided by the Twitcident framework proves to generate more valuable representations of the Twitter messages and therefore allows for faceted search functionality that clearly outperforms the two hashtag-based strategies.

The performance of the different faceted search strategies is listed in Figure 8. The performance of those strategies that benefit from the semantic enrichment significantly exceeds the performance of the hashtag-based strategy in predicting appropriate facet-value pairs. A detailed review of the results shows that a key success factor of the semantic faceted search strategies is given by their ability of disambiguating facet-value pairs. While the hashtag-based strategy would, for example, treat *#Tahrir* and *#TahrirSquare* as different facet values, the semantic faceted search strategies would—in context of the *"Egyptian evacuation"* incident which is one of the TREC topics—map both values to the same concept (namely *dbpedia:Tahrir_Square*) and therefore facilitate the faceted search for the user.

Figure 8 furthermore shows that both personalization and temporal contextualization lead to significant improvements over the frequency-based strategy. In fact, regarding MRR the performance of the personalized and time-sensitive strate-

---

[16]Statistical significance was tested with a two-tailed *t*-Test where the significance level was set to $\alpha = 0.01$.

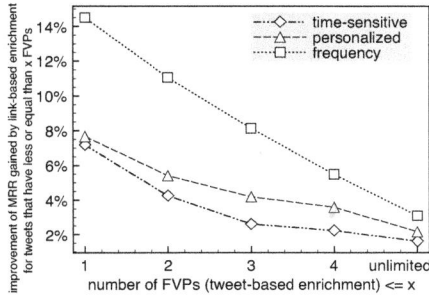

Figure 9: Impact of link-based semantic enrichment on faceted search performance. The y-axis shows the improvement with respect to the mean reciprocal rank (MRR) of the first relevant FVP that is gained when using link-based enrichment in addition to solely tweet-based enrichment averaged for those search settings where the target tweet features x or less than x FVPs.

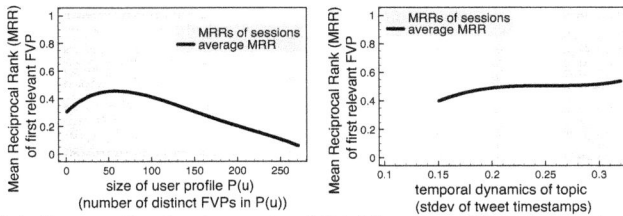

(a) Personalized: impact of profile size

(b) Time-sensitive: impact of topic dynamics

Figure 10: Impact of (a) profile size on the search performance of the personalized faceted search strategy and correlation between (b) search performance and temporal dynamics of the topic within which a user is searching. Temporal dynamics is measured by means of the standard deviation of the timestamps of Twitter messages that are published within one topic, i.e. a high standard deviation indicates strong temporal dynamics.

gies is 39.7% and 36.8% better than the one of the faceted search strategy that ranks the facet-value pairs according to their occurrence frequency in the current search result set.

By enriching the tweet profiles with facet-value pairs extracted from external Web resources that are referenced from the Twitter messages (link-based semantic enrichment), one can further improve the performance of the semantic faceted search strategies (see Figure 9). The level of improvement depends on the characteristics of the tweet profiles. Those search settings where the target tweet contains exactly one facet-value pair benefit most from the link-based enrichment. For these settings, the performance increases by 14.5% for the frequency-based strategy and around 7% for the personalized and time-sensitive strategies.

Figure 10 allows us to study how the performance of the personalized and time-sensitive search strategies depends on the characteristics of the user and incident profiles. Therefore, Figure 10(a) plots the MRR scores of the personalized strategy in relation to the size of the profile of the user who performed the corresponding search activity. It is interesting to observe how the average performance varies with changing profile sizes: the average MRR for profiles with less then 10 distinct FVPs is 0.328. The personalized strategy achieves its maximum average MRR performance for

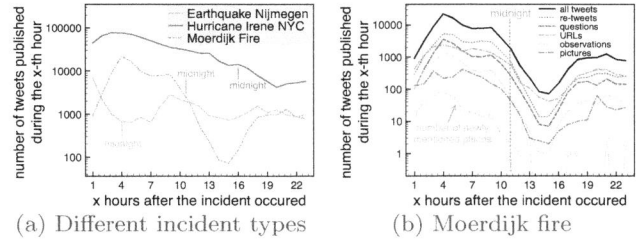

(a) Different incident types

(b) Moerdijk fire

Figure 11: Posting behavior about incidents within the first 24 hours of an incident: (a) comparison of different types of incidents and (b) type of information posted during a fire incident in Moerdijk.

profiles that feature between 50 and 70 FVPs while for the few user profiles which feature more than 150 FVPs the performance drops—possibly because those profiles feature too much diversity.

The time-sensitive faceted search strategy, which promotes those facet-value pairs that are currently trending, performs best for those search settings that are performed within a topic that is characterized by strong temporal dynamics (see Figure 10(b)). Here, the dynamics of a topic are described by means of the standard deviation of the creation times of tweets which are considered to be relevant for the topic. Figure 10(b) depicts that the performance slightly increases the more a topic underlies temporal changes. Hence, the more distributed the messages are posted over time the more important it is to adapt to the temporal context.

5.3 Synopsis

Given the experimental results, we can answer the research questions raised at the beginning of this section:

1. Faceted search strategies allow for significantly higher search performance than the hashtag-based keyword search strategies. They enable users to more precisely filter tweets and therefore retrieve relevant information.

2. Personalized and time-sensitive faceted search strategies that adapt to the profile of a user and to the temporal context respectively allow for the best search performance and lead to significant improvements over the standard semantic faceted search strategy. Further exploitation of links posted in tweets allows us to further enrich the semantic representation of tweets and moreover induces additional improvements of the search performance.

3. The performance of the personalized faceted search strategy is influenced by the size of a user's profile and achieves the highest performance for medium-sized profiles. The quality of the time-sensitive strategy depends on the temporal dynamics within an incident: the more temporal changes the more important it is to adapt to the temporal context.

6. DISCUSSION

With Twitcident we introduce a system that allows users to explore, search and analyze information about incidents available on the Social Web and Twitter in particular. During the last ten months we tested the Twitcident system in practice to monitor various incidents, specifically to support emergency services such as the Dutch police and fire department. Given these experiences, we identify that different types of incidents imply different types of posting behavior

293

on the Social Web. For example, Figure 11(a) compares the number of Twitter messages posted about three different types of incidents within the first 24 hours: a large-scale fire at a chemical factory in Moerdijk (Jan 5th 2011), an earthquake with its epicenter close to Nijmegen (Sep 8th 2011) and the so-called hurricane *Irene* which caused floodings in New York (Aug 28th 2011). One can see that all incidents reach their maximum peak within the first 4 hours after the incident occurred. For the fire and hurricane the amount of tweets gradually grows until it reaches its peak while for the unexpected earthquake most tweets are already published within the first hour after the incident. In fact, the hurricane Irene did not hit New York City unexpectedly, but was forecasted already weeks ahead which caused Twitter traffic already before the hurricane appeared.

Twitcident thus has to process huge amounts of messages within the first hours of an incident. To handle ten thousands of messages per hour, Twitcident parallelizes the semantic enrichment of Twitter messages which is the most time-intensive procedure. In particular, following URLs and processing the corresponding Web sites may take seconds. Therefore, Twitcident applies heuristics to decide whether the link of a tweet should be processed in realtime or marked for later processing (e.g. during the night when the amount of messages to be processed decreases; see Figure 11(a)). For example, URLs posted in tweets for which the tweet-based enrichment—which takes on average between 100 and 300 milliseconds—detects already two or more facet-value pairs are not processed immediately because for these tweets the link-based enrichment improves the search performance only slightly (see Figure 9).

Figure 11(b) illustrates for the fire at the chemical factory in Moerdijk the kind of information that is posted on Twitter within the first 24 hours after the fire started. It is interesting to see that the number of questions that are being asked is exceptionally high when the overall number of tweets reaches its maximum. At that point, questions such as *"What about the toxic cloud?"* or *"Is there a chance that the smoke is going to Leiden?"* are prominent and exceed the amount of URLs and pictures which may reveal answers to these questions. Emergency services are often interested in *new* information and question, for example, whether the impact area of an incident is exceeding (cf. "number of newly mentioned places" in Figure 11(b)).

Twitcident allows people to find answers to such questions and allows emergency services to analyze the information that people publish on the Social Web.

7. CONCLUSIONS

In this paper we introduced Twitcident, a framework for filtering, searching and analyzing information about incidents that people publish in their Social Web streams. Triggered by an incident detection module that monitors emergency broadcasting services, our framework automatically collects and filters relevant information from Twitter. It enriches the semantics of Twitter messages to adapt and improve the incident profiling and filtering over time. Semantic enrichment is also the foundation for faceted search and realtime analytics provided by the Twitcident framework. In our evaluations we proved that semantic enrichment boosts the performance of both the filtering of Twitter messages for a given incident and the search for relevant information about an incident within the filtered messages significantly.

8. ACKNOWLEDGEMENTS

This work is co-funded by the EU FP7 project ImREAL (http://imreal-project.eu).

9. REFERENCES

[1] F. Abel, I. Celic, G.-J. Houben, and P. Siehndel. Leveraging the Semantics of Tweets for Adaptive Faceted Search on Twitter. In *ISWC*, pages 1–17, 2011. Springer.

[2] M. S. Bernstein, B. Suh, L. Hong, J. Chen, S. Kairam, and E. H. Chi. Eddi: interactive topic-based browsing of social status streams. In *UIST*, pages 303–312, 2010. ACM.

[3] C. Bizer, J. Lehmann, G. Kobilarov, S. Auer, C. Becker, R. Cyganiak, and S. Hellmann. DBpedia - A crystallization point for the Web of Data. *Web Semantics*, 2009.

[4] J. Chen, R. Nairn, and E. H. Chi. Speak Little and Well: Recommending Conversations in Online Social Streams. In *CHI*, 2011. ACM.

[5] J. Chen, R. Nairn, L. Nelson, M. Bernstein, and E. Chi. Short and tweet: experiments on recommending content from information streams. In *Proc. of CHI*, pages 1185–1194, 2010. ACM.

[6] A. Dong, R. Zhang, P. Kolari, J. Bai, F. Diaz, Y. Chang, Z. Zheng, and H. Zha. Time is of the essence: improving recency ranking using twitter data. In *Proc. of WWW*, pages 331–340, 2010. ACM.

[7] D. Gaffney. iranelection: quantifying online activism. In *WebScience*, 2010. ACM.

[8] A. Java, X. Song, T. Finin, and B. Tseng. Why we twitter: understanding microblogging usage and communities. In *Proc. of WebKDD/SNA-KDD*, pages 56–65, 2007. ACM.

[9] J. Koren, Y. Zhang, and X. Liu. Personalized interactive faceted search. In *WWW*, pages 477–486, 2008. ACM.

[10] H. Kwak, C. Lee, H. Park, and S. Moon. What is twitter, a social network or a news media? In *Proc. of WWW*, pages 591–600, 2010. ACM.

[11] V. Lavrenko and W. B. Croft. Relevance based language models. In *Proc. of SIGIR*, pages 120–127, 2001.

[12] C. Lee, H. Kwak, H. Park, and S. Moon. Finding influentials based on the temporal order of information adoption in Twitter. In *Proc. of WWW*, pages 1137–1138, 2010. ACM.

[13] K. Lerman and R. Ghosh. Information contagion: an empirical study of spread of news on Digg and Twitter social networks. In *Proc. of ICWSM*, 2010. AAAI Press.

[14] A. Marcus, M. S. Bernstein, O. Badar, D. R. Karger, S. Madden, and R. C. Miller. Twitinfo: Aggregating and visualizing microblogs for event exploration. In *Proc. of CHI*, 2011. ACM.

[15] M. Mathioudakis and N. Koudas. Twittermonitor: trend detection over the twitter stream. In *Proc. of SIGMOD*, pages 1155–1158, 2010. ACM.

[16] B. Meeder, B. Karrer, A. Sayedi, R. Ravi, C. Borgs, and J. Chayes. We Know Who You Followed Last Summer: Inferring Social Link Creation Times In Twitter. In *Proc. of WWW*, 2011. ACM.

[17] M. Pennacchiotti and A.-M. Popescu. A Machine Learning Approach to Twitter User Classification. In *Proc. of ICWSM*, 2011. AAAI Press.

[18] D. M. Romero, B. Meeder, and J. Kleinberg. Differences in the mechanics of information diffusion across topics: Idioms, political hashtags, and complex contagion on twitter. In *Proc. of WWW*, 2011. ACM.

[19] T. Sakaki, M. Okazaki, and Y. Matsuo. Earthquake shakes Twitter users: real-time event detection by social sensors. In *Proc. of WWW*, pages 851–860, 2010. ACM.

[20] J. Sankaranarayanan, H. Samet, B. E. Teitler, M. D. Lieberman, and J. Sperling. Twitterstand: news in tweets. In *Proc. of GIS*, pages 42–51, 2009. ACM.

[21] R. Stronkman. Exploiting Twitter to fulfill information needs during incidents. Master thesis, TU Delft, 2011. http://wis.ewi.tudelft.nl/twitcident/thesis.pdf.

[22] J. Teevan, D. Ramage, and M. R. Morris. #TwitterSearch: a comparison of microblog search and web search. In *Proc. of WSDM*, pages 35–44, 2011. ACM.

[23] J. Weng and B.-S. Lee. Event Detection in Twitter. In *Proc. of ICWSM*, 2011. AAAI Press.

Finding and Exploring Memes in Social Media

Hohyon Ryu, Matthew Lease, and Nicholas Woodward
School of Information
University of Texas at Austin
hohyon@utexas.edu, ml@ischool.utexas.edu, nwoodward@mail.utexas.edu

ABSTRACT

Critical literacy challenges us to question how what we read has been shaped by external context, especially when information comes from less established sources. While cross-checking multiple sources provides a foundation for critical literacy, trying to keep pace the constant deluge of new online information is a daunting proposition, especially for casual readers. To help address this challenge, we propose a new form of technological assistance which automatically discovers and displays underlying *memes*: ideas embodied by similar phrases which are found in multiple sources. Once detected, these underlying memes are revealed to users via generated hypertext, allowing memes to be explored in context. Given the massive volume of online information today, we propose a highly-scalable system architecture based on MapReduce, extending work by Kolak and Schilit [11]. To validate our approach, we report on using our system to process and browse a 1.5 TB collection of crawled social media. Our contributions include a novel technological approach to support critical literacy and a highly-scalable system architecture for meme discovery optimized for Hadoop [25]. Our source code and *Meme Browser* are both available online.

Categories and Subject Descriptors

H.5.4 [**Information Interfaces and Presentation**]: Hypertext/Hypermedia—*Architectures*; H.4.3 [**Information Systems Applications**]: Communications Applications—*Information browsers*; H.3.1 [**Information Storage and Retrieval**]: Content Analysis and Indexing—*Miscellaneous*

General Terms

Algorithm, Design, Experimentation, Measurement

Keywords

automatic hypertext, critical literacy, memes, MapReduce

1. INTRODUCTION

Web 2.0 technologies have broken down many traditional barriers to authorship, enabling greater democratization of

information exchange via online social media, where hypertext can blur distinctions between readers and writers [15]. However, the massive growth of information produced by less established sources has created significant new *critical literacy*[1] challenges for helping people effectively interpret and assess online information [24, 5]. Our vision is to complement traditional forms of critical literacy education with additional technological support in the form of smarter browsing technology. Such technology has additional promise for providing new paths for discovering and exploring collections [19], as well as integrating information expressed across multiple sources. Instead of understanding online narrative through only a single source, we can instead explore how broader community discourse has shaped its development [2] or facilitates greater social engagement [9].

Our analysis centers on fine-grained discovery and display of *memes*: ideas represented by one or more similar phrases which occur across multiple collection documents. While our work is inspired by Leskovec et al.'s system for meme detection and visualizion [12], their notion of memes was restricted to explicit quotations only, ignoring the vast majority of text. This assumption is limiting with social media, which often eschews use of quotations for reasons ranging from innocuous social norms to more insidious "messaging" campaigns which flood social media with repeated stock phrases while obfuscating their central originating source.

Of course, mining complete texts instead of quotations represents a significant scalability challenge. To address this, we propose an adaption of Kolak and Schilit (K&S)'s scalable architecture for finding "popular passages" in scanned books [11]. While their approach centered on use of the MapReduce paradigm for data-intensive, distibuted computing [7], they utilized Google's proprietary version of MapReduce and omitted some important practical details. We instead adopt the open-source Hadoop version of MapReduce [25] and discuss practical implementation issues and design patterns [14] for building scalable Hadoop systems for tasks such as ours. Because the K&S algorithm generates a quadratic data increase in what is already a data-intensive problem, requiring aggressive filtering, we describe an alternative approach which avoids this problem.

To validate our approach, we report on using our system to discover and browse memes in a 1.5 TB collection of 28 million crawled blogs. Our primary contributions include: 1) a novel approach and browser design for supporting critical literacy; and 2) a highly-scalable system architecture for meme discovery, providing a solid foundation for further system extensions and refinements. Our discussion of Hadoop algorithms and design patterns used should also be helpful

---

[1] http://en.wikipedia.org/wiki/Critical_literacy

| Feb | Mar | Apr | May | Jun | Jul | Aug | Sep | Oct | Nov | Dec | Jan |

Meme

laura bush and cindy mccain

▼ Other Mentions (Same Source)
2008: 09/02   09/03   09/06

▼ Other Mentions (General)
04/21/2008 www.perrspectives.com
09/03/2008 www.blogher.com
09/03/2008 d-day.blogspot.com
                                        More

▼ Meme Related Phrases
laura bush and cindy mccain
16 mentions, 04/21/2008 - 09/25/2008

laura bush and cindy mccain's speech
8 mentions, 09/03/2008 - 09/18/2008

the first lady and cindy mccain
5 mentions, 09/04/2008 - 11/02/2008

▼ Memes of the Day

1. laura bush and cindy mccain
2. eight deaths were attributed to the storm in the
3. on this labor day weekend
4. the great threat to the obama biden

Tonight's line-up will feature a speech delivered via video by President George Bush, whose Monday night address was canceled due to the storm while **Laura Bush and Cindy McCain** stepped in. Also speaking will be Democratic senator and former vice president candidate Joe Lieberman, who is supporting presumptive GOP nominee John McCain over Democratic nominee Barack Obama. Former Tennessee Sen. Fred Thompson also will speak. While Backyard Conservative attends the event with videographer Leah Peterson, BlogHer will host a live-blog tonight by Chilihead.

The RNC held some programs Monday, including this leadership summit for young women videoblogged by Backyard Conservative for BlogHer. In addition, CNN reports that nearly 300 protesters were arrested after a march by about 5,000 people.

Other than Blogger Nice Deb, who is not a fan of protests, you wouldn't know about the protests from reading too many political blogs by women. Most are still talking about Alaska Gov. Sarah Palin, who is Sen. McCain's pick for vice president. On Monday Palin confirmed that her 17-year-old daughter is pregnant. In the past 24 hours, that discussion has evolved into an emotional conversation in the BlogHersphere about her personal decision to seek and hold elected office while being a mother of five children -- while other BlogHers question other peoples' willingness to judge Palin's decisions and still others ask

Feedback

Does the highlighted phrase reveal an interesting connection between the sources?

👍 Yes   👎 No

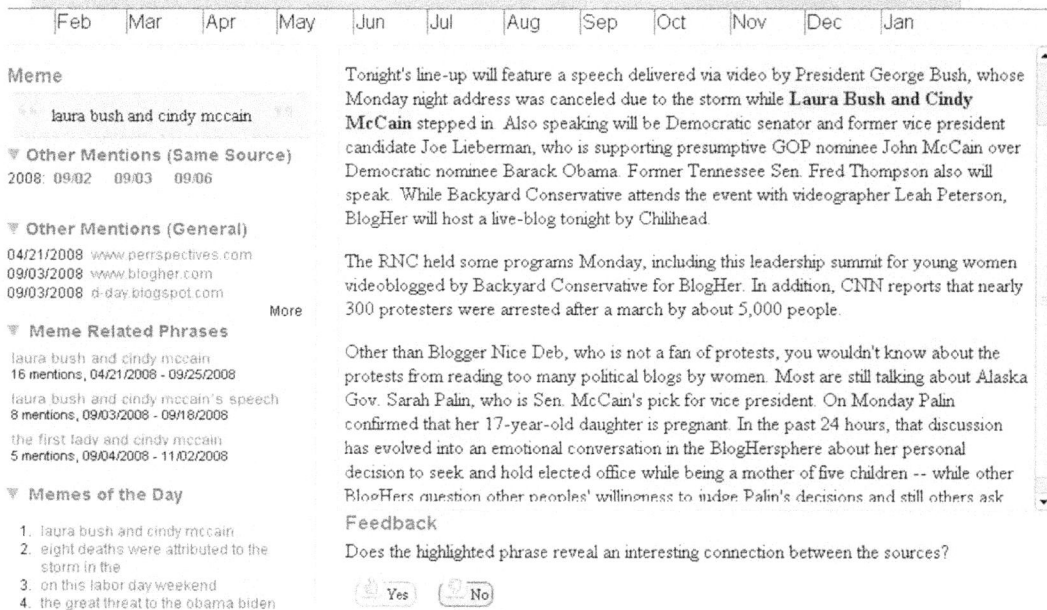

Figure 1: The **Meme Browser** makes readers aware of (discovered) underlying memes via highlighting. Navigation links let the reader explore detected memes in context, investigating connections they reveal between different documents. A *common phrase* (CP) is any phrase seen to occur in multiple documents, while a *meme* is a cluster a similar CPs. At all times, there exists an Active CP (ACP) and associated Active Meme (AM), for which relevant information is shown.

At top: The **Timeline Navigator** 1) indicates the date of the current document being read; 2) shows the temporal profile of mentions of the AM and 3) supports access and navigation to top memes on other days.

Below the timeline: The **Content Pane** 1) highlights a specific ACP for the AM in the context of the the current document; and 2) marks in gray any other highly-ranked memes present in the document. The reader may select a new AM at any time.

At left: The **Faceted Browsing Pane** provides information and navigation links relevant to the ACP and AM. From top-to-bottom, the pane shows 1) "Phrase": the ACP; 2) "Other Mentions (Same Source)": links to other mentions of the ACP by the same *source* (i.e. information provider); 3) "Other Mentions (General)": links to other mentions of the ACP by other sources; 4) "Meme Related Phrases": other CPs belonging to the AM; and 5) "Memes of the Day": an automatically-generated ranking of the the most informative memes for the current date.

At bottom: A **Feedback Widget** invites simple user feedback on meme quality to collect labels for training and evaluation.

for those more generally interested in data-intensive computing and effective use of Hadoop. Our source code[2] and *Meme Browser*[3] are both freely available online.

2. ENVISIONED USER EXPERIENCE

A screen shot of our *Meme Browser* interface is shown in Figure 1. A reader's experience with our system might start by opening a document and finding memes displayed, selecting a meme from opening the *Top Memes of the Day* page, or selecting some other date from the *Timeline Navigator*. Imagine the reader selects September 3, 2008 and its top meme, "laura bush and cindy mccain". The names might be familiar, but the reader might wonder why they are occurring together on this day. After selecting the meme, a

[2]https://bitbucket.org/softbass/meme-extractor
[3]http://odyssey.ischool.utexas.edu/mb/

representative document opens to a paragraph where the phrase is found highlighted:

> God loves Republicans because he allowed **Laura Bush and Cindy McCain** show how classy they were. Either of these women has more class in her little finger than Thunder Rodent Thighs has in her whole body.

At this point, the reader may become even more curious: what happened that day and why was the blogger so excited? He notices gray bars above the timeline indicating when the current meme was mentioned and its popularity in mentions over time. He then selects the first day where the peak is observed and finds a document with the following paragraph:

> Cindy McCain and first lady Laura Bush will appear before the Republican convention Monday to encourage people to donate to the relief efforts

in the Gulf region, a senior McCain campaign official told reporters in a conference call.

Depending on the reader's familiarity with world events at that time, more questions might come to mind. "What happened in the Gulf area?"; "What did other politicians think about this?"; and "What was the public reaction?" The readers realizes that the highlighted phrases lead to other documents where the given phrase is mentioned. They see that "Hurricane Gustav slammed into the Louisiana coast," and "all political activity will be suspended for the time being."

Glancing at the *Meme Related Phrases* section, the reader can find additional phrases related to this same meme, along with how often they were mentioned and the time period in which they were most active. In this case, additional phrases include "laura bush and cindy mccain's speech" and "the first lady and cindy mccain", providing further points for exploration. Looking at the *Memes of the Day* section, the reader begins discerning relationships between other popular phrases and can continue to explore further.

3. SYSTEM ARCHITECTURE

Figure 2 presents our system's overall processing architecture. Initial preprocessing extracts and normalizes textual content (e.g. filtering out advertisements and HTML tags), as well as non-English documents and extremely short documents (see Section 4 for preprocessing details). Our subsequent processing follows Kolak and Schilit's high-level approach for finding "popular passages" in scanned books [11]. First, near-duplicate documents are identified and removed (Section 3.1). Next, we utilize a multi-stage, scalable MapReduce process to automatically find common phrases (CPs) that occur in multiple documents. We then rank CPs to identify the most informative ones to display to the user (Section 3.3). A clustering phase then groups similar CPs to form memes (Section 3.4). We report efficiency statistics in Section 4 and design of the *Meme Browser* in Section 5.

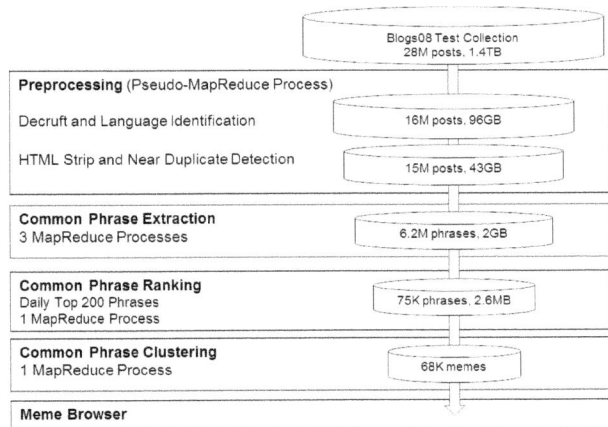

Figure 2: Our meme detection architecture involves preprocessing, near-duplicate detection, then finding, ranking, and clustering common phrases (CPs) to form memes.

3.1 Near-Duplicate Removal

Social media and news collections often contain many minor variants of the same document, e.g. different editors'

versions of the same Associated Press story [1]. Because brute force near-duplicate document detection (NDD) requires $O(n^2)$ comparison of all document pairs, we developed several simple heuristics to reduce the search space and speed up comparison which served our immediate need. While secondary to our core work, we describe our approach here and refer the interested reader to other well-known NDD methods (cf. [23, 8]) and MapReduce approaches for performing efficient document comparison [13].

To reduce the number of comparisons required, we partition the document space to only compare documents which begin with the same character and have total word length within ± a parameter *window_size* of each other. To speed up the remaining comparisons, we: 1) reduce the vocabulary size by conflating all terms starting with the same four characters; 2) build a dictionary hashmap for mapping these (4-character) "terms" to numeric indices; 3) ignore term frequencies and record only binary presence vs. absence of each term; and 4) represent each document by a bit-vector for fast intersection operations. Note this representation of documents is used only for NDD.

Building the collection dictionary for the reduced vocabulary represents a minor variant on the cannonical **word count** example in the original MapReduce paper [7]. To reduce intermediate output, rather than emitting all tokens, we instead collected the document-specific vocabulary for each document in the Mapper and then output this vocabulary after the entire document has been processed (i.e. in-Mapper combiner pattern [14]). We also save all document-specific vocabulary from the Mapper (along with the document's length and first character) directly to HDFS. The hashmap is trivially built from the vocabulary and then shared with an *embarrassingly parallel* processing stage which partitions the collection (i.e. the document-specific vocabulary for each document) across the cluster and uses the shared hashmap to convert each document to a bit vector.

Next, all documents with the same first character and word length are grouped together. The Mapper simply emits (character,length) as the primary key for each document, using the document ID as a secondary key. MapReduce secondary sorting [14] then groups documents by the primary key and sorts them by the secondary key. The reducer is just the identity function, outputting a sorted list of document IDs for each (character, length) primary key. A second hashmap is then trivially built for fast lookup.

Algorithm 1 details our NDD method. For each (character, length) bucket, we load the sorted list of document IDs plus document IDs in buckets within ±*window_size*. By symmetry, we need only consider longer lengths, as well as only compare documents with smaller IDs to those with larger. If document similarity is below the *dsim_threshold* parameter, the document with greater ID is identified as a near-duplicate and output for deletion.

As a slight variant to Jaccard similarity and Dice's coefficient, we compute document similarity by:

$$dsim(A, B) = \frac{|A \cap B|}{min(|A|, |B|)} \qquad (1)$$

As an example, if one document has vocabulary [**a**, b, **f, g, h, i**] and another has [**a, f, g, h, i**, j, k, l], the resulting similarity is $\frac{5}{6}$. While this strict coefficient could be problematic were the document lengths considerably different, the parameter *window_size* prevents this case from occurring.

Algorithm 1 Near-Duplicate Document Removal

Parameter: $t \leftarrow dsim\_threshold$
Parameter: $\Delta \leftarrow window\_size$
Parameter: $map \leftarrow$ (character c, length l) $hashmap$

1: **for each** (c, l) bucket $\in map$ **do**
2:      Sorted List $L \leftarrow \emptyset$
3:      **for each** $i \in [0 : \Delta]$ **do**
4:          $L.add$(all document IDs $\in map(c, l + i)$)
5:      **for each** $d \in L$ **do**
6:          **for each** $(d2.ID > d1.ID) \in L$ **do**
7:              **if** $dsim(d1, d2) > t$ **then**
8:                  $output(d2)$
9:                  $L.remove(d2)$

3.2 Finding Common Phrases

Our definition of *memes* was ideas represented by similar phrases that occur across multiple documents. Based upon the Kolak and Schilit (K&S) approach for finding "popular passages" in scanned books [11], we find identical phrases occurring in multiple documents, then group similar phrases into memes. While we adopt a similar 3-stage MapReduce architecture for finding the common phrases (CPs), our second and third stages differ markedly. As we shall further discuss, Stage 2 of the original K&S algorithm generates quadratic growth of data in an already data-intensive computation. While this growth can be mitigated by aggressive filtering, such reduction comes at the cost of increasing the false positive rate. Consequently, we describe an alternative formulation which finds CPs while avoiding this scalability tradeoff. We also replace the loosely-defined *grouping* phase of K&S with a well-specified method based on established clustering techniques (Section 3.4).

Algorithm 2 Stage 1: Shingle Table Generation

Parameter: $shingle\_size$
1: **method** MAP(doc_id, $text$)
2:      $position \leftarrow 0$
3:      **for each** $shingle\_size$ shingle in $text$ **do**
4:          EMIT($shingle$, pair(doc_id, $position$))
5:          $position \leftarrow position + 1$

Parameter: min_count
Parameter: max_count ▷ Maximum bucket size
1: **method** REDUCE($shingle$, $[(doc\_id, i)]$)
2:      $shingle\_count \leftarrow$ count($[(doc\_id, index)]$)
3:      **if** ($min\_count \leq shingle\_count \leq max\_count$) **then**
4:          EMIT ($shingle$, $[(doc\_id, i)]$)

Stage 1: Shingle Table Generation. K&S begin by *shingling* each collection document, i.e. extracting sequential n-grams which overlap like roof shingles. For example, bigram shingling of "a man a plan" would yield three bigram shingles: "a man", "man a", and "a plan". For each observed shingle, a *bucket* is maintained tracking all (document ID, word position) pairs in which the shingle is seen to occur. The set of all observed shingles and their associated buckets defines the *shingle table*. Creating this table requires a single pass over the corpus, followed by a massive MapReduce sort for grouping bucket entries by shingle. To reduce the size of the shingle table, K&S describe two pruning optimizations:

1) discarding singleton shingles occurring only once in the collection (which cannot contribute to a match across multiple documents); 2) discarding very frequent shingles which would generate very large buckets (though the upper-limit they use is not specified). We adopt this shingle table generation process largely unmodified, although we do specify a more general lower-bound parameter for discarding rare shingles. A complete description of our shingle table generation process appears in Algorithm 2.

In the K&S approach, the bucket size upper-limit must be set aggressively to keep data small enough for practical processing in subsequent stages. While only the size of the output shingle table is affected at this stage, we shall describe the greater impact of bucket size on Stage 2 & 3.

As a final note on Stage 1 processing, an important point of Hadoop programming is not obvious from the canonical form of MapReduce pseudo-code shown in Algorithm 2: the Reducer does not actually load the entire bucket for a given shingle into memory. Instead, the Hadoop run-time provides an iteration mechanism to sequentially process each bucket entry one-at-a-time, avoiding this potential memory bottleneck. However, this raises the question of how we can implement an upper-limit constraint on bucket size shown in Line 2 of the Reducer.

The simplest, but memory-intensive, option is *Buffering*, which means retaining all bucket entries during iteration and only emitting entries after ensuring the upper-limit is not violated. The *Unbuffered* approach instead emits each bucket entry as we iterate but keeps count as we go. If the bucket size limit is ever violated, we record the shingle and ignore any subsequent bucket entries for it. After termination, we then go back and iterate over the list of recorded shingle IDs to prune them (and their associated buckets) from the shingle table. Such options are indicative of a common tradeoff in Hadoop programming. *Buffering* approaches are typically more efficient if the size of memory required is manageable; when data-intensive computing precludes this, however, we instead adopt an *Unbuffered* approaches. Between these extremes, one can alternatively specify a limited-size buffer and flush to disk whenever the buffer is filled. Since we assume a relatively large limit on bucket size, we do not buffer.

Algorithm 3 Stage 2: Grouping Shingles by Document

1: **method** MAP($shingle$, $[(doc\_id, i)]$)
2:      **for each** (doc_id, i) in $[(doc\_id, i)]$ **do**
3:          EMIT(doc_id, $(shingle, i)$)

1: **method** REDUCE(doc_id, $[(shingle, i)]$)   ▷ Identity
2:      EMIT (doc_id, $[(shingle, i)]$)

Stage 2: Grouping Shingles by Document. Our approach to Stage 2 marks a significant departure from that of K&S; we simply perform a trivial a re-sort of the shingle table by document ID. In contrast, K&S output the shingle buckets for every shingle occurring in every document. To give a simple example, assume we have D documents which each contain S unique shingles, where each shingle occurs in some constant fraction of the D total documents (i.e. has bucket size $\frac{D}{k}$, for some k). For the $D \times S$ shingles to be output, we must output a total of $\frac{D^2 \times S}{k}$ bucket entries. This quadratic number of bucket entries to output as a function of the collection size D can be problematic for scaling the method to realistic collection sizes.

At this stage, the challenge is I/O intensive rather than memory intensive, impacting the amount of intermediate and persistent data which must be transferred over the network, buffered to/from disk, written persistently (end of Stage 2), then redistributed by HDFS over the network and read-in for Stage 3. As mentioned, K&S implicitly address this issue by aggressively restricting maximum bucket size. By using only positional information from the buckets for Stage 3 matching, they also cleverly avoid having to output shingle strings. Because we do not output buckets, we instead do output the shingle strings for Stage 3 matching.

In either approach, document shingles must be sorted by position for sequential processing in Stage 3. As before, we encounter another Hadoop space vs. time tradeoff. We could simply perform this sort in-memory with *Buffering*, or we could instead utilize slower *secondary sorting* to let the Hadoop run-time perform this sorting for us [25]. While large limit on bucket size led us to avoid buffering before, here we can buffer because documents are relatively short. A complete description of our Stage 2 appears in Algorithm 3.

Algorithm 4 Stage 3: Common Phrases (CP) Detection

Parameter: max_gap_length
1: **method** MAP(doc_id, [($shingle$, i)])
2:    $cp \leftarrow$ first $shingle$
3:    $prev\_i \leftarrow$ first i
4:    **for each** ($shingle$, i) in rest of ($shingle$, i) **do**
5:       **if** $(i - prev\_i) \leq max\_gap\_length$ **then**
6:          $start = end - (i - prev\_i)$
7:          $cp \leftarrow cp + shingle_{start:shingle\_size}$
8:       **else**
9:          EMIT (cp, doc_id)
10:         $cp \leftarrow shingle$
11:       $prev\_i \leftarrow i$
12:    EMIT (cp, doc_id)

Parameter: min_doc_count
1: **method** REDUCE(cp, [doc_id])
2:    **if** (count([doc_id]) $\geq min\_doc\_count$) **then**
3:       EMIT (cp, [doc_id])

Stage 3: Common Phrase (CP) Detection. Stage 3, shown in Algorithm 4, marks a complete departure from the K&S approach [11]. Whereas they find phrase matches based on shingle buckets, we use shingle strings instead for scalability. Moreover, without aggressive bucket size filtering, large bucket sizes become a problem of memory as well as I/O in their Stage 3 since large buckets lead to large numbers of active alignments buffered while iterating over document shingles . Finally, they give a "free pass" to any shingle pruned by the bucket size limit; because this limit is set aggressively to reduce quadratic data growth, an increasing number of spurious alignments will be made.

Our Mapper effectively just concatenates consecutive shingles, giving our "free passes" only to shingle gaps of length at most max_gap_length. Because scalability of our method allows us to adopt a conservative upper-limit on bucket size, we do not encounter many gaps from pruning of frequent shingles. At the other extreme, whereas K&S only prune singleton shingles in Stage 1, we prune rare shingles occur-

ring less than min_count times (see Algorithm 2). However, singleton shingles always break phrases for K&S, even if the shingle is the only minor divergence from a longer alignment that ought to be captured. In contrast, our max_gap_length parameter allows us to preserve running phrases provided we do not miss too many shingles in a row, in which case such a gap is likely warranted anyway.

Whereas K&S find CPs by explicit sequence alignment across documents, we simply use the MapReduce sort phase to group together multiple occurrences of the same phrase. Because by default we find many CPs that are not interesting, we prune rare CPs (later ranking will further reduce this set). Buffering CPs in the reducer until the minimum threshold is met is trivial, after which we simply flush the buffer and emit all subsequent occurrences directly.

3.3 Common Phrase (CP) Ranking

As with the "popular passages" found by Kolak and Schilit (K&S) [11], the complete set of all CPs we find contains many phrases that are unlikely to be interesting to a reader. K&S perform ranking via a weighted geometric mean of length and frequency statistics. Our different social media data and usage context lead us to another formulation.

First and foremost, we are interested in developing a notion of information *source*, where multiple documents are agreed to originate from the same source. One challenge is conceptual: with news posts, for example, is the source an individual reporter, the reporter's local news organization, its umbrella corporation, or some other equivalence class we define over individuals or organizations. Another challenge is practical: how can we automatically infer this source (however source is defined), given the observable data? In this work, we make a simple assumption of treating each domain address as a unique source. For example, for a document with URL http://copiouschatter.blogspot.com/2009/02/grumpy-old-men.html, we take as source copiouschatter.blogspot.com. In general, a long tail of different URL naming patterns used by different social sites makes this a challenging mining problem [6].

For our context of usage, we want to rank some top set of CPs for each day to reveal to the reader. Unlike K&S, we do not use length statistics, but rather use a variant of TF-IDF style ranking. We use the number of unique sources the CP appears (S) and the number of documents (DF_{date}) for a given date, with an IDF-like effect from the number of documents across all dates in which the CP occurs (DF):

$$score_{date} = \frac{S \cdot DF_{date}}{DF} \qquad (2)$$

Algorithm 5 illustrates our MapReduce procedure of extracting daily top k common phrases from CPs.

An interesting tradeoff to explore in future work is use of greater Map-side local aggregation to reduce intermediate data [14]. In particular, since we only want to output the top k values per day, this is an associative and commutative operation for which we could potentially filter in the Mapper without any approximation to correctness. The problem is that the Mapper here uses CPs as keys rather than dates, so the Mapper would be required to buffer data over all collection dates; more importantly, distribution of CPs for the same date across Mappers loses the critical locality needed. Another MapReduce process would be needed to re-sort the CPs by date, potentially negating any subsequent savings.

Algorithm 5 Rank top-k Common Phrases (CPs)

1: **method** MAP(cp, [(doc_id, $source$)])
2:    Map[$date \mapsto source$] $sources \leftarrow \emptyset$
3:    Multiset $dates \leftarrow \emptyset$
4:    **for each** (doc_id, $source$) in [(doc_id, $source$)] **do**
5:       $dates.add(date(doc\_id))$
6:       $sources[date(doc\_id)].add(source)$
7:    Set $uniqdates \leftarrow set(dates)$
8:    $DF \leftarrow |dates|$
9:    **for each** $date$ in $uniqdates$ **do**
10:      $S_{date} \leftarrow |sources[date]|$
11:      **if** $S_{date} > 1$ **then**
12:        $DF_{date} \leftarrow |dates[date]|$
13:        EMIT ($date$, (cp, $score_{date}$))

Parameter: top_k
1: **method** REDUCE($date$, [(cp, ms)])
2:    $ranked\_cps \leftarrow sort([(cp, ms)]$ by $ms)$
3:    **for each** $i \in [1, top\_k]$ **do**
4:       EMIT ($date$, $ranked\_cps[i]$)

3.4 Common Phrase (CP) Clustering

Section 3.2 described how we find CPs at scale, while the previous section discussed how to filter out less interesting CPs. We now discuss how we cluster similar (unranked) CPs to form *memes*. Our approach here replaces the loosely-defined *grouping* phase of K&S with a well-specified method based on more standard clustering techniques.

In comparison to traditional clustering, our task is somewhat unusual. First, term vectors are far sparser vs. traditional document clustering since CPs are much shorter. Second, manual analysis suggests we are looking for many memes with few CPs, rather than a more traditional assigning of many examples to few clusters. We perform single-linkage hierarchical clustering [21] with cosine similarity:

$$cos(A, B) = \frac{\sum_{i=1}^{n} A_i B_i}{\sqrt{\sum_{i=1}^{n} A_i^2} \sqrt{\sum_{i=1}^{n} B_i^2}} \quad (3)$$

Terms in vectors A and B are weighted by standard TF-IDF in which the weight w of a term t in CP p is given by

$$w_{tp} = TF_{tp} \times \log \frac{N}{DF_t} \quad (4)$$

where TF denotes the frequency of term t in CP p, N denotes the total number of CPs, and DF denotes the number of CPs in which term t appears.

Like near-duplicate detection (Section 3.1), clustering is also naively an $O(n^2)$ problem, involving similarity comparisons between all pairs of CP vectors. In this case, we adopt a standard information retrieval (IR) approach of using inverted indexing to efficiently restrict similarity comparisons to only those vectors which share one or more common terms. Efficient inverted indexing with Hadoop has been described in depth elsewhere [14]. We also use the standard IR method of stopwords to reduce vocabulary for further efficiency, though the set of stopwords is determined via a parameter $p\_threshold$, where the stoplist = $\{w | \frac{f_w}{N} < p\_threshold\}$. Crucially, stopwords are excluded from the in-

dex but not the CPs; if at least one non-stopword is shared between vectors, then similarity will be computed over the complete vocabulary. We refer to our approach as Indexed Hierarchical Clustering with MapReduce (IHCMR).

The Mapper algorithm is shown in Algorithm 6. Initialization begins by reading in all CPs (cp) from a shared file and the inverted index. The set of CPs is partitioned such that each node receives a subset of input IDs as input for Map invocations, while all CPs are considered as candidates (via the inverted index) to which the inputs CP may be compared. Due to symmetry, the input CP is only compared to candidate CPs with larger IDs. For each non-stopword in the input CP, we lookup the postings list in the inverted index and entries to the candidate set. Finally, the set of candidates are evalated. Only if the cosine similarity is greater than a parameter $sim\_threshold$ will a key-value pair of (sim, ($cp1$, $cp2$)) be emitted, where sim denotes the cosine similarity, and $cp1$ and $cp2$ denote the CPs compared. If a CP does not have any match above this threshold, then $(0.0, cp1)$ is emitted instead (creating a singleton cluster).

Algorithm 6 Cluster Common Phrases (Mapper)

Parameter: $t \leftarrow similarity\_threshold$

1: $index \leftarrow$ read from disk   ▷ Inverted Index
2: $cp \leftarrow$ read from disk   ▷ Vector of Common Phrases

3: **method** MAP(id)   ▷ Common Phrase ID
4:    Set $candidates \leftarrow \emptyset$
5:    **for each** $w \in (cp[id] \cap index)$ **do**
6:       **for each** $(cand\_id < id) \in index[w]$ **do**
7:          $candidates.add(cand\_id)$
8:    **for each** $cand\_id \in candidates$ **do**
9:       $sim \leftarrow cos(cp[id], cp[cand\_id])$ ▷ Cosine Sim.
10:      $emit\_flag \leftarrow False$
11:      **if** $sim > t$ **then**
12:        EMIT(sim, ($cp[id]$, $cp[cand\_id]$))
13:        $emit\_flag \leftarrow True$
14:    **if** $emit\_flag = False$ **then**
15:       EMIT(0.0, ($cp[id]$, null))

The Reducer, shown in Algorithm 7, is initialized with an empty cluster list. While the sort phase between Map and Reduce stages cannonically provides only "group-by" functionality (i.e. grouping together values with the same keys prior to invoking the Reducer), we utilize Hadoop's ability to sort the (floating point) keys in decreasing order. The Reducer is then iteratively invoked on decreasing similarity values, adding and merging clusters as appropriate. Final clusters are emitted at Reducer termination.

4. CASE STUDY: ANALYZING BLOGS08

This section reports a case study for using our system to discover memes in a large collection of crawled blogs. We begin by describing the dataset, computing infrastructure, parameter settings, and pre-processing. We then report empirical results of processing efficiency (time and space).

Dataset. We utilize the TREC[4] BLOGS08 collection[5] of Web Logs (blogs) crawled from January 14, 2008 to February 10, 2009. 1.3 million RSS feeds were polled weekly during

---
[4] http://trec.nist.gov
[5] http://ir.dcs.gla.ac.uk/test_collections/blogs08info.html

Algorithm 7 Cluster Common Phrases (Reducer)
```
1:  cl_list ← ArrayList
2:  method REDUCE(sim, [(cp1, cp2)])
3:     if sim = 0.0 then
4:         Add cp1 to cl_list as a new cluster
5:     else
6:         if cp1 in cl_list and cp2 in cl_list then
7:             Merge clusters
8:         else if cp1 in cl_list then
9:             Add cp2 to cluster containing cp1
10:        else if cp2 in cl_list then
11:            Add cp1 to cluster containing cp2
12:        else
13:            Add new cluster(cp1, cp2) to cl_list

14: method CLOSE()
15:    EMIT(cl_list)
```

the period, and "permalink" documents (blog pages) were downloaded every two weeks. Each document includes all the components of a blog page as would be presented to a web browser. The collection consists of a total of 28,488,766 documents whose uncompressed size is 1445GB. Each document has a unique identifier and an associated crawl date. We have anecdotally observed differences of about 2-3 days between the crawl date and the posting date as indicated in the document text. At present, we simply use the crawl date for document dating; accuracy of dating could be further improved by either more frequent crawling or by extracting document dates from the text (e.g. via HeidelTime [22]).

Pre-processing. Because the BLOGS08 collection contains many non-English blog posts, advertisements, as well as HTML tags, we perform the following preprocessing to prepare documents for subsequent processing:

1. To extract meaningful content from a blog page (i.e. filtering out navigation links, advertisements, sidebar contents, and links to other sites), we apply Decruft, a Python implementation of ARC90's readability project[6].

2. To filter out non-English content, we utilize NLTK[7]'s language identification module.

3. For text analysis, HTML tags are removed with Beautiful Soup[8] and all text is converted to lowercase.

4. Short documents (fewer than five words) are removed

5. Documents are tokenized by words as follows (leading punctuation: ampersand, middle punctuation: back quote; final punctuation: apostrophe. "&" and ";" are included to preserve HTML entries such as "&" or ">." Aposrophe is used as a grammatical marker.

Compute Cluster. Experiments reported below were performed on a local Hadoop cluster at the Texas Advanced Computing Center[9] having 48 nodes, each having 8 2.53 GHz cores with 48GB RAM. When all 48 nodes are used, a total of 376 mappers and reducers can run simultaneously, using one Namenode and 47 Datanodes.

[6] http://www.minvolai.com/blog/decruft-arc90s-readability-in-python
[7] http://www.nltk.org
[8] http://www.crummy.com/software/BeautifulSoup
[9] http://www.tacc.utexas.edu

Parameter Settings. Table 1 lists our system parameters, the processing module in which each is used, and the parameter settings yielding the empirical results reported below. Current settings reflect heuristic tuning; our future work will investigate this parameter space in greater detail.

Process	Parameter	Value
Deduplication	$dsim\_threshold$	0.85
	$window\_size$	5
CP Finding: Stage 1	$shingle\_size$	5
	min_count	5
	max_count	225,000
CP Finding: Stage 3	min_doc_count	5
	max_gap_length	5
Ranking	top_k	200
Clustering	$p\_threshold$	0.01
	$sim\_threshold$	0.7

Table 1: System parameters and settings used.

Our parameters for $shingle\_size = 5$ and $min\_count = 5$ and $max\_count = 225,000$ differ from those of Kolak and Schilit (K&S) [11] (8, 1, and unspecified, respectively). While K&S were interested in finding long quotations in books, we are interested in shorter expressions such as "putting lipstick on a pig" and "the biggest financial fraud in history."

4.1 Processing Efficiency

Preprocessing. Initial filtering of extraneous page content and non-English posts significantly reduces collection size to 16,674,981 posts (totaling 96 GB). While HTML tags are filtered out for meme discovery, we do preserve tags for display in the Meme Browser (Section 5). HTML tag removal further reduces collection size to 47 GB.

Near-duplicate Detection (NDD). 1,577,525 documents (9.5%) were identified as near-duplicates, leaving 15,097,456 documents (43GB) after their removal. Unlike other experiments, NDD was performed early in our project using only a single 6-core server. With Hadoop pseudo-distributed mode, it required 6.5 days to complete. While this was sufficient for our proof-of-concept and could be further sped up via greater parallelism, our future work will instead pursue more efficient methods as discussed in Section 3.1.

Finding Common Phrases (CPs). Table 2 reports run time and volume of data generated by each MapReduce process in finding CPs. These results reflect use of 1 namenode and 17 datanodes, allowing 136 simultaneous mappers and reducers. A total of 5,631,742 CPs were found.

Stage	Mappers	Reducers	Time	Output
Stage 1	867	270	23:49	56GB
Stage 2	954	364	9:18	95GB
Stage 3	1786	364	4:03	2.0GB

Table 2: The total running time, number of mappers and reducers used, and size of output data generated by each MapReduce process in CP Finding.

Our lower-bound shingle frequency parameter $min\_count = 5$ for Stage 1 was quite aggressive, filtering out the vast majority of shingles observed (4,608,276,420, accounting for 98.27% of all shingles). In contrast, our upper-bound parameter of $max\_count = 225,000$ was very conservative and had very limited impact on performance. We plan to explore the tradeoff of more moderate settings in future work. After filtering, a total of 81,099,356 shingles remained. Stage 3 produces a total of 6,224,087 CPs.

Common Phrase (CP) Ranking. From the top 200 daily CPs, we gathered 75,039 unique phrases. The MapReduce process took 2 minutes and 51 seconds on a cluster of 18 nodes capable of 136 simultaneous mappers and reducers. Our job used 480 Mappers and 86 Reducers, and 6.2 million common phrases (2.0 GB) were processed.

Trial	Indexed	# Cores	Time
WEKA	-	1	> 96 hours
IHCMR	no	1	10:59:11
IHCMR	no	136	33:43
IHCMR	yes	1	16:20
IHCMR	yes	136	2:51

Table 3: Performance of alternative hierarchical clustering approaches for meme generation.

Common Phrase Clustering. Savings shown include:

1. Without indexing, our sparse vector representation over WEKA's off-the-shelf clustering using single core: from > 96 hours down to 11 hours

2. Indexed vs. unindexed: from 11 hours to 16 minutes (single core), from 34 to 3 minutes (136 cores)

3. Distributed vs. single core: from 11 hours to 34 minutes (unindexed) to 16 minutes to 3 minutes (indexed)

IHCMR is optimized to process extremely sparse data. The average length of the extracted common phrases is only 6.08 words while the vector space includes 28,694 words. When the dataset is converted into Attribute-Relation File Format (ARFF), 2.4MB of meme list data becomes 11GB in dense matrix ARFF, and 8.5MB in sparse matrix ARFF. We first tried to use WEKA COBWEB Hierarchical Clustering[10] with default settings. 2.5GB of memory was assigned to WEKA, and the clustering was run on a single processor at 2.67GHz. WEKA took more than 96 hours to finish the clustering. WEKA generates and processes the full dense matrix even from the sparse ARFF input, thus while WEKA compares the vectors of 28,694 dimensions, IHCMR compares the vectors of 6.08 dimensions in average.

Indexing and stopword removal. As discussed earlier, terms occurring more that 1% ($p\_threshold$) of documents are not indexed (a total of 60 terms). Indexing and stopword removal reduce comparisons to only 411.78 per CP on average ($\sigma = 441.25$, range $[0 - 10, 996]$ out of 75,034 phrases).

5. MEME BROWSER

As a first step toward our larger vision of enabling people to achieve greater critical literacy via technological assistance, we have designed a prototype *Meme Browser* for viewing and exploring detected memes in context. By visibly displaying underlying memes, readers become explicitly aware of their presence and have an opportunity to investigate them and the connections they reveal between sources. In addition to supporting critical literacy, the browser also

---

[10]http://www.cs.waikato.ac.nz/ml/weka

allows readers to explore how such memes develop and propagate across sources and time. The browser serves both a casual reader, with limited time for independently finding reading many sources for connections, as well as a more motivated reader, who requires technological assistance to cope with the vast scale of diverse information sources today.

The Meme Browser (Figure 1) accesses collection documents via a `DocID` index, and an Apache-PHP-MySQL server provides database access to discovered memes. The browser interface is written in PHP with CSS, Javascript, and jQuery used for layout and dynamic presentation.

The Meme Browser's interface layout is informed by prior eye-tracking studies for faceted browsers and sponsored search results, which have shown typical heat-map distributions of user attention focused on top and left with exponential decay moving down and right [16]. Recall that a *common phrase* (CP) is any (unfiltered) phrase found in multiple documents, while a *meme* clusters similar CPs. The Browser's state maintains at all times an Active CP (ACP) and associated Active Meme (AM), for which relevant information is shown. We describe each component in detail below.

Timeline Navigator. At top, the Timeline Navigator 1) indicates the date of the current document being read; 2) shows the temporal profile of mentions of the AM and 3) supports access and navigation to top memes on other days.

If the mouse cursor hovers over the dateline, the date below the cursor is shown to assist in correct date selection. A click on the timeline reveals a pop-up display showing a *Top 10 Memes of* `<DATE>` listing, from which the user may then select a given meme. The selected meme then becomes the AM, a representative ACP for the AM selected, and a representative document for that day is opened.

Content Pane. Below the Timeline Navigator, the Content Pane 1) highlights a specific ACP for the AM in the context of the the current document; and 2) marks in gray any other highly-ranked memes present in the document. A new AM may be selected at any time.

The Content Pane displays the document (with its original formatting and layout) and any CPs found in it. The five most common CPs in the document are visibly marked to provide the user with multiple avenues for exploration. Any CPs other than the ACP are marked in a lighter gray color, which visibly indicates their presence while preserving the ACP as the primary focus. If the user has arrived at the document via a meme of CP-based navigation, the selected CP becomes the ACP and the document is automatically scrolled to vertically center the ACP and its surrounding context. If the user arrived at the document via traditional document-based navigation, then the document view opens at the beginning of the document. In this case, the first-occurring CP in the document is selected as the ACP, though it may not be visible until it is scrolled into view during the course of reading the document. If the user hovers the mouse cursor over the ACP, a pop-up window invites feedback on the ACP, similar to the *Feedback Widget* (see below).

Faceted Browsing Pane. Along the left side of the interface, the Faceted Browsing Pane provides information and navigation links relevant to the ACP and AM. From top to bottom, the following panes are provided:

- **Phrase** shows the Active Common Phrase (ACP).
- **Other Mentions (Same Source)** lists other (dated) documents from the same source which also contain the ACP. This allows the user to quickly assess the

level of association between source and phrase. Navigation via this list demonstrates how the phrase context changes (or stays the same) over time.

- **Other Mentions (General)** takes a slightly broader approach, giving the user a list of other sources that also mention the ACP. Using this list, one can make several rough determinations of relationships across sources by looking at the dates in which they mention the same phrase. For example, if *Source A* mentions a meme and it consistently appears in the documents of *Source B* afterwards then the user may decide that the former "feeds" the latter information. Similarly, if different memes appear first in one source and then another, the relationship may be more bidirectional.

- **Meme Related Phrases** shows a different relationship than that between sources. Here, the focus is on the cluster of phrases itself. The selector displays a list of phrases that are similar to the ACP, along with when they first appear in the collection. Again, the user is able to quickly develop a rough idea of how the cluster of related phrases has evolved, particularly how the the meme text appeared and changed over time.

- **Memes of the Day** focuses less on relationships between sources and phrases and more on time and popularity. The selector shows a list of the 10 most frequently mentioned phrases on the same day of the viewed ACP. This list serves more as a "pulse" of the news by providing a snapshot of the topics that were trending on a given day. The user is able to jump to any of the most popular phrases and immediately see their relationships across sources and related phrases.

Feedback Widget. At bottom, a *Feedback Widget* invites user feedback on meme quality to collect labels for training and evaluation. It is located directly below the *Timeline Navigator* and above the *Content Pane*. Inspired by volunteer-based crowdsourcing approaches [3], it collects feedback on the quality and nature of discovered memes, generating "gold" labels to evaluate accuracy of discovered memes and training data for further improving this accuracy. A second benefit is making explicit to the reader that automation is imperfect, and that the quality and usefulness of detected memes should be critically assessed as should anything being read. The widget also promotes greater reader engagement through increased interaction.

To alert the reader to the Widget and invite their participation, a simple question asks, *Does the highlighted phrase reveal an interesting connection between the sources mentioning it?* Simple "Thumbs Up" and "Thumbs Down" icons fun, easy interaction. On clicking either button, a pop-up window offers thanks and invites the reader to answer one further question (shown in Figure 3). Prior work has shown the benefit of designing for such staged feedback [10].

Because the definition and nature of memes requires careful explanation, the questions asked in Figure 3 reflect careful scrutiny of (correct and incorrect) memes identified by our system, as well as iterative revision, in order to provide annotators with clear guidelines for data labeling (e.g. to distinguish near-duplicate documents erroneous missed in earlier process vs. memes occurring in distinct documents). In addition to inviting readers to provide such feedback, our future work will also investigate use of Amazon Mechanical Turk to perform pay-based annotation work [18].

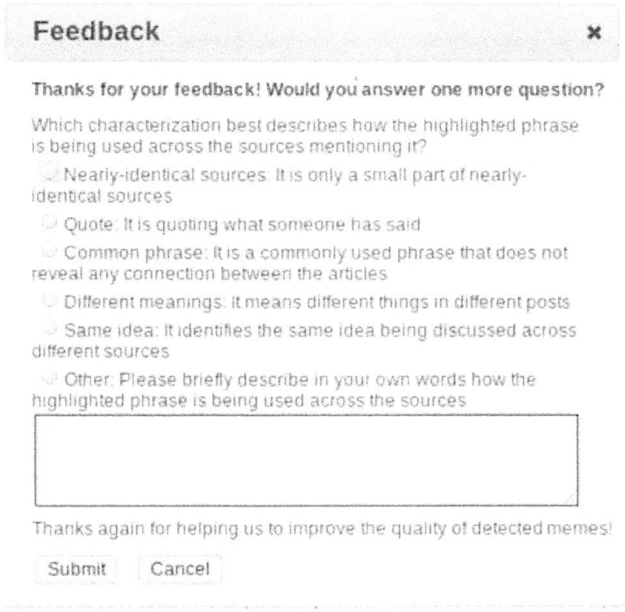

Figure 3: Whenever the Feedback Widget is used to provide yes/no feedback on meme quality, a pop-up dialog offers thanks and invites the reader to answer one further question.

6. RELATED WORK

Leskovec et al. [12] detect and analyze reuse of quotations online, but they do not address cases of text reuse beyond quotations (e.g. how shared experience of contemporary events can lead to to reuse of common phrases). Kolak and Schilit [11] mine full texts in entirety, but their approach was focused on scanned books, reflecting a different task and usage scenario. Plagiarism detection [4] is clearly related, though tends to focus on classifying documents rather than identifying and exploring examples of reuse. Somewhat farther afield, multiple sequence alignment methods from computational biology [17] may also be used to align variant phrases, though again our problem context and data differ.

Seo and Croft[20] detect local text reuse across newswire and blogs by breaking documents into sequences of words and measuring the frequency of shared phrases. Their DCT fingerprinting approach appears to be especially robust against small word variations within phrases, and they also exploit the idea that less common components are more important than higher frequency components. They show that DCT fingerprinting is both effective and efficient on blog data.

Kolak and Schilit [11]'s work, as our own, is made possible by the MapReduce framework was pioneered at Google in 2004 for effectively processing massive amounts of data using distributed computing, i.e. *data-intensive* computing [7]. MapReduce is designed to distribute data and computational tasks across a cluster of computers that all work simultaneously. Google's MapReduce architecture uses its proprietary distributed GoogleFS filesystem to replicate data in chunks across multiple computers and distribute it for locality of computation, bringing computation to the data as much as possible. The model is ideal for some forms of computation which can be divided into individual units that operate largely independently, unlike alternative message-passing approaches supporting greater synchronization.

Hadoop is an open-source Java implementation of the MapReduce programming model that operates on the Hadoop Distributed File System (HDFS) [25]. Inspired by similar work at Google, Hadoop offers developers a framework for parallel computation of large-scale data analysis. As an open-source system, Hadoop has gained tremendous popularity across industry and research environments in recent years, especially as "big data" grows even bigger and more common every day. As more researchers and practioners have begun working with Hadoop, there has been increased interest in developing and disseminating effective design patterns for efficient and easier data-intensive programming [14].

7. CONCLUSION AND FUTURE WORK

The question of how to effectively find relevant information has driven decades of information retrieval (IR) research. Relatively less attention has been directed toward helping people to more easily and effectively contextualize, interpret, assess information once it is found. The scale of information overload today threatens effective sense-making as well search. More research is needed to develop effective technologies for helping us better analyze and evaluate what we read, e.g. to support critical decision making.

As a modest step in this direction, we utilized MapReduce (Hadoop) and IR methods to identify and rank informative memes in a large-scale blog collection. These memes can then be browsed and explored in context via our *Meme Browser*. In future work, we are particularly interested in tracking and letting the user interactively explore how similar phrases in a meme cluster evolve over time, as well as showing the individuals and communities involved in disseminating, altering, and responding to memes. Readers should be able to see how sources follow others in using the same meme, or memes that commonly appear together. By recognizing inter-connection of sources through common meme flow patterns, we can become more critical readers.

8. ACKNOWLEDGMENTS

We thank the anonymous reviewers and Luis Francisco-Revilla for their valuable feedback. Prateek Maheshwari contributed to our literature review. This work was partially supported by Science and Technology Foundation of Portugal (FCT) grant UTA Est/MAI/0006/2009, a John P. Commons fellowship, a Longhorn Innovation Fund for Technology (LIFT) award, and Amazon Web Services. Any opinions, findings, conclusions or recommendations expressed in this material are those of the authors and do not necessarily reflect the views of their institution or funding agencies.

9. REFERENCES

[1] R. Barzilay and L. Lee. Learning to paraphrase: An unsupervised approach using multiple-sequence alignment. In *Proc. NAACL HLT*, pages 16–23, 2003.

[2] M. Bernstein. On Hypertext Narrative. In *HyperText*, pages 5–14, 2009.

[3] A. Brew, D. Greene, and P. Cunningham. Using crowdsourcing and active learning to track sentiment in online media. In *ECAI 2010*, pages 145–150, 2010.

[4] S. Eissen and B. Stein. Intrinsic plagiarism detection. *Advances in Info. Retrieval*, pages 565–569, 2006.

[5] R. Ennals, B. Trushkowsky, and J. Agosta. Highlighting disputed claims on the web. In *Proc. of WWW*, pages 341–350, 2010.

[6] G. Forman, E. Kirshenbaum, and S. Rajaram. A novel traffic analysis for identifying search fields in the long tail of web sites. In *WWW*, pages 361–370, 2010.

[7] S. Ghemawat and J. Dean. Mapreduce: Simplified data processing on large clusters. In *Proc. of OSDI*, pages 137–149, 2004.

[8] A. Gionis, P. Indyk, and R. Motwani. Similarity search in high dimensions via hashing. In *Proc. of VLDB 1999*, pages 518–529, 1999.

[9] M. A. Hearst. Emerging trends in search user interfaces. In *Proc. HyperText*, pages 5–6, 2011.

[10] R. Kohavi, R. Longbotham, D. Sommerfield, and R. Henne. Controlled experiments on the web: survey and practical guide. *Data Mining and Knowledge Discovery*, 18(1):140–181, 2009.

[11] O. Kolak and B. N. Schilit. Generating links by mining quotations. *HyperText*, pages 117–126, 2008.

[12] J. Leskovec, L. Backstrom, and J. Kleinberg. Meme-tracking and the dynamics of the news cycle. *Proc. of ACM SIGKDD '09*, page 497, 2009.

[13] J. Lin. Brute force and indexed approaches to pairwise document similarity comparisons with mapreduce. In *Proceedings of ACM SIGIR*, pages 155–162, 2009.

[14] J. Lin and C. Dyer. Data-intensive text processing with mapreduce. *Synthesis Lectures on Human Language Technologies*, 3(1):1–177, 2010.

[15] S. Moulthrop. What The Geeks Know: Hypertext and the problem of literacy. In *Proceedings of ACM HyperText*, pages 227–231, 2005.

[16] V. Navalpakkam, J. Rao, and M. Slaney. Using gaze patterns to study and predict reading struggles due to distraction. In *ACM CHI*, pages 1705–1710, 2011.

[17] C. Notredame. Recent evolutions of multiple sequence alignment algorithms. *PLoS computational biology*, 3(8):1405–1408, Aug. 2007.

[18] H. Ryu and M. Lease. Crowdworker Filtering with Support Vector Machine. In *Proc. ASIS&T*, 2011.

[19] B. N. Schilit and O. Kolak. Exploring a digital library through key ideas. In *JCDL*, pages 177–186, 2008.

[20] J. Seo and W. Croft. Local text reuse detection. In *Proc. of ACM SIGIR*, pages 571–578. ACM, 2008.

[21] R. Sibson. SLINK: an optimally efficient algorithm for the single-link cluster method. *The Computer Journal*, 16(1):30–34, 1973.

[22] J. Strötgen and M. Gertz. HeidelTime: High quality rule-based extraction and normalization of temporal expressions. In *SemEval*, pages 321–324, July 2010.

[23] M. Theobald, J. Siddharth, and A. Paepcke. Spotsigs: robust and efficient near duplicate detection in large web collections. In *SIGIR*, pages 563–570, 2008.

[24] J. Valenza. Web 2.0 meets information fluency: Evaluating blogs, 2010. January 20.
`http://21cif.com/rkitp/assessment/v1n5/valenza1.5_blogeval.html`.

[25] T. White. *Hadoop: The Definitive Guide*. O'Reilly Media, Inc., 2nd edition, 2010.

On the Rise of Artificial Trending Topics in Twitter

[Extended Abstract]

Raquel Recuero
UCPel
Rua Goncalves Chaves, 373
Pelotas - RS - Brazil
raquel@raquelrecuero.com

Ricardo Araújo
UFPel
Rua Gomes Carneiro, 1
Pelotas - RS - Brazil
ricardo.araujo@gmail.com

ABSTRACT

We present a quanti-qualitative research about Trending Topics in Twitter. Our goal was to investigate how social networks can interfere in Trending Topics seeking for visibility and based on social capital, using bridging and bonding ties. We collected, analyzed and classified 460 topics from the Brazilian Trending Topics' List and the social networks associated to 40 of those. Our results point to two types of topics: artificial topics, created by groups of users consciously acting to put their message among the Trending Topics, usually to make statements and gain visibility to their causes; and organic topics, which emerge without effortful coordination by a group of people. While organic topics rely on values such as novelty and spread through bridging ties, artificial topics are based on bonding ties, with associated values such as engagement, cooperation and trust among the actors.

Categories and Subject Descriptors

J.4 [**Social and Behavioral Sciences**]: Sociology

General Terms

Human Factors

Keywords

Trending Topics, Twitter, Social Capital, Social Networks

1. INTRODUCTION

We report on an analysis of Twitter's [4] *Trending Topics*, a feature that automatically detects and emphasizes topics that are worth noting from the public stream of tweets. Since topics that appear in this list are seen by a large audience, there might be an incentive for users to try and find ways to manipulate the list, showing topics that are only of interest to a small group of users.

In this paper, we test this hypothesis, showing that indeed there are evidences of the creation of such Artificial Trending Topics. We further show characteristics of the social networks behind this type of trending topic, comparing to topics that are more organic in nature. We show that the social networks associated to each type of trending topic

have unique features that may allow for the automatic identification of such manipulations.

To test our hypothesis, we collected a sample of 460 Trending Topics, between November 2011 and January 2012. These topics were collected from Twitter's list of Brazil's Trending Topics, by manually inspecting them over the specified period of time. We didn't explicitly make a distinction between, or filtered for, topics that trended for a longer or shorter time. Nonetheless, topics that stayed in the list for a longer time (i.e. "trended" more strongly) had a higher probability of being spotted and included in the set using our methodology.

For each topic, we observed users' interactions behind it over time, collecting tweets containing that topic. By qualitatively analyzing the interactions, we concluded that there are two strikingly different types of trending topics, those that arise organically and those that are artificially inflated to make it to the trending topics (we discuss our reasoning in the next section). We then further gathered data on the social network of the users behind each collected tweet, for 20 organic topics and 20 artificial ones, extracting features of each network and relating them to the the type of topic behind it. This data was collected using NodeXL and contained users and their relations.

2. RESULTS

2.1 Artificial and Organic Trending Topics

By analyzing the textual content of tweets behind each topic, it became clear that for some topics users behind them were actively trying to make the topic "trend", creating an **Artificial Trending Topic**. These users were typically part of some community and often part of *fandoms* [1]. Two strategies could be devised from their interactions. The first was to actively ask followers to talk about the topic and use the chosen hashtag or some specific combination of words and retweet their tweets. The second strategy was to include the hashtag or words in any tweet written, in any context.

Users would incentivize followers to talk about the topic by explicitly mentioning that they wanted to make it to trending topics, but often this was not necessary as the community was already organized and understood what they were trying to accomplish. Hence, most of the time all that was needed was for some user to ask others to use some specific set of words. A common observed practice was for users to specify some period of the day where they would use the topic in their tweets. For example: "Use the words 'We need Lovato back' starting tomorrow 3pm!

Spread among lovactics!". Some tweets would even include advices to supposedly elude Twitter's spam detection algorithms (e.g. "Guys, don't forget to not tweet only the tag or you will get caught!"). These rules seem to have been devised from trial and error, rather than some knowledge of Twitter's inner workings.

Getting many users to talk about the topic was only part of the strategy. Since only a limited number of users would respond to their call to action, mostly those part of their community, they had to compensate with a greater volume of tweets per user. This was attained by having the community use the topic in all of their tweets in a given period of time. The common use for hashtags, for instance, is to summarize or characterize what the tweet is about. However, users acting to artificially trend a topic would use a specific hashtag in all of their tweets, independent of the context or content of the tweet. For an example of this strategy, one hashtag that trended was "BrasilComSaudadesdoLuanS" (which translates to "Brazil misses LuanS", where LuanS is a short name for a popular singer); users would then proceed to use this hashtag, rendering tweets such as "I'll be right back! BrasilComSaudadesdoLuanS" or "Just had my lunch. It was so good. BrasilComSaudadesdoLuanS".

The effect of these two strategies was the ability of these communities to quickly impose a topic of their choice on the trending topics list. Some communities became so good in artificially trending topics that, at times, we also witnessed battles between two communities to see who could make their topic trend higher.

In contrast, **Organic Trending Topics** did not exhibit any of these interactions. Users used these topic in a very specific context and many users would mention the topic only a few times. There were no signs of community or the presence of users incentivizing others to talk about these topics.

2.2 Features of Trending Topic Types

According to the type of interaction present, we marked each of the 460 topics as Artificial or Organic. We classified as Artificial any topic that showed signs of the above strategies and Organic otherwise.

We found that 60% (276) topics were being artificially created, while only 40% (184) could be considered organic. We further classified topics by themes; organic topics were mostly internet memes (38%), about events (38%) or about personalities, such as musicians and actors (24%). Artificial topics, on the other hand, were mostly about personalities (87.6%), with a small share being about protests (4.3%) or marketing promotions (4.3%). Therefore, fandoms around some personality (mostly musicians) seem to be the most responsible for artificial trending topics.

By analyzing the social networks behind each type of trending topic, some trends became evident. Artificial topics exhibited much more dense and clustered networks (9.3 edges/node, clustering coefficient = 0.219) than organic topics (2.24 edges/node, clustering coefficient = 0.081). The in-degree of networks behind artificial trending topics was found to be on average much higher (9.46) than in the organic case (2.10). These are evidences that artificial trending topics benefit from having a tight community behind them, as is the case with fandoms.

The average number of tweets per node in networks behind

artificial topics was found to be much higher (12.8) than in organic topics (4.2). This is due to artificial topic networks having about 50% less nodes than organic topic networks and producing almost twice as many tweets on average. This corroborates our observation that users would include the topic even when tweeting about something else.

2.3 Motivations and Social Capital

The Trending Topics list seems to be highly valued by some users as a place where they can gain visibility and promote their views. Since the Trending Topics list allows only 10 topics, it is difficult to get in it, making it a very scarce resource that becomes highly valuable due to its visibility. This is the value users seem to seek when they cooperate to artificially trend a topic.

Artificial topics can be seen as a form of collective action, where the social network cooperates to reach benefits and resources that are harder to achieve without this cooperation. Artificial topics seem to rely on *bonding ties* [6], since these networks activate fewer nodes, requiring more engagement and cooperation to achieve their goals. These networks are based on mutual identification with some cause. People work together because they share the same values and the same vision. As Burt [2] and Lin [5] argued, homophily is a characteristic associated with bonding rather than bridging ties.

Organic topics, on the other hand, seem to travel through bridging ties [6]. Rather than being represented by an organized movement to reach visibility, they emerge from discussions and conversations about events, personalities and memes. They don't need users to cooperate. The value of propagating a topic is connected to the novelty and the hotness of the topic rather than a statement made by a group. Organic topics are more naturally related to the essence of how we believe Twitter perceives Trending Topics. Thus, information here is the type of social capital [3], rather than cooperation and engagement.

While artificial trending topics are a group strategy to obtain resources in a war for visibility and attention, organic trending topics are not. However, our research shows that artificially created topics are, quite often, winning over the Trending Topic's list from organic topics. More and more artificial topics are becoming a central part of the list, sometimes eradicating topics that are actually trending among a larger population.

3. REFERENCES

[1] N. K. Baym. The new shape of online community: The example of swedish independent music fandom. *First Monday*, 12(8), 2007.

[2] R. Burt. *Structural Holes: The Social Structure of Competition*. Harvard University Press, 1995.

[3] J. S. Coleman. Social capital and the creation of human capital. *American Journal of Sociology*, 94:S95–S120, 1988.

[4] B. A. Huberman, D. M. Romero, and F. Wu. Social networks that matter: Twitter under the microscope. *First Monday*, 14(1), January 2009.

[5] N. Lin. *Social Capital: A Theory of Social Structure and Action*. Cambridge University Press, 2002.

[6] R. D. Putnam. E pluribus unum: Diversity and community in the twenty-first century. *Scandinavian Political Studies*, 30(2), June 2007.

QualityRank: Assessing Quality of Wikipedia Articles by Mutually Evaluating Editors and Texts

Yu Suzuki
Information Technology Center, Nagoya University
Furo, Chikusa, Nagoya
Aichi 4648601, Japan
suzuki@db.itc.nagoya-u.ac.jp

Masatoshi Yoshikawa
Graduate School of Informatics, Kyoto University
Yoshida Honmachi, Sakyo, Kyoto
Kyoto 6068501, Japan
yoshikawa@i.kyoto-u.ac.jp

ABSTRACT

In this paper, we propose a method to identify high-quality Wikipedia articles by mutually evaluating editors and texts. A major approach for assessing articles using edit history is a text survival ratio based approach. However, the problem is that many high-quality articles are identified as low quality, because many vandals delete high-quality texts, then the survival ratios of high-quality texts are decreased by vandals. Our approach's strongest point is its resistance to vandalism. Using our method, if we calculate text quality values using editor quality values, vandals do not affect any quality values of the other editors, then the accuracy of text quality values should improve. However, the problem is that editor quality values are calculated by text quality values, and text quality values are calculated by editor quality values. To solve this problem, we mutually calculate editor and text quality values until they converge. Using this method, we can calculate a quality value of a text that takes into consideration that of its editors. From experimental evaluation, we confirmed that the proposed method can improve the accuracy of quality values for articles.

Categories and Subject Descriptors

H.1.2 [**Models and Principles**]: User/Machine Systems

Keywords

Quality, Peer Review, Edit History, Link Analysis

1. INTRODUCTION

Wikipedia is one of the most successful and well-known User Generated Content (UGC) websites. However, a dramatic increase in the number of editors causes an increase in the number of low-quality articles. Therefore, automatic or semi-automatic systems should be developed to identify which parts of articles are high-quality and which are not.

If editors find low-quality texts, the editors reject and delete them. This means that if a text survives beyond

multiple edits by the other editors, the text should be high-quality. Therefore, using the *survival ratio* of texts, the system calculates the quality value of a text.

However, the problem is that many high-quality articles are identified as low-quality, because they assume all editors delete only low-quality texts. In this paper, we propose a method for mutually calculating quality values of texts using both survival ratios of texts and quality degrees of editors who delete the texts. We assume that vandals rarely submit high-quality texts, whereas high-quality editors frequently submit high-quality texts. We define an editor quality value as the average quality value of the text written by the editor.

Text quality values are calculated on the basis of editor quality values. In short, one quality value is calculated by another quality value. Therefore, it is hard to calculate the quality value of a text by using those of its editors. To solve this problem, we first set an editor quality value as a constant value and calculate a text quality value. Next, we calculate the quality value of an editor by using those of his/her texts. Again, we calculate the quality value of a text by using those of its editors. In this way, we repeatedly calculate editor and text quality values. Using this method, we can calculate a quality value of a text that takes into consideration that of its editors.

2. RELATED WORK

Adler et al. [1], Hu et al. [2], and Wilkinson et al. [3] proposed a method for calculating quality values from edit histories. This method is based on survival ratios of texts. However, these authors did not consider editor quality values. Thus, if vandals delete articles frequently, the quality values of deleted texts decrease, and so the system cannot calculate appropriate quality values. In addition, this method cannot calculate the quality values for new, up-to-date texts. In our method, we use editor quality values as well as text quality values. Therefore, we can calculate quality values for new texts by using the quality values of editors of the text.

3. PROPOSED METHOD

Our key idea is that we adjust text quality values by using editor quality values. We assume that vandals rarely write high-quality texts, so their quality values should be low. Therefore, if an editor deletes a text and has a low quality value, we adjust the decreased survival ratio of this text so that it increases, because this deletion should be considered inappropriate. However, if the editor's quality is high, we do not adjust the survival ratio of a text, because

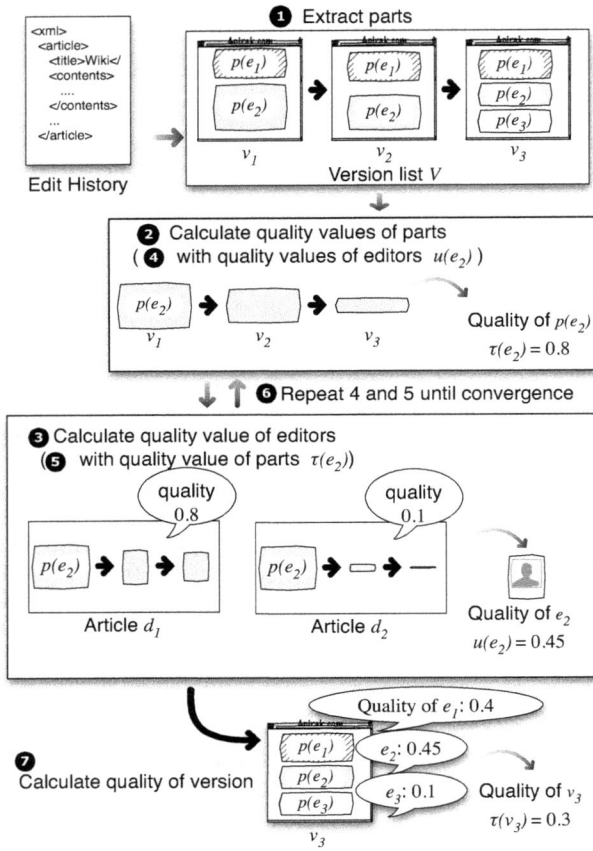

Figure 1: Overview of our proposed method.

this deletion should be considered appropriate. In this way, when we calculate text quality values, we use not only survival ratios of the text but use the quality values of editors who delete the text. By using our proposed method, the accuracy of text quality values should improve.

Figure 1 shows the overview of calculating quality value. We calculate the quality values of parts using quality values of editors at the step of (4) in Figure 1. In this phase, we integrate the survival ratio of parts and those of the editors who delete them using weighted summation, whereas the initial quality value calculation method only use the survival ratio of parts.

We calculate the quality value $\tau_k(e)$ of part $p(e)$ as follows:

$$\tau_k(e) = \alpha \cdot \tau_0(e) - (1 - \alpha) \cdot \sum_{e' \in E'} u'_{k-1}(e')|\delta(e')| \quad (1)$$

$$\tau_0(e) = \sum_{p(e) \in \bar{P}} \log_2(|p(e)| + 1) \quad (2)$$

where $\tau_0(e)$ is an initial quality value of a part $p(e)$ added by the editor e, E' is a set of editors who delete $p(e)$, $\delta(e')$ is the letters in $p(e)$ deleted by e', $|\delta(e')|$ is the number of letters in $\delta(e')$, and α ($0 < \alpha \leq 1$) is the parameter to control the effect of editor quality value. The first part of this expression means the initial part quality values using raw survival ratio based method, and the second part of this expression means the number of deleted letters with

quality values of editors who delete them. If an editor who has a low-quality value deletes a part $p(e)$, then the value of the second expression is high, then the value of $\tau_k(e)$ is almost the same as $\tau_{k-1}(e)$. Therefore, the editor quality value does not affect the part quality value. In this case, if the editor who deletes the part has a high-quality value, the second expression has a high value. Thus, the value of $\tau_k(e)$ decreases more than $\tau_{k-1}(e)$.

At step 5. of Figure 1, we calculate the quality values of editor as the average value of the part quality values which are edited by the editor. Then, we normalize $u_k(e)$ to range between 0 and 1. Using these equations, we mutually calculate editor quality values and part quality values until converge.

Our proposed method is resistant to vandalism. The behavior of vandals, such as inappropriately adding and deleting high-quality texts, is not permitted by the other editors, so many non-vandal editors try to counter the behavior of vandals. In our proposed system, if the behavior of an editor is permitted by the other editors, the quality value of the editor increase. As a result, vandals do not affect the quality values of the other editors.

4. CONCLUSION

Wikipedia is the most popular and highest quality encyclopedia to be created by many editors. The information on Wikipedia keeps expanding, but its quality is not proportional to its quantity. In this paper, we propose a method to identify high-quality articles mutually evaluating editors and text to improve the accuracy of quality values of versions.

This editor quality value is not always distinct because the frequency of editing is different for each editor. We suppose that if an editor rarely edits articles, the editor may just happen to obtain a high quality value, but vagueness of the editor quality value should be high. Therefore, we should develop a method to calculate vagueness of editor quality values that does not depend on editor quality value.

5. ACKNOWLEDGMENTS

This work was partially supported by Japan Society for the Promotion of Science, Grants-in-Aid for Scientific Research (20300036, 23700113).

6. REFERENCES

[1] B.T. Adler, K. Chatterjee, L. de Alfaro, M. Faella, I. Pye, and V. Raman. Measuting Author Contributions to the Wikipedia. In *Procee ings of the International Symposium on   i is   i iSym* , 2008.

[2] M. Hu, E. Lim, A. Sun, H. W. Lauw, and B. Vuong. Measuring Article Quality in Wikipedia: Models and Evaluation. In *Procee ings of ACM International Conference on Information an Kno le ge Management CIKM   7* , pages 243–252, 2007.

[3] D. M. Wilkinson and B. A. Huberman. Cooperation and quality in wikipedia. In *Procee ings of the   7 international symposium on   i is   i iSym 7* , pages 157–164. ACM, 2007.

A Real-Time Architecture for Detection of Diseases using Social Networks: Design, Implementation and Evaluation

Mustafa Sofean
University of Hannover
Schlosswender Str. 5
Hannover, Germany
sofean@dcsec.uni-hannover.de

Matthew Smith
University of Hannover
Schlosswender Str. 5
Hannover, Germany
smith@dcsec.uni-hannover.de

ABSTRACT

In this work we developed a surveillance architecture to detect diseases-related postings in social networks using Twitter as an example for a high-traffic social network. Our real-time architecture uses Twitter streaming API to crawl Twitter messages as they are posted. Data mining techniques have been used to index, extract and classify postings. Finally, we evaluate the performance of the classifier with a dataset of public health postings and also evaluate the run-time performance of whole system with respect to latency and throughput.

Categories and Subject Descriptors

H.3.3 [**Information search and Retrieval**]: Information filtering

General Terms

Design, Experimentation, Performance, Data Mining

Keywords

Disease Surveillance, Twitter, Real Time Search

1. INTRODUCTION

Recently, the big challenge for detecting diseases using social networks is how to deal with a huge amount of messages which are generated every day and how to get more discriminative data. Sophisticated filtering methods are required to identify relevant postings. Due to the characteristics of social networks, they are extremely important to become integral to public health surveillance. Previous work such as Culotta [2], Lampos and Cristianini [3] or Paul and Dredze [4] studied the possibility of detecting disease outbreaks by Twitter. People in social networks can connect with family and friends, share or get information and write about their feeling and diseases. Therefore, we want to develop a real-time architecture which collects pure disease-related postings. In more details, we focus on the tracking status updates of people and identify if they are disease-reportings. This includes all disease postings where people report about symptoms, claim that they have a certain disease or indicate that there is outbreak somewhere; a list of disease which we are interested is presented in our previous

Figure 1: The Real-time Architecture

work [1]. We use social networks to monitor disease-related postings because the social networks could be faster and cheaper than public health providers and the public health data are coming directly from population. In particular, we use Twitter as an example for a high-traffic social network because of public conversations, real-time nature, increasing volume of data and simplicity. In this work, we design, implement and evaluate a real-time architecture for collecting and filtering disease-related postings, this architecture tracks the status of people in real-time. The metric is using state of the art text classification to filter postings into disease-related or non-related and the ability to distinguish between real disease-related postings, shot or vaccine-related postings, and Bieber fever-related postings. Furthermore, the architecture removes most undesired words and symbols in postings because Twitter contains so much chatter.

2. THE REAL-TIME ARCHITECTURE

In this section, we briefly present the design and the description the different components of the real-time architecture (figure 1) as follows: The Crawler component uses the Twitter streaming API [5] to crawl status updates of Twitter users filtered by medical keywords and saves the returned data into pool called Main-Pool; The Indexer component is used to index each post with its metadata (e.g., user location, Geolocation, time,..etc) into pool called Index-

Pool. The Extractor component is the search engine executes queries on the Index-Pool to retrieve postings and stores them in the temporary repository; the extractor works as a scanner to remove all tweets which contain medical conditions but they actually do not related to our interest; for instance, tweets contain Bieber fever (e.g., *I think I'm getting a case of Bieber fever*), tweets contain vaccine or shot (e.g., *Getting my last shot of hepatitis B vaccine today*), tweets containing Typhoid Mary or Beadles Measles (e.g., *I HAVE BEADLES MEASLES lol*), and tweets contain love (e.g., *I'm infected. I have a virus. My virus is serious and contagious. I am in love*). The Collector component is the entry point in the architecture which communicates between all other components. Because of misspellings and slang in Twitter, The Cleansing component is used to clean each post from undesired tokens; The Classifier component is working as a gate keeper to filter all pure disease-reporting postings, it uses support vector machines (SVM) for classification and saves disease-postings in the central repository. Finally, the Stream Handler component used to control the scalability of the architecture by determined a threshold for amount of data which can be processing.

3. IMPLEMENTATION

The real-time architecture was implemented in Java under Ubuntu Linux 11.04 operating system. We implemented each component as independent Java package after that we combined all of them in one system else Crawler which is working independently over time and returns data in JSON file format, each one contains 1000 postings with their metadata; then we used Apache Lucene [6] to parse and index data of JSON files into structured data. Apache Lucene also used by Extractor component as a search engine to extract or ignore postings. Furthermore we used the classification model [1] in Classifier component for filtering postings. Multi-threading technique has been used to make the components working at same time as a non-stop processes. We also used MySQL to create two databases temporary and central repository and used Java Vectors to transport and store data during processing.

4. EVALUATION

Classifier Performance: we used 10-fold cross-validation method with support vector machine (SVM) to assess the accuracy of our classification model [1] and the results show that we can identify medical tweets with up to 89% of accuracy. In addition, we collected 200 tweets, all these tweets belong to the same domain of public health and contain different names of symptoms and diseases. 111 tweets were annotated manually as disease-related (Positive) and 89 tweets annotated as non disease-related (Negative). After applied the classification model [1] on this data; for the positive tweets, 99 tweets assigned correctly by the model and 12 tweets assigned incorrectly. Negative tweets on the other hand, 72 tweets assigned correctly by the model and 17 tweets assigned incorrectly. Therefore, the classification model achieved a performance of 85.5% accuracy with crucial dataset.

Run Time Performance: the overall performance for execution is important metric. We run our system on Intel Xeon 2.40GHZ (8 processors) with 2G of memory; running a 32-bit version of Ubuntu Linux 11.04 and we measured the latency and throughput: **(1)latency** we have measured the

Component	Run Time(Millisecond)
Indexer	0.487
Extractor	11
Classifier	0.975
Total	12.462

Table 1: The processing time for single tweet

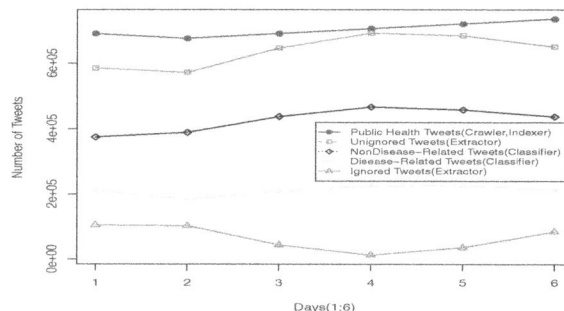

Figure 2: Number of tweets for 6 day

execution time in our system from when the system receives a tweet from Crawler until the real-time architecture decides whether that tweet is disease-related or non-related. Table 1 shows the processing time for single tweet, We found that each tweet takes on average 12.46 Milliseconds to process from start to finish. **(2)throughput** we run our system over time for 6 days and we measured number of tweets in each process of the system as shown in the figure 2. Using this small deployment, we can process more than 6 millions tweets per day.

5. CONCLUSIONS

In this work, we designed, implemented and evaluated a real-time architecture for collecting and filtering disease-related tweets; It is using state of the art text classification for classifying tweets and has ability to distinguish the ambiguous tweets(e.g., Bieber fever-related tweets). The architecture has been implemented and evaluated. In future work we study named entity recognition on tweets.

6. REFERENCES

[1] Mustafa Sofean,Kerstin Denecke, Avare Stewart, Matthew Smith. Medical Case-Driven Classification of Microblogs: Characteristics and Annotation. IHI2012. ACM, USA

[2] A. Culotta. Towards detecting influenza epidemics by analyzing twitter messages.2010.ACM.

[3] Vasileios Lampos, Nello Cristianini. Tracking the flu pandemic by monitoring the Social Web. Cognitive Information Processing (CIP), 2010

[4] Michael J. Paul and Mark Dredze. You Are What You Tweet: Analyzing Twitter for Public Health. nternational AAAI Conference (ICWSM 2011)

[5] Twitter API wiki. http://apiwiki.twitter.com/Twitter-APIDocumentation.

[6] Apache Lucene. http://lucene.apache.org/.

SHI3LD: an Access Control Framework
for the Mobile Web of Data

Luca Costabello, Serena Villata,* Nicolas Delaforge, Fabien Gandon
INRIA Sophia Antipolis, France
firstname.lastname@inria.fr

ABSTRACT

We present Shi3ld, a context-aware access control framework for consuming the Web of Data from mobile devices.

Categories and Subject Descriptors

H.3.5 [**Information Storage and Retrieval**]: Online Information Services

Keywords

Linked Data, Ubiquitous Web, Access Control

1. INTRODUCTION

The Web is evolving from an information space for sharing textual documents into a medium for publishing structured data. Recent developments in the Semantic Web field leverage on the RDF uniform data model and on URIs to merge and identify structured data of heterogeneous nature. The Linked Data[1] initiative aims at fostering the publication and interlink of data on the Web, giving birth to the *Web of Data*, an interconnected global dataspace where data providers publish their content publicly [6].
In this paper we describe Shi3ld[2], an access control framework for querying RDF datastores in mobile environments. The open nature of current Web of Data information and the consumption of web resources from mobile devices may give providers the impression that their content is not safe, thus preventing further publication of datasets, at the expense of the growth of the Web of Data itself. Access control is therefore necessary, and mobile context must be part of the access control evaluation. For a comparison with the related work [1, 5, 7, 8], see [3].
We protect RDF stores by changing the semantics of incoming SPARQL queries, whose scope is restricted to triples included in accessible Named Graphs only [2]. We determine the list of accessible graphs by evaluating pre-defined access policies against the actual mobile context of the requester. Beyond the support for context in control enforcement, our proposal has the advantage of being a pluggable filter for

generic SPARQL endpoints, with no need to modify the endpoint itself. We adopt exclusively Semantic Web languages and reuse existing proposals, thus we do not add new policy definition languages, parsers nor validation procedures. We provide protection up to triple level. Our work does not provide yet another context ontology: our model includes base classes and properties only, as we delegate refinements and extensions to domain specialists, in the light of the Web of Data philosophy. For the time being, our framework assumes the trustworthiness of the information sent by the mobile consumer, including data describing context (e.g. location, device features, etc). We do not provide any privacy-preserving mechanism yet, although we are aware that sensible data such as current location must be handled appropriately.

2. THE FRAMEWORK

The access control model is built over the notion of Named Graph [2], thus supporting fine-grained access control policies, including the triple level. We rely on named graphs to avoid depending on documents (one document can serialize several named graphs, one named graph can be split over several documents, and not all graphs come from documents. The model is grounded on two ontologies: S4AC deals with core access control concepts and PRISSMA focuses on the mobile context. The main component of the S4AC model is the Access Policy which defines the constraints that must be satisfied to access a given named graph or a set of named graphs. If the Access Policy is *satisfied* the data consumer is allowed to access the data. Otherwise, access is denied. The constraints specified by the Access Policies concern the data consumer, the device, the environment, or any given combination of these dimensions. We express Access Conditions as SPARQL ASK queries. Each Access Policy is associated to an Access Evaluation Context, an explicit link between the policy and the actual context data used to evaluate the Access Policy. The Shi3ld framework adopts PRISSMA which provides classes and properties to model core mobile context concepts, but is not meant to deliver yet another mobile contextual model: instead, well-known Web of Data vocabularies and recent W3C recommendations are reused. We agree on the widely-accepted proposal by Dey [4] and, more specifically, on the work by Fonseca et al.[3]. The mobile context is seen as an encompassing term, an information space defined as the sum of three different dimensions: the mobile *User* model, the *Device* features and the *Environment* in which the action is performed.

*Acknowledge support of the DataLift Project ANR-10-CORD-09 founded by the French National Research Agency.
[1] http://linkeddata.org
[2] http://wimmics.inria.fr/projects/shi3ld

HT'12, June 25–28, 2012, Milwaukee, Wisconsin, USA.
ACM 978-1-4503-1335-3/12/06.

[3] http://bit.ly/XGR-mbui

```
:policy1 a  s4ac:AccessPolicy;  ACCESS POLICY
           s4ac:appliesTo :alice_reviews;  RESOURCE TO PROTECT
           s4ac:hasAccessPrivilege [a s4ac:Read];  ACCESS PRIVILEGE
           s4ac:hasAccessConditionSet :acs1.

:acs1 a s4ac:AccessConditionSet;
        s4ac:ConjunctiveAccessConditionSet;
        s4ac:hasAccessCondition :ac1,:ac2.  ACCESS CONDITIONS
                                            TO VERIFY

:ac1 a s4ac:AccessCondition;
       s4ac:hasQueryAsk
       """ASK {?context a prissma:Context.
               ?context prissma:user ?u.
               ?u foaf:knows ex:alice#me.}""".

:ac2 a s4ac:AccessCondition;
       s4ac:hasQueryAsk
       """ASK {?context a prissma:Context.
               ?context prissma:environment ?env.
               ?env prissma:based_near ?p.
               FILTER (!(?p=ex:ACME_boss#me))}""".
```

(a)

```
:bobCtx{
:ctx1 a prissma:Context;
       prissma:user :usr1;
       prissma:device :dev1;           THE CONSUMER'S
       prissma:environment :env1.      CONTEXT

:usr1 a prissma:User;
       foaf:name "Bob";                THE USER DIMENSION
       foaf:knows ex:alice#me.

:dev1 a prissma:Device;
       soft:deviceSoftware :dev1sw.
:dev1sw a soft:DeviceSoftware;
       soft:operatingSystem :dev1os.   THE DEVICE DIMENSION
:dev1os a soft:OperatingSystem;
       common:name "Android".

:env1 a prissma:Environment;
       prissma:motion "no";
       prissma:nearbyEntity :ACME_boss#me;
       prissma:currentPOI :ACMEoffice.  THE ENVIRONMENT
:ACMEoffice a prissma:POI;              DIMENSION
       prissma:poiCategory example:Office;
       prissma:poiLabel example:ACMECorp.
}
```

(b)

Figure 1: The Access Policy protecting :alice_data (a) and Bob's sample mobile context in TriG notation (b).

An example of Access Policy associated to a Read privilege is shown in Figure 1a. The policy protects the named graph :alice_data and allows the access to the named graph only if the consumer (i) knows Alice, and (ii) is not located near Alice's boss. Figure 1b visualizes a sample mobile context featuring all the dimensions described above. The user, Bob, knows Alice and is currently at work, near his and Alice's boss. Bob is using an Android device and is not moving.

Our Access Control Manager is designed as a pluggable component for SPARQL endpoints. As mobile consumer query the SPARQL endpoint to access content, context data is sent with the query and cached as a named graph using SPARQL 1.1 update language statements. Each time a context element is added we use an INSERT DATA, while we rely on a DELETE/INSERT when the contextual information is already stored and has to be updated. Summarizing, the mobile client sends two SPARQL queries: the first is the client query to the datastore, the second provides contextual information (e.g. Figure 1b). The client query is filtered by the Access Control Manager instead of being directly executed on the SPARQL endpoint. The Access Control Manager selects the set of policies affecting the client query, i.e. those with a matching Access Privilege. The Access

```
PREFIX bibo: <http://purl.org/ontology/bibo/>
SELECT *
WHERE {?review a bibo:Article}
```

(a)

```
PREFIX bibo: <http://purl.org/ontology/bibo/>
SELECT *                              NAMED GRAPH
FROM :peter_reviews                   ACCESSIBLE BY
FROM NAMED :peter_reviews             THE CONSUMER
WHERE {?review a bibo:Article}
```

(b)

Figure 2: Bob's SPARQL query (a) and the secured one (b).

Conditions (SPARQL ASK queries) included in the selected policies are executed. For each verified policy, the associated named graph is added to the set of accessible named graphs. The client query is sent to the SPARQL endpoint with the addition of the FROM and FROM NAMED clauses (the latter protects from the GRAPH clause). Query execution is therefore performed only on the accessible named graphs, given the consumer contextual information. The result of the query is returned to the consumer.

An example of client query is shown in Figure 2a, where Bob wants to access all the datastore (including Alice data) from the context described in Figure 1b. The Access Conditions included in the policies are evaluated against the actual context data of the mobile consumer.In our example, the identification of the named graph(s) accessible by Bob returns only the graph :peter_data. Alice data is forbidden because Access Conditions evaluation leads to a false answer with Bob's context (Bob is near Alice's boss). The Manager adds the FROM clause to constrain the execution of the client query only on the allowed named graph. The "secured" client query is shown in Figure 2b. For the implementation details of Shi3ld and its evaluation, see [3].

3. REFERENCES

[1] F. Abel, J. L. De Coi, N. Henze, A. W. Koesling, D. Krause, and D. Olmedilla. Enabling Advanced and Context-Dependent Access Control in RDF Stores. In *Procs of ISWC-2007, LNCS 4825*, pages 1–14, 2007.

[2] J. J. Carroll, C. Bizer, P. J. Hayes, and P. Stickler. Named graphs. *J. Web Sem.*, 3(4):247–267, 2005.

[3] L. Costabello, S. Villata, N. Delaforge, and F. Gandon. Ubiquitous access control for sparql endpoints: Lessons learned and future challenges. In *Procs of WWW Companion*, 2012.

[4] A. K. Dey. Understanding and using context. *Personal Ubiquitous Computing*, 5:4–7, 2001.

[5] G. Flouris, I. Fundulaki, M. Michou, and G. Antoniou. Controlling Access to RDF Graphs. In *Procs of FIS-2010, LNCS 6369*, pages 107–117, 2010.

[6] T. Heath and C. Bizer. *Linked Data: Evolving the Web into a Global Data Space*. Morgan & Claypool, 2011.

[7] O. Sacco and A. Passant. A Privacy Preference Ontology (PPO) for Linked Data. In *Procs of LDOW-2011*, 2011.

[8] A. Toninelli, R. Montanari, L. Kagal, and O. Lassila. A semantic context-aware access control framework for secure collaborations in pervasive computing environments. In *Procs of ISWC-2006, LNCS 4273*, pages 473–486, 2006.

Adaptive Spatial Hypermedia in Computational Journalism

Luis Francisco-Revilla
School of Information
1 University Station D7000
Austin, TX, 78715-0390
+1-512-471-3821

revilla@ischool.utexas.edu

Alvaro Figueira
CRACS & INESC TEC – Universidade do Porto
Rua do Campo Alegre, 1021/1055
4169-007 Porto, Portugal
+351-220-402-932

arf@dcc.fc.up.pt

ABSTRACT

Computational journalism allows journalists to collect large collections of information *chunks* from separate sources. The analysis of these collections can reveal hidden relationships between of relationships, but due to their size, diversity, and varying nuances it is necessary to use both computational and human analysis. Breadcrumbs PDL is an adaptive spatial hypermedia system that brings together human cognition and machine computation in order to analyze a collection of user-generated news clips. The project demonstrates the effectiveness of spatial hypermedia in the domain of computational journalism.

Categories and Subject Descriptors

H.5.4 [**Information Interfaces and Presentation**]: Hypertext/ Hypermedia - *Architectures, Navigation, User issues.*

General Terms

Design, Experimentation, Human Factors.

Keywords

Computational journalism, spatial hypermedia.

1. INTRODUCTION

A central point of interest in computational journalism is enabling journalists to collect and analyze large sets of information chunks. Accordingly, an important body of work within computational journalism has focused on developing automatic mechanisms that can provide insights about the impact of specific stories and journalistic practices. For example, tracking how *memes* travel over the Web [4] helps to identify "hot" news stories as well as the sources that tend to report them before anyone else. This allows journalists to focus on the best of the blogosphere instead of having to read numerous individual blogs [6].

Ironically, the growing availability of computational tools for collecting information is making the investigational activities of information workers increasingly more complex [5]. While computational journalism provides many automatic mechanisms, it also recognizes the need for humans to explore and analyze the information because they can identify and make sense of relationships between elements in ways that computers cannot. Promoting human participation in the computational journalism (e.g., identifying relevant phrases for meme tracking) requires designing systems that make their inferences unobtrusively by "looking" at the actions that the users perform to accomplish their own goals (e.g., sharing an interesting quote with their friends).

As evidenced by the success of social bookmarking systems (e.g., delicious, digg, and reddit), people like to track and collect information items such that they can be used or reviewed later. Project Breadcrumbs [2] capitalizes on this behavior, allowing users to make *clips* from text fragments in online news media, annotate them with comments and tags, and collect them a Personal Digital Library (PDL). Specifically, Breadcrumbs' PDL is a spatial hypermedia system designed to:

- Facilitate and encourage the human organization of a collection of user-generated clips of online newspapers
- Infer connections between various clips unobtrusively
- Combine human and machine perspectives about the organization of a collection

2. PROJECT BREADCRUMBS

Breadcrumbs has three main components: Clipper, CCE, and PDL (Figure 1). Clipper supports collecting, tagging and commenting of clips (Figure 2). The Classification and Clustering Engine (CCE) organizes the clips based on semantic proximity of content, tags and comments. PDL provides a workspace that supports the human-based organization of the personal collection of clips

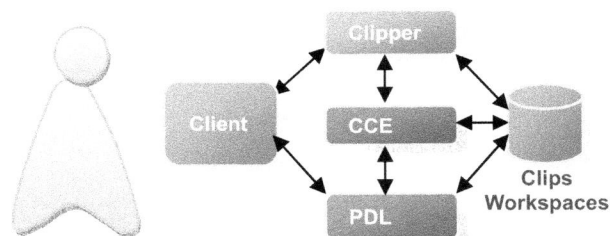

Figure 1. Overall diagram of the system

CCE creates a social network of news clips by organizing the user-selected fragments at the PDL level, and then aggregating all PDLs at the system level using text mining and social filtering techniques. The social network and its correspondent graph help journalists and news agencies to: learn which stories and phrases resonate with the readers; identify undetectable connections between apparently disconnected information sources; identify user communities; and provide readers with reading suggestions.

Figure 2. Clipper Interface

PDL uses WARP [3], a Web-based spatial hypermedia platform, to present users with a personal workspace that allows them to read, manipulate and organize their collections. The workspace is populated automatically with all the clips that the user created with Clipper.

As users organize their workspace following the typical patterns of interaction for spatial hypermedia (i.e., moving *clips*, creating piles and annotating the workspace using *labels* and explicit *groups*) they find and express relationships between clips, and develop a better understanding of their collection as whole. Figure 3 shows an example.

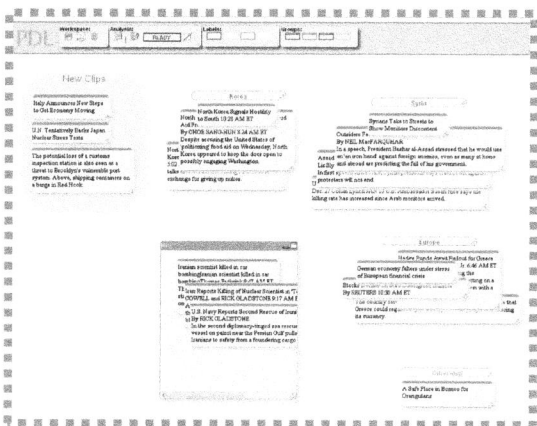
Figure 3. Clipper Interface

In order to integrating new clips into the existing organization, PDL **recommends where to move individual clips**. Based on CCE's automatic analyses PDL also **recommends alternative organizations for the whole workspace** (Figure 4).

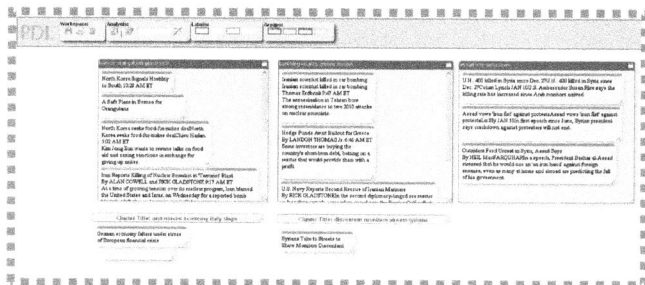
Figure 4. Alternative Workspace Organization

PDL can also recommend related clips based on the PDLs of other users. This use of the users' workspace organization for suggesting content is similar to Garnet's functionality [1].

3. CONCLUSIONS

PDL demonstrates that spatial hypermedia provides the foundational support for establishing a collaborative enterprise in computational journalism systems by integrating human and machine computation. By allowing users to interact with their collections of clips, PDL harnesses the users' ability to identify relationships that computers cannot easily detect.

However, the design and development of PDL points at the need for spatial hypermedia platforms to acclimatize to their domain, even if this implies modifying to a relatively high degree some of their intrinsic functionality. Building PDL required modifying some of the intrinsic features of the spatial hypermedia platform, including:

- Limiting the editing of the content of clips
- Limiting the editing of the appearance of clips
- Limiting the visual effects
- Editing of the clip's metadata
- Limiting the maximum organizational hierarchy in order to match the hierarchical structures used by CCE
- Constraining the vocabulary of the spatial parser to only two visual constructs: the pile, and vertical list
- Adjusting the spatial parser's parameters to target the same type of relationships

Overall, the Breadcrumbs project helps readers and journalists to express and discover hidden relationships between articles, understand the perspective of other readers better, and learn which memes *click better* with various user communities.

4. ACKNOWLEDGMENTS

This work is financed by the European Regional Development Fund through the COMPETE Programme (operational programme for competitiveness) and by National Funds through the FCT – Fundação para a Ciência e a Tecnologia (Portuguese Foundation for Science and Technology), project UTA-Est/MAI/0007/2009.

5. REFERENCES

[1] Buchanan, G., Blandford, A., Thimbleby, H., and Jones, M. 2004. Integrating information seeking and structuring: exploring the role of spatial hypertext in a digital library. In *Proc. of the 15th ACM Conference on Hypertext and Hypermedia* (HT '04). ACM, New York, NY, USA, 225-234.

[2] Figueira, A. 2011. A Social Network Built from Clips of Online News. In *Proc. of International Conf. on Internet Technologies & Society* (ITS 2011), Shanghai, China.

[3] Francisco-Revilla, L. and Shipman, F. 2004. WARP: a web-based dynamic spatial hypertext. In *Proc. of the 15th ACM conference on Hypertext and hypermedia* (HT '04). ACM, New York, NY, USA, 235-236.

[4] Li, Q, Wang, J., Chen, Y.P., and Lin, Z. 2010. User comments for news recommendation in forum-based social media. *Inf. Sci.* 180, 24 (December 2010), 4929-4939.

[5] WIKI. Memetrakers. 2012. http://en.wikipedia.org/wiki/Memetracker

Structuring Folksonomies with Implicit Tag Relations

Florian Matthes
Technische Universität
München
Boltzmannstraße 3
85748 Garching bei München,
Germany
matthes@tum.de

Christian Neubert
Technische Universität
München
Boltzmannstraße 3
85748 Garching bei München,
Germany
christian.neubert@tum.de

Alexander Steinhoff
Technische Universität
München
Boltzmannstraße 3
85748 Garching bei München,
Germany
alexander.steinhoff@tum.de

ABSTRACT

Tagging systems allow users to assign arbitrary text labels (i.e., tags) to various types of resources, such as photos or web pages, to facilitate future retrieval and selective sharing of contents. The resulting system of classification is referred to as a folksonomy. The uncontrolled nature of tags leads to inconsistencies in the usage of terms which impairs the utility of the system. Approaches to this problem that map tags to concepts of external knowledge representations, such as ontologies, are often inapplicable since they require that corresponding concepts exist and that they reflect the meaning of tags as intended by the users. In this paper, we present the notion of implicit tag relations. Our aim is to improve the accessibility of contents in tagging systems without significantly reducing the flexibility and universal applicability of tags. Instead of explicitly relating tags to each other, we propose to give users the ability to retroactively alter folksonomies by changing the tags of many resources with a single operation. This way, the usage of tags can be harmonized and it can be controlled how they are used in combination. We highlight the benefits of our approach compared to explicit tag relations and discuss important implications as well as its limitations.

Categories and Subject Descriptors

H.3.2 [**Information Storage and Retrieval**]: Information Storage—*File Organization*; H.5.4 [**Information Interfaces And Presentation**]: Hypertext/Hypermedia—*Navigation*

General Terms

Design, Theory

Keywords

Social tagging, folksonomies, organization structures

1. INTRODUCTION

To manage large collections of information resources, it is practical to relate these resources to concepts in taxonomies. In information systems, these taxonomies are often represented as hierarchical menus or nested folders. While the term *taxonomy* often refers to a purely hierarchical structure [1], we use it in a broader sense to denote a classification scheme that is primarily organized by generalization-specialization relationships. This includes faceted classification schemes [3] that are composed of several hierarchies and it allows one concept to have several generalizations.

In contrast to such rigid structures, in recent years it became popular to allow users to tag resources with freely-chosen textl abels, particularly on web platforms containing user generated content for which it is generally not practical to apply such static schemes. The structures that dynamically emerge from the users' tagging activities are usually referred to as *folksonomies* [4]. In the following we will also use the term *tagging system* to refer to an application with the purpose of managing and navigating a folksonomy.

While tagging has many advantages, such as increased flexibility, tagging systems suffer from the inconsistent usage of tags and the lack of clear tag relations makes it difficult to provide the user with helpful navigation options when browsing a collection of resources. Usually users have to resort to so-called *tag clouds* simply displaying the most frequently used tags in a collection.

In this paper, we present our approach of enabling users to establish *implicit* relations between tags by retroactively harmonizing their usage, more precisely how they are used in combination. Thereby, our aim is to combine the flexibility of tagging with the advantages of more structured classification schemes. We introduce our approach in Section 2 and discuss its benefits and limitations in Section 3.

2. IMPLICIT TAG RELATIONS

We distinguish three different kinds of implicit tag relations that users can establish in a folksonomy by assigning tags accordingly. This means that users can consciously alter the state of the system in such a way that the assignment of tags reflects the intended implicit tag relations.

Subsumption: We say a tag a *subsumes* another tag b when b is never used without a. Establishing such a relationship in a folksonomy is for example useful if a is a hypernym of b (e.g., "project" and "research project") or a holonym (like "wisconsin" and "milwaukee"). It can be compared to the generalization-specialization relationship in a classic taxonomy. When both, a specific and a respective general tag, are used in a folksonomy, it is in principle desirable that the general one is assigned to all resources being tagged with the more specific one. Otherwise a search for the general tag misses relevant resources. A tag can be subsumed by several other tags not being in a subsumption relation with each other.

Equivalence: *Equivalence* of two tags *a* and *b* simply means that for each information resource it holds that either *a* and *b* are both assigned or neither of them. The most obvious reason for this type of co-occurrence relationship is that *a* and *b* are semantically equivalent, i.e., synonyms.

Mutual exclusion: We say that two tags *a* and *b* are *mutually exclusive* if they are never used in combination. While it is a particular strength of tagging systems that one resource can be assigned to several categories, there are tags naturally not being combined with each other. If a photo is tagged "summer 2011", it is unlikely that the tags "summer 2012" or "winter 2011" apply, too. Typically, the tags in such sets belong to the same facet [2], i.e., the same dimension of classification (such as time, place, etc.).

Close to our approach is the concept of *tag gardening* which is elaborately depicted by Weller and Peters [5]. They discuss which activities are required to retroactively organize a folksonomy and manage the usage of tags. However, while they suggest that tags can be deleted or new tags can be "seeded" by the tag gardener, for the expression of tag relations they rely on explicit knowledge representations.

3. DISCUSSION

The following short discussion of our approach is based on theoretical considerations as well as on experiences gained during the work with a prototypical implementation.

3.1 The benefits of implicit tag relations

Increased recall for searches: The most obvious benefit of the application of subsumption and equivalence relations is that a general tag is systematically applied to all information resources tagged with more specific or synonym tags. In effect, it is assigned to all resources that it actually applies to. If for example the tag "terrier" is used for some resources in the folksonomy, it can be assigned to all resources tagged "welsh terrier", "irish terrier", etc. as well. This practice clearly increases the recall of tag searches.

Improved navigation options: Being able to derive tag relations for a set of resources offers various opportunities to improve the presentation of navigation options and to summarize a search result with a tag cloud: If tags *a* and *b* are both contained in a tag cloud and *a* subsumes *b*, then *b* can be hidden. The user can first select *a* to narrow the search and then add *b* to the search filter in a subsequent step. Equivalent tags can be hidden as well. Furthermore, when facets are discovered, the respective tags can be grouped.

Emergent organization structures: Users can start to harmonize the usage of tags in manageable subsets of resources (e.g., their own resources, or resources they care about) without considering whether a particular relation is adequate in general. Having established relationships in the small, they can be adopted in other contexts or they can be gradually generalized.

Portability and universal applicability: Since tag relations are not explicitly stored but embodied in the usage of tags, they can be theoretically applied in all systems that allow the assignment of arbitrary tags to resources.

3.2 Challenges and limitations

Limited expressivity: Although quite complex structures can emerge when implicit tag relations are applied, the basic modeling primitives are very restricted. It is for example not possible to distinguish part-whole relations from subtype relations since both are expressed as subsumption.

Unintended tag relations: One of the major challenges resulting from the lack of *explicit* relations is that incidental, meaningless co-occurrences of tags have to be distinguished from such relations that have been consciously established (false positives).

Scalability and applicability: It is technically challenging to scale our approach to millions or even billions of resources. Furthermore, if tag consolidation activities are not limited to a user's personal resources, it has to be regulated how the tags of foreign resources can be modified and how disagreement on particular relations is handled.

Usability: Finally, it is not obvious how to design a user interface that on the one hand allows to exploit the full flexibility of our approach and on the other hand offers a clear and understandable way of browsing and managing a folksonomy. For our prototype, we developed a simple interface that allows to browse a collection of tagged information resources as well as to establish implicit tag relations by assigning and removing tags in particular subsets of such resources. However, further improvements are necessary in order to make it transparent for users how they can introduce implicit relations and how those relations are exploited.

4. OUTLOOK

To overcome some of the limitations discussed in Section 3.2, we are currently experimenting with a combination of implicit tag relations and explicit context-dependent relations. Additionally, we plan to examine the effectiveness of implicit tag-based taxonomies, i.e., to what extent they can increase findability compared to plain tagging systems and hierarchical folder structures. Finally, we have to observe the social dynamics emerging when several users work on the same content base and independently employ implicit tag relations.

5. REFERENCES

[1] P. Lambe. *Organising Knowledge: Taxonomies, Knowledge and Organisational Effectiveness: Taxonomies, Knowledge and Organization Effectiveness.* Chandos Publishing (Oxford) Ltd, 1st edition edition, 2007.

[2] S. R. Ranganathan. *The colon classification.* Rutgers University Press, New Brunswick, 1965.

[3] G. M. Sacco and Y. Tzitzikas. *Dynamic Taxonomies and Faceted Search.* Springer, 1st edition edition, 2009.

[4] T. Vander Wal. Folksonomy definition and wikipedia. http://www.vanderwal.net/random/entrysel.php?blog=1750, 2005. accessed February 8th, 2012.

[5] K. Weller and I. Peters. Seeding, weeding, fertilizing. different tag gardening activities for folksonomy maintenance and enrichment. In *Proceedings of I-SEMANTICS '08*, pages 100–117, 2008.

Following the Follower: Detecting Communities with Common Interests on Twitter

Kwan Hui Lim and Amitava Datta
School of Computer Science and Software Engineering
The University of Western Australia
Crawley, WA 6009, Australia
kwanhui@graduate.uwa.edu.au, datta@csse.uwa.edu.au

ABSTRACT

We propose an efficient approach for detecting communities that share common interests on Twitter, based on linkages among followers of celebrities representing an interest category. This approach differs from existing ones that detects all communities before determining the interest of these communities, a computationally intensive process given the large scale of online social networks. In addition, we also study the characteristics of these communities and the effects of deepening or specialization of interest.

Categories and Subject Descriptors

J.4 [**Computer Applications**]: Social and behavioral sciences

General Terms

Theory

Keywords

Twitter, Social Networks, Community Detection, Graph Mining

1. INTRODUCTION

One important problem in the application of target advertising and viral marketing to online social networks is the efficient identification of communities with common interests. Current approaches involve detecting all communities, then determining the interests of these communities [2, 5]. These approaches involve a lengthy and intensive process of detecting communities for the entire social network and many of the detected communities may not share the interest we are looking for. We propose a method to identify communities comprising like-minded individuals with common interests on Twitter. Also, our method does not unnecessarily detect communities that do not share any specific interest.

2. DATASET AND METHODS

The Twitter dataset collected by Kwak et al. [1] is used for our experimentations. A followership link (i, j) indicates that user i is a follower of user j, while a friendship link $Fr_{i,j}$ indicates $(i, j) = (j, i)$. We define celebrities as users with more than 10,000 followers. The interest of a user, Int_{cat} is inferred by the number of celebrities (of category cat) that the user follows.

Suppose we identify a set of k celebrities $c_1, c_2, ..., c_k$. We next identify all the followership links for the individual celebrities in this set. Consider celebrity $c_j, 1 \leqslant j \leqslant k$, and all the followership links for this celebrity $\bigcup_i link(i, c_j)$. We construct the set:

$$\mathcal{P} = \bigcap_i (\bigcup link(i, c_j)), for\ 1 \leqslant j \leqslant k$$

$\mathcal{P}$ is the set of fans who follow all the k celebrities in the set $\bigcup c_j, for\ 1 \leqslant j \leqslant k$. We consider only friendship links for community detection as friendship links are stronger and more reflective of real-life interactions. Next, we try to detect communities among the members of $\mathcal{P}$ using the Infomap algorithm and Clique Percolation Method (CPM) at a k-value of 3. Refer to [3] and [4] for more details on the CPM and Infomap respectively.

3. INVESTIGATING COMMON INTERESTS

For our study, we selected Film & TV, Music, Hosting, News and Blogging as categories of interest due to their popularity. For each category, we selected the six most popular celebrities based on their number of followers. The categories that these celebrities represent were determined using information from Google and Wikipedia. Following which, we selected users with $Int_{cat} = 6$, for $cat \in \{Film\&TV, Music, Hosting, News, Blogging\}$. As a control group, we randomly chose 200,858 users to represent the group with no shared interest. We now use our approach and compare the detected communities with common interests against the control group in terms of the total number of communities, size of largest community, and average community size.

Fig. 1 and 2 show that users with common interests form larger and more communities than users without a common interest. Similarly, users with common interests form larger communities on average as shown in Fig. 3. The exception is the News category detected using CPM as many cliques of three nodes were detected as communities thus decreasing the average community size.

Table 1: Network statistics of the communities

Category	Control	Film/TV	Music	Hosting	News	Blogging
Path Length	2.83	3.03	2.82	3.09	3.35	3.09
Clustering Coefficient	0.60	0.62	0.63	0.59	0.58	0.62
Diameter	6	7	8	8	8	7
Average Degree	7.81	6.80	7.29	8.17	9.15	7.51

Users with common interests also form communities that are more cohesive than those without common interest. Table 1 shows this trend where the communities with common interest have a higher clustering coefficient than our control group with no common interest, except the Hosting and News categories. However, users interested in Hosting and News have a higher average degree of links which shows that these users are better connected than users in the control group. These results show that our community detection approach finds communities that are larger, more cohesive and share common interests.

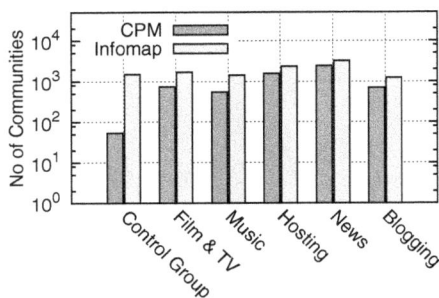

Figure 1: Total Communities

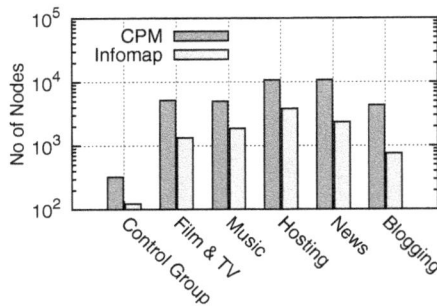

Figure 2: Size of Largest Community

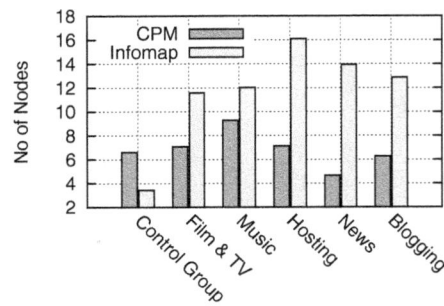

Figure 3: Average Size of Communities

4. SPECIALIZING/DEEPENING INTERESTS

We show that users sharing a specialized interest (i.e. Country Music) form a more tightly-coupled community than users sharing a general interest (i.e. Music). The control group is the users interested in the general Music category as discussed in Section 3. The celebrities representing the Country Music category are seven Country Music singers who have won various awards at the Country Music Awards between 2001 to 2008 and have more than 10,000 followers.

We investigate the changes in community formation as users specialize in their common interest (from Music to Country Music). The results are normalized by the number of users in each respective group to give an accurate representation of the community characteristics of each interest group. This Normalized Average Community Size (NACS) allows us to compare if users with specialized interests form larger communities than users with a general interest, without the biases of the base population size. We observe that the NACS of the $Int_{Country} = 6$ group is 23 and 28 times larger than the $Int_{Music} = 6$ group using CPM and Infomap respectively as shown in Table 2. In addition, users with a lower level of interest in a specialized category are also more likely to form larger communities on average compared to users with a higher level of interest in a general category.

Table 2: Comparison of General and Specialized Interest

Statistic	General (Music)	Specialized (Country)
NACS (CPM)	0.00032	0.00750
NACS (Infomap)	0.00041	0.01151
Path Length	2.82	2.10
Clustering Coefficient	0.63	0.76
Diameter	8	4
Avg. Degree	7.29	5.52

Communities comprising users with a specialized interest are also more cohesive and well-connected than those with a general interest. Table 2 best illustrates this where users with a specialized interest in Country Music form communities with a shorter average path length and diameter but higher clustering coefficient compared to those with a general interest in Music.

Next, we investigate the changes in communities as their interest in a category grows deeper, which is indicated by an increasing Int_{cat} value. Specifically, we report on the changes in number of communities, community size, clustering coefficient and path length among users as their interest deepens. The size and number of communities show how likely users with common interests form communities while clustering coefficient and path length give an indication of connectedness within the communities.

An increase in interest level among users corresponds to an increase in their average community size. We observe an increasing NACS with increasing $Int_{Country}$ values. This result supports our original observation that communities are more likely to be formed among like-minded individuals. In addition, the average size and number of communities formed increases as the interest level of the users increases.

Communities comprising users with a common interest get more tightly coupled as their level of interest increases. We observe a gradual increase in clustering coefficient among the largest communities with increasing $Int_{Country}$ values. Similarly, the largest communities at varying values of $Int_{Country}$ have an average path length of 1.7 to 3.0 hops, illustrating that users sharing common interests form communities that are better connected.

Even considering only friendship links for community detection, the communities detected still display the characteristics of scale-free networks. Upon closer examination, we observe that many individuals with large degree distribution are also country music artists but with less fans than the celebrities we have chosen. The fact that there are other minor country singers among these communities shows that our method effectively detects communities comprising users with a common interest.

In conclusion, we proposed a method to efficiently detect communities comprising individuals with common interests for application in target advertising and viral marketing. As Twitter has no explicit options for users to state their interest, we derived a measurement of interest based on the number of celebrities in an interest category that the user follows. Our approach detects communities that are larger, more cohesive and only comprise users that share a common interest. Also, we observed how their community structures become more connected and cohesive with specializing or deepening of interest in a given category.

5. ACKNOWLEDGMENTS

Kwan Hui Lim was supported by the Australian Government, University of Western Australia (UWA) and School of Computer Science and Software Engineering (CSSE) under the International Postgraduate Research Scholarship, Australian Postgraduate Award, UWA CSSE Ad-hoc Top-up Scholarship and UWA Safety Net Top-Up Scholarship.

6. REFERENCES

[1] H. Kwak, C. Lee, H. Park, and S. Moon. What is Twitter, a social network or a news media? In *Proc. of WWW*, pages 591–600, 2010.

[2] D. Li, B. He, Y. Ding, J. Tang, C. Sugimoto, Z. Qin, E. Yan, J. Li, and T. Dong. Community-based topic modeling for social tagging. In *Proc. of CIKM*, pages 1565–1568, 2010.

[3] G. Palla, I. Derényi, I. Farkas, and T. Vicsek. Uncovering the overlapping community structure of complex networks in nature and society. *Nature*, 435:814–818, 2005.

[4] M. Rosvall and C. T. Bergstrom. Maps of random walks on complex networks reveal community structure. *PNAS*, 105(4):1118–1123, 2008.

[5] S. H. Yang, B. Long, A. Smola, N. Sadagopan, Z. Zheng, and H. Zha. Like like alike - Joint friendship and interest propagation in social networks. In *Proc. of WWW*, pages 537–546, 2011.

Towards Real-Time Summarization of Scheduled Events from Twitter Streams

[Extended Abstract]

Arkaitz Zubiaga
Queens College & Graduate Center
City University of New York
New York, NY, USA
arkaitz.zubiaga@qc.cuny.edu

Damiano Spina, Enrique Amigó, Julio Gonzalo
NLP&IR Group
ETSI Informática UNED
Madrid, Spain
{damiano,enrique,julio}@lsi.uned.es

ABSTRACT

We deal with shrinking the stream of tweets for scheduled events in real-time, following two steps: (i) sub-event detection, which determines if something new has occurred, and (ii) tweet selection, which picks a tweet to describe each sub-event. By comparing summaries in three languages to live reports by journalists, we show that simple text analysis methods which do not involve external knowledge lead to summaries that cover 84% of the sub-events on average, and 100% of key types of sub-events (such as goals in soccer)[1].

Categories and Subject Descriptors

H.3.3 [**Information Storage and Retrieval**]: Information Search and Retrieval; H.1.2 [**Models and Principles**]: User/Machine Systems—*Human information processing*

General Terms

Experimentation

Keywords

twitter, real-time, events, summarization

1. INTRODUCTION

Twitter users exhaustively share messages about (all kinds of) events they are following live, occasionally giving rise to related trending topics [4]. The community of users live *tweeting* generates rich contents describing sub-events that occur during a scheduled event, where the time is known [1]. However, the overwhelming amount of information makes difficult for the user: (i) to follow the full stream while finding out about new sub-events, and (ii) to retrieve from Twitter the main, summarized information about which are the key things happening at the event. In the context of exploring the potential of Twitter as a means to follow an event, we address the (yet largely unexplored) task of summarizing Twitter contents by providing the user with a summed up stream that describes the key sub-events. We propose a two-step process for the real-time summarization of events –sub-event detection and tweet selection–, and analyze and evaluate different approaches for each of these two steps. To the best of our knowledge, our work is the first to provide an approach to generate real-time summaries of events from Twitter streams without making use of external knowledge. Thus, our approach might be straightforwardly applied to other kinds of scheduled events.

2. REAL-TIME EVENT SUMMARIZATION

We define real-time event summarization as the task that provides new information about an event every time a relevant sub-event occurs. To tackle the task, we define a two-step process that enables to report summaries in different languages. The first step identifies at all times whether a specific sub-event just occurred. The output will be a boolean value determining if something relevant occurred; if so, the second step chooses a representative tweet that describes the sub-event in the language preferred by the user. These two processes will in turn provide a set of tweets as a summary of the game. We study the case of tweets sent during the games of the soccer competition *Copa America 2011*. For the 26 games, we retrieved 1,425,858 unique tweets sent by 290,716 different users. As a reference for evaluation, we collected the live reports for all the games given by Yahoo! Sports. These reports include annotations of the most relevant sub-events during a game –goals, penalties, red cards, disallowed goals, and games starts, ends, stops and resumptions–, and the minute when it happened. On average, each game comprises 7.42 annotations.

2.1 First Step: Sub-Event Detection

The sub-event detection step has to determine at all times whether a relevant sub-event has occurred, clueless of how the stream will continue to evolve. Before the beginning of an event, the system is provided with the scheduled start time. We rely on the fact that relevant sub-events trigger a massive tweeting activity of the community. We assume that the more important a sub-event is, the more users will tweet about it almost immediately. In the process of detecting sub-events, we compare 2 different ideas: (i) considering only sudden increase with respect to the recent tweeting activity (*increase* approach [3]), and (ii) considering also the previous activity seen during a game, so that the system learns from the evolution of the audience (*outliers* approach). Here, a time frame is reported as a sub-event when

---

[1]Further experimental details about this work can be found at: http://arxiv.org/abs/1204.3731

its tweeting rate is above 90% of all the previously seen tweeting rates (not only from the previous time frame).

Table 1 shows precision (P), recall (R), F-measure (F1), and average number (#) of reported sub-events as compared to the reference. Our outliers approach clearly outperforms the baseline, improving both precision (75.8% improvement) and recall (3.7%) for an overall 40% gain in F1, while the compression rate for the outliers approach almost doubles that of the baseline (56.4%). The outperformance of the outlier-based approach shows the importance of taking into account the audience of a specific game, as well as the helpfulness of learning from previous activity throughout a game.

	P	R	F1	#
Increase	0.29	0.81	0.41	45.4
Outliers	0.51	0.84	0.63	25.6

Table 1: Evaluation of sub-event detection.

2.2 Second Step: Tweet Selection

We rely on the outputs of the outlier-based sub-event detection, as the best approach for the first step. When the first step detects a new sub-event, the tweet selector has to choose a tweet as descriptive of the sub-event. To this end, we select the tweet that maximizes the sum of term weights. To define the values of terms, we compare two methods: one relying only on the information contained within the minute of the sub-event (term frequency considering the tweets generated in that minute, TF), and another considering the knowledge acquired during the game. For the latter we use Kullback-Leibler divergence (KLD) [2] to measure how frequent is a term t within the sub-event (H), but also considering how frequent it has been during the game until the previous minute (G): $D_{\mathrm{KL}}(H\|G) = H(t) \log \frac{H(t)}{G(t)}$.

With weights given to all tweets, we create a ranking of tweets sent during the sub-event. We create a ranking for each of the languages we work on. The tweet ranked first for a language is selected to show in the summary in that language. The two term weighting methods were applied to create summaries in the three most frequent languages in our dataset: Spanish (76.2% of the tweets), Portuguese (7.8%) and English (6.2%). Thus, we got six summaries for each game, i.e., TF and KLD-based summaries for the three languages, and they were manually evaluated by comparing them to the reference. In the manual evaluation process, each tweet in a system summary is classified as *correct* if it can be associated to a sub-event in the reference and is descriptive enough (note that there might be more than one correct tweet associated to the same sub-event). Alternatively, tweets are classified as *novel* (they contain relevant information for the summary which is not in the reference) or *noisy*. From these annotations, we computed the following values for analysis and evaluation: (i) precision, given by the ratio of correct + novel tweets from a whole summary; and (ii) recall, given by the ratio of sub-events in the reference which are covered by a correct tweet in the summary (note that redundancy is not penalized by any of these measures).

Table 2 shows precision values as the ratio of useful tweets and recall values as the coverage of identified sub-events for the six generated summaries. The results show that a simple TF approach is relatively good for the selection of a repre-

	P(es)	P(pt)	P(en)	R(es)	R(pt)	R(en)
TF	0.79	0.79	0.74	0.79	0.78	0.74
KLD	0.84	0.83	0.79	0.84	0.82	0.77

Table 2: Precision and Recall of summaries in Spanish (es), Portuguese (pt) and English (en).

sentative tweet, with precision values above 70% for all three languages. However, KLD does better than TF, with precision values near 80%. This shows that taking advantage of the differences between the current sub-event and tweets shared before considerably helps in the tweet selection. Note also that English summaries reach 0.79 precision even if the tweet stream is, in that case, an order of magnitude smaller than their Spanish counterpart, suggesting that the method works well at very different tweeting rates.

These results also corroborate that simple state-of-the-art approaches like TF and KLD score outstanding recall values. Nevertheless, KLD shows to be slightly superior than TF for recall. Regarding the averages of all kinds of sub-events, recall values are near or above 80% for all the languages.

3. CONCLUSIONS

Using simple text analysis methods, our system generates real-time summaries with precision and recall values above 80% when compared to manual reports. The fact that users tweet at the same time with overlapping vocabulary helps not only detect that a sub-event occurs, but also select a tweet to describe it. Our study also shows that considering previous information seen during the event is helpful to this end, outperforming methods that only consider the most recent activity. The activity for the soccer games studied in this work varies from 11k to 74k tweets sent, showing that regardless of the audience tweeting about an event, our method effectively reports the key sub-events occurred during a game. The most relevant types of sub-events, such as goals and game ends, are reported almost perfectly.

4. ACKNOWLEDGMENTS

This work has been part-funded by MA2VICMR (S-2009/TIC-1542), the Holopedia project (TIN2010-21128-C02-01), the European Community's Seventh Framework Programme (FP7/ 2007-2013) under grant agreement nr. 288024 (LiMoSINe project) and the Spanish Ministry of Education for a doctoral grant (AP2009-0507).

5. REFERENCES

[1] H. Becker, D. Iter, M. Naaman, and L. Gravano. Identifying Content for Planned Events Across Social Media Sites. In *WSDM 2012*, pages 533–542, 2012.

[2] S. Kullback and R. Leibler. On information and sufficiency. *The Annals of Mathematical Statistics*, 22(1):79–86, 1951.

[3] S. Zhao, L. Zhong, J. Wickramasuriya, and V. Vasudevan. Human as Real-Time Sensors of Social and Physical Events: A Case Study of Twitter and Sports Games. *Arxiv preprint arXiv:1106.4300*, 2011.

[4] A. Zubiaga, D. Spina, V. Fresno, and R. Martínez. Classifying Trending Topics: A Typology of Conversation Triggers on Twitter. In *CIKM 2011*, pages 2461–2464, 2011.

Linked Open Corpus Models, Leveraging the Semantic Web for Adaptive Hypermedia

Ian O'Keeffe, Alexander O'Connor, Philip Cass, Séamus Lawless and Vincent Wade

Centre for Next Generation Localisation

Knowledge and Data Engineering Group

School of Computer Science and Statistics

Trinity College Dublin, Ireland

{Ian.OKeeffe,Alex.OConnor,casspm,Seamus.Lawless,Vincent.Wade}@scss.tcd.ie

ABSTRACT

Despite the recent interest in extending Adaptive Hypermedia beyond the closed corpus domain and into the open corpus world of the web, many current approaches are limited by their reliance on closed metadata model repositories. The need to produce large quantities of high quality metadata is an expensive task which results in silos of high quality metadata. These silos are often underutilized due to the proprietary nature of the content described by the metadata and the perceived value of the metadata itself. Meanwhile, the Linked Open Data movement is promoting a pragmatic approach to exposing, sharing and connecting pieces of machine-readable data and knowledge on the WWW using an agreed set of best practices. In this paper we identify the potential issues that arise from building personalization systems based on Linked Open Data.

Categories and Subject Descriptors

H.5.4 [**Hypertext/Hypermedia**]: Architectures;

H.3.5 [**Online Information Services**]: Web-based services;

Keywords

Adaptive Hypermedia, Personalization, Linked Open Data

1. INTRODUCTION

In the traditional, closed model approach to Adaptive Hypermedia (AH), proprietary models that describe aspects of the system and the environment including the user, the domain and the presentation strategy all need to be defined in advance. These systems also need the content which will be used in the generation of presentations to be in a defined format and described using a specific metadata standard. This reliance upon bespoke, proprietary content and models restricts the ease of adoption, scalability and accessibility of such technologies. This paper describes a "speed of web" experiment carried out to assess the concern that the use of Linked Open Data for adaptivity could negatively impact upon responsiveness and reliability.

The Open Model for AH described by this paper proposes utilizing the vast volume of data available on the WWW to address the issues described above. It is proposed to not only

gather content from the web, but also to gather the data which describes that content. A number of web technologies have emerged in recent years which make this Open Model achievable. Linked Open Data (LOD) is a practical approach to exposing, sharing and connecting content via the WWW. The structure and links exposed in LOD repositories can be leveraged quickly. This structure potentially has real value in AH as it describes both the content and the domain, which are both basic requirements of AH systems.

2. Evaluation

The inclusion of distributed information sources in any user-facing application can reduce usability by introducing delays, unreliability and distortion in the interface. In particular, because adaptive applications seek to perform rich transformations on the web experience of the user based on their attributes, it is vital that the adaptive system be responsive and reliable. These concerns arise directly in the use of Linked Open Data for adaptivity, because such systems depend on querying remote knowledge bases with differing infrastructure and with often-complex query expressions. In order to address this concern an experiment was carried out to assess, at a qualitative level, what kind of delay remote querying introduces.

The relatively high cost of querying linked open data remotely presents an important design consideration, particularly for knowledge-intensive applications such as Adaptive Hypermedia environments. The prototype used in this experiment demonstrates a system which uses one repository, the Linked Movie Database. However, the nature of the web dictates that different linked data endpoints for different content and platforms will have different performance profiles. In order to gain a qualitative perspective on the cost of remote linked data querying, two representative queries were chosen and executed on a number of repositories, chosen from across the LOD cloud. While these results are not statistically representative, they do provide an initial view of the "speed of the LOD web".

The SPARQL queries executed were designed to be representative of the kinds of operation relevant to a LOD AH environment, specifically two tasks: retrieving a long list of entities, and retrieving the detail of particular entities. These queries are represented graphically in Figure 1. One of the key challenges for creating representative queries was to define queries of approximately equivalent semantics. In order to achieve this, the three linked data sources chosen were examined to locate somewhat equivalent entities and attributes of similar cardinality and relationship to the entities.

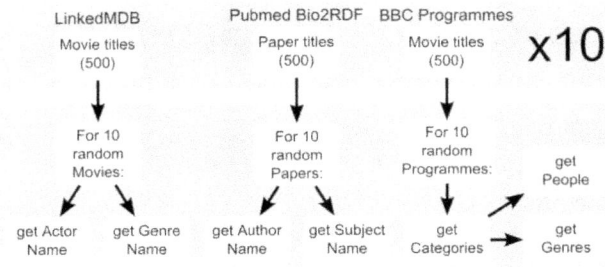

Figure 1: Schematic representation of SPARQL queries used to measure response of different LOD repositories.

For the LinkedMDB data source, Movie entities were chosen as the basic object for retrieval. A query for 500 titles for entities of the Movie type were retrieved. This query was repeated ten times, and the aggregate time recorded.

From this list of retrieved titles, ten Movies were chosen at random, and the list of Actor names and Genre names for the Movie of a particular title were retrieved.

Similarly, for Pubmed Bio2RDF [1], JournalArticle entities were chosen for retrieval, with paper authors and subject keywords were selected. These are approximately similar attributes in terms of cardinality and semantics to the Movie entities.

The BBC Programme data source [2] differed slightly in the way it represented the categorizations. The basic entity under investigation was the Episode, but the graph differed from the other two data sources by having one category relationship, and the difference between Persons and Genres was decided by type inference. This also accounts for a high variance in the result timings because of a higher variance in the cardinality of the results. This is a good example of the challenges of attempting to uniformly assess different data sets: modeling differences can make equivalence only approximate. The query procedures on each Linked Data source were repeated three times, on separate days. The results were serialized as JSON. The architecture for this test harness was based on the SPARQL Endpoint Interface for Python [3] and used Python's built-in Timer library.

There are many inherent difficulties with effective performance testing, particularly with regard to http-based interfaces, where caching, proxies, network issues and other factors complicate the repetition of trials. Because of this, aggregate times for repetitions of individual times were recorded separately. This provides an informative, rather than objective guide to likely timing for queries. The results are shown in Figure 2 and Figure 3.

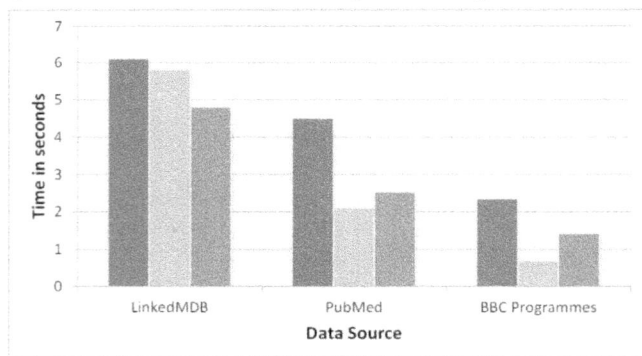

Figure 2 Time for sequences of genres for 10 random items

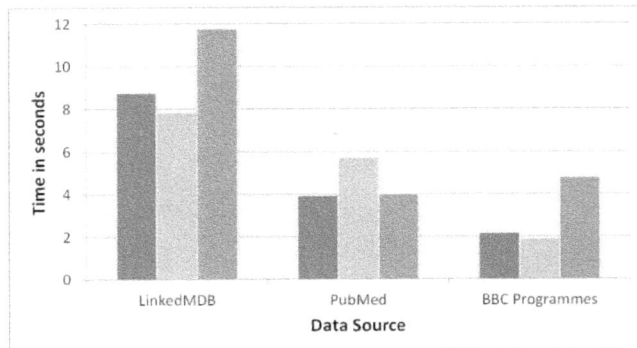

Figure 3 Time for 10 sequences of 500 title queries

These results show that the performance of remote semantic querying can vary depending on a complex series of known and unknown effects. This has implications for the design of adaptive systems, which point towards a need for caching strategies for complex or repetitive queries. Another factor observed was the limitation of connection rates by the end-points. One endpoint returned rate limits after 10 successive queries in a 12 second period. This points to another key non-functional design parameter: supporting rate limited access to end-points.

3. CONCLUSION AND FUTURE WORK

There are also some important practical considerations to be taken into account in implementing effective Open Model AH systems. The high variability of the response performance of LOD repositories motivates further research into repository and client performance, particularly through caching. It is important for future architectures for Open Model AH, and LOD in general, to be resistant to variable responses and which are able to avoid excessive load on LOD repositories. The personalized nature of Open Adaptive Hypermedia means that it is an interesting example of the general problem of deciding how to store portions of large Linked Data sets to improve client performance. The challenges of personalization are also applicable to other LOD use cases.

4. ACKNOWLEDGMENTS

This research is supported by the Science Foundation Ireland (Grant 07/CE/I1142) as part of the Centre for Next Generation Localisation (www.cngl.ie) at Trinity College Dublin

5. REFERENCES

[1] Nolin, M.-A., Ansell, P., Belleau, F., Idehen, K., Rigault, P., Tourigny, N., Roe, P., Hogan, J.M. and Dumontier, M. 2008. Bio2RDF Network of Linked Data. *Semantic Web Challenge at International Semantic Web Conference (ISWC 2008)*. Karlsruhe, Germany

[2] BBC Backstage programmes API http://backstage.bbc.co.uk (accessed April 2012)

[3] SPARQL Endpoint interface to Python, http://sparql-wrapper.sourceforge.net (accessed April 2012)

A Gender Based Study of Tagging Behavior in Twitter

Evandro Cunha[1], Gabriel Magno[1], Virgilio Almeida[1], Marcos André Gonçalves[1], Fabrício Benevenuto[2]

[1]Computer Science Department, Federal University of Minas Gerais (UFMG), Brazil
[2]Computer Science Department, Federal University of Ouro Preto (UFOP), Brazil

{evandrocunha, magno, virgilio, mgoncalv, fabricio}@dcc.ufmg.br

ABSTRACT

Gender plays a key role in the process of language variation. Men and women use language in different ways, according to the expected behavior patterns associated with their status in the communities. In this paper, we present a first description of gender distinctions in the usage of Twitter hashtags. After analyzing data collected from more than 650,000 tagged tweets concerning three different subjects, we concluded that gender can be considered a social factor that influences the user's choice of particular hashtags about a given topic. This study aims to increase knowledge about human behavior in free tagging environments and may be useful to the development of tag recommendation systems based on users' collective preferences.

Categories and Subject Descriptors

K.4.2 [**Computers and Society**]: Social Issues

General Terms

Human Factors

Keywords

Twitter, tagging, gender studies.

1. INTRODUCTION

Behavioral differences between men and women have been studied in many fields of knowledge. Knowing them can help us to better understand not only the characteristics of individuals, but also the properties of the communities in which they take part and especially the social dynamics between genders. Studying the behavior of Web and social networks users is also a major field of study in social informatics. The Web reflects interests and values of human society, operating as a mirror to which scientists may look to analyze communities across an extremely large information space. In addition, the description of the behaviors of individuals on the Web may be useful to offer more tailored services according to their characteristics, preferences and requirements. Supported by studies showing that men and women tend to deal with linguistic elements and innovations in different ways, we investigate the conduct of both genders regarding a specific the use of hashtags in Twitter.

The fact that any term can be turned into a hashtag and disseminate through the network generates interest in studying the dynamics of its creation, use and propagation, as a way to understand the behavior of users in free tagging environments. Our aim is to complement the experimental studies regarding

HT'12, June 25–28, 2012, Milwaukee, Wisconsin, USA.
ACM 978-1-4503-1335-3/12/06.

these dynamics in the light of linguistics and gender theory, looking for a description of the roles that men and women have in the life process of this kind of linguistic element.

The analysis of social factors that influence the choice of a linguistic variant is an important goal within sociolinguistics research. Many studies correlated gender to linguistic variation [2] and found significant differences in the way men and women speak and interact using language. These results support that the correlation between gender and linguistic variation must be associated with the social organization of the communities.

Our findings show that it is possible to recognize gendered hashtags. We identified linguistic characteristics that these elements may share and verified oppositions between different categories of tags. We noticed that transparent hashtags, which carry full and clear information about the topic, are more frequent among women. On the other hand, men seem more comfortable to use innovative (and sometimes more opaque) forms. We also show that male and female users adopt different persuasive strategies in the domain of Twitter communication, reflecting their behaviors in offline communities.

2. GENDER ANALYSIS

In this work, the main question we address is if male and female Twitter users choose the same tags when talking about the same topic. We expect to answer this question and, if there are "neutral", "male" and "female" forms, then we aim to identify some of the features that distinguish these three groups of tags.

For this study, we use three datasets to verify the behavior of both genders regarding topics of different natures. Our datasets consist of hashtags related to specific topics and their frequencies of utilization by male and female users. We selected the following topics: a) the 2010 Brazilian presidential election (dataset BE); b) the death of Michael Jackson, in 2009 (dataset MJ); and c) the swine flu outbreak of 2009 (dataset SF). Dataset BE has been built using data obtained by the National Institute of Science and Technology for the Web using a Twitter API. Datasets MJ and SF have been created from data collected by the Twitter Project at Max Planck Institute [1].

Dataset BE has also been divided into four sub-datasets. The purpose of this split is that we intend to investigate the choices of users of each gender in situations that admit linguistic variation – that is, the usage of different forms (in this case, hashtags) even when the semantic and the functional values are equivalent. Then, we created sub-datasets formed by hashtags related to the following topics: Dilma's supporters (BE-1); Serra's supporters (BE-2); Dilma's opposers (BE-3); and Serra's opposers (BE-4) (Dilma and Serra were the main candidates during 2010 Brazilian presidential election).

As our datasets include users' given names, we assigned to each user a gender based on his/her name. For doing this, we used lists of the most common male and female names in Brazil (for dataset BE) and in the United States (for datasets MJ and SF).

For each hashtag, we calculated the percentage of occurrences generated by male and female users. As the total number of occurrences of hashtags used by men and women are different for all datasets, we converted the raw scores to the same unit of measurement using z-scores, which represent the number of standard deviation units a raw score is above or below the mean. High raw scores are above the mean and have positive z-scores; low raw scores, thus, have negative z-scores. Here, the use of z-scores does not operate as a test of statistical significance, but as a scaling factor so that comparisons between male and female users can take place using a common yard stick.

In this way, for a given hashtag, we obtain two z-scores: the "female z-score" indicates the correspondent weight of the female usage, and the "male z-score" indicates the weight of the male usage regarding that specific hashtag. "Female" and "male z-scores" are complementary, so their sum is always equal to zero. For convenience, all z-scores presented in this study will be associated to the female z-scores. Therefore, positive z-scores will indicate a prevalence of female users and negative z-scores will indicate a prevalence of male users. We found that neutral hashtags correspond to great part of the corpus, but also that there is a significant presence of gendered tags.

Inspired by linguistic and social studies, we analyzed four different opposite categories and observed the average z-scores obtained for the hashtags that belong to them. Several classic studies [2] show that, in general, women tend to use more standard and stigma-free forms than men, who usually feel more comfortable than female speakers to use substandard and sometimes innovative variants. We checked if the opposition between standard and substandard hashtags might be a factor that affects their acceptation by male and female users.

We decided to consider as "standard forms" the most used hashtags, as we noticed that they tend to be very transparent about the topic to which they refer. For instance, the most used hashtags in the datasets MJ and SF are respectively #michaeljackson and #swineflu. On the other hand, we considered the less common – and generally more opaque – hashtags among those related to a given topic as the most innovative and "substandard forms". For each dataset, we evaluated the average z-scores of the 20% most and less common hashtags. The results are displayed in Table 1.

Table 1. Average z-scores of the most common (standard forms) and less common (substandard forms) hashtags

Dataset	Z-scores	
	Standard forms	Substandard forms
BE-1	0.974	-0.145
BE-2	0.450	-0.215
BE-3	1.024	-1.512
BE-4	0.885	0.031
MJ	1.467	-0.024
SF	0.002	0.079

We found that, in all datasets, female users are more likely to use the most common hashtags, which we consider here as the standard forms, than male users. With the exception of the dataset SF, women also use more frequently the standard forms than the substandard ones. This outcome is consistent to the ones reported by the classical sociolinguistic studies.

When analyzing the dataset BE, especially the sub-datasets BE-1 and BE-2 (supporters of the candidates), we could distinguish some hashtags between two categories: those which included personal and direct user's involvement, and those which contained pure voting instructions to the readers of the message. We consider that these two different discursive strategies have the same objective, that is, try to convince readers to vote for a specific candidate. However, linguistically speaking, they are very different, because the usage of a more personal approach brings the reader to a closer position with respect to the author and may be desirable in particular situations.

"Personal involvement" tags are those written in singular 1st person, e.g. #votodilma/#votoserra ("I vote for Dilma/Serra") and #euquerodilma/#euqueroserra ("I want Dilma/Serra"). Persuasive ones are those produced using the 3rd person imperative mood, expressing a command urging the audience to act a certain way, as in #vote13/#vote45 (13/45=Dilma's/Serra's number) and #sejamais1dilma ("Be one more for Dilma"). Table 2 shows the average z-scores of the hashtags of each category.

Table 2. Average z-scores of hashtags including "personal involvement" and "clear persuasion" discursive strategies

Dataset	Z-scores	
	Personal involvement	Voting instruction
BE-1	0.601	-1.894
BE-2	1.477	-0.957

In this case, the "personal involvement" strategy appears to be more common among female users. Male users, on the other hand, tend to be adopters of the "clear persuasion" strategy. Previous studies have found that men are more confident about their ability to persuade, which can be a reason to let them be more confident about using such clear and straightforward strategies. Other studies have also found that female managers, when attempting to convince a subordinate, rely more often on altruism than male managers. Considering that the "personal involvement" strategy reduces the distance between the author and the reader, we could also state that this strategy is related to the altruistic behavior of female managers.

3. CONCLUSIONS AND FUTURE WORK

We present an initial gender based analysis on the usage of hashtags in Twitter. The main purpose of this work is to verify if and how the behavior of male and female users differ in the usage of these specific linguistic elements. This study provides evidence that, although the majority of the hashtags seem to be neutral, some of them are, to some extent, gendered. We have also analyzed different categories of hashtags and found that certain social roles occupied by each gender in offline communities are equally performed in online social networks. Future work will involve the improvement of the statistical analysis and the investigation of other aspects that might act as factors to influence users to employ particular hashtags.

4. REFERENCES

[1] Cha, M., Haddadi, H., Benevenuto, F., and Gummadi, K.P. 2010. Measuring User Influence in Twitter: The Million Follower Fallacy. *Proc.* ICWSM, May 2010.

[2] Labov, W. 2001. *Principles of Linguistic Change: Social Factors.* Blackwell, Malden, MA.

Query Prediction with Context Models
for Populating Personal Linked Data Caches

Olaf Hartig
Humboldt-Universität zu Berlin
Unter den Linden 6, 10099 Berlin, Germany
hartig@informatik.hu-berlin.de

Tom Heath
Talis Education Ltd.
43 Temple Row, Birmingham, B2 5LS, UK
tom.heath@talis.com

ABSTRACT

The emergence of a Web of Linked Data [2] enables new forms of application that require expressive query access, for which mature, Web-scale information retrieval techniques may not be suited. Rather than attempting to deliver expressive query capabilities at Web-scale, we propose the use of smaller, pre-populated data caches whose contents are personalized to the needs of an individual user. Such caches can act as personal data stores supporting a range of different applications. In this paper we formally introduce a strategy for predicting queries that can then be used to inform an *a priori* population of a personal cache of Linked Data harvested from Web. Based on a comprehensive user evaluation we demonstrate that our approach can accurately predict queries and their execution probability, thereby optimizing the cache population process.

Categories and Subject Descriptors

H.3.m [**Information Storage and Retrieval**]: Miscellaneous;
K.8.m [**Personal Computing**]: Miscellaneous

Keywords

Query Prediction, Context, Cache Population, Linked Data

1. INTRODUCTION

In earlier work we introduce an approach to *pro-actively* populate a personalized Linked Data cache for a particular, forthcoming usage context [1]. Such caches present an alternative to maintaining a centralized infrastructure that aims to serve the needs of all users in all situations. By accessing a personalized cache in the context for which it was populated, software applications may efficiently support a particular user in satisfying context-specific information needs. An important step of our cache population process is the prediction of SPARQL queries [4] that applications may execute over the cache in a given, future context. The predicted queries may then be used as a basis for the actual cache population strategy [1].

Each of the predicted queries is associated with an *execution probability* which represents the likelihood that the query is actually executed in the given context. Formally, we define predicted queries as follows:

Definition 1. A **predicted query** is a pair (q, ep) where: q is a SPARQL query; $ep \in [0, 1]$ is an estimated execution probability.

Note that the *actual* execution probability of predicted queries is unknown during the process of pre-populating a cache. Accord-

ingly, the value ep associated with a predicted query (q, ep) represents an assumed (i.e. predicted) probability, computed as part of the query prediction itself. Since execution probabilities indicate the relevancy of queries for our cache population approach we require a prediction strategy that forecasts the execution probability for predicted queries as accurately as possible.

The main contributions of this paper are the precise definition of our query prediction strategy and a user based evaluation thereof.

2. PRELIMINARIES

The basis of our approach is a generic context model which represents a context by a set C of *context attribute*s (CA). Each CA is a tuple (t, v, r) where t denotes the type of the CA, v is an RDF term [3] which denotes the value of the CA, and $r \in [0, 1]$ is a relevancy score which denotes the degree to which the CA is relevant in the corresponding context. We deliberately refrain from defining a particular set of CA types for our model; a multitude of works exist that aim to capture the notion of context by defining relevant concepts (e.g. location, user interest) and their relationships. Depending on the application domain, any collection of such concepts may be suitable (and can be selected) as possible types for CAs.

In addition to a (future) context, our query prediction strategy depends on a specification of user tasks: People aim to meet their information needs by performing certain tasks. Software applications may support the performance of some of these tasks, in which case we call such a task a *supported task*. For example, an application may enable a user to perform the task of finding transport options to nearby places of interest.

The actual performance of supported tasks is context-specific. To capture this dependency formally we model a supported task as a pair (P, cat) where P is a set of symbols that denote context dependent properties (CDP) of the task and cat is a total mapping from P to the set of all CA types in the application domain. In any possible, context-specific performance of such a task, each CDP of the task will always be instantiated by CAs of a certain type. Mapping cat specifies this type. Formally, we define the performance of a supported task in a particular context as follows: Let $st = (P, cat)$ be a supported task and let C be a set of CAs. A C-*specific performance of* st is a total, injective mapping $perf : P \to C$ such that $\forall cdp \in P : \big(perf(cdp) = (t, v, r) \Rightarrow cat(cdp) = t \big)$.

When a person interacts with an application in order to perform a supported task, some of the user actions will cause the application to issue queries that will be evaluated over the user's personal cache. We assume that applications generate such queries by instantiating prepared templates for queries. To denote the set of *query template*s an application may instantiate when used to perform a supported task $st = (P, cat)$ we write $QT(st)$. Furthermore, each such query template $qt \in QT(st)$ is modeled as a tuple

$qt = (q, ip, sub)$ consisting of a SPARQL query q, an instantiation probability $ip \in [0, 1]$, and a partial, injective mapping sub : $\text{vars}_{\text{where}}(q) \rightarrow P$ where $\text{vars}_{\text{where}}(q)$ denotes the set of query variables that occur only in the WHERE clause of q. The variables in the domain of sub act as placeholders. If an application instantiates a query template during a context-specific performance of a supported task, then it replaces each placeholder of the template by the value of the CA that instantiates the corresponding CDP. Formally, we define such an instantiation as follows: Let $st = (P, cat)$ be a supported task; let $qt = (q, ip, sub) \in QT(st)$ be a query template of st; and let $\text{dom}(sub)$ denote the domain of mapping sub. Furthermore, let $perf$ be a C-specific performance of st. The $perf$-based instantiation of qt, denoted by $\text{inst}(qt, perf)$, is a SPARQL query that we obtain from q when for each query variable $?v \in \text{dom}(sub)$ we replace all occurrences of $?v$ in q by v where v is the value in CA $perf(sub(?v)) = (t, v, r)$.

3. QUERY PREDICTION

The general idea of our query prediction strategy is to generate all possible instantiations of those query templates that applications may instantiate in a future context given by a set C_{fut} of CAs[1]. To allow for an automated implementation of this idea, we assume a complete specification of all tasks supported by all applications that may access the personal cache; in particular, the specified list of query templates for these supported tasks is assumed to be complete. Hence, an additional input to our approach (in addition to C_{fut}) is a (full) set of supported tasks ST_{input} which is given as part of a usage scenario specification [1].

To predict any query that is possible w.r.t. C_{fut} and ST_{input}, we consider all query templates of all supported tasks in ST_{input}. For each of these templates we generate all instantiations that are possible in the context represented by C_{fut}. Formally, the complete set of queries that we may generate is given as follows:

$$\{ \text{inst}(qt, perf) \mid st \in ST_{\text{input}} \text{ and } qt \in QT(st) \text{ and}$$
$$perf \text{ is a } C_{\text{fut}}\text{-specific performance of } st \}$$

For all queries that we generate we have to estimate an execution probability. Our estimation is based on the following assumption: The likelihood that a query $q = \text{inst}(qt, perf)$ generated for a task $st \in ST_{\text{input}}$ is executed in the context represented by C_{fut} depends on i) the general instantiation probability ip of $qt \in QT(st)$ and ii) the likelihood of $perf$. The first of these parameters is given as part of ST_{input}. For computing the second parameter we introduce the notion of a $performance\ estimation\ method$, that is, a function that, for any finite set C of CAs and any supported task st, maps any possible C-specific performance $perf$ of st to a value $\xi(perf) \in [0, 1]$ such that $\xi(perf)$ is an estimate for the likelihood that st, in the context represented by C, is actually performed as specified by $perf$. Examples for such functions are ξ_{min} and ξ_{avg}:

$$\xi_{\text{min}}(perf) = \min\big(\Phi(perf)\big) \; ; \; \xi_{\text{avg}}(perf) = \frac{1}{|\Phi(perf)|} \sum_{r \in \Phi(perf)} r$$

where

$$\Phi(perf) = \{r \mid cdp \in \text{dom}(perf) \text{ and } perf(cdp) = (t, v, r)\}$$

Given the concept of performance estimation methods we now define the construction of a predicted query:

Definition 2. Let C be a set of CAs; let $st = (P, cat)$ be a supported task; let $qt = (q, ip, sub) \in QT(st)$ be a query template;

---

let $perf$ be a C-specific performance of st; and let ξ be a performance estimation method. The ξ-**based query prediction result for** qt **and** $perf$, denoted by $\text{qp}^\xi(qt, perf)$, is a predicted query:

$$\text{qp}^\xi(qt, perf) = \Big(\text{inst}(qt, perf), \text{p}^{w_{\text{ip}}, w_{\text{perf}}}\big(ip, \xi(perf)\big)\Big)$$

where $w_{\text{ip}}, w_{\text{perf}} \in \mathbb{N}^+$ are weights and

$$\text{p}^{w_{\text{ip}}, w_{\text{perf}}}\big(ip, \xi(perf)\big) = (w_{\text{ip}} \cdot ip) \cdot \big(w_{\text{perf}} \cdot \xi(perf)\big)$$

Given Definition 2, the complete set of predicted queries that can be computed with our query prediction strategy (for C_{fut}, ST_{input}, and a performance estimation method ξ) is the following:

$$\big\{ \text{qp}^\xi(qt, perf) \mid st \in ST_{\text{input}} \text{ and } qt \in QT(st) \text{ and}$$
$$perf \text{ is a } C_{\text{fut}}\text{-specific performance of } st \big\}$$

4. EVALUATION

We evaluated the accuracy of our prediction of execution probabilities by assessing their degree of correlation with participants' ratings of the likelihood of executing each query; we refer to the $per\ query$ aggregate of these ratings as $actual\ execution\ probabilities$. This was achieved by presenting participants with a concrete description of a $stranded\ traveller$ scenario and asked to rate (on a scale of 0-10) the likelihood that, if stranded at a specific airport with access to our hypothetical application, they would ask various questions involving certain locations near the airport. The degree of correlation between the predicted and actual execution probabilities was calculated on a per-airport basis (and for each permutation of weights $w_{\text{ip}}, w_{\text{perf}} \in \{1, 2, 10\}$ and aggregation functions ξ_{min} and ξ_{avg} used in computing these probabilities) using $Spearman's$ $rank\ correlation\ coefficient\ \rho$. Table 1 shows the highest and lowest values of ρ for all queries across each airport. Comparison of each ρ to the critical values (taken from [5]) in the final column shows that all permutations of weights and aggregation functions produced correlations that are statistically significant at the 5% alpha level ($\alpha=0.05$), for all airports. Therefore, we conclude that our approach is able to predict, with a high degree of accuracy, the actual execution probability of queries instantiated with a wide range of values in the stranded traveller scenario.

Airport	N	Lowest ρ	Highest ρ	Crit. Val. at α=0.05
Coleman	151	0.216	0.328	0.165
Edmonton	122	0.289	0.566	0.165
Halifax	86	0.321	0.660	0.179

Table 1: Highest and lowest values of Spearman's rank correlation coefficient ρ for all queries across each group.

5. REFERENCES

[1] O. Hartig and T. Heath. Populating Personal Linked Data Caches using Context Models. In *Proceedings of WWW*, 2012.

[2] T. Heath and C. Bizer. *Linked Data: Evolving the Web into a Global Data Space*. Morgan & Claypool, 1st edition, 2011.

[3] G. Klyne and J. J. Carroll (eds.). Resource Description Framework (RDF): Concepts and Abstract Syntax. W3C Recommendation, Feb. 2004.

[4] E. Prud'hommeaux and A. Seaborne (eds.). SPARQL Query Language for RDF. W3C Recommendation, Jan. 2008.

[5] P. H. Ramsey. Critical Values for Spearman's Rank Order Correlation. *Journal of Educational Statistics*, 14(3), 1989.

---

[1] In our cache population approach [1], C_{fut} results from an enrichment process applied to a given set of forecasted CAs. Due to space constraints we omit the definition of that process in this paper.

Author Index